RULES OF CONTRACT LAW

**Selections from the Restatement (Second) of
Contracts and Other Restatements, the Uniform
Commercial Code, the CISG, and the UNIDROIT
Principles, with Materials and Commentary on
Electronic Contracting, Commercial, Employment,
and Consumer Arbitration, and Contract
Drafting, 2017-2018**

RULES OF CONTRACT LAW

Selections from the Restatement (Second) of Contracts and Other Restatements, the Uniform Commercial Code, the CISG, and the UNIDROIT Principles, with Materials and Commentary on Electronic Contracting, Commercial, Employment, and Consumer Arbitration, and Contract Drafting, 2017-2018

Charles L. Knapp
Emeritus Joseph W. Cotchett Distinguished Professor of Law
University of California, Hastings College of the Law
Max E. Greenberg Professor Emeritus of Contract Law
New York University School of Law

Nathan M. Crystal
Adjunct Professor of Law
New York University School of Law
Distinguished Professor Emeritus
University of South Carolina School of Law

Harry G. Prince
Professor of Law
University of California, Hastings College of the Law

Keith A. Rowley
William S. Boyd Professor of Law
University of Nevada Las Vegas, William S. Boyd School of Law

Published by Wolters Kluwer in New York.

Wolters Kluwer Legal & Regulatory U.S. serves customers worldwide with CCH, Aspen Publishers, and Kluwer Law International products. (www.WKLegaledu.com)

To contact Customer Service, e-mail customer.service@wolterskluwer.com, call 1-800-234-1660, fax 1-800-901-9075, or mail correspondence to:

Wolters Kluwer
Attn: Order Department
PO Box 990
Frederick, MD 21705

Printed in the United States of America.

4 5 6 7 8 9 0

ISBN 978-1-4548-7534-5

ISSN 1556-0058

About Wolters Kluwer Legal & Regulatory U.S.

Wolters Kluwer Legal & Regulatory U.S. delivers expert content and solutions in the areas of law, corporate compliance, health compliance, reimbursement, and legal education. Its practical solutions help customers successfully navigate the demands of a changing environment to drive their daily activities, enhance decision quality and inspire confident outcomes.

Serving customers worldwide, its legal and regulatory portfolio includes products under the Aspen Publishers, CCH Incorporated, Kluwer Law International, ftwilliam.com, and MediRegs names. They are regarded as exceptional and trusted resources for general legal and practice-specific knowledge, compliance and risk management, dynamic workflow solutions, and expert commentary.

Contents

RULES OF CONTRACT LAW

Selections from the Restatement (Second) of Contracts and Other Restatements, the Uniform Commercial Code, the CISG, and the UNIDROIT Principles, with Materials and Commentary on Electronic Contracting, Commercial, Employment, and Consumer Arbitration, and Contract Drafting, 2017-2018

Restatement (Second) of Contracts (1981)

EDITORS' NOTE[1]

For centuries, critics of the legal system have complained of its delay, uncertainty, and complexity, and each generation has attempted to devise solutions to these problems. In the early part of the twentieth century, prominent members of the legal profession created an institution to study the legal system and to offer proposals for reform. Formed in 1923, the American Law Institute (ALI) remains today a private, nonprofit corporation, funded by grants principally from foundations.

While the Institute has undertaken a variety of projects since its formation, its best-known work has been the preparation of "Restatements" of the common law. Begun in the 1920s and 1930s, the Restatements are black-letter pronouncements, in statute-like form, of the rules of major common law subjects, such as contracts, property, torts, and agency. The ALI appointed Professor Samuel Williston of Harvard Law School, the best-known contracts scholar of his day, as Chief Reporter for the first Restatement of Contracts. Professor Arthur Corbin of Yale Law School, whose contracts treatise would later surpass Williston's treatise in influence (if only briefly in size), acted as a special advisor for the remedies section of the first Restatement.

Adopted by the ALI in 1932, the first Restatement of Contracts — the ALI's first completed Restatement — generated both respect and ridicule. Thousands of courts cited provisions of the Restatement to support their decisions. Yet some scholars, particularly those whose jurisprudential approach has tended toward "legal realism" or one of its later offshoots, have attacked the Restatements. Writing in 1933, Dean Charles Clark of the Yale Law School criticized the Restatement's attempt to simplify contract law by preparing an authoritative statement of rules.

---

1. For further discussion of the Restatements, see Grant Gilmore, The Death of Contract (1974); John Honnold, The Life of the Law 144-180 (1964); Nathan M. Crystal, Codification and the Rise of the Restatement Movement, 54 Wash. L. Rev. 239 (1979). For a discussion and assessment of various critiques of the Restatement movement, see Kristen David Adams, The Restatements and the Common Law: Blaming the Mirror, 40 Ind. L. Rev. 205 (2007).

... [T]he resulting statement is the law nowhere and in its unreality only deludes and misleads. It is either a generality so obvious as immediately to be accepted, or so vague as not to offend, or of such antiquity as to be unchallenged as a statement of past history.

.... There are a large number of purely bromidic sections. ... [n]o one would wish to dissent from. ... They cannot be used in deciding cases; nor are they now useful in initiating students into contract law, for the present teaching mode is to start with case study, not abstract definition. They may afford convenient citations to a court, but that is all.

Charles E. Clark, The Restatement of the Law of Contracts, 42 Yale L.J. 643, 654-655 (1933).

In the 1950s and 1960s, the Institute began work on the second generation of Restatements. The ALI chose Professor Robert Braucher of Harvard Law School as Chief Reporter for the Restatement (Second) of Contracts. After Professor Braucher's appointment to the Supreme Judicial Court of Massachusetts in 1971, Professor Allan Farnsworth of Columbia Law School became Chief Reporter. Originally issued in 14 installments labeled "tentative drafts," the ALI adopted the final version (revised and renumbered) in 1979 (although it bears a 1981 publication date).

While the Restatement (Second) continued the black-letter approach of its predecessor, it also represented a shift in several respects. Stylistically, the black-letter text was rewritten and supplemented with extensive commentary and case citations. Substantively, influenced by the publication of the Uniform Commercial Code, the Restatement (Second) added several new provisions not found in the first Restatement. These include Restatement (Second) §205, which imposes on each party to a contract a duty of good faith and fair dealing (compare UCC §1-304 (formerly §1-203)); Restatement (Second) §208, which provides that a court may refuse to enforce an agreement or any of its terms that the court finds to be unconscionable (compare UCC §2-302); and Restatement (Second) §251, allowing a party concerned about the other party's willingness or ability to perform when performance comes due to seek adequate assurances (compare UCC §2-609). Many other rules carried forward from the first Restatement were modified to reflect the Code's influence. See, e.g., Restatement (Second) §33 (reformulating the certainty requirement for contract terms based on UCC §2-204); Restatement (Second) §222 (modeling usage of trade on former UCC §1-205, now UCC §1-303).

Unlike a statute or a court decision, the Restatements do not have the force of law. They are generally regarded, however, as authoritative by courts and commentators. Judge Herbert Goodrich, former Director of the ALI, characterized the Restatements as "common law 'persuasive authority' with a high degree of persuasion." Herbert Goodrich, Restatement and Codification, in David Dudley Field Centenary Essays 242, 244-45 (Alison Reppy ed. 1949). Indeed, many cases have used the Restatement (Second) provisions as the framework for analyzing contract problems. See, e.g., Alaska Democratic Party v. Rice, 934 P.2d 1313 (Alaska 1997) (applying §139 to determine when an oral promise is enforceable under the doctrine of promissory estoppel notwithstanding statute of frauds); Lenawee County Board of Health v. Messerly, 331 N.W.2d 203 (Mich. 1982) (adopting §152 to analyze mutual mistake). Courts are zealous in protecting their independence, however, and may sometimes bristle at the suggestion that they should blindly follow the Restatement. For example, in Rowe v. Montgomery Ward & Co., 473 N.W.2d 268 (Mich. 1991), the Michigan Supreme Court, which nine years earlier had relied on the Restatement (Second) in *Lenawee*, offered this response to the argument that it should follow Restatement (Second) §33, dealing with contractual certainty:

> While we acknowledge the Restatement as persuasive authority on the subject of contracts, this Court is not, nor is any other court, bound to follow any of the rules set out in the Restatement. Moreover, even assuming . . . that our ruling is inconsistent with the Restatement, the writings of the American Law Institute do not control the rulings of this Court, nor is the contract law of this state necessarily written to be consistent with the Restatement.

Id. at 278.

The ALI has a number of other Restatement projects, and a Principles project, that overlap substantively with contract law. You will note in the editors' casebook, Problems in Contract Law, that there are repeated references to the Restatement (Second) of Torts in the section on fraud or misrepresentation, as well as, elsewhere, to the Restatement (Third) of Agency, the Restatement of Employment Law, and the Restatement (Third) of Restitution and Unjust Enrichment. Selected excerpts from the latter three, as well as the Restatement (Second) of Conflict of Laws and the Principles of the Law of Software Contracts, appear later in this Supplement.

Two more recent ALI projects involve specific contract law areas. The Restatement of the Law of Liability Insurance, launched in 2010, addresses many areas of insurance contract law, including interpretation, waiver and estoppel, good faith, and enforceability of policy limits. Originally scheduled for final approval at the May 2017 ALI Annual Meeting, the Restatement of the Law of Liability Insurance project has been carried over for another year to allow the reporters to address a handful of issues before seeking a final vote in 2018. The Restatement of the Law of Consumer Contracts, launched in 2011, focuses on distinctive aspects of business-to-consumer contracts that justify greater predictability for businesses and greater protection for consumers than current law provides – or, at least, articulates – across a broad spectrum of business-to-consumer contracts. The reporters presented a discussion draft of the Restatement of the Law of Consumer Contracts at the May 2017 ALI Annual Meeting. Although prognostication is a tricky undertaking, it appears that this project is unlikely to receive final approval before 2019. Because both of these restatements are at least a year from final approval, your editors decided not to include them in the current Supplement. For the status of current ALI projects, see www.ali.org.

* * *

Unlike prior editions, this Supplement contains the black-letter text of the entire Restatement (Second) of Contracts, as well as selected comments and illustrations accompanying some of the black-letter provisions. The unabridged version of the Restatement (Second), published by the American Law Institute in three volumes, provides extensive comments, illustrations, and Reporter's Notes, referring the reader to additional cases and commentary, for each black-letter provision, as well as introductory notes preceding each of the Restatement (Second)'s sixteen chapters and the various topics within those chapters.

CHAPTER 1.   MEANING OF TERMS

CHAPTER 2.   FORMATION OF CONTRACTS — PARTIES AND CAPACITY

CHAPTER 3.   FORMATION OF CONTRACTS — MUTUAL ASSENT

Topic 1.   In General

Topic 2.   Manifestation of Assent in General

Topic 3.   Making of Offers

CHAPTER 4.   FORMATION OF CONTRACTS — CONSIDERATION

Topic 1.   The Requirement of Consideration

CHAPTER 7.   MISREPRESENTATION, DURESS AND UNDUE INFLUENCE

Topic 1.   Misrepresentation

Topic 2.   Duress and Undue Influence

CHAPTER 8.   UNENFORCEABILITY ON GROUNDS OF PUBLIC POLICY

Topic 1.   Unenforceability in General

Topic 2.   Restraint of Trade

CHAPTER 1.   MEANING OF TERMS

§1.   Contract Defined

A contract is a promise or a set of promises for the breach of which the law gives a remedy, or the performance of which the law in some way recognizes as a duty.

Comment

a. Other meanings. The word "contract" is often used with meanings different from that given here. It is sometimes used as a synonym for "agreement" or "bargain." It may refer to legally ineffective agreements, or to wholly executed transactions such as conveyances; it may refer indifferently to the acts of the parties, to a document which evidences those acts, or to the resulting legal relations. In a statute the word may be given still other meanings by context or explicit definition. As is indicated in the Introductory Note to the Restatement of this Subject, definition in terms of "promise" excludes wholly executed transactions in which no promises are made; such a definition also excludes analogous obligations imposed by law rather than by virtue of a promise.

b. Act and resulting legal relations. As the term is used in the Restatement of this Subject, "contract," like "promise," denotes the act or acts of promising. But, unlike the term "promise," "contract" applies only to those acts which have legal effect as stated in the definition given. Thus the word "contract" is commonly and quite properly also used to refer to the resulting legal obligation, or to the entire resulting complex of legal relations. Compare Uniform Commercial Code §1-201[(b)(12)], defining "contract" in terms of "the total legal obligation which results from the parties' agreement." . . .

§2. Promise; Promisor; Promisee; Beneficiary

(1) A promise is a manifestation of intention to act or refrain from acting in a specified way, so made as to justify a promisee in understanding that a commitment has been made.

(2) The person manifesting the intention is the promisor.

(3) The person to whom the manifestation is addressed is the promisee.

(4) Where performance will benefit a person other than the promisee, that person is a beneficiary.

Comment

a. Acts and resulting relations. "Promise" as used in the Restatement of this Subject denotes the act of the promisor. If by virtue of other operative facts there is a legal duty to perform, the promise is a contract; but the word "promise" is not limited to acts having legal effect. Like "contract," however, the word "promise" is commonly and quite properly also used to refer to the complex of human relations which results from the promisor's words or acts of assurance, including the justified expectations of the promisee and any moral or legal duty which arises to make good the assurance by performance. The performance may be specified either in terms describing the action of the promisor or in terms of the result which that action or inaction is to bring about.

b. Manifestation of intention. Many contract disputes arise because different people attach different meanings to the same words and conduct. The phrase "manifestation of intention" adopts an external or objective standard for interpreting conduct; it means the external expression of intention as distinguished from undisclosed intention. A promisor manifests an intention if he believes or has reason to believe that the promisee will infer that intention from his words or conduct. Rules governing cases where the promisee could reasonably draw more than one inference as to the promisor's intention are stated in connection with the acceptance of offers (see §§19 and 20), and the scope of contractual obligations (see §§201, 219). . . .

e. Illusory promises; mere statements of intention. Words of promise which by their terms make performance entirely optional with the "promisor" whatever may happen, or whatever course of conduct in other respects he may pursue, do not constitute a promise. Although such words are often referred to as forming an illusory promise, they do not fall within the present definition of promise. They may not even manifest any intention on the part of the promisor. Even if a present intention is manifested, the reservation of an option to change that intention means that there can be no promisee who is justified in an expectation of performance. . . .

§3. Agreement Defined; Bargain Defined

An agreement is a manifestation of mutual assent on the part of two or more persons. A bargain is an agreement to exchange promises or to exchange a promise for a performance or to exchange performances.

Comment

a. Agreement distinguished from bargain. Agreement has in some respects a wider meaning than contract, bargain or promise. On the other hand, there are contracts which do not require agreement. See, e.g., §§82-90, 94, 104. The word "agreement" contains no implication that legal consequences are or are not produced. It applies to transactions executed on one or both sides, and also to those that are wholly executory. The word contains no implication of mental agreement. Such agreement usually but not always exists where the parties manifest assent to a transaction. . . .

§4. How a Promise May Be Made

A promise may be stated in words either oral or written, or may be inferred wholly or partly from conduct.

§5. Terms of Promise, Agreement, or Contract

(1) A term of a promise or agreement is that portion of the intention or assent manifested which relates to a particular matter.

(2) A term of a contract is that portion of the legal relations resulting from the promise or set of promises which relates to a particular matter, whether or not the parties manifest an intention to create those relations.

§6. Formal Contracts

The following types of contracts are subject in some respects to special rules that depend on their formal characteristics and differ from those governing contracts in general:

(a) Contracts under seal,
(b) Recognizances,
(c) Negotiable instruments and documents,
(d) Letters of credit.

§7. Voidable Contracts

A voidable contract is one where one or more parties have the power, by a manifestation of election to do so, to avoid the legal relations created by the contract, or by ratification of the contract to extinguish the power of avoidance.

Comment

. . . .

e. Power of ratification. The propriety of calling a transaction a voidable contract rests primarily on the traditional view that the transaction is valid and has its usual legal consequences until the power of avoidance is exercised. Where each party has a power of avoidance, there is no legal duty of performance; but the term voidable contract is appropriate if ratification by one of the parties would terminate his power of avoidance and make the contract enforceable against him. See §85. . . .

§8. Unenforceable Contracts

An unenforceable contract is one for the breach of which neither the remedy of damages nor the remedy of specific performance is available, but which is recognized in some other way as creating a duty of performance, though there has been no ratification.

CHAPTER 2. FORMATION OF
CONTRACTS — PARTIES AND CAPACITY

§9. Parties Required

There must be at least two parties to a contract, a promisor and a promisee, but there may be any greater number.

§10. Multiple Promisors and Promisees of the Same Performance

(1) Where there are more promisors than one in a contract, some or all of them may promise the same performance, whether or not there are also promises of separate performances.

(2) Where there are more promisees than one in a contract, a promise may be made to some or all of them as a unit, whether or not the same or another performance is separately promised to one or more of them.

§11. When a Person May Be Both Promisor and Promisee

A contract may be formed between two or more persons acting as a unit and one or more but fewer than all of these persons, acting either singly or with other persons.

§12. Capacity to Contract

(1) No one can be bound by contract who has not legal capacity to incur at least voidable contractual duties. Capacity to contract may be partial and its existence in respect of a particular transaction may depend upon the nature of the transaction or upon other circumstances.

(2) A natural person who manifests assent to a transaction has full legal capacity to incur contractual duties thereby unless he is

    (a) under guardianship, or

    (b) an infant, or

    (c) mentally ill or defective, or

    (d) intoxicated.

Comment

a. Total and partial incapacity. Capacity, as here used, means the legal power which a normal person would have under the same circumstances. . . . Incapacity may be total, as in cases where extreme physical or mental disability prevents manifestation of assent to the transaction, or in cases of mental illness after a guardian has been appointed. Often, however, lack of capacity merely renders contracts voidable. See §7. Incapacity sometimes relates only to particular types of transactions; on the other hand, persons whose capacity is limited in most circumstances may be bound by particular types of transactions. In cases of partial disability, the law of mistake or of misrepresentation, duress and undue influence may be relevant. . . .

c. Inability to manifest assent. In order to incur a contractual duty, a party must make a promise, manifesting his intention; in most cases he must manifest assent to a bargain. See §§2, 17, 18. The conduct of a party is not effective as a manifestation of his assent unless he intends to engage in the conduct. See §19. Hence if physical disability prevents a person from acting, or if mental disability is so extreme that he cannot form the necessary intent, there is no contract. Similarly, even if he intends to engage in the conduct, there is no contract if the other party knows or has reason to know that he does not intend the resulting appearance of assent. See §20. In such cases it is proper to say that incapacity prevents the formation of a contract. . . .

f. Necessaries. Persons having no capacity or limited capacity to contract are often liable for necessaries furnished to them or to their wives or children. Though often treated as contractual, such liabilities are quasi-contractual: the liability is measured by the value of the necessaries rather than by the terms of the promise. . . .

§13. Persons Affected by Guardianship

A person has no capacity to incur contractual duties if his property is under guardianship by reason of an adjudication of mental illness or defect.

§14. Infants

Unless a statute provides otherwise, a natural person has the capacity to incur only voidable contractual duties until the beginning of the day before the person's eighteenth birthday.

Comment

. . . .

c. Restoration of consideration. An infant need not take any action to disaffirm his contracts until he comes of age. If sued upon the contract, he may defend on the ground of infancy without returning the consideration received. His disaffirmance revests in the other party the title to any property received by the infant under the contract. If the consideration received by the infant has been dissipated by him, the other party is without remedy unless the infant ratifies the contract after coming of age or is under some non-contractual obligation. But some states, by statute or decision, have restricted the power of disaffirmance, either generally or under particular circumstances, by requiring restoration of the consideration received. Where the infant seeks to enforce the contract, the conditions of the other party's promise must be fulfilled. . . .

§15. Mental Illness or Defect

(1) A person incurs only voidable contractual duties by entering into a transaction if by reason of mental illness or defect

(a) he is unable to understand in a reasonable manner the nature and consequences of the transaction, or

(b) he is unable to act in a reasonable manner in relation to the transaction and the other party has reason to know of his condition.

(2) Where the contract is made on fair terms and the other party is without knowledge of the mental illness or defect, the power of avoidance under Subsection (1) terminates to the extent that the contract has been so performed in whole or in part or the circumstances have so changed that avoidance would be unjust. In such a case a court may grant relief as justice requires.

Comment

a. Rationale. A contract made by a person who is mentally incompetent requires the reconciliation of two conflicting policies: the protection of justifiable expectations and of the security of transactions, and the protection of persons unable to protect themselves against imposition. Each policy has sometimes prevailed to a greater extent than is stated in this Section. At one extreme, it has been said that a lunatic has no capacity to contract because he has no mind; this view has given way to a better understanding of mental phenomena and to the doctrine that contractual obligation depends on manifestation of assent rather than on mental assent. See §§2, 19. At the other extreme, it has been asserted that mental incompetency has no effect on a contract unless other grounds of avoidance are present, such as fraud, undue influence, or gross inadequacy of consideration; it is now widely believed that such a rule gives inadequate protection to the incompetent and his family, particularly where the contract is entirely executory. . . .

§16.   Intoxicated Persons

A person incurs only voidable contractual duties by entering into a transaction if the other party has reason to know that by reason of intoxication
    (a) he is unable to understand in a reasonable manner the nature and consequences of the transaction, or
    (b) he is unable to act in a reasonable manner in relation to the transaction.

Comment

a. Rationale. Compulsive alcoholism may be a form of mental illness; and when a guardian is appointed for the property of a habitual drunkard, his transactions are treated like those of a person under guardianship by reason of mental illness. See §§13, 15. If drunkenness is so extreme as to prevent any manifestation of assent, there is no capacity to contract. See §§2, 12, 19. It would be possible to treat voluntary intoxication as a temporary mental disorder in all cases, but voluntary intoxication not accompanied by any other disability has been thought less excusable than mental illness. Compare Model Penal Code §2.08 and Comment. Hence a contract made by an intoxicated person is enforceable by the other party . . . unless the other person has reason to know that the intoxicated person lacks capacity. Elements of overreaching or other unfair advantage may be relevant on the issues of competency, of the other party's reason to know, and of the appropriate remedy. . . . Use of drugs may raise similar problems.

b. What contracts are voidable. The standard of competency in intoxication cases is the same as that in cases of mental illness. If the intoxication is so extreme as to prevent any manifestation of assent, there is no contract. Otherwise the other party is affected only by intoxication of which he has reason to know. A contract made by a person who is so drunk he does not know what he is doing is voidable if the other party has reason to know of the intoxication. Where there is some understanding of the transaction despite intoxication, avoidance depends on a showing that the other party induced the drunkenness or that the consideration was inadequate or that the transaction departed from the normal pattern of similar transactions; if the particular transaction in its result is one which a reasonably competent person might have made, it cannot be avoided even though entirely executory. . . .

c. Ratification and avoidance. Where a contract is voidable on the ground of intoxication, the rules as to ratification and avoidance are much the same as in cases of misrepresentation. See Chapter 7. On becoming sober, the intoxicated person must act promptly to disaffirm and must offer to restore consideration received. Such an offer may be excused, however, if the consideration has been dissipated during the period of drunkenness. . . .

CHAPTER 3.   FORMATION OF CONTRACTS — MUTUAL ASSENT

Topic 1.   In General

§17.   Requirement of a Bargain

(1) Except as stated in Subsection (2), the formation of a contract requires a bargain in which there is a manifestation of mutual assent to the exchange and a consideration.

(2) Whether or not there is a bargain a contract may be formed under special rules applicable to formal contracts or under the rules stated in §§82-94.

Comment

. . . .

c. "Meeting of the minds." The element of agreement is sometimes referred to as a "meeting of the minds." The parties to most contracts give actual as well as apparent assent, but it is clear that a mental reservation of a party to a bargain does not impair the obligation he purports to undertake. The phrase used here, therefore, is "manifestation of mutual assent," as in the definition of "agreement" in §3. . . .

d. "Sufficient consideration." The element of exchange is embodied in the concept of consideration. In some cases a promise is not binding for want of consideration, despite the presence of an element of exchange. "Consideration" has sometimes been used to refer to the element of exchange, without regard to whether it is sufficient to make an informal promise legally binding; the consideration which satisfies the legal requirement has then been called "sufficient consideration." As the term "consideration" is used here, however, it refers to an element of exchange which is legally sufficient, and the word "sufficient" would therefore be redundant. . . .

   e. *Informal contract without bargain.* There are numerous atypical cases where informal promises are binding though not made as part of a bargain. In such cases it is often said that there is consideration by virtue of reliance on the promise or by virtue of some circumstance, such as a "past consideration," which does not involve the element of exchange. In this Restatement, however, "consideration" is used only to refer to the element of exchange, and contracts not involving that element are described as promises binding without consideration. There is no requirement of agreement for such contracts. They are the subject of §§82-94.

Topic 2.   *Manifestation of Assent in General*

§18.   Manifestation of Mutual Assent

Manifestation of mutual assent to an exchange requires that each party either make a promise or begin or render a performance.

Comment

   . . . .

   c. *Sham or jest.* Where all the parties to what would otherwise be a bargain manifest an intention that the transaction is not to be taken seriously, there is no such manifestation of assent to the exchange as is required by this Section. In some cases the setting makes it clear that there is no contract, as where a business transaction is simulated on a stage during a dramatic performance. In other cases, there may be doubt as to whether there is a joke, or one of the parties may take the joke seriously. If one party is deceived and has no reason to know of the joke the law takes the joker at his word. Even if the deceived party had reason to know of the joke, there may be a claim for fraud or unjust enrichment by virtue of the promise made. Where the parties to a sham transaction intend to deceive third parties, considerations of public policy may sometimes preclude a defense of sham. . . .

§19.   Conduct as Manifestation of Assent

   (1) The manifestation of assent may be made wholly or partly by written or spoken words or by other acts or by failure to act.

(2) The conduct of a party is not effective as a manifestation of his assent unless he intends to engage in the conduct and knows or has reason to know that the other party may infer from his conduct that he assents.

(3) The conduct of a party may manifest assent even though he does not in fact assent. In such cases a resulting contract may be voidable because of fraud, duress, mistake, or other invalidating cause.

Comment

. . . .

b. *"Reason to know."* A person has reason to know a fact, present or future, if he has information from which a person of ordinary intelligence would infer that the fact in question does or will exist. A person of superior intelligence has reason to know a fact if he has information from which a person of his intelligence would draw the inference. There is also reason to know if the inference would be that there is such a substantial chance of the existence of the fact that, if exercising reasonable care with reference to the matter in question, the person would predicate his action upon the assumption of its possible existence.

Reason to know is to be distinguished from knowledge and from "should know." Knowledge means conscious belief in the truth of a fact; reason to know need not be conscious. "Should know" imports a duty to others to ascertain facts; the words "reason to know" are used both where the actor has a duty to another and where he would not be acting adequately in the protection of his own interests were he not acting with reference to the facts which he has reason to know. See . . . Uniform Commercial Code §1-[202]. . . .

§20. Effect of Misunderstanding

(1) There is no manifestation of mutual assent to an exchange if the parties attach materially different meanings to their manifestations and
(a) neither party knows or has reason to know the meaning attached by the other; or
(b) each party knows or each party has reason to know the meaning attached by the other.
(2) The manifestations of the parties are operative in accordance with the meaning attached to them by one of the parties if
(a) that party does not know of any different meaning attached by the other, and the other knows the meaning attached by the first party; or
(b) that party has no reason to know of any different meaning attached by the other, and the other has reason to know the meaning attached by the first party.

Comment

. . . .

b. *The need for interpretation.* The meaning given to words or other conduct depends to a varying extent on the context and on the prior experience of the parties. Almost never are all the connotations of a bargain exactly identical for both parties; it is enough that there is a core of common meaning sufficient to determine their performances with reasonable certainty or to give a reasonably certain basis for an appropriate legal remedy. See §33. But material differences of meaning are a standard cause of contract disputes, and the decision of such disputes necessarily requires interpretation of the language and other conduct of the parties in the light of the circumstances.

   c. *Interpretation and agreement.* There is a problem of interpretation in determining whether a contract has been made as well as in determining what obligations a contract imposes. Where one party makes a precise and detailed offer and the other accepts it, or where both parties sign the same written agreement, there may be an "integrated" agreement (see §209) and the problem is then one of interpreting the offer or written agreement. In other cases agreement may be found in a jumble of letters, telegrams, acts and spoken words. In either type of case, the parties may have different understandings, intentions and meanings. Even though the parties manifest mutual assent to the same words of agreement, there may be no contract because of a material difference of understanding as to the terms of the exchange. . . .

   d. *Error in expression.* The basic principle governing material misunderstanding is stated in Subsection (1): no contract is formed if neither party is at fault or if both parties are equally at fault. Subsection (2) deals with cases where both parties are not equally at fault. If one party knows the other's meaning and manifests assent intending to insist on a different meaning, he may be guilty of misrepresentation. Whether or not there is such misrepresentation as would give the other party a power of avoidance, there is a contract under Subsection (2)(a), and the mere negligence of the other party is immaterial. See §166 as to reformation of a written contract in such a case. Under Subsection (2)(b) a party may be bound by a merely negligent manifestation of assent, if the other party is not negligent. The question whether such a contract is voidable for mistake is dealt with in §§151-58. . . .

§21. Intention to Be Legally Bound

Neither real nor apparent intention that a promise be legally binding is essential to the formation of a contract, but a manifestation of intention that a promise shall not affect legal relations may prevent the formation of a contract.

§22. Mode of Assent: Offer and Acceptance

   (1) The manifestation of mutual assent to an exchange ordinarily takes the form of an offer or proposal by one party followed by an acceptance by the other party or parties.

   (2) A manifestation of mutual assent may be made even though neither offer nor acceptance can be identified and even though the moment of formation cannot be determined.

§23. Necessity That Manifestations Have Reference to Each Other

It is essential to a bargain that each party manifest assent with reference to the manifestation of the other.

Comment

a. Mutuality of assent. Two manifestations of willingness to make a bargain, though having the same terms, do not constitute a bargain unless each is made with reference to the other. Ordinarily one party, by making an offer, assents in advance; the other, upon learning of the offer, assents by accepting it and thereby forms the contract. The offer may be communicated directly or through an agent; but information received by one party that another is willing to enter into a bargain is not necessarily an offer. The test is whether the offer is so made as to justify the accepting party in a belief that the offer is made to him. . . .

Topic 3.   Making of Offers

§24.   Offer Defined

An offer is the manifestation of willingness to enter into a bargain, so made as to justify another person in understanding that his assent to that bargain is invited and will conclude it.

Comment

a. Offer as promise. An offer may propose an executed sale or barter rather than a contract, or it may propose the exchange of a promise for a performance or an exchange of promises, or it may propose two or more such transactions in combination or in the alternative. In the normal case of an offer of an exchange of promises, or in the case of an offer of a promise for an act, the offer itself is a promise, revocable until accepted. There may also be an offer of a performance, to be exchanged either for a return promise (§55) or for a return performance; in such cases the offer is not necessarily a promise, but there are often warranties or other incidental promises. . . .

§25.   Option Contracts

An option contract is a promise which meets the requirements for the formation of a contract and limits the promisor's power to revoke an offer.

Comment

. . . .

b. The need for irrevocable offers. To provide the offeree with a dependable basis for decision whether or not to accept, the rule in many legal systems is that an offer is irrevocable unless it provides otherwise. The common-law rule, on the other hand, resting on the requirement of consideration, permits the revocation of offers even though stated to be firm. See Comment *a* to §42. The offeree's need for a dependable basis for decision is met in part by the common-law rule that mailed acceptance prevents revocation. See §63. Where more is needed, the option contract is available. . . .

§26. Preliminary Negotiations

A manifestation of willingness to enter into a bargain is not an offer if the person to whom it is addressed knows or has reason to know that the person making it does not intend to conclude a bargain until he has made a further manifestation of assent.

Comment

a. Interpretation of proposals for exchange. The rule stated in this Section is a special application of the definition in §24 and of the principles governing the interpretation of manifestations of assent. See §20 and Chapter 9. Conduct which resembles an offer may not be so intended either because there is an intent not to affect legal relations (see §18), or because the actor does not intend to engage in the conduct (see §19), or because the proposal is not addressed to the recipient or is not received by the addressee (see §23), or because the proposal contemplates a gift rather than a bargain (see Comment *b* to §24). This Section deals rather with the case where the actor intends to make a bargain in the future, but only if he makes some further manifestation of assent. If the addressee of a proposal has reason to know that no offer is intended, there is no offer even though he understands it to be an offer. "Reason to know" depends not only on the words or other conduct, but also on the circumstances, including previous communications of the parties and the usages of their community or line of business.

b. Advertising. Business enterprises commonly secure general publicity for the goods or services they supply or purchase. Advertisements of goods by display, sign, handbill, newspaper, radio or television are not ordinarily intended or understood as offers to sell. The same is true of catalogues, price lists and circulars, even though the terms of suggested bargains may be stated in some detail. It is of course possible to make an offer by an advertisement directed to the general public (see §29), but there must ordinarily be some language of commitment or some invitation to take action without further communication. . . .

c. Quotation of price. A "quotation" of price is usually a statement of price per unit of quantity; it may omit the quantity to be sold, time and place of delivery, terms of payment, and other terms. It is sometimes associated with a price list or circular, but the word "quote" is commonly understood as inviting an offer rather than as making one, even when directed to a particular customer. But just as the word "offer" does not necessarily mean that an offer is intended, so the word "quote" may be used in an offer. In determining whether an offer is made relevant factors include the terms of any previous inquiry, the completeness of the terms of the suggested bargain, and the number of persons to whom a communication is addressed. . . .

d. Invitation of bids or other offers. Even though terms are specified in detail, it is common for one party to request the other to make an offer. The words "Make me an offer" would normally indicate that no offer is being made, and other conduct such as the announcement of an auction may have similar effect. See §28. A request for bids on a construction project is similar, even though the practice may be to accept the lowest bid conforming to specifications and other requirements. And forms used or statements made by a traveling salesman may make it clear that the customer is making an offer to be accepted at the salesman's home office. See §69. . . .

§27. Existence of Contract Where Written Memorial Is Contemplated

Manifestations of assent that are in themselves sufficient to conclude a contract will not be prevented from so operating by the fact that the parties also manifest an intention to prepare and adopt a written memorial thereof; but the circumstances may show that the agreements are preliminary negotiations.

Comment

a. Parties who plan to make a final written instrument as the expression of their contract necessarily discuss the proposed terms of the contract before they enter into it and often, before the final writing is made, agree upon all the terms which they plan to incorporate therein. This they may do orally or by exchange of several writings. It is possible thus to make a contract the terms of which include an obligation to execute subsequently a final writing which shall contain certain provisions. If parties have definitely agreed that they will do so, and that the final writing shall contain these provisions and no others, they have then concluded the contract.

b. On the other hand, if either party knows or has reason to know that the other party regards the agreement as incomplete and intends that no obligation shall exist until other terms are assented to or until the whole has been reduced to another written form, the preliminary negotiations and agreements do not constitute a contract. . . .

§28. Auctions

(1) At an auction, unless a contrary intention is manifested,

(a) the auctioneer invites offers from successive bidders which he may accept or reject;

(b) when goods are put up without reserve, the auctioneer makes an offer to sell at any price bid by the highest bidder, and after the auctioneer calls for bids the goods cannot be withdrawn unless no bid is made within a reasonable time;

(c) whether or not the auction is without reserve, a bidder may withdraw his bid until the auctioneer's announcement of completion of the sale, but a bidder's retraction does not revive any previous bid.

(2) Unless a contrary intention is manifested, bids at an auction embody terms made known by advertisement, posting or other publication of which bidders are or should be aware, as modified by any announcement made by the auctioneer when the goods are put up.

Comment

a. Manifestation of contrary intention. The rules stated in this Section reflect the usual understanding at an auction sale. Established auctions often have their own customary rules, made known by publication or by announcement at the commencement of the auction. Such rules prevail even though they are contrary to the rules stated here. Compare the phrase, "unless otherwise agreed," explained in the Introductory Note to this Restatement; see Uniform Commercial Code §§1-[302], 1-[303], 2-328. But where an auction is held pursuant to statute or court order, there may be requirements or terms which cannot be varied by private agreement.

b. Auction with reserve. An auction as ordinarily conducted furnishes an illustration of the principle stated in §26. The auctioneer, by beginning to auction property, does not impliedly say: "I offer to sell this property to which ever of you makes the highest bid," but rather requests that the bidders make offers to him, as indeed he frequently states in his remarks to those before him. Hence, it is understood that he may reject all bids and withdraw the goods from sale until he announces completion of the sale. Similarly, under §42, a bidder may withdraw his bid at any time before the announcement of completion. See Uniform Commercial Code §2-328(3). . . .

§29. To Whom an Offer Is Addressed

(1) The manifested intention of the offeror determines the person or persons in whom is created a power of acceptance.

(2) An offer may create a power of acceptance in a specified person or in one or more of a specified group or class of persons, acting separately or together, or in anyone or everyone who makes a specified promise or renders a specified performance.

Comment

a. Terms of offer control. .... The offeror is the master of his offer; just as the making of any offer at all can be avoided by appropriate language or other conduct, so the power of acceptance can be narrowly limited. The offeror is bound only in accordance with his manifested assent; he is not bound just because he receives a consideration as good as or better than the one he bargained for. But if he knows or has reason to know that he is creating an appearance of assent, he may be bound by that appearance. These considerations apply to the identity of the offeree or offerees as well as to the mode of manifesting acceptance (see §30) and the substance of the exchange (see §§31, 32, 58).

b. General offers. An offer may create separate powers of acceptance in an unlimited number of persons, and the exercise of the power by one person may or may not extinguish the power of another. Where one acceptor only is to be selected, various methods of selection are possible: for example, "first come, first served" ... , the highest bidder ... , or the winner of a contest. Who can accept, and how, is determined by interpretation of the offer. ...

§30.   Form of Acceptance Invited

(1) An offer may invite or require acceptance to be made by an affirmative answer in words, or by performing or refraining from performing specified act, or may empower the offeree to make a selection of terms in his acceptance.

(2) Unless otherwise indicated by the language or the circumstances, an offer invites acceptance in any manner and by any medium reasonable in the circumstances.

§31.   Offer Proposing a Single Contract or a Number of Contracts

An offer may propose the formation of a single contract by a single acceptance or the formation of a number of contracts by successive acceptances from time to time.

§32.   Invitation of Promise or Performance

In case of doubt an offer is interpreted as inviting the offeree to accept either by promising to perform what the offer requests or by rendering the performance, as the offeree chooses.

Comment

a. Promise or performance. In the ordinary commercial bargain a party expects to be bound only if the other party either renders the return performance or binds himself to do so either by express words or by part performance or other conduct. Unless the language or the circumstances indicate that one party is to have an option, therefore, the usual offer invites an acceptance which either amounts to performance or constitutes a promise. The act of acceptance may be merely symbolic of assent and promise, or it may also be part or all of the performance bargained for. See §§2, 4, 18, 19. In either case notification of the offeror may be necessary. See §§54, 56.

The rule of this Section is a particular application of the rule stated in §30(2). The offeror is often indifferent as to whether acceptance takes the form of words of promise or acts of performance, and his words literally referring to one are often intended and understood to refer to either. Where performance takes time, however, the beginning of performance may constitute a promise to complete it. See §62. . . .

b. Offer limited to acceptance by performance only. Language or circumstances sometimes make it clear that the offeree is not to bind himself in advance of performance. His promise may be worthless to the offeror, or the circumstances may make it unreasonable for the offeror to expect a firm commitment from the offeree. In such cases, the offer does not invite a promissory acceptance, and a promise is ineffective as an acceptance. Examples are found in offers of reward or of prizes in a contest, made to a large number of people but to be accepted by only one. See §29. Non-commercial arrangements among relatives and friends . . . and offers which leave important terms to be fixed by the offeree in the course of performance (see §§33, 34) provide other examples.

It is a separate question whether the offeree undertakes any responsibility to complete performance once begun, or whether he takes any responsibility for the quality of the performance when completed. . . .

§33. Certainty

(1) Even though a manifestation of intention is intended to be understood as an offer, it cannot be accepted so as to form a contract unless the terms of the contract are reasonably certain.

(2) The terms of a contract are reasonably certain if they provide a basis for determining the existence of a breach and for giving an appropriate remedy.

(3) The fact that one or more terms of a proposed bargain are left open or uncertain may show that a manifestation of intention is not intended to be understood as an offer or as an acceptance.

Comment

a. Certainty of terms. It is sometimes said that the agreement must be capable of being given an exact meaning and that all the performances to be rendered must be certain. Such statements may be appropriate in determining whether a manifestation of intention is intended to be understood as an offer. But the actions of the parties may show conclusively that they have intended to conclude a binding agreement, even though one or more terms are missing or are left to be agreed upon. In such cases courts endeavor, if possible, to attach a sufficiently definite meaning to the bargain.

An offer which appears to be indefinite may be given precision by usage of trade or by course of dealing between the parties. Terms may be supplied by factual implication, and in recurring situations the law often supplies a term in the absence of agreement to the contrary. . . . Where the parties have intended to conclude a bargain, uncertainty as to incidental or collateral matters is seldom fatal to the existence of the contract. If the essential terms are so uncertain that there is no basis for deciding whether the agreement has been kept or broken, there is no contract. But even in such cases partial performance or other action in reliance on the agreement may reinforce it under §34.

b. Certainty in basis for remedy. The rule stated in Subsection (2) reflects the fundamental policy that contracts should be made by the parties, not by the courts, and hence that remedies for breach of contract must have a basis in the agreement of the parties. . . .

§34. Certainty and Choice of Terms; Effect of Performance or Reliance

(1) The terms of a contract may be reasonably certain even though it empowers one or both parties to make a selection of terms in the course of performance.

(2) Part performance under an agreement may remove uncertainty and establish that a contract enforceable as a bargain has been formed.

(3) Action in reliance on an agreement may make a contractual remedy appropriate even though uncertainty is not removed.

Topic 4. Duration of the Offeree's Power of Acceptance

§35. The Offeree's Power of Acceptance

(1) An offer gives to the offeree a continuing power to complete the manifestation of mutual assent by acceptance of the offer.

(2) A contract cannot be created by acceptance of an offer after the power of acceptance has been terminated in one of the ways listed in §36.

§36. Methods of Termination of the Power of Acceptance

(1) An offeree's power of acceptance may be terminated by
  (a) rejection or counter-offer by the offeree, or
  (b) lapse of time, or
  (c) revocation by the offeror, or
  (d) death or incapacity of the offeror or offeree.

(2) In addition, an offeree's power of acceptance is terminated by the nonoccurrence of any condition of acceptance under the terms of the offer.

§37. Termination of Power of Acceptance Under Option Contract

Notwithstanding §§38-49, the power of acceptance under an option contract is not terminated by rejection or counter-offer, by revocation, or by death or incapacity of the offeror, unless the requirements are met for the discharge of a contractual duty.

§38. Rejection

(1) An offeree's power of acceptance is terminated by his rejection of the offer, unless the offeror has manifested a contrary intention.

(2) A manifestation of intention not to accept an offer is a rejection unless the offeree manifests an intention to take it under further advisement.

Comment

a. The probability of reliance. The legal consequences of a rejection rest on its probable effect on the offeror. An offeror commonly takes steps to prepare for performance in the event that the offer is accepted. If the offeree states in effect that he declines to accept the offer, it is highly probable that the offeror will change his plans in reliance on the statement. . . . To protect the offeror in such reliance, the power of acceptance is terminated without proof of reliance. This rule also protects the offeree in accordance with his manifested intention that his subsequent conduct is not to be understood as an acceptance. . . .

b. Contrary statement of offeror or offeree. The rule of this Section is designed to give effect to the intentions of the parties, and a manifestation of intention on the part of either that the offeree's power of acceptance is to continue is effective. Thus if the offeree states that he rejects the offer for the present but will reconsider it at a future time, . . . under Subsection (2) there is no rejection. Similarly a statement in the offer that it will continue in effect despite a rejection is effective. . . .

. . . . If the offeror is justified in inferring from the words or conduct of the offeree, interpreted in light of the offeror's prior words or conduct, that the offeree intends not to accept the offer and not take it under further advisement, the power of acceptance is terminated. Compare §39.

§39. Counter-offers

(1) A counter-offer is an offer made by an offeree to his offeror relating to the same matter as the original offer and proposing a substituted bargain differing from that proposed by the original offer.

(2) An offeree's power of acceptance is terminated by his making of a counter-offer, unless the offeror has manifested a contrary intention or unless the counter-offer manifests a contrary intention of the offeree.

Comment

a. Counter-offer as rejection. It is often said that a counter-offer is a rejection, and it does have the same effect in terminating the offeree's power of acceptance. But in other respects a counter-offer differs from a rejection. A counter-offer must be capable of being accepted; it carries negotiations on rather than breaking them off. The termination of the power of acceptance by a counter-offer merely carries out the usual understanding of bargainers that one proposal is dropped when another is taken under consideration; if alternative proposals are to be under consideration at the same time, warning is expected.

Illustration

    1. A offers B to sell him a parcel of land for $5,000, stating that the offer will remain open for thirty days. B replies, "I will pay $4,800 for the parcel," and on A's declining that, B writes, within the thirty day period, "I accept your offer to sell for $5,000." There is no contract unless A's offer was [an option supported by consideration], or unless A's reply to the counter-offer manifested an intention to renew his original offer.

b. Qualified acceptance, inquiry or separate offer. A common type of counter-offer is the qualified or conditional acceptance, which purports to accept the original offer but makes acceptance expressly conditional on assent to additional or different terms. See §59. Such a counter-offer must be distinguished from an unqualified acceptance which is accompanied by a proposal for modification of the agreement or for a separate agreement. A mere inquiry regarding the possibility of different terms, a request for a better offer, or a comment upon the terms of the offer, is ordinarily not a counter-offer. Such responses to an offer may be too tentative or indefinite to be offers of any kind; or they may deal with new matters rather than a substitution for the original offer; or their language may manifest an intention to keep the original offer under consideration.

Illustration

    2. A makes the same offer to B as that stated in Illustration 1, and B replies, "Won't you take less?" A answers, "No." An acceptance thereafter by B within the thirty-day period is effective. B's inquiry was not a counter-offer, and A's original offer stands.

c. Contrary statement of offeror or offeree. An offeror may state in his offer that it shall continue for a stated time in any event and that in the meanwhile he will be glad to receive counter-offers. Likewise an offeree may state that he is holding the offer under advisement, but that if the offeror desires to close a bargain at once the offeree makes a specific counter-offer. Such an answer will not extend the time that the original offer remains open, but will not cut that time short. Compare §38.

Illustration

    3. A makes the same offer to B as that stated in Illustration 1. B replies "I am keeping your offer under advisement, but if you wish to close the matter at once I will give you $4,800." A does not reply, and within the thirty-day period B accepts the original offer. B's acceptance is effective.

§40. Time When Rejection or Counter-offer Terminates the Power of Acceptance

Rejection or counter-offer by mail or telegram does not terminate the power of acceptance until received by the offeror, but limits the power so that a letter or telegram of acceptance started after the sending of an otherwise effective rejection or counter-offer is only a counter-offer unless the acceptance is received by the offeror before he receives the rejection or counter-offer.

Comment

a. Receipt essential. A rejection terminates the offeree's power of acceptance because of the probability of reliance by the offeror, and there is no possibility of reliance until the rejection is received. See §38. Hence the power continues until receipt. The same rule is applied by analogy to a counter-offer, although the reason is somewhat different: a counter-offer cannot be taken under consideration as a substitute proposal until it is received. See §39. As to when a rejection is received, see §68. . . .

b. Subsequent acceptance. Since a rejection or counter-offer is not effective until received, it may until that time be superseded by an acceptance. But the probability remains that the offeror will rely on the rejection or counter-offer if it is received before the acceptance. To protect the offeror in such reliance, the offeree who has dispatched a rejection is deprived of the benefit of the rule that an acceptance may take effect on dispatch (§63). . . .

§41. Lapse of Time

(1) An offeree's power of acceptance is terminated at the time specified in the offer, or, if no time is specified, at the end of a reasonable time.

(2) What is a reasonable time is a question of fact, depending on all the circumstances existing when the offer and attempted acceptance are made.

(3) Unless otherwise indicated by the language or the circumstances, and subject to the rule stated in §49, an offer sent by mail is seasonably accepted if an acceptance is mailed at any time before midnight on the day on which the offer is received.

Comment

. . . .

b. Reasonable time. In the absence of a contrary indication, just as acceptance may be made in any manner and by any medium which is reasonable in the circumstances (§30), so it may be made at any time which is reasonable in the circumstances. The circumstances to be considered . . . include the nature of the proposed contract, the purposes of the parties, the course of dealing between them, and any relevant usages of trade. In general, the question is what time would be thought satisfactory to the offeror by a reasonable man in the position of the offeree. . . .

d. Direct negotiations. Where the parties bargain face to face or over the telephone, the time for acceptance does not ordinarily extend beyond the end of the conversation unless a contrary intention is indicated. A contrary intention may be indicated either by express words or by the circumstances. . . .

f. Speculative transactions. The rule that an offer becomes irrevocable when an acceptance is mailed (§§42, 63) in effect imposes a risk of commitment on the offeror during the period required for communication of the acceptance, although during that period the offeror has no assurance that the bargain has been concluded. The rule that the power of acceptance is terminated by the lapse of a reasonable time serves to limit this risk. The more significant the risk, the greater is the need for limitation, and hence the shorter is the time which is reasonable. . . .

The reasonable time for acceptance in a speculative transaction is brief not only because the offeror does not ordinarily intend to assume an extended risk without compensation but also because he does not intend to give the offeree an extended opportunity for speculation at the offeror's expense. If the offeree makes use for speculative purposes of time allowed for communication, there may be a lack of good faith, and an acceptance may not be timely even though it arrives within the time contemplated by the offeror. Compare Uniform Commercial Code [§1-304]. . . .

§42. Revocation by Communication from Offeror Received by Offeree

An offeree's power of acceptance is terminated when the offeree receives from the offeror a manifestation of an intention not to enter into the proposed contract.

§43. Indirect Communication of Revocation

An offeree's power of acceptance is terminated when the offeror takes definite action inconsistent with an intention to enter into the proposed contract and the offeree acquires reliable information to that effect.

§44. Effect of Deposit on Revocability of Offer

An offeror's power of revocation is not limited by the deposit of money or other property to be forfeited in the event of revocation, but the deposit may be forfeited to the extent that it is not a penalty.

§45. Option Contract Created by Part Performance or Tender

(1) Where an offer invites an offeree to accept by rendering a performance and does not invite a promissory acceptance, an option contract is created when

the offeree tenders or begins the invited performance or tenders a beginning of it.

(2) The offeror's duty of performance under any option contract so created is conditional on completion or tender of the invited performance in accordance with the terms of the offer.

Comment

. . . .

b. *Manifestation of contrary intention.* The rule of this Section is designed to protect the offeree in justifiable reliance on the offeror's promise, and the rule yields to a manifestation of intention which makes reliance unjustified. A reservation of power to revoke after performance has begun means that as yet there is no promise and no offer. . . .

d. *Beginning to perform.* If the invited performance takes time, the invitation to perform necessarily includes an invitation to begin performance. In most such cases the beginning of performance carries with it an express or implied promise to complete performance. See §62. In the less common case where the offer does not contemplate or invite a promise by the offeree, the beginning of performance nevertheless completes the manifestation of mutual assent and furnishes consideration for an option contract. See §25. . . .

e. *Completion of performance.* Where part performance or tender by the offeree creates an option contract, the offeree is not bound to complete performance. The offeror alone is bound, but his duty of performance is conditional on completion of the offeree's performance. . . .

f. *Preparations for performance.* What is begun or tendered must be part of the actual performance invited in order to preclude revocation under this Section. Beginning preparations, though they may be essential to carrying out the contract or to accepting the offer, is not enough. Preparations to perform may, however, constitute justifiable reliance sufficient to make the offeror's promise binding under §87(2).

In many cases what is invited depends on what is a reasonable mode of acceptance. See §30. The distinction between preparing for performance and beginning performance in such cases may turn on many factors: the extent to which the offeree's conduct is clearly referable to the offer, the definite and substantial character of that conduct, and the extent to which it is of actual or prospective benefit to the offeror rather than the offeree, as well as the terms of the communications between the parties, their prior course of dealing, and any relevant usages of trade. . . .

§46. Revocation of General Offer

Where an offer is made by advertisement in a newspaper or other general notification to the public or to a number of persons whose identity is unknown to the offeror, the offeree's power of acceptance is terminated when a notice of termination is given publicity by advertisement or other general notification equal to that given to the offer and no better means of notification is reasonably available.

§47. Revocation of Divisible Offer

An offer contemplating a series of independent contracts by separate acceptances may be effectively revoked so as to terminate the power to create future contracts, though one or more of the proposed contracts have already been formed by the offeree's acceptance.

§48. Death or Incapacity of Offeror or Offeree

An offeree's power of acceptance is terminated when the offeree or offeror dies or is deprived of legal capacity to enter into the proposed contract.

Comment

a. Death of offeror. The offeror's death terminates the power of the offeree without notice to him. . . .

b. Incapacity of offeror. . . . The offeror's permanent lack of capacity to enter into a contract terminates the offeree's power to accept in the same manner as [does] the offeror's death. . . .

c. Death or incapacity of offeree. Only the offeree can accept an offer. . . . See §52. When the offeree dies or lacks capacity, therefore, acceptance is impossible. . . . By the terms of the offer, however, the personal representative or [successor] of the offeree may be made an additional offeree. . . .

§49. Effect of Delay in Communication of Offer

If communication of an offer to the offeree is delayed, the period within which a contract can be created by acceptance is not thereby extended if the offeree knows or has reason to know of the delay, though it is due to the fault of the offeror; but if the delay is due to the fault of the offeror or to the means of transmission adopted by him, and the offeree neither knows nor has reason to know that there has been delay, a contract can be created by acceptance within the period which would have been permissible if the offer had been dispatched at the time that its arrival seems to indicate.

Topic 5. Acceptance of Offers

§50. Acceptance of Offer Defined; Acceptance by Performance; Acceptance by Promise

(1) Acceptance of an offer is a manifestation of assent to the terms thereof made by the offeree in a manner invited or required by the offer.

(2) Acceptance by performance requires that at least part of what the offer requests be performed or tendered and includes acceptance by a performance which operates as a return promise.

(3) Acceptance by a promise requires that the offeree complete every act essential to the making of the promise.

Comment

. . . .

b. *Acceptance by performance.* Where the offer requires acceptance by performance and does not invite a return promise, as in the ordinary case of an offer of a reward, a contract can be created only by the offeree's performance. . . . In such cases the act requested and performed as consideration for the offeror's promise ordinarily also constitutes acceptance; under §45 the beginning of performance or the tender of part performance of what is requested may both indicate assent and furnish consideration for an option contract. In some other cases the offeree may choose to create a contract either by making a promise or by rendering or tendering performance; in most such cases the beginning of performance or a tender of part performance operates as a promise to render complete performance. See §§32, 62. Mere preparation to perform, however, is not acceptance, although in some cases preparation may make the offeror's promise binding under §87(2). . . .

c. *Acceptance by promise.* The typical contract consists of mutual promises and is formed by an acceptance constituting a return promise by the offeree. A promissory acceptance may be explicitly required by the offer, or may be the only type of acceptance which is reasonable under the circumstances, or the offeree may choose to accept by promise an offer which invites acceptance either by promise or by performance. See §§30, 32. The promise may be made in words or other symbols of assent, or it may be implied from conduct, other than acts of performance, provided only that it is in a form invited or required by the offer. An act of performance may also operate as a return promise, but the acceptance in such a case is treated as an acceptance by performance rather than an acceptance by promise; thus the requirement of notification is governed by §54 rather than by §56. As appears from §63, acceptance by promise may be effective when a written promise is started on its way, but the offeree must complete the acts necessary on his part to constitute a promise by him. Similarly, in cases where communication to the offeror is unnecessary under §69, the acts constituting the promise must be complete. . . .

§51.   Effect of Part Performance Without Knowledge of Offer

Unless the offeror manifests a contrary intention, an offeree who learns of an offer after he has rendered part of the performance requested by the offer may accept by completing the requested performance.

§52.   Who May Accept an Offer

An offer can be accepted only by a person whom it invites to furnish the consideration.

Comment

. . . .

c. *Agency.* The rules stated in the Restatement of this Subject are supplemented by the law of agency, and in the absence of contrary statement it is assumed that any necessary act may be performed on behalf of a contracting party by his agent. Thus an offer may be accepted by an agent of the offeree. . . . Even an acceptance by a purported agent, acting without agency power, may in appropriate cases be ratified by the offeree. . . . Ratification must occur, however, before the offeror manifests withdrawal from the transaction and before the termination of the offeree's power of acceptance. . . .

Under the law of agency, an offeree who purports to act on his own behalf may in fact be acting for an undisclosed principal, and the undisclosed principal may be bound by the contract and may have rights under it. . . .

§53. Acceptance by Performance; Manifestation of Intention Not to Accept

(1) An offer can be accepted by the rendering of a performance only if the offer invites such an acceptance.

(2) Except as stated in §69, the rendering of a performance does not constitute an acceptance if within a reasonable time the offeree exercises reasonable diligence to notify the offeror of non-acceptance.

(3) Where an offer of a promise invites acceptance by performance and does not invite a promissory acceptance, the rendering of the invited performance does not constitute an acceptance if before the offeror performs his promise the offeree manifests an intention not to accept.

§54. Acceptance by Performance; Necessity of Notification to Offeror

(1) Where an offer invites an offeree to accept by rendering a performance, no notification is necessary to make such an acceptance effective unless the offer requests such a notification.

(2) If an offeree who accepts by rendering a performance has reason to know that the offeror has no adequate means of learning of the performance with reasonable promptness and certainty, the contractual duty of the offeror is discharged unless

(a) the offeree exercises reasonable diligence to notify the offeror of acceptance, or

(b) the offeror learns of the performance within a reasonable time, or

(c) the offer indicates that notification of acceptance is not required.

Comment

a. Rationale. In the usual commercial bargain the offeror expects and receives prompt notification of acceptance, and such notification is ordinarily essential to an acceptance by promise. See §56. But where an offer invites the offeree to accept by rendering a performance, the offeree needs a dependable basis for his decision whether to accept. Compare §63 and Comment *a*. When the offeree performs or begins to perform in response to such an offer, there is need for protection of his justifiable reliance. Compare §45. Those needs are met by giving the performance the effect of temporarily barring revocation of the offer; but ordinarily notification of the offeror must follow in due course. . . .

b. Performance operating as return promise. This Section applies only to offers which invite acceptance by performance. Where the offeree is empowered to choose between acceptance by performance and acceptance by promise (see §32), this Section applies only if he chooses to accept by performance. See §50(2). In such a case the acceptance often carries with it a return commitment (see §62), and it is rare that the offer dispenses with notification of such a commitment. Compare §§56, 69. Unless the performance will come to the offeror's attention in normal course, it is not likely to be a reasonable mode of acceptance. See §30. In the exceptional case where acceptance is invited by a performance which will not come promptly to the offeror's attention, Subsection (2) usually requires notification of acceptance. . . . [I]f no notification is sent within a reasonable time in such a case, the offeror may treat the offer as having lapsed before acceptance. . . .

c. Where no return promise is contemplated. Performance may be invited as an alternative mode of acceptance or as the exclusive mode of acceptance. See §§30, 32. Where no return commitment is involved, the only notification of acceptance called for is often that necessarily involved in performance by the offeree, or that which accompanies the offeree's request for performance by the offeror. Performance itself both manifests assent and furnishes consideration. Notification is requisite only where the offeror has no convenient means of ascertaining whether the requisite performance has taken place. Even then, it is not the notification which creates the contract, but lack of notification which ends the duty. Compare §224. Moreover, the offeror may effectively waive notification either before or after the time when it would otherwise be due. See §84. . . .

§55. Acceptance of Non-Promissory Offers

Acceptance by promise may create a contract in which the offeror's performance is completed when the offeree's promise is made.

§56. Acceptance by Promise; Necessity of Notification to Offeror

Except as stated in §69 or where the offer manifests a contrary intention, it is essential to an acceptance by promise either that the offeree exercise reasonable diligence to notify the offeror of acceptance or that the offeror receive the acceptance seasonably.

Comment

a. Necessity of notification. Where the offeree has performed in whole or in part, notification to the offeror is not essential to acceptance, although failure to notify may discharge the offeror's duty of performance. See §54. Similarly, where the offeror has rendered a performance and the offeree has taken the benefit of that performance, the offeree may be bound without notification to the offeror. See §69. In such cases the enforcement of the promise rests in part on a change of position in justifiable reliance on a promise, often reinforced by a corresponding benefit received by the promisor. . . .

§57. Effect of Equivocal Acceptance

Where notification is essential to acceptance by promise, the offeror is not bound by an acceptance in equivocal terms unless he reasonably understands it as an acceptance.

§58. Necessity of Acceptance Complying with Terms of Offer

An acceptance must comply with the requirements of the offer as to the promise to be made or the performance to be rendered.

Comment

a. Scope. This rule applies to the substance of the bargain the basic principle that the offeror is the master of his offer. . . . That principle rests on the concept of private autonomy underlying contract law. It is mitigated by the interpretation of offers, in accordance with common understanding, as inviting acceptance in any reasonable manner unless there is contrary indication. See §§20, 30(2), 32. . . .

§59. Purported Acceptance Which Adds Qualifications

A reply to an offer which purports to accept it but is conditional on the offeror's assent to terms additional to or different from those offered is not an acceptance but is a counter-offer.

Comment

a. Qualified acceptance. A qualified or conditional acceptance proposes an exchange different from that proposed by the original offeror. Such a proposal is a counter-offer and ordinarily terminates the power of acceptance of the original offeree. See §39. The effect of the qualification or condition is to deprive the purported acceptance of effect. But a definite and seasonable expression of acceptance is operative despite the statement of additional or different terms if the acceptance is not made to depend on assent to the additional or different terms. See §61; Uniform Commercial Code §2-207(1). The additional or different terms are then to be construed as proposals for modification of the contract. See Uniform Commercial Code §2-207(2). Such proposals may sometimes be accepted by the silence of the original offeror. See §69. . . .

   b. Statement of conditions implied in offer. To accept, the offeree must assent unconditionally to the offer as made, but the fact that the offeree makes a conditional promise is not sufficient to show that his acceptance is conditional. The offer itself may either expressly or by implication propose that the offeree make a conditional promise as his part of the exchange. By assenting to such a proposal the offeree makes a conditional promise, but his acceptance is unconditional. The offeror's promise may also be conditional on the same or a different fact or event. . . .

§60. Acceptance of Offer Which States Place, Time, or Manner of Acceptance

If an offer prescribes the place, time or manner of acceptance its terms in this respect must be complied with in order to create a contract. If an offer merely suggests a permitted place, time or manner of acceptance, another method of acceptance is not precluded.

Comment

   a. Interpretation of offer. If the offeror prescribes the only way in which his offer may be accepted, an acceptance in any other way is a counter-offer. But frequently in regard to the details of methods of acceptance, the offeror's language, if fairly interpreted, amounts merely to a statement of a satisfactory method of acceptance, without positive requirement that this method shall be followed. . . .

§61. Acceptance Which Requests Change of Terms

An acceptance which requests a change or addition to the terms of the offer is not thereby invalidated unless the acceptance is made to depend on an assent to the changed or added terms.

§62. Effect of Performance by Offeree Where Offer Invites Either Performance or Promise

   (1) Where an offer invites an offeree to choose between acceptance by promise and acceptance by performance, the tender or beginning of the invited performance or a tender of a beginning of it is an acceptance by performance.
   (2) Such an acceptance operates as a promise to render complete performance.

Comment

a. The offeree's power to choose. The offeror normally invites a promise by the offeree for the purpose of obtaining performance of the promise. Full performance fulfills that purpose more directly than the promise invited, and hence constitutes a reasonable mode of acceptance. The offeror can insist on any mode of acceptance, but ordinarily he invites acceptance in any reasonable manner; in case of doubt, an offer is interpreted as inviting the offeree to choose between acceptance by promise and acceptance by performance. See §§30, 32, 58.

b. Part performance or tender. Where acceptance by performance is invited and no promise is invited, the beginning of performance or the tender of part performance creates an option contract and renders the offer irrevocable. See §§37, 45. Under Subsection (1) of this Section the offer is similarly rendered irrevocable where it invites the offeree to choose between acceptance by promise and acceptance by performance. In both types of cases, if the invited performance takes time, the invitation to perform necessarily includes an invitation to begin performance; if performance requires cooperation by the offeror, there is an offer only if acceptance can be completed by tender of performance. But unless an option contract is contemplated, the offeree is expected to be bound as well as the offeror, and Subsection (2) of this Section states the implication of promise which results from that expectation. . . . In such standard cases as the shipment of goods in response to an order, the acceptance will come to the offeror's attention in normal course; in other cases, the rule of §54(2) ordinarily requires prompt notification. . . .

d. Preparations for performance. As under §45, what is begun or tendered must be part of the actual performance invited, rather than preparation for performance, in order to make the rule of this Section applicable. See Comment *f* to §45. But preparations to perform may bring the case within §87(2) on justifiable reliance. . . .

§63. Time When Acceptance Takes Effect

Unless the offer provides otherwise,

(a) an acceptance made in a manner and by a medium invited by an offer is operative and completes the manifestation of mutual assent as soon as put out of the offeree's possession, without regard to whether it ever reaches the offeror; but

(b) an acceptance under an option contract is not operative until received by the offeror.

Comment

. . . .

b. Loss or delay in transit. In the interest of simplicity and clarity, the rule [that an acceptance is effective on dispatch] has been extended [in Section 63] to cases where an acceptance is lost or delayed in the course of transmission. The convenience of the rule is less clear in such cases than in cases of attempted revocation of the offer, however, and the language of the offer is often properly interpreted as making the offeror's duty of performance conditional upon receipt of the acceptance. Indeed, where the receipt of notice is essential to enable the offeror to perform, such a condition is normally implied. See Comment *c* to §226. . . .

   c. Revocation of acceptance. The fact that the offeree has power to reclaim his acceptance from the post office or telegraph company does not prevent the acceptance from taking effect on dispatch. Nor, in the absence of additional circumstances, does the actual recapture of the acceptance deprive it of legal effect, though as a practical matter the offeror cannot assert his rights unless he learns of them. An attempt to revoke the acceptance by an overtaking communication is similarly ineffective, even though the revocation is received before the acceptance is received. After mailing an acceptance of a revocable offer, the offeree is not permitted to speculate at the offeror's expense during the time required for the letter to arrive.

   A purported revocation of acceptance may, however, affect the rights of the parties. It may amount to an offer to rescind the contract or to a repudiation of it, or it may bar the offeree by estoppel from enforcing it. . . .

   f. Option contracts. . . . Option contracts are commonly subject to a definite time limit, and the usual understanding is that the notification that the option has been exercised must be received by the offeror before that time. Whether or not there is such a time limit, in the absence of a contrary provision in the option contract, the offeree . . . remains free to revoke the acceptance until it arrives. . . .

§64.   Acceptance by Telephone or Teletype

Acceptance given by telephone or other medium of substantially instantaneous two-way communication is governed by the principles applicable to acceptances where the parties are in the presence of each other.

§65.   Reasonableness of Medium of Acceptance

Unless circumstances known to the offeree indicate otherwise, a medium of acceptance is reasonable if it is the one used by the offeror or one customary in similar transactions at the time and place the offer is received.

Comment

   a. Significance of use of reasonable medium. Under §30 an offer invites acceptance by any reasonable medium unless there is contrary indication; under §63 an acceptance so invited is ordinarily effective upon dispatch. If an unreasonable medium of acceptance is used, on the other hand, the governing rule is that stated in §67. . . .

§66. Acceptance Must Be Properly Dispatched

An acceptance sent by mail or otherwise from a distance is not operative when dispatched, unless it is properly addressed and such other precautions taken as are ordinarily observed to insure safe transmission of similar messages.

Comment

a. Rationale. Under §50, acceptance by promise is not effective until the offeree has completed every act essential to the making of the promise. Reasonable diligence to notify is essential under §56, except as stated in §69. It follows that, notwithstanding §63, acceptance by mail or telegram is not effective on dispatch unless the acceptor exercises reasonable diligence to notify the offeror. . . .

b. Proper address. The offeree may fulfill the requirement that an acceptance be properly addressed by using a return address indicated in the offer, whether in a letterhead or otherwise. But any other place held out by the offeror as the place for receipt of such communications will do as well. . . . If the acceptance is duly received despite misdirection, the rule of §67 may apply. . . .

§67. Effect of Receipt of Acceptance Improperly Dispatched

Where an acceptance is seasonably dispatched but the offeree uses means of transmission not invited by the offer or fails to exercise reasonable diligence to insure safe transmission, it is treated as operative upon dispatch if received within the time in which a properly dispatched acceptance would normally have arrived.

§68. What Constitutes Receipt of Revocation, Rejection, or Acceptance

A written revocation, rejection, or acceptance is received when the writing comes into the possession of the person addressed, or of some person authorized by him to receive it for him, or when it is deposited in some place which he has authorized as the place for this or similar communications to be deposited for him.

§69. Acceptance by Silence or Exercise of Dominion

(1) Where an offeree fails to reply to an offer, his silence and inaction operate as an acceptance in the following cases only:

(a) Where an offeree takes the benefit of offered services with reasonable opportunity to reject them and reason to know that they were offered with the expectation of compensation.

(b) Where the offeror has stated or given the offeree reason to understand that assent may be manifested by silence or inaction, and the offeree in remaining silent and inactive intends to accept the offer.

(c) Where because of previous dealings or otherwise, it is reasonable that the offeree should notify the offeror if he does not intend to accept.

(2) An offeree who does any act inconsistent with the offeror's ownership of offered property is bound in accordance with the offered terms unless they are manifestly unreasonable. But if the act is wrongful as against the offeror it is an acceptance only if ratified by him.

Comment

. . . .

c. Intent to accept. The mere fact that an offeror states that silence will constitute acceptance does not deprive the offeree of his privilege to remain silent without accepting. But the offeree is entitled to rely on such a statement if he chooses. The case for acceptance is strongest when the reliance is definite and substantial or when the intent to accept is objectively manifested though not communicated to the offeror. Compare §§54, 87(2). Even though the intent to accept is manifested only by silent inaction, however, the offeror who has invited such an acceptance cannot complain of the resulting uncertainty in his position. . . .

d. Prior conduct of the offeree. Explicit statement by the offeree, usage of trade, or a course of dealing between the parties may give the offeror reason to understand that silence will constitute acceptance. In such a situation the offer may tacitly incorporate that understanding, and if the offeree intends to accept the case then falls within Subsection (1)(b). Under Subsection (1)(c) the offeree's silence is acceptance, regardless of his actual intent, unless both parties understand that no acceptance is intended. See §20. . . .

§70. Effect of Receipt by Offeror of a Late or Otherwise Defective Acceptance

A late or otherwise defective acceptance may be effective as an offer to the original offeror, but his silence operates as an acceptance in such a case only as stated in §69.

CHAPTER 4. FORMATION OF CONTRACTS — CONSIDERATION

Topic 1. The Requirement of Consideration

§71. Requirement of Exchange; Types of Exchange

(1) To constitute consideration, a performance or a return promise must be bargained for.

(2) A performance or return promise is bargained for if it is sought by the promisor in exchange for his promise and is given by the promisee in exchange for that promise.

(3) The performance may consist of
    (a) an act other than a promise, or
    (b) a forbearance, or
    (c) the creation, modification, or destruction of a legal relation.
(4) The performance or return promise may be given to the promisor or to some other person. It may be given by the promisee or by some other person.

Comment

. . . .

b. *"Bargained for."* In the typical bargain, the consideration and the promise bear a reciprocal relation of motive or inducement: the consideration induces the making of the promise and the promise induces the furnishing of the consideration. Here, as in the matter of mutual assent, the law is concerned with the external manifestation rather than the undisclosed mental state: it is enough that one party manifests an intention to induce the other's response and to be induced by it and that the other responds in accordance with the inducement. . . . But it is not enough that the promise induces the conduct of the promisee or that the conduct of the promisee induces the making of the promise; both elements must be present, or there is no bargain. Moreover, a mere pretense of bargain does not suffice, as where there is a false recital of consideration or where the purported consideration is merely nominal. . . .

e. *Consideration moving from or to a third person.* It matters not from whom the consideration moves or to whom it goes. If it is bargained for and given in exchange for the promise, the promise is not gratuitous. . . .

§72. Exchange of Promise for Performance

Except as stated in §§73 and 74, any performance which is bargained for is consideration.

Comment

. . . .

b. *Substantive bases for enforcement; the half-completed exchange.* Bargains are widely believed to be beneficial to the community in the provision of opportunities for freedom of individual action and exercise of judgment and as a means by which productive energy and product are apportioned in the economy. The enforcement of bargains rests in part on the common belief that enforcement enhances that utility. Where one party has performed, there are additional grounds for enforcement. Where, for example, one party has received goods from the other and has broken his promise to pay for them, enforcement of the promise not only encourages the making of socially useful bargains; it also reimburses the seller for a loss incurred in reliance on the promise and prevents the unjust enrichment of the buyer at the seller's expense. Each of these three grounds of enforcement, bargain, reliance and unjust enrichment, has independent force, but the bargain element alone satisfies the requirement of consideration except in the cases covered by §§73, 74, 76 and 77. Cases of promises binding by virtue of reliance or unjust enrichment are dealt with in §§82-94.

c. Formality. Consideration furnishes a substantive rather than a formal basis for the enforcement of a promise. Many bargains, particularly when fully performed on one side, involve acts in the course of performance which satisfy some or all of the functions of form and thus may be thought of as natural formalities. Four principal functions have been identified which legal formalities in general may serve: the *evidentiary* function, to provide evidence of the existence and terms of the contract; the *cautionary* function, to guard the promisor against ill-considered action; the *deterrent* function, to discourage transactions of doubtful utility; and the *channeling* or signalizing function, to distinguish a particular type of transaction from other types and from tentative or exploratory expressions of intention in the way that coinage distinguishes money from other metal. But formality is not essential to consideration; nor does formality supply consideration where the element of exchange is absent. Rules under which formality makes binding a promise not supported by consideration are stated in §§82-94. . . .

§73. Performance of Legal Duty

Performance of a legal duty owed to a promisor which is neither doubtful nor the subject of honest dispute is not consideration; but a similar performance is consideration if it differs from what was required by the duty in a way which reflects more than a pretense of bargain.

Comment

a. Rationale. A claim that the performance of a legal duty furnished consideration for a promise often raises a suspicion that the transaction was gratuitous or mistaken or unconscionable. . . . [T]he rule of this Section renders unnecessary any inquiry into the existence of such an invalidating cause, and denies enforcement to some promises which would otherwise be valid. Because of the likelihood that the promise was obtained by an express or implied threat to withhold performance of a legal duty, the promise does not have the presumptive social utility normally found in a bargain. Enforcement must therefore rest on some substantive or formal basis other than the mere fact of bargain. . . .

b. Public duties; torts and crimes. A legal duty may be owed to the promisor as a member of the public, as when the promisee is a public official. . . . A bargain by a public official to obtain private advantage for performing his duty is therefore unenforceable as against public policy. . . . And under this Section performance of the duty is not consideration for a promise.

. . . . The performance of legal duty is not consideration for a promise . . . if the duty is owed to the promisor. If the legal duty is not owed to the promisor, there is consideration. . . .

.... The requirement of consideration is satisfied if the duty is doubtful or is the subject of honest dispute, or if the consideration includes a performance in addition to or materially different from the performance of the duty. . . .

d. Contractual duty to third person. [I] n cases involving a contractual duty owed to a person other than the promisor . . . , there is less likelihood of economic coercion or other unfair pressure than there is if the duty is owed to the promisee. In some cases consideration can be found in the fact that the promisee gives up his right to propose to the third person the rescission or modification of the contractual duty. But the tendency of the law has been simply to hold that performance of contractual duty can be consideration if the duty is not owed to the promisor. . . .

e. Voidable and unenforceable duties. . . . One who may at will avoid a legal relation or refrain from any performance without legal consequences, or against whom all remedies appropriate to the enforcement of his duty have become barred, is not under a duty within the meaning of the Section. . . .

f. Doubtful, disputed and unliquidated duties. Such duties are not within this Section. They are the subject of §74.

§74. Settlement of Claims

(1) Forbearance to assert or the surrender of a claim or defense which proves to be invalid is not consideration unless

(a) the claim or defense is in fact doubtful because of uncertainty as to the facts or the law, or

(b) the forbearing or surrendering party believes that the claim or defense may be fairly determined to be valid.

(2) The execution of a written instrument surrendering a claim or defense by one who is under no duty to execute it is consideration if the execution of the written instrument is bargained for even though he is not asserting the claim or defense and believes that no valid claim or defense exists.

Comment

a. Relation to legal-duty rule. Subsection (1) elaborates a limitation on the scope of the legal-duty rule stated in §73. That limitation is based on the traditional policy of favoring compromises of disputed claims in order to reduce the volume of litigation. . . .

b. Requirement of good faith. The policy favoring compromise of disputed claims is clearest, perhaps, where a claim is surrendered at a time when it is uncertain whether it is valid or not. Even though the invalidity later becomes clear, the bargain is to be judged as it appeared to the parties at the time; if the claim was then doubtful, no inquiry is necessary as to their good faith. Even though the invalidity should have been clear at the time, the settlement of an honest dispute is upheld. But a mere assertion or denial of liability does not make a claim doubtful, and the fact that invalidity is obvious may indicate that it was known. In such cases Subsection (1)(b) requires a showing of good faith.

c. Unliquidated obligations. An undisputed obligation may be unliquidated, that is, uncertain or disputed in amount. The settlement of such a claim is governed by the same principles as settlement of a claim the existence of which is doubtful or disputed. The payment of any definite sum of money on account of a single claim which is entirely unliquidated is consideration for a return promise. An admission by the obligor that a minimum amount is due does not liquidate the claim even partially unless he is contractually bound to the admission. But payment of less than is admittedly due may in some circumstances tend to show that a partial defense or offset was not asserted in good faith.

Payment of an obligation which is liquidated and undisputed is not consideration for a promise to surrender an unliquidated claim which is wholly distinct. See §73. Whether in a particular case there is a single unliquidated claim or a combination of separate claims, some liquidated and some not, depends on the circumstances and the agreements of the parties. If there are no circumstances of unfair pressure or economic coercion and a disputed item is closely related to an undisputed item, the two are treated as making up a single unliquidated claim; and payment of the amount admittedly due can be consideration for a promise to surrender the entire claim. . . .

e. Execution of release or quit-claim deed. Subsection (2) provides for the situation where the party who would be subject to a claim or defense, if one existed, wants assurance of its non-existence. Such assurance may be useful, for example, to enable him to obtain credit or to sell property. Although surrender of a non-existent claim by one who knows he has no claim is not consideration for a promise, the execution of an instrument of surrender may be consideration if there is no improper pressure or deception. See §79. But there is no consideration if the surrendering party is under a duty to execute the instrument. . . .

§75. Exchange of Promise for Promise

Except as stated in §§76 and 77, a promise which is bargained for is consideration if, but only if, the promised performance would be consideration.

§76. Conditional Promise

(1) A conditional promise is not consideration if the promisor knows at the time of making the promise that the condition cannot occur.

(2) A promise conditional on a performance by the promisor is a promise of alternative performances within §77 unless occurrence of the condition is also promised.

Comment

. . . .

d. Conditions within the promisor's control. Words of promise do not constitute a promise if they make performance entirely optional with the purported promisor. See Comment *e* to §2. Such words, often referred to as forming an illusory promise, do not constitute consideration for a return promise. See §77.

But a promise may be conditional on an event within the control of the promisor. Such a promise may be consideration if he has also promised that the condition will occur. Similarly, even though he does not promise occurrence of the condition, there may be consideration if forbearance from causing the condition to occur would itself have been consideration if it alone had been bargained for. In such a case, there is in effect a promise in the alternative, and the rules stated in §77 apply. . . .

§77. Illusory and Alternative Promises

A promise or apparent promise is not consideration if by its terms the promisor or purported promisor reserves a choice of alternative performances unless
    (a) each of the alternative performances would have been consideration if it alone had been bargained for; or
    (b) one of the alternative performances would have been consideration and there is or appears to the parties to be a substantial possibility that before the promisor exercises his choice events may eliminate the alternatives which would not have been consideration.

Comment

a. Illusory promises. Words of promise which by their terms make performance entirely optional with the "promisor" do not constitute a promise. See Comment *e* to §2; compare §76. In such cases there might theoretically be a bargain to pay for the utterance of the words, but in practice it is performance which is bargained for. Where the apparent assurance of performance is illusory, it is not consideration for a return promise. . . .

§78. Voidable and Unenforceable Promises

The fact that a rule of law renders a promise voidable or unenforceable does not prevent it from being consideration.

Comment

a. Rationale. The value of a promise depends on its terms and on the probability that it will be performed. The value is not necessarily affected adversely by the fact that no legal remedy will be available in the event of breach; the probability of performance may be greater for a voidable or unenforceable promise, or even for a promise which is not binding or is against public policy, than for the judgment or decree of a court. In general the law of contracts leaves to the parties the valuation of a promise in the formation of a bargain. See §79. The fact that no legal remedy is available for breach of a promise does not prevent it from being a part of a bargain or remove the bargain from the scope of the general principle that bargains are enforceable. See §§17, 71. . . .

b. *Voidable promises.* A contract may be voidable by one party by reason of his incapacity or mistake, or by reason of the fraud, breach or other fault of the other party. See §7. In many such cases a reservation of a similar power by the terms of the agreement would mean that he had made no promise or that his promise was not consideration for a return promise. See §77. But where the power of avoidance is given by the law to protect one party from actual or possible imposition, he often regards himself as bound in conscience if not in law. He may in some circumstance lose the power by ratification without consideration. See §85. Until the power is exercised, it does not prevent enforcement of a return promise. . . .

§79. Adequacy of Consideration; Mutuality of Obligation

If the requirement of consideration is met, there is no additional requirement of
    (a) a gain, advantage, or benefit to the promisor or a loss, disadvantage, or detriment to the promisee; or
    (b) equivalence in the values exchanged; or
    (c) "mutuality of obligation."

Comment

. . . .

c. *Exchange of unequal values.* To the extent that the apportionment of productive energy and product in the economy are left to private action, the parties to transactions are free to fix their own valuations. The resolution of disputes often requires a determination of value in the more general sense of market value, and such values are commonly fixed as an approximation based on a multitude of private valuations. But in many situations there is no reliable external standard of value, or the general standard is inappropriate to the precise circumstances of the parties. Valuation is left to private action in part because the parties are thought to be better able than others to evaluate the circumstances of particular transactions. . . .

d. *Pretended exchange.* Disparity in value, with or without other circumstances, sometimes indicates that the purported consideration was not in fact bargained for but was a mere formality or pretense. Such a sham or "nominal" consideration does not satisfy the requirement of §71. . . .

e. *Effects of gross inadequacy.* Although the requirement of consideration may be met despite a great difference in the values exchanged, gross inadequacy of consideration may be relevant in the application of other rules. . . .

§80. Multiple Exchanges

(1) There is consideration for a set of promises if what is bargained for and given in exchange would have been consideration for each promise in the set if exchanged for that promise alone.

(2) The fact that part of what is bargained for would not have been consideration if that part alone had been bargained for does not prevent the whole from being consideration.

§81.   Consideration as Motive or Inducing Cause

(1) The fact that what is bargained for does not of itself induce the making of a promise does not prevent it from being consideration for the promise.

(2) The fact that a promise does not of itself induce a performance or return promise does not prevent the performance or return promise from being consideration for the promise.

Topic 2.   Contracts Without Consideration

§82.   Promise to Pay Indebtedness; Effect on the Statute of Limitations

(1) A promise to pay all or part of an antecedent contractual or quasi-contractual indebtedness owed by the promisor is binding if the indebtedness is still enforceable or would be except for the effect of a statute of limitations.

(2) The following facts operate as such a promise unless other facts indicate a different intention:

(a) A voluntary acknowledgement to the obligee, admitting the present existence of the antecedent indebtedness; or

(b) A voluntary transfer of money, a negotiable instrument, or other thing by the obligor to the obligee, made as interest on or part payment of or collateral security for the antecedent indebtedness; or

(c) A statement to the obligee that the statute of limitations will not be pleaded as a defense.

§83.   Promise to Pay Indebtedness Discharged in Bankruptcy

An express promise to pay all or part of an indebtedness of the promisor, discharged or dischargeable in bankruptcy proceedings begun before the promise is made, is binding.

§84.   Promise to Perform a Duty in Spite of Non-occurrence of a Condition

(1) Except as stated in Subsection (2), a promise to perform all or part of a conditional duty under an antecedent contract in spite of the non-occurrence of the condition is binding, whether the promise is made before or after the time for the condition to occur, unless

(a) occurrence of the condition was a material part of the agreed exchange for the performance of the duty and the promisee was under no duty that it occur; or

(b) uncertainty of the occurrence of the condition was an element of the risk assumed by the promisor.

(2) If such a promise is made before the time for the occurrence of the condition has expired and the condition is within the control of the promisee or a beneficiary, the promisor can make his duty again subject to the condition by notifying the promisee or beneficiary of his intention to do so if

(a) the notification is received while there is still a reasonable time to cause the condition to occur under the antecedent terms or an extension given by the promisor; and

(b) reinstatement of the requirement of the condition is not unjust because of a material change of position by the promisee or beneficiary; and

(c) the promise is not binding apart from the rule stated in Subsection (1).

Comment

. . . .

b. *"Waiver" and "estoppel".* . . . "Waiver" is often inexactly defined as "the voluntary relinquishment of a known right." When the waiver is reinforced by reliance, enforcement is often said to rest on "estoppel." Compare §§89, 90. . . . The common definition of waiver may lead to the incorrect inference that the promisor must know his legal rights and must intend the legal effect of the promise. But . . . it is sufficient if he has reason to know the essential facts. . . .

c. *Conditions material to the exchange or risk.* A promise is often conditional on the receipt of some performance regarded as the equivalent of the performance promised, as in the case of an option contract to sell a horse if the promisee pays $500 for him. A promise may also be conditional on a fortuitous event, and the risk or burden assumed by the promisor may depend on the probability that the condition will occur, as in a promise to insure a house against fire. In both types of cases, where a promise to disregard the non-occurrence of the condition materially affects the value received by the promisor or the burden or risk assumed by him, the promise is not binding under Subsection (1). Such a promise may be binding by virtue of reliance or for some other reason. See §§89, 90. See also §246. But a waiver of the price of a horse or of the fire required by an insurance policy is not within this Section. . . .

d. *Conditions which may be waived.* The rule of Subsection (1) applies primarily to conditions which may be thought of as procedural or technical, or to instances in which the non-occurrence of condition is comparatively minor. Examples are conditions which merely relate to the time or manner of the return performance or provide for the giving of notice or the supplying of proofs. Insurance policies ordinarily contain conditions of notice and proof of loss and of time for suit; and guarantors, indorsers and other sureties may be discharged by an agreement varying the duty of the principal debtor, by failure of diligence in presentment or prosecution, or by failure to give a required notice. In such cases, even though a promise to disregard the non-occurrence of the condition subjects the promisor to a new duty, the new duty is not regarded as significantly different from the old and the promise is binding without consideration, reliance, or formality. . . .

Illustrations

. . . .

3. A employs B to build a house, promising to pay therefor $10,000 on the production of a certificate from A's architect, C, stating that the work has been satisfactorily completed. B builds the house but the work is defective in certain trivial particulars. C refuses to give B a certificate. A says to B, "My architect rightfully refuses to give you a certificate but the defects are not serious; I will pay you the full price which I promised." A is bound to do so, and has no power to restore the requirement of the condition.

4. A, an insurance company, insures B's house for $5000 against loss by fire. The insurance policy provides that it shall be payable only if B gives written notification of any loss within thirty days after its occurrence. An insured loss occurs and B gives only oral notification thereof within thirty days. A tells him, either before or after the lapse of thirty days from the loss, that this notification is sufficient. A cannot thereafter rely upon B's failure to give written notification as an excuse for failure to pay for the loss. . . .

f. Reinstatement after waiver. If the requirement of a condition has been eliminated from a contract by an agreement supported by consideration it cannot be reinstated by unilateral action of the promisor. Nor can it be reinstated if a new unconditional duty has been created by a promise made after the original duty was discharged by non-occurrence of the condition, or if reinstatement would be unjust in view of a change of position by the other party. Compare Uniform Commercial Code §2-209(5); Restatement of Restitution §142. But where the requirement of a condition is waived in advance, the promisor may reinstate the requirement by giving notice to the other party before the latter has materially changed his position. Whether delay alone makes reinstatement unjust depends upon the circumstances: in some cases a reasonable extension of time sufficiently protects the other party; in others the extension may be required to be both definite and reasonable; in some no extension can put him in as good a position to perform as before the waiver. . . .

§85. Promise to Perform a Voidable Duty

Except as stated in §93, a promise to perform all or part of an antecedent contract of the promisor, previously voidable by him, but not avoided prior to the making of the promise, is binding.

§86. Promise for Benefit Received

(1) A promise made in recognition of a benefit previously received by the promisor from the promisee is binding to the extent necessary to prevent injustice.

(2) A promise is not binding under Subsection (1)

(a) if the promisee conferred the benefit as a gift or for other reasons the promisor has not been unjustly enriched; or

(b) to the extent that its value is disproportionate to the benefit.

Comment

a. "Past consideration"; "moral obligation." Enforcement of promises to pay for benefit received has sometimes been said to rest on "past consideration" or on the "moral obligation" of the promisor, and there are statutes in such terms in a few states. Those terms are not used here: "past consideration" is inconsistent with the meaning of consideration stated in §71, and there seems to be no consensus as to what constitutes a "moral obligation." The mere fact of promise has been thought to create a moral obligation, but it is clear that not all promises are enforced. Nor are moral obligations based solely on gratitude or sentiment sufficient of themselves to support a subsequent promise.

Illustrations

1. A gives emergency care to B's adult son while the son is sick and without funds far from home. B subsequently promises to reimburse A for his expenses. The promise is not binding under this Section.

2. A lends money to B, who later dies. B's widow promises to pay the debt. The promise is not binding under this Section. . . .

b. Rationale. Although in general a person who has been unjustly enriched at the expense of another is required to make restitution, restitution is denied in many cases in order to protect persons who have had benefits thrust upon them. . . . In other cases restitution is denied by virtue of rules designed to guard against false claims, stale claims, claims already litigated, and the like. In many such cases a subsequent promise to make restitution removes the reason for the denial of relief, and the policy against unjust enrichment then prevails. . . .

d. Emergency services and necessaries. The law of restitution in the absence of promise severely limits recovery for necessaries furnished to a person under disability and for emergency services. . . . A subsequent promise in such a case may remove doubt as to the reality of the benefit and as to its value, and may negate any danger of imposition or false claim. . . . [A]n intention to make, a gift must be shown to defeat restitution . . . .

f. Benefit conferred pursuant to contract. By virtue of the policy of enforcing bargains, the enrichment of one party as a result of an unequal exchange is not regarded as unjust, and this Section has no application to a promise to pay or perform more or to accept less than is called for by a pre-existing bargain between the same parties. Compare §§79, 89. Similarly, if a third person receives a benefit as a result of the performance of a bargain, this Section does not make binding the subsequent promise of the third person to pay extra compensation to the performing party. But a promise to pay in substitution for the return performance called for by the bargain may be binding under this Section. . . .

i. Partial enforcement. . . . [W]here a benefit received is a liquidated sum of money, a promise is not enforceable under this Section beyond the amount of the benefit. Where the value of the benefit is uncertain, a promise to pay the value is binding and a promise to pay a liquidated sum may serve to fix the amount due if in all the circumstances it is not disproportionate to the benefit. . . . A promise which is excessive may sometimes be enforced to the extent of the value of the benefit, and the remedy may be thought of as quasi-contractual rather than contractual. . . .

Illustrations

12. A, a married woman of sixty, has rendered household services without compensation over a period of years for B, a man of eighty living alone and having no close relatives. B has a net worth of three million dollars and has often assured A that she will be well paid for her services, whose reasonable value is not in excess of $6,000. B executes and delivers to A a written promise to pay A $25,000 "to be taken from my estate." The promise is binding.

13. The facts being otherwise as stated in Illustration 12, B's promise is made orally and is to leave A his entire estate. A cannot recover more than the reasonable value of her services.

§87. Option Contract

(1) An offer is binding as an option contract if it

(a) is in writing and signed by the offeror, recites a purported consideration for the making of the offer, and proposes an exchange on fair terms within a reasonable time; or

(b) is made irrevocable by statute.

(2) An offer which the offeror should reasonably expect to induce action or forbearance of a substantial character on the part of the offeree before acceptance and which does induce such action or forbearance is binding as an option contract to the extent necessary to avoid injustice.

Comment

a. Consideration and form. The traditional common-law devices for making a firm offer or option contract are the giving of consideration and the affixing of a seal. See §§25, 95. But the firm offer serves a useful purpose even though no preliminary bargain is made: it is often a necessary step in the making of the main bargain proposed, and it partakes of the natural formalities inherent in business transactions. The erosion of the formality of the seal has made it less and less satisfactory as a universal formality. As literacy has spread, the personal signature has become the natural formality and the seal has become more and more anachronistic. The rules stated in this section reflect the judicial and legislative response to this situation.

b. Nominal consideration. . . . [A] comparatively small payment may furnish consideration for the irrevocability of an offer proposing a transaction involving much larger sums. . . .

[S]uch a nominal consideration is regularly held sufficient to support a short-time option proposing an exchange on fair terms. The fact that the option is an appropriate preliminary step in the conclusion of a socially useful transaction provides a sufficient substantive basis for enforcement, and a signed writing taking a form appropriate to a bargain satisfies the desiderata of form. . . .

e. Reliance. Subsection (2) states the application of §90 to reliance on an unaccepted offer, with qualifications which would not be appropriate in some other types of cases covered by §90. It is important chiefly in cases of reliance that is not part performance. If the beginning of performance is a reasonable mode of acceptance, it makes the offer fully enforceable under §45 or §62; if not, the offeror commonly has no reason to expect part performance before acceptance. But circumstances may be such that the offeree must undergo substantial expense, or undertake substantial commitments, or forego alternatives, in order to put himself in a position to accept by either promise or performance. The offer may be made expressly irrevocable in contemplation of reliance by the offeree. If reliance follows in such cases, justice may require a remedy. Compare Restatement, Second, Torts §325; Restatement, Second, Agency §378. But the reliance must be substantial as well as foreseeable.

Full-scale enforcement of the offered contract is not necessarily appropriate in such cases. Restitution of benefits conferred may be enough, or partial or full reimbursement of losses may be proper. Various factors may influence the remedy: the formality of the offer, its commercial or social context, the extent to which the offeree's reliance was understood to be at his own risk, the relative competence and the bargaining position of the parties, the degree of fault on the part of the offeror, the ease and certainty of proof of particular items of damage and the likelihood that unprovable damages have been suffered. . . .

§88. Guaranty

A promise to be surety for the performance of a contractual obligation, made to the obligee, is binding if

(a) the promise is in writing and signed by the promisor and recites a purported consideration; or

(b) the promise is made binding by statute; or

(c) the promisor should reasonably expect the promise to induce action or forbearance of a substantial character on the part of the promisee or a third person, and the promise does induce such action or forbearance.

§89. Modification of Executory Contract

A promise modifying a duty under a contract not fully performed on either side is binding

(a) if the modification is fair and equitable in view of circumstances not anticipated by the parties when the contract was made; or

(b) to the extent provided by statute; or

(c) to the extent that justice requires enforcement in view of material change of position in reliance on the promise.

Comment

a. Rationale. This Section relates primarily to adjustments in on-going transactions. Like offers and guaranties, such adjustments are ancillary to exchanges and have some of the same presumptive utility. See §§72, 87, 88. Indeed, paragraph (a) deals with bargains which are without consideration only because of the rule that performance of a legal duty to the promisor is not consideration. See §73. This Section is also related to §84 on waiver of conditions: it may apply to cases in which §84 is inapplicable because a condition is material to the exchange or risk. As in cases governed by §84, relation to a bargain tends to satisfy the cautionary and channeling functions of legal formalities. See Comment *c* to §72. The Statute of Frauds may prevent enforcement in the absence of reliance. See §§149-50. Otherwise formal requirements are at a minimum.

b. Performance of legal duty. The rule of §73 finds its modern justification in cases of promises made by mistake or induced by unfair pressure. Its application to cases where those elements are absent has been much criticized and is avoided if paragraph (a) of this Section is applicable. The limitation to a modification which is "fair and equitable" goes beyond absence of coercion and requires an objectively demonstrable reason for seeking a modification. Compare Uniform Commercial Code §2-209 Comment. The reason for modification must rest in circumstances not "anticipated" as part of the context in which the contract was made, but a frustrating event may be unanticipated for this purpose if it was not adequately covered, even though it was foreseen as a remote possibility. When such a reason is present, the relative financial strength of the parties, the formality with which the modification is made, the extent to which it is performed or relied on and other circumstances may be relevant to show or negate imposition or unfair surprise.

The same result called for by paragraph (a) is sometimes reached on the ground that the original contract was "rescinded" by mutual agreement and that new promises were then made which furnished consideration for each other. That theory is rejected here because it is fictitious when the "rescission" and new agreement are simultaneous, and because if logically carried out it might uphold unfair and inequitable modifications. . . .

d. Reliance. Paragraph (c) states the application of §90 to modification of an executory contract in language adapted from Uniform Commercial Code §2-209. Even though the promise is not binding when made, it may become binding in whole or in part by reason of action or forbearance by the promisee or third persons in reliance on it. In some cases the result can be viewed as based either on estoppel to contradict a representation of fact or on reliance on a promise. Ordinarily reliance by the promisee is reasonably foreseeable and makes the modification binding with respect to performance by the promisee under it and any return performance owed by the promisor. But as under §84 the original terms can be reinstated for the future by reasonable notification received by the promisee unless reinstatement would be unjust in view of a change of position on his part. Compare Uniform Commercial Code §2-209(5). . . .

§90. Promise Reasonably Inducing Action or Forbearance

(1) A promise which the promisor should reasonably expect to induce action or forbearance on the part of the promisee or a third person and which does induce such action or forbearance is binding if injustice can be avoided only by enforcement of the promise. The remedy granted for breach may be limited as justice requires.

(2) A charitable subscription or a marriage settlement is binding under Subsection (1) without proof that the promise induced action or forbearance.

Comment

a. Relation to other rules. . . . It is fairly arguable that the enforcement of informal contracts in the action of assumpsit rested historically on justifiable reliance on a promise. Certainly reliance is one of the main bases for enforcement of the half-completed exchange, and the probability of reliance lends support to the enforcement of the executory exchange. See Comments to §§72, 75. This Section thus states a basic principle which often renders inquiry unnecessary as to the precise scope of the policy of enforcing bargains. Sections 87-89 state particular applications of the same principle to promises ancillary to bargains, and it also applies in a wide variety of non-commercial situations. See, e.g., §94. . . .

b. Character of reliance protected. The principle of this Section is flexible. The promisor is affected only by reliance which he does or should foresee, and enforcement must be necessary to avoid injustice. Satisfaction of the latter requirement may depend on the reasonableness of the promisee's reliance, on its definite and substantial character in relation to the remedy sought, on the formality with which the promise is made, on the extent to which the evidentiary, cautionary, deterrent and channeling functions of form are met by the commercial setting or otherwise, and on the extent to which such other policies as the enforcement of bargains and the prevention of unjust enrichment are relevant. Compare Comment to §72. . . .

d. Partial enforcement. A promise binding under this section is a contract, and full-scale enforcement by normal remedies is often appropriate. But the same factors which bear on whether any relief should be granted also bear on the character and extent of the remedy. In particular, relief may sometimes be limited to restitution or to damages or specific relief measured by the extent of the promisee's reliance rather than by the terms of the promise. . . .

§91. Effect of Promises Enumerated in §§82-90 When Conditional

If a promise within the terms of §§82-90 is in terms conditional or performable at a future time the promisor is bound thereby, but performance becomes due only upon the occurrence of the condition or upon the arrival of the specified time.

§92. To Whom Promises Enumerated in §§82-85 Must Be Made

The new promise referred to in §§82-85 is not binding unless it is made to a person who is then an obligee of the antecedent duty.

§93. Promises Enumerated in §§82-85 Made in Ignorance of Facts

A promise within the terms of §§82-85 is not binding unless the promisor knew or had reason to know the essential facts of the previous transaction to which the promise relates, but his knowledge of the legal effect of the facts is immaterial.

§94. Stipulations

A promise or agreement with reference to a pending judicial proceeding, made by a party to the proceeding or his attorney, is binding without consideration. By statute or rule of court such an agreement is generally binding only
    (a) if it is in writing and signed by the party or attorney, or
    (b) if it is made or admitted in the presence of the court, or
    (c) to the extent that justice requires enforcement in view of material change of position in reliance on the promise or agreement.

Topic 3. Contracts Under Seal; Writing as a Statutory Substitute for the Seal

§95. Requirements for Sealed Contract or Written Contract or Instrument

(1) In the absence of statute a promise is binding without consideration if
    (a) it is in writing and sealed; and
    (b) the document containing the promise is delivered; and
    (c) the promisor and promisee are named in the document or so described as to be capable of identification when it is delivered.

(2) When a statute provides in effect that a written contract or instrument is binding without consideration or that lack of consideration is an affirmative defense to an action on a written contract or instrument, in order to be subject to the statute a promise must either
    (a) be expressed in a document signed or otherwise assented to by the promisor and delivered; or
    (b) be expressed in a writing or writings to which both promisor and promisee manifest assent.

§96. What Constitutes a Seal

(1) A seal is a manifestation in tangible and conventional form of an intention that a document be sealed.

(2) A seal may take the form of a piece of wax, a wafer or other substance affixed to the document or of an impression made on the document.

(3) By statute or decision in most States in which the seal retains significance a seal may take the form of a written or printed seal, word, scrawl or other sign.

§97. When a Promise Is Sealed

A written promise is sealed if the promisor affixes or impresses a seal on the document or adopts a seal already thereon.

§98. Adoption of a Seal by Delivery

Unless extrinsic circumstances manifest a contrary intention, the delivery of a written promise by the promisor amounts to the adoption of any seal then on the document which has apparent reference to his signature or to the signature of another party to the document.

§99. Adoption of the Same Seal by Several Parties

Any number of parties to the same instrument may adopt one seal.

§100. Recital of Sealing or Delivery

A recital of the sealing or of the delivery of a written promise is not essential to its validity as a contract under seal and is not conclusive of the fact of sealing or delivery unless a statute makes a recital of sealing the equivalent of a seal.

§101. Delivery

A written promise, sealed or unsealed, may be delivered by the promisor in escrow, conditionally to the promisee, or unconditionally.

§102. Unconditional Delivery

A written promise is delivered unconditionally when the promisor puts it out of his possession and manifests an intention that it is to take effect at once according to its terms.

§103. Delivery in Escrow; Conditional Delivery to the Promisee

(1) A written promise is delivered in escrow by the promisor when he puts it into the possession of a person other than the promisee without reserving a power

of revocation and manifests an intention that the document is to take effect according to its terms upon the occurrence of a stated condition but not otherwise.

(2) A written promise is delivered conditionally to the promisee when the promisor puts it into the possession of the promisee without reserving a power of revocation and manifests an intention that the document is to take effect according to its terms upon the occurrence of a stated condition but not otherwise.

(3) Delivery of a written promise in escrow or its conditional delivery to the promisee has the same effect as unconditional delivery would have if the requirement of the condition were expressed in the writing.

(4) In the absence of a statute modifying the significance of a seal, delivery of a sealed promise in escrow or its conditional delivery to the promisee is irrevocable for the time specified by the promisor for the occurrence of the condition, or, if no time is specified, for a reasonable time.

§104. Acceptance or Disclaimer by the Promisee

(1) Neither acceptance by the promisee nor knowledge by him of the existence of a promise is essential to the formation of a contract by the delivery of a written promise which is binding without consideration.

(2) A promisee who has not manifested assent to a written promise may, within a reasonable time after learning of its existence and terms, render it inoperative by disclaimer.

(3) Acceptance or disclaimer is irrevocable.

§105. Acceptance Where Return Promise Is Contemplated

Where a conveyance or a document containing a promise also purports to contain a return promise by the grantee or promisee, acceptance by the grantee or promisee is essential to create any contractual obligation other than an option contract binding on the grantor or promisor.

§106. What Amounts to Acceptance of Instrument

Acceptance of a conveyance or of a document containing a promise is a manifestation of assent to the terms thereof made, either before or after delivery, in accordance with any requirements imposed by the grantor or promisor. If the acceptance occurs before delivery and is not binding as an option contract, it is revocable until the moment of delivery.

§107. Creation of Unsealed Contract by Acceptance by Promisee

Where a grantee or promisee accepts a sealed document which purports to contain a return promise by him, he makes the return promise. But if he does not sign or seal the document his promise is not under seal, and whether it is binding depends on the rules governing unsealed contracts.

§108. Requirement of Naming or Describing Promisor and Promisee

A promise under seal is not binding without consideration unless both the promisor and the promisee are named in the document or so described as to be capable of identification when it is delivered.

§109. Enforcement of a Sealed Contract by Promisee Who Does Not Sign or Seal It

The promisee of a promise under seal is not precluded from enforcing it as a sealed contract because he has not signed or sealed the document, unless his doing so was a condition of the delivery, whether or not the document contains a promise by him.

CHAPTER 5.   THE STATUTE OF FRAUDS

§110. Classes of Contracts Covered

(1) The following classes of contracts are subject to a statute, commonly called the Statute of Frauds, forbidding enforcement unless there is a written memorandum or an applicable exception:

(a) a contract of an executor or administrator to answer for a duty of his decedent (the executor-administrator provision);

(b) a contract to answer for the duty of another (the suretyship provision);

(c) a contract made upon consideration of marriage (the marriage provision);

(d) a contract for the sale of an interest in land (the land contract provision);

(e) a contract that is not to be performed within one year from the making thereof (the one-year provision).

(2) The following classes of contracts, which were traditionally subject to the Statute of Frauds, are now governed by Statute of Frauds provisions of the Uniform Commercial Code:

(a) a contract for the sale of goods for the price of $500 or more (Uniform Commercial Code §2-201);

(b) a contract for the sale of securities (Uniform Commercial Code §8-319);

(c) a contract for the sale of personal property not otherwise covered, to the extent of enforcement by way of action or defense beyond $5,000 in amount of value of remedy (Uniform Commercial Code §1-206).*

(3) In addition the Uniform Commercial Code requires a writing signed by the debtor for an agreement which creates or provides for a security

---

* [Eds. note] Former UCC §1-206 was deleted when Article 1 was revised in 2001. It has no counterpart in the versions of Article 1 enacted in every state and the District of Columbia since 2001.

interest in personal property or fixtures not in the possession of the secured party.**

(4) Statutes in most states provide that no acknowledgment or promise is sufficient evidence of a new or continuing contract to take a case out of the operation of a statute of limitations unless made in some writing signed by the party to be charged, but that the statute does not alter the effect of any payment of principal or interest.

(5) In many states other classes of contracts are subject to a requirement of a writing.

Topic 1.   The Executor-Administrator Provision

§111.   Contract of Executor or Administrator

A contract of an executor or administrator to answer personally for a duty of his decedent is within the Statute of Frauds if a similar contract to answer for the duty of a living person would be within the Statute as a contract to answer for the duty of another.

Topic 2.   The Suretyship Provision

§112.   Requirement of Suretyship

A contract is not within the Statute of Frauds as a contract to answer for the duty of another unless the promisee is an obligee of the other's duty, the promisor is a surety for the other, and the promisee knows or has reason to know of the suretyship relation.

§113.   Promises of the Same Performance for the Same Consideration

Where promises of the same performance are made by two persons for a consideration which inures to the benefit of only one of them, the promise of the other is within the Statute of Frauds as a contract to answer for the duty of another, whether or not the promise is in terms conditional on default by the one to whose benefit the consideration inures, unless

(a) the other is not a surety for the one to whose benefit the consideration inures; or

(b) the promises are in terms joint and do not create several duties or joint and several duties; or

---

** [Eds. note] See UCC §9-203(b).

(c) the promisee neither knows nor has reason to know that the consideration does not inure to the benefit of both promisors.

§114. Independent Duty of Promisor

A contract to perform or otherwise to satisfy all or part of a duty of a third person to the promisee is not within the Statute of Frauds as a contract to answer for the duty of another if, by the terms of the promise when it is made, performance thereof can involve no more than

(a) the application of funds or property held by the promisor for the purpose, or

(b) performance of any other duty owing, irrespective of his promise, by the promisor to the promisee, or

(c) performance of a duty which is either owing, irrespective of his promise, by the promisor to the third person, or which the promisee reasonably believes to be so owing.

§115. Novation

A contract that is itself accepted in satisfaction of a previously existing duty of a third person to the promisee is not within the Statute of Frauds as a contract to answer for the duty of another.

§116. Main Purpose; Advantage to Surety

A contract that all or part of a duty of a third person to the promisee shall be satisfied is not within the Statute of Frauds as a promise to answer for the duty of another if the consideration for the promise is in fact or apparently desired by the promisor mainly for his own economic advantage, rather than in order to benefit the third person. If, however, the consideration is merely a premium for insurance, the contract is within the Statute.

§117. Promise to Sign a Written Contract of Suretyship

A promise to sign a written contract as a surety for the performance of a duty owed to the promisee or to sign a negotiable instrument for the accommodation of a person other than the promisee is within the Statute of Frauds.

§118. Promise to Indemnify a Surety

A promise to indemnify against liability or loss made to induce the promisee to become a surety is not within the Statute of Frauds as a contract to answer for the duty of another.

§119. Assumption of Duty by Another

A contract not within the Statute of Frauds as a contract to answer for the duty of another when made is not brought within it by a subsequent promise of another person to assume performance of the duty as principal obligor.

§120. Obligations on Negotiable Instruments

(1) An obligation on a negotiable instrument or a guaranty written on the instrument is not within the Statute of Frauds.

(2) A promise to pay a negotiable instrument, made by a party to it who has been or may be discharged by the holder's failure or delay in making presentment or giving notice of dishonor or in making protest, is not within the Statute of Frauds.

§121. Contract of Assignor or Factor

(1) A contract by the assignor of a right that the obligor of the assigned right will perform his duty is not within the Statute of Frauds as a contract to answer for the duty of another.

(2) A contract by an agent with his principal that a purchaser of the principal's goods through the agent will pay their price to the principal is not within the Statute of Frauds as a contract to answer for the duty of another.

§122. Contract to Buy a Right From the Obligee

A contract to purchase a right which the promisee has or may acquire against a third person is not within the Statute of Frauds as a contract to answer for the duty of another.

§123. Contract to Discharge the Promisee's Duty

A contract to discharge a duty owed by the promisee to a third person is not within the Statute of Frauds as a contract to answer for the duty of another.

Topic 3. The Marriage Provision

§124. Contract Made Upon Consideration of Marriage

A promise for which all or part of the consideration is either marriage or a promise to marry is within the Statute of Frauds, except in the case of an agreement which consists only of mutual promises of two persons to marry each other.

Topic 4.   The Land Contract Provision

§125.   Contract to Transfer, Buy, or Pay for an Interest in Land

(1) A promise to transfer to any person any interest in land is within the Statute of Frauds.

(2) A promise to buy any interest in land is within the Statute of Frauds, irrespective of the person to whom the transfer is to be made.

(3) When a transfer of an interest in land has been made, a promise to pay the price, if originally within the Statute of Frauds, ceases to be within it unless the promised price is itself in whole or in part an interest in land.

(4) Statutes in most states except from the land contract and one-year provisions of the Statute of Frauds short-term leases and contracts to lease, usually for a term not longer than one year.

§126.   Contract to Procure Transfer or to Act as Agent

(1) A contract to procure the transfer of an interest in land by a person other than the promisor is within the Statute of Frauds.

(2) A contract to act as agent for another in endeavoring to procure the transfer of any interest in land by someone other than the promisor is not within the Statute of Frauds as a contract for the sale of an interest in land.

§127.   Interest in Land

An interest in land within the meaning of the Statute is any right, privilege, power or immunity, or combination thereof, which is an interest in land under the law of property and is not "goods" within the Uniform Commercial Code.

§128.   Boundary and Partition Agreements

(1) A contract between owners of adjoining tracts of land fixing a dividing boundary is within the Statute of Frauds but if the location of the boundary was honestly disputed the contract becomes enforceable notwithstanding the Statute when the agreed boundary has been marked or has been recognized in the subsequent use of the tracts.

(2) A contract by joint tenants or tenants in common to partition land into separate tracts for each tenant is within the Statute of Frauds but becomes enforceable notwithstanding the Statute as to each tract when possession of it is taken in severalty in accordance with the agreement.

§129.   Action in Reliance; Specific Performance

A contract for the transfer of an interest in land may be specifically enforced notwithstanding failure to comply with the Statute of Frauds if it is established that the party seeking enforcement, in reasonable reliance on the contract and on the continuing assent of the party against whom enforcement is sought, has so changed his position that injustice can be avoided only by specific enforcement.

Topic 5. The One-Year Provision

§130. Contract Not to Be Performed Within a Year

(1) Where any promise in a contract cannot be fully performed within a year from the time the contract is made, all promises in the contract are within the Statute of Frauds until one party to the contract completes his performance.

(2) When one party to a contract has completed his performance, the one-year provision of the Statute does not prevent enforcement of the promises of other parties.

Comment

a. Possibility of performance within one year. . . . [T]he enforceability of a contract under the one-year provision does not turn on the actual course of subsequent events, nor on the expectations of the parties as to the probabilities. Contracts of uncertain duration are simply excluded; the provision covers only those contracts whose performance cannot possibly be completed within a year. . . .

b. Discharge within a year. Any contract may be discharged by a subsequent agreement of the parties, and performance of many contracts may be excused by supervening events or by the exercise of a power to cancel granted by the contract. The possibility that such a discharge or excuse may occur within a year is not a possibility that the contract will be "performed" within a year. This is so even though the excuse is articulated in the agreement. This distinction between performance and excuse for nonperformance is sometimes tenuous; it depends on the terms and the circumstances, particularly on whether the essential purposes of the parties will be attained. Discharge by death of the promisor may be the equivalent of performance in case of a promise to forbear, such as a contract not to compete. . . .

d. Full performance on one side. If either party promises a performance that cannot be completed within a year, the Statute applies to all promises in the contract, including those which can or even must be performed within a year. But unlike other provisions of the Statute, the one-year provision does not apply to a contract which is performed on one side at the time it is made, such as a loan of money, nor to any contract which has been fully performed on one side, whether the performance is completed within a year or not. This rule, by permitting an action for the agreed price, avoids the problem of valuation which would otherwise arise in an action for the value of benefits conferred; but the rule goes further and makes available the usual contract remedies. . . .

Topic 6.   Satisfaction of the Statute by a Memorandum

§131.   General Requisites of a Memorandum

Unless additional requirements are prescribed by the particular statute, a contract within the Statute of Frauds is enforceable if it is evidenced by any writing, signed by or on behalf of the party to be charged, which
(a) reasonably identifies the subject matter of the contract,
(b) is sufficient to indicate that a contract with respect thereto has been made between the parties or offered by the signer to the other party, and
(c) states with reasonable certainty the essential terms of the unperformed promises in the contract.

Comment

. . . .

c. Rationale. The primary purpose of the Statute is evidentiary, to require reliable evidence of the existence and terms of the contract and to prevent enforcement through fraud or perjury of contracts never in fact made. The contents of the writing must be such as to make successful fraud unlikely, but the possibility need not be excluded that some other subject matter or person than those intended will also fall within the words of the writing. Where only an evidentiary purpose is served, the requirement of a memorandum is read in the light of the dispute which arises and the admissions of the party to be charged; there is no need for evidence on points not in dispute. . . .

§132.   Several Writings

The memorandum may consist of several writings if one of the writings is signed and the writings in the circumstances clearly indicate that they relate to the same transaction.

Comment

a. Rationale. . . . A memorandum of a contract need only give assurance that the contract enforced was in fact made and provide evidence of its terms. It may consist of several separate documents, even though not all of them are signed and even though no one of them is itself a sufficient memorandum. At least one must be signed by the party to be charged, and the documents and circumstances must be such that the documents can be read together as "some memorandum or note" of the agreement. Explicit incorporation by reference is unnecessary, but if the connection depends on evidence outside the writings, the evidence of connection must be clear and convincing.

b. Several signed writings. Where two or more documents are signed by the party to be charged, they may be read together even though neither contains any reference to the other. The question whether they constitute a sufficient memorandum is substantially the same as if they had been incorporated in a single document. . . .

c. Reference to unsigned writing: physical connection. Where the signature of the party to be charged is made or adopted with reference to an unsigned writing, the signed and unsigned writings together may constitute a memorandum. It is sufficient that the signed writing refers to the unsigned writing explicitly or by implication, or that the party to be charged physically attaches one document to the other or encloses them in the same envelope. Even if there is no internal reference or physical connection, the documents may be read together if in the circumstances they clearly relate to the same transaction and the party to be charged has acquiesced in the contents of the unsigned writing.

§133. Memorandum Not Made as Such

Except in the case of a writing evidencing a contract upon consideration of marriage, the Statute may be satisfied by a signed writing not made as a memorandum of a contract.

§134. Signature

The signature to a memorandum may be any symbol made or adopted with an intention, actual or apparent, to authenticate the writing as that of the signer.

§135. Who Must Sign

Where a memorandum of a contract within the Statute is signed by fewer than all parties to the contract and the Statute is not otherwise satisfied, the contract is enforceable against the signers but not against the others.

§136. Time of Memorandum

A memorandum sufficient to satisfy the Statute may be made or signed at any time before or after the formation of the contract.

§137. Loss or Destruction of a Memorandum

The loss or destruction of a memorandum does not deprive it of effect under the Statute.

Comment

a. Not a rule of evidence. Although the Statute of Frauds was designed to serve an evidentiary purpose, it is not a rule of evidence. In cases of loss or destruction, the contents of a memorandum may be shown by an unsigned copy or by oral evidence. . . .

Topic 7. Consequences of Non-Compliance

§138. Unenforceability

Where a contract within the Statute of Frauds is not enforceable against the party to be charged by an action against him, it is not enforceable by a set-off or counterclaim in an action brought by him, or as a defense to a claim by him.

§139. Enforcement by Virtue of Action in Reliance

(1) A promise which the promisor should reasonably expect to induce action or forbearance on the part of the promisee or a third person and which does induce the action or forbearance is enforceable notwithstanding the Statute of Frauds if injustice can be avoided only by enforcement of the promise. The remedy granted for breach is to be limited as justice requires.

(2) In determining whether injustice can be avoided only by enforcement of the promise, the following circumstances are significant:

(a) the availability and adequacy of other remedies, particularly cancellation and restitution;

(b) the definite and substantial character of the action or forbearance in relation to the remedy sought;

(c) the extent to which the action or forbearance corroborates evidence of the making and terms of the promise, or the making and terms are otherwise established by clear and convincing evidence;

(d) the reasonableness of the action or forbearance;

(e) the extent to which the action or forbearance was foreseeable by the promisor.

Comment

a. Relation to other rules. This Section is complementary to §90, which dispenses with the requirement of consideration if the same conditions are met, but it also applies to promises supported by consideration. Like §90, this Section . . . states a basic principle which sometimes renders inquiry unnecessary as to the precise scope of other policies. . . .

b. Avoidance of injustice. Like §90, this Section states a flexible principle, but the requirement of consideration is more easily displaced than the requirement of a writing. . . . Subsection (2) lists some of the relevant factors in applying the latter requirement. Each factor relates either to the extent to which reliance furnishes a compelling substantive basis for relief in addition to the expectations created by the promise or to the extent to which the circumstances satisfy the evidentiary purpose of the Statute [of Frauds] and fulfill any cautionary, deterrent and channeling functions it may serve. . . .

§140. Defense of Failure to Perform

The Statute of Frauds does not invalidate defenses based on the plaintiff's failure to perform a condition of his claim or defenses based on his present or prospective breach of the contract he seeks to enforce.

§141. Action for Value of Performance Under Unenforceable Contract

(1) In an action for the value of performance under a contract, except as stated in Subsection (2), the Statute of Frauds does not invalidate any defense which would be available if the contract were enforceable against both parties.

(2) Where a party to a contract which is unenforceable against him refuses either to perform the contract or to sign a sufficient memorandum, the other party is justified in suspending any performance for which he has not already received the agreed return, and such a suspension is not a defense in an action for the value of performance rendered before the suspension.

§142. Tort Liability for Acts Under Unenforceable Contract

Where because of the existence of a contract conduct would not be tortious, unenforceability of the contract under the Statute of Frauds does not make the conduct tortious if it occurs without notice of repudiation of the contract.

§143. Unenforceable Contract as Evidence

The Statute of Frauds does not make an unenforceable contract inadmissible in evidence for any purpose other than its enforcement in violation of the Statute.

§144. Effect of Unenforceable Contract as to Third Parties

Only a party to a contract or a transferee or successor of a party to the contract can assert that the contract is unenforceable under the Statute of Frauds.

§145. Effect of Full Performance

Where the promises in a contract have been fully performed by all parties, the Statute of Frauds does not affect the legal relations of the parties.

§146. Rights of Competing Transferees of Property

(1) Where a contract to transfer property or a transfer was unenforceable against the transferor under the Statute of Frauds but subsequently becomes enforceable, the contract or transfer has whatever priority it would have had aside from the Statute of Frauds over an intervening contract by the transferor to transfer the same property to a third person.

(2) If the third person obtains title to the property by an enforceable transaction before the prior contract becomes enforceable, the prior contract is unenforceable against him and does not affect his title.

§147. Contract Containing Multiple Promises

(1) Where performance of the promises in a contract which subject it to the Statute of Frauds is exclusively beneficial to one party, that party by agreeing to forego the performance may render the remainder of the contract enforceable, but this rule does not apply to a contract to transfer property on the promisor's death.

(2) Where the promises in a contract which subject it to the Statute have become enforceable or where the duty to perform them has been discharged by performance or otherwise, the Statute does not prevent enforcement of the remaining promises.

(3) Except as stated in this Section, where some of the unperformed promises in a contract are unenforceable against a party under the Statute of Frauds, all the promises in the contract are unenforceable against him.

§148. Rescission by Oral Agreement

Notwithstanding the Statute of Frauds, all unperformed duties under an enforceable contract may be discharged by an oral agreement of rescission. The Statute may, however, apply to a contract to rescind a transfer of property.

§149. Oral Modification

(1) For the purpose of determining whether the Statute of Frauds applies to a contract modifying but not rescinding a prior contract, the second contract is treated as containing the originally agreed terms as modified. The Statute may, however, apply independently of the original terms to a contract to modify a transfer of property.

(2) Where the second contract is unenforceable by virtue of the Statute of Frauds and there has been no material change of position in reliance on it, the prior contract is not modified.

§150. Reliance on Oral Modification

Where the parties to an enforceable contract subsequently agree that all or part of a duty need not be performed or of a condition need not occur, the Statute of Frauds does not prevent enforcement of the subsequent agreement if reinstatement of the original terms would be unjust in view of a material change of position in reliance on the subsequent agreement.

Comment

a. Relation to other rules. This Section states a particular application of the broader principle stated in §139. . . . Enforcement of a promise or agreement under the present rule is often said to rest on "waiver" or "estoppel," or on excuse by prevention or hindrance. See §§84, 153; Uniform Commercial Code §2-209(5).

b. Waiver. Where a contract is modified by subsequent agreement and the contract as modified is within a provision of the Statute of Frauds, the modified contract is unenforceable unless the Statute is satisfied. In such a case, if the original contract was enforceable it is not rescinded or modified but remains enforceable. See §149. But the unenforceable modification may operate as a waiver. See Uniform Commercial Code §2-209(4). To the extent that the waiver is acted on before it is revoked, it excuses the other party from performance of his own duty and of conditions of the duty of the waiving party. . . .

c. Reinstatement after waiver. Where an unenforceable modification of an enforceable contract operates as a waiver affecting an executory portion of the contract, the waiving party may retract the waiver by reasonable notification received by the other party. The original terms are then reinstated unless reinstatement would be unjust in view of a material change of position in reliance on the waiver. . . .

CHAPTER 6. MISTAKE

§151. Mistake Defined

A mistake is a belief that is not in accord with the facts.

§152. When Mistake of Both Parties Makes a Contract Voidable

(1) Where a mistake of both parties at the time a contract was made as to a basic assumption on which the contract was made has a material effect on the agreed

exchange of performances, the contract is voidable by the adversely affected party unless he bears the risk of the mistake under the rule stated in §154.

(2) In determining whether the mistake has a material effect on the agreed exchange of performances, account is taken of any relief by way of reformation, restitution, or otherwise.

Comment

a. Rationale. Before making a contract, a party ordinarily evaluates the proposed exchange of performances on the basis of a variety of assumptions with respect to existing facts. Many of these assumptions are shared by the other party, in the sense that the other party is aware that they are made. The mere fact that both parties are mistaken with respect to such an assumption does not, of itself, afford a reason for avoidance of the contract by the adversely affected party. Relief is only appropriate in situations where a mistake of both parties has such a material effect on the agreed exchange of performances as to upset the very basis for the contract. . . .

b. Basic assumption. A mistake of both parties does not make the contract voidable unless it is one as to a basic assumption on which both parties made the contract. The term "basic assumption" has the same meaning here as it does in Chapter 11 in connection with impracticability (§§261, 266(1)) and frustration (§§265, 266(2)). See Uniform Commercial Code §2-615(a). For example, market conditions and the financial situation of the parties are ordinarily not such assumptions, and, generally, just as shifts in market conditions or financial ability do not effect discharge under the rules governing impracticability, mistakes as to market conditions or financial ability do not justify avoidance under the rules governing mistake. . . . The parties may have had such a "basic assumption," even though they were not conscious of alternatives. . . . Where, for example, a party purchases an annuity on the life of another person, it can be said that it was a basic assumption that the other person was alive at the time, even though the parties never consciously addressed themselves to the possibility that he was dead. . . .

c. Material effect on agreed exchange. A party cannot avoid a contract merely because both parties were mistaken as to a basic assumption on which it was made. He must, in addition, show that the mistake has a material effect on the agreed exchange of performances. It is not enough for him to prove that he would not have made the contract had it not been for the mistake. He must show that the resulting imbalance in the agreed exchange is so severe that he cannot fairly be required to carry it out. Ordinarily he will be able to do this by showing that the exchange is not only less desirable to him but is also more advantageous to the other party. . . . In exceptional cases the adversely affected party may be able to show that the effect on the agreed exchange has been material simply on the ground that the exchange has become less desirable for him, even though there has been no effect on the other party. Cases of hardship that result in no advantage to the other party are, however, ordinarily appropriately left to the rules on impracticability and frustration. . . . The standard of materiality here, as elsewhere in this Restatement (e.g., §237), is a flexible one to be applied in the light of all the circumstances. . . .

h. Mistakes as to different assumptions. The rule stated in this Section applies only where both parties are mistaken as to the same basic assumption. Their mistakes need not be, and often they will not be, identical. If, however, the parties are mistaken as to different assumptions, the rule stated in §153, rather than that stated in this Section, applies.

§153. When Mistake of One Party Makes a Contract Voidable

Where a mistake of one party at the time a contract was made as to a basic assumption on which he made the contract has a material effect on the agreed exchange of performances that is adverse to him, the contract is voidable by him if he does not bear the risk of the mistake under the rule stated in §154, and

(a) the effect of the mistake is such that enforcement of the contract would be unconscionable, or

(b) the other party had reason to know of the mistake or his fault caused the mistake.

Comment

a. Rationale. Courts have traditionally been reluctant to allow a party to avoid a contract on the ground of mistake, even as to a basic assumption, if the mistake was not shared by the other party. Nevertheless, relief has been granted where the other party actually knew (see §§160, 161) or had reason to know of the mistake at the time the contract was made or where his fault caused the mistake. There has, in addition, been a growing willingness to allow avoidance where the consequences of the mistake are so grave that enforcement of the contract would be unconscionable. This Section states a rule that permits avoidance on this latter basis, as well as on the more traditional grounds. . . . The parol evidence rule does not preclude the use of prior or contemporaneous agreements or negotiations to establish that a party was mistaken. See §214(d). Nevertheless, because mistakes are the exception rather than the rule, the trier of the facts should examine the evidence with particular care when a party attempts to avoid liability by proving mistake. See Comment *c* to §155. The rule stated in this Section is subject to that stated in §157 on fault of the party seeking relief. It is also subject to the rules on exercise of the power of avoidance stated in §§380-85.

b. Similarity to rule where both are mistaken. In order for a party to have the power to avoid a contract for a mistake that he alone made, he must at least meet the same requirements that he would have had to meet had both parties been mistaken (§152). The mistake must be one as to a basic assumption on which the contract was made; it must have a material effect on the agreed exchange of performances; and the mistaken party must not bear the risk of the mistake. The most common sorts of such mistakes occur in bids on construction contracts and result from clerical errors in the computation of the price or in the omission of component items. . . . The rule stated in this Section is not, however, limited to such cases. It also applies, for example, to a misreading of specifications . . . or such misunderstanding as does not prevent a manifestation of mutual assent. . . . Where only one party is mistaken, however, he must meet either the additional requirement stated in Subparagraph (a) or one of the additional requirements stated in Subparagraph (b).

c. Additional requirement of unconscionability. Under Subparagraph (a), the mistaken party must in addition show that enforcement of the contract would be unconscionable. The reason for this additional requirement is that, if only one party was mistaken, avoidance of the contract will more clearly disappoint the expectations of the other party than if he too was mistaken. . . . The mistaken party bears the substantial burden of establishing unconscionability and must ordinarily show not only the position he would have been in had the facts been as he believed them to be but also the position in which he finds himself as a result of his mistake. For example, in the typical case of a mistake as to the price in a bid, the builder must show the profit or loss that will result if he is required to perform, as well as the profit that he would have made had there been no mistake. . . .

d. Effect of reliance on unconscionability. Reliance by the other party may make enforcement of a contract proper although enforcement would otherwise be unconscionable. . . . If, however, the court can adequately protect the other party by compensating him for his reliance under the rules stated in §158, avoidance is not then precluded on this ground. . . .

e. Had reason to know of or caused the mistake. If the other party had reason to know of the mistake, the mistaken party can avoid the contract regardless of whether its enforcement would be unconscionable. . . . Similar results follow where the other party's fault caused the mistake. (If the mistake was the fault of both parties, it was not caused by the other party within the meaning of this Section and the court may exercise its discretion under the rule stated in §158(2). See Comment *c* to §158.) . . . .

§154. When a Party Bears the Risk of a Mistake

A party bears the risk of a mistake when

(a) the risk is allocated to him by agreement of the parties, or

(b) he is aware, at the time the contract is made, that he has only limited knowledge with respect to the facts to which the mistake relates but treats his limited knowledge as sufficient, or

(c) the risk is allocated to him by the court on the ground that it is reasonable in the circumstances to do so.

Comment

a. Rationale. . . . A party . . . bears the risk of many mistakes as to existing circumstances even though they upset basic assumptions and unexpectedly affect the agreed exchange of performances. For example, it is commonly understood that the seller of farm land generally cannot avoid the contract of sale upon later discovery by both parties that the land contains valuable mineral deposits, even though the price was negotiated on the basic assumption that the land was suitable only for farming and the effect on the agreed exchange of performances is material. In such a case a court will ordinarily allocate the risk of the mistake to the seller, so that he is under a duty to perform regardless of the mistake. . . .

b. Allocation by agreement. The most obvious case of allocation of the risk of a mistake is one in which the parties themselves provide for it by their agreement. . . .

c. Conscious ignorance. Even though the mistaken party did not agree to bear the risk, he may have been aware when he made the contract that his knowledge with respect to the facts to which the mistake relates was limited. If he was not only so aware that his knowledge was limited but undertook to perform in the face of that awareness, he bears the risk of the mistake. It is sometimes said in such a situation that, in a sense, there was not mistake but "conscious ignorance." . . . .

§155. When Mistake of Both Parties as to Written Expression Justifies Reformation

Where a writing that evidences or embodies an agreement in whole or in part fails to express the agreement because of a mistake of both parties as to the contents or effect of the writing, the court may at the request of a party reform the writing to express the agreement, except to the extent that rights of third parties such as good faith purchasers for value will be unfairly affected.

§156. Mistake as to Contract Within the Statute of Frauds

If reformation of a writing is otherwise appropriate, it is not precluded by the fact that the contract is within the Statute of Frauds.

§157. Effect of Fault of Party Seeking Relief

A mistaken party's fault in failing to know or discover the facts before making the contract does not bar him from avoidance or reformation under the rules stated in this Chapter, unless his fault amounts to a failure to act in good faith and in accordance with reasonable standards of fair dealing.

Comment

a. Rationale. The mere fact that a mistaken party could have avoided the mistake by the exercise of reasonable care does not preclude either avoidance

(§§152, 153) or reformation (§155). . . . Nevertheless, in extreme cases the mistaken party's fault is a proper ground for denying him relief for a mistake that he otherwise could have avoided. Although the critical degree of fault is sometimes described as "gross" negligence, that term is not well defined and is avoided in this Section. . . . Instead, the rule is stated in terms of good faith and fair dealing. The general duty of good faith and fair dealing, imposed under the rule stated in §205, extends only to the performance and enforcement of a contract and does not apply to the negotiation stage prior to the formation of the contract. See Comment c to §205. . . . Nevertheless, under the rule stated in this Section, . . . [d]uring the negotiation stage each party is held to a degree of responsibility appropriate to the justifiable expectations of the other. . . .

b. *Failure to read writing.* Generally, one who assents to a writing is presumed to know its contents and cannot escape being bound by its terms merely by contending that he did not read them; his assent is deemed to cover unknown as well as known terms. See Comment b to §23; Comment b to §211. But see the special rule of §211(3) for the case of standardized agreements. The exceptional rule stated in the present Section with regard to reformation has no application to the common case in which the term in question was not the subject of prior negotiations. It only affects cases that come within the scope of §155, under which there must have been an agreement that preceded the writing. In such a case, a party's negligence in failing to read the writing does not preclude reformation if the writing does not correctly express the prior agreement. . . . Where there was no prior agreement, however, this Section does not apply because reformation is not available under §155. . . .

§158. Relief Including Restitution

(1) In any case governed by the rules stated in this Chapter, either party may have a claim for relief including restitution under the rules stated in §§240 and 376.

(2) In any case governed by the rules stated in this Chapter, if those rules together with the rules stated in Chapter 16 will not avoid injustice, the court may grant relief on such terms as justice requires including protection of the parties' reliance interests.

Comment

a. *Scope.* A court may use several techniques to adjust the rights of the parties after discovery of a mistake. Subsection (1) speaks to claims for relief such as that provided by the rule on part performances as agreed equivalents stated in §240 and those on restitution and other relief stated in Chapter 16. Subsection (2) speaks to supplying a term to avoid injustice. See the analogous rule stated in §272.

b. Relief including restitution. Avoidance of a contract ideally involves a reversal of any steps that the parties may have taken by way of performance, so that each party returns such benefit as he may have received. This is not, however, possible in all cases. Occasionally a party who has performed may be entitled to recover on the contract for the part that he has performed under the rule on part performances as agreed equivalents (§240). Even where this is not so, it may be appropriate to permit avoidance coupled with a money claim for restitution to the extent that one party's performance has benefited the other. Such claims are governed by the rules stated in §§370-77. A party may also have a claim that goes beyond mere restitution and includes elements of reliance by the claimant. . . .

c. Supplying a term to avoid injustice. Under the rule stated in §204, when the parties have not agreed with respect to a term that is essential to a determination of their rights and duties, the court will supply a term that is reasonable in the circumstances. Ordinarily the rules stated in this Chapter, coupled with those stated in Chapter 16, will be adequate to allow the court to arrive at a just result. See Subsection (1). If, however, these rules will not suffice to avoid injustice, the court may supply a term just as it may in cases of impracticability of performance and frustration of purpose. See §272(2) and Comment *c* to that section. Here, as there, a particularly significant application occurs when the just solution is to "sever" the agreement and require that some unexecuted part of it be performed on both sides, rather than to relieve both parties of all their duties. The situation differs from that envisioned in §240, under which the court merely allows recovery at the contract rate for performance that has already been rendered. The question under this Section is whether the court can salvage a part of the agreement that is still executory on both sides. . . .

Sometimes the party who is not adversely affected by a mistake can, by assenting to a modification of the contract, eliminate the effect of the mistake on the agreed exchange. He should generally be allowed to do so and thereby to preclude avoidance by the party who would otherwise be adversely affected. A court may, under Subsection (2), grant the party who has not been adversely affected what is, in effect, an option to enforce the contract on new terms. . . .

The Court may also exercise its discretion under Subsection (2) where both parties have been responsible for the mistake. It may do so, for example, where a mistake of one party resulted both from his failure to act in good faith and in accordance with reasonable standards of fair dealing (§157) and from the fault of the other party (§153(b)). See Comment *f* to §153. Furthermore, for the sake of simplicity, the rules stated in this Chapter have been formulated in terms of the typical contract based on an exchange of consideration by two parties, and it does not, therefore, deal exhaustively with problems of mistake involving several parties (§9) including intended beneficiaries (§302), promises enforceable because of reliance (§90), promises enforceable because under seal (§95), and other less typical situations. In such cases, the court will apply rules analogous to those stated in this Chapter. See Comments *b*, *d*, and *e* to §155. The situations dealt with in Subsection (2) are to be distinguished from those envisioned by §155, where a writing is reformed to carry out the intentions of the parties. . . .

CHAPTER 7.   MISREPRESENTATION, DURESS AND UNDUE INFLUENCE

Topic 1.   Misrepresentation

§159.   Misrepresentation Defined

A misrepresentation is an assertion that is not in accord with the facts.

Comment

a. Nature of the assertion. . . . Whether a statement is false depends on the meaning of the words in all the circumstances, including what may fairly be inferred from them. An assertion may also be inferred from conduct other than words. Concealment or even non-disclosure may have the effect of a misrepresentation under the rules stated in §§160 and 161. Whether a misrepresentation is fraudulent is determined by the rule stated in §162(1). However, an assertion need not be fraudulent to be a misrepresentation. Thus a statement intended to be truthful may be a misrepresentation because of ignorance or carelessness, as when the word "not" is inadvertently omitted or when inaccurate language is used. But a misrepresentation that is not fraudulent has no consequences under this Chapter unless it is material. . . .

b. Half-truths. A statement may be true with respect to the facts stated, but may fail to include qualifying matter necessary to prevent the implication of an assertion that is false with respect to other facts. For example, a true statement that an event has recently occurred may carry the false implication that the situation has not changed since its occurrence. Such a half-truth may be as misleading as an assertion that is wholly false. . . .

c. Meaning of "fact." An assertion must relate to something that is a fact at the time the assertion is made in order to be a misrepresentation. Such facts include past events as well as present circumstances but do not include future events. An assertion limited to future events (see §2), may be a basis of liability for breach of contract, but not of relief for misrepresentation. However, a promise or a prediction of future events may by implication involve an assertion that facts exist from which the promised or predicted consequences will follow, which may be a misrepresentation as to those facts. Thus, from a statement that a particular machine will attain a specified level of performance when it is used, it may be inferred that its present design and condition make it capable of such a level. Such an inference may be drawn even if the statement is not legally binding as a promise. . . .

d. State of mind as a fact. A person's state of mind is a fact, and an assertion as to one's opinion or intention, including an intention to perform a promise, is a misrepresentation if the state of mind is other than as asserted. The extent to which the recipient is justified in relying on an assertion of opinion or intention is dealt with in §§168, 169 and 171. . . .

§160. When Action Is Equivalent to an Assertion (Concealment)

Action intended or known to be likely to prevent another from learning a fact is equivalent to an assertion that the fact does not exist.

Comment

a. Scope. Concealment is an affirmative act intended or known to be likely to keep another from learning of a fact of which he would otherwise have learned. Such affirmative action is always equivalent to a misrepresentation and has any effect that a misrepresentation would have under the rules stated in §§163, 164 and 166. The rule stated in the following section applies to non-disclosure, where one person simply fails to inform another of a fact relating to the transaction. Non-disclosure is equivalent to a misrepresentation only in the circumstances enumerated in that section. . . .

§161. When Non-Disclosure Is Equivalent to an Assertion

A person's non-disclosure of a fact known to him is equivalent to an assertion that the fact does not exist in the following cases only:

(a) where he knows that disclosure of the fact is necessary to prevent some previous assertion from being a misrepresentation or from being fraudulent or material.

(b) where he knows that disclosure of the fact would correct a mistake of the other party as to a basic assumption on which that party is making the contract and if non-disclosure of the fact amounts to a failure to act in good faith and in accordance with reasonable standards of fair dealing.

(c) where he knows that disclosure of the fact would correct a mistake of the other party as to the contents or effect of a writing, evidencing or embodying an agreement in whole or in part.

(d) where the other person is entitled to know the fact because of a relation of trust and confidence between them.

Comment

a. Concealment distinguished. Like concealment, non-disclosure of a fact may be equivalent to a misrepresentation. Concealment necessarily involves an element of non-disclosure, but it is the act of preventing another from learning of a fact that is significant and this act is always equivalent to a misrepresentation (§160). Non-disclosure without concealment is equivalent to a misrepresentation only in special situations. A party making a contract is not expected to tell all that he knows to the other party, even if he knows that the other party lacks knowledge on some aspects of the transaction. His nondisclosure, as such, has no legal effect except in the situations enumerated in this Section. He may not, of course, tell half-truths and his assertion of only some of the facts without the inclusion of such additional matters as he knows or believes to be necessary to prevent it from being misleading is itself a misrepresentation. See Comment *a* to §159. ... [I]t is not enough, where disclosure is expected, merely to make reasonable efforts to disclose the relevant facts. Actual disclosure is required. ...

b. Fraudulent or material. In order to make the contract voidable under the rule stated in §164(1), the non-disclosure must be either fraudulent or material. The notion of disclosure necessarily implies that the fact in question is known to the person expected to disclose it. But the failure to disclose the fact may be unintentional, as when one forgets to disclose a known fact, and it is then equivalent to an innocent misrepresentation. Furthermore, one is expected to disclose only such facts as he knows or has reason to know will influence the other in determining his course of action. See §162(2). Therefore, he need not disclose facts that the ordinary person would regard as unimportant unless he knows of some peculiarity of the other person that is likely to lead him to attach importance to them. There is, however, no such requirement of materiality if it can be shown that the non-disclosure was actually fraudulent. If a fact is intentionally withheld for the purpose of inducing action, this is equivalent to a fraudulent misrepresentation.

c. Failure to correct. One who has made an assertion that is neither a fraudulent nor a material misrepresentation may subsequently acquire knowledge that bears significantly on his earlier assertion. He is expected to speak up and correct the earlier assertion in three cases. First, if his assertion was not a misrepresentation because it was true, he may later learn that it is no longer true. ... Second, his assertion may have been a misrepresentation but may not have been fraudulent. If this was because he believed that it was true, he may later learn that it was not true. ... Third, if his assertion was a misrepresentation but was not material because he had no reason to know of the other's special characteristics that made reliance likely, he may later learn of such characteristics. If a person fails to correct his earlier assertion in these situations, the result is the same as it would have been had he had his newly acquired knowledge at the time he made the assertion. The rule stated in Clause (a), like that stated in Clause (d), extends to non-disclosure by persons who are not parties to the transaction. ...

d. Known mistake as to a basic assumption. In many situations, if one party knows that the other is mistaken as to a basic assumption, he is expected to disclose the fact that would correct the mistake. A seller of real or personal property is, for example, ordinarily expected to disclose a known latent defect of quality or title that is of such a character as would probably prevent the buyer from buying at the contract price. An owner is ordinarily expected to disclose a known error in a bid that he has received from a contractor. See Comment *e* to §153. The mistake must be as to a basic assumption. ... The rule stated in Clause (b), is, however, broader than these rules for mistake because it does not require a showing of a material effect on the agreed exchange and is not affected by the fact that the party seeking relief bears the risk of the mistake (§154). Nevertheless, a party need not correct all mistakes of the other and is expected only to act in good faith and in accordance with reasonable standards of fair dealing, as reflected in prevailing business ethics. A party may, therefore, reasonably expect the other to take normal steps to inform himself and to draw his own conclusions. If the other is indolent, inexperienced or ignorant, or if his judgment is bad or he lacks access to adequate information, his adversary is not generally expected to compensate for these deficiencies. A buyer of property, for example, is not ordinarily expected to disclose circumstances that make the property more valuable than the seller supposes. . . . In contrast to the rules stated in Clauses (a) and (d), that stated in Clause (b) is limited to non-disclosure by a party to the transaction. Actual knowledge is required for the application of the rule stated in Clause (b). The case of a party who does not know but has reason to know of a mistake is governed by the rule stated in §153(b). As to knowledge in the case of an organization, see the analogous rule in Uniform Commercial Code §1-[202]. . . .

Illustrations

. . . .

5. A, seeking to induce B to make a contract to buy A's house, knows that B does not know that the house is riddled with termites but does not disclose this to B. B makes the contract. A's non-disclosure is equivalent to an assertion that the house is not riddled with termites, and this assertion is a misrepresentation. Whether the contract is voidable by B is determined by the rule stated in §164.

6. A, seeking to induce B to make a contract to buy a food-processing business, knows that B does not know that the health department has given re-peated warnings that a necessary license will not be renewed unless expensive improvements are made but does not disclose this to B. B makes the contract. A's non-disclosure is equivalent to an assertion that no warnings have been given by the health department, and this assertion is a misrepresentation. Whether the contract is voidable by B is determined by the rule stated in §164. . . .

10. A, seeking to induce B to make a contract to sell A land, learns from government surveys that the land contains valuable mineral deposits and knows that B does not know this, but does not disclose this to B. B makes the contract. A's non-disclosure does not amount to a failure to act in good faith and in accordance with reasonable standards of fair dealing and is therefore not equivalent to an assertion that the land does not contain valuable mineral deposits. The contract is not voidable by B. . . .

e. Known mistake as to a writing. One party cannot hold the other to a writing if he knew that the other was mistaken as to its contents or as to its legal effect. He is expected to correct such mistakes of the other party and his failure to do so is equivalent to a misrepresentation, which may be grounds either for avoidance under §164 or for reformation under §166. . . . The failure of a party to use care in reading the writing so as to discover the mistake may not preclude such relief (§172). In the case of standardized agreements, these rules Supplement that of §211(3), which applies, regardless of actual knowledge, if there is reason to believe that the other party would not manifest assent if he knew that the writing contained a particular term. Like the rule stated in Clause (b), that stated in Clause (c) requires actual knowledge and is limited to non-disclosure by a party to the transaction. See Comment *d.* . . .

f. Relation of trust and confidence. The rule stated in Clause (d) Supplements that stated in §173 with respect to contracts between parties in a fiduciary relation. Where the latter rule applies, as in the case of a trustee, an agent, a guardian, or an executor or administrator, its more stringent requirements govern. Even where a party is not, strictly speaking, a fiduciary, he may stand in such a relation of trust and confidence to the other as to give the other the right to expect disclosure. Such a relationship normally exists between members of the same family and may arise, in other situations as, for example, between physician and patient. In addition, some types of contracts, such as those of suretyship or guaranty, marine insurance and joint adventure, are recognized as creating in themselves confidential relations and hence as requiring the utmost good faith and full and fair disclosure. . . .

§162. When a Misrepresentation Is Fraudulent or Material

(1) A misrepresentation is fraudulent if the maker intends his assertion to induce a party to manifest his assent and the maker
    (a) knows or believes that the assertion is not in accord with the facts, or
    (b) does not have the confidence that he states or implies in the truth of the assertion, or
    (c) knows that he does not have the basis that he states or implies for the assertion.
(2) A misrepresentation is material if it would be likely to induce a reasonable person to manifest his assent, or if the maker knows that it would be likely to induce the recipient to do so.

Comment

. . . .

c. Meaning of "material." Although a fraudulent misrepresentation need not be material in order to entitle the recipient to relief under the rule stated in §164, a non-fraudulent misrepresentation will not entitle him to relief unless it is material. The materiality of a misrepresentation is determined from the viewpoint of the maker, while the justification of reliance is determined from the viewpoint of the recipient. (Contrast also the concept of a "material" failure to perform. See §241.) The requirement of materiality may be met in either of two ways. First, a misrepresentation is material if it would be likely to induce a reasonable person to manifest his assent. Second, it is material if the maker knows that for some special reason it is likely to induce the particular recipient to manifest his assent. There may be personal considerations that the recipient regards as important even though they would not be expected to affect others in his situation, and if the maker is aware of this the misrepresentation may be material even though it would not be expected to induce a reasonable person to make the proposed contract. One who preys upon another's known idiosyncrasies cannot complain if the contract is held voidable when he succeeds in what he is endeavoring to accomplish. Cf. Restatement, Second, Torts §538. . . .

§163. When a Misrepresentation Prevents Formation of a Contract

If a misrepresentation as to the character or essential terms of a proposed contract induces conduct that appears to be a manifestation of assent by one who neither knows nor has reasonable opportunity to know of the character or essential terms of the proposed contract, his conduct is not effective as a manifestation of assent.

Comment

a. Rationale. Under the general principle stated in §19(2), a party's conduct is not effective as a manifestation of his assent unless he knows or has reason to know that the other party may infer from it that he assents. . . . If, because of a misrepresentation as to the character or essential terms of a proposed contract, a party does not know or have reasonable opportunity to know of its character or essential terms, then he neither knows nor has reason to know that the other party may infer from his conduct that he assents to that contract. In such a case there is no effective manifestation of assent and no contract at all. Compare §174. This result only follows, however, if the misrepresentation relates to the very nature of the proposed contract itself and not merely to one of its non-essential terms. The party may believe that he is not assenting to any contract or that he is assenting to a contract entirely different from the proposed contract. . . . It is immaterial under the rule stated in this Section whether the misrepresentation is made by a party to the transaction or by a third person. See Comment *e* to §164. . . .

§164. When a Misrepresentation Makes a Contract Voidable

(1) If a party's manifestation of assent is induced by either a fraudulent or a material misrepresentation by the other party upon which the recipient is justified in relying, the contract is voidable by the recipient.

(2) If a party's manifestation of assent is induced by either a fraudulent or a material misrepresentation by one who is not a party to the transaction upon which the recipient is justified in relying, the contract is voidable by the recipient, unless the other party to the transaction in good faith and without reason to know of the misrepresentation either gives value or relies materially on the transaction.

§165. Cure by Change of Circumstances

If a contract is voidable because of a misrepresentation and, before notice of an intention to avoid the contract, the facts come into accord with the assertion, the contract is no longer voidable unless the recipient has been harmed by relying on the misrepresentation.

§166. When a Misrepresentation as to a Writing Justifies Reformation

If a party's manifestation of assent is induced by the other party's fraudulent misrepresentation as to the contents or effect of a writing evidencing or embodying in whole or in part an agreement, the court at the request of the recipient may reform the writing to express the terms of the agreement as asserted,

(a) if the recipient was justified in relying on the misrepresentation, and

(b) except to the extent that rights of third parties such as good faith purchasers for value will be unfairly affected.

§167. When a Misrepresentation Is an Inducing Cause

A misrepresentation induces a party's manifestation of assent if it substantially contributes to his decision to manifest his assent.

§168. Reliance on Assertions of Opinion

(1) An assertion is one of opinion if it expresses only a belief, without certainty, as to the existence of a fact or expresses only a judgment as to quality, value, authenticity, or similar matters.

(2) If it is reasonable to do so, the recipient of an assertion of a person's opinion as to facts not disclosed and not otherwise known to the recipient may properly interpret it as an assertion

(a) that the facts known to that person are not incompatible with his opinion, or

(b) that he knows facts sufficient to justify him in forming it.

Comment

a. Knowledge and opinion. A statement of opinion is also a statement of fact because it states that a person has a particular state of mind concerning the matter to which his opinion relates. But it also implies that he does not have such definite information, that he is not certain enough of what he says, to make an assertion of his own knowledge as to that matter. It implies at most that he knows of no facts incompatible with the belief or that he knows of facts that justify him in holding it. The difference is that between "This is true," and "I think this is true, but I am not sure." The important distinction is between assertions of knowledge and those of opinion, rather than assertions of fact and those of opinion. The person whose opinion is asserted is usually the maker of the assertion himself, but the opinion may also be that of a third person. See Comment *b* to §169. . . .

d. Implication of a statement of opinion. In some circumstances the recipient may reasonably understand a statement of opinion to be more than an assertion as to the maker's state of mind. Under the rule stated in Subsection (2), if the statement of opinion relates to facts not known to the recipient, he may be justified in inferring that there are facts that justify the opinion, or at least that there are no facts that are incompatible with it. In such a case, the statement of opinion becomes, in effect, an assertion as to those facts and may be relied on as such. The rule is, however, applied in the light of the realities of the market place. The propensity of sellers and buyers to exaggerate the advantages to the other party of the bargains they promise is well recognized, and to some extent their assertions of opinion must be discounted. Nevertheless, while some allowance must be made for seller's puffing and buyer's depreciation, the other party is entitled to assume that a statement of opinion is not so far removed from the truth as to be incompatible with the facts known to the maker. Where circumstances justify it, a statement of opinion may also be reasonably understood as carrying with it an assertion that the maker knows facts sufficient to justify him in forming it. However, the rule stated in Subsection (2) applies only when the facts to which the opinion relates are not disclosed and not otherwise known to the recipient. An assertion of opinion that does not fall within Subsection (2) is one of opinion only. As to the circumstances in which reliance on such an assertion is justified, see §169. . . .

§169. When Reliance on an Assertion of Opinion Is Not Justified

To the extent that an assertion is one of opinion only, the recipient is not justified in relying on it unless the recipient

    (a) stands in such a relation of trust and confidence to the person whose opinion is asserted that the recipient is reasonable in relying on it, or

    (b) reasonably believes that, as compared with himself, the person whose opinion is asserted has special skill, judgment or objectivity with respect to the subject matter, or

    (c) is for some other special reason particularly susceptible to a misrepresentation of the type involved.

Comment

. . . .

b. Rationale. . . . The law assumes that the ordinary person is reasonably competent to form his own opinions as to the advisability of entering into those transactions that form part of the ordinary routine of life. The mere fact that one of the parties is less astute than the other does not justify him in relying on the other's opinion. This is true even though one party knows that the other is somewhat more conversant with the value and quality of the subject matter, since expressions of opinion by the other party are generally to be discounted. It may be assumed, for example, that a seller will express a favorable opinion concerning what he has to sell. When he praises it in general terms, commonly known as "puffing" or "sales talk," without specific content or reference to facts, buyers are expected to understand that they are not entitled to rely. See Uniform Commercial Code §2-313(2). A similar assumption applies to deprecating statements by buyers. See Comment *d* to §168. . . .

§170. Reliance on Assertions as to Matters of Law

If an assertion is one as to a matter of law, the same rules that apply in the case of other assertions determine whether the recipient is justified in relying on it.

Comment

a. Law as fact. A statement as to a matter of law is subject to the same rules as are other assertions. Such a statement may or may not be one of opinion. Thus, an assertion that a particular statute has been enacted or repealed or that a particular decision has been rendered by a court is generally not a statement of opinion. The rules that determine the consequences of a misrepresentation of such a matter of law are the same as those that determine the consequences of a similar misrepresentation of any other fact. . . .

b. Law as opinion. Many statements of law involve assertions as to what a court would determine to be the legal consequences of a dispute if it were litigated, and such a statement is one of opinion. Such a statement may, as may any other statement of opinion, carry with it the assertion that the facts known to the maker are not incompatible with his opinion, or that he does know facts that justify him in forming it. See §168(2). However, a statement that is limited to the maker's opinion as to the legal consequences of a state of facts and does not amount to an assertion as to the facts themselves is an assertion of opinion only. This is particularly true if all of the facts are known to both parties or are assumed by both of them to exist. . . .

§171. When Reliance on an Assertion of Intention Is Not Justified

(1) To the extent that an assertion is one of intention only, the recipient is not justified in relying on it if in the circumstances a misrepresentation of intention is consistent with reasonable standards of dealing.

(2) If it is reasonable to do so, the promisee may properly interpret a promise as an assertion that the promisor intends to perform the promise.

Comment

a. Assertions of intention. A statement as to the intention of either the maker or a third person is an assertion of a fact, his state of mind, just as a statement of his opinion is such an assertion. It is therefore a misrepresentation if that state of mind is not as asserted. However, the truth of a statement as to a person's intention depends on his intention at the time that the statement is made and is not affected if he subsequently, for any reason, changes his mind. In order for reliance on an assertion of intention to be justified, the recipient's expectation that the maker's intention will be carried out must be reasonable. If he knows facts that will make it impossible for the maker to carry out his intention, then his reliance cannot be justified. . . .

b. A promise as a statement of intention. It is ordinarily reasonable for the promisee to infer from the making of a promise that the promisor intends to perform it. If, therefore, the promise is made with the intention of not performing it, this implied assertion is false and is a misrepresentation. . . . The promisor's intention not to perform his promise cannot be established merely by proof of its non-performance. Nevertheless, . . . [i]f the promisor knows or should know that he cannot at least substantially perform his promise, this is strong although not conclusive evidence of an intent not to carry it out. . . . If a party is entitled to avoid the contract on this ground, he may do so immediately and need not await the time for performance. The application of the rule stated in Subsection (2) does not turn on whether the promisor is the offeror or the offeree. When the parties exchange promises as consideration for each other, each promise is properly regarded as the inducement for the other. Therefore, if the offeree has no intention of performing his promise when he accepts, the contract is voidable by the offeror on the ground that his promise was made in reliance on that of the offeree. . . . As with other assertions, the recipient's reliance must be justified. It is not justified if the promisor has disclosed his intention not to perform or if performance is known not to be within his control. . . .

§172. When Fault Makes Reliance Unjustified

A recipient's fault in not knowing or discovering the facts before making the contract does not make his reliance unjustified unless it amounts to a failure to act in good faith and in accordance with reasonable standards of fair dealing.

§173. When Abuse of a Fiduciary Relation Makes a Contract Voidable

If a fiduciary makes a contract with his beneficiary relating to matters within the scope of the fiduciary relation, the contract is voidable by the beneficiary, unless
(a) it is on fair terms, and
(b) all parties beneficially interested manifest assent with full understanding of their legal rights and of all relevant facts that the fiduciary knows or should know.

Topic 2. Duress and Undue Unfluence

§174. When Duress by Physical Compulsion Prevents Formation of a Contract

If conduct that appears to be a manifestation of assent by a party who does not intend to engage in that conduct is physically compelled by duress, the conduct is not effective as a manifestation of assent.

Comment

a. Rationale. Under the general principle stated in §21(2), a party's conduct is not effective as a manifestation of his assent if he does not intend to engage in it. This Section involves an application of that principle to those relatively rare situations in which actual physical force has been used to compel a party to appear to assent to a contract. Compare §163. The essence of this type of duress is that a party is compelled by physical force to do an act that he has no intention of doing. . . . The result is that there is no contract at all, or a "void contract" as distinguished from a voidable one. See Comment *a* to §7. . . .

§175. When Duress by Threat Makes a Contract Voidable

(1) If a party's manifestation of assent is induced by an improper threat by the other party that leaves the victim no reasonable alternative, the contract is voidable by the victim.

(2) If a party's manifestation of assent is induced by one who is not a party to the transaction, the contract is voidable by the victim unless the other party to the transaction in good faith and without reason to know of the duress either gives value or relies materially on the transaction.

Comment

. . . .

b. No reasonable alternative. A threat, even if improper, does not amount to duress if the victim has a reasonable alternative to succumbing and fails to take advantage of it. It is sometimes said that the threat must arouse such fear as precludes a party from exercising free will and judgment or that it must be such as would induce assent on the part of a brave man or a man of ordinary firmness. . . . It is enough if the threat actually induces assent (see Comment *c*) on the part of one who has no reasonable alternative. The alternative may take the form of a legal remedy. For example, the threat of commencing an ordinary civil action to enforce a claim to money may be improper. See §176(1)(c). However, it does not usually amount to duress because the victim can assert his rights in the threatened action, and this is ordinarily a reasonable alternative to succumbing to the threat, making the proposed contract, and then asserting his rights in a later civil action. . . . This alternative may not, however, be reasonable if the threat involves, for instance, the seizure of property, the use of oppressive tactics, or the possibility of emotional consequences. . . . The standard is a practical one under which account must be taken of the exigencies in which the victim finds himself, and the mere availability of a legal remedy is not controlling if it will not afford effective relief to one in the victim's circumstances. . . . The alternative to succumbing to the threat need not, however, involve a legal remedy at all. In the case of a threatened denial of needed goods or services, the availability on the market of similar goods or services may afford a reasonable means of avoiding the threat. . . . Whether the victim has a reasonable alternative is a mixed question of law and fact, to be answered in clear cases by the court. . . .

c. *Subjective test of inducement.* . . . [T]he improper threat must induce the making of the contract. The rule for causation in cases of misrepresentation stated in §167 is also applied to analogous cases of duress. . . . A party's manifestation of assent is induced by duress if the duress substantially contributes to his decision to manifest his assent. . . . The test is subjective and the question is, did the threat actually induce assent on the part of the person claiming to be the victim of duress. Threats that would suffice to induce assent by one person may not suffice to induce assent by another. All attendant circumstances must be considered, including such matters as the age, background and relationship of the parties. Persons of a weak or cowardly nature are the very ones that need protection; the courageous can usually protect themselves. Timid and inexperienced persons are particularly subject to threats, and it does not lie in the mouths of the unscrupulous to excuse their imposition on such persons on the ground of their victims' infirmities. . . . [S]uch factors as the availability of disinterested advice and the length of time that elapses between the making of the threat and the assent may . . . be relevant in determining whether the threat actually induced the assent. . . .

e. *Duress by a third person.* If a party's assent has been induced by the duress of a third person, rather than that of the other party to the contract, the contract is nevertheless voidable by the victim. There is, however, an important exception if the other party has, in good faith and without reason to know of the duress, given value or changed his position materially in reliance on the transaction. . . . The rule stated in this Section does not, however, protect a party to whom the duress is attributable under the law of agency. The rule is similar to that for misrepresentation (§163) and is analogous to the rule that protects against the original owner the good faith purchaser of property from another who obtained it by duress. . . .

§176. When a Threat Is Improper

(1) A threat is improper if
    (a) what is threatened is a crime or a tort, or the threat itself would be a crime or a tort if it resulted in obtaining property,
    (b) what is threatened is a criminal prosecution,
    (c) what is threatened is the use of civil process and the threat is made in bad faith, or
    (d) the threat is a breach of the duty of good faith and fair dealing under a contract with the recipient.
(2) A threat is improper if the resulting exchange is not on fair terms, and
    (a) the threatened act would harm the recipient and would not significantly benefit the party making the threat,

(b) the effectiveness of the threat in inducing the manifestation of assent is significantly increased by prior unfair dealing by the party making the threat, or

(c) what is threatened is otherwise a use of power for illegitimate ends.

Comment

a. Rationale. An ordinary offer to make a contract commonly involves an implied threat by one party, the offeror, not to make the contract unless his terms are accepted by the other party, the offeree. Such threats are an accepted part of the bargaining process. A threat does not amount to duress unless it is so improper as to amount to an abuse of that process. Courts first recognized as improper threats of physical violence and later included wrongful seizure or detention of goods. Modern decisions have recognized as improper a much broader range of threats, notably those to cause economic harm. . . .

c. Threat of prosecution. Under the rule stated in Clause (1)(b), a threat of criminal prosecution is improper as a means of inducing the recipient to make a contract. An explanation in good faith of the criminal consequences of another's conduct may not involve a threat. But if a threat is made, the fact that the one who makes it honestly believes that the recipient is guilty is not material. The threat involves a misuse, for personal gain, of power given for other legitimate ends. See Comment *f.* . . . The guilt or innocence of the person whose prosecution is threatened is immaterial in determining whether the threat is improper, although it may be easier to show that the threat actually induced assent in the case of guilt. A bargain to suppress prosecution may be unenforceable on grounds of public policy. . . .

d. Threat of civil process. The policy in favor of free access to the judicial system militates against the characterization as improper of threats to commence civil process, even if the claim on which the process is based eventually proves to be without foundation. Nevertheless, if the threat is shown to have been made in bad faith, it is improper. Bad faith may be shown by proving that the person making the threat did not believe there was a reasonable basis for the threatened process, that he knew the threat would involve a misuse of the process or that he realized the demand he made was exorbitant. . . .

Illustrations

. . . .

7. A, who has a valid claim for damages against B, threatens to attach a shipment of perishable goods unless B makes a contract to sell a machine to A. As A knows, other non-perishable goods are available for attachment. B, having no reasonable alternative, is induced by A's threat to make the contract. Since A knows that the threatened attachment would involve a misuse of that process to force a settlement rather than to preserve assets, his threat is made in bad faith. A's threat is improper and the contract is voidable by B.

e. Breach of contract. A threat by a party to a contract not to perform his contractual duty is not, of itself, improper. Indeed, a modification induced by such a threat may be binding, even in the absence of consideration, if it is fair and equitable in view of unanticipated circumstances. See §89. The mere fact that the modification induced by the threat fails to meet this test does not mean that the threat is necessarily improper. However, the threat is improper if it amounts to a breach of the duty of good faith and fair dealing imposed by the contract. See §205. . . .

f. Other improper threats. The proper limits of bargaining are difficult to define with precision. Hard bargaining between experienced adversaries of relatively equal power ought not to be discouraged. Parties are generally held to the resulting agreement, even though one has taken advantage of the other's adversity, as long as the contract has been dictated by general economic forces. . . . Where, however, a party has been induced to make a contract by some power exercised by the other for illegitimate ends, the transaction is suspect. For example, absent statute, a threat of refusal to deal with another party is ordinarily not duress, but if other factors are present an agreement that results from such a threat may be called into question. Subsection (2) deals with threats that are improper if the resulting exchange is not on fair terms. Clause (a) is concerned with cases in which a party threatens to do an act that would not significantly benefit him but would harm the other party. If, on the recipient's refusal to contract, the maker of the threat were to do the threatened act, it would therefore be done maliciously and unconscionably, out of pure vindictiveness. A typical example is a threat to make public embarrassing information concerning the recipient unless he makes a proposed contract. . . . Clause (b) is concerned with cases in which the party making the threat has by unfair dealing achieved an advantage over the recipient that makes his threat unusually effective. Typical examples involve manipulative conduct during the bargaining stage that leaves one person at the mercy of the other. . . . Clause (c) is concerned with other cases in which the threatened act involves the use of power for illegitimate ends. Many of the situations encompassed by clauses (1)(b), (1)(c), (2)(a) and (2)(b) involve extreme applications of this general rule, but it is more broadly applicable to analogous cases. . . . If, in any of these cases, the threat comes within Subsection (1), as where the threatened act or the threat itself is criminal or tortious (Clause (1)(a)), it is improper without an inquiry into the fairness of the resulting exchange under Subsection 2. See Comment *a*. . . .

§177. When Undue Influence Makes a Contract Voidable

(1) Undue influence is unfair persuasion of a party who is under the domination of the person exercising the persuasion or who by virtue of the relation between them is justified in assuming that that person will not act in a manner inconsistent with his welfare.

(2) If a party's manifestation of assent is induced by undue influence by the other party, the contract is voidable by the victim.

(3) If a party's manifestation of assent is induced by one who is not a party to the transaction, the contract is voidable by the victim unless the other party to the transaction in good faith and without reason to know of the undue influence either gives value or relies materially on the transaction.

Comment

a. Required domination or relation. The rule stated in this Section protects a person only if he is under the domination of another or is justified, by virtue of his relation with another in assuming that the other will not act inconsistently with his welfare. Relations that often fall within the rule include those of parent and child, husband and wife, clergyman and parishioner, and physician and patient. In each case it is a question of fact whether the relation is such as to give undue weight to the other's attempts at persuasion. The required relation may be found in situations other than those enumerated. However, the mere fact that a party is weak, infirm or aged does not of itself suffice, although it may be a factor in determining whether the required relation existed.

b. Unfair persuasion. Where the required domination or relation is present, the contract is voidable if it was induced by any unfair persuasion on the part of the stronger party. The law of undue influence therefore affords protection in situations where the rules on duress and misrepresentation give no relief. The degree of persuasion that is unfair depends on a variety of circumstances. The ultimate question is whether the result was produced by means that seriously impaired the free and competent exercise of judgment. Such factors as the unfairness of the resulting bargain, the unavailability of independent advice, and the susceptibility of the person persuaded are circumstances to be taken into account in determining whether there was unfair persuasion, but they are not in themselves controlling. Compare §173. . . .

CHAPTER 8. UNENFORCEABILITY ON GROUNDS OF PUBLIC POLICY

Topic 1. Unenforceability in General

§178. When a Term Is Unenforceable on Grounds of Public Policy

(1) A promise or other term of an agreement is unenforceable on grounds of public policy if legislation provides that it is unenforceable or the interest in its enforcement is clearly outweighed in the circumstances by a public policy against the enforcement of such terms.

(2) In weighing the interest in the enforcement of a term, account is taken of

    (a) the parties' justified expectations,

    (b) any forfeiture that would result if enforcement were denied, and

    (c) any special public interest in the enforcement of the particular term.

(3) In weighing a public policy against enforcement of a term, account is taken of

    (a) the strength of that policy as manifested by legislation or judicial decisions,

    (b) the likelihood that a refusal to enforce the term will further that policy,

(c) the seriousness of any misconduct involved and the extent to which it was deliberate, and

(d) the directness of the connection between that misconduct and the term.

Comment

. . . .

b. Balancing of interests. Only infrequently does legislation, on grounds of public policy, provide that a term is unenforceable. When a court reaches that conclusion, it usually does so on the basis of a public policy derived either from its own perception of the need to protect some aspect of the public welfare or from legislation that is relevant to that policy although it says nothing explicitly about unenforceability. See §179. In some cases the contravention of public policy is so grave, as when an agreement involves a serious crime or tort, that unenforceability is plain. In other cases the contravention is so trivial as that it plainly does not preclude enforcement. In doubtful cases, however, a decision as to enforceability is reached only after a careful balancing, in the light of all the circumstances, of the interest in the enforcement of the particular promise against the policy against the enforcement of such terms. . . . Enforcement will be denied only if the factors that argue against enforcement clearly outweigh the law's traditional interest in protecting the expectations of the parties, its abhorrence of any unjust enrichment, and any public interest in the enforcement of the particular term.

c. Strength of policy. The strength of the public policy involved is a critical factor in the balancing process. Even when the policy is one manifested by legislation, it may be too insubstantial to outweigh the interest in the enforcement of the term in question. . . . A court should be particularly alert to this possibility in the case of minor administrative regulations or local ordinances that may not be indicative of the general welfare. A disparity between a relatively modest criminal sanction provided by the legislature and a much larger forfeiture that will result if enforcement of the promise is refused may suggest that the policy is not substantial enough to justify the refusal. . . .

f. Effect on rest of agreement. The rules stated in this Section determine only whether a particular promise or other term is unenforceable. The question of the effect of such a determination on the rest of the agreement is sometimes a complex one. If there is only one promise in the transaction and it is unenforceable, then the question will not arise. . . . Furthermore, even when there is another promise, it too is often unenforceable under the rules stated in this Section. This is the case, for example, where one party's promise is unenforceable because the promised conduct offends public policy and the other party's return promise is unenforceable because it tends to induce that conduct. . . . There are, however, situations in which only one party's promise is unenforceable while the other party's return promise is enforceable. . . . Finally, there are circumstances in which the unenforceability of one part of an agreement does not entail the unenforceability of the rest of the agreement. . . .

§179. Bases of Public Policies Against Enforcement

A public policy against the enforcement of promises or other terms may be derived by the court from

    (a) legislation relevant to such a policy, or

    (b) the need to protect some aspect of the public welfare, as is the case for the judicial policies against, for example,

        (i) restraint of trade (§§186-188),

        (ii) impairment of family relations (§§189-191), and

        (iii) interference with other protected interests (§§192-196, 356).

§180. Effect of Excusable Ignorance

If a promisee is excusably ignorant of facts or of legislation of a minor character, of which the promisor is not excusably ignorant and in the absence of which the promise would be enforceable, the promisee has a claim for damages for its breach but cannot recover damages for anything that he has done after he learns of the facts or legislation.

Comment

a. Excusable ignorance. At the time a promise is made, the promisee may be excusably ignorant of facts that contravene the public policy in question. Furthermore, although for the purposes of this Chapter, parties are generally charged with knowledge of policies affecting enforceability, this Section states a limited exception for a party who is excusably ignorant of legislation of a minor character from which the policy is derived. Such ignorance is more likely to be excusable where the legislation is of a local, specialized or technical nature and where the other party may be assumed to have knowledge as to such matters. In determining whether ignorance of fact or law is excusable, any misrepresentations made by the other party are relevant. However, good faith is expected on the part of the party who claims ignorance and he cannot blind his eyes because he does not wish to see. Furthermore, the matter of which he is ignorant must not be one as to which he is expected to have knowledge because of his expertise or his relation to the transaction.

b. Promisor must not be excusably ignorant. The promisee's excusable ignorance is not by itself enough to give him the right to enforce the promise under this Section. The promisor must not be excusably ignorant as to the matter in question. (That an unenforceable promise can be consideration for a return promise, see §78.) If the promisor has specialized knowledge of the field involved, he is likely to be charged with knowledge as to legislation of even a minor character. It is not necessary that the promisor make any misrepresentation, although a misrepresentation by him may be significant as bearing on whether the promisee's ignorance is excusable. See Comment *a*. Furthermore, on learning the truth, the promisee is expected promptly to withdraw from the transaction and render no further performance. . . .

§181. Effect of Failure to Comply with Licensing or Similar Requirement

If a party is prohibited from doing an act because of his failure to comply with a licensing, registration or similar requirement, a promise in consideration of his doing that act or of his promise to do so it is unenforceable on grounds of public policy if
(a) the requirement has a regulatory purpose, and
(b) the interest in the enforcement of the promise is clearly outweighed by the public policy behind the requirement.

§182. Effect of Performance if Intended Use Is Improper

If the promisee has substantially performed, enforcement of a promise is not precluded on grounds of public policy because of some improper use that the promisor intends to make of what he obtains unless the promisee
(a) acted for the purpose of furthering the improper use, or
(b) knew of the use and the use involves grave social harm.

§183. When Agreement Is Enforceable as to Agreed Equivalents

If the parties' performances can be apportioned into corresponding pairs of part performances so that the parts of each pair are properly regarded as agreed equivalents and one pair is not offensive to public policy, that portion of the agreement is enforceable by a party who did not engage in serious misconduct.

§184. When Rest of Agreement Is Enforceable

(1) If less than all of an agreement is unenforceable under the rule stated in §178, a court may nevertheless enforce the rest of the agreement in favor of a party who did not engage in serious misconduct if the performance as to which the agreement is unenforceable is not an essential part of the agreed exchange.

(2) A court may treat only part of a term as unenforceable under the rule stated in Subsection (1) if the party who seeks to enforce the term obtained it in good faith and in accordance with reasonable standards of fair dealing.

Comment

a. Refusal to enforce a promise. . . . If the performance as to which the agreement is unenforceable is an essential part of the agreed exchange, the inequality will be so great as to make the entire agreement unenforceable. Under Subsection (1), however, if that performance is not an essential part of the agreed exchange, a court may enforce all but the part that contravenes public policy. For example, a promise not to compete that is unreasonably in restraint of trade will often not invalidate the entire agreement of which it is a part. Whether the performance is an essential part of the agreed exchange depends on its relative importance in the light of the entire agreement between the parties. A party who has engaged in such serious misconduct that the entire agreement is unenforceable cannot take advantage of the rule stated in Subsection (1). . . .

b. Refusal to enforce part of a term. Sometimes a term is unenforceable on grounds of public policy because it is too broad, even though a narrower term would be enforceable. In such a situation, under Subsection (2), the court may refuse to enforce only part of the term, while enforcing the other part of the term as well as the rest of the agreement. . . . A court will not exercise this discretion in favor of a party unless it appears that he made the agreement in good faith and in accordance with reasonable standards of fair dealing. Compare §§157, 205. For example, a court will not aid a party who has taken advantage of his dominant bargaining power to extract from the other party a promise that is clearly so broad as to offend public policy by redrafting the agreement so as to make a part of the promise enforceable. The fact that the term is contained in a standard form supplied by the dominant party argues against aiding him in this request. Whether a particular dispute involves a single term, so that it comes under Subsection (2), or separate terms, so that it comes under Subsection (1), will be determined from the substance of the agreement as well as from its language. . . .

§185. Excuse of a Condition on Grounds of Public Policy

To the extent that a term requiring the occurrence of a condition is unenforceable under the rule stated in §178, a court may excuse the non-occurrence of the condition unless its occurrence was an essential part of the agreed exchange.

Topic 2.   Restraint of Trade

§186. Promise in Restraint of Trade

(1) A promise is unenforceable on grounds of public policy if it is unreasonably in restraint of trade.

(2) A promise is in restraint of trade if its performance would limit competition in any business or restrict the promisor in the exercise of a gainful occupation.

Comment

a. Rule of reason. Every promise that relates to business dealings or to a professional or other gainful occupation operates as a restraint in the sense that it restricts the promisor's future activity. Such a promise is not, however, unenforceable unless the restraint that it imposes is unreasonably detrimental to the smooth operation of a freely competitive private economy. A rule of reason of this kind necessarily has somewhat vague outlines. Whether a restraint is reasonable is determined in the light of the circumstances of the transaction, including not only the particular facts but general social and economic conditions as well. The promise is viewed in terms of the effects that it could have had and not merely what actually occurred. Account is taken of such factors as the protection that it affords for the promisee's legitimate interests, the hardship that it imposes on the promisor, and the likely injury to the public. See §188 and Comments *b* and *c* to that Section. A restraint that is reasonable in some circumstances may be unreasonable in others. . . .

§187. Non-Ancillary Restraints on Competition

A promise to refrain from competition that imposes a restraint that is not ancillary to an otherwise valid transaction or relationship is unreasonably in restraint of trade.

Comment

. . . .

b. Non-ancillary restraints. In order for a promise to refrain from competition to be reasonable, the promisee must have an interest worthy of protection that can be balanced against the hardship on the promisor and the likely injury to the public. See §188 and Comments *b* and *c* to that Section. The restraint must, therefore, be subsidiary to an otherwise valid transaction or relationship that gives rise to such an interest. A restraint that is not so related to an otherwise valid transaction or relationship is necessarily unreasonable. The promisee's interest may arise out of his acquisition from the promisor of a business. See §188(2)(a). It may arise out of a relation between himself as employer or principal and the promisor as employee or agent. See §188(2)(b). Or it may arise out of a relation between himself and the promisor as partners. See §188(2)(c). This enumeration does not purport to be exhaustive, but a promise not to *compete* that is not ancillary to some such transaction or relationship as these is unreasonable because it protects no legitimate interest of the promisee. This is so even though the promise would be enforceable if it were an ancillary promise. In order for a restraint to be ancillary to a transaction or relationship the promise that imposes it must be made as part of that transaction or relationship. A promise made subsequent to the transaction or relationship is not ancillary to it. In the case of an ongoing transaction or relationship, however, it is enough if the promise is made before its termination, as long as it is supported by consideration and meets the other requirements of enforceability. . . .

§188. Ancillary Restraints on Competition

(1) A promise to refrain from competition that imposes a restraint that is ancillary to an otherwise valid transaction or relationship is unreasonably in restraint of trade if

(a) the restraint is greater than is needed to protect the promisee's legitimate interest, or

(b) the promisee's need is outweighed by the hardship to the promisor and the likely injury to the public.

(2) Promises imposing restraints that are ancillary to a valid transaction or relationship include the following:

(a) a promise by the seller of a business not to compete with the buyer in such a way as to injure the value of the business sold;

(b) a promise by an employee or other agent not to compete with his employer or other principal;

(c) a promise by a partner not to compete with the partnership.

Comment

. . . .

d. Extent of the restraint. The extent of the restraint . . . may be limited in three ways: by type of activity, by geographical area, and by time. If the promise proscribes types of activity more extensive than necessary to protect those engaged in by the promisee, it goes beyond what is necessary to protect his legitimate interests and is unreasonable. If it covers a geographical area more extensive than necessary to protect his interests, it is also unreasonable. And if the restraint is to last longer than is required in light of those interests, taking account of such factors as the permanent or transitory nature of technology and information, it is unreasonable. Since, in any of these cases, the restraint is too broad to be justified by the promisee's need, a court may hold it to be unreasonable without the necessity of weighing the countervailing interests of the promisor and the public. What limits as to activity, geographical area, and time are appropriate in a particular case depends on all the circumstances. . . .

f. Promise by seller of a business. A promise to refrain from competition made in connection with a sale of a business may be reasonable in the light of the buyer's need to protect the value of the good will that he has acquired. In effect, the seller promises not to act so as to diminish the value of what he has sold. An analogous situation arises when the value of a corporation's business depends largely on the good will of one or more of the officers or shareholders. In that situation, officers or shareholders, either on the sale of their shares or on the sale of the corporation's business, may make an enforceable promise not to compete with the corporation or with the purchaser of its business, just as the corporation itself could on sale of its business make an enforceable promise to refrain from competition. . . .

g. Promise by employee or agent. The employer's interest in exacting from his employee a promise not to compete after termination of the employment is usually explained on the ground that the employee has acquired either confidential trade information relating to some process or method or the means to attract customers away from the employer. Whether the risk that the employee may do injury to the employer is sufficient to justify a promise to refrain from competition after the termination of the employment will depend on the facts of the particular case. Post-employment restraints are scrutinized with particular care because they are often the product of unequal bargaining power and because the employee is likely to give scant attention to the hardship he may later suffer through loss of his livelihood. This is especially so where the restraint is imposed by the employer's standardized printed form. Cf. §208. A line must be drawn between the general skills and knowledge of the trade and information that is peculiar to the employer's business. If the employer seeks to justify the restraint on the ground of the employee's knowledge of a process or method, the confidentiality of that process or method and its technological life may be critical. . . . The court will take account of any diminution in competition likely to result from slowing down the dissemination of ideas and of any impairment of the function of the market in shifting manpower to areas of greatest productivity. If the employer seeks to justify the restraint on the ground of the employee's ability to attract customers, the nature, extent and locale of the employee's contacts with customers are relevant. A restraint is easier to justify if it is limited to one field of activity among many that are available to the employee. The same is true if the restraint is limited to the taking of his former employer's customers as contrasted with competition in general. A restraint may be ancillary to a relationship although, as in the case of an employment at will, no contract of employment is involved. . . .

Topic 3. Impairment of Family Relations

§189. Promise in Restraint of Marriage

A promise is unenforceable on grounds of public policy if it is unreasonably in restraint of marriage.

§190. Promise Detrimental to Marital Relationship

(1) A promise by a person contemplating marriage or by a married person, other than as part of an enforceable separation agreement, is unenforceable on grounds of public policy if it would change some essential incident of the marital relationship in a way detrimental to the public interest in the marriage relationship. A separation agreement is unenforceable on grounds of public policy unless it is made after separation or in contemplation of an immediate separation and is fair in the circumstances.

(2) A promise that tends unreasonably to encourage divorce or separation is unenforceable on grounds of public policy.

§191. Promise Affecting Custody

A promise affecting the right of custody of a minor child is unenforceable on grounds of public policy unless the disposition as to custody is consistent with the best interest of the child.

Topic 4.   *Interference with Other Protected Interests*

§192.   Promise Involving Commission of a Tort

A promise to commit a tort or to induce the commission of a tort is unenforceable on grounds of public policy.

§193.   Promise Inducing Violation of Fiduciary Duty

A promise by a fiduciary to violate his fiduciary duty or a promise that tends to induce such a violation is unenforceable on grounds of public policy.

§194.   Promise Interfering With Contract With Another

A promise that tortiously interferes with performance of a contract with a third person or a tortiously induced promise to commit a breach of contract is unenforceable on grounds of public policy.

§195.   Term Exempting From Liability for Harm Caused Intentionally, Recklessly or Negligently

(1) A term exempting a party from tort liability for harm caused intentionally or recklessly is unenforceable on grounds of public policy.

(2) A term exempting a party from tort liability for harm caused negligently is unenforceable on grounds of public policy if

(a) the term exempts an employer from liability to an employee for injury in the course of his employment;

(b) the term exempts one charged with a duty of public service from liability to one to whom that duty is owed for compensation for breach of that duty, or

(c) the other party is similarly a member of a class protected against the class to which the first party belongs.

(3) A term exempting a seller of a product from his special tort liability for physical harm to a user or consumer is unenforceable on grounds of public policy unless the term is fairly bargained for and is consistent with the policy underlying that liability.

Comment

a. Rationale. The law of torts imposes standards of conduct for the protection of others against unreasonable risk of harm. One cannot exempt himself from such liability for harm that is caused either intentionally or recklessly. . . . However, a party to a contract can ordinarily exempt himself from liability for harm caused by his failure to observe the standard of reasonable care imposed by the law of negligence. . . . This rule is subject to an exception if the other party is a member of a protected class. Two examples of this exception are widely recognized. First, an employer is not permitted to exempt himself from liability to his employee for negligently caused injury (paragraph (a)). Second, one who is charged with a duty of public service, such as a common carrier or a public utility, and who undertakes to perform it for compensation, is not permitted to exempt himself from liability to the one to be served for negligent breach of that duty (paragraph (b)). The rigor of this rule may, however, be mitigated by a fairly bargained for agreement to limit liability to a reasonable agreed value in return for a lower rate. In most jurisdictions legislation has altered the rule in specific situations, usually by restricting the power to limit liability. The two examples given under Subsection (2) are not intended as an exhaustive list of situations in which such terms are unenforceable. If, for example, a statute imposes a standard of conduct, a court may decide on the basis of an analysis of the statute, that a term exempting a party from liability for failure to conform to that standard is unenforceable. See §179(a). . . .

b. *Relation to other rules.* Language inserted by a party in an agreement for the purpose of exempting him from liability for negligent conduct is scrutinized with particular care and a court may require specific and conspicuous reference to negligence under the general principle that language is interpreted against the draftsman. See §206. Furthermore, a party's attempt to exempt himself from liability for negligent conduct may fail as unconscionable. See §208. The rule stated in this Section does not apply to an agreement by a third person to indemnify a party against liability in tort. The effect of a term purporting to exempt a party from the consequences of a misrepresentation is governed by the rule stated in §196. . . .

§196. Term Exempting From Consequences of Misrepresentation

A term unreasonably exempting a party from the legal consequences of a misrepresentation is unenforceable on grounds of public policy.

Topic 5. Restitution

§197. Restitution Generally Unavailable

Except as stated in §§198 and 199, a party has no claim in restitution for performance that he has rendered under or in return for a promise that is unenforceable on grounds of public policy unless denial of restitution would cause disproportionate forfeiture.

§198. Restitution in Favor of Party Who Is Excusably Ignorant or Is Not Equally in the Wrong

A party has a claim in restitution for performance that he has rendered under or in return for a promise that is unenforceable on grounds of public policy if

(a) he was excusably ignorant of the facts or of legislation of a minor character, in the absence of which the promise would be enforceable, or

(b) he was not equally in the wrong with the promisor.

§199. Restitution Where Party Withdraws or Situation Is Contrary to Public Interest

A party has a claim in restitution for performance that he has rendered under or in return for a promise that is unenforceable on grounds of public policy if he did not engage in serious misconduct and

(a) he withdraws from the transaction before the improper purpose has been achieved, or

(b) allowance of the claim would put an end to a continuing situation that is contrary to the public interest.

CHAPTER 9.   THE SCOPE OF CONTRACTUAL OBLIGATIONS

Topic 1.   The Meaning of Agreements

§200.   Interpretation of Promise or Agreement

Interpretation of a promise or agreement or a term thereof is the ascertainment of its meaning.

Comment

a. Formation of contract. Questions of interpretation arise in determining whether there is a contract as well as in determining rights and duties under a contract. . . .

b. Manifestation of intention. [T]he intention of a party that is relevant to formation of a contract is the intention manifested by him rather than any different undisclosed intention. . . . It follows that the meaning of the words or other conduct of a party is not necessarily the meaning he expects or understands. He is not bound by a meaning unless he has reason to know of it, but the expectation and understanding of the other party must also be taken into account. See §201.

c. Interpretation and legal operation. Interpretation is not a determination of the legal effect of words or other conduct. Properly interpreted, an agreement may not be enforceable as a contract, or a term such as a promise to pay a penalty may be denied legal effect, or it may have a legal effect different from that agreed upon, as in a case of employment at less than a statutory minimum wage.

§201. Whose Meaning Prevails

(1) Where the parties have attached the same meaning to a promise or agreement or a term thereof, it is interpreted in accordance with that meaning.

(2) Where the parties have attached different meanings to a promise or agreement or a term thereof, it is interpreted in accordance with the meaning attached by one of them if at the time the agreement was made

    (a) that party did not know of any different meaning attached by the other, and the other knew the meaning attached by the first party; or

    (b) that party had no reason to know of any different meaning attached by the other, and the other had reason to know the meaning attached by the first party.

(3) Except as stated in this Section, neither party is bound by the meaning attached by the other, even though the result may be a failure of mutual assent.

Comment

a. The meaning of words. Words are used as conventional symbols of mental states, with standardized meanings based on habitual or customary practice. Unless a different intention is shown, language is interpreted in accordance with its generally prevailing meaning. See §202(3). Usages of varying degrees of generality are recorded in dictionaries, but there are substantial differences between English and American usages and between usages in different parts of the United States. Differences of usage also exist in various localities and in different social, economic, religious and ethnic groups. All these usages change over time, and persons engaged in transactions with each other often develop temporary usages peculiar to themselves. Moreover, most words are commonly used in more than one sense.

b. The problem of context. Uncertainties in the meaning of words are ordinarily greatly reduced by the context in which they are used. The same is true of other conventional symbols, and the meaning of conduct not used as a conventional symbol is even more dependent on its setting. But the context of words and other conduct is seldom exactly the same for two different people, since connotations depend on the entire past experience and the attitudes and expectations of the person whose understanding is in question. In general, the context relevant to interpretation of a bargain is the context common to both parties. More precisely, the question of meaning in cases of misunderstanding depends on an inquiry into what each party knew or had reason to know, as stated in Subsections (2) and (3). See §20 . . . . Ordinarily a party has reason to know of meanings in general usage.

c. Mutual understanding. Subsection (1) makes it clear that the primary search is for a common meaning of the parties, not a meaning imposed on them by the law. . . . The objective of interpretation in the general law of contracts is to carry out the understanding of the parties rather than to impose obligations on them contrary to their understanding: "the courts do not make a contract for the parties." Ordinarily, therefore, the mutual understanding of the parties prevails even where the contractual term has been defined differently by statute or administrative regulation. But parties who used a standardized term in an unusual sense obviously run the risk that their agreement will be misinterpreted in litigation. . . .

d. Misunderstanding. Subsection (2) follows the terminology of §20, referring to the understanding of each party as the meaning "attached" by him to a term of a promise or agreement. Where the rules stated in Subsections (1) and (2) do not apply, neither party is bound by the understanding of the other. The result may be an entire failure of agreement or a failure to agree as to a term. There may be a binding contract despite failure to agree as to a term, if the term is not essential or if it can be supplied. See §204. In some cases a party can waive the misunderstanding and enforce the contract in accordance with the understanding of the other party. . . .

§202.   Rules in Aid of Interpretation

(1) Words and other conduct are interpreted in the light of all the circumstances, and if the principal purpose of the parties is ascertainable it is given great weight.

(2) A writing is interpreted as a whole, and all writings that are part of the same transaction are interpreted together.

(3) Unless a different intention is manifested,

(a) where language has a generally prevailing meaning, it is interpreted in accordance with that meaning;

(b) technical terms and words of art are given their technical meaning when used in a transaction within their technical field.

(4) Where an agreement involves repeated occasions for performance by either party with knowledge of the nature of the performance and opportunity for objection to it by the other, any course of performance accepted or acquiesced in without objection is given great weight in the interpretation of the agreement.

(5) Wherever reasonable, the manifestations of intention of the parties to a promise or agreement are interpreted as consistent with each other and with any relevant course of performance, course of dealing, or usage of trade.

Comment

a. Scope of special rules. The rules in this Section are applicable to all manifestations of intention and all transactions. The rules are general in character, and serve merely as guides in the process of interpretation. They do not depend upon any determination that there is an ambiguity, but are used in determining what meanings are reasonably possible as well as in choosing among possible meanings.

b. Circumstances. The meaning of words and other symbols commonly depends on their context; the meaning of other conduct is even more dependent on the circumstances. In interpreting the words and conduct of the parties to a contract, a court seeks to put itself in the position they occupied at the time the contract was made. When the parties have adopted a writing as a final expression of their agreement, interpretation is directed to the meaning of that writing in the light of the circumstances. See §§209, 212. The circumstances for this purpose include the entire situation, as it appeared to the parties, and in appropriate cases may include facts known to one party of which the other had reason to know. See §201. . . .

c. Principal purpose. The purposes of the parties to a contract are not always identical; particularly in business transactions, the parties often have divergent or even conflicting interests. But up to a point they commonly join in a common purpose of attaining a specific factual or legal result which each regards as necessary to the attainment of his ultimate purposes. Moreover, one party may know or have reason to know the purpose of the other and thus that his meaning is one consistent with that purpose. Determination that the parties have a principal purpose in common requires interpretation, but if such a purpose is disclosed further interpretation is guided by it. Even language which is otherwise explicit may be read with a modification needed to make it consistent with such a purpose. . . .

d. Interpretation of the whole. Meaning is inevitably dependent on context. A word changes meaning when it becomes part of a sentence, the sentence when it becomes part of a paragraph. A longer writing similarly affects the paragraph, other related writings affect the particular writing, and the circumstances affect the whole. Where the whole can be read to give significance to each part, that reading is preferred; if such a reading would be unreasonable, a choice must be made. See §203. To fit the immediate verbal context or the more remote total context particular words or punctuation may be disregarded or supplied; clerical or grammatical errors may be corrected; singular may be treated as plural or plural as singular. . . .

e. General usage. . . . English words are read as having the meaning given them by general usage, if there is one. This rule is a rule of interpretation in the absence of contrary evidence, not a rule excluding contrary evidence. It may also yield to internal indications such as inconsistency, absurdity, or departure from normal grammar, punctuation, or word order. . . .

f. Technical terms. Parties to an agreement often use the vocabulary of a particular place, vocation or trade, in which new words are coined and common words are assigned new meanings. But technical terms are often misused, and it may be shown that a technical word or phrase was used in a non-technical sense. Moreover, the same word may have a variety of technical and other meanings. "Mules" may mean animals, shoes or machines; a "ram" may mean an animal or a hydraulic ram; "zebra" may refer to a mammal, a butterfly, a lizard, a fish, a type of plant, tree or wood, or merely to the letter "Z". . . .

g. Course of performance. The parties to an agreement know best what they meant, and their action under it is often the strongest evidence of their meaning. But such "practical construction" is not conclusive of meaning. Conduct must be weighed in the light of the terms of the agreement and their possible meanings. Where it is unreasonable to interpret the contract in accordance with the course of performance, the conduct of the parties may be evidence of an agreed modification or of a waiver by one party. . . .

§203. Standards of Preference in Interpretation

In the interpretation of a promise or agreement or a term thereof, the following standards of preference are generally applicable:

(a) an interpretation which gives a reasonable, lawful, and effective meaning to all the terms is preferred to an interpretation which leaves a part unreasonable, unlawful, or of no effect;

(b) express terms are given greater weight than course of performance, course of dealing, and usage of trade, course of performance is given greater weight than course of dealing or usage of trade, and course of dealing is given greater weight than usage of trade;

(c) specific terms and exact terms are given greater weight than general language;

(d) separately negotiated or added terms are given greater weight than standardized terms or other terms not separately negotiated.

Comment

a. Scope. The rules of this Section are applicable to all manifestations of intention and all transactions. They apply only in choosing among reasonable interpretations. They do not override evidence of the meaning of the parties, but aid in determining meaning or prescribe legal effect when meaning is in doubt.

b. Superfluous terms. Since an agreement is interpreted as a whole, it is assumed in the first instance that no part of it is superfluous. . . . [P]articularly in cases of integrated agreements, terms are rarely agreed to without reason. Where an integrated agreement has been negotiated with care and in detail and has been expertly drafted for the particular transaction, an interpretation is very strongly negated if it would render some provisions superfluous. On the other hand, a standard form may include provisions appropriate only to some of the transactions in which the form is to be used; or the form may be used for an inappropriate transaction. Even agreements tailored to particular transactions sometimes include overlapping or redundant or meaningless provisions.

The preference for an interpretation which gives meaning to every part of an agreement does not mean that every part is assumed to have legal consequences. Parties commonly direct their attention to performance rather than breach, and it is enough that each provision has meaning to them as a guide to performance. Stipulations against particular legal consequences are not uncommon. Thus it is not unusual to define the intended performance with precision and then to provide for tolerances within which variation is permitted. . . .

c. Unreasonable and unlawful terms. In the absence of contrary indication, it is assumed that each term of an agreement has a reasonable rather than an unreasonable meaning, and that the agreement is intended to be lawful rather than unconscionable, fraudulent or otherwise illegal. But parties are free to make agreements which seem unreasonable to others, and circumstances may show that even an agreement innocent on its face has an illegal purpose. The search is for the manifested intention of the parties. If a term or a contract is unconscionable or otherwise against public policy, it should be dealt with directly rather than by spurious interpretation. See §208 and Uniform Commercial Code §2-302. . . .

d. Priority of express terms. Just as parties to agreements often depart from general usage as to the meaning of words or other conduct, so they may depart from a usage of trade. Similarly, they may change a pattern established by their own prior course of dealing. Their meaning in such cases is ordinarily to be ascertained as a fact; no penalty is attached by the law of contracts to their failure to conform to the usages of others or to their own prior usage. Course of performance may establish meaning, or it may show mistake or oversight or modification or waiver. . . . The priorities stated in Subsection (b) are those stated in Uniform Commercial Code §[1-303], rephrased to fit the different context of the Restatement.

e. General and specific terms. People commonly use general language without a clear consciousness of its full scope and without awareness that an exception should be made. Attention and understanding are likely to be in better focus when language is specific or exact, and in case of conflict the specific or exact term is more likely to express the meaning of the parties with respect to the situation than the general language. If the specific or exact can be read as an exception or qualification of the general, both are given some effect, in accordance with the rule stated in Subsection (a). . . . But the rule yields to manifestation of a contrary intention.

f. Superseded standard terms. The rule stated in Subsection (d) has frequent application in cases of standardized documents. Printed forms are often misused, and there may be a question whether the parties manifested assent to a printed term on a writing. A printed provision that is clearly part of an integrated contract is normally to be interpreted as consistent with other terms, but in cases of inconsistency a handwritten or typewritten term inserted in connection with the particular transaction ordinarily prevails. Similarly, a typewritten term may be superseded by drawing a line through it, modified by interlineation, or controlled by an inconsistent handwritten insertion in another part of the agreement. It is sometimes said generally that handwritten terms control typewritten and printed terms, and typewritten control printed. . . . But the rule yields to manifestation of a contrary intention. . . .

§204. Supplying an Omitted Essential Term

When the parties to a bargain sufficiently defined to be a contract have not agreed with respect to a term which is essential to a determination of their rights and duties, a term which is reasonable in the circumstances is supplied by the court.

Comment

a. Scope; relation to other rules. This Section states a principle governing the legal effect of a binding agreement. The supplying of an omitted term is not technically interpretation, but the two are closely related; courts often speak of an "implied" term. . . .

b. How omission occurs. The parties to an agreement may entirely fail to foresee the situation which later arises and gives rise to a dispute; they then have no expectations with respect to that situation, and a search for their meaning with respect to it is fruitless. Or they may have expectations but fail to manifest them, either because the expectation rests on an assumption which is unconscious or only partly conscious, or because the situation seems to be unimportant or unlikely, or because discussion of it might be unpleasant or might produce delay or impasse.

c. Interpretation and omission. Interpretation may be necessary to determine that the parties have not agreed with respect to a particular term, but the supplying of an omitted term is not within the definition of interpretation in §200. . . . [I]nterpretation may result in the conclusion that there was in fact no agreement on a particular point, and that conclusion should be accepted even though the omitted term could be supplied by giving agreed language a meaning different from the meaning or meanings given it by the parties.

d. Supplying a term. The process of supplying an omitted term has sometimes been disguised as a literal or a purposive reading of contract language directed to a situation other than the situation that arises. Sometimes it is said that the search is for the term the parties would have agreed to if the question had been brought to their attention. Both the meaning of the words used and the probability that a particular term would have been used if the question had been raised may be factors in determining what term is reasonable in the circumstances. But where there is in fact no agreement, the court should supply a term which comports with community standards of fairness and policy rather than analyze a hypothetical model of the bargaining process. Thus where a contract calls for a single performance such as the rendering of a service or the delivery of goods, the parties are most unlikely to agree explicitly that performance will be rendered within a "reasonable time;" but if no time is specified, a term calling for performance within a reasonable time is supplied. . . .

e. Effect of the parol evidence rule. The fact that an essential term is omitted may indicate that the agreement is not integrated or that there is partial rather than complete integration. In such cases the omitted term may be supplied by prior negotiations or a prior agreement. See §216. But omission of a term does not show conclusively that integration was not complete and a completely integrated agreement, if binding, discharges prior agreements within its scope. See §213. Where there is complete integration and interpretation of the writing discloses a failure to agree on an essential term, evidence of prior negotiations or agreements is not admissible to supply the omitted term, but such evidence may be admissible, if relevant, on the question of what is reasonable in the circumstances. . . .

Topic 2.   Considerations of Fairness and the Public Interest

§205.   Duty of Good Faith and Fair Dealing

Every contract imposes upon each party a duty of good faith and fair dealing in its performance and its enforcement.

Comment

a. Meanings of "good faith." Good faith is defined in Uniform Commercial Code §1-201(19) as "honesty in fact in the conduct or transaction concerned." "In the case of a merchant" Uniform Commercial Code §2-103(1)(b) provides that good faith means "honesty in fact and the observance of reasonable commercial standards of fair dealing in the trade."*** The phrase "good faith" is used in a variety of contexts, and its meaning varies somewhat with the context. Good faith performance or enforcement of a contract emphasizes faithfulness to an agreed common purpose and consistency with the justified expectations of the other party; it excludes a variety of types of conduct characterized as involving "bad faith" because they violate community standards of decency, fairness or reasonableness. The appropriate remedy for a breach of the duty of good faith also varies with the circumstances.

b. Good faith purchase. In many situations a good faith purchaser of property for value can acquire better rights in the property than his transferor had. See, e.g., §342. In this context "good faith" focuses on the honesty of the purchaser, as distinguished from his care or negligence. Particularly in the law of negotiable instruments inquiry may be limited to "good faith" under what has been called "the rule of the pure heart and the empty head." When diligence or inquiry is a condition of the purchaser's right, it is said that good faith is not enough. This focus on honesty is appropriate to cases of good faith purchase; it is less so in cases of good faith performance.

c. Good faith in negotiation. This Section, like Uniform Commercial Code §1-[304], does not deal with good faith in the formation of a contract. . . . In cases of negotiation for modification of an existing contractual relationship, the rule stated in this Section may overlap with more specific rules requiring negotiation in good faith. See §§73, 89; Uniform Commercial Code §2-209 and Comment.

d. Good faith performance. Subterfuges and evasions violate the obligation of good faith in performance even though the actor believes his conduct to be justified. But the obligation goes further: bad faith may be overt or may consist of inaction, and fair dealing may require more than honesty. A complete catalogue of types of bad faith is impossible, but the following types are among those which have been recognized in judicial decisions: evasion of the spirit of the bargain, lack of diligence and slacking off, willful rendering of imperfect performance, abuse of a power to specify terms, and interference with or failure to cooperate in the other party's performance. . . .

e. Good faith in enforcement. The obligation of good faith and fair dealing extends to the assertion, settlement and litigation of contract claims and defenses. See, e.g., §§73, 89. The obligation is violated by dishonest conduct

---

*** [Eds. note] The comprehensive revision of UCC Article 1 in 2001 included a new definition of good faith that combined former §1-201(19) and §2-103(1)(b) into a single standard applicable to all parties, merchant and non-merchant alike. See UCC §1-201(b)(20). As of June 1, 2017, thirty-eight states and the District of Columbia had adopted the new, unified good faith standard, while twelve states retained the bifurcated standard to which the Comment to Restatement (Second) §205 refers.

such as conjuring up a pretended dispute, asserting an interpretation contrary to one's own understanding, or falsification of facts. It also extends to dealing which is candid but unfair, such as taking advantage of the necessitous circumstances of the other party to extort a modification of a contract for the sale of goods without legitimate commercial reason. See Uniform Commercial Code §2-209, Comment 2. Other types of violation have been recognized in judicial decisions: harassing demands for assurances of performance, rejection of performance for unstated reasons, willful failure to mitigate damages, and abuse of a power to determine compliance or to terminate the contract. . . .

§206. Interpretation Against the Draftsman

In choosing among the reasonable meanings of a promise or agreement or a term thereof, that meaning is generally preferred which operates against the party who supplies the words or from whom a writing otherwise proceeds.

Comment

a. Rationale. Where one party chooses the terms of a contract, he is likely to provide more carefully for the protection of his own interests than for those of the other party. He is also more likely than the other party to have reason to know of uncertainties of meaning. Indeed, he may leave meaning deliberately obscure, intending to decide at a later date what meaning to assert. In cases of doubt, therefore, so long as other factors are not decisive, there is substantial reason for preferring the meaning of the other party. The rule is often invoked in cases of standardized contracts and in cases where the drafting party has the stronger bargaining position, but it is not limited to such cases. It is in strictness a rule of legal effect, sometimes called construction, as well as interpretation: its operation depends on the positions of the parties as they appear in litigation, and sometimes the result is hard to distinguish from a denial of effect to an unconscionable clause. . . .

§207. Interpretation Favoring the Public

In choosing among the reasonable meanings of a promise or agreement or a term thereof, a meaning that serves the public interest is generally preferred.

Comment

a. Scope. Th[is] rule . . . applies only to agreements which affect a public interest. . . . It has often been relied on to justify narrow construction of a grant of a public franchise or an agreement for a tax exemption. In general, it does not prefer the interest of a governmental agency as a party to a contract . . . .

§208. Unconscionable Contract or Term

If a contract or term thereof is unconscionable at the time the contract is made a court may refuse to enforce the contract, or may enforce the remainder of the contract without the unconscionable term, or may so limit the application of any unconscionable term as to avoid any unconscionable result.

Comment

a. Scope. . . . The determination that a contract or term is or is not unconscionable is made in the light of its setting, purpose and effect. Relevant factors include weaknesses in the contracting process like those involved in more specific rules as to contractual capacity, fraud, and other invalidating causes; the policy also overlaps with rules which render particular bargains or terms unenforceable on grounds of public policy. Policing against unconscionable contracts or terms has sometimes been accomplished "by adverse construction of language, by manipulation of the rules of offer and acceptance or by determinations that the clause is contrary to public policy or to the dominant purpose of the contract." Uniform Commercial Code §2-302 Comment 1. Particularly in the case of standardized agreements, the rule of this Section permits the court to pass directly on the unconscionability of the contract or clause rather than to avoid unconscionable results by interpretation. Compare §211. . . .

c. Overall imbalance. Inadequacy of consideration does not of itself invalidate a bargain, but gross disparity in the values exchanged may be an important factor in a determination that a contract is unconscionable and may be sufficient ground, without more, for denying specific performance. . . . Such a disparity may also corroborate indications of defects in the bargaining process. . . . Theoretically it is possible for a contract to be oppressive taken as a whole, even though there is no weakness in the bargaining process and no single term which is in itself unconscionable. Ordinarily, however, an unconscionable contract involves other factors as well as overall imbalance. . . .

d. Weakness in the bargaining process. A bargain is not unconscionable merely because the parties to it are unequal in bargaining position, nor even because the inequality results in an allocation of risks to the weaker party. But gross inequality of bargaining power, together with terms unreasonably favorable to the stronger party, may confirm indications that the transaction involved elements of deception or compulsion, or may show that the weaker party had no meaningful choice, no real alternative, or did not in fact assent or appear to assent to the unfair terms. Factors which may contribute to a finding of unconscionability in the bargaining process include the following: belief by the stronger party that there is no reasonable probability that the weaker party will fully perform the contract; knowledge of the stronger party that the weaker party will be unable to receive substantial benefits from the contract; knowledge of the stronger party that the weaker party is unable reasonably to protect his interests by reason of physical or mental infirmities, ignorance, illiteracy or inability to understand the language of the agreement, or similar factors. . . .

Topic 3. Effect of Adoption of a Writing

§209. Integrated Agreements

(1) An integrated agreement is a writing or writings constituting a final expression of one or more terms of an agreement.

(2) Whether there is an integrated agreement is to be determined by the court as a question preliminary to determination of a question of interpretation or to application of the parol evidence rule.

(3) Where the parties reduce an agreement to a writing which in view of its completeness and specificity reasonably appears to be a complete agreement, it is taken to be an integrated agreement unless it is established by other evidence that the writing did not constitute a final expression.

Comment

a. Significance of integration. Where the parties to an agreement have reduced a term of the agreement to specific words or other symbols, interpretation of that term relates to the meaning of the words and symbols used. See §212. An integrated agreement supersedes contrary prior statements, and a completely integrated agreement supersedes even consistent additional terms. See §§213-16. But both integrated and unintegrated agreements are to be read in the light of the circumstances and may be explained or supplemented by operative usages of trade, by the course of dealing between the parties, and by the course of performance of the agreement.

b. Form of integrated agreement. No particular form is required for an integrated agreement. Written contracts, signed by both parties, may include an explicit declaration that there are no other agreements between the parties, but such a declaration may not be conclusive. The intention of the parties may also be manifested without explicit statement and without signature. A letter, telegram or other informal document written by one party may be orally assented to by the other as a final expression of some or all of the terms of their agreement. Indeed, the parties to an oral agreement may choose their words with such explicit precision and completeness that the same legal consequences follow as where there is a completely integrated agreement. . . .

c. Proof of integration. Whether a writing has been adopted as an integrated agreement is a question of fact to be determined in accordance with all relevant evidence. . . . Ordinarily the issue whether there is an integrated agreement is determined by the trial judge in the first instance as a question preliminary to an interpretative ruling or to the application of the parol evidence rule. . . .

§210. Completely and Partially Integrated Agreements

(1) A completely integrated agreement is an integrated agreement adopted by the parties as a complete and exclusive statement of the terms of the agreement.

(2) A partially integrated agreement is an integrated agreement other than a completely integrated agreement.

(3) Whether an agreement is completely or partially integrated is to be determined by the court as a question preliminary to determination of a question of interpretation or to application of the parol evidence rule.

Comment

a. Complete integration. The definition in Subsection (1) is to be read with the definition of integrated agreement in §209, to reject the assumption sometimes made that because a writing has been worked out which is final on some matters, it is to be taken as including all the matters agreed upon. Even though there is an integrated agreement, consistent additional terms not reduced to writing may be shown, unless the court finds that the writing was assented to by both parties as a complete and exclusive statement of all the terms. . . .

b. Proof of complete integration. That a writing was or was not adopted as a completely integrated agreement may be proved by any relevant evidence. A document in the form of a written contract, signed by both parties and apparently complete on its face, may be decisive of the issue in the absence of credible contrary evidence. But a writing cannot of itself prove its own completeness, and wide latitude must be allowed for inquiry into circumstances bearing on the intention of the parties. . . .

c. Partial integration. It is often clear from the face of a writing that it is incomplete and cannot be more than a partially integrated agreement. Incompleteness may also be shown by other writings, which may or may not become part of a completely or partially integrated agreement. Or it may be shown by any relevant evidence, oral or written, that an apparently complete writing never became fully effective, or that it was modified after initial adoption. . . .

§211. Standardized Agreements

(1) Except as stated in Subsection (3), where a party to an agreement signs or otherwise manifests assent to a writing and has reason to believe that like writings are regularly used to embody terms of agreements of the same type, he adopts the writing as an integrated agreement with respect to the terms included in the writing.

(2) Such a writing is interpreted wherever reasonable as treating alike all those similarly situated, without regard to their knowledge or understanding of the standard terms of the writing.

(3) Where the other party has reason to believe that the party manifesting such assent would not do so if he knew that the writing contained a particular term, the term is not part of the agreement.

Comment

. . . .

b. Assent to unknown terms. A party who makes regular use of a standardized form of agreement does not ordinarily expect his customers to understand or even to read the standard terms. One of the purposes of standardization is to eliminate bargaining over details of individual transactions, and that purpose would not be served if a substantial number of customers retained counsel and reviewed the standard terms. Employees regularly using a form often have only a limited understanding of its terms and limited authority to vary them. Customers do not in fact ordinarily understand or even read the standard terms. They trust to the good faith of the party using the form and to the tacit representation that like terms are being accepted regularly by others similarly situated. But they understand that they are assenting to the terms not read or not understood, subject to such limitations as the law may impose.

c. *Review of unfair terms.* . . . The obvious danger of overreaching has resulted in government regulation of insurance policies, bills of lading, retail installment sales, small loans, and other particular types of contracts. . . . Apart from such regulation, standard terms imposed by one party are enforced. But standard terms may be superseded by separately negotiated or added terms . . . , they are construed against the draftsman . . . , and they are subject to the overriding obligation of good faith . . . and to the power of the court to refuse to enforce an unconscionable contract or term (§208). . . .

d. *Non-contractual documents.* The same document may serve both contractual and other purposes, and a party may assent to it for other purposes without understanding that it embodies contract terms. He may nevertheless be bound if he has reason to know that it is used to embody contract terms. Insurance policies, steamship tickets, bills of lading, and warehouse receipts are commonly so obviously contractual in form as to give the customer reason to know their character. But baggage checks or automobile parking lot tickets may appear to be mere identification tokens, and a party without knowledge or reason to know that the token purports to be a contract is then not bound by terms printed on the token. Documents such as invoices, instructions for use, and the like, delivered after a contract is made, may raise similar problems. . . .

f. *Terms excluded.* Subsection (3) applies to standardized agreements the general principles stated in §§20 and 201. Although customers typically adhere to standardized agreements and are bound by them without even appearing to know the standard terms in detail, they are not bound to unknown terms which are beyond the range of reasonable expectation. A debtor who delivers a check to his creditor with the amount blank does not authorize the insertion of an infinite figure. Similarly, a party who adheres to the other party's standard terms does not assent to a term if the other party has reason to believe that the adhering party would not have accepted the agreement if he had known that the agreement contained the particular term. Such a belief or assumption may be shown by the prior negotiations or inferred from the circumstances. Reason to believe may be inferred from the fact that the term is bizarre or oppressive, from the fact that it eviscerates the non-standard terms explicitly agreed to, or from the fact that it eliminates the dominant purpose of the transaction. The inference is reinforced if the adhering party never had an opportunity to read the term, or if it is illegible or otherwise hidden from view. This rule is closely related to the policy against unconscionable terms and the rule of interpretation against the draftsman. . . .

§212. Interpretation of Integrated Agreement

(1) The interpretation of an integrated agreement is directed to the meaning of the terms of the writing or writings in the light of the circumstances, in accordance with the rules stated in this Chapter.

(2) A question of interpretation of an integrated agreement is to be determined by the trier of fact if it depends on the credibility of extrinsic evidence or on a choice among reasonable inferences to be drawn from extrinsic evidence. Otherwise a question of interpretation of an integrated agreement is to be determined as a question of law.

Comment

a. "Objective" and "subjective" meaning. Interpretation of contracts deals with the meaning given to language and other conduct by the parties rather than with meanings established by law. But the relevant intention of a party is that manifested by him rather than any different undisclosed intention. In cases of misunderstanding, there may be a contract in accordance with the meaning of one party if the other knows or has reason to know of the misunderstanding and the first party does not. See §§200, 201. The meaning of one party may prevail as to one term and the meaning of the other as to another term; thus the contract as a whole may not be entirely in accordance with the understanding of either. When a party is thus held to a meaning of which he had reason to know, it is sometimes said that the "objective" meaning of his language or other conduct prevails over his "subjective" meaning. Even so, the operative meaning is found in the transaction and its context rather than in the law or in the usages of people other than the parties. . . .

b. Plain meaning and extrinsic evidence. It is sometimes said that extrinsic evidence cannot change the plain meaning of a writing, but meaning can almost never be plain except in a context. Accordingly, the rule stated in Subsection (1) is not limited to cases where it is determined that the language used is ambiguous. Any determination of meaning or ambiguity should only be made in the light of the relevant evidence of the situation and relations of the parties, the subject matter of the transaction, preliminary negotiations and statements made therein, usages of trade, and the course of dealing between the parties. . . .

e. Evaluation of extrinsic evidence. Even though an agreement is not integrated, or even though the meaning of an integrated agreement depends on extrinsic evidence, a question of interpretation is not left to the trier of fact where the evidence is so clear that no reasonable person would determine the issue in any way but one. But if the issue depends on evidence outside the writing, and the possible inferences are conflicting, the choice is for the trier of fact.

§213. Effect of Integrated Agreement on Prior Agreements (Parol Evidence Rule)

(1) A binding integrated agreement discharges prior agreements to the extent that it is inconsistent with them.

(2) A binding completely integrated agreement discharges prior agreements to the extent that they are within its scope.

(3) An integrated agreement that is not binding or that is voidable and avoided does not discharge a prior agreement. But an integrated agreement, even though not binding, may be effective to render inoperative a term which would have been part of the agreement if it had not been integrated.

Comment

a. Parol evidence rule. This Section states what is commonly known as the parol evidence rule. It is not a rule of evidence but a rule of substantive law. Nor is it a rule of interpretation; it defines the subject matter of interpretation. It renders inoperative prior written agreements as well as prior oral agreements. . . .

b. Inconsistent terms. Whether a binding agreement is completely integrated or partially integrated, it supersedes inconsistent terms of prior agreements. To apply this rule, the court must make preliminary determinations that there is an integrated agreement and that it is inconsistent with the term in question. See §209. Those determinations are made in accordance with all relevant evidence, and require interpretation both of the integrated agreement and of the prior agreement. The existence of the prior agreement may be a circumstance which sheds light on the meaning of the integrated agreement, but the integrated agreement must be given a meaning to which its language is reasonably susceptible when read in the light of all the circumstances. See §§212, 214. . . .

c. Scope of a completely integrated agreement. Where the parties have adopted a writing as a complete and exclusive statement of the terms of the agreement, even consistent additional terms are superseded. See §216. But there may still be a separate agreement between the same parties which is not affected. To apply the rule of Subsection (2) the court in addition to determining that there is an integrated agreement and that it is completely integrated, must determine that the asserted prior agreement is within the scope of the integrated agreement. Those determinations are made in accordance with all relevant evidence, and require interpretation both of the integrated agreement and of the prior agreement. . . .

§214. Evidence of Prior or Contemporaneous Agreements and Negotiations

Agreements and negotiations prior to or contemporaneous with the adoption of a writing are admissible in evidence to establish

(a) that the writing is or is not an integrated agreement;

(b) that the integrated agreement, if any, is completely or partially integrated;

(c) the meaning of the writing, whether or not integrated;

(d) illegality, fraud, duress, mistake, lack of consideration, or other invalidating cause;

(e) ground for granting or denying rescission, reformation, specific performance, or other remedy.

Comment

a. Integrated agreement and completely integrated agreement. Whether a writing has been adopted as an integrated agreement and, if so, whether the agreement is completely or partially integrated are questions determined by the court preliminary to determination of a question of interpretation or to application of the parol evidence rule. See §§209-13. Writings do not prove themselves; ordinarily, if there is dispute, there must be testimony that there was a signature or other manifestation of assent. The preliminary determination is made in accordance with all relevant evidence, including the circumstances in which the writing was made or adopted. It may require preliminary interpretation of the writing; the court must then consider the evidence which is relevant to the question of interpretation.

b. Interpretation. Words, written or oral, cannot apply themselves to the subject matter. The expressions and general tenor of speech used in negotiations are admissible to show the conditions existing when the writing was made, the application of the words, and the meaning or meanings of the parties. Even though words seem on their face to have only a single possible meaning, other meanings often appear when the circumstances are disclosed. In cases of misunderstanding, there must be inquiry into the meaning attached to the words by each party and into what each knew or had reason to know. See §201.

Illustrations

. . . .

2. In an integrated contract with A, B promises to buy "your wool." Previous negotiations of the parties related to both wool from A's sheep and wool that A had contracted to buy from other persons. The negotiations are admissible to establish both classes as the meaning of the words "your wool" in the contract.

3. A, in an integrated contract with B, promises B to sell certain goods to be manufactured by A, and B promises to pay the "total cost." Previous negotiations may establish the meaning of "total cost.". . .

c. Invalidating cause. What appears to be a complete and binding integrated agreement may be a forgery, a joke, a sham, or an agreement without consideration, or it may be voidable for fraud, duress, mistake, or the like, or it may be illegal. Such invalidating causes need not and commonly do not appear on the face of the writing. They are not affected even by a "merger" clause. See Comment *e* to §216. . . .

§215. Contradiction of Integrated Terms

Except as stated in the preceding Section, where there is a binding agreement, either completely or partially integrated, evidence of prior or contemporaneous agreements or negotiations is not admissible in evidence to contradict a term of the writing.

Comment

a. Relation to other rules. Like §216, this Section states an evidentiary consequence of §213. A binding integrated agreement discharges inconsistent prior agreements, and evidence of a prior agreement is therefore irrelevant to the rights of the parties when offered to contradict a term of the writing. The same evidence may be properly considered on the preliminary issues whether there is an integrated agreement and whether it is completely or partially integrated. See §§209, 210. If there is a finding that there is an integrated agreement or a completely integrated agreement, the evidence may nevertheless be relevant to a question of interpretation, to a question of invalidating cause, or to a question of remedy. See §214. But the earlier agreement, no matter how clear, cannot override a later agreement which supersedes or amends it. . . .

§216. Consistent Additional Terms

(1) Evidence of a consistent additional term is admissible to Supplement an integrated agreement unless the court finds that the agreement was completely integrated.

(2) An agreement is not completely integrated if the writing omits a consistent additional agreed term which is

(a) agreed to for separate consideration, or

(b) such a term as in the circumstances might naturally be omitted from the writing.

Comment

a. Relation to other rules. Like §215, this Section states an evidentiary consequence of §213. It also limits the concept of a completely integrated agreement set forth in §210. Compare Uniform Commercial Code §2-202(b). Where the limitation is not applicable, the court must decide whether the agreement is completely integrated on the basis of all relevant evidence, including the evidence of consistent additional terms.

b. Consistency. Terms of prior agreements are superseded to the extent that they are inconsistent with an integrated agreement, and evidence of them is not admissible to contradict a term of the integration. See §§213, 215. The determination whether an alleged additional term is consistent or inconsistent with the integrated agreement requires interpretation of the writing in the light of all the circumstances, including the evidence of the additional term. For this purpose, the meaning of the writing includes not only the terms explicitly stated but also those fairly implied as part of the bargain of the parties in fact. It does not include a term supplied by a rule of law designed to fill gaps where the parties have not agreed otherwise, unless it can be inferred that the parties contracted with reference to the rule of law. There is no clear line between implications of fact and rules of law filling gaps; although fairly clear examples of each can be given, other cases will involve almost imperceptible shadings. See §204. . . .

d. Terms omitted naturally. If it is claimed that a consistent additional term was omitted from an integrated agreement and the omission seems natural in the circumstances, it is not necessary to consider further the questions whether the agreement is completely integrated and whether the omitted term is within its scope, although factual questions may remain. This situation is especially likely to arise when the writing is in a standardized form which does not lend itself to the insertion of additional terms. . . . Even though the omission does not seem natural, evidence of the consistent additional terms is admissible unless the court finds that the writing was intended as a complete and exclusive statement of the terms of the agreement. See §210.

Illustrations

    4. A owes B $1,000. They agree orally that A will sell B Blackacre for $3,000 and that the $1,000 will be credited against the price, and then sign a written agreement, complete on its face, which does not mention the $1,000 debt or the credit. The written agreement is not completely integrated, and the oral agreement for a credit is admissible in evidence to Supplement the written agreement. . . .

e. Written term excluding oral terms ("merger" clause). Written agreements often contain clauses stating that there are no representations, promises or agreements between the parties except those found in the writing. Such a clause . . . if agreed to is likely to conclude the issue whether the agreement is completely integrated. Consistent additional terms may then be excluded even though their omission would have been natural in the absence of such a clause. But such a clause does not control the question whether the writing was assented to as an integrated agreement, the scope of the writing if completely integrated, or the interpretation of the written terms.

§217. Integrated Agreement Subject to Oral Requirement of a Condition

Where the parties to a written agreement agree orally that performance of the agreement is subject to the occurrence of a stated condition, the agreement is not integrated with respect to the oral condition.

Comment

. . . .

b. Requirement of a condition inconsistent with a written term. The rule of this Section may be regarded as a particular application of the rule of §216(2)(b), giving effect to consistent additional terms omitted naturally from a writing. So regarded, it has sometimes been limited to requirements of conditions consistent with the written terms. But an oral requirement of a condition is never completely consistent with a signed written agreement which is complete on its face; in such cases evidence of the oral requirement bears directly on the issues whether the writing was adopted as an integrated agreement and if so whether the agreement was completely integrated or partially integrated. Inconsistency is merely one factor in the preliminary determination of those issues. If the parties orally agreed that performance of the written agreement was subject to a condition, either the writing is not an integrated agreement or the agreement is only partially integrated until the condition occurs. Even a "merger" clause in the writing, explicitly negating oral terms, does not control the question whether there is an integrated agreement or the scope of the writing. See Comment *e* to §216. . . .

§218. Untrue Recitals; Evidence of Consideration

(1) A recital of a fact in an integrated agreement may be shown to be untrue.

(2) Evidence is admissible to prove whether or not there is consideration for a promise, even though the parties have reduced their agreement to a writing which appears to be a completely integrated agreement.

Comment

. . . .

b. Effect of recital. A recital of fact in an integrated agreement is evidence of the fact, and its weight depends on the circumstances. Contrary facts may be proved. The result may be that the integrated agreement is not binding, or that it has a different effect from the effect if the recital had been true. In the absence of estoppel, the true facts have the same operation as if stated in the writing. . . .

d. Omission of consideration. Where a written agreement requires consideration and none is stated in the writing, a finding that the writing is a completely integrated agreement would mean that it is not binding for want of consideration. Since only a binding integrated agreement brings the parol evidence rule into operation, evidence is admissible to show that there was consideration and what it was. . . .

e. Incorrect recital of consideration. Where a writing shows a promise in consideration of a return promise and it is determined that the writing is a binding integrated agreement, inconsistent prior agreements are discharged. See §213. But an integrated agreement which is not binding does not ordinarily discharge prior agreements, and the parol evidence rule does not apply to recitals of facts. Where consideration is required, the requirement is not satisfied by a false recital of consideration, although in some circumstances a recital of consideration may make a promise binding without consideration. See §§71, 87, 88. An incorrect statement of a consideration does not prevent proof either that there was no consideration or that there was a consideration different from that stated. In some such cases the recital may imply a promise not explicitly stated. . . .

Topic 4. Scope as Affected by Usage

§219. Usage

Usage is habitual or customary practice.

§220.   Usage Relevant to Interpretation

(1) An agreement is interpreted in accordance with a relevant usage if each party knew or had reason to know of the usage and neither party knew or had reason to know that the meaning attached by the other was inconsistent with the usage.

(2) When the meaning attached by one party accorded with a relevant usage and the other knew or had reason to know of the usage, the other is treated as having known or had reason to know the meaning attached by the first party.

Comment

. . . .

b. Interpretation of language. An agreement may have a legal effect not intended by either party, but interpretation is limited to meanings intended by at least one party. Neither party is bound by a meaning unless he knows or has reason to know of it. See §§200, 201. Usage is subject to the same rule: a party is not bound by a usage unless he knows or has reason to know of it. Hence a party who asserts a meaning based on usage must show either that the other party knew of the usage or that the other party had reason to know of it. Analytically, the meaning of language is a question of fact, but in the absence of extrinsic evidence the meaning of language in an integrated writing is to be determined as a question of law. See §212. Where a usage of words is sufficiently well known, a court will take judicial cognizance of it without proof; otherwise the burden of establishing a usage is on the party asserting it. See §202. Ordinarily there is no requirement that a usage relevant to the interpretation of language be pleaded, but a party against whom evidence of usage is offered may be entitled to a continuance or to notice sufficient to prevent unfair surprise. See Uniform Commercial Code §1-[303(g)]. . . .

c. Agreed but unstated terms. An agreement or term thereof need not be stated in words if the parties manifest assent to it by other conduct, and such assent is often manifested by conduct in accordance with usage. Where there is an integrated agreement, an agreed but unstated term may be annexed by usage on the same principle which controls consistent additional terms generally. See §216. But it is so common to contract with reference to usage, leaving the usage unstated, that no inquiry is necessary as to whether it is natural in the particular circumstances to omit the term from the writing. See Uniform Commercial Code §2-202(a). Where it is claimed that the usage contradicts the express terms, the issue is resolved as a question of interpretation. See §203(b). Whether a usage is reasonable may bear on the issue whether the parties contracted with reference to it, but if they did they are not in general forbidden to make agreements which seem unreasonable to others. . . .

d. Ambiguity and contradiction. Language and conduct are in general given meaning by usage rather than by the law, and ambiguity and contradiction likewise depend upon usage. Hence usage relevant to interpretation is treated as part of the context of an agreement in determining whether there is ambiguity or contradiction as well as in resolving ambiguity or contradiction. There is no requirement that an ambiguity be shown before usage can be shown, and no prohibition against showing that language or conduct have a different meaning in the light of usage from the meaning they might have apart from the usage. The normal effect of a usage on a written contract is to vary its meaning from the meaning it would otherwise have. . . .

§221. Usage Supplementing an Agreement

An agreement is supplemented or qualified by a reasonable usage with respect to agreements of the same type if each party knows or has reason to know of the usage and neither party knows or has reason to know that the other party has an intention inconsistent with the usage.

Comment

a. Agreed terms and omitted terms. . . . This Section [applies] to cases where the parties did not advert to the problem with which the usage deals, or where one or each separately foresaw the problem but failed to manifest any intention with respect to it. In such cases, in the absence of usage, the court would supply a reasonable term. . . . But if there is a reasonable usage which supplies an omitted term and the parties know or have reason to know of the usage, it is a surer guide than the court's own judgment of what is reasonable. Thus a usage may make it unnecessary to inquire into or prove what the actual intentions of the parties were with respect to an unstated term. . . .

b. Reason to know and reasonableness. The more general and well-established a usage is, the stronger is the inference that a party knew or had reason to know of it. Similarly, the fact that a usage is reasonable may tend to show that the parties contracted with reference to it or that a particular party knew or had reason to know of it. Where the parties in fact agree to a usage, there is no general requirement that their usage seem reasonable to others; but where there is no agreement only a reasonable usage supplies an omitted term. What is reasonable for this purpose depends on the circumstances. . . .

c. Effect of usage on law. It is often said that usage cannot change a rule of law, but a distinction must be drawn. If the rule of law is one which overrides contrary agreement, it also overrides usage; but if the law merely supplies a term in the absence of contrary agreement, usage can have the same effect as contrary agreement. See Uniform Commercial Code §1-201[(b)](3). . . .

d. Intention inconsistent with usage. The parties to an agreement are not bound to follow the usages of others or their own prior usages. If either party has reason to know that the other has an intention inconsistent with a particular usage, the usage is not applicable. Such an intention need not be manifested in any particular way; whether the parties contracted with reference to a usage is determined on the basis of all the circumstances, and a usage may be excluded by the same type of proof which would include it. . . .

§222. Usage of Trade

(1) A usage of trade is a usage having such regularity of observance in a place, vocation, or trade as to justify an expectation that it will be observed with respect to a particular agreement. It may include a system of rules regularly observed even though particular rules are changed from time to time.

(2) The existence and scope of a usage of trade are to be determined as questions of fact. If a usage is embodied in a written trade code or similar writing the interpretation of the writing is to be determined by the court as a question of law.

(3) Unless otherwise agreed, a usage of trade in the vocation or trade in which the parties are engaged or a usage of trade of which they know or have reason to know gives meaning to or Supplements or qualifies their agreement.

Comment

a. Relation to other rules. This Section follows Uniform Commercial Code §1-[303] and states a particular application of the rules stated in §§220 and 221. As to conflicting usages of words, see §202; as to conflict between usage of trade and express terms, course of performance or course of dealing, see §203.

b. Regularity of observance. A usage of trade need not be "ancient or immemorial," "universal," or the like. Unless agreed to in fact, it must be reasonable, but commercial acceptance by regular observance makes out a prima facie case that a usage of trade is reasonable. There is no requirement that an agreement be ambiguous before evidence of a usage of trade can be shown, nor is it required that the usage of trade be consistent with the meaning the agreement would have apart from the usage. When the usage consists of a system of rules, the parties need not be aware of a particular rule if they know or have reason to know the system and the particular rule is within the scheme of the system. A change within the system may have effect promptly, even though there has been no time for regular observance of the change.

Illustrations

. . . .

2. A contracts to sell B 1,000 feet of San Domingo mahogany. By usage of dealers in mahogany, known to A and B, good figured mahogany of a certain density is known as San Domingo mahogany, though it does not come from San Domingo. Unless otherwise agreed, the usage is part of the contract. . . .

c. Local usages of trade. Where usages vary from place to place, there may be a problem in deciding which usage is applicable. Even though local residents regularly contract with reference to a local usage of trade, others are not bound by the usage unless they know or have reason to know of it. If that condition is satisfied and no contrary intention is shown, a usage of trade in a particular place is ordinarily used to interpret the agreement as to that part of the performance which is to occur there. See Uniform Commercial Code §1-[303(d)].

Illustrations

7. A contracts to employ B for 20 days. In the kind of work to which the employment relates, in the place where both reside and the work is to be

performed, a day's work is eight hours. Unless otherwise agreed, B's employment is for 20 eight-hour days. . . .

    9. A promises B to keep certain premises "fully insured." At the time and place where the contract is made and to be performed and where the parties reside, insurance companies will not insure such premises for more than three-fourths of their value, and such premises insured for three-fourths of their value are called "fully insured." Unless otherwise agreed, the local usage is part of the contract. . . .

§223. Course of Dealing

(1) A course of dealing is a sequence of previous conduct between the parties to an agreement which is fairly to be regarded as establishing a common basis of understanding for interpreting their expressions and other conduct.

(2) Unless otherwise agreed, a course of dealing between the parties gives meaning to or Supplements or qualifies their agreement.

Comment

    a. Relation to other rules. This Section follows Uniform Commercial Code §1-[303] and states a particular application of the rules stated in §§220 and 221. As to conflict between course of dealing and express terms, course of performance or usage of trade, see §203.

    b. Common basis of understanding. Course of dealing may become part of an agreement either by explicit provision or by tacit recognition, or it may guide the court in supplying an omitted term. Like usage of trade, it may determine the meaning of language or it may annex an agreed but unstated term. There is no requirement that an agreement be ambiguous before evidence of a course of dealing can be shown, nor is it required that the course of dealing be consistent with the meaning the agreement would have apart from the course of dealing. . . .

Topic 5.   *Conditions and Similar Events*

§224. Condition Defined

A condition is an event, not certain to occur, which must occur, unless its non-occurrence is excused, before performance under a contract becomes due.

Comment

   . . . .

    b. Uncertainty of event. Whether the reason for making an event a condition is to shift to the obligee the risk of its non-occurrence, or whether it is to induce the obligee to cause the event to occur, there is inherent in the concept of condition some degree of uncertainty as to the occurrence of the event.

Therefore, the mere passage of time, as to which there is no uncertainty, is not a condition and a duty is unconditional if nothing but the passage of time is necessary to give rise to a duty of performance. Moreover, an event is not a condition, even though its occurrence is uncertain, if it is referred to merely to measure the passage of time after which an obligor is to perform. See Comment *b* to §227. Performance under a contract becomes due when all necessary events, including any conditions and the passage of any required time, have occurred so that a failure of performance will be a breach. See §§231-43.

The event need not, in order to be a condition, be one that is to occur after the making of the contract, although that is commonly the case. It may relate to the present or even to the past, as is the case where a marine policy insures against a loss that may already have occurred. Furthermore, a duty may be conditioned upon the failure of something to happen rather than upon its happening, and in that case its failure to happen is the event that is the condition. . . .

§225. Effects of the Non-Occurrence of a Condition

(1) Performance of a duty subject to a condition cannot become due unless the condition occurs or its non-occurrence is excused.

(2) Unless it has been excused, the non-occurrence of a condition discharges the duty when the condition can no longer occur.

(3) Non-occurrence of a condition is not a breach by a party unless he is under a duty that the condition occur.

Comment

a. Two effects. The unexcused non-occurrence of a condition has two possible effects on the duty subject to that condition. The first effect always follows and the second often does. The first, stated in Subsection (1), is that of preventing performance of the duty from becoming due. This follows from the definition of "condition" in §224. Performance of the duty may still become due, however, if the condition occurs later within the time for its occurrence. The non-occurrence of the condition within that time has the additional effect, stated in Subsection (2), of discharging the duty. The time within which the condition can occur in order for the performance of the duty to become due may be fixed by a term of the agreement or, in the absence of such a term, by one supplied by the court. . . .

b. Excuse. The non-occurrence of a condition of a duty is said to be "excused" when the condition need no longer occur in order for performance of the duty to become due. The non-occurrence of a condition may be excused . . . . by a subsequent promise, even without consideration, to perform the duty in spite of the non-occurrence of the condition. . . . It may be excused by acceptance of performance in spite of the non-occurrence of the condition, or by rejection following its non-occurrence accompanied by an inadequate statement of reasons. See §§246-48. It may be excused by a repudiation of the conditional duty or by a manifestation of an inability to perform it. See §255; §§250-51. It may be excused by prevention or hindrance of its occurrence through a breach of the duty of good faith and fair dealing (§205). See §239. And it may be excused by impracticability. See §271. . . .

c. *Effect of excuse.* When the non-occurrence of a condition of a duty is excused, the damages for breach of the duty will depend on whether or not the occurrence of the condition was also part of the performances to be exchanged under the exchange of promises. If it was not part of the agreed exchange, the obligor is liable for the same damages for which he would have been liable had the duty originally been unconditional. If it was part of the agreed exchange, however, the saving to the obligee resulting from the non-occurrence of the condition must be subtracted in determining the obligor's liability for damages. . . . If the obligee is under a duty that the condition occur, the ground for the excuse of the non-occurrence of the condition may not be a ground for discharge of that duty. He may therefore be liable for breach of the duty in spite of the excuse of the non-occurrence of the condition . . . .

§226. How an Event May Be Made a Condition

An event may be made a condition either by the agreement of the parties or by a term supplied by the court.

Comment

a. By agreement of the parties. No particular form of language is necessary to make an event a condition, although such words as "on condition that," "provided that" and "if" are often used for this purpose. An intention to make a duty conditional may be manifested by the general nature of an agreement, as well as by specific language. . . .

c. By a term supplied by court. When the parties have omitted a term that is essential to a determination of their rights and duties, the court may supply a term which is reasonable in the circumstances (§204). Where that term makes an event a condition, it is often described as a "constructive" (or "implied in law") condition. This serves to distinguish it from events which are made conditions by the agreement of the parties, either by their words or by other conduct, and which are described as "express" and as "implied in fact" (inferred from fact) conditions. . . .

§227. Standards of Preference with Regard to Conditions

(1) In resolving doubts as to whether an event is made a condition of an obligor's duty, and as to the nature of such an event, an interpretation is preferred that will reduce the obligee's risk of forfeiture, unless the event is within the obligee's control or the circumstances indicate that he has assumed the risk.

(2) Unless the contract is of a type under which only one party generally undertakes duties, when it is doubtful whether

    (a) a duty is imposed on an obligee that an event occur, or

    (b) the event is made a condition of the obligor's duty, or

    (c) the event is made a condition of the obligor's duty and a duty is imposed on the obligee that the event occur,

the first interpretation is preferred if the event is within the obligee's control.

(3) In case of doubt, an interpretation under which an event is a condition of an obligor's duty is preferred over an interpretation under which the non-occurrence of the event is a ground for discharge of that duty after it has become a duty to perform.

Comment

. . . .

b. Condition or not. The non-occurrence of a condition of an obligor's duty may cause the obligee to lose his right to the agreed exchange after he has relied substantially on the expectation of that exchange, as by preparation or performance. The word "forfeiture" is used in this Restatement to refer to the denial of compensation that results in such a case. The policy favoring freedom of contract requires that, within broad limits (see §229), the agreement of the parties should be honored even though forfeiture results. When, however, it is doubtful whether or not the agreement makes an event a condition of an obligor's duty, an interpretation is preferred that will reduce the risk of forfeiture. . . . When the nature of the condition is such that the uncertainty as to the event will be resolved before either party has relied on its anticipated occurrence, both parties can be entirely relieved of their duties, and the obligee risks only the loss of his expectations. When, however, the nature of the condition is such that the uncertainty is not likely to be resolved until after the obligee has relied by preparing to perform or by performing at least in part, he risks forfeiture. If the event is within his control, he will often assume this risk. If it is not within his control, it is sufficiently unusual for him to assume the risk that, in case of doubt, an interpretation is preferred under which the event is not a condition. The rule is, of course, subject to a showing of a contrary intention, and even without clear language, circumstances may show that he assumed the risk of its non-occurrence.

Although the rule is consistent with a policy of avoiding forfeiture and unjust enrichment, it is not directed at the avoidance of actual forfeiture and unjust enrichment. Since the intentions of the parties must be taken as of the time the contract was made, the test is whether a particular interpretation would have avoided the risk of forfeiture viewed as of that time, not whether it will avoid actual forfeiture in the resolution of a dispute that has arisen later. . . .

c. Nature of event. In determining the nature of the event that is made a condition by the agreement, as in determining whether the agreement makes an event a condition in the first place . . . , it will not ordinarily be supposed that a party has assumed the risk of forfeiture. Where the language is doubtful, an interpretation is generally preferred that will avoid this risk. This standard of preference finds an important application in the case of promises to pay for work done if some independent third party, such as an architect, surveyor or engineer, is satisfied with it, where the risk of forfeiture in the case of a judgment that is dishonest or based on a gross mistake as to the facts is substantial. The standard does not, however, help a party if the condition is within his control or if the circumstances otherwise indicate that he assumed that risk.

Illustrations

. . . .

5. A contracts with B to repair B's building for $20,000, payment to be made "on the satisfaction of C, B's architect, and the issuance of his certificate." A makes the repairs, but C refuses to issue his certificate, and explains why he is not satisfied. Other experts in the field consider A's performance to be satisfactory and disagree with C's explanation. A has no claim against B. . . . If C is honestly not satisfied, B is under no duty to pay A, and it makes no difference if his dissatisfaction was not reasonable.

6. The facts being otherwise as stated in Illustration 5, C refuses to issue his certificate although he admits that he is satisfied. A has a claim against B for $20,000. The quoted language will be interpreted so that the requirement of the certificate is merely evidentiary and the condition occurs when there is, as here, adequate evidence that C is honestly satisfied. . . .

§228. Satisfaction of the Obligor as a Condition

When it is a condition of an obligor's duty that he be satisfied with respect to the obligee's performance or with respect to something else, and it is practicable to determine whether a reasonable person in the position of the obligor would be satisfied, an interpretation is preferred under which the condition occurs if such a reasonable person in the position of the obligor would be satisfied.

Comment

a. Conditions of satisfaction. This Section sets out a special standard of preference for a type of condition that has long been of particular interest and importance – the satisfaction of the obligor himself, rather than a third party. Usually it is the obligee's performance as to which the obligor is to be satisfied, but it may also be something else, such as the propitiousness of circumstances for his enterprise. The agreement will often use language such as "satisfaction" or "complete satisfaction," without making it clear that the test is merely one of honest satisfaction rather than of reasonable satisfaction. Under any interpretation, the exercise of judgment must be in accordance with the duty of good faith and fair dealing (§205), and for this reason, the agreement is not illusory (§77). If the agreement leaves no doubt that it is only honest satisfaction that is meant and no more, it will be so interpreted, and the condition does not occur if the obligor is honestly, even though unreasonably, dissatisfied. Even so, the dissatisfaction must be with the circumstance and not with the bargain and the mere statement of the obligor that he is not satisfied is not conclusive on the question of his honest satisfaction. . . .

b. Preference for objective standard. When, however, the agreement does not make it clear that it requires merely honest satisfaction, it will not usually be supposed that the obligee has assumed the risk of the obligor's unreasonable, even if honest, dissatisfaction. In such a case, to the extent that it is practicable to apply an objective test of reasonable satisfaction, such a test will be applied. The situation differs from that where the satisfaction of a third party such as an architect, surveyor or engineer is concerned. See Comment *c* to §227. These professionals, even though employed by the obligor, are assumed to be capable of independent judgment, free from the selfish interests of the obligor. But if the obligor would subject the obligee's right to compensation to his own idiosyncrasies, he must use clear language. When, as is often the case, the preferred interpretation will reduce the obligee's risk of forfeiture, so that §227(1) also applies, there is an additional argument in its favor. This argument is particularly strong where the obligor will be left with a benefit which he cannot return. If, however, the circumstance with respect to which a party is to be satisfied is such that the application of an objective test is impracticable, the rule of this Section is not applicable. A court will then, for practical reasons, apply a subjective test of honest satisfaction, even if the agreement admits of doubt on the point and even if the result will be to increase the obligee's risk of forfeiture. . . .

§229. Excuse of a Condition to Avoid Forfeiture

To the extent that the non-occurrence of a condition would cause disproportionate forfeiture, a court may excuse the non-occurrence of that condition unless its occurrence was a material part of the agreed exchange.

Comment

a. Relation to other rules. . . . Although both this Section and §208, on unconscionable contract or term, limit freedom of contract, they are designed to reach different types of situations. While §208 speaks of unconscionability "at the time the contract is made," this Section is concerned with forfeiture that would actually result if the condition were not excused. It is intended to deal with a term that does not appear to be unconscionable at the time the contract is made but that would, because of ensuing events, cause forfeiture.

b. Disproportionate forfeiture. The rule stated in the present Section is, of necessity, a flexible one, and its application is within the sound discretion of the court. Here, as in §227(1), "forfeiture" is used to refer to the denial of compensation that results when the obligee loses his right to the agreed exchange after he has relied substantially, as by preparation or performance on the expectation of that exchange. See Comment *b* to §227. The extent of the forfeiture in any particular case will depend on the extent of that denial of compensation. In determining whether the forfeiture is "disproportionate," a court must weigh the extent of the forfeiture by the obligee against the importance to the obligor of the risk from which he sought to be protected and the degree to which that protection will be lost if the non-occurrence of the condition is excused to the extent required to prevent forfeiture. The character of the agreement may, as in the case of insurance agreements, affect the rigor with which the requirement is applied.

Illustrations

1. A contracts to build a house for B, using pipe of Reading manufacture. In return, B agrees to pay $75,000 in progress payments, each payment to be made "on condition that no pipe other than that of Reading manufacture has been used." Without A's knowledge, a subcontractor mistakenly uses pipe of Cohoes manufacture which is identical in quality and is distinguishable only by the name of the manufacturer which is stamped on it. The mistake is not discovered until the house is completed, when replacement of the pipe will require destruction of substantial parts of the house. B refuses to pay the unpaid balance of $10,000. A court may conclude that the use of Reading rather than Cohoes pipe is so relatively unimportant to B that the forfeiture that would result from denying A the entire balance would be disproportionate, and may allow recovery by A subject to any claim for damages for A's breach of his duty to use Reading pipe.

2. A, an ocean carrier, carries B's goods under a contract providing that it is a condition of A's liability for damage to cargo that "written notice of claim for loss or damage must be given within 10 days after removal of goods." B's cargo is damaged during carriage and A knows of this. On removal of the goods, B notes in writing on the delivery record that the cargo is damaged, and five days later informs A over the telephone of a claim for that damage and invites A to participate in an inspection within the ten day period. A inspects the goods within the period, but B does not give written notice of its claim until 25 days after removal of the goods. Since the purpose of requiring the condition of written notice is to alert the carrier and enable it to make a prompt investigation, and since this purpose had been served by the written notice of damage and the oral notice of claim, the court may excuse the non-occurrence of the condition to the extent required to allow recovery by B. . . .

§230. Event That Terminates a Duty

(1) Except as stated in Subsection (2), if under the terms of the contract the occurrence of an event is to terminate an obligor's duty of immediate performance or one to pay damages for breach, that duty is discharged if the event occurs.

(2) The obligor's duty is not discharged if occurrence of the event

(a) is the result of a breach by the obligor of his duty of good faith and fair dealing, or

(b) could not have been prevented because of impracticability and continuance of the duty does not subject the obligor to a materially increased burden. . . .

Illustrations

1. A, an insurance company, insures the property of B under a policy providing that no recovery can be had if suit is not brought on the policy within two years after a loss. A loss occurs and B lets two years pass before bringing suit. A's duty to pay B for the loss is discharged and B cannot maintain the action on the policy.

2. The facts being otherwise as stated in Illustration 1, B lives in a foreign country and is prevented by the outbreak of war from bringing suit against A

for two years. A's duty to pay B for the loss is not discharged and B can maintain an action on the policy when the war is ended. . . .

CHAPTER 10.   PERFORMANCE AND NON-PERFORMANCE

Topic 1.   *Performances to Be Exchanged Under an Exchange of Promises*

§231.   Criterion for Determining When Performances Are to Be Exchanged Under an Exchange of Promises

Performances are to be exchanged under an exchange of promises if each promise is at least part of the consideration for the other and the performance of each promise is to be exchanged at least in part for the performance of the other.

Comment

a. Expectation of an exchange of performances. Agreements involving an exchange of promises play a vital role in an economically advanced society. Ordinarily when parties make such an agreement, they not only regard the promises themselves as the subject of an exchange (§71(2)), but they also intend that the performances of those promises shall subsequently be exchanged for each other. Even without a showing of such an actual intention, a court will often, out of a sense of fairness, assume that it was their expectation that there would be a subsequent exchange of the performance of each party for that of the other. Cf. §204. This Chapter consists, in substantial part, of rules designed to secure that expectation of a subsequent exchange of performances. . . .

§232.   When It Is Presumed That Performances Are to Be Exchanged Under an Exchange of Promises

Where the consideration given by each party to a contract consists in whole or in part of promises, all the performances to be rendered by each party taken collectively are treated as performances to be exchanged under an exchange of promises, unless a contrary intention is clearly manifested.

§233.   Performance at One Time or in Installments

(1) Where performances are to be exchanged under an exchange of promises, and the whole of one party's performance can be rendered at one time, it is due at one time, unless the language or the circumstances indicate the contrary.

(2) Where only a part of one party's performance is due at one time under Subsection (1), if the other party's performance can be so apportioned that there is a comparable part that can also be rendered at that time, it is due at that time, unless the language or the circumstances indicate the contrary.

§234. Order of Performances

(1) Where all or part of the performances to be exchanged under an exchange of promises can be rendered simultaneously, they are to that extent due simultaneously, unless the language or the circumstances indicate the contrary.

(2) Except to the extent stated in Subsection (1), where the performance of only one party under such an exchange requires a period of time, his performance is due at an earlier time than that of the other party, unless the language or the circumstances indicate the contrary.

Comment

a. Advantages of simultaneous performance. A requirement that the parties perform simultaneously where their performances are to be exchanged under an exchange of promises is fair for two reasons. First, it offers both parties maximum security against disappointment of their expectations of a subsequent exchange of performances by allowing each party to defer his own performance until he has been assured that the other will perform. . . . Second, it avoids placing on either party the burden of financing the other before the latter has performed. . . .

b. When simultaneous performance possible under agreement. . . . Cases in which simultaneous performance is possible under the terms of the contract can be grouped into five categories: (1) where the same time is fixed for the performance of each party; (2) where a time is fixed for the performance of one of the parties and no time is fixed for the other; (3) where no time is fixed for the performance of either party; (4) where the same period is fixed within which each party is to perform; (5) where different periods are fixed within which each party is to perform. The requirement of simultaneous performance applies to the first four categories. The requirement does not apply to the fifth category, even if simultaneous performance is possible, because in fixing different periods for performance the parties must have contemplated the possibility of performance at different times under their agreement. Therefore in cases in the fifth category the circumstances show an intention contrary to the rule stated in Subsection (1).

Illustrations

1. A promises to sell land to B, delivery of the deed to be on July 1. B promises to pay A $50,000, payment to be made on July 1. Delivery of the deed and payment of the price are due simultaneously.

2. A promises to sell land to B, the deed to be delivered on July 1. B promises to pay A $50,000, no provision being made for the time of payment. Delivery of the deed and payment of the price are due simultaneously.

3. A promises to sell land to B and B promises to pay A $50,000, no provision being made for the time either of delivery of the deed or of payment. Delivery of the deed and payment of the price are due simultaneously.

4. A promises to sell land to B, delivery of the deed to be on or before July 1. B promises to pay A $50,000, payment to be on or before July 1. Delivery of the deed and payment of the price are due simultaneously.

5. A promises to sell land to B, delivery of the deed to be on or before July 1. B promises to pay A $50,000, payment to be on or before August 1. Delivery of the deed and payment of the price[] are not due simultaneously. . . .

e. Where performance requires a period of time. Where the performance of one party requires a period of time and the performance of the other party does not, their performance can not be simultaneous. Since one of the parties must perform first, he must forego the security that a requirement of simultaneous performance affords against disappointment of his expectation of an exchange of performances, and he must bear the burden of financing the other party before the latter has performed. See Comment *a*. Of course the parties can by express provision mitigate the harshness of a rule that requires that one completely perform before the other perform at all. They often do this, for example, in construction contracts by stating a formula under which payment is to be made at stated intervals as work progresses. But it is not feasible for courts to devise such formulas for the wide variety of such cases that come before them in which the parties have made no provision. . . .

f. Applicability of rule. The rule stated in Subsection (2) usually finds its application to contracts involving services, such as construction and employment contracts. The common practice of making express provision for progress payments has diminished its importance with regard to the former, and the widespread enactment of state wage statutes giving the employee a right to the frequent periodic payment of wages has lessened its significance with regard to the latter. Nevertheless, it is a helpful rule for residual cases not otherwise provided for. . . .

Topic 2.   *Effect of Performance and Non-Performance*

§235.   Effect of Performance as Discharge and of Non-Performance as Breach

(1) Full performance of a duty under a contract discharges the duty.

(2) When performance of a duty under a contract is due any non-performance is a breach.

Comment

. . . .

b. Effect of non-performance. Non-performance is not a breach unless performance is due. Performance may not be due because a required period of time has not passed, or because a condition has not occurred (§225), or because the duty has already been discharged (Chapter 12) as, for example, by impracticability of performance (Chapter 11). In such a case non-performance is justified. When performance is due, however, anything short of full performance is a breach, even if the party who does not fully perform was not at fault and even if the defect in his performance was not substantial. . . . Non-performance includes defective performance as well as an absence of performance. . . .

§236. Claims for Damages for Total and for Partial Breach

(1) A claim for damages for total breach is one for damages based on all of the injured party's remaining rights to performance.

(2) A claim for damages for partial breach is one for damages based on only part of the injured party's remaining rights to performance.

Comment

. . . .

b. Total and partial breach distinguished. Although every breach gives rise to a claim for damages, not every claim for damages is one for damages based on all of the injured party's remaining rights to performance under the contract. Such a claim is said to be one for damages for total breach. . . . If the injured party elects to or is required to await the balance of the other party's performance under the contract, his claim is said instead to be one for damages for partial breach. . . . Rules for determining whether a particular breach gives rise to a claim for damages for partial breach, for total breach, or for either partial or total breach at the election of the injured party are stated in §§243 and 253. . . .

§237. Effect on Other Party's Duties of a Failure to Render Performance

Except as stated in §240, it is a condition of each party's remaining duties to render performances to be exchanged under an exchange of promises that there be no uncured material failure by the other party to render any such performance due at an earlier time.

Comment

a. Effect of non-occurrence of condition. . . . [A] material failure of performance [prevents] the other party's remaining duties of performance with respect to the exchange. . . . from becoming due, at least temporarily, and it discharges those duties if it has not been cured during the time in which performance can occur. The occurrence of conditions of the type dealt with in this Section is required out of a sense of fairness rather than as a result of the agreement of the parties. Such conditions are therefore sometimes referred to as "constructive conditions of exchange." Cf. §204. . . .

b. *First material failure of performance.* . . . In determining whether a failure of performance is material, the circumstances listed in §241 should be considered. Even if the failure is material, it may still be possible to cure it by subsequent performance without a material failure. In the event of cure the injured party may still have a claim for any remaining non-performance as well as for any delay. In determining when it is too late to cure a failure of performance, the circumstances listed in §242 should be considered. In making all of these determinations the situation of the parties is to be viewed as of the time for performance and in terms of the actual failure. . . .

d. *Substantial performance.* In an important category of disputes over failure of performance, one party asserts the right to payment on the ground that he has completed his performance, while the other party refuses to pay on the ground that there is an uncured material failure of performance. . . . If there has been substantial although not full performance, the [obligee] has a claim for the unpaid balance and the [obligor] has a claim only for damages. If there has not been substantial performance, the [obligee] has no claim for the unpaid balance, although he may have a claim in restitution (§374). The considerations in determining whether performance is substantial are those listed in §241 for determining whether a failure is material. If, however, . . . the agreement makes full performance a condition, substantial performance is not sufficient and if relief is to be had under the contract, it must be through excuse of the non-occurrence of the condition to avoid forfeiture. . . .

§238. Effect on Other Party's Duties of a Failure to Offer Performance

Where all or part of the performances to be exchanged under an exchange of promises are due simultaneously, it is a condition of each party's duties to render such performance that the other party either render or, with manifested present ability to do so, offer performance of his part of the simultaneous exchange.

Comment

a. *Effect of offer to perform.* Where the performances are to be exchanged simultaneously under an exchange of promises, each party is entitled to refuse to proceed with that simultaneous exchange until he is reasonably assured that the other party will perform at the same time. If a party actually performs, his performance both discharges his own duty (5235(1)) and amounts to the occurrence of a condition of the other party's duty (§237). But it . . . . is enough that he make an appropriate offer to perform, since it is a condition of each party's duties of performance with respect to the exchange that there be no uncured material failure by the other party at least to offer performance. . . .

b. *What amounts to an offer to perform.* An offer of performance meets the requirement stated in this Section even though it is conditional on simultaneous performance by the other party. The offer must be accompanied with manifested present ability to make it good, but the offeror need not go so far as actually to hold out that which he is to deliver. . . .

§239. Effect on Other Party's Duties of a Failure Justified by Non-Occurrence of a Condition

(1) A party's failure to render or to offer performance may, except as stated in Subsection (2), affect the other party's duties under the rules stated in §§237 and 238 even though failure is justified by the non-occurrence of a condition.

(2) The rule stated in Subsection (1) does not apply if the other party assumed the risk that he would have to perform in spite of such a failure.

§240. Part Performances as Agreed Equivalents

If the performances to be exchanged under an exchange of promises can be apportioned into corresponding pairs of part performances so that the parts of each pair are properly regarded as agreed equivalents, a party's performance of his part of such a pair has the same effect on the other's duties to render performance of the agreed equivalent as it would have if only that pair of performances had been promised.

Comment

a. Mitigating effect of the rule. . . . This Section . . . reduces the risk of forfeiture in that important class of cases in which it is proper to regard corresponding parts of the performances of each party as agreed equivalents. Its effect is to give a party who has performed one of these parts the right to its agreed equivalent just as if the parties had made a separate contract with regard to that pair of corresponding parts. A failure as to some other part does not affect this right. . . . Substantial performance of such a part has the same effect with regard to such a pair of agreed equivalents as substantial performance of the whole has under §237 with respect to the entire contract. . . .

d. Apportionment. The rule stated in this Section cannot be applied unless the parties' performances can be apportioned into corresponding pairs of part performances. The process of apportionment is essentially one of calculation and the rule can only be applied where calculation is feasible. It is enough, however, if the price of separate items is separately stated in the agreement itself or in a price list on which the agreement was based, or can be reliably ascertained from stated prices for components or from a total price for similar items. . . .

e. Agreed equivalents. [C]orresponding pairs of performances . . . only come within the rule stated in this Section if it is proper to regard the parts of each pair as agreed equivalents. . . . [T]his Section . . . requires that the parts of a pair be of roughly equivalent value to the injured party in terms of his expectation with respect to the total agreed exchange. This is because fairness requires that a party, having received only a fraction of the performance that he expected under a contract, not be asked to pay an identical fraction of the price that he originally promised on the expectation of full performance, unless it appears that the performance that he actually received is worth to him roughly that same fraction of what full performance would have been worth to him. . . . The injured party will not be required to pay for a part of the performance that he has received if he cannot make full use of that part without the remainder of the performance, as, for example, where a buyer has received a machine but not an attachment necessary for its operation. In deciding whether the injured party can make full use of only part, a court must, of course, take account of the possibility that the remainder of the performance can be easily obtained from some other source, as, for example, where the attachment is available on the market. . . .

§241. Circumstances Significant in Determining Whether a Failure Is Material

In determining whether a failure to render or to offer performance is material, the following circumstances are significant:

(a) the extent to which the injured party will be deprived of the benefit which he reasonably expected;

(b) the extent to which the injured party can be adequately compensated for the part of that benefit of which he will be deprived;

(c) the extent to which the party failing to perform or to offer to perform will suffer forfeiture;

(d) the likelihood that the party failing to perform or to offer to perform will cure his failure, taking account of all the circumstances including any reasonable assurances;

(e) the extent to which the behavior of the party failing to perform or to offer to perform comports with standards of good faith and fair dealing.

Comment

a. Nature of significant circumstances. The application of the rules stated in §§237 and 238 turns on a standard of materiality that is necessarily imprecise and flexible. . . . The standard of materiality. . . . is to be applied in the light of the facts of each case in such a way as to further the purpose of securing for each party his expectation of an exchange of performances. This Section therefore states circumstances, not rules, which are to be considered in determining whether a particular failure is material. A determination that a failure is not material means only that it does not have the effect of the non-occurrence of a condition under §§237 and 238. Even if not material, the failure may be a breach and give rise to a claim for damages for partial breach (§§236, 243). . . .

b. Loss of benefit to injured party. . . . [A]n important circumstance in determining whether a failure is material is the extent to which the injured party will be deprived of the benefit which he reasonably expected from the exchange (Subsection (a)). If the consideration given by either party consists partly of some performance and only partly of a promise (see Comment *a* to §232), regard must be had to the entire exchange, including that performance, in applying this criterion. Although the relationship between the monetary loss to the injured party as a result of the failure and the contract price may be significant, no simple rule based on the ratio of the one to the other can be laid down, and here, as elsewhere under this Section, all relevant circumstances must be considered. In construction contracts, for example, defects affecting structural soundness are ordinarily regarded as particularly significant. . . .

c. Adequacy of compensation for loss. The second circumstance, the extent to which the injured party can be adequately compensated for his loss of benefit (Subsection (b)), is a corollary of the first. Difficulty that he may have in proving with sufficient certainty the amount of that loss will affect the adequacy of compensation. If the failure is a breach, the injured party always has a claim for damages, and the question becomes one of the adequacy of that claim to compensate him for the lost benefit. Where the failure is not a breach, the question becomes one of the adequacy of any claim, such as one in restitution, to which the injured party may be entitled. This is a particularly important circumstance when the party in breach seeks specific performance. Such relief may be granted if damages can adequately compensate the injured party for the defect in performance. See Comment *c* to §242.

d. Forfeiture by party who fails. [T]he same risk of forfeiture obtains as in the case of conditions generally if the party who fails to perform or tender has relied substantially on the expectation of the exchange, as through preparation or performance. . . . [A] failure is less likely to be regarded as material if it occurs late, after substantial preparation or performance, and more likely to be regarded as material if it occurs early, before such reliance. For the same reason the failure is more likely to be regarded as material if such preparation or performance as has taken place can be returned to and salvaged by the party failing to perform or tender, and less likely to be regarded as material if it cannot. These factors argue against a finding of material failure and in favor of one of substantial performance where a builder has completed performance under a construction contract and, because the building is on the owner's land, can salvage nothing if he is denied recovery of the balance of the price. Even in such a case, however, the potential forfeiture may be mitigated if the builder has a claim in restitution (§§370-77, especially §374) or if he has already received progress payments under a provision of the contract. The same factors argue for a finding of material failure where a seller tenders goods and can salvage them by resale to others if they are rejected and he is denied recovery of the price. This helps to explain the severity of the rule as applied to the sale of goods. See Comment *b.* Even in such a case, however, the potential forfeiture may be aggravated if the seller has manufactured the goods specially for the buyer or has spent substantial sums in shipment. . . .

e. Uncertainty. A material failure by one party gives the other party the right to withhold further performance as a means of securing his expectation of an exchange of performances. To the extent that that expectation is already reasonably secure, in spite of the failure, there is less reason to conclude that the failure is material. The likelihood that the failure will be cured is therefore a significant circumstance in determining whether it is material (Subsection (d)). The fact that the injured party already has some security for the other party's performance argues against a determination that the failure is material. So do reasonable assurances of performance given by the other party after his failure. So does a shift in the market that makes performance of the contract more favorable to the other party. On the other hand, defaults by the other party under other contracts or as to other installments under the same contract argue for a determination of materiality. So does such financial weakness of the other party as suggests an inability to cure. This circumstance differs from the notion of reasonable grounds for insecurity (§251), in that the former can become relevant only after there has been an actual failure to perform or to tender. On discharge by repudiation, see §253(2). . . .

f. Absence of good faith or fair dealing. A party's adherence to standards of good faith and fair dealing (§205) will not prevent his failure to perform a duty from amounting to a breach (§236(2)). Nor will his adherence to such standards necessarily prevent his failure from having the effect of the non-occurrence of a condition (§237; cf. §238). The extent to which the behavior of the party failing to perform or to offer to perform comports with standards of good faith and fair dealing is, however, a significant circumstance in determining whether the failure is material (Subsection (e)). In giving weight to this factor courts have often used such less precise terms as "wilful." Adherence to the standards stated in Subsection (e) is not conclusive, since other circumstances may cause a failure to be material in spite of such adherence. Nor is non-adherence conclusive, and other circumstances may cause a failure not to be material in spite of such non-adherence. . . .

§242. Circumstances Significant in Determining When Remaining Duties Are Discharged

In determining the time after which a party's uncured material failure to render or to offer performance discharges the other party's remaining duties to render performance under the rules stated in §§237 and 238, the following circumstances are significant:

(a) those stated in §241;

(b) the extent to which it reasonably appears to the injured party that delay may prevent or hinder him in making reasonable substitute arrangements;

(c) the extent to which the agreement provides for performance without delay, but a material failure to perform or to offer to perform on a stated day does not of itself discharge the other party's remaining duties unless the circumstances, including the language of the agreement, indicate that performance or an offer to perform by that day is important.

Comment

a. Cure. . . . [A] party's uncured material failure to perform or to offer to perform not only has the effect of suspending the other party's duties (§225(1)) but, when it is too late for the performance or the offer to perform to occur, the failure also has the effect of discharging those duties (§225(2)). Ordinarily there is some period of time between suspension and discharge, and during this period a party may cure his failure. Even then, since any breach gives rise to a claim, a party who has cured a material breach has still committed a breach, by his delay, for which he is liable in damages. Furthermore, in some instances timely performance is so essential that any delay immediately results in discharge and there is no period of time during which the injured party's duties are merely suspended and the other party can cure his failure.

b. Significant circumstances. This Section states circumstances which are to be considered in determining whether there is still time to cure a particular failure, or whether the period of time for discharge has expired. They are similar to the circumstances stated in the preceding section. The importance of delay to the injured party will depend on the extent to which it will deprive him of the benefit which he reasonably expected (§241(a)) and on the extent to which he can be adequately compensated (§241(b)). The extent of the forfeiture by the party failing to perform or to offer to perform (§241(c)) is also significant in determining the importance of delay. The likelihood that the injured party's withholding of performance will induce the other party to cure his failure is particularly important (§241(d)), because the very reason for suspending rather than immediately discharging the injured party's duties is that this will induce cure. The reasonableness of the injured party's conduct in communicating his grievances and in seeking satisfaction is a factor to be considered in this connection. Where performance is to extend over a period of time, as where delivery of goods is to be in installments, so that a continuing relationship between the parties is contemplated, the injured party may be expected to give more opportunity for cure than in the case of an isolated exchange. . . . Finally, the nature of the behavior of the party failing to perform or to offer to perform may be considered here as under the preceding section (§241(e)). . . .

c. Substitute arrangements. . . . Under any contract, the extent to which it reasonably appears to the injured party that delay may prevent or hinder him from making reasonable substitute arrangements is a consideration in determining the effect of delay. . . . [A] party in breach who seeks specific performance may be granted relief with compensation for the delay, in circumstances where he would have no claim for damages. . . .

d. Effect of agreement. The agreement of the parties often contains a provision for the time of performance or tender. It may simply provide for performance on a stated date. In that event, a material breach on that date entitles the injured party to withhold his performance and gives him a claim for damages for delay, but it does not of itself discharge the other party's remaining duties. Only if the circumstances, viewed as of the time of the breach, indicate that performance or tender on that day is of genuine importance are the injured party's remaining duties discharged immediately, with no period of time during which they are merely suspended. It is, of course, open to the parties to make performance or tender by a stated date a condition by their agreement, in which event, absent excuse . . . delay beyond that date results in discharge. . . . Such stock phrases as "time is of the essence" do not necessarily have this effect, although under Subsection (c) they are to be considered along with other circumstances in determining the effect of delay. . . .

e. Excuse and reinstatement. Just as a party may under §84 promise to perform in spite of the complete non-occurrence of a condition, he may under that section promise to perform in spite of a delay in its occurrence. If he places no limit on the delay, his power to impose a time limit by later notification of the other party is subject to the rules on reinstatement stated in §84(2).

§243. Effect of a Breach by Non-Performance as Giving Rise to a Claim for Damages for Total Breach

(1) With respect to performances to be exchanged under an exchange of promises, a breach by non-performance gives rise to a claim for damages for total breach only if it discharges the injured party's remaining duties to render such performance, other than a duty to render an agreed equivalent under §240.

(2) Except as stated in Subsection (3), a breach by non-performance accompanied or followed by a repudiation gives rise to a claim for damages for total breach.

(3) Where at the time of the breach the only remaining duties of performance are those of the party in breach and are for the payment of money in installments not related to one another, his breach by non-performance as to less than the whole, whether or not accompanied or followed by a repudiation, does not give rise to a claim for damages for total breach.

(4) In any case other than those stated in the preceding subsections, a breach by non-performance gives rise to a claim for total breach only if it so substantially impairs the value of the contract to the injured party at the time of the breach that it is just in the circumstances to allow him to recover damages based on all his remaining rights to performance.

Comment

a. Promises exchanged in an expectation of an exchange of performances. . . . [If] performances are to be exchanged under an exchange of promises, and the breach occurs before the injured party has fully performed . . . , the breach, if it is material (§241), will operate as the non-occurrence of a condition of those remaining duties (§237). This will at least justify the injured party in suspending his performance (§225(1)), and will, if the breach is not cured in time (§242), discharge his remaining duties of performance (§225(2)). Under the rule stated in Subsection (1), the injured party has a claim for damages for total breach if, but only if, those remaining duties are discharged . . . . There is, of course, an exception where the injured party has already, at the time of the breach, come under a duty to render performance of an agreed equivalent under the rule stated in §240. Such a duty is not discharged, even if there is a material breach, and its survival does not prevent the injured party from claiming damages for total breach under Subsection (1). . . . [T]he injured party has a choice in the situation contemplated in Subsection (1). If, in spite of the breach, he wishes to await performance by the party in breach and to have merely a claim for damages for partial breach rather than for total breach, he can excuse the non-occurrence of the condition of his remaining duties (§237) by promising to perform them in spite of its non-occurrence (§84). His remaining duties are then not discharged, and the rule stated in Subsection (1) does not apply. The injured party need not do this expressly . . . , but may do so by his actions in the course of performance. See §§246, 247. . . .

b. Effect of repudiation. Under the rule stated in Subsection (2), if a repudiation (§250) accompanies or follows a breach by non-performance, the injured party generally has a claim for damages for total breach. A repudiation does not, however, have this effect in those circumstances in which, under the rule stated in Subsection (3), nothing less than a breach as to the whole gives rise to such a claim. . . . An injured party who has a claim for damages for total breach as a result of a repudiation, and who asserts a claim merely for damages for partial breach, runs the risk that if he prevails he will be barred under the doctrine of merger from further recovery, even in the event of a subsequent breach, because he has "split a cause of action." See Restatement, Second, Judgments §§24-26. . . . If the repudiator nullifies his repudiation (§256(1)), the injured party still has a claim for damages for the breach by nonperformance but it may then be a claim merely for damages for partial breach (see Comment *a* to §256). . . .

d. Avoiding harsh results of limitations. Dissatisfaction with the rule stated in Subsection (3) often manifests itself by the inclusion in the agreement of an acceleration clause under which the remaining installments become due, either automatically or at the option of the injured party, on a breach as to one installment, so that such non-performance gives rise to a claim for damages for total breach. Even when the injured party has no claim for damages for total breach, he may be entitled to equitable relief, a declaratory judgment, an installment judgment, or restitution (see Comment *b* to §359), to the extent that these remedies are permitted. The degree to which the limitation might yield on a showing of manifest injustice, as where the refusal to pay is not in good faith or where fraud on creditors is involved, is unclear. Problems of assuring performance of such obligations to pay in installments on the debtor's death, dissolution, or bankruptcy arise even where no breach by non-performance has occurred, and are not dealt with in this Restatement. See Comment *c* to §250. . . .

e. General criterion. [W]hether the breach so substantially impairs the value of the contract to the injured party at the time of the breach that it is just to allow him to recover damages based on all his remaining rights to performance . . . is to be [determined] in the light of all the circumstances, taking account of the difficulty of calculating damages for total breach and of any uncertainties that could be avoided if the injured party were given a claim merely for damages for partial breach. . . . Although the considerations listed in §§241 and 242 are intended for use in determining whether the injured party is discharged, not in determining whether he has a claim for damages for total breach, some of them are relevant to this latter determination. Among these are the extent to which the injured party will be deprived of the benefit that he reasonably expected (§241(a)), the likelihood that the party in breach will cure his breach (§241(d)), the extent to which the behavior of the party in breach comports with standards of good faith and fair dealing (§241(e)), and the extent to which further delay will prevent or hinder the injured party in making reasonable substitute arrangements (§242(b))....

§244. Effect of Subsequent Events on Duty to Pay Damages

A party's duty to pay damages for total breach by non-performance is discharged if it appears after the breach that there would have been a total failure by the injured party to perform his return promise.

§245. Effect of a Breach by Non-Performance as Excusing the Non-Occurrence of a Condition

Where a party's breach by non-performance contributes materially to the non-occurrence of a condition of one of his duties, the non-occurrence is excused.

Comment

a. Excuse of non-occurrence of condition. Where a duty of one party is subject to the occurrence of a condition, the additional duty of good faith and fair dealing imposed on him under §205 may require some cooperation on his part, either by refraining from conduct that will prevent or hinder the occurrence of that condition or by taking affirmative steps to cause its occurrence. Under §235(2), non-performance of that duty when performance is due is a breach. ... Under this Section it has the further effect of excusing the non-occurrence of the condition itself, so that performance of the duty that was originally subject to its occurrence can become due in spite of its non-occurrence. ... The rule stated in this Section only applies, however, where the lack of cooperation constitutes a breach, either of a duty imposed by the terms of the agreement itself or of a duty imposed by a term supplied by the court. There is no breach if the risk of such a lack of cooperation was assumed by the other party or if the lack of cooperation is justifiable. ...

b. Contribute materially. Although it is implicit in the rule that the condition has not occurred, it is not necessary to show that it would have occurred but for the lack of cooperation. ... [I]f it can be shown that the condition would not have occurred regardless of the lack of cooperation, the failure of performance did not contribute materially to its non-occurrence and the rule does not apply. The burden of showing this is properly thrown on the party in breach. ...

§246. Effect of Acceptance as Excusing the Non-Occurrence of a Condition

(1) Except as stated in Subsection (2), an obligor's acceptance or his retention for an unreasonable time of the obligee's performance, with knowledge of or reason to know of the non-occurrence of a condition of the obligor's duty,

operates as a promise to perform in spite of that non-occurrence, under the rules stated in §84.

(2) If at the time of its acceptance or retention the obligee's performance involves such attachment to the obligor's property that removal would cause material loss, the obligor's acceptance or retention of that performance operates as a promise to perform in spite of the non-occurrence of the condition, under the rules stated in §84, only if the obligor with knowledge of or reason to know of the defects manifests assent to the performance.

§247. Effect of Acceptance of Part Performance as Excusing the Subsequent Non-Occurrence of a Condition

An obligor's acceptance of part of the obligee's performance, with knowledge or reason to know of the non-occurrence of a condition of the obligor's duty, operates as a promise to perform in spite of a subsequent non-occurrence of the condition under the rules stated in §84 to the extent that it justifies the obligee in believing that subsequent performances will be accepted in spite of that non-occurrence.

§248. Effect of Insufficient Reason for Rejection as Excusing the Non-Occurrence of a Condition

Where a party rejecting a defective performance or offer of performance gives an insufficient reason for rejection, the non-occurrence of a condition of his duty is excused only if he knew or had reason to know of that non-occurrence and then only to the extent that the giving of an insufficient reason substantially contributes to a failure by the other party to cure.

§249. When Payment Other Than by Legal Tender Is Sufficient

Where the payment or offer of payment of money is made a condition of an obligor's duty, payment or offer of payment in any manner current in the ordinary course of business satisfies the requirement unless the obligee demands payment in legal tender and gives any extension of time reasonably necessary to procure it.

Topic 3. Effect of Prospective Non-Performance

§250. When a Statement or an Act Is a Repudiation

A repudiation is
(a) a statement by the obligor to the obligee indicating that the obligor will commit a breach that would of itself give the obligee a claim for damages for total breach under §243, or
(b) a voluntary affirmative act which renders the obligor unable or apparently unable to perform without such a breach.

Comment

a. Consequences of repudiation. A statement by a party to the other that he will not or cannot perform without a breach, or a voluntary affirmative act that renders him unable or apparently unable to perform without a breach may impair the value of the contract to the other party. It may have several consequences under this Restatement. If it accompanies a breach by non-performance that would otherwise give rise to only a claim for damages for partial breach, it may give rise to a claim for damages for total breach instead (§243). Even if it occurs before any breach by non-performance, it may give rise to a claim for damages for total breach (§253(1)), discharge the other party's duties (§253(2)), or excuse the non-occurrence of a condition (§255).

b. Nature of statement. In order to constitute a repudiation, a party's language must be sufficiently positive to be reasonably interpreted to mean that the party will not or cannot perform. Mere expression of doubt as to his willingness or ability to perform is not enough to constitute a repudiation, although such an expression may give an obligee reasonable grounds to believe that the obligor will commit a serious breach and may ultimately result in a repudiation under the rule stated in §251. However, language that under a fair reading "amounts to a statement of intention not to perform except on conditions which go beyond the contract" constitutes a repudiation. Comment 2 to Uniform Commercial Code §2-610. Language that is accompanied by a breach by non-performance may amount to a repudiation even though, standing alone, it would not be sufficiently positive. See §243(2). The statement must be made to an obligee under the contract [or their agent]. . . .

c. Nature of act. In order to constitute a repudiation, a party's act must be both voluntary and affirmative, and must make it actually or apparently impossible for him to perform. An act that falls short of these requirements may, however, give reasonable grounds to [seek assurances] for the purposes of the rule stated in §251. . . .

d. Gravity of threatened breach. [F]or a statement or an act to be a repudiation, the threatened breach must be of sufficient gravity that, if the breach actually occurred, it would . . . give the obligee a claim for damages for total breach under §243(1). Generally, a party acts at his peril if, insisting on what he mistakenly believes to be his rights, he refuses to perform his duty. His statement is a repudiation if the threatened breach would, without more, have given the injured party a claim for damages for total breach. . . . [W]here a party wrongfully states that he will not perform at all unless the other party consents to a modification of his contract rights, the statement is a repudiation even though the concession that he seeks is a minor one, because the breach that he threatens in order to exact it is a complete refusal of performance. . . .

§251. When a Failure to Give Assurance May Be Treated as a Repudiation

(1) Where reasonable grounds arise to believe that the obligor will commit a breach by non-performance that would of itself give the obligee a claim for

damages for total breach under §243, the obligee may demand adequate assurance of due performance and may, if reasonable, suspend any performance for which he has not already received the agreed exchange until he receives such assurance.

(2) The obligee may treat as a repudiation the obligor's failure to provide within a reasonable time such assurance of due performance as is adequate in the circumstances of the particular case.

Comment

a. Rationale. Ordinarily an obligee has no right to demand reassurance by the obligor that the latter will perform when his performance is due. However, a contract "imposes an obligation on each party that the other's expectation of receiving due performance will not be impaired." Uniform Commercial Code §2-609(1). When, therefore, an obligee reasonably believes that the obligor will commit a breach by non-performance that would of itself give him a claim for damages for total breach (§243), he may, under the rule stated in this Section, be entitled to demand assurance of performance. . . . The rule stated in this Section may be modified by agreement of the parties. . . .

b. Relation to other rules. An obligee who believes . . . that the obligor will not or cannot perform without a breach, is always free to act on that belief. If he is not himself under a duty to perform before the obligor, he may simply await the obligor's performance and, if his belief is confirmed, he will have a claim for damages for breach by non-performance. . . . If, however, the obligee's belief is incorrect, his own failure to perform or his making of alternate arrangements may subject him to a claim for damages for total breach. This Section affords him an opportunity, in appropriate cases, to demand assurance of due performance and thereby avoid the uncertainties that would otherwise inhere in acting on his belief. . . . If the obligee does not, within a reasonable time, obtain adequate assurance of due performance, he may under Subsection (2) treat the obligor's failure to provide such an assurance as a repudiation. . . . [T]he obligee may choose not to treat the failure to provide assurances as a repudiation and may continue to perform without affecting his right to recover damages for subsequent loss that he could have avoided by so treating it. . . .

c. Reasonable grounds for belief. Whether "reasonable grounds" have arisen for an obligee's belief that there will be a breach must be determined in the light of all the circumstances of the particular case. The grounds for his belief must have arisen after the time when the contract was made and cannot be based on facts known to him at that time. . . . [M]inor breaches may give reasonable grounds for a belief that there will be more serious breaches, and the mere failure of the obligee to press a claim for damages for those minor breaches will not preclude him from basing a demand for assurances on them. Compare §241(d), Comment *e* to that section, and Comment *b* to §242. Even circumstances that do not relate to the particular contract, such as defaults under other contracts, may give reasonable grounds for such a belief. . . . Conduct by a party that indicates his doubt as to his willingness or ability to perform but that is not sufficiently positive to amount to a repudiation (see Comment *b* to §250) may give reasonable grounds for such a belief. And events that indicate a party's apparent inability, but do not amount to a repudiation because they are not voluntary acts, may also give reasonable grounds for such a belief. . . .

d. Nature of demand. A party who demands assurances must do so in accordance with his duty of good faith and fair dealing in the enforcement of the contract (§205). Whether a particular demand for assurance conforms to that duty will depend on the circumstances. The demand need not be in writing. Although a written demand is usually preferable to an oral one, if time is of particular importance the additional time required for a written demand might necessitate an oral one. . . . Harassment by means of frequent unjustified demands may amount to a violation of the duty of good faith and fair dealing. . . .

e. Nature and time of assurance. Whether an assurance of due performance is "adequate" depends on what it is reasonable to require in a particular case taking account of the circumstances of that case. The relationship between the parties, any prior dealings that they have had, the reputation of the party whose performance has been called into question, the nature of the grounds for insecurity, and the time within which the assurance must be furnished are all relevant factors. . . . What is a "reasonable time" within which to give assurance under Subsection (2) will also depend on the particular circumstances. Like the demand, the assurance is subject to the general requirement of good faith and fair dealing in the enforcement of the contract (§205; see Comment *d*). . . .

§252. Effect of Insolvency

(1) Where the obligor's insolvency gives the obligee reasonable grounds to believe that the obligor will commit a breach under the rule stated in §251, the obligee may suspend any performance for which he has not already received the agreed exchange until he receives assurance in the form of performance itself, an offer of performance, or adequate security.

(2) A person is insolvent who either has ceased to pay his debts in the ordinary course of business or cannot pay his debts as they become due or is insolvent within the meaning of the federal bankruptcy law.

§253. Effect of a Repudiation as a Breach and on Other Party's Duties

(1) Where an obligor repudiates a duty before he has committed a breach by non-performance and before he has received all of the agreed exchange for it, his repudiation alone gives rise to a claim for damages for total breach.

(2) Where performances are to be exchanged under an exchange of promises, one party's repudiation of a duty to render performance discharges the other party's remaining duties to render performance.

Comment

a. Breach. An obligee under a contract is ordinarily entitled to the protection of his expectation that the obligor will perform. For this reason, a repudiation by the obligor under §250 or §251 generally gives rise to a claim for damages for total breach even though it is not accompanied or preceded by a breach by non-performance. Such a repudiation is sometimes elliptically called an "anticipatory breach," meaning a breach by anticipatory repudiation, because it occurs before there is any breach by non-performance. If there is a breach by non-performance, in addition to the repudiation . . . the breach is not one by repudiation alone and the rules stated in §243 rather than those stated in Subsection (1) apply. . . .

b. Discharge. . . . [A] breach by repudiation alone can only give rise to a claim for total breach. . . . Subsection (2) states a corollary of this rule that a breach by repudiation always gives rise to a claim for damages for total breach: where performances are to be exchanged under an exchange of promises, one party's repudiation discharges any remaining duties of performance of the other party with respect to the expected exchange. . . .

§254. Effect of Subsequent Events on Duty to Pay Damages

(1) A party's duty to pay damages for total breach by repudiation is discharged if it appears after the breach that there would have been a total failure by the injured party to perform his return promise.

(2) A party's duty to pay damages for total breach by repudiation is discharged if it appears after the breach that the duty that he repudiated would have been discharged by impracticability or frustration before any breach by non-performance.

Comment

. . . .

b. Impracticability or frustration after repudiation. Under the rule stated in §253(1), a party's breach by anticipatory repudiation immediately gives rise to a claim for damages for total breach. If it subsequently appears that the duty that he repudiated would have been discharged by supervening impracticability (§261) or frustration (§265) before any breach by non-performance, his duty to pay damages is discharged. Impracticability or frustration that would have occurred after breach by non-performance may affect the measure of damages but does not discharge the duty to pay damages. . . .

§255. Effect of a Repudiation as Excusing the Non-Occurrence of a Condition

Where a party's repudiation contributes materially to the non-occurrence of a condition of one of his duties, the non-occurrence is excused.

Comment

a. Rationale. This Section accords the same effect to a repudiation that §245 accords to a breach by non-performance. No one should be required to do a useless act, and if, because of a party's repudiation, it appears that the occurrence of a condition of a duty would not be followed by performance of the duty, the non-occurrence of the condition is generally excused. In judging whether occurrence of the condition would be followed by performance of the duty the obligee may take the obligor at his word. Nevertheless, the repudiation must contribute materially to the non-occurrence of the condition, and if the condition would not have occurred in any event, its non-occurrence is not excused. In such a case both parties are discharged. . . .

§256. Nullification of Repudiation or Basis for Repudiation

(1) The effect of a statement as constituting a repudiation under §250 or the basis for a repudiation under §251 is nullified by a retraction of the statement if notification of the retraction comes to the attention of the injured party before he materially changes his position in reliance on the repudiation or indicates to the other party that he considers the repudiation to be final.

(2) The effect of events other than a statement as constituting a repudiation under §250 or the basis for a repudiation under §251 is nullified if, to the knowledge of the injured party, those events have ceased to exist before he materially changes his position in reliance on the repudiation or indicates to the other party that he considers the repudiation to be final.

Comment

a. Effect of nullification. A repudiation . . . may give rise to a claim for damages for total breach (§253(1)), discharge duties (§253(2)), and excuse the non-occurrence of a condition (§255). A party's manifestation of doubt or apparent inability may entitle the other party to demand adequate assurance of due performance and to treat a failure to give such assurance as a repudiation under the rule stated in §251. If, however, the effect of the statement or other events constituting the repudiation under §250 or the basis for the repudiation under §251 is nullified as provided in this Section, none of these consequences follows. . . . If the repudiation is wholly anticipatory, nullification leaves the injured party with no claim at all. . . .

b. Manner of retraction. It is not necessary for the repudiator to use words in order to retract his statement. Conduct, such as an offer of performance, may be adequate to convey the idea of retraction to the injured party.

c. Time for nullification. Once the injured party has materially changed his position in reliance on the repudiation, nullification would clearly be unjust. In the interest of certainty, however, it is undesirable to make the injured party's rights turn exclusively on such a vague criterion, and he may therefore prevent subsequent nullification by indicating to the other party that he considers the repudiation final. . . . Cancellation of the contract or the commencement of an action claiming damages for total breach would be sufficient. . . .

§257. Effect of Urging Performance in Spite of Repudiation

The injured party does not change the effect of a repudiation by urging the repudiator to perform in spite of his repudiation or to retract his repudiation.

Comment

a. Effects of rule. . . . [A] repudiation operates until nullified not only as a breach (§253(1)), but as a ground for discharge (§253(2)) and for excuse of the non-occurrence of a condition (§255). Under the rule stated in this Section, these effects continue although the injured party has urged that the repudiator perform or that he retract his repudiation . . . . Any possibility that the injured party might unfairly mislead the repudiator is avoided by the duty of good faith and fair dealing (§205). An injured party who continues to perform in spite of a repudiation may, however, be precluded under §350 from claiming damages for loss that he could have avoided. . . .

Topic 4. Application of Performances

§258. Obligor's Direction of Application

(1) Except as stated in Subsection (2), as between two or more contractual duties owed by an obligor to the same obligee, a performance is applied according to a direction made by the obligor to the obligee at or before the time of performance.

(2) If the obligor is under a duty to a third person to devote a performance to the discharge of a particular duty that the obligor owes to the obligee and the obligee knows or has reason to know this, the obligor's performance is applied to that duty.

§259. Creditor's Application

(1) Except as stated in Subsections (2) and (3), if the debtor has not directed application of a payment as between two or more matured debts, the payment is applied according to a manifestation of intention made within a reasonable time by the creditor to the debtor.

(2) A creditor cannot apply such a payment to a debt if
    (a) the debtor could not have directed its application to that debt, or
    (b) a forfeiture would result from a failure to apply it to another debt and the creditor knows or has reason to know this, or
    (c) the debt is disputed or is unenforceable on grounds of public policy.

(3) If a creditor is owed one such debt in his own right and another in a fiduciary capacity, he cannot, unless empowered to do so by the beneficiary, effectively apply to the debt in his own right a greater proportion of a payment than that borne by the unsecured portion of that debt to the unsecured portions of both claims.

§260. Application of Payments Where Neither Party Exercises His Power

(1) If neither the debtor nor the creditor has exercised his power with respect to the application of a payment as between two or more matured debts, the payment is applied to debts to which the creditor could have applied it with just regard to the interests of third persons, the debtor and the creditor.

(2) In applying payments under the rule stated in Subsection (1), a payment is applied to the earliest matured debt and ratably among debts of the same maturity, except that preference is given

    (a) to a debt that the debtor is under a duty to a third person to pay immediately, and

    (b) if he is not under such a duty,

(i) to overdue interest rather than principal, and

(ii) to an unsecured or precarious debt rather than one that is secured or certain of payment.

CHAPTER 11. IMPRACTICABILITY OF PERFORMANCE AND FRUSTRATION OF PURPOSE

§261. Discharge by Supervening Impracticability

Where, after a contract is made, a party's performance is made impracticable without his fault by the occurrence of an event the non-occurrence of which was a basic assumption on which the contract was made, his duty to render that performance is discharged, unless the language or the circumstances indicate the contrary.

Comment

. . . .

d. Impracticability. Events that come within the rule stated in this Section are generally due either to "acts of God" or to acts of third parties. If the event that prevents the obligor's performance is caused by the obligee, it will ordinarily amount to a breach by the latter and the situation will be governed by the rules stated in Chapter 10, without regard to this Section. . . . If the event is due to the fault of the obligor himself, this Section does not apply. As used here "fault" may include not only "willful" wrongs, but such other types of conduct as that amounting to breach of contract or to negligence. See Comment 1 to Uniform Commercial Code §2-613. Although the rule stated in this Section is sometimes phrased in terms of "impossibility," it has long been recognized that it may operate to discharge a party's duty even though the event has not made performance absolutely impossible. This Section, therefore, uses "impracticable," the term employed by Uniform Commercial Code §2-615(a), to describe the required extent of the impediment to performance. Performance may be impracticable because extreme and unreasonable difficulty, expense, injury, or loss to one of the parties will be involved. A severe shortage of raw materials or of supplies due to war, embargo, local crop failure, unforeseen shutdown of major sources of supply, or the like, which either causes a marked increase in cost or prevents performance altogether may bring the case within the rule stated in this Section. Performance may also be impracticable because it will involve a risk of injury to person or to property, of one of the parties or of others, that is disproportionate to the ends to be attained by performance. However, "impracticability" means more than "impracticality." A mere change in the degree of difficulty or expense due to such causes as increased wages, prices of raw materials, or costs of construction, unless well beyond the normal range, does not amount to impracticability since it is this sort of risk that a fixed-price contract is intended to cover. Furthermore, a party is expected to use reasonable efforts to surmount obstacles to performance (see §205), and a performance is impracticable only if it is so in spite of such efforts. . . .

§262. Death or Incapacity of Person Necessary for Performance

If the existence of a particular person is necessary for the performance of a duty, his death or such incapacity as makes performance impracticable is an event the non-occurrence of which was a basic assumption on which the contract was made.

§263. Destruction, Deterioration or Failure to Come into Existence of Thing Necessary for Performance

If the existence of a specific thing is necessary for the performance of a duty, its failure to come into existence, destruction, or such deterioration as makes performance impracticable is an event the non-occurrence of which was a basic assumption on which the contract was made.

§264. Prevention by Governmental Regulation or Order

If the performance of a duty is made impracticable by having to comply with a domestic or foreign governmental regulation or order, that regulation or order is an event the non-occurrence of which was a basic assumption on which the contract was made.

§265. Discharge by Supervening Frustration

Where, after a contract is made, a party's principal purpose is substantially frustrated without his fault by the occurrence of an event the non-occurrence of which was a basic assumption on which the contract was made, his remaining duties to render performance are discharged, unless the language or the circumstances indicate the contrary.

Comment

a. Rationale. This Section deals with the problem that arises when a change in circumstances makes one party's performance virtually worthless to the other, frustrating his purpose in making the contract. It is distinct from the problem of impracticability dealt with in the four preceding sections because there is no impediment to performance by either party. Although there has been no true failure of performance in the sense required for the application of the rule stated in §237, the impact on the party adversely affected will be similar. The rule stated in this Section sets out the requirements for the discharge of that party's duty. First, the purpose that is frustrated must have been a principal purpose of that party in making the contract. It is not enough that he had in mind some specific object without which he would not have made the contract. The object must be so completely the basis of the contract that, as both parties understand, without it the transaction would make little sense. Second, the frustration must be substantial. It is not enough that the transaction has become less profitable for the affected party or even that he will sustain a loss. The frustration must be so severe that it is not fairly to be regarded as within the risks that he assumed under the contract. Third, the non-occurrence of the frustrating event must have been a basic assumption on which the contract was made. This involves essentially the same sorts of determinations that are involved under the general rule on impracticability. See Comments *b* and *c* to §261. The foreseeability of the event is here, as it is there, a factor in that determination, but the mere fact that the event was foreseeable does not compel the conclusion that its non-occurrence was not such a basic assumption.

Illustrations

1. A and B make a contract under which B is to pay A $1,000 and is to have the use of A's window on January 10 to view a parade that has been scheduled for that day. Because of the illness of an important official, the parade is cancelled. B refuses to use the window or pay the $1,000. B's duty to pay $1,000 is discharged, and B is not liable to A for breach of contract.

2. A contracts with B to print an advertisement in a souvenir program of an international yacht race, which has been scheduled by a yacht club, for a price of $10,000. The yacht club cancels the race because of the outbreak of war. A has already printed the programs, but B refuses to pay the $10,000. B's duty to pay $10,000 is discharged, and B is not liable to A for breach of contract. A may have a claim under the rule stated in §272(1). . . .

b. Limitations on scope. The rule stated in this Section is subject to limitations similar to those stated in §261 with respect to impracticability. It applies only when the frustration is without the fault of the party who seeks to take advantage of the rule, and it does not apply if the language or circumstances indicate the contrary. Frustration by circumstances existing at the time of the making of the contract rather than by supervening circumstances is governed by the similar rule stated in §266(2). . . .

§266. Existing Impracticability or Frustration

(1) Where, at the time a contract is made, a party's performance under it is impracticable without his fault because of a fact of which he has no reason to know and the non-existence of which is a basic assumption on which the contract is made, no duty to render that performance arises, unless the language or circumstances indicate the contrary.

(2) Where, at the time a contract is made, a party's principal purpose is substantially frustrated without his fault by a fact of which he has no reason to know and the non-existence of which is a basic assumption on which the contract is made, no duty of that party to render performance arises, unless the language or circumstances indicate the contrary.

§267. Effect on Other Party's Duties of a Failure Justified by Impracticability or Frustration

(1) A party's failure to render or to offer performance may, except as stated in Subsection (2), affect the other party's duties under the rules stated in §§237 and 238 even though the failure is justified under the rules stated in this Chapter.

(2) The rule stated in Subsection (1) does not apply if the other party assumed the risk that he would have to perform despite such a failure.

§268. Effect on Other Party's Duties of a Prospective Failure Justified by Impracticability or Frustration

(1) A party's prospective failure of performance may, except as stated in Subsection (2), discharge the other party's duties or allow him to suspend performance under the rules stated in §§251(1) and 253(2) even though the failure would be justified under the rules stated in this Chapter.

(2) The rule stated in Subsection (1) does not apply if the other party assumed the risk that he would have to perform in spite of such a failure.

Comment

. . . .

b. *Statement or voluntary act.* If a party properly states that he will not perform because of impracticability of his performance or frustration of his purpose, the other party cannot treat that statement as a repudiation under the rule stated in §250(a) because the threatened non-performance would not be a breach. It therefore gives him no claim for breach of contract. Nevertheless, under the rule stated in this Section it discharges his remaining duties to render the agreed exchange. The same rule applies to a voluntary affirmative act that would otherwise be a repudiation under the rule stated in §250(b). The rules on nullification of a repudiation (§256) and urging performance (§257) also apply to situations that come under this Section. . . .

   c. Failure to give assurances. If reasonable grounds arise to believe that a party will not perform because of impracticability of his performance or frustration of his purpose, the other party cannot demand assurances and treat a failure to give them as a repudiation under the rule stated in §251, because the prospective non-performance would not be a breach. It therefore gives him no claim for breach of contract. Nevertheless, under the rule stated in this Section, he may in a proper case suspend his own performance and treat a failure to give assurance as discharging any remaining duties that he has to render the agreed exchange. . . .

§269. Temporary Impracticability or Frustration

Impracticability of performance or frustration of purpose that is only temporary suspends the obligor's duty to perform while the impracticability or frustration exists but does not discharge his duty or prevent it from arising unless his performance after the cessation of the impracticability or frustration would be materially more burdensome than had there been no impracticability or frustration.

Comment

   a. Rationale. Impracticability of performance or frustration of purpose may be only temporary. While it lasts, the affected party's duty is at least suspended. When the circumstances giving rise to the impracticability or frustration cease to exist, he must then perform. He is usually expected to perform in full and is entitled to an appropriate extension of time for performance. When the delay has made full performance impracticable, the rules stated in §270 for partial impracticability and in §272(2) on supplying a term apply. In some cases, however, delay will make his performance materially more burdensome for him than had there been no impracticability or frustration, and when it appears that this will be so, his duty is discharged and not merely suspended. In applying the standard of materiality, a court will consider whether the delay has seriously upset the allocation of risks under the agreement of the parties. The rule stated in this Section is, of course, subject to contrary agreement. It applies only to the duty of the party adversely affected by the impracticability or frustration; the effect on the duty of the other party, as to a performance to be exchanged under an exchange of promises, is governed by the rules stated in §§267, 268, 237 and 238. . . .

§270. Partial Impracticability

Where only part of an obligor's performance is impracticable, his duty to render the remaining part is unaffected if

(a) it is still practicable for him to render performance that is substantial, taking account of any reasonable substitute performance that he is under a duty to render; or

(b) the obligee, within a reasonable time, agrees to render any remaining performance in full and to allow the obligor to retain any performance that has already been rendered.

§271. Impracticability as Excuse for Non-Occurrence of a Condition

Impracticability excuses the non-occurrence of a condition if the occurrence of the condition is not a material part of the agreed exchange and forfeiture would otherwise result.

Comment

a. Relation to other rules. . . . Under the rule stated in this Section, if the non-occurrence of the condition is the result of impracticability, it is excused if forfeiture, even if not extreme, would otherwise result. The impracticability must, of course, be such as would suffice to discharge a duty or prevent it from arising. See §§261, 262, 263, 264, 266(1). Here, as in §§227 and 229, "forfeiture" is used to refer to the denial of compensation that results when the obligee loses his right to the agreed exchange, after he has relied substantially on the expectation of that exchange, as by preparation or performance. See Comment *b* to §227 and Comment *b* to §229.

Illustrations

1. A contracts with B to repair B's building for $20,000, payment to be made "on the satisfaction of C, B's architect, and the issuance of his certificate." A properly makes the repairs, but C dies before he is able to give a certificate. Since presentation of the architect's certificate is not a material part of the agreed exchange and forfeiture would otherwise result, the occurrence of the condition is excused, and A has a claim against B for $20,000. . . .

2. A, an insurance company, issues to B a policy of accidental injury insurance which provides that notice within 14 days of an accident is a condition of A's duty. B is injured as a result of an accident covered by the policy but is so mentally deranged that he is unable to give notice for 20 days. B gives notice as soon as he is able. Since the giving of notice within 14 days is not a material part of the agreed exchange, and forfeiture would otherwise result, the non-occurrence of the condition is excused and B has a claim against A under the policy. . . .

§272. Relief Including Restitution

(1) In any case governed by the rules stated in this Chapter, either party may have a claim for relief including restitution under the rules stated in §§240 and 377.

(2) In any case governed by the rules stated in this Chapter, if those rules together with the rules stated in Chapter 16 will not avoid injustice, the court may grant relief on such terms as justice requires including protection of the parties' reliance interests.

Comment

. . . .

c. Supplying a term to avoid injustice. Under the rule stated in §204, when the parties have not agreed with respect to a term that is essential to a determination of their rights and duties, the court will supply a term that is reasonable in the circumstances. Since it is the rationale of this Chapter that, in a case of impracticability or frustration, the contract does not cover the case that has arisen, the court's function can be viewed generally as that set out in §204 of supplying a term to deal with that omitted case. . . . Ordinarily the rules stated in this Chapter, coupled with those stated in Chapter 16, will be adequate to allow the court to arrive at a just result (Subsection (1)). In some instances, however, these rules will not suffice to avoid injustice. A particularly significant example occurs where the just solution is to "sever" the agreement and require that some unexecuted part of it be performed on both sides, rather than to relieve both parties of all of their duties. This situation differs from that envisioned in §240, under which the court merely allows recovery at the contract rate for performance that has already been rendered. The question under this Section is whether the court can salvage a part of the agreement that is still executory on both sides. . . . The rule stated in Subsection (2) makes it clear that it can do so by supplying a term which is reasonable in the circumstances when the rules stated in this Chapter together with those stated in Chapter 16 will not avoid injustice. The rule operates in other situations as well and may, for example, be invoked to require an obligor to prorate among several obligees that part of his performance that remains practicable. . . .

CHAPTER 12. DISCHARGE BY ASSENT OR ALTERATION

Topic 1. The Requirement of Consideration

§273. Requirement of Consideration or a Substitute

Except as stated in §§274-77, an obligee's manifestation of assent to a discharge is not effective unless
(a) it is made for consideration,
(b) it is made in circumstances in which a promise would be enforceable without consideration, or
(c) it has induced such action or forbearance as would make a promise enforceable.

§274. Cancellation, Destruction or Surrender of a Writing

An obligee's cancellation, destruction or surrender to the obligor of a writing of a type customarily accepted as a symbol or as evidence of his right discharges without consideration the obligor's duty if it is done with the manifested intention to discharge it.

§275. Assent to Discharge Duty of Return Performance

If a party, before he has fully performed his duty under a contract, manifests to the other party his assent to discharge the other party's duty to render part or all of the agreed exchange, the duty is to that extent discharged without consideration.

§276. Assent to Discharge Duty to Transfer Property

A duty of an obligor in possession of identified personal property to transfer an interest in that property is discharged without consideration if the obligee manifests to the obligor his assent to the discharge of that duty.

§277. Renunciation

(1) A written renunciation signed and delivered by the obligee discharges without consideration a duty arising out of a breach of contract.

(2) A renunciation by the obligee on his acceptance from the obligor of some performance under a contract discharges without consideration a duty to pay damages for a breach that gives rise only to a claim for damages for partial breach of contract.

Topic 2. Substituted Performance, Substituted Contract, Accord and Account Stated

§278. Substituted Performance

(1) If an obligee accepts in satisfaction of the obligor's duty a performance offered by the obligor that differs from what is due, the duty is discharged.

(2) If an obligee accepts in satisfaction of the obligor's duty a performance offered by a third person, the duty is discharged, but an obligor who has not previously assented to the performance for his benefit may in a reasonable time after learning of it render the discharge inoperative from the beginning by disclaimer.

§279. Substituted Contract

(1) A substituted contract is a contract that is itself accepted by the obligee in satisfaction of the obligor's existing duty.

(2) The substituted contract discharges the original duty and breach of the substituted contract by the obligor does not give the obligee a right to enforce the original duty.

§280. Novation

A novation is a substituted contract that includes as a party one who was neither the obligor nor the obligee of the original duty.

§281. Accord and Satisfaction

(1) An accord is a contract under which an obligee promises to accept a stated performance in satisfaction of the obligor's existing duty. Performance of the accord discharges the original duty.

(2) Until performance of the accord, the original duty is suspended unless there is such a breach of the accord by the obligor as discharges the new duty of the obligee to accept the performance in satisfaction. If there is such a breach, the obligee may enforce either the original duty or any duty under the accord.

(3) Breach of the accord by the obligee does not discharge the original duty, but the obligor may maintain a suit for specific performance of the accord, in addition to any claim for damages for partial breach.

§282. Account Stated

(1) An account stated is a manifestation of assent by debtor and creditor to a stated sum as an accurate computation of an amount due the creditor. A party's retention without objection for an unreasonably long time of a statement of account rendered by the other party is a manifestation of assent.

(2) The account stated does not itself discharge any duty but is an admission by each party of the facts asserted and a promise by the debtor to pay according to its terms.

Topic 3. *Agreement of Rescission, Release and Contract not to Sue*

§283. Agreement of Rescission

(1) An agreement of rescission is an agreement under which each party agrees to discharge all of the other party's remaining duties of performance under an existing contract.

(2) An agreement of rescission discharges all remaining duties of performance of both parties. It is a question of interpretation whether the parties also agree to make restitution with respect to performance that has been rendered.

§284. Release

(1) A release is a writing providing that a duty owed to the maker of the release is discharged immediately or on the occurrence of a condition.

(2) The release takes effect on delivery as stated in §§101-03 and, subject to the occurrence of any condition, discharges the duty.

§285. Contract Not to Sue

(1) A contract not to sue is a contract under which the obligee of a duty promises never to sue the obligor or a third person to enforce the duty or not to do so for a limited time.

(2) Except as stated in Subsection (3), a contract never to sue discharges the duty and a contract not to sue for a limited time bars an action to enforce the duty during that time.

(3) A contract not to sue one co-obligor bars levy of execution on the property of the promisee during the agreed time but does not bar an action or the recovery of judgment against any co-obligor.

Topic 4.   Alteration

§286. Alteration of Writing

(1) If one to whom a duty is owed under a contract alters a writing that is an integrated agreement or that satisfies the Statute of Frauds with respect to that contract, the duty is discharged if the alteration is fraudulent and material.

(2) An alteration is material if it would, if effective, vary any party's legal relations with the maker of the alteration or adversely affect that party's legal relations with a third person. The unauthorized insertion in a blank space in a writing is an alteration.

§287. Assent to or Forgiveness of Alteration

(1) If a party, knowing of an alteration that discharges his duty, manifests assent to the altered terms, his manifestation is equivalent to an acceptance of an offer to substitute those terms.

(2) If a party, knowing of an alteration that discharges his duty, asserts a right under the original contract or otherwise manifests a willingness to remain subject to the original contract or to forgive the alteration, the original contract is revived.

CHAPTER 13.   JOINT AND SEVERAL PROMISORS AND PROMISEES

Topic 1.   Joint and Several Promisors

§288.   Promises of the Same Performance

(1) Where two or more parties to a contract make a promise or promises to the same promisee, the manifested intention of the parties determines whether they promise that the same performance or separate performances shall be given.

(2) Unless a contrary intention is manifested, a promise by two or more promisors is a promise that the same performance shall be given.

§289.   Joint, Several, and Joint and Several Promisors of the Same Performance

(1) Where two or more parties to a contract promise the same performance to the same promisee, each is bound for the whole performance thereof, whether his duty is joint, several, or joint and several.

(2) Where two or more parties to a contract promise the same performance to the same promisee, they incur only a joint duty unless an intention is manifested to create several duties or joint and several duties.

(3) By statute in most states some or all promises which would otherwise create only joint duties create joint and several duties.

§290.   Compulsory Joinder of Joint Promisors

(1) By statute in most states where the distinction between joint duties and joint and several duties retains significance, an action can be maintained against one or more promisors who incur only a joint duty, even though other promisors subject to the same duty are not served with process.

(2) In the absence of statute, an action can be maintained against promisors who incur only a joint duty without joinder of those beyond the jurisdiction of the court, the representatives of deceased promisors, or those against whom the duty is not enforceable at the time of suit.

§291.   Judgment in an Action Against Co-promisors

In an action against promisors of the same performance, whether their duties are joint, several, or joint and several, judgment can properly be entered for or against one even though no judgment or a different judgment is entered with respect to another, except that judgment for one and against another is improper where there has been a determination on the merits and the liability of one cannot exist without the liability of the other.

§292. Effect of Judgment for or Against Co-promisors

(1) A judgment against one or more promisors does not discharge other promisors of the same performance unless joinder of the other promisors is required by the rule stated in §290. By statute in most states judgment against one promisor does not discharge co-promisors even where such joinder is required.

(2) The effect of judgment for one or more promisors of the same performance is determined by the rules of res judicata relating to suretyship or vicarious liability.

§293. Effect of Performance or Satisfaction on Co-promisors

Full or partial performance or other satisfaction of the contractual duty of a promisor discharges the duty to the obligee of each other promisor of the same performance to the extent of the amount or value applied to the discharge of the duty of the promisor who renders it.

§294. Effect of Discharge on Co-promisors

(1) Except as stated in §295, where the obligee of promises of the same performance discharges one promisor by release, rescission or accord and satisfaction,

    (a) co-promisors who are bound only by a joint duty are discharged unless the discharged promisor is a surety for the co-promisor;

    (b) co-promisors who are bound by joint and several duties or by several duties are not discharged except to the extent required by the law of suretyship.

(2) By statute in many states a discharge of one promisor does not discharge other promisors of the same performance except to the extent required by the law of suretyship.

(3) Any consideration received by the obligee for discharge of one promisor discharges the duty of each other promisor of the same performance to the extent of the amount or value received. An agreement to the contrary is not effective unless it is made with a surety and expressly preserves the duty of his principal.

§295. Effect of Contract Not to Sue; Reservation of Rights

(1) Where the obligee of promises of the same performance contracts not to sue one promisor, the other promisors are not discharged except to the extent required by the law of suretyship.

(2) Words which purport to release or discharge a promisor and also to reserve rights against other promisors of the same performance have the effect of a contract not to sue rather than a release or discharge.

(3) Any consideration received by the obligee for a contract not to sue one promisor discharges the duty of each other promisor of the same performance to the extent of the amount or value received. An agreement to the contrary is not

effective unless it is made with a surety and expressly preserves the duty of his principal.

§296. Survivorship of Joint Duties

On the death of one of two or more promisors of the same performance in a contract, the estate of the deceased promisor is bound by the contract, whether the duty was joint, several, or joint and several.

Topic 2. Joint and Several Promisees

§297. Obligees of the Same Promised Performance

(1) Where a party to a contract makes a promise to two or more promisees or for the benefit of two or more beneficiaries, the manifested intention of the parties determines whether he promises the same performance to all, a separate performance to each, or some combination.

(2) Except to the extent that a different intention is manifested or that the interests of the obligees in the performance or in the remedies for breach are distinct, the rights of obligees of the same performance are joint.

§298. Compulsory Joinder of Joint Obligees

(1) In an action based on a joint right created by a promise, the promisor by making appropriate objection can prevent recovery of judgment against him unless there are joined either as plaintiffs or as defendants all the surviving joint obligees.

(2) Except in actions on negotiable instruments and except as stated in §300, any joint obligee unless limited by agreement may sue in the name of all the joint obligees for the enforcement of the promise by a money judgment.

§299. Discharge by or Tender to One Joint Obligee

Except where the promise is made in a negotiable instrument and except as stated in §300, any joint obligee, unless limited by agreement, has power to discharge the promisor by receipt of the promised performance or by release or otherwise, and tender to one joint obligee is equivalent to a tender to all.

§300. Effect of Violation of Duty to a Co-Obligee

(1) If an obligee attempts or threatens to discharge the promisor in violation of his duty to a co-obligee of the same performance, the co-obligee may obtain an injunction forbidding the discharge.

(2) A discharge of the promisor by an obligee in violation of his duty to a co-obligee of the same performance is voidable to the extent necessary to protect the co-obligee's interest in the performance, except to the extent that the promisor has given value or otherwise changed his position in good faith and without knowledge or reason to know of the violation.

§301. Survivorship of Joint Rights

On the death of a joint obligee, unless a contrary intention was manifested, the surviving obligees are solely entitled as against the promisor to receive performance, to discharge the promisor, or to sue for the enforcement of the promise by a money judgment. On the death of the last surviving obligee, only his estate is so entitled.

CHAPTER 14.   CONTRACT BENEFICIARIES

§302. Intended and Incidental Beneficiaries

(1) Unless otherwise agreed between promisor and promisee, a beneficiary of a promise is an intended beneficiary if recognition of a right to performance in the beneficiary is appropriate to effectuate the intention of the parties and either
(a) the performance of the promise will satisfy an obligation of the promisee to pay money to the beneficiary; or
(b) the circumstances indicate that the promisee intends to give the beneficiary the benefit of the promised performance.
(2) An incidental beneficiary is a beneficiary who is not an intended beneficiary.

Comment

a. Promisee and beneficiary. This Section distinguishes an "intended" beneficiary, who acquires a right by virtue of a promise, from an "incidental" beneficiary, who does not. See §§304, 315. Section 2 defines "promisee" as the person to whom a promise is addressed, and "beneficiary" as a person other than the promisee who will be benefitted by performance of the promise. Both terms are neutral with respect to rights and duties: either or both or neither may have a legal right to performance. Either promisee or beneficiary may but need not be connected with the transaction in other ways: neither promisee nor beneficiary is necessarily the person to whom performance is to be rendered, the person who will receive economic benefit, or the person who furnished the consideration.

b. Promise to pay the promisee's debt. The type of beneficiary covered by Subsection (1)(a) is often referred to as a "creditor beneficiary." In such cases the promisee is surety for the promisor, the promise is an asset of the promisee, and a direct action by beneficiary against promisor is normally appropriate to carry out the intention of promisor and promisee, even though no intention is manifested to give the beneficiary the benefit of the promised performance. . . .

A suretyship relation may exist even though the duty of the promisee is voidable or is unenforceable by reason of the statute of limitations, the Statute of Frauds, or a discharge in bankruptcy, and Subsection (1)(a) covers such cases. The term "creditor beneficiary" has also sometimes been used with reference to promises to satisfy a supposed or asserted duty of the promisee, but there is no suretyship if the promisee has never been under any duty to the beneficiary. Hence such cases are not covered by Subsection (1)(a). The beneficiary of a promise to discharge a lien on the promisee's property, or of a promise to satisfy a duty of a third person, is similarly excluded from Subsection (1)(a). Such beneficiaries may, however, be "intended beneficiaries" under Subsection (1)(b). . . .

c. *Gift promise.* Where the promised performance is not paid for by the recipient, discharges no right that he has against anyone, and is apparently designed to benefit him, the promise is often referred to as a "gift promise." The beneficiary of such a promise is often referred to as a "donee beneficiary"; he is an intended beneficiary under Subsection (1)(b). The contract need not provide that performance is to be rendered directly to the beneficiary: a gift may be made to the beneficiary, for example, by payment of his debt. Nor is any contact or communication with the beneficiary essential. . . .

d. *Other intended beneficiaries.* Either a promise to pay the promisee's debt to a beneficiary or a gift promise involves a manifestation of intention by the promisee and promisor sufficient, in a contractual setting, to make reliance by the beneficiary both reasonable and probable. Other cases may be quite similar in this respect. Examples are a promise to perform a supposed or asserted duty of the promisee, a promise to discharge a lien on the promisee's property, or a promise to satisfy the duty of a third person. In such cases, if the beneficiary would be reasonable in relying on the promise as manifesting an intention to confer a right on him, he is an intended beneficiary. Where there is doubt whether such reliance would be reasonable, considerations of procedural convenience and other factors not strictly dependent on the manifested intention of the parties may affect the question whether under Subsection (1) recognition of a right in the beneficiary is appropriate. In some cases an overriding policy, which may be embodied in a statute, requires recognition of such a right without regard to the intention of the parties. . . .

e. *Incidental beneficiaries.* Performance of a contract will often benefit a third person. But unless the third person is an intended beneficiary as here defined, no duty to him is created. See §315. . . .

§303. Conditional Promises; Promises Under Seal

The statements in this Chapter are applicable to both conditional and unconditional promises and to sealed and unsealed promises.

§304. Creation of Duty to Beneficiary

A promise in a contract creates a duty in the promisor to any intended beneficiary to perform the promise, and the intended beneficiary may enforce the duty.

Comment

. . . .

b. Creation and termination of duty. This Section reflects the basic principle that the parties to a contract have the power, if they so intend, to create a right in a third person. The requirements for formation of a contract must of course be met, and the right of the beneficiary, like that of the promisee, may be conditional, voidable, or unenforceable. See §309. Whether the right of the beneficiary can be varied without his consent by action taken by the promisee or by agreement between promisee and promisor is a separate question which depends on the terms of the contract. See §311.

c. Promise to pay the promisee's debt. Where the performance of the promise will satisfy an obligation of the promisee to pay money to the beneficiary, the promisee is surety for the promisor. The contract is an asset of the promisee, and on grounds of simplicity and convenience of remedy the beneficiary is allowed a direct action against the promisor without joining the promisee, instead of a procedure like garnishment or a suit to realize on an asset of the debtor not available to seizure by ordinary legal process. The direct remedy also protects the beneficiary in reliance on the promise; his reliance is likely to take the form of inaction and to be difficult or impossible to prove. Promises to render performances other than the payment of money may be similar but require a manifestation of intention to give the benefit of the performance to the beneficiary. . . .

d. Gift promise. Where the promisee manifests an intention to make a gift of the promised performance to a beneficiary, recognition of a duty to the beneficiary means that the beneficiary has available for his own benefit the usual remedies for breach of contract. An action by the beneficiary is commonly a convenient way to enforce the right of the promisee as well as to redress any injury to the beneficiary. This is so even though the promisee has reserved a power to vary the beneficiary's right, so long as that power has not been exercised. . . .

e. Other intended beneficiaries. . . . Where the promisee clearly manifests an intention to confer on the beneficiary a legal right to enforce the contract, recognition of the beneficiary's right rests on the same grounds as recognition of the promisee's right. In cases of doubt, the question whether such an intention is to be attributed to the promisee may be influenced by the likelihood that recognition of the right will further the legitimate expectations of the promisee, make available a simple and convenient procedure for enforcement, or protect the beneficiary in his reasonable reliance on the promise. . . .

§305. Overlapping Duties to Beneficiary and Promisee

(1) A promise in a contract creates a duty in the promisor to the promisee to perform the promise even though he also has a similar duty to an intended beneficiary.

(2) Whole or partial satisfaction of the promisor's duty to the beneficiary satisfies to that extent the promisor's duty to the promisee.

§306. Disclaimer by a Beneficiary

A beneficiary who has not previously assented to the promise for his benefit may in a reasonable time after learning of its existence and terms render any duty to himself inoperative from the beginning by disclaimer.

§307. Remedy of Specific Performance

Where specific performance is otherwise an appropriate remedy, either the promisee or the beneficiary may maintain a suit for specific enforcement of a duty owed to an intended beneficiary.

Comment

a. Suit by beneficiary. . . . Where a contract creates a duty to a beneficiary under the rule stated in §304, the beneficiary is a proper party plaintiff either in an action for damages or in a suit for specific performance. He is the real party in interest within the meaning of any statute requiring suit to be brought by such a party. There is no general requirement that the promisee be made a party, but the promisee is ordinarily a proper party and the circumstances may be such that a final decree should await joinder of the promisee. . . .

b. Suit by promisee. Even though a contract creates a duty to a beneficiary, the promisee has a right to performance. See §305. The promisee cannot recover damages suffered by the beneficiary, but the promisee is a proper party to sue for specific performance if that remedy is otherwise appropriate under the rules stated in §§357-69. . . . There is no general requirement that the beneficiary be joined in such a suit; whether he should or must be made a party depends on the circumstances.

c. Promise to pay the promisee's debt. Where the promised performance will satisfy an obligation of the promisee to pay money to the beneficiary, the promisee may suffer substantial damages as a result of breach. He is entitled to recover such damages so long as there is no conflict with rights of the beneficiary or the promisor. But the promisee as surety for the promisor is not permitted to compete with the beneficiary for the assets of the promisor, and the promisor is ordinarily entitled to protection against enforced double liability. See §§305, 310. . . .

d. Gift promise. Where the promisee intends to make a gift of the promised performance to the beneficiary, the beneficiary ordinarily has an economic interest in the performance but the promisee does not. Thus the promisee may suffer no damages as the result of breach by the promisor. In such cases the promisee's remedy in damages is not an adequate remedy, within the rules stated in §§359 and 360, and specific performance may be appropriate. . . .

§308. Identification of Beneficiaries

It is not essential to the creation of a right in an intended beneficiary that he be identified when a contract containing the promise is made.

§309. Defenses Against the Beneficiary

(1) A promise creates no duty to a beneficiary unless a contract is formed between the promisor and the promisee; and if a contract is voidable or unenforceable at the time of its formation the right of any beneficiary is subject to the infirmity.

(2) If a contract ceases to be binding in whole or in part because of impracticability, public policy, non-occurrence of a condition, or present or prospective failure of performance, the right of any beneficiary is to that extent discharged or modified.

(3) Except as stated in Subsections (1) and (2) and in §311 or as provided by the contract, the right of any beneficiary against the promisor is not subject to the promisor's claims or defenses against the promisee or to the promisee's claims or defenses against the beneficiary.

(4) A beneficiary's right against the promisor is subject to any claim or defense arising from his own conduct or agreement.

§310. Remedies of the Beneficiary of a Promise to Pay the Promisee's Debt; Reimbursement of Promisee

(1) Where an intended beneficiary has an enforceable claim against the promisee, he can obtain a judgment or judgments against either the promisee or the promisor or both based on their respective duties to him. Satisfaction in whole or in part of either of these duties, or of a judgment thereon, satisfies to that extent the other duty or judgment, subject to the promisee's right of subrogation.

(2) To the extent that the claim of an intended beneficiary is satisfied from assets of the promisee, the promisee has a right of reimbursement from the promisor, which may be enforced directly and also, if the beneficiary's claim is fully satisfied, by subrogation to the claim of the beneficiary against the promisor, and to any judgment thereon and to any security therefor.

§311. Variation of a Duty to a Beneficiary

(1) Discharge or modification of a duty to an intended beneficiary by conduct of the promisee or by a subsequent agreement between promisor and promisee is ineffective if a term of the promise creating the duty so provides.

(2) In the absence of such a term, the promisor and promisee retain power to discharge or modify the duty by subsequent agreement.

(3) Such a power terminates when the beneficiary, before he receives notification of the discharge or modification, materially changes his position in justifiable reliance on the promise or brings suit on it or manifests assent to it at the request of the promisor or promisee.

(4) If the promisee receives consideration for an attempted discharge or modification of the promisor's duty which is ineffective against the beneficiary, the beneficiary can assert a right to the consideration so received. The promisor's duty is discharged to the extent of the amount received by the beneficiary.

Comment

a. The power to create an irrevocable duty. The parties to a contract cannot by agreement preclude themselves from varying their duties to each other by subsequent agreement. Nor can they force a right on an unwilling beneficiary, or prevent the beneficiary from joining with them in an agreement varying the duty to him. . . . But they can by agreement create a duty to a beneficiary which cannot be varied without the beneficiary's consent. Compare §104. . . .

b. Express and implied terms. Agreements precluding variation of a duty to a beneficiary before the beneficiary knows of the promise are unusual and would often be unwise. See Comment *f.* But the power of the parties to make such an agreement is not restricted by special formal requirements. The agreement need not be explicit: omission of a standard clause reserving a power of modification may manifest an intention to preclude modification; reservation of a limited power may negate a broader power; usage of trade or course of dealing may supply a term precluding modification. See §5, defining "term." . . .

f. The power to vary. Under the rule stated in Subsection (1), a promisor and a promisee can by agreement create a duty to a beneficiary which cannot be varied without his consent. But in the absence of such an agreement the parties retain control over the contractual relation they have created. Loss of control over a policy of life insurance, for example, may prevent perfectly proper readjustments in the light of misconduct of the beneficiary or the birth of children, or a family financial crisis; the practice of reserving a power to change the beneficiary has therefore become almost universal. Other types of contracts normally remain subject to variation by the parties without express provision at least until there is some possibility of reliance by the beneficiary. . . .

g. Reliance. In the absence of some contrary indication, an intended beneficiary is justified in relying on the promise. It is immaterial whether he learns of the promise from the promisor, the promisee or a third party, and whether the promise is one to satisfy the promisee's duty or is a gift promise or is neither. If there is a material change of position in justifiable reliance on the promise, the change of position precludes discharge or modification of the contract without the beneficiary's consent. In the case of a promise to pay a debt of the promisee or another person, it is not necessary that the beneficiary enter into a novation with the promisor, though a novation would *a fortiori* be effective. See §280. As to what constitutes receipt of a notification sufficient to preclude reliance, see §68. . . .

h. Assent. Even though there is no novation and no change of position by the beneficiary, the power of promisor and promisee to vary the promisor's duty to an intended beneficiary is terminated when the beneficiary manifests assent to the promise in a manner invited by the promisor or promisee. This rule rests in part on an analogy to the law of offer and acceptance and in part on the probability that the beneficiary will rely in ways difficult or impossible to prove. . . . The bringing of suit against the promisor is a sufficient manifestation of assent to preclude discharge or modification. . . .

j. The beneficiary's right to proceeds. Where a promise creates rights in a beneficiary, the promisee may retain power to discharge or modify the promisor's duty. Whether the exercise of such a power is rightful or wrongful may depend on facts other than the promise. If it is wrongful, the promisee is under a duty of restitution to the beneficiary for any amount received by him therefor. . . . Subsection (4) applies a similar principle to cases where the beneficiary's right against the promisor is not discharged or modified. In the latter type of case, the promisor may also have a right of restitution. . . . Which right prevails in the event of conflict and the extent to which assertion of the right against the promisee bars a claim against the promisor depends on what is equitable in the circumstances.

§312.   Mistake as to Duty to Beneficiary

The effect of an erroneous belief of the promisor or promisee as to the existence or extent of a duty owed to an intended beneficiary is determined by the rules making contracts voidable for mistake.

§313.   Government Contracts

(1) The rules stated in this Chapter apply to contracts with a government or governmental agency except to the extent that application would contravene the policy of the law authorizing the contract or prescribing remedies for its breach.

(2) In particular, a promisor who contracts with a government or governmental agency to do an act for or render a service to the public is not subject to contractual liability to a member of the public for consequential damages resulting from performance or failure to perform unless

(a) the terms of the promise provide for such liability; or

(b) the promisee is subject to liability to the member of the public for the damages and a direct action against the promisor is consistent with the terms of the contract and with the policy of the law authorizing the contract and prescribing remedies for its breach.

§314.   Suretyship Defenses

An intended beneficiary who has an enforceable claim against the promisee is affected by the incidents of the suretyship of the promisee from the time he has knowledge of it.

§315.   Effect of a Promise of Incidental Benefit

An incidental beneficiary acquires by virtue of the promise no right against the promisor or the promisee.

CHAPTER 15. ASSIGNMENT AND DELEGATION

§316. Scope of This Chapter

(1) In this Chapter, references to assignment of a right or delegation of a duty or condition, to the obligee or obligor of an assigned right or delegated duty, or to an assignor or assignee, are limited to rights, duties, and conditions arising under a contract or for breach of a contract.

(2) The statements in this Chapter are qualified in some respects by statutory and other rules governing negotiable instruments and documents, relating to interests in land, and affecting other classes of contracts.

Comment

. . . .

c. Assignment and delegation. In this Chapter rights are said to be "assigned"; duties are said to be "delegated." The phrase "assignment of the contract," which may refer to either or both, is avoided because "contract" is defined in §1 in terms of the act or acts of promising. See §328. "Assignment" is the transfer of a right by the owner (the obligee or assignor) to another person (the assignee). See §317. A person subject to a duty (the obligor) does not ordinarily have such a power to substitute another in his place without the consent of the obligee; this is what is meant when it is said that duties cannot be assigned. "Delegation" of performance may be effective to empower a substitute to perform on behalf of the obligor, but the obligor remains subject to the duty until it has been discharged by performance or otherwise. Compare the usage of terms in Uniform Commercial Code §2-210. Delegation of performance of a condition is similar in effect to delegation of performance of duty.

d. Involuntary transfer. In accordance with common usage, assignment and delegation in this Chapter include only transfers made or powers created by virtue of a manifestation of intention of the assignor or obligor. The manifestation may be made to the assignee or the person delegated or to another person on his behalf, but transfers made and powers created by operation of law are excluded. Such transfers and powers, including transfers to and powers of an executor, administrator, trustee in bankruptcy or receiver by virtue of his office, are in general beyond the scope of this Restatement. . . .

Topic 1. What Can Be Assigned or Delegated

§317. Assignment of a Right

(1) An assignment of a right is a manifestation of the assignor's intention to transfer it by virtue of which the assignor's right to performance by the obligor is extinguished in whole or in part and the assignee acquires a right to such performance.

(2) A contractual right can be assigned unless

(a) the substitution of a right of the assignee for the right of the assignor would materially change the duty of the obligor, or materially increase the burden or risk imposed on him by his contract, or materially impair his chance of obtaining return performance, or materially reduce its value to him, or

(b) the assignment is forbidden by statute or is otherwise inoperative on grounds of public policy, or

(c) assignment is validly precluded by contract.

Comment

a. "Assignment." The word "assignment" is sometimes used to refer to the act of the owner of a right (the obligee or assignor) purporting to transfer it, sometimes to the resulting change in legal relations, sometimes to a document evidencing the act or change. In this Chapter "assign" and "assignment" refer to an act which has the effect stated in Subsection (1). To avoid ambiguity, such an assignment is said to be "effective"; a similar act which does not have the stated effect is referred to as an "attempted" or "purported" assignment. In either case the actor is referred to as the "assignor" and the transferee or intended or purported transferee is referred to as the "assignee." . . .

d. Material variation. What is a material variation, an increase in burden or risk, or an impairment of the obligor's expectation of counter-performance under paragraph (2)(a) depends on the nature of the contract and on the circumstances. Both assignment of rights and delegation of performance are normal and permissible incidents of many types of contracts. See, for example, as to contracts for the sale of goods, Uniform Commercial Code §2-210 Comment. When the obligor's duty is to pay money, a change in the person to whom the payment is to be made is not ordinarily material. . . . But if the duty is to depend on the personal discretion of one person, substitution of the personal discretion of another is likely to be a material change. The clause on material impairment of the chance of obtaining return performance operates primarily in cases where the assignment is accompanied by an improper delegation under §318 or §319: if the obligor is to perform in exchange for the promise of one person to render a return performance at a future time, substitution of the return promise of another impairs the obligor's expectation of counter-performance. But in cases of doubt, adequate assurance of due performance may prevent such an impairment. Compare §251; Uniform Commercial Code §2-609. . . .

f. Contractual prohibition. The effect of a term in a contract forbidding the assignment of rights arising under the contract is the subject of §322. Such a term may resolve doubts as to whether an assignment violates paragraph (2)(a) of this Section. Where it seems to forbid an assignment clearly outside the scope of paragraph (2)(a), it may be read restrictively to permit the assignment, or to give the obligor a claim against the assignor rather than a defense against the assignee, or the term may be invalid by statute or decision. See Uniform Commercial Code §§2-210, 9-[404 to 9-406]. Even if the term gives the obligor a defense against the assignee, the assignment is usually partially effective as an assignment conditional on the assent of the obligor.

§318.   Delegation of Performance of Duty

(1) An obligor can properly delegate the performance of his duty to another unless the delegation is contrary to public policy or the terms of his promise.

(2) Unless otherwise agreed, a promise requires performance by a particular person only to the extent that the obligee has a substantial interest in having that person perform or control the acts promised.

(3) Unless the obligee agrees otherwise, neither delegation of performance nor a contract to assume the duty made with the obligor by the person delegated discharges any duty or liability of the delegating obligor.

Comment

. . . .

c. Non-delegable duties. Delegation of performance is a normal and permissible incident of many types of contract. See Uniform Commercial Code §2-210, Comment. The principal exceptions relate to contracts for personal services and to contracts for the exercise of personal skill or discretion. . . . Even where delegation is normal, a particular contract may call for personal performance. . . . In the absence of contrary agreement, Subsection (2) precludes delegation only where a substantial reason is shown why delegated performance is not as satisfactory as personal performance.

Illustrations

5. A, a teacher employed in a public or private school, attempts to delegate the performance of his duties to B, a competent person. An offer by B to perform A's duties need not be accepted, and actual performance by B without the assent of the employer will create no right in either A or B to the salary stated in A's contract.

6. A contracts . . . to sing three songs over the radio as part of an advertisement of B's product. A's performance is not delegable unless B assents.

7. A contracts with B that A will personally cut the grass on B's meadow. A cannot effectively delegate performance of the duty to C, however competent C may be. . . .

d. Delegation and novation. An obligor is discharged by the substitution of a new obligor only if the contract so provides or if the obligee makes a binding manifestation of assent, forming a novation. See §§280, 328 and 329. Otherwise, the obligee retains his original right against the obligor, even though the obligor manifests an intention to substitute another obligor in his place and the other purports to assume the duty. The obligee may, however, have rights against the other as an intended beneficiary of the promise to assume the duty. See Chapter 14. . . .

§319.   Delegation of Performance of Condition

(1) Where a performance by a person is made a condition of a duty, performance by a person delegated by his satisfies that requirement unless the delegation is contrary to public policy or the terms of the agreement.

(2) Unless otherwise agreed, an agreement requires performance of a condition by a particular person only to the extent that the obligor has a substantial interest in having that person perform or control the acts required.

Comment

. . . .

b. Non-delegable performance. The propriety of delegation of performance that is made a condition is in general governed by the same standard as the propriety of delegation of performance of a duty. Indeed, the same delegation may involve both. See, e.g., Illustration 5 to §318. Delegation is generally permissible unless otherwise agreed, but performance of personal services and the exercise of personal skill and discretion are not ordinarily delegable. Where the condition consists of the making of a promise, delegation substituting a different promisor is ordinarily not effective. . . .

§320. Assignment of Conditional Rights

The fact that a right is created by an option contract or is conditional on the performance of a return promise or is otherwise conditional does not prevent its assignment before the condition occurs.

§321. Assignment of Future Rights

(1) Except as otherwise provided by statute, an assignment of a right to payment expected to arise out of an existing employment or other continuing business relationship is effective in the same way as an assignment of an existing right.

(2) Except as otherwise provided by statute and as stated in Subsection (1), a purported assignment of a right expected to arise under a contract not in existence operates only a promise to assign the right when it arises and as a power to enforce it.

§322. Contractual Prohibition of Assignment

(1) Unless the circumstances indicate the contrary, a contract term prohibiting assignment of "the contract" bars only the delegation to an assignee of the performance by the assignor of a duty or condition.

(2) A contract term prohibiting assignment of rights under the contract, unless a different intention is manifested,

(a) does not forbid assignment of a right to damages for breach of the whole contract or a right arising out of the assignor's due performance of his entire obligation;

(b) gives the obligor a right to damages for breach of the terms forbidding assignment but does not render the assignment ineffective;

(c) is for the benefit of the obligor, and does not prevent the assignee from acquiring rights against the assignor or the obligor from discharging his duty as if there were no such prohibition.

Comment

a. Rationale. In the absence of statute or other contrary public policy, the parties to a contract have power to limit the rights created by their agreement. The policy against restraints on the alienation of property has limited application to contractual rights. . . . A term in a contract prohibiting assignment of the rights created may resolve doubts as to whether assignment would materially change the obligor's duty or whether he has a substantial interest in personal performance by the obligee (see §§317-19); or it may serve to protect the obligor against conflicting claims and the hazard of double liability (see §§338-43). But as assignment has become a common practice, the policy which limits the validity of restraints on alienation has been applied to the construction of contractual terms open to two or more possible constructions. . . .

c. Construction. The rules stated in this Section do not exhaust the factors to be taken into account in construing and applying a prohibition against assignment. "Not transferable" has a clear meaning in a theatre ticket; in a certificate of deposit the same words may refer to negotiability rather than assignability. Where there is a promise not to assign but no provision that an assignment is ineffective, the question whether breach of the promise discharges the obligor's duty depends on all the circumstances. See §§237, 241.

§323. Obligor's Assent to Assignment or Delegation

(1) A term of a contract manifesting an obligor's assent to the future assignment of a right or an obligee's assent to the future delegation of the performance of a duty or condition is effective despite any subsequent objection.

(2) A manifestation of such assent after the formation of a contract is similarly effective if made for consideration or in circumstances in which a promise would be binding without consideration, or if a material change of position takes place in reliance on the manifestation.

Comment

a. Effect of assent. The assent of the obligor is not ordinarily necessary to make an assignment effective. But his assent may operate to preclude objection based on a change in his duty, burden or risk or in his chance of obtaining return performance. See §317. It may permit a separate action by a partial assignee. See §326. It may be an offer of a new contract by novation, or the acceptance of an offer of novation, and may thus terminate the assignor's power to revoke a gratuitous assignment (see §332), or may discharge or modify a duty of the assignor or a condition of the right assigned (see §§318-19). Which of these effects is produced depends on the circumstances and the scope of the assent manifested.

b. *Promises to or by "assigns."* Contracts often refer to the "assigns" of one or both parties. A purported promise by a promisor "and his assigns" does not mean that the promisor can terminate his duty by making an assignment, nor does it of itself show an assumption of duties by any assignee. It tends to indicate that the promised performance is not personal, just as a promise to a promisee "and his assigns" tends to indicate that the promisor is willing to render performance to an assignee. Whether there is a manifestation of assent to assignment or delegation, however, depends on the interpretation of the contract as a whole. Notwithstanding references to "assigns," other terms and the circumstances may show that the assent is limited or even that there is no assent. . . .

Topic 2.   Mode of Assignment or Delegation

§324.   Mode of Assignment in General

It is essential to an assignment of a right that the obligee manifest an intention to transfer the right to another person without further action or manifestation of intention by the obligee. The manifestation may be made to the other or to a third person on his behalf and, except as provided by statute or by contract, may be made either orally or by a writing.

§325.   Order as Assignment

(1) A written order drawn upon an obligor and signed and delivered to another person by the obligee is an assignment if it is conditional on the existence of a duty of the drawee to the drawer to comply with the order and the drawer manifests an intention that a person other than the drawer is to retain the performance.

(2) An order which directs the drawee to render a performance without reference to any duty of the drawee is not of itself an assignment, even though the drawee is under a duty to the drawer to comply with the order and even though the order indicates a particular account to be debited or any other fund or source from which reimbursement is expected.

§326.   Partial Assignment

(1) Except as stated in Subsection (2), an assignment of a part of a right, whether the part is specified as a fraction, as an amount, or otherwise, is operative as to that part to the same extent and in the same manner as if the part had been a separate right.

(2) If the obligor has not contracted to perform separately the assigned part of a right, no legal proceeding can be maintained by the assignor or assignee against the obligor over his objection, unless all the persons entitled to the promised performance are joined in the proceeding, or unless joinder is not feasible and it is equitable to proceed without joinder.

§327. Acceptance or Disclaimer by the Assignee

(1) A manifestation of assent by an assignee to the assignment is essential to make it effective unless
    (a) a third person gives consideration for the assignment, or
    (b) the assignment is irrevocable by virtue of the delivery of a writing to a third person.
(2) An assignee who has not manifested assent to an assignment may, within a reasonable time after learning of its existence and terms, render it inoperative from the beginning by disclaimer.

Comment

a. Necessity of acceptance. Sale of a contractual right, like sale of goods, requires a bargain in which there is a manifestation of mutual assent to the exchange. Ordinarily the person who furnishes the consideration is the transferee of the right sold, but where consideration is given by one person for an assignment to another, it is not necessary that the assignee know of the bargain or assent to it. Compare §§17, 71(2). Where there is no bargain, an irrevocable gift can be made without the assent of the donee by the delivery of a written assignment or a symbolic or evidentiary writing to a third person. Compare §§104, 306. . . . The circumstances in which such a delivery makes the assignment irrevocable are stated in §332. . . .

b. Disclaimer. As in other cases of rights created without the assent of the obligee, an assignee is entitled to reject the right, whether or not there is a related burden. Compare §§38, 104, 306. No particular formality is required for disclaimer, and its usual effect is the same as if no assignment had been made. But it cannot make tortious acts lawful when done, and in some cases it may give rise to a right of restitution. . . .

§328. Interpretation of Words of Assignment; Effect of Acceptance of Assignment

(1) Unless the language or the circumstances indicate the contrary, as in an assignment for security, an assignment of "the contract" or of "all my rights under the contract" or an assignment in similar general terms is an assignment of the assignor's rights and a delegation of his unperformed duties under the contract.
(2) Unless the language or the circumstances indicate the contrary, the acceptance by an assignee of such an assignment operates as a promise to the

assignor to perform the assignor's unperformed duties, and the obligor of the assigned rights is an intended beneficiary of the promise.

Caveat: The Institute expresses no opinion as to whether the rule stated in Subsection (2) applies to an assignment by a purchaser of his rights under a contract for the sale of land.

Comment

a. "Assignment" of duty. A duty cannot be "assigned" in the sense in which "assignment" is used in this Chapter. The parties to an assignment, however, may not distinguish between assignment of rights and delegation of duties. A purported "assignment" of duties may simply manifest an intention that the assignee shall be substituted for the assignor. Such an intention is not completely effective unless the obligor of the assigned right joins in a novation, but the rules of this Section give as full effect as can be given without the obligor's assent. As to contracts for the sale of goods, see Uniform Commercial Code §2-210. . . .

b. Contrary agreement. . . . This Section states rules of presumptive interpretation which yield to a manifestation of a different intention. In particular delegation and assumption of the assignor's duties is not ordinarily implied where the contract calls for personal performance by the assignor. . . .

c. Land contracts. By virtue of the right of either party to obtain specific performance of a contract for the sale of land, such contracts are treated for many purposes as creating a property interest in the purchaser and thus as partially executed. The vendor's interest resembles the interest of a mortgagee under a mortgage given as security for the purchase price. An assignment of the vendor's rights under the contract is similar to an assignment of a right to payment for goods or services: ordinarily no assumption of the vendor's duties by the assignee is implied merely from the acceptance of the assignment.

When the purchaser under a land contract assigns his rights, the assignment has commonly been treated like a sale of land "subject to" a mortgage. In this view acceptance of the assignment does not amount to an assumption of the assignor's duties unless the contract of assignment so provides either expressly or by implication. . . . Decisions refusing to infer an assumption of duties by the assignee have been influenced by doctrinal difficulties in the recognition of rights of assignees and beneficiaries. Those difficulties have now been overcome, and it is doubtful whether adherence to such decisions carries out the probable intention of the parties in the usual case. But since the shift in doctrine has not yet produced any definite change in the body of decisions, the Institute expresses no opinion on the application of Subsection (2) to an assignment by a purchaser under a land contract. . . .

§329. Repudiation by Assignor and Novation With Assignee

(1) The legal effect of a repudiation by an assignor of his duty to the obligor of the assigned right is not limited by the fact that the assignee is a competent person and has promised to perform the duty.

(2) If the obligor, with knowledge of such a repudiation, accepts any performance from the assignee without reserving his rights against the assignor, a novation arises by which the duty of the assignor is discharged and a similar duty of the assignee is substituted.

Comment

a. Repudiation and its effects. In some cases a repudiation by one party to a contract discharges the duty of the other party; in some cases it requires the other to treat as total a breach which might otherwise be partial, or it may itself be a total breach. See §253; Uniform Commercial Code §2-610. For these purposes repudiation includes a positive statement by an assignor that he will not or cannot substantially perform his duties, or any voluntary affirmative action which renders substantial performance apparently impossible. In some circumstances a statement that he doubts whether he will substantially perform, or that he takes no responsibility for performance, or even a failure to give adequate assurance of performance may have a similar effect. See §§250-51.

b. Scope of obligor's assent. The assignment of a contractual right and delegation to the assignee of the assignor's duty is often a matter of course. The obligor of the assigned right may then have a right to withhold performance until he receives adequate assurance of performance by the assignee. Section 251. Failure to demand such assurance and acceptance of performance by the assignee manifest the obligor's assent to the assignment and delegation (see §323), but not to the discharge of the assignor's duty. However, when the obligor knows that the delegating assignor has repudiated his duty he has reason to know that the performance of the assignee is offered by way of novation, and his silent acceptance of the performance operates as acceptance of the offer of novation. Compare §69. . . .

c. Reservation of rights. The obligor of an assigned right cannot be forced to assent to a repudiation by the assignor or to an offer of a substituted contract with the assignee. To avoid the implication that his silence gives assent, he must manifest either to the assignor or to the assignee his intention to retain unimpaired his rights against the assignor, but no particular form is required. See Uniform Commercial Code §§1-207, 3-606; §281. If the terms of the assignment so provide, the delegation or assumption of duty may be defeated in such a case, and the repudiation may be retracted before it has been acted on. See Uniform Commercial Code §2-611. Where the assignee continues performance, the reservation of rights by the obligor means that the assignor, if compelled to pay for the assignee's default, will have a right over against the assignee. . . .

§330. Contracts to Assign in the Future, or to Transfer Proceeds to Be Received

(1) A contract to make a future assignment of a right, or to transfer proceeds to be received in the future by the promisor, is not an assignment.

(2) Except as provided by statute, the effect of such a contract on the rights and duties of the obligor and third persons is determined by the rules relating to specific performance of contracts.

Topic 3. Effect Between Assignor and Assignee

§331. Partially Effective Assignments

An assignment may be conditional, revocable, or voidable by the assignor, or unenforceable by virtue of a Statute of Frauds.

Comment

a. Assignor's power to destroy assignee's right. In this Restatement "assignment" is used to refer to an act which extinguishes in whole or in part the assignor's right and creates a similar right in the assignee. See §§317, 324. On proof of an unconditional assignment, the assignee can recover on an assigned right; the assignor cannot. The assignor may be entitled to revoke the assignment because it is gratuitous or by virtue of a reserved power, or the assignment may be voidable for fraud or other invalidating cause. Even if destruction of the assignee's right is a violation of the assignor's duty, he retains by virtue of his former ownership certain powers which may have that effect. See §§338, 342. . . .

§332. Revocability of Gratuitous Assignments

(1) Unless a contrary intention is manifested, a gratuitous assignment is irrevocable if

    (a) the assignment is in a writing either signed or under seal that is delivered by the assignor; or

    (b) the assignment is accompanied by delivery of a writing of a type customarily accepted as a symbol or as evidence of the right assigned.

(2) Except as stated in this Section, a gratuitous assignment is revocable and the right of the assignee is terminated by the assignor's death or incapacity, by a subsequent assignment by the assignor, or by notification from the assignor received by the assignee or by the obligor.

(3) A gratuitous assignment ceases to be revocable to the extent that before the assignee's right is terminated he obtains

    (a) payment or satisfaction of the obligation, or

    (b) judgment against the obligor, or

    (c) a new contract of the obligor by novation.

(4) A gratuitous assignment is irrevocable to the extent necessary to avoid injustice where the assignor should reasonably expect the assignment to induce action or forbearance by the assignee or a subassignee and the assignment does induce such action or forbearance.

(5) An assignment is gratuitous unless it is given or taken

(a) in exchange for a performance or return promise that would be consideration for a promise; or

(b) as security for or in total or partial satisfaction of a pre-existing debt or other obligation.

§333. Warranties of an Assignor

(1) Unless a contrary intention is manifested, one who assigns or purports to assign a right by assignment under seal or for value warrants to the assignee

(a) that he will do nothing to defeat or impair the value of the assignment and has no knowledge of any fact which would do so;

(b) that the right, as assigned, actually exists and is subject to no limitations or defenses good against the assignor other than those stated or apparent at the time of the assignment;

(c) that any writing evidencing the right which is delivered to the assignee or exhibited to him to induce him to accept the assignment is genuine and what it purports to be.

(2) An assignment does not of itself operate as a warranty that the obligor is solvent or that he will perform his obligation.

(3) An assignor is bound by affirmations and promises to the assignee with reference to the right assigned in the same way and to the same extent that one who transfers goods is bound in like circumstances.

(4) An assignment of a right to a subassignee does not operate as an assignment of the assignee's rights under his assignor's warranties unless an intention is manifested to assign the rights under the warranties.

Topic 4.   Effect on the Obligor's Duty

§334. Variation of Obligor's Duty by Assignment

(1) If the obligor's duty is conditional on the personal cooperation of the original obligee or another person, an assignee's right is subject to the same condition.

(2) If the obligor's duty is conditional on cooperation which the obligee could properly delegate to an agent, the condition may occur if there is similar cooperation by an assignee.

Comment

. . . .

b. *Terms of assignment.* Whether there is a material change in the obligor's duty depends not only on the terms of the contract creating the duty and on the circumstances, but also on the terms of the assignment. Commonly an assignment manifests an intention that the obligor render performance to the assignee rather than to the assignor. Such a change is immaterial in the usual case of a duty to pay money, but material where personal cooperation is made a condition of the duty. Even in the latter case, however, it is at least theoretically possible to assign the right without departing from the requirement. . . .

§335. Assignment by a Joint Obligee

A joint obligee may effectively assign his right, but the assignee can enforce it only in the same manner and to the same extent as the assignor could have enforced it.

§336. Defenses Against an Assignee

(1) By an assignment the assignee acquires a right against the obligor only to the extent that the obligor is under a duty to the assignor; and if the right of the assignor would be voidable by the obligor or unenforceable against him if no assignment had been made, the right of the assignee is subject to the infirmity.

(2) The right of an assignee is subject to any defense or claim of the obligor which accrues before the obligor receives notification of the assignment, but not to defenses or claims which accrue thereafter except as stated in this Section or as provided by statute.

(3) Where the right of an assignor is subject to discharge or modification in whole or in part by impracticability, public policy, non-occurrence of a condition, or present or prospective failure of performance by an obligee, the right of the assignee is to that extent subject to discharge or modification even after the obligor receives notification of the assignment.

(4) An assignee's right against the obligor is subject to any defense or claim arising from his conduct or to which he was subject as a party or a prior assignee because he had notice.

Comment

. . . .

b. Accrued defenses. . . . [T]he assignment of a non-negotiable contractual right ordinarily transfers what the assignor has but only what he has. The assignee's right depends on the validity and enforceability of the contract creating the right, and is subject to limitations imposed by the terms of that contract and to defenses which would have been available against the obligee had there been no assignment. Until the obligor receives notification of an assignment, he is entitled to treat the obligee as owner of the right, and the assignee's right is subject to defenses and claims arising from dealings between assignor and obligor in relation to the contract before notification. See §338. . . .

f. Agreement not to assert defenses. The obligor may undertake a greater obligation to an assignee than to the assignor by direct contract with the assignee, and may confer on the assignor an agency power to bind him to such an agreement. Section 9-[403] of the Uniform Commercial Code gives effect to an agreement by a buyer or lessee that he will not assert against an assignee any claim or defense which he may have against the seller or lessor, making it enforceable by a good faith assignee for value without notice of a claim or defense, except as to defenses of a type which may be asserted against a holder in due course of a negotiable instrument. The Assignment of Claims Act of 1940, 31 U.S.C. §203 (1979), contains a more limited authorization for a no-setoff agreement by the United States. The Code provision is subject to any statute or decision which establishes a different rule for buyers or lessees of consumer goods, and a number of retail installment sales acts limit the power of a buyer to make such an agreement. In addition, the Federal Trade Commission has issued a Trade Regulation Rule barring such agreements with respect to consumers. See 16 C.F.R. §§433.1-.3 (1975). In the absence of statute, administrative rule or court decision, such an agreement can take effect to give the assignee greater rights than the assignor as to matters governed by the terms of the contract; but if the agreement not to assert defenses or claims is itself voidable or unenforceable, the assignee takes subject to the defect. . . .

g. *Estoppel.* Even though an obligor's agreement not to assert a defense or claim is not binding or is voidable or unenforceable, he may be estopped to assert the claim or defense against an assignee. Where he makes a representation of fact with the intention of inducing an assignee or prospective assignee to act in reliance on the representation, and an assignee does so act, the doctrine of estoppel bars the obligor from contradicting the representation in litigation against the assignee if contradiction would be inequitable. Compare §90. Application of the doctrine depends on all the circumstances. The representation may be express or it may be implied from conduct, in unusual cases even from failure to act. In some circumstances estoppel may rest on the obligor's reason to know that the assignee may rely, even though there is no intention to induce reliance. . . .

h. *Conduct of the assignee.* The conduct of the assignee or his agents may, like that of any obligee, give rise to defenses and claims which may be asserted against him by the obligor. An obligee who is subject to such a defense or claim cannot improve his position by assigning the right to an assignee who is not subject to the defense or claim and then taking a reassignment. . . .

§337. Elimination of Defenses by Subsequent Events

Where the right of an assignor is limited or voidable or unenforceable or subject to discharge or modification, subsequent events which would eliminate the limitation or defense have the same effect on the right of the assignee.

§338. Discharge of an Obligor After Assignment

(1) Except as stated in this Section, notwithstanding an assignment, the assignor retains his power to discharge or modify the duty of the obligor to the extent that the obligor performs or otherwise gives value until but not after the obligor receives notification that the right has been assigned and that performance is to be rendered to the assignee.

(2) So far as an assigned right is conditional on the performance of a return promise, and notwithstanding notification of the assignment, any modification of or substitution for the contract made by the assignor and obligor in good faith and in accordance with reasonable commercial standards is effective against the

assignee. The assignee acquires corresponding rights under the modified or substituted contract.

(3) Notwithstanding a defect in the right of an assignee, he has the same power his assignor had to discharge or modify the duty of the obligor to the extent that the obligor gives value or otherwise changes his position in good faith and without knowledge or reason to know of the defect.

(4) Where there is a writing of a type customarily accepted as a symbol or as evidence of the right assigned, a discharge or modification is not effective

(a) against the owner or an assignor having a power of avoidance, unless given by him or by a person in possession of the writing with his consent and any necessary indorsement or assignment;

(b) against a subsequent assignee who takes possession of the writing and gives value in good faith and without knowledge or reason to know of the discharge or modification.

Comment

a. *Discharge by true obligee.* Rules governing the discharge of a contractual right by one who is actually the owner of the right are stated in Chapter 12. Such a discharge is effective against the obligee who gives it, whether he is the original promisee, a beneficiary, or an assignee, and against any person who has no greater rights. Under §336 a subsequent assignee is ordinarily such a person; but the law governing negotiable instruments and documents in some circumstances gives to a bona fide holder a greater right than his transferor had. . . . Estoppel and related doctrines have a similar effect. See Subsection (4) (b); §336 Comments *f, g.* . . .

b. *Discharge by apparent obligee.* This Section covers discharge by one who reasonably seems to the obligor to own the right, though in fact he does not. The obligor is ordinarily protected in such a case of a discharge wrongfully given, but only if he renders performance or otherwise gives value or changes his position in good faith and without knowledge or reason to know that the appearance is false. . . .

§339. Protection of Obligor in Cases of Adverse Claims

Where a claim adverse to that of an assignee subjects the obligor to a substantial risk beyond that imposed on him by his contract, the obligor will be granted such relief as is equitable in the circumstances.

Topic 5. *Priorities Between Assignee and Adverse Claimants*

§340. Effect of Assignment on Priority and Security

(1) An assignee is entitled to priority of payment from the obligor's insolvent estate to the extent that the assignor would have been so entitled in the absence of assignment.

(2) Where an assignor holds collateral as security for the assigned right and does not effectively transfer the collateral to the assignee, the assignor is a constructive trustee of the collateral for the assignee in accordance with the rules stated for pledges in §§29-34 of the Restatement of Security.

§341. Creditors of an Assignor

(1) Except as provided by statute, the right of an assignee is superior to a judicial lien subsequently obtained against the property of the assignor, unless the assignment is ineffective or revocable or is voidable by the assignor or by the person obtaining the lien or is in fraud of creditors.

(2) Notwithstanding the superiority of the right of an assignee, an obligor who does not receive notification of the assignment until after he has lost his opportunity to assert the assignment as a defense in the proceeding in which the judicial lien was obtained is discharged from his duty to the assignee to the extent of his satisfaction of the lien.

§342. Successive Assignees From the Same Assignor

Except as otherwise provided by statute, the right of an assignee is superior to that of a subsequent assignee of the same right from the same assignor, unless

(a) the first assignment is ineffective or revocable or is voidable by the assignor or by the subsequent assignee; or

(b) the subsequent assignee in good faith and without knowledge or reason to know of the prior assignment gives value and obtains

(i) payment or satisfaction of the obligation,

(ii) judgment against the obligor,

(iii) a new contract with the obligor by novation, or

(iv) possession of a writing of a type customarily accepted as a symbol or as evidence of the right assigned.

Comment

. . . .

d. Defective assignment. If the prior assignment is revocable or voidable by the assignor a subsequent assignment is an effective manifestation of an intent to revoke or avoid. The subsequent assignment therefore has priority. A subsequent assignment may be similarly used to effectuate a power of avoidance of the subsequent assignee. . . .

§343. Latent Equities

If an assignor's right against the obligor is held in trust or constructive trust for or subject to a right of avoidance or equitable lien of another than the obligor, an assignee does not so hold it if he gives value and becomes an assignee in good faith and without notice of the right of the other.

CHAPTER 16.   REMEDIES

Topic 1.   In General

§344.   Purposes of Remedies

Judicial remedies under the rules stated in this Restatement serve to protect one or more of the following interests of a promisee:

(a) his "expectation interest," which is his interest in having the benefit of his bargain by being put in as good a position as he would have been in had the contract been performed,

(b) his "reliance interest," which is his interest in being reimbursed for loss caused by reliance on the contract by being put in as good a position as he would have been in had the contract not been made, or

(c) his "restitution interest," which is his interest in having restored to him any benefit that he has conferred on the other party.

Comment

a. Three interests. The law of contract remedies implements the policy in favor of allowing individuals to order their own affairs by making legally enforceable promises. Ordinarily, when a court concludes that there has been a breach of contract, it enforces the broken promise by protecting the expectation that the injured party had when he made the contract. It does this by attempting to put him in as good a position as he would have been in had the contract been performed, that is, had there been no breach. The interest protected in this way is called the "expectation interest." It is sometimes said to give the injured party the "benefit of the bargain." This is not, however, the only interest that may be protected.

The promisee may have changed his position in reliance on the contract by, for example, incurring expenses in preparing to perform, in performing, or in foregoing opportunities to make other contracts. In that case, the court may recognize a claim based on his reliance rather than on his expectation. It does this by attempting to put him back in the position in which he would have been had the contract not been made. The interest protected in this way is called "reliance interest." Although it may be equal to the expectation interest, it is ordinarily smaller because it does not include the injured party's lost profit.

In some situations a court will recognize yet a third interest and grant relief to prevent unjust enrichment. This may be done if a party has not only changed his own position in reliance on the contract but has also conferred a benefit on the other party by, for example, making a part payment or furnishing services under the contract. The court may then require the other party to disgorge the benefit that he has received by returning it to the party who conferred it. The interest of the claimant protected in this way is called the "restitution interest." Although it may be equal to the expectation or reliance interest, it is ordinarily smaller because it includes neither the injured party's lost profit nor that part of his expenditures in reliance that resulted in no benefit to the other party. . . .

b. Expectation interest. In principle, at least, a party's expectation interest represents the actual worth of the contract to him rather than to some reasonable third person. Damages based on the expectation interest therefore take account of any special circumstances that are peculiar to the situation of the injured party, including his personal values and even his idiosyncracies, as well as his own needs and opportunities. . . . In practice, however, the injured party is often held to a more objective valuation of his expectation interest because he may be barred from recovering for loss resulting from such special circumstances on the ground that it was not foreseeable or cannot be shown with sufficient certainty. See §§351 and 352. Furthermore, since he cannot recover for loss that he could have avoided by arranging a substitute transaction on the market (§350), his recovery is often limited by the objective standard of market price. . . . The expectation interest is not based on the injured party's hopes when he made the contract but on the actual value that the contract would have had to him had it been performed. . . . It is therefore based on the circumstances at the time for performance and not those at the time of the making of the contract. . . .

c. Reliance interest. If it is reliance that is the basis for the enforcement of a promise, a court may enforce the promise but limit the promisee to recovery of his reliance interest. See §§87, 89, 90, 139. There are also situations in which a court may grant recovery based on the reliance interest even though it is consideration that is the basis for the enforcement of the promise. These situations are dealt with in §§349 and 353.

d. Restitution interest. [P]roblems of restitution . . . arise in connection with contracts . . . when a party, instead of seeking to enforce an agreement, claims relief on the ground that the other party has been unjustly enriched as a result of some benefit conferred under the agreement. In some cases a party's choice of the restitution interest is dictated by the fact that the agreement is not enforceable . . . Occasionally a party chooses the restitution interest even though the contract is enforceable because it will give a larger recovery than will enforcement based on either the expectation or reliance interest. . . .

§345. Judicial Remedies Available

The judicial remedies available for the protection of the interests stated in §344 include a judgment or order

(a) awarding a sum of money due under the contract or as damages,

(b) requiring specific performance of a contract or enjoining its non-performance,

(c) requiring restoration of a specific thing to prevent unjust enrichment,

(d) awarding a sum of money to prevent unjust enrichment,

(e) declaring the rights of the parties, and

(f) enforcing an arbitration award.

Topic 2.   Enforcement by Award of Damages

§346.   Availability of Damages

(1) The injured party has a right to damages for any breach by a party against whom the contract is enforceable unless the claim for damages has been suspended or discharged.

(2) If the breach caused no loss or if the amount of the loss is not proved under the rules stated in this Chapter, a small sum fixed without regard to the amount of loss will be awarded as nominal damages.

Comment

a. Right to damages. Every breach of contract gives the injured party a right to damages against the party in breach, unless the contract is not enforceable against that party, as where he is not bound because of the Statute of Frauds. The resulting claim may be one for damages for total breach of one for damages for only partial breach. See §236. Although a judgment awarding a sum of money as damages is the most common judicial remedy for breach of contract, other remedies, including equitable relief in the form of specific performance or an injunction, may be also available, depending on the circumstances. See Topic 3. In the exceptional situation of a contract for transfer of an interest in land that is unenforceable under the Statute of Frauds, action in reliance makes the contract enforceable by specific performance even though it gives rise to no claim for damages for breach. See Comment *c* to §129. A duty to pay damages may be suspended or discharged by agreement or otherwise, and if it is discharged the claim for damages is extinguished. See Introductory Note to Chapter 12. When this happens, the right to enforcement by other means such as specific performance or an injunction is also extinguished. . . . If the duty of performance, as distinguished from the duty to pay damages, has been suspended or discharged, as by impracticability of performance or frustration of purpose, there is then no breach and this Section is not applicable.

The parties can by agreement vary the rules stated in this Section, as long as the agreement is not invalid for unconscionability (§208) or on other grounds. The agreement may provide for a remedy such as repair or replacement in substitution for damages. See Uniform Commercial Code §2-719.

b. Nominal damages. Although a breach of contract by a party against whom it is enforceable always gives rise to a claim for damages, there are instances in which the breach causes no loss. See Illustration 1. There are also instances in which loss is caused but recovery for that loss is precluded because it cannot be proved with reasonable certainty or because of one of the other limitations stated in this Chapter. See §§350-53. In all these instances the injured party will nevertheless get judgment for nominal damages, a small sum usually fixed by judicial practice in the jurisdiction in which the action is brought. Such a judgment may, in the discretion of the court, carry with it an award of court costs. Costs are generally awarded if a significant right was involved or the claimant made a good faith effort to prove damages, but not if the maintenance of the action was frivolous or in bad faith. Unless a significant right is involved, a court will not reverse and remand a case for a new trial if only nominal damages could result.

Illustration

1. A contracts to sell to B 1,000 shares of stock in X Corporation for $10 a share to be delivered on June 1, but breaks the contract by refusing on that date to deliver the stock. B sues A for damages, but at trial it is proved that B could have purchased 1,000 shares of stock in X Corporation on the market on June 1 for $10 a share and therefore has suffered no loss. In an action by B against A, B will be awarded nominal damages.

c. Beneficiaries of gift promises. If a promisee makes a contract, intending to give a third party the benefit of the promised performance, the third party may be an intended beneficiary who is entitled to enforce the contract. See §302(1)(b). Such a gift promise creates overlapping duties, one to the beneficiary and the other to the promisee. If the performance is not forthcoming, both the beneficiary and the promisee have claims for damages for breach. If the promisee seeks damages, however, he will usually be limited to nominal damages: although the loss to the beneficiary may be substantial, the promisee cannot recover for that loss and he will ordinarily have suffered no loss himself. In such a case the remedy of specific performance will often be an appropriate one for the promisee. See §307. . . .

§347. Measure of Damages in General

Subject to the limitations stated in §§350-53, the injured party has a right to damages based on his expectation interest as measured by

(a) the loss in the value to him of the other party's performance caused by its failure or deficiency, plus

(b) any other loss, including incidental or consequential loss, caused by the breach, less

(c) any cost or other loss that he has avoided by not having to perform.

Comment

a. Expectation interest. Contract damages are ordinarily based on the injured party's expectation interest and are intended to give him the benefit of his bargain by awarding him a sum of money that will, to the extent possible, put him in as good a position as he would have been in had the contract been performed. See §344(1)(a). In some situations the sum awarded will do this adequately as, for example, where the injured party has simply had to pay an additional amount to arrange a substitute transaction and can be adequately compensated by damages based on that amount. In other situations the sum awarded cannot adequately compensate the injured party for his disappointed expectation as, for example, where a delay in performance has caused him to miss an invaluable opportunity. The measure of damages stated in this Section is subject to the agreement of the parties, as where they provide for liquidated damages (§356) or exclude liability for consequential damages.

b. Loss in value. The first element that must be estimated in attempting to fix a sum that will fairly represent the expectation interest is the loss in the value to the injured party of the other party's performance that is caused by the failure of, or deficiency in, that performance. If no performance is rendered, the loss in value caused by the breach is equal to the value that the performance would have had to the injured party. . . . If defective or partial performance is rendered, the loss in value caused by the breach is equal to the difference between the value that the performance would have had if there had been no breach and the value of such performance as was actually rendered. In principle, this requires a determination of the values of those performances to the injured party himself and not their values to some hypothetical reasonable person or on some market. . . . They therefore depend on his own particular circumstances or those of his enterprise, unless consideration of these circumstances is precluded by the limitation of foreseeability (§351). Where the injured party's expected advantage consists largely or exclusively of the realization of profit, it may be possible to express this loss in value in terms of money with some assurance. In other situations, however, this is not possible and compensation for lost value may be precluded by the limitation of certainty. See §352. In order to facilitate the estimation of loss with sufficient certainty to award damages, the injured party is sometimes given a choice between alternative bases of calculating his loss in value. The most important of these are stated in §348. See also §§349 and 373. . . .

c. Other loss. Subject to the limitations stated in §§350-53, the injured party is entitled to recover for all loss actually suffered. Items of loss other than loss in value of the other party's performance are often characterized as incidental or consequential. Incidental losses include costs incurred in a reasonable effort, whether successful or not, to avoid loss, as where a party pays brokerage fees in arranging or attempting to arrange a substitute transaction. . . . Consequential losses include such items as injury to person or property resulting from defective performance. . . . The terms used to describe the type of loss are not, however, controlling, and the general principle is that all losses, however described, are recoverable. . . .

d. Cost or other loss avoided. Sometimes the breach itself results in a saving of some cost that the injured party would have incurred if he had had to perform. See Illustration 5. Furthermore, the injured party is expected to take reasonable steps to avoid further loss. See §350. Where he does this by discontinuing his own performance, he avoids incurring additional costs of performance. See Illustration 6. This cost avoided is subtracted from the loss in value caused by the breach in calculating his damages. If the injured party avoids further loss by making substitute arrangements for the use of his resources that are no longer needed to perform the contract, the net profit from such arrangements is also subtracted. . . . The value to him of any salvageable materials that he has acquired for performance is also subtracted. See Illustration 7. Loss avoided is subtracted only if the saving results from the injured party not having to perform rather than from some unrelated event. . . . If no cost or other loss has been avoided, however, the injured party's damages include the full amount of the loss in value with no subtraction, subject to the limitations stated in §§350-53. . . . The intended "donee" beneficiary of a gift promise usually suffers loss to the full extent of the value of the promised performance, since he is ordinarily not required to do anything, and so avoids no cost on breach. See §302(1)(b).

Illustrations

5. A contracts to build a hotel for B for $500,000 and to have it ready for occupancy by May 1. B's occupancy of the hotel is delayed for a month because of a breach by A. The cost avoided by B as a result of not having to operate the hotel during May is subtracted from the May rent lost in determining B's damages.

6. A contracts to build a house for B for $100,000. When it is partly built, B repudiates the contract and A stops work. A would have to spend $60,000 more to finish the house. The $60,000 cost avoided by A as a result of not having to finish the house is subtracted from the $100,000 price lost in determining A's damages. A has a right to $40,000 in damages from B, less any progress payments that he has already received. . . .

7. The facts being otherwise as stated in Illustration 6, A has bought materials that are left over and that he can use for other purposes, saving him $5,000. The $5,000 cost avoided is subtracted in determining A's damages, resulting in damages of only $35,000 rather than $40,000. . . .

e. Actual loss caused by breach. The injured party is limited to damages based on his actual loss caused by the breach. If he makes an especially favorable substitute transaction, so that he sustains a smaller loss than might have been expected, his damages are reduced by the loss avoided as a result of that transaction. . . . If he arranges a substitute transaction that he would not have been expected to do under the rules on avoidability (§350), his damages are similarly limited by the loss so avoided. . . . Recovery can be had only for loss that would not have occurred but for the breach. See §346. If, after the breach, an event occurs that would have discharged the party in breach on grounds of impracticability of performance or frustration of purpose, damages are limited to the loss sustained prior to that event. . . . Compare §254(2). The principle that a party's liability is not reduced by payments or other benefits received by the injured party from collateral sources is less compelling in the case of a breach of contract than in the case of a tort. . . . The effect of the receipt of unemployment benefits by a discharged employee will turn on the court's perception of legislative policy rather than on the rule stated in this Section. . . .

f. Lost volume. Whether a subsequent transaction is a substitute for the broken contract sometimes raises difficult questions of fact. If the injured party could and would have entered into the subsequent contract, even if the contract had not been broken, and could have had the benefit of both, he can be said to have "lost volume" and the subsequent transaction is not a substitute for the broken contract. The injured party's damages are then based on the net profit that he has lost as a result of the broken contract. Since entrepreneurs try to operate at optimum capacity, however, it is possible that an additional transaction would not have been profitable and that the injured party would not have chosen to expand his business by undertaking it had there been no breach. It is sometimes assumed that he would have done so, but the question is one of fact to be resolved according to the circumstances of each case. . . . See Uniform Commercial Code §2-708(2).

§348. Alternatives to Loss in Value of Performance

(1) If a breach delays the use of property and the loss in value to the injured party is not proved with reasonable certainty, he may recover damages based on the rental value of the property or on interest on the value of the property.

(2) If a breach results in defective or unfinished construction and the loss in value to the injured party is not proved with sufficient certainty, he may recover damages based on

(a) the diminution in the market price of the property caused by the breach, or

(b) the reasonable cost of completing performance or of remedying the defects if that cost is not clearly disproportionate to the probable loss in value to him.

(3) If a breach is of a promise conditioned on a fortuitous event and it is uncertain whether the event would have occurred had there been no breach, the injured party may recover damages based on the value of the conditional right at the time of breach.

Comment

a. Reason for alternative bases. Although in principle the injured party is entitled to recover based on the loss in value to him caused by the breach, in practice he may be precluded from recovery on this basis because he cannot show the loss in value to him with sufficient certainty. See §352. In such a case, if there is a reasonable alternative to loss in value, he may claim damages based on that alternative. . . .

b. Breach that delays the use of property. If the breach is one that prevents for a period of time the use of property from which profits would have been made, the loss in value to the injured party is based on the profits that he would have made during that period. If those profits cannot be proved with reasonable certainty (§352), two other bases for recovery are possible. One is the fair rental value of the property during the period of delay. Damages based on fair rental value include an element of profit since the fair rental value of property depends on what it would command on the market and this turns on the profit that would be derived from its use. For this reason, uncertainty as to profits may result in uncertainty in fair rental value. Another possible basis for recovery, as a last resort, is the interest on the value of the property that has been made unproductive by the breach, if that value can be shown with reasonable certainty. Although these two other bases will ordinarily give a smaller recovery than loss in value, it is always open to the party in breach to show that this is not so and to hold the injured party to a smaller recovery based on loss in value to him. . . .

c. Incomplete or defective performance. If the contract is one for construction, including repair or similar performance affecting the condition of property, and the work is not finished, the injured party will usually find it easier to prove what it would cost to have the work completed by another contractor than to prove the difference between the values to him of the finished and the unfinished performance. Since the cost to complete is usually less than the loss in value to him, he is limited by the rule on avoidability to damages based on cost to complete. See §350(1). If he has actually had the work completed, damages will be based on his expenditures if he comes within the rule stated in §350(2).

Sometimes, especially if the performance is defective as distinguished from incomplete, it may not be possible to prove the loss in value to the injured party with reasonable certainty. In that case he can usually recover damages based on the cost to remedy the defects. Even if this gives him a recovery somewhat in excess of the loss in value to him, it is better that he receive a small windfall than that he be undercompensated by being limited to the resulting diminution in the market price of his property.

Sometimes, however, such a large part of the cost to remedy the defects consists of the cost to undo what has been improperly done that the cost to remedy the defects will be clearly disproportionate to the probable loss in value to the injured party. Damages based on the cost to remedy the defects would then give the injured party a recovery greatly in excess of the loss in value to him and result in a substantial windfall. Such an award will not be made. It is sometimes said that the award would involve "economic waste," but this is a misleading expression since an injured party will not, even if awarded an excessive amount of damages, usually pay to have the defects remedied if to do so will cost him more than the resulting increase in value to him. If an award based on the cost to remedy the defects would clearly be excessive and the injured party does not prove the actual loss in value to him, damages will be based instead on the difference between the market price that the property would have had without the defects and the market price of the property with the defects. This diminution in market price is the least possible loss in value to the injured party, since he could always sell the property on the market even if it had no special value to him. . . .

§349. Damages Based on Reliance Interest

As an alternative to the measure of damages stated in §347, the injured party has a right to damages based on his reliance interest, including expenditures made in preparation for performance or in performance, less any loss that the party in breach can prove with reasonable certainty the injured party would have suffered had the contract been performed.

Comment

a. Reliance interest where profit uncertain. . . . Under the rule stated in this Section, the injured party may, if he chooses, ignore the element of profit and recover as damages his expenditures in reliance. He may choose to do this if he cannot prove his profit with reasonable certainty. He may also choose to do this in the case of a losing contract, one under which he would have had a loss rather than a profit. In that case, however, it is open to the party in breach to prove the amount of the loss, to the extent that he can do so with reasonable certainty under the standard stated in §352, and have it subtracted from the injured party's damages. The resulting damages will then be the same as those under the rule stated in §347 . . . .

§350. Avoidability as a Limitation on Damages

(1) Except as stated in Subsection (2), damages are not recoverable for loss that the injured party could have avoided without undue risk, burden or humiliation.

(2) The injured party is not precluded from recovery by the rule stated in Subsection (1) to the extent that he has made reasonable but unsuccessful efforts to avoid loss.

Comment

. . . .

b. Effect of failure to make efforts to mitigate damages. As a general rule, a party cannot recover damages for loss that he could have avoided by reasonable efforts. Once a party has reason to know that performance by the other party will not be forthcoming, he is ordinarily expected to stop his own performance to avoid further expenditure. . . . Furthermore, he is expected to take such affirmative steps as are appropriate in the circumstances to avoid loss by making substitute arrangements or otherwise. It is sometimes said that it is the "duty" of the aggrieved party to mitigate damages, but this is misleading because he incurs no liability for his failure to act. The amount of loss that he could reasonably have avoided by stopping performance, making substitute arrangements or otherwise is simply subtracted from the amount that would otherwise have been recoverable as damages.

Illustrations

1. A contracts to build a bridge for B for $100,000. B repudiates the contract shortly after A has begun work on the bridge, telling A that he no longer has need for it. A nevertheless spends an additional $10,000 in continuing to perform. A's damages for breach of contract do not include the $10,000. . . .

c. Substitute transactions. When a party's breach consists of a failure to deliver goods or furnish services, for example, it is often possible for the injured party to secure similar goods or services on the market. If a seller of goods repudiates, the buyer can often buy similar goods elsewhere. . . . If an employee quits his job, the employer can often find a suitable substitute. . . . Similarly, when a party's breach consists of a failure to receive goods or services, for example, it is often possible for the aggrieved party to dispose of the goods or services on the market. If a buyer of goods repudiates, the seller can often sell the goods elsewhere. . . . If an employer fires his employee, the employee can often find a suitable job elsewhere. . . . In such cases as these, the injured party is expected to make appropriate efforts to avoid loss by arranging a substitute transaction. If he does not do so, the amount of loss that he could have avoided by doing so is subtracted in calculating his damages. In the case of the sale of goods, this principle has inspired the standard formulas under which a buyer's or seller's damages are based on the difference between the contract price and the market price on that market where the injured party could have arranged a substitute transaction for the purchase or sale of similar goods. See Uniform Commercial Code §§2-708, 2-713. Similar rules are applied to other contracts, such as contracts for the sale of securities, where there is a well-established market for the type of performance involved, but the principle extends to other situations in which a substitute transaction can be arranged, even if there is no well-established market for the type of performance. However, in those other situations, the burden is generally put on the party in breach to show that a substitute transaction was available, as is done in the case in which an employee has been fired by his employer.

Illustrations:

> 6. A contracts to supervise the production of B's crop for $10,000, but breaks his contract and leaves at the beginning of the season. By appropriate efforts, B could obtain an equally good supervisor for $11,000, but he does not do so and the crop is lost. B's damages for A's breach of contract do not include the loss of his crop, but he can recover $1,000 from A. . . .

> 8. A contracts to employ B for $10,000 to supervise the production of A's crop, but breaks his contract by firing B at the beginning of the season. By appropriate efforts, B could obtain an equally good job as a supervisor at $100 less than A had contracted to pay him, but he does not do so and remains unemployed. B's damages for A's breach of contract do not include his $10,000 loss of earnings, but he can recover $100 from A. . . .

d. *"Lost volume."* The mere fact that an injured party can make arrangements for the disposition of the goods or services that he was to supply under the contract does not necessarily mean that by doing so he will avoid loss. If he would have entered into both transactions but for the breach, he has "lost volume" as a result of the breach. See Comment f to §347. In that case the second transaction is not a "substitute" for the first one. . . .

Illustrations

> . . .

> 10. A contracts to pay B $20,000 for paving A's parking lot, which would give B a net profit of $3,000. A breaks the contract by repudiating it before B begins work. If B would have made the contract with A in addition to other contracts, B's efforts to obtain other contracts do not affect his damages. B's damages for A's breach of contract include his $3,000 loss of profit. . . .

f. *Time for arranging substitute transaction.* The injured party is expected to arrange a substitute transaction within a reasonable time after he learns of the breach. He is expected to do this even if the breach takes the form of an anticipatory repudiation, since under the rule stated in Subsection (2) he is then protected against the possibility of a change in the market before the time for performance. . . . The injured party may, however, make appropriate efforts to urge the repudiating party to perform in spite of his repudiation or to retract his repudiation, and these efforts will be taken into account in determining what is a reasonable time. Although the injured party is expected to arrange a substitute transaction without unreasonable delay following the anticipatory repudiation, the time for performance under the substitute transaction will ordinarily be the same time as it would have been under the original contract. . . .

h. *Actual efforts to mitigate damages.* Sometimes the injured party makes efforts to avoid loss but fails to do so. The rule stated in Subsection (2) protects the injured party in that situation if the efforts were reasonable. . . . The rule stated in Subsection (2) reflects the policy . . . encouraging the injured party to make reasonable efforts to avoid loss by protecting him even when his efforts fail. To this extent, his failure to avoid loss does not have the effect stated in Subsection (1). Under the rule stated in §347, costs incurred in a reasonable but unsuccessful effort to avoid loss are recoverable as incidental losses. See Comment *c* to §347. . . .

§351.   Unforeseeability and Related Limitations on Damages

(1) Damages are not recoverable for loss that the party in breach did not have reason to foresee as a probable result of the breach when the contract was made.

(2) Loss may be foreseeable as a probable result of a breach because it follows from the breach

(a) in the ordinary course of events, or

(b) as a result of special circumstances, beyond the ordinary course of events, that the party in breach had reason to know.

(3) A court may limit damages for foreseeable loss by excluding recovery for loss of profits, by allowing recovery only for loss incurred in reliance, or otherwise if it concludes that in the circumstances justice so requires in order to avoid disproportionate compensation.

Comment

a. Requirement of foreseeability. A contracting party is generally expected to take account of those risks that are foreseeable at the time he makes the contract. He is not, however, liable in the event of breach for loss that he did not at the time of contracting have reason to foresee as a probable result of such a breach. The mere circumstance that some loss was foreseeable, or even that some loss of the same general kind was foreseeable, will not suffice if the loss that actually occurred was not foreseeable. It is enough, however, that the loss was foreseeable as a probable, as distinguished from a necessary, result of his breach. Furthermore, the party in breach need not have made a "tacit agreement" to be liable for the loss. Nor must he have had the loss in mind when making the contract, for the test is an objective one based on what he had reason to foresee. There is no requirement of foreseeability with respect to the injured party. In spite of these qualifications, the requirement of foreseeability is a more severe limitation of liability than is the requirement of substantial or "proximate" cause in the case of an action in tort or for breach of warranty. Compare Restatement, Second, Torts §431; Uniform Commercial Code §2-715(2)(b). Although the recovery that is precluded by the limitation of foreseeability is usually based on the expectation interest and takes the form of lost profits (see Illustration 1), the limitation may also preclude recovery based on the reliance interest . . . .

Illustrations

1. A, a carrier, contracts with B, a miller, to carry B's broken crankshaft to its manufacturer for repair. B tells A when they make the contract that the crankshaft is part of B's milling machine and that it must be sent at once, but not that the mill is stopped because B has no replacement. Because A delays in carrying the crankshaft, B loses profit during an additional period while the mill is stopped because of the delay. A is not liable for B's loss of profit. That loss was not foreseeable by A as a probable result of the breach at the time the contract was

made because A did not know that the broken crankshaft was necessary for the operation of the mill. . . .

b. *"General" and "special" damages.* Loss that results from a breach in the ordinary course of events is foreseeable as the probable result of the breach. . . . Such loss is sometimes said to be the "natural" result of the breach, in the sense that its occurrence accords with the common experience of ordinary persons. For example, a seller of a commodity to a wholesaler usually has reason to foresee that his failure to deliver the commodity as agreed will probably cause the wholesaler to lose a reasonable profit on it. . . . Similarly, a seller of a machine to a manufacturer usually has reason to foresee that his delay in delivering the machine as agreed will probably cause the manufacturer to lose a reasonable profit from its use, although courts have been somewhat more cautious in allowing the manufacturer recovery for loss of such profits than in allowing a middleman recovery for loss of profits on an intended resale. . . . The damages recoverable for such loss that results in the ordinary course of events are sometimes called "general" damages.

If loss results other than in the ordinary course of events, there can be no recovery for it unless it was foreseeable by the party in breach because of special circumstances that he had reason to know when he made the contract. See Uniform Commercial Code §2-715(2)(a). For example, . . . a seller who delays in delivering a machine to a manufacturer is not liable for the manufacturer's loss of profit to the extent that it results from an intended use that was abnormal unless the seller had reason to know of this special circumstance. . . . In the case of a written agreement, foreseeability is sometimes established by the use of recitals in the agreement itself. The parol evidence rule (§213) does not, however, preclude the use of negotiations prior to the making of the contract to show for this purpose circumstances that were then known to a party. The damages recoverable for loss that results other than in the ordinary course of events are sometimes called "special" or "consequential" damages. These terms are often misleading, however, and it is not necessary to distinguish between "general" and "special" or "consequential" damages for the purpose of the rule stated in this Section. . . .

c. *Litigation or settlement caused by breach.* Sometimes a breach of contract results in claims by third persons against the injured party. The party in breach is liable for the amount of any judgment against the injured party together with his reasonable expenditures in the litigation, if the party in breach had reason to foresee such expenditures as the probable result of his breach at the time he made the contract. . . . A failure to notify the party in breach in advance of the litigation may prevent the result of the litigation from being conclusive as to him. But to the extent that the injured party's loss resulting from litigation is reasonable, the fact that the party in breach was not notified does not prevent the inclusion of that loss in the damages assessed against him. In furtherance of the policy favoring private settlement of disputes, the injured party is also allowed to recover the reasonable amount of any settlement made to avoid litigation, together with the costs of settlement. . . .

d. *Unavailability of substitute.* . . . Sometimes a loss would not have occurred if the injured party had been able to make substitute arrangements after breach, as, for example, by "cover" through purchase of substitute goods in the case of a buyer of goods (see Uniform Commercial Code §2-712). If the inability of the injured party to make such arrangements was foreseeable by the party in breach at the time he made the contract, the resulting loss was foreseeable. . . .

e. Breach of contract to lend money. The limitation of foreseeability is often applied in actions for damages for breach of contracts to lend money. Because credit is so widely available, a lender often has no reason to foresee at the time the contract is made that the borrower will be unable to make substitute arrangements in the event of breach. See Comment *d.* In most cases, then, the lender's liability will be limited to the relatively small additional amount that it would ordinarily cost to get a similar loan from another lender. However, in the less common situation in which the lender has reason to foresee that the borrower will be unable to borrow elsewhere or will be delayed in borrowing elsewhere, the lender may be liable for much heavier damages based on the borrower's inability to take advantage of a specific opportunity . . . , his having to postpone or abandon a profitable project . . . , or his forfeiture of security for failure to make prompt payment . . . .

f. Other limitations on damages. It is not always in the interest of justice to require the party in breach to pay damages for all of the foreseeable loss that he has caused. There are unusual instances in which it appears from the circumstances either that the parties assumed that one of them would not bear the risk of a particular loss or that, although there was no such assumption, it would be unjust to put the risk on that party. One such circumstance is an extreme disproportion between the loss and the price charged by the party whose liability for that loss is in question. The fact that the price is relatively small suggests that it was not intended to cover the risk of such liability. Another such circumstance is an informality of dealing, including the absence of a detailed written contract, which indicates that there was no careful attempt to allocate all of the risks. The fact that the parties did not attempt to delineate with precision all of the risks justifies a court in attempting to allocate them fairly. The limitations dealt with in this Section are more likely to be imposed in connection with contracts that do not arise in a commercial setting. Typical examples of limitations imposed on damages under this discretionary power involve the denial of recovery for loss of profits and the restriction of damages to loss incurred in reliance on the contract. Sometimes these limits are covertly imposed, by means of an especially demanding requirement of foreseeability or of certainty. The rule stated in this Section recognizes that what is done in such cases is the imposition of a limitation in the interests of justice.

Illustrations

> 17. A, a private trucker, contracts with B to deliver to B's factory a machine that has just been repaired and without which B's factory, as A knows, cannot reopen. Delivery is delayed because A's truck breaks down. In an action by B against A for breach of contract the court may, after taking into consideration such factors as the absence of an elaborate written contract and the extreme disproportion between B's loss of profits during the delay and the price of the trucker's services, exclude recovery for loss of profits. . . .
>
> 19. A, a plastic surgeon, makes a contract with B, a professional entertainer, to perform plastic surgery on her face in order to improve her appearance. The result of the surgery is, however, to disfigure her face and to require a second operation. In an action by B against A for breach of contract, the court may limit damages by allowing recovery only for loss incurred by B in reliance on the

contract, including the fees paid by B and expenses for hospitalization, nursing care and medicine for both operations, together with any damages for the worsening of B's appearance if these can be proved with reasonable certainty, but not including any loss resulting from the failure to improve her appearance.

§352. Uncertainty as a Limitation on Damages

Damages are not recoverable for loss beyond an amount that the evidence permits to be established with reasonable certainty.

Comment

a. Requirement of certainty. A party cannot recover damages for breach of a contract for loss beyond the amount that the evidence permits to be established with reasonable certainty. . . . Courts have traditionally required greater certainty in the proof of damages for breach of a contract than in the proof of damages for a tort. The requirement does not mean, however, that the injured party is barred from recovery unless he establishes the total amount of his loss. It merely excludes those elements of loss that cannot be proved with reasonable certainty. The main impact of the requirement of certainty comes in connection with recovery for lost profits. Although the requirement of certainty is distinct from that of foreseeability (§351), its impact is similar in this respect. Although the requirement applies to damages based on the reliance as well as the expectation interest, there is usually little difficulty in proving the amount that the injured party has actually spent in reliance on the contract, even if it is impossible to prove the amount of profit that he would have made. In such a case, he can recover his loss based on his reliance interest instead of on his expectation interest. See §349 . . . .

Doubts are generally resolved against the party in breach. A party who has, by his breach, forced the injured party to seek compensation in damages should not be allowed to profit from his breach where it is established that a significant loss has occurred. A court may take into account all the circumstances of the breach, including willfulness, in deciding whether to require a lesser degree of certainty, giving greater discretion to the trier of the facts. Damages need not be calculable with mathematical accuracy and are often at best approximate. . . . This is especially true for items such as loss of good will as to which great precision cannot be expected. . . . Furthermore, increasing receptiveness on the part of courts to proof by sophisticated economic and financial data and by expert opinion has made it easier to meet the requirement of certainty. . . .

b. Proof of profits. The difficulty of proving lost profits varies greatly with the nature of the transaction. If, for example, it is the seller who claims lost profit on the ground that the buyer's breach has caused him to lose a sale, proof of lost profit will ordinarily not be difficult. If, however, it is the buyer who claims lost profit on the ground that the seller's breach has caused him loss in other transactions, the task of proof is harder. Furthermore, if the transaction is more complex and extends into the future, as where the seller agrees to furnish all of the buyer's requirements over a period of years, proof of the loss of profits caused by the seller's breach is more difficult. If the breach prevents the injured party from carrying on a well-established business, the resulting loss of profits can often be proved with sufficient certainty. Evidence of past performance will form the basis for a reasonable prediction as to the future. See Illustration 5. However, if the business is a new one or if it is a speculative one that is subject to great fluctuations in volume, costs or prices, proof will be more difficult. Nevertheless, damages may be established with reasonable certainty with the aid of expert testimony, economic and financial data, market surveys and analyses, business records of similar enterprises, and the like. See Illustration 6. Under a contract of exclusive agency for the sale of goods on commission, the agent can often prove with sufficient certainty the profits that he would have made had he not been discharged. Proof of the sales made by the agent in the agreed territory before the breach, or of the sales made there by the principal after the breach, may permit a reasonably accurate estimate of the agent's loss of commissions. However, if the agency is not an exclusive one, so that the agent's ability to withstand competition is in question, such a showing will be more difficult, although the agent's past record may give a sufficient basis for judging this. See Illustration 7.

Illustrations

5. A contracts with B to remodel B's existing outdoor drive-in theatre, work to be completed on June 1. A does not complete the work until September 1. B can use records of the theatre's prior and subsequent operation, along with other evidence, to prove his lost profits with reasonable certainty.

6. A contracts with B to construct a new outdoor drive-in theatre, to be completed on June 1. A does not complete the theatre until September 1. Even though the business is a new rather than an established one, B may be able to prove his lost profits with reasonable certainty. B can use records of the theatre's subsequent operation and of the operation of similar theatres in the same locality, along with other evidence including market surveys and expert testimony, in attempting to do this.

7. A contracts with B to make B his exclusive agent for the sale of machine tools in a specified territory and to supply him with machine tools at stated prices. After B has begun to act as A's agent, A repudiates the agreement and replaces him with C. B can use evidence as to sales and profits made by him before the repudiation and made by C after the repudiation in attempting to prove his lost profits with reasonable certainty. It would be more difficult, although not necessarily impossible, for B to succeed in this attempt if his agency were not exclusive.

c. *Alternative remedies*. The necessity of proving damages can be avoided if another remedy, such as a decree of specific performance or an injunction, is granted instead of damages. Although the availability of such a remedy does not preclude an award of damages as an alternative, it may justify a court in requiring greater certainty of proof if damages are to be awarded. . . .

§353. Loss Due to Emotional Disturbance

Recovery for emotional disturbance will be excluded unless the breach also caused bodily harm or the contract or the breach is of such a kind that serious emotional disturbance was a particularly likely result.

Comment

a. Emotional disturbance. Damages for emotional disturbance are not ordinarily allowed. Even if they are foreseeable, they are often particularly difficult to establish and to measure. There are, however, two exceptional situations where such damages are recoverable. In the first, the disturbance accompanies a bodily injury. In such cases the action may nearly always be regarded as one in tort. . . . In the second exceptional situation, the contract or the breach is of such a kind that serious emotional disturbance was a particularly likely result. Common examples are contracts of carriers and innkeepers with passengers and guests, contracts for the carriage or proper disposition of dead bodies, and contracts for the delivery of messages concerning death. Breach of such a contract is particularly likely to cause serious emotional disturbance. Breach of other types of contracts, resulting for example in sudden impoverishment or bankruptcy, may by chance cause even more severe emotional disturbance, but, if the contract is not one where this was a particularly likely risk, there is no recovery for such disturbance. . . .

§354. Interest as Damages

(1) If the breach consists of a failure to pay a definite sum in money or to render a performance with fixed or ascertainable monetary value, interest is recoverable from the time for performance on the amount due less all deductions to which the party in breach is entitled.

(2) In any other case, such interest may be allowed as justice requires on the amount that would have been just compensation had it been paid when performance was due.

§355. Punitive Damages

Punitive damages are not recoverable for a breach of contract unless the conduct constituting the breach is also a tort for which punitive damages are recoverable.

§356. Liquidated Damages and Penalties

(1) Damages for breach by either party may be liquidated in the agreement but only at an amount that is reasonable in the light of the anticipated or actual loss caused by the breach and the difficulties of proof of loss. A term fixing unreasonably large liquidated damages is unenforceable on grounds of public policy as a penalty.

(2) A term in a bond providing for an amount of money as a penalty for non-occurrence of the condition of the bond is unenforceable on grounds of public policy to the extent that the amount exceeds the loss caused by such non-occurrence.

Comment

a. Liquidated damages or penalty. The parties to a contract may effectively provide in advance the damages that are to be payable in the event of breach as long as the provision does not disregard the principle of compensation. The enforcement of such provisions for liquidated damages saves the time of courts, juries, parties and witnesses and reduces the expense of litigation. . . . However, the parties to a contract are not free to provide a penalty for its breach. The central objective behind the system of contract remedies is compensatory, not punitive. Punishment of a promisor for having broken his promise has no justification on either economic or other grounds and a term providing such a penalty is unenforceable on grounds of public policy. See Chapter 8. The rest of the agreement remains enforceable, however, under the rule stated in §184(1), and the remedies for breach are determined by the rules stated in this Chapter. . . . A term that fixes an unreasonably small amount as damages may be unenforceable as unconscionable. See §208. As to the liquidation of damages and modification or limitation of remedies in contracts of sale, see Uniform Commercial Code §§2-718, 2-719.

b. Test of penalty. Under the test stated in Subsection (1), two factors combine in determining whether an amount of money fixed as damages is so unreasonably large as to be a penalty. The first factor is the anticipated or actual loss caused by the breach. The amount fixed is reasonable to the extent that it approximates the actual loss that has resulted from the particular breach, even though it may not approximate the loss that might have been anticipated under other possible breaches. . . . Furthermore, the amount fixed is reasonable to the extent that it approximates the loss anticipated at the time of the making of the contract, even though it may not approximate the actual loss. . . . The second factor is the difficulty of proof of loss. The greater the difficulty either of proving that loss has occurred or of establishing its amount with the requisite certainty (see §351), the easier it is to show that the amount fixed is reasonable. To the extent that there is uncertainty as to the harm, the estimate of the court or jury may not accord with the principle of compensation any more than does the advance estimate of the parties. A determination whether the amount fixed is a penalty turns on a combination of these two factors. If the difficulty of proof of loss is great, considerable latitude is allowed in the approximation of anticipated or actual harm. If, on the other hand, the difficulty of proof of loss is slight, less latitude is allowed in that approximation. If, to take an extreme case, it is clear that no loss at all has occurred, a provision fixing a substantial sum as damages is unenforceable. . . .

c. Disguised penalties. Under the rule stated in this Section, the validity of a term providing for damages depends on the effect of that term as interpreted according to the rules stated in Chapter 9. Neither the parties' actual intention as to its validity nor their characterization of the term as one for liquidated damages or a penalty is significant in determining whether the term is valid. Sometimes parties attempt to disguise a provision for a penalty by using language that purports to make payment of the amount an alternative performance under the contract, that purports to offer a discount for prompt performance, or that purports to place a valuation on property to be delivered. Although the parties may in good faith contract for alternative performances and fix discounts or valuations, a court will look to the substance of the agreement to determine whether this is the case or whether the parties have attempted to disguise a provision for a penalty that is unenforceable under this Section. In determining whether a contract is one for alternative performances, the relative value of the alternatives may be decisive. . . .

d. Related types of provisions. This Section does not purport to cover the wide variety of provisions used by parties to control the remedies available to them for breach of contract. A term that fixes as damages an amount that is unreasonably small does not come within the rule stated in this Section, but a court may refuse to enforce it as unconscionable under the rule stated in §208. A mere recital of the harm that may occur as a result of a breach of contract does not come within the rule stated in this Section, but may increase damages by making that harm foreseeable under the rule stated §351. As to the effect of a contract provision on the right to equitable relief, see Comment *a* to §359. As to the effect of a term requiring the occurrence of a condition where forfeiture would result, see §229. Although attorneys' fees are not generally awarded to the winning party, if the parties provide for the award of such fees the court will award a sum that it considers to be reasonable. If, however, the parties specify the amount of such fees, the provision is subject to the test stated in this Section. . . .

Topic 3. *Enforcement By Specific Performance and Injunction*

§357. Availability of Specific Performance and Injunction

(1) Subject to the rules stated in §§359-69, specific performance of a contract duty will be granted in the discretion of the court against a party who has committed or is threatening to commit a breach of the duty.

(2) Subject to the rules stated in §§359-69, an injunction against breach of a contract duty will be granted in the discretion of the court against a party who has committed or is threatening to commit a breach of the duty if

(a) the duty is one of forbearance, or

(b) the duty is one to act and specific performance would be denied only for reasons that are inapplicable to an injunction.

Comment

a. Specific performance. An order of specific performance is intended to produce as nearly as is practicable the same effect that the performance due under a contract would have produced. It usually, therefore, orders a party to render the performance that he promised. (On the form of the order, see §358.) Such relief is seldom granted unless there has been a breach of contract, either by non-performance or by repudiation. In unusual circumstances, however, it may be granted where there is merely a threatened breach. . . .

b. Injunction. A court may by injunction direct a party to refrain from doing a specified act. This is appropriate in two types of cases.

In the first, the performance due under the contract consists simply of forbearance, and the injunction in effect orders specific performance. See Paragraph (2)(a). Duties of forbearance are often imposed not as a matter of agreement but as a matter of law, as is usually the case for the duty not to interfere with the other party's performance of the contract. Duties of forbearance are ordinarily accompanied by other duties that require affirmative action by both parties. The presence of such other duties does not, of itself, preclude issuance of an injunction ordering forbearance only, but an injunction will not be issued if the performance of those other duties cannot be secured. See §363.

In the second type of case, the performance due under the contract consists of the doing of an act rather than of forbearance, and the injunction is used as an indirect means of enforcing the duty to act. See Paragraph (2)(b). Instead of ordering that the act be done, the court orders forbearance from inconsistent action. This is appropriate in situations where an injunction will afford a measure of relief and the duty to act would have been specifically enforced were it not for some objection that can be avoided by ordering forbearance from inconsistent action. For example, the difficulties involved in supervising compliance with the order may be less in the case of an injunction that in the case of specific performance. See §366. An injunction will not be issued, however, if the reason for refusing specific performance is not merely that the practical difficulties of such relief are too great but that compelling performance of the duty is itself undesirable. For example, an injunction is not ordinarily appropriate as an indirect means of enforcing a duty to render personal service. See Comment *c* to §367. . . .

c. Discretionary nature of relief. The granting of equitable relief has traditionally been regarded as within judicial discretion. The exercise of that discretion is subject to the rules stated in §§359-69. It is also subject to general principles of equity that are not peculiar to contract disputes, such as those that bar relief to one who has been guilty of laches or who has come into court with unclean hands. Furthermore, it is subject to principles of common sense so that, for example, a court will not order a performance that is impossible. In granting relief, as well as in denying it, a court may take into consideration the public interest.

§358.   Form of Order and Other Relief

(1) An order of specific performance or an injunction will be so drawn as best to effectuate the purposes for which the contract was made and on such terms as justice requires. It need not be absolute in form and the performance that it requires need not be identical with that due under the contract.

(2) If specific performance or an injunction is denied as to part of the performance that is due, it may nevertheless be granted as to the remainder.

(3) In addition to specific performance or an injunction, damages and other relief may be awarded in the same proceeding and an indemnity against future harm may be required.

Comment

. . . .

c. Damages and other relief. In addition to any equitable relief granted, a court may also award damages or other relief. Since an order seldom results in performance within the time the contract requires, damages for the delay will usually be appropriate. A seller of land who cannot perform as agreed because of a deficiency in area or a defect in title may be ordered to transfer all that he can, with compensation for the resulting claim for partial breach. The compensation may take the form of damages, restitution of money already paid or an abatement of the price not yet paid. A claimant who sues for specific performance or an injunction and who is denied that relief, may be awarded damages or restitution in the same proceeding. In appropriate cases, an indemnity may be required against future harm, and in some cases such an indemnity may be the only remedy that is necessary.

Illustrations

. . . .

4. A contracts to transfer land to B and to make specified repairs and complete an unfinished building on the land. A repudiates and B sues for specific performance. Specific performance of A's duty to transfer the land may be granted with an abatement in the price or other compensation sufficient to enable him to make the repairs and complete the building himself.

§359. Effect of Adequacy of Damages

(1) Specific performance or an injunction will not be ordered if damages would be adequate to protect the expectation interest of the injured party.

(2) The adequacy of the damage remedy for failure to render one part of the performance due does not preclude specific performance or injunction as to the contract as a whole.

(3) Specific performance or an injunction will not be refused merely because there is a remedy for breach other than damages, but such a remedy may be considered in exercising discretion under the rule stated in §357.

Comment

a. Bases for requirement. The underlying objective in choosing the form of relief to be granted is to select a remedy that will adequately protect the legally recognized interest of the injured party. If, as is usually the case, that interest is the expectation interest, the remedy may take the form either of damages or of specific performance or an injunction. As to the situation in which the interest to be protected is the restitution interest, see §373.

During the development of the jurisdiction of courts of equity, it came to be recognized that equitable relief would not be granted if the award of damages at law was adequate to protect the interests of the injured party. There is, however, a tendency to liberalize the granting of equitable relief by enlarging the classes of cases in which damages are not regarded as an adequate remedy. This tendency has been encouraged by the adoption of the Uniform Commercial Code, which "seeks to further a more liberal attitude than some courts have shown in connection with the specific performance of contracts of sale." Comment 1 to Uniform Commercial Code §2-716. In accordance with this tendency, if the adequacy of the damage remedy is uncertain, the combined effect of such other factors as uncertainty of terms (§362), insecurity as to the agreed exchange (§363) and difficulty of enforcement (§366) should be considered. Adequacy is to some extent relative, and the modern approach is to compare remedies to determine which is more effective in serving the ends of justice. Such a comparison will often lead to the granting of equitable relief. Doubts should be resolved in favor of the granting of specific performance or injunction. . . .

§360. Factors Affecting Adequacy of Damages

In determining whether the remedy in damages would be adequate, the following circumstances are significant:
   (a) the difficulty of proving damages with reasonable certainty,
   (b) the difficulty of procuring a suitable substitute performance by means of money awarded as damages, and
   (c) the likelihood that an award of damages could not be collected.

Comment

. . . .

b. *Difficulty in proving damages.* The damage remedy may be inadequate to protect the injured party's expectation interest because the loss caused by the breach is too difficult to estimate with reasonable certainty. . . . If the injured party has suffered loss but cannot sustain the burden of proving it, only nominal damages will be awarded. If he can prove some but not all of his loss, he will not be compensated in full. In either case damages are an inadequate remedy. Some types of interests are by their very nature incapable of being valued in money. Typical examples include heirlooms, family treasures and works of art that induce a strong sentimental attachment. Examples may also be found in contracts of a more commercial character. The breach of a contract to transfer shares of stock may cause a loss in control over the corporation. The breach of a contract to furnish an indemnity may cause the sacrifice of property and financial ruin. The breach of a covenant not to compete may cause the loss of customers of an unascertainable number or importance. The breach of a requirements contract may cut off a vital supply of raw materials. In such situations, equitable relief is often appropriate. . . .

c. *Difficulty of obtaining substitute.* If the injured party can readily procure by the use of money a suitable substitute for the promised performance, the damage remedy is ordinarily adequate. Entering into a substitute transaction is generally a more efficient way to prevent injury than is a suit for specific performance or an injunction and there is a sound economic basis for limiting the injured party to damages in such a case. Furthermore, the substitute transaction affords a basis for proving damages with reasonable certainty, eliminating the factor stated in Paragraph (a). The fact that the burden of financing the transaction is cast on the injured party can usually be sufficiently compensated for by allowing interest. There are many situations, however, in which no suitable substitute is obtainable, and others in which its procurement would be unreasonably difficult or inconvenient or would impose serious financial burdens or risks on the injured party. A suitable substitute is never available for a performance that consists of forbearance, such as that under a contract not to compete. If goods are unique in kind, quality or personal association, the purchase of an equivalent elsewhere may be impracticable, and the buyer's "inability to cover is strong evidence of" the propriety of granting specific performance. Comment 2 to Uniform Commercial Code §2-716. Shares of stock in a corporation may not be obtainable elsewhere. Patents and copyrights are unique. In all these situations, damages may be regarded as inadequate. . . .

   e. Contracts for the sale of land. Contracts for the sale of land have traditionally been accorded a special place in the law of specific performance. A specific tract of land has long been regarded as unique and impossible of duplication by the use of any amount of money. Furthermore, the value of land is to some extent speculative. Damages have therefore been regarded as inadequate to enforce a duty to transfer an interest in land, even if it is less than a fee simple. Under this traditional view, the fact that the buyer has made a contract for the resale of the land to a third person does not deprive him of the right to specific performance. If he cannot convey the land to his purchaser, he will be held for damages for breach of the resale contract, and it is argued that these damages cannot be accurately determined without litigation. Granting him specific performance enables him to perform his own duty and to avoid litigation and damages. . . .

§361. Effect of Provision for Liquidated Damages

Specific performance or an injunction may be granted to enforce a duty even though there is a provision for liquidated damages for breach of that duty.

Comment

   a. Rationale. A contract provision for payment of a sum of money as damages may not afford an adequate remedy even though it is valid as one for liquidated damages and not a penalty (§356). Merely by providing for liquidated damages, the parties are not taken to have fixed a price to be paid for the privilege not to perform. The same uncertainty as to the loss caused that argues for the enforceability of the provision may also argue for the inadequacy of the remedy that it provides. . . . If equitable relief is granted, damages for such breach as has already occurred may also be awarded in accordance with the rule stated in

§358. These damages will ordinarily be limited to the actual loss suffered unless the provision for liquidated damages affords a suitable basis for calculating such damages. . . .

§362. Effect of Uncertainty of Terms

Specific performance or an injunction will not be granted unless the terms of the contract are sufficiently certain to provide a basis for an appropriate order.

Comment

. . . .

b. Degree of certainty required. If specific performance or an injunction is to be granted, it is important that the terms of the contract are sufficiently certain to enable the order to be drafted with precision because of the availability of the contempt power for disobedience. Before concluding that the required certainty is lacking, however, a court will avail itself of all of the usual aids in determining the scope of the agreement. . . . Apparent difficulties of enforcement due to uncertainty may disappear in the light of courageous common sense. Expressions that at first appear incomplete may not appear so after resort to usage (§221) or the addition of a term supplied by law (§204). A contract is not too uncertain merely because a promisor is given a choice of performing in several ways, whether expressed as alternative performances or otherwise. He may be ordered to make the choice and to perform accordingly, and, if he fails to make the choice, the court may choose for him and order specific performance. Even though subsidiary terms have been left to determination by future agreement, if performance has begun by mutual consent, equitable relief may be appropriate with the court supplying the missing terms so as to assure the promisor all advantages that he reasonably expected. . . .

§363. Effect of Insecurity as to the Agreed Exchange

Specific performance or an injunction may be refused if a substantial part of the agreed exchange for the performance to be compelled is unperformed and its performance is not secured to the satisfaction of the court.

§364. Effect of Unfairness

(1) Specific performance or an injunction will be refused if such relief would be unfair because

(a) the contract was induced by mistake or by unfair practices,

(b) the relief would cause unreasonable hardship or loss to the party in breach or to third persons, or

(c) the exchange is grossly inadequate or the terms of the contract are otherwise unfair.

(2) Specific performance or an injunction will be granted in spite of a term of the agreement if denial of such relief would be unfair because it would cause unreasonable hardship or loss to the party seeking relief or to third persons.

Comment

a. Types of unfairness. Courts have traditionally refused equitable relief on grounds of unfairness . . . in situations where they would not necessarily refuse to award damages. Some of these situations involve . . . elements of substantive unfairness in the exchange itself or in its terms that fall short of what is required for unenforceability on grounds of unconscionability (§208). . . .

b. Unfairness in the exchange. Unfairness in the exchange does not of itself make an agreement unenforceable. See comment *c* to §208. If it is extreme, however, it may be a sufficient ground, without more, for denying specific performance or an injunction. . . .

§365. Effect of Public Policy

Specific performance or an injunction will not be granted if the act or forbearance that would be compelled or the use of compulsion is contrary to public policy.

Comment

. . . .

b. Compulsion against public policy. Even though the act or forbearance that would be compelled is not contrary to public policy, the use of compulsion to require that act or forbearance may be contrary to public policy. One example of this general principle is the rule under which a court. . . . will refuse to grant specific performance of a promise to render personal services or supervision (§367). . . .

§366. Effect of Difficulty in Enforcement or Supervision

A promise will not be specifically enforced if the character and magnitude of the performance would impose on the court burdens in enforcement or supervision that are disproportionate to the advantages to be gained from enforcement and to the harm to be suffered from its denial.

§367. Contracts for Personal Service or Supervision

(1) A promise to render personal service will not be specifically enforced.

(2) A promise to render personal service exclusively for one employer will not be enforced by an injunction against serving another if its probable result will be to compel a performance involving personal relations the enforced continuance of which is undesirable or will be to leave the employee without other reasonable means of making a living.

Comment

a. Rationale of refusal of specific performance. A court will refuse to grant specific performance of a contract for service or supervision that is personal in nature. The refusal is based in part upon the undesirability of compelling the continuance of personal association after disputes have arisen and confidence and loyalty are gone and, in some instances, of imposing what might seem like involuntary servitude. . . .

b. What is personal service. A performance is not a personal service under the rule stated in Subsection (1) unless it is personal in the sense of being non-delegable (§318). However, not every non-delegable performance is properly described as a service. An act such as the writing of an autograph or the signing of a diploma may be personal in the sense of being non-delegable even though it is not a personal service, and if that is so specific performance is not precluded. In determining what is a personal service, the . . . importance of trust and confidence in the relation between the parties, the difficulty of judging the quality of the performance rendered and the length of time required for performance are significant factors. Among the parties that have been held to render what are personal services within the rule stated in Subsection (1) are actors, singers and athletes, and the rule applies generally to contracts of employment that create the intimate relation traditionally known as master and servant. . . .

The rule that bars specific enforcement of the employee's promise to render personal service has sometimes been extended to bar specific enforcement of the employer's promise where personal supervision is considered to be involved. The policies against compelling an employer to retain an employee have not, however, prevented courts from ordering reinstatement of employees discharged in contravention of statutes prohibiting discrimination or in violation of collective bargaining agreements.

Illustrations

1. A, a noted opera singer, contracts with B to sing exclusively at B's opera house during the coming season. A repudiates the contract before the time for performance in order to sing at C's competing opera house, and B sues A for specific performance. Even though A's singing at C's opera house will cause B great loss that he cannot prove with reasonable certainty, and even though A can find suitable jobs singing at opera houses not in competition with B's, specific performance will be refused.

2. The facts being otherwise as stated in Illustration 1, B discharges A and A sues for specific performance. Even though singing at B's opera house would have greatly enhanced A's reputation and earning power in an amount that A cannot prove with reasonable certainty, specific performance will be refused. . . .

§368. Effect of Power of Termination

(1) Specific performance or an injunction will not be granted against a party who can substantially nullify the effect of the order by exercising a power of termination or avoidance.

(2) Specific performance or an injunction will not be denied merely because the party seeking relief has a power to terminate or avoid his duty unless the power could be used, in spite of the order, to deprive the other party of reasonable security for the agreed exchange for his performance.

§369. Effect of Breach by Party Seeking Relief

Specific performance or an injunction may be granted in spite of a breach by the party seeking relief, unless the breach is serious enough to discharge the other party's remaining duties of performance.

Topic 4. Restitution

§370. Requirement That Benefit Be Conferred

A party is entitled to restitution under the rules stated in this Restatement only to the extent that he has conferred a benefit on the other party by way of part performance or reliance.

Comment

a. Meaning of requirement. A party's restitution interest is his interest in having restored to him any benefit that he has conferred on the other party. See §344(2). Restitution is, therefore, available to a party only to the extent that he has conferred a benefit on the other party. The benefit may result from the transfer of property or from services, including forbearance. . . . The benefit is ordinarily conferred by performance by the party seeking restitution, and receipt by the other party of performance that he bargained for is regarded as a benefit. However, a benefit may also be conferred if the party seeking restitution relies on the contract in some other way, as where he makes improvements on property that does not ultimately become his. However, a party's expenditures in preparation for performance that do not confer a benefit on the other party do not give rise to a restitution interest. . . . If, for example, the performance consists of the manufacture and delivery of goods and the buyer wrongfully prevents its completion, the seller is not entitled to restitution because no benefit has been conferred on the buyer. See Illustration 2. The injured party may, however, have an action for damages, including one for recovery based on his reliance interest (§349). The requirement of this Section is generally satisfied if a benefit has been conferred, and it is immaterial that it was later lost, destroyed or squandered. . . . The benefit must have been conferred by the party claiming restitution. It is not enough that it was simply derived from the breach. . . . The other party is considered to have had a benefit conferred on him if a performance was rendered at his request to a third person. See Illustration 5. If the contract is for the benefit of a third person, the promisee is entitled to restitution unless the duty to the beneficiary cannot be varied under the rule stated in §311.

Illustrations

. . . .

2. A contracts to sell B a machine for $100,000. After A has spent $40,000 on the manufacture of the machine but before its completion, B repudiates the contract. A cannot get restitution of the $40,000 because no benefit was conferred on B. . . .

5. A, a social worker, promises B to render personal services to C in return for B's promise to educate A's children. B repudiates the contract after A has rendered part of the services. A can get restitution from B for the services, even though they were not rendered to B, because they conferred a benefit on B. . . .

§371. Measure of Restitution Interest

If a sum of money is awarded to protect a party's restitution interest, it may as justice requires be measured by either
    (a) the reasonable value to the other party of what he received in terms of what it would have cost him to obtain it from a person in the claimant's position, or
    (b) the extent to which the other party's property has been increased in value or his other interests advanced.

Comment

a. Measurement of benefit. Under the rules stated in §§344 and 370, a party who is liable in restitution for a sum of money must pay an amount equal to the benefit that has been conferred upon him. If the benefit consists simply of a sum of money received by the party from whom restitution is sought, there is no difficulty in determining this amount. If the benefit consists of something else, however, such as services or property, its measurement in terms of money may pose serious problems. . . .

A particularly significant circumstance is whether the benefit has been conferred by way of performance or by way of reliance in some other way. . . . Recovery is ordinarily more generous for a benefit that has been conferred by performance. To the extent that the benefit may reasonably be measured in different ways, the choice is within the discretion of the court. Thus a court may take into account the value of opportunities for benefit even if they have not been fully realized in the particular case.

An especially important choice is that between the reasonable value to a party of what he received in terms of what it would have cost him to obtain it from a person in the claimant's position and the addition to the wealth of that party as measured by the extent to which his property has been increased in value or his other interests advanced. In practice, the first measure is usually based on the market price of such a substitute. Under the rule stated in this

Section, the court has considerable discretion in making the choice between these two measures of benefit. Under either choice, the court may properly consider the purposes of the recipient of the benefit when he made the contract, even if those purposes were later frustrated or abandoned.

b. Choice of measure. The reasonable value to the party against whom restitution is sought (Paragraph (a)) is ordinarily less than the cost to the party seeking restitution, since his expenditures are excluded to the extent that they conferred no benefit. See Comment *a* to §344. Nor can the party against whom restitution is sought reduce the amount for which he may himself be liable by subtracting such expenditures from the amount of the benefit that he has received. . . . The reasonable value to the party from whom restitution is sought (Paragraph (a)), is, however, usually greater than the addition to his wealth (Paragraph (b)). If this is so, a party seeking restitution for part performance is commonly allowed the more generous measure of reasonable value, unless that measure is unduly difficult to apply, except when he is in breach (§374). . . . In the case of services rendered in an emergency or to save life, however, restitution based on addition to wealth will greatly exceed that based on expense saved and recovery is invariably limited to the smaller amount. . . . In the case of services rendered to a third party as the intended beneficiary of a gift promise, restitution from the promisee based on his enrichment is generally not susceptible of measurement and recovery based on reasonable value is appropriate. . . .

Illustrations

1. A, a carpenter, contracts to repair B's roof for $3,000. A does part of the work at a cost of $2,000, increasing the market price of B's house by $1,200. The market price to have a similar carpenter do the work done by A is $1,800. A's restitution interest is equal to the benefit conferred on B. That benefit may be measured either by the addition to B's wealth from A's services in terms of the $1,200 increase in the market price of B's house or the reasonable value to B of A's services in terms of the $1,800 that it would have cost B to engage a similar carpenter to do the same work. If the work was not completed because of a breach by A . . . $1,200 is appropriate. If the work was not completed because of a breach by B . . . $1,800 is appropriate. . . .

§372. Specific Restitution

(1) Specific restitution will be granted to a party who is entitled to restitution, except that:

(a) specific restitution based on a breach by the other party under the rule stated in §373 may be refused in the discretion of the court if it would unduly interfere with the certainty of title to land or otherwise cause injustice, and

(b) specific restitution in favor of the party in breach under the rule stated in §374 will not be granted.

(2) A decree of specific restitution may be made conditional on return of or compensation for anything that the party claiming restitution has received.

(3) If specific restitution, with or without a sum of money, will be substantially as effective as restitution in money in putting the party claiming restitution in the position he was in before rendering any performance, the other party can dis-

charge his duty by tendering such restitution before suit is brought and keeping his tender good.

§373. Restitution When Other Party Is in Breach

(1) Subject to the rule stated in Subsection (2), on a breach by non-performance that gives rise to a claim for damages for total breach or on a repudiation, the injured party is entitled to restitution for any benefit that he has conferred on the other party by way of part performance or reliance.

(2) The injured party has no right to restitution if he has performed all of his duties under the contract and no performance by the other party remains due other than payment of a definite sum of money for that performance.

Comment

a. Restitution as alternative remedy for breach. An injured party usually seeks, through protection of either his expectation or his reliance interest, to enforce the other party's broken promise. See §344(1). However, he may, as an alternative, seek, through protection of his restitution interest, to prevent the unjust enrichment of the other party. See §344(2). This alternative is available to the injured party as a remedy for breach under the rule stated in this Section. It is available regardless of whether the breach is by non-performance or by repudiation. If, however, the breach is by non-performance, restitution is available only if the breach gives rise to a claim for damages for total breach and not merely to a claim for damages for partial breach. . . . A party who has lost the right to claim damages for total breach by, for example, acceptance or retention of performance with knowledge of defects (§246), has also lost the right to restitution. Restitution is available on repudiation by the other party, even in those exceptional situations in which no claim for damages for total breach arises as a result of repudiation alone. See Comment *d* to §253. . . . The rule stated in this Section applies to all enforceable promises, including those that are enforceable because of reliance. . . . An injured party's right to restitution may be barred by election under the rules stated in §§378 and 379. . . .

b. When contract price is a limit. The rule stated in Subsection (1) is subject to an important exception. If, after one party has fully performed his part of the contract, the other party then refuses to pay a definite sum of money that has been fixed as the price for that performance, the injured party is barred from recovery of a greater sum as restitution under the rule stated in Subsection (2). Since he is entitled to recover the price in full together with interest, he has a remedy that protects his expectation interest by giving him the very thing that he was promised. Even if he asserts that the benefit he conferred on the other party exceeds the price fixed by the contract, justice does not require that he have the right to recover this larger sum in restitution. To give him that right would impose on the court the burden of measuring the benefit in terms of money in spite of the fact that this has already been done by the parties themselves when they made their contract. . . . If, however, the performance to be rendered by the party in breach is something other than the payment of a definite sum in money, this burden is less of an imposition on the court since, even if damages were sought by the injured party, the court would have to measure the value to him of the performance due from the party in breach. . . . [T]he rule stated in Subsection (2) is limited to the situation where the only remaining performance due from the party in breach is the payment of a definite sum of money. . . . If the performance promised by the party in breach consists in part of money and in part of something else, full performance by the injured party does not bar him from restitution unless the party in breach has rendered all of his performance except a money payment. . . .

d. *Losing contracts.* An injured party who has performed in part will usually prefer to seek damages based on his expectation interest (§347) instead of a sum of money based on his restitution interest because such damages include his net profit and will give him a larger recovery. Even if he cannot prove what his net profit would have been, he will ordinarily seek damages based on his reliance interest (§34[9]), since this will compensate him for all of his expenditures, regardless of whether they resulted in a benefit to the party in breach. See Comment *a* to §344. In the case of a contract on which he would have sustained a loss instead of having made a profit, however, his restitution interest may give him a larger recovery than would damages on either basis. . . . He is entitled to such recovery even if the contract price is stated in terms of a rate per unit of work and the recovery exceeds that rate. There are, however, two important limitations. The first limitation is one that is applicable to any claim for restitution: the party in breach is liable only to the extent that he has benefited from the injured party's performance. If he has, for example, taken advantage of the injured party's part performance by having the rest of the work completed after his breach, the extent of his benefit is easy to measure in terms of the reasonable value of the injured party's performance. . . . If, however, he has abandoned the project and not completed the work, that measurement will be more difficult. . . . In that situation, the court may exercise its sound discretion in choosing between the two measures stated in §371. In doing so it will take account of all the circumstances including the observance by the parties of standards of good faith and fair dealing during any negotiations leading up to the rupture of contractual relations (§208). . . . Since a contract that is a losing one for the injured party is often an advantageous one for the party in breach, the possibility should not be overlooked that the breach was provoked by the injured party in order to avoid having to perform. The second limitation is that stated in Subsection (2). If the injured party has completed performance and nothing remains for the party in breach to do but to pay him the price, his recovery is limited to the price. See Comment *b*.

Illustrations

10. A, a plumbing subcontractor, contracts with B, a general contractor, to install the plumbing in a factory being built by B for C. B promises to pay A $100,000. After A has spent $40,000, B repudiates the contract and has the plumbing finished by another subcontractor at a cost of $80,000. The market price to have a similar plumbing subcontractor do the work done by A is $40,000. A can recover the $40,000 from B in restitution. . . .

§374. Restitution in Favor of Party in Breach

(1) Subject to the rule stated in Subsection (2), if a party justifiably refuses to perform on the ground that his remaining duties of performance have been discharged by the other party's breach, the party in breach is entitled to restitution for any benefit that he has conferred by way of part performance or reliance in excess of the loss that he has caused by his own breach.

(2) To the extent that, under the manifested assent of the parties, a party's performance is to be retained in the case of breach, that party is not entitled to restitution if the value of the performance as liquidated damages is reasonable in the light of the anticipated or actual loss caused by the breach and the difficulties of proof of loss.

Comment

a. Restitution in spite of breach. The rule stated in this Section applies where a party, after having rendered part performance, commits a breach by either non-performance or repudiation that justifies the other party in refusing further performance. It is often unjust to allow the injured party to retain the entire benefit of the part performance rendered by the party in breach without paying anything in return. The party in breach is, in any case, liable for the loss caused by his breach. If the benefit received by the injured party does not exceed that loss, he owes nothing to the party in breach. If the benefit received exceeds that loss, the rule stated in this Section generally gives the party in breach the right to recover the excess in restitution. If the injured party has a right to specific performance and remains willing and able to perform, he may keep what he has received and sue for specific performance of the balance. . . .

§375. Restitution When Contract Is Within Statute of Frauds

A party who would otherwise have a claim in restitution under a contract is not barred from restitution for the reason that the contract is unenforceable by him because of the Statute of Frauds unless the Statute provides otherwise or its purpose would be frustrated by allowing restitution.

§376. Restitution When Contract Is Voidable

A party who has avoided a contract on the ground of lack of capacity, mistake, misrepresentation, duress, undue influence or abuse of a fiduciary relation is entitled to restitution for any benefit that he has conferred on the other party by way of part performance or reliance.

Comment

a. Recovery of benefit on avoidance. A party who exercises his power of avoidance is entitled to recover in restitution for any benefit that he has conferred on the other party through part performance of or reliance on the contract. The benefit from his part performance includes that resulting from the use by the other party of whatever he has received up to the time that it is returned on avoidance. Furthermore, under the rule stated in §384, a party seeking restitution must generally return any benefit that he has himself received. If he has received and must return land, for example, he may have made improvements on the land in reliance on the contract and he is entitled, on avoidance and return of the land, to recover the reasonable value of those improvements (§371(b)). The rule stated in this Section applies to avoidance on any ground, including lack of capacity (§§14-16), mistake (§§152, 153), misrepresentation (§164), duress (§175), undue influence (§177) or abuse of a fiduciary relation (§173). Uncertainties in measuring the benefit, however, are more likely to be resolved in favor of the party seeking restitution if the other party engaged in misconduct, as in cases of fraudulent misrepresentation, duress or undue influence. In cases of mental incompetency the rule stated in this Section is supplemented by that stated in §15(2) and in cases of mistake it is supplemented by that stated in §158. . . .

§377. Restitution in Cases of Impracticability, Frustration, Non-Occurrence of Condition or Disclaimer by Beneficiary

A party whose duty of performance does not arise or is discharged as a result of impracticability of performance, frustration of purpose, non-occurrence of a condition or disclaimer by a beneficiary is entitled to restitution for any benefit that he has conferred on the other party by way of part performance or reliance.

Comment

a. Scope. A party whose duty of performance is discharged on grounds of supervening impracticability of performance (§261) or frustration of purpose (§265) may already have performed in part or otherwise relied on the contract before the occurrence of the supervening event. A party whose duty never arises on those grounds (§266) may have taken similar action before discovery of the relevant circumstances. Under the rule stated in this Section such a party is entitled to restitution. Furthermore, in cases of impracticability or frustration the other party is also ordinarily relieved of any obligation of rendering the return performance that he has promised on the ground of failure of performance (§267). Under the rule stated in this Section that party is also entitled to restitution. The same is true where the parties are relieved of their obligations on the ground of the non-occurrence of a condition (§225) or because of a disclaimer by a beneficiary (§306). If both parties have rendered some performance, each is entitled to restitution against the other. The rule stated in this Section is subject to contrary agreement to the extent that the agreement does not violate the rules relating to unfairness (§364), unconscionability (§208) and forfeiture (§229). . . .

b. Measure of benefit. Cases of impracticability and frustration may pose particularly difficult problems of adjustment after the occurrence of a disrupting event that was ordinarily unforeseeable when the contract was made. The rule stated in §272(2) gives a court discretion in an extreme case to do justice by supplying a term that is reasonable in the circumstance. In most cases, however, restitution is all that is required, given the choice open to the court in measuring benefit (§371). Usually the measure of reasonable value is appropriate. A benefit may be found if it was conferred before the occurrence of the event even though the event later resulted in its destruction, and in that case recovery may be limited to the measure of increase in wealth prior to the event, if this is less than reasonable value. . . . A party cannot, however, recover his reliance interest under the rule stated in this Section, and his expenditures in reliance are not subtracted from what he has received in calculating the benefit for which he is liable. . . . Furthermore, to the extent that the contract price can be roughly apportioned to the work done, recovery will not be allowed in excess of the appropriate amount of the price. . . .

Topic 5. Preclusion by Election and Affirmance

§378. Election Among Remedies

If a party has more than one remedy under the rules stated in this Chapter, his manifestation of a choice of one of them by bringing suit or otherwise is not a bar to another remedy unless the remedies are inconsistent and the other party materially changes his position in reliance on the manifestation.

§379. Election to Treat Duties of Performance Under Aleatory Contract as Discharged

If a right or duty of the injured party is conditional on an event that is fortuitous or is supposed by the parties to be fortuitous, he cannot treat his remaining duties to render performance as discharged on the ground of the other party's breach by non-performance if he does not manifest to the other party his intention to do so before any adverse change in the situation of the injured party resulting from the occurrence of that event or a material change in the probability of its occurrence.

§380. Loss of Power of Avoidance by Affirmance

(1) The power of a party to avoid a contract for incapacity, duress, undue influence or abuse of a fiduciary relation is lost if, after the circumstances that made the contract voidable have ceased to exist, he manifests to the other party his intention to affirm it or acts with respect to anything that he has received in a manner inconsistent with disaffirmance.

(2) The power of a party to avoid a contract for mistake or misrepresentation is lost if after he knows or has reason to know of the mistake or of the misrepresentation if it is non-fraudulent or knows of the misrepresentation if it is fraudulent, he manifests to the other party his intention to affirm it or acts with respect to anything that he has received in a manner inconsistent with disaffirmance.

(3) If the other party rejects an offer by the party seeking avoidance to return what he has received, the party seeking avoidance if entitled to restitution can, after the lapse of a reasonable time, enforce a lien on what he has received by selling it and crediting the proceeds toward his claim in restitution.

§381.   Loss of Power of Avoidance by Delay

(1) The power of a party to avoid a contract for incapacity, duress, undue influence or abuse of a fiduciary relation is lost if, after the circumstances that made it voidable have ceased to exist, he does not within a reasonable time manifest to the other party his intention to avoid it.

(2) The power of a party to avoid a contract for misrepresentation or mistake is lost if after he knows of a fraudulent misrepresentation or knows or has reason to know of a non-fraudulent misrepresentation or mistake he does not within a reasonable time manifest to the other party his intention to avoid it. The power of a party to avoid a contract for non-fraudulent misrepresentation or mistake is also lost if the contract has been so far performed or the circumstances have otherwise so changed that avoidance would be inequitable and if damages will be adequate compensation.

(3) In determining what is a reasonable time, the following circumstances are significant:

(a) the extent to which the delay enabled or might have enabled the party with the power of avoidance to speculate at the other party's risk;

(b) the extent to which the delay resulted or might have resulted in justifiable reliance by the other party or by third persons;

(c) the extent to which the ground for avoidance was the result of any fault by either party; and

(d) the extent to which the other party's conduct contributed to the delay.

(4) If a right or duty of the party who has the power of avoidance for non-fraudulent misrepresentation or mistake is conditional on an event that is fortuitous or is supposed by the parties to be fortuitous, a manifestation of intention under Subsection (1) or (2) is not effective unless it is made before any adverse change in his situation resulting from the occurrence of that event or a material change in the probability of its occurrence.

§382.   Loss of Power to Affirm by Prior Avoidance

(1) If a party has effectively exercised his power of avoidance, a subsequent manifestation of intent to affirm is inoperative unless the other party manifests his assent to affirmance by refusal to accept a return of his performance or otherwise.

(2) A party has not exercised his power of avoidance under the rule stated in Subsection (1) until

(a) he has regained all or a substantial part of what he would be entitled to by way of restitution on avoidance,

(b) he has obtained a final judgment of or based on avoidance, or

(c) the other party has materially relied on or manifested his assent to a statement of disaffirmance.

§383. Avoidance in Part

A contract cannot be avoided in part except that where one or more corresponding pairs of part performances have been fully performed by one or both parties the rest of the contract can be avoided.

§384. Requirement That Party Seeking Restitution Return Benefit

(1) Except as stated in Subsection (2), a party will not be granted restitution unless

(a) he returns or offers to return, conditional on restitution, any interest in property that he has received in exchange in substantially as good condition as when it was received by him, or

(b) the court can assure such return in connection with the relief granted.

(2) The requirement stated in Subsection (1) does not apply to property

(a) that was worthless when received or that has been destroyed or lost by the other party or as a result of its own defects,

(b) that either could not from the time of receipt have been returned or has been used or disposed or without knowledge of the grounds for restitution if justice requires that compensation be accepted in its place and the payment of such compensation can be assured, or

(c) as to which the contract apportions the price if that part of the price is not included in the claim for restitution.

§385. Effect of Power of Avoidance on Duty of Performance or on Duty Arising Out of Breach

(1) Unless an offer to restore performance received is a condition of avoidance, a party has no duty of performance while his power of avoidance exists.

(2) If an offer to restore performance received is a condition of avoidance, a duty to pay damages is terminated by such an offer made before the power of avoidance is lost.

Restatement (Third) of Agency (2006)

EDITORS' NOTE

The first Restatement of Agency, published in 1933, was the second restatement completed by the American Law Institute (ALI), coming to fruition a year after the first Restatement of Contracts (1932). Professors Floyd Meachem (University of Chicago Law School) and Warren Seavey (Harvard Law School), served as reporters for the first Restatement of Agency, and Professor Seavey reprised his role for the Restatement (Second), published in 1958. Professor Deborah DeMott (Duke University School of Law) served as reporter for the current Restatement (Third), published in 2006.[1]

Once a staple of the required law school curriculum, agency (somewhat like restitution and unjust enrichment, the most recent restatement of which we excerpt later in this Supplement) was subsumed by other courses, including torts, employment law, business associations, but the principles of agency relationships and the rights and duties they create remain important across a broad swath of law, including the law of contracts. Corporations and other entities cannot form contracts; they do so through the actions of one or more agents. Most people purchase, sell, or lease real property with the assistance of an agent. Many employees find or change employment and many employers acquire talent with an agent's assistance. Creative and performing artists, athletes and coaches, models and endorsers, among others, generally use agents to identify and negotiate the terms of their contracts. And, at the front end of many contemplated transactions, and the back end of many transactions that have not worked out as planned, there are attorneys – agents acting on behalf of their principals (that is, their clients) – to pursue the latter's goals and protect their interests.

The Restatement (Third) of Agency includes provisions that reach beyond contract law's scope. Consequently, we present only selected sections, comments, and illustrations addressing important contract questions: When does an agent have

---

1. See Lance Liebman, Foreword, Restatement (Third) of Agency xi (2006).

authority (a form of capacity) to contract on behalf of a (purported) principal with a third party and how does the agent acquire that authority? When and how may a purported principal be bound after the fact by an agreement a non-agent or an agent acting outside the scope of her authority forms? Who may be liable on an agreement an agent forms on behalf of a principal or purported principal?

For interesting discussions of the Restatement (Third), the issues underlying it, and perceived strengths and weaknesses of the Restatement's approach, see, e.g., Deborah A. DeMott, The Contours and Composition of Agency Doctrine: Perspectives from History and Theory on Inherent Agency Power, 2014 U. Ill. L. Rev. 1813; Paula J. Dalley, A Theory of Agency Law, 72 U. Pitt. L. Rev. 495 (2011). For an insightful discussion of agency issues in the attorney-client setting, see Grace M. Giesel, Client Responsibility for Lawyer Conduct: Examining the Agency Nature of the Lawyer-Client Relationship, 86 Neb. L. Rev. 346 (2007).

CHAPTER 1.   INTRODUCTORY MATTERS

Topic 1.   Definitions and Terminology

CHAPTER 2.   PRINCIPLES OF ATTRIBUTION

Topic 1.   Actual Authority

Topic 2.   Apparent Authority

Topic 4.   Related Doctrines

CHAPTER 3.   CREATION AND TERMINATION OF AUTHORITY AND AGENCY RELATIONSHIPS

Topic 1.   Creating and Evidencing Actual Authority

Topic 2.   Creating Apparent Authority

Topic 3.   Capacity to Act as Principal or Agent

CHAPTER 4.   RATIFICATION

CHAPTER 1.   INTRODUCTORY MATTERS

Topic 1.   Definitions and Terminology

§1.01. Agency Defined

Agency is the fiduciary relationship that arises when one person (a "principal") manifests assent to another person (an "agent") that the agent shall act on the principal's behalf and subject to the principal's control, and the agent manifests assent or otherwise consents so to act.

Comment

. . . .

c. Elements of agency. [A]gency posits a consensual relationship in which one person, to one degree or another or respect or another, acts as a representative of or otherwise acts on behalf of another person with power to affect the legal rights and duties of the other person. The person represented has a right to control the actions of the agent. Agency thus entails inward-looking consequences, operative as between the agent and the principal, as well as outward-looking consequences, operative as among the agent, the principal, and third parties with whom the agent interacts. Only interactions that are within the scope of an agency relationship affect the principal's legal position. . . .

The common-law definition requires that an agent hold power, a concept that encompasses authority but is broader in scope and connotation. The terminology of "power" is neutral in that it states a result but not the justification for the result. An agent who has actual authority holds power as a result of a voluntary conferral by the principal and is privileged, in relation to the principal, to exercise that power. Actual authority is defined in §2.01. Actual authority does not exhaust the circumstances under which the legal consequences of one person's actions may be attributed to another person. An agent also has power to affect the principal's legal relations through the operation of apparent authority, as stated in §2.03. Additionally, a person may be estopped to deny the existence of an agency relationship, as stated in §2.05. Separately, a person may, through ratification, create the consequences of actual authority with respect to an actor's prior act. . . .

Agency encompasses a wide and diverse range of relationships and circumstances. The elements of common-law agency are present in the relationships between employer and employee, corporation and officer, client and lawyer, and partnership and general partner. People often retain agents to perform specific services. Common real-estate transactions, for example, involve the use of agents by buyers, sellers, lessors, and lessees. Authors, performers, and athletes often retain specialized agents to represent their interests in dealing with third parties. Some industries make frequent use of nonemployee agents to communicate with customers and enter into contracts that bind the customer and a vendor. Agents who lack authority to bind their principals to contracts nevertheless often have authority to negotiate or to transmit or receive information on their behalf. . . .

Not all relationships in which one person provides services to another satisfy the definition of agency. It has been said that a relationship of agency always "contemplates three parties – the principal, the agent, and the third party with whom the agent is to deal." 1 Floyd R. Mechem, A Treatise on the Law of Agency §27 (2d ed. 1914). It is important to define the concept of "dealing" broadly rather than narrowly. For example, a principal might employ an agent who acquires information from third parties on the principal's behalf but does not "deal" in the sense of entering into transactions on the principal's account. In contrast, if a service provider simply furnishes advice and does not interact with third parties as the representative of the recipient of the advice, the service provider is not acting as an agent. The adviser may be subject to a fiduciary duty of loyalty even when the adviser is not acting as an agent. . . .

Despite their agency relationship, a principal and an agent retain separate legal personalities. . . . The fact that an agent acts on behalf of, or represents, another person implies the existence of limits on the scope of the agency relationship and on the extent to which the principal is accountable for the agent's acts. . . .

A relationship is not one of agency within the common-law definition unless the agent consents to act on behalf of the principal, and the principal has the right throughout the duration of the relationship to control the agent's acts. A principal's manifestation may be such that an agency relationship will exist without any communication from the agent to the principal explicitly stating the agent's consent. If the principal requests another to act on the principal's behalf, indicating that the action should be taken without further communication and the other consents so to act, an agency relationship exists. If the putative agent does the requested act, it is appropriate to infer that the action was taken as agent for the person who requested the action unless the putative agent manifests an intention to the contrary or the circumstances so indicate.

A principal's right to control the agent is a constant across relationships of agency, but the content or specific meaning of the right varies. Thus, a person may be an agent although the principal lacks the right to control the full range of the agent's activities, how the agent uses time, or the agent's exercise of professional judgment. A principal's failure to exercise the right of control does not eliminate it, nor is it eliminated by physical distance between the agent and principal. . . . The common-law definition of agency presupposes a principal who exists and who has legal capacity throughout the duration of the relationship; otherwise the principal will not be able on an ongoing basis to assess the agent's performance in relationship to the principal's interests. . . . The requirement that an agent be subject to the principal's control assumes that the principal is capable of providing instructions to the agent and of terminating the agent's authority. . . . The chief justifications for the principal's account-ability for the agent's acts are the principal's ability to select and control the agent and to terminate the agency relationship, together with the fact that the agent has agreed expressly or implicitly to act on the principal's behalf. . . .

§1.04. Terminology

. . . .

(2) *Disclosed, undisclosed, and unidentified principals.*

(a) *Disclosed principal.* A principal is disclosed if, when an agent and a third party interact, the third party has notice that the agent is acting for a principal and has notice of the principal's identity.

(b) *Undisclosed principal.* A principal is undisclosed if, when an agent and a third party interact, the third party has no notice that the agent is acting for a principal.

(c) *Unidentified principal.* A principal is unidentified if, when an agent and a third party interact, the third party has notice that the agent is acting for a principal but does not have notice of the principal's identity. . . .

Comment

. . . .

b. Disclosed, unidentified, and undisclosed principal. These distinctions are relevant to the legal position of principal and agent in relation to third parties. . . . Whether a principal is disclosed, undisclosed, or unidentified depends on the manifestations of the principal and the agent and the notice received by the other party at the time of that party's transaction with the agent. The principal is no longer undisclosed if the agent discloses either the principal's identity or the fact that the agent represents a principal without identifying the principal. The principal is no longer undisclosed even if such disclosure is contrary to the principal's instructions.

The terms "partially undisclosed" principal and "unnamed" principal are synonyms for "unidentified" principal. The terminology "unidentified" principal is preferable. "Partially disclosed" misleadingly suggests that some portion of the principal's identity is known to the third party. "Unnamed principal" is too restrictive because a third party may know the principal's identity but not know the principal's name.

Manifestations of a principal or an agent may reasonably indicate to a third party that the agent acts on behalf of a principal and the principal's identity. If so, the principal is disclosed although the third party subjectively believes that the agent acts alone and represents no one. If the third party has notice that an agent acts on behalf of a principal, even though the agent has represented otherwise, the principal is not undisclosed but is either disclosed or unidentified, depending on the facts of which the third party has notice. If manifestations as to the principal's existence or identity are ambiguous, the third party's belief is conclusive if it is reasonable. These distinctions are relevant to whether an agent becomes a party to a contract made on the principal's behalf. . . .

CHAPTER 2.   PRINCIPLES OF ATTRIBUTION

Topic 1.   Actual Authority

§2.01.   Actual Authority

An agent acts with actual authority when, at the time of taking action that has legal consequences for the principal, the agent reasonably believes, in accordance with the principal's manifestations to the agent, that the principal wishes the agent so to act.

Comment

. . . .

b. *Terminology.* . . . The definition in this section does not attempt to classify different types of actual authority on the basis of the degree of detail in the principal's manifestation, which may consist of written or spoken words or other conduct. . . . As commonly used, the term "express authority" often means actual authority that a principal has stated in very specific or detailed language.

The term "implied authority" has more than one meaning. "Implied authority" is often used to mean actual authority either (1) to do what is necessary, usual, and proper to accomplish or perform an agent's express responsibilities or (2) to act in a manner in which an agent believes the principal wishes the agent to act based on the agent's reasonable interpretation of the principal's manifestation in light of the principal's objectives and other facts known to the agent. These meanings are not mutually exclusive. Both fall within the definition of actual authority. . . .

c. *Rationale.* Actual authority is a consequence of a principal's expressive conduct toward an agent, through which the principal manifests assent to be affected by the agent's action, and the agent's reasonable understanding of the principal's manifestation. An agent's actions establish the agent's consent to act on the principal's behalf, as does any separate manifestation of assent by the agent. When an agent acts with actual authority, the agent's power to affect the principal's legal relations with third parties is coextensive with the agent's right to do so, which actual authority creates. In contrast, although an agent who acts with only apparent authority also affects the principal's legal relations, the agent lacks the right to do so, and the agent's act is not rightful as toward the principal. Actual authority often overlaps with the presence of apparent authority. . . .

[A]ctual authority requires that an agent's belief be reasonable at the time the agent acts. It is also necessary that the agent in fact believes that the principal desires the action taken by the agent. . . .

§2.02. Scope of Actual Authority

(1) An agent has actual authority to take action designated or implied in the principal's manifestations to the agent and acts necessary or incidental to achieving the principal's objectives, as the agent reasonably understands the principal's manifestations and objectives when the agent determines how to act.

(2) An agent's interpretation of the principal's manifestations is reasonable if it reflects any meaning known by the agent to be ascribed by the principal and, in the absence of any meaning known to the agent, as a reasonable person in the agent's position would interpret the manifestations in light of the context, including circumstances of which the agent has notice and the agent's fiduciary duty to the principal.

(3) An agent's understanding of the principal's objectives is reasonable if it accords with the principal's manifestations and the inferences that a reasonable person in the agent's position would draw from the circumstances creating the agency.

Comment

. . . .

c. Rationale. Actual authority is an agent's power to affect the principal's legal relations in accord with the agent's reasonable understanding, at the time the agent acts, of the principal's manifestations to the agent. . . . If an agent's understanding is reasonable, the agent has actual authority to act in accordance with the understanding, although the principal subsequently establishes that the agent was mistaken. The agent's belief must be grounded in a manifestation of the principal, including but not limited to the principal's written or spoken words. See §3.01. . . .

. . . . [A]ctual authority differs from a promise or an agreement, although promises and agreements that are constitutive elements of a contract between a principal and an agent may coincide with a manifestation of assent by the principal that creates actual authority under §3.01. . . . [T]he focal point for determining whether an agent's interpretation of the principal's manifestation was reasonable is the time the agent decides what action to take. This inquiry determines whether the agent acted with actual authority because the agent reasonably believed the principal consented to the agent's action. In contrast, . . . resolving questions of contractual interpretation, the primary inquiry is ascertaining the parties' shared meaning to determine whether there is a contract and what rights and duties it creates. Moreover, questions of interpretation that determine whether an agent acted with actual authority have a temporal focus that moves through time as the agent decides how to act, while questions of contractual interpretation focus on the parties' shared meaning as of the time of a promise or agreement.

d. Acts necessary or incidental to achieving principal's objectives. If a principal's manifestation to an agent expresses the principal's wish that something be done, it is natural to assume that the principal [also] wishes . . . that the agent take the steps necessary [to achieve the principal's objectives]. . . . The underlying assumptions are that the principal does not wish to authorize what cannot be achieved if necessary steps are not taken by the agent, and that the principal's manifestation often will not specify all steps necessary to translate it into action. . . .

e. Agent's reasonable understanding of principal's manifestation. An agent does not have actual authority to do an act if the agent does not reasonably believe that the principal has consented to its commission. . . . Lack of actual authority is established by showing either that the agent did not believe, or could not reasonably have believed, that the principal's grant of actual authority encompassed the act in question. This standard requires that the agent's belief be reasonable, an objective standard, and that the agent actually hold the belief, a subjective standard. . . .

Interactions between principal and agent do not occur in a vacuum. Prior dealings between them are relevant to the reasonableness of the agent's understanding of the principal's manifestation. If a principal and an agent share an idiosyncratic understanding of what is meant by the principal's manifestation, that understanding controls the scope of the agent's actual authority, not the understanding that a reasonable person would have. Unlike a party dealing at arm's length with another, the focus for an agent is interpreting the principal's manifestations so as to further the principal's objectives. . . .

In determining whether an agent's action reflected a reasonable understanding of the principal's manifestations of consent, it is relevant whether the principal knew of prior similar actions by the agent and acquiesced in them. . . .

The context in which principal and agent interact will often include customs and usages that are particular to a type of business or a geographic locale. A person carrying on business has reason to know of such customs and usages and thus has notice of them. . . . If an agent has notice that the principal does not know of a custom or usage, the agent is not authorized to act in accordance with it if doing so would result in a transaction different from that which the agent has notice is desired by the principal.

If a principal states the agent's authority in terms that contemplate that the agent will use substantial discretion to determine the particulars, it is ordinarily reasonable for the agent to believe that following usage and custom will be acceptable to the principal. In contrast, if a principal's express statement of authority is highly detailed, it is not reasonable for the agent to believe the principal intended that the agent should follow a custom or usage that is at odds with the terms of the principal's express authorization. . . .

Topic 2. Apparent Authority

§2.03. Apparent Authority

Apparent authority is the power held by an agent or other actor to affect a principal's legal relations with third parties when a third party reasonably believes the actor has authority to act on behalf of the principal and that belief is traceable to the principal's manifestations.

Comment

. . . .

b. Terminology. The doctrine stated in this section applies to agents and other actors who purport to act as agents on a principal's behalf. The doctrine also applies to the "apparent authority" of actors who are agents but whose actions exceed their actual authority. . . .

The definition of apparent authority in this section . . . requires that the third party reasonably believe the agent to be authorized and that such belief be traceable to a manifestation of the principal's manifestation. . . .

c. Rationale. Apparent authority holds a principal accountable for the results of third-party beliefs about an actor's authority to act as an agent when the belief is reasonable and is traceable to a manifestation of the principal. As to the third person, apparent authority when present trumps restrictions that the principal has privately imposed on the agent. The relevant appearance is that the principal has conferred authority on an agent. . . . Apparent authority is distinct from the circumstances of an agency relationship known to agent and principal, which may not be observable by a third party, even though the course of dealing between agent and principal will often be observed at least in part by third parties. . . .

The doctrine stated in this section applies to any set of circumstances under which it is reasonable for a third party to believe that an agent has authority, so long as the belief is traceable to manifestations of the principal. . . . A third party's reasonable understanding of the principal's conduct will reflect general business custom as well as usage that is particular to the principal's industry and prior dealings between the parties. A belief that results solely from the statements or other conduct of the agent, unsupported by any manifestations traceable to the principal, does not create apparent authority. . . .

. . . [A] principal may permit an agent to acquire a reputation of authority in an area or endeavor by acquiescing in conduct by the agent under circumstances likely to lead to a reputation. Third parties may continue reasonably to believe that the agent is authorized even after the agency relationship has been terminated if they are unaware of the termination. . . .

Apparent authority has been said to be "based upon the principle which has led to the objective theory of contracts, namely, that in contractual relations one should ordinarily be bound by what he says rather than by what he intends, so that the contract which results from the acceptance of an offer is that which the offeree reasonably understands, rather than what the offeror means."

Restatement, Second, Agency §8, Comment *d*. The principal's manifestation as to the agent's authority empowers the agent to affect the principal's legal relations. Restrictions on an agent's authority that are known only to the principal and the agent do not defeat or supersede the consequences of apparent authority for the principal's legal relations, apart from the principal's legal relations with the agent. In the principal's relations with third parties, restrictions that the principal has placed on the agent's authority are inoperative if apparent authority is present just as, by analogy, an offeror's unexpressed meaning that is unknown to the offeree is inoperative as to the offeror's contractual relations with the offeree. *See* Restatement, Second, Contracts §19, Comment *c*. To establish apparent authority, it is not necessary for a third party to establish fault on the part of the principal, just as it is not necessary for an offeree to establish fault on the part of an offeror to hold the offeror to the manifested intention to enter into a bargain with the offeree. If apparent authority is present, it is irrelevant that its presence or continued presence eluded the principal's exercise of due care to prevent or defeat it. . . .

Topic 4. Related Doctrines

§2.05. Estoppel to Deny Existence of Agency Relationship

A person who has not made a manifestation that an actor has authority as an agent and who is not otherwise liable as a party to a transaction purportedly done by the actor on that person's account is subject to liability to a third party who justifiably is induced to make a detrimental change in position because the transaction is believed to be on the person's account, if
   (1) the person intentionally or carelessly caused such belief, or
   (2) having notice of such belief and that it might induce others to change their positions, the person did not take reasonable steps to notify them of the facts.

Comment

. . . .
   c. In general. . . . [T]his section protects third parties who justifiably rely on a belief that an actor is an agent and who act on that belief to their detriment. The doctrine is applicable when the person against whom estoppel is asserted . . . is responsible for the third party's belief that an actor is an agent and the third party has justifiably been induced by that belief to undergo a detrimental change in position. . . . If the scope of the actor's power to bind the person estopped is in issue, the doctrine of apparent authority, stated in §2.03, governs. The operative question is whether a reasonable person in the position of the third party would believe such an agent, as the actor appears to be, to have authority to do a particular act.
   d. Rationale. The agency-law doctrines of actual authority and apparent authority attribute the legal consequences of an actor's actions to a person when the person has made a manifestation of authority, either to the actor, thereby

creating actual authority under §2.01, or to a third party, thereby creating apparent authority under §2.03. Estoppel links the legal consequences of the actor's actions to the person estopped on different bases. These are the third party's justifiable and detrimental change in position and the third party's belief in the actor's relationship to the person estopped, which induced the change in position for which the person estopped is held responsible. . . .

When a relationship of agency exists, a principal is often estopped to deny the existence of authority when the origin of the third party's belief, or the explanation for it, demarcates between the elements requisite to estoppel and those requisite to proving apparent authority as defined in §2.03. Apparent authority is not present unless the third party's belief is traceable to the principal's own manifestations, which may include placing the agent in a position that leads third parties to believe the agent has authority consistent with the position. See §3.03, comment *b*. Estoppel does not require as close a fit between affirmative acts of the principal and the third party's belief. Instead, it protects third parties who reasonably believe an actor to be authorized as an agent when the belief cannot be shown to follow directly or indirectly from the principal's own manifestations. . . .

CHAPTER 3.   CREATION AND TERMINATION OF AUTHORITY AND AGENCY RELATIONSHIPS

Topic 1.   Creating and Evidencing Actual Authority

§3.01.   Creation of Actual Authority

Actual authority, as defined in §2.01, is created by a principal's manifestation to an agent that, as reasonably understood by the agent, expresses the principal's assent that the agent take action on the principal's behalf.

Comment

. . . .

b. Manifestation an essential requirement. . . . [A]n agent's actual authority originates with expressive conduct by the principal toward the agent by which the principal manifests assent to action by the agent with legal consequences for the principal. A principal's unexpressed willingness that another act as agent does not create actual authority. . . . The manifestation may be made directly by the principal to the agent or may reach the agent through a more circuitous route. The principal's unexpressed reservations and qualifications do not reduce the agent's actual authority. . . .

Actual authority may exist although there is no contract between a principal and agent; a relationship of agency does not require that the principal or the agent receive consideration from the other. . . . It is not necessary to the existence of actual authority that an actor promise or otherwise undertake to act as agent. However, an actor is not an agent as defined in §1.01 unless the actor manifests assent or otherwise consents to a relationship of agency. The agent's manifestation need not be made explicitly, nor be made directly to the principal. . . .

Topic 2.   Creating Apparent Authority

§3.03.   Creation of Apparent Authority

Apparent authority, as defined in §2.03, is created by a person's manifestation that another has authority to act with legal consequences for the person who makes the manifestation, when a third party reasonably believes the actor to be authorized and the belief is traceable to the manifestation.

Comment

. . . .

b. Manifestation an essential requirement. . . . Apparent authority is present only when a third party's belief is traceable to manifestations of the principal. . . .

A principal may make manifestations regarding an agent's authority in many ways. In some settings, the principal's acts speak so loudly that explicit verbal communication is unnecessary. Similarly, an indirect route of communication between a principal and third party may suffice, especially when it is consistent with practice in the relevant industry. . . .

A principal may also make a manifestation by placing an agent in a defined position in an organization or by placing an agent in charge of a transaction or situation. Third parties who interact with the principal through the agent will naturally and reasonably assume that the agent has authority to do acts consistent with the agent's position or role unless they have notice of facts suggesting that this may not be so. . . .

. . . . The determinative question is whether a third party can establish a linkage between statements of authority by the agent and a manifestation of assent by the principal to the making of such statements. If no such linkage can be established, the third party may be able nonetheless to estop the principal from denying the agent's authority under the doctrine stated in §2.05 if the principal is responsible for the agent's representation. . . .

A principal's inaction creates apparent authority when it provides a basis for a third party reasonably to believe the principal intentionally acquiesces in the agent's representations or actions. . . . If the third party has observed prior interactions between the agent and the principal, the third party may reasonably believe that a subsequent act or representation by the agent is authorized because it conforms to the prior pattern observed by the third party. . . .

If a principal has given an agent general authority to engage in a class of transactions, subject to limits known only to the agent and the principal, third parties may reasonably believe the agent to be authorized to conduct such transactions and need not inquire into the existence of undisclosed limits on the agent's authority. The agent's apparent authority does not disappear when, unbeknownst to the third party, the agent errs in performing tasks requisite to completing a transaction. Similarly, if a principal has authorized an agent to communicate the principal's decisions to a third party, the third party may reasonably believe the agent's reports. . . .

   c. Organizational principals. Apparent authority is [] essential . . . in enabling third parties to deal effectively with organizations. Actual authority . . . is often less important to those who interact with the organization than is the regular-looking appearance of authority. Apparent authority enables persons who interact with the organization to treat the agent's act or statement as dispositive, without further inquiry directed elsewhere within the organization, in the absence of circumstances suggestive of self-dealing or other irregularity. . . .

   . . . . Most organizations are operated by their officers and managers; the governing body often plays no direct role in the myriad of decisions and transactions required for the organization's routine operation. As a consequence, delegation of authority is significant in the organizational context because it reflects a sensible accommodation of agency doctrine to the common operating practices of organizations. Most people proceed on many matters on the assumption that ordinary-looking instances of delegation are effective. For example, it is not necessary to see an exemplified resolution of the board of directors of a car-rental company reasonably to conclude that a counter agent has authority to bind the company to the rental agreement. . . .

   The reasonableness of a third party's belief in an agent's authority is often a matter of degree. That is, the fact that an organization has authorized an agent to do specific acts does not always make it reasonable for a third party to believe that the agent is authorized to do other acts as well. The nature of the agent's act, or the subject matter of a transaction to which the agent purports to commit the organization, is often a dispositive circumstance. The magnitude or scope of the agent's actual authority is also relevant. If the transaction is of a type that typically requires the approval of the organization's governing body, a third party would not be reasonable in believing that the agent has complete authority to bind the organization. For example, the fact that an organization has entrusted an officer with keys to a building does not warrant a third party's belief that the officer has been authorized to sell the building. . . .

Topic 3.   *Capacity to Act as Principal or Agent*

§3.05.   Capacity to Act as Agent

Any person may ordinarily be empowered to act so as to affect the legal relations of another. The actor's capacity governs the extent to which, by so acting, the actor becomes subject to duties and liabilities to the person whose legal relations are affected or to third parties.

Comment

. . . .

b. Capacity to affect the legal relations of another. As a general matter, any person able to act may do so with actual authority as defined in §2.01 or apparent authority as defined in §2.03. An agent's power to affect the principal's legal relations is usually limited only by the agent's ability to take action. If an agent is an individual, ability to act is a function of physical and mental ability. However, in some contexts the requisites for capacity to act as an agent are more exacting. Representing another person as a lawyer requires that the representative be a lawyer. . . .

If an agent is not an individual, ability to act is a function of the law through which the agent has legal personality. It is not necessary for an agent, as to the action taken, to have capacity to hold legal rights or be subject to liabilities.

Illustration

> 1. P permits A, P's 12-year-old child, to use P's computer, for which P has arranged Internet access. P has configured the computer such that, once the user is inside the website of T.com, a retailer of books, it is possible to order any particular book title by clicking on a button labeled "Buy It Now." Clicking on "Buy It Now" transmits the order to T.com, along with P's e-mail address, credit-card number, and password, all of which P has registered with T.com.
>
> With P's consent, A enters an order for many books from T.com. P is bound to a contract with T.com, although A lacks capacity to make contracts that are enforceable against A because A is a minor. . . .

In Illustration 1, A acted with actual authority as defined by §2.01. In contrast, if A uses the computer to order books from T.com without P's consent, A acts without actual authority. By permitting A to have access to the computer, loaded as it is with the "Buy It Now" feature, P has created the risk that A will use the feature without P's consent and without actual authority. Some uses of the facility that A may make may be so extravagant that human agents of T.com, or even T.com's own computer system, would be able to recognize that the new purchases depart from P's established purchasing pattern. Such a recognition is not compatible with the presence of apparent authority, as defined in §2.03. On the other hand, P affirmatively chose to enable the "Buy It Now" feature, which made A's unauthorized spree much easier for A to effect. Whether A acted with actual or apparent authority in so using P's computer, the contract that results between P and T may be subject to rescission if P returns the books to T and requests a refund. . . .

Power is a broader concept than authority. One who holds power is not necessarily an agent as defined in §1.01. For example, . . . a person who acts with apparent authority as defined in §2.03 has power to affect the legal relations of another person even though actual authority as defined in §2.01 is not present. A former agent, all of whose actual authority has been revoked by the principal, may act with apparent authority as defined in §2.03. . . .

CHAPTER 4.   RATIFICATION

§4.01.   Ratification Defined

(1) Ratification is the affirmance of a prior act done by another, whereby the act is given effect as if done by an agent acting with actual authority.

(2) [Subject to §§4.03-4.07, a] person ratifies an act by

(a) manifesting assent that the act shall affect the person's legal relations, or

(b) conduct that justifies a reasonable assumption that the person so consents. . . .

Comment

. . . .

b. The nature and effect of ratification. . . . [R]atification consists of an externally observable manifestation of assent to be bound by the prior act of another person. When the prior act did not otherwise affect the legal relations of the ratifier, ratification provides the basis on which the ratifier's legal relations are affected by the act. . . . [W]hen a person ratifies another's act, the legal consequence is that the person's legal relations are affected as they would have been had the actor been an agent acting with actual authority at the time of the act. . . .

Ratification often serves the function of clarifying situations of ambiguous or uncertain authority. A principal's ratification confirms or validates an agent's right to have acted as the agent did. . . . [B]y replicating the effects of actual authority, the principal's ratification eliminates claims the principal would otherwise have against the agent for acting without actual authority. . . . The principal's ratification. . . . is effective even when the third party knew that the agent lacked authority to bind the principal but nonetheless dealt with the agent.

. . . . Although ratification creates the legal effects of actual authority, it reverses in time the sequence between an agent's conduct and the principal's manifestation of assent. If the principal ratifies, the relevant time for determining legal consequences is the time of the agent's act. See §4.02, Comment *b*. Thus, if the agent purported to commit the principal to a transaction, the principal and third party become bound as of the time of the agent's commitment when the principal ratifies. . . . If the agent receives a notification, or learns information relevant to the action the agent takes, the notification is effective as to the principal, and knowledge of the information is imputed to the principal, as of the time of the agent's act if the principal ratifies it. . . .

. . . . In most cases in which the outcome turns on whether a principal has ratified, the claim of ratification is asserted by a third party who seeks to bind the principal in the absence of other bases to attribute the legal consequences of an agent's act to the principal. It is fair to hold the principal to such consequences when the principal has, after the fact, assented to the agent's act. The principal's ability to ratify also enables the principal to create a clear basis on which to hold the third party to transactions that are desirable from the principal's perspective. . . .

. . . . Ratification is an all-or-nothing proposition in two basic respects. First, in most cases, by ratifying the principal eliminates claims the principal might otherwise have against the agent for acting without actual authority. . . . Were the doctrine otherwise, the principal could speculate at the agent's expense by ratifying a transaction as against the third party, but holding the agent accountable if, after the time of ratification, the transaction turned out to be a losing proposition for the principal. Second, a principal must ratify a single transaction in its entirety, thereby becoming subject to its burdens as well as enjoying its benefits. . . .

d. Actions that constitute ratification. Ratification requires an objectively or externally observable indication that a person consents that another's prior act shall affect the person's legal relations. To constitute ratification, the consent need not be communicated to the third party or the agent. . . .

Conduct demonstrates consent to becoming subject to the legal consequences of another's act in [] two situations. . . . First, a person may ratify an act by manifesting assent that the act affect the person's legal relations. Second, the person may ratify the act through conduct justifiable only on the assumption that the person consents to be bound by the act's legal consequences. For example, knowing acceptance of the benefit of a transaction ratifies the act of entering into the transaction. This is so even though the person also manifests dissent to becoming bound by the act's legal consequences. . . .

It is a question of fact whether conduct is sufficient to indicate consent. Conduct that can be otherwise explained may not effect ratification. For example, a principal's failure to terminate or reprimand an employee by itself is not likely to ratify the employee's unauthorized action because the employer may have varied reasons for failing to take action adverse to an employee. On the other hand, if the employer is aware of ongoing conduct encompassing numerous acts by the employee, failure to terminate may constitute ratification, as in some circumstances may the promotion or celebration of such an employee. . . .

f. Failure to act as ratification. A principal may ratify an act by failing to object to it or to repudiate it. . . . when the [principal] has notice that others are likely to draw such an inference from silence. . . .

Delay in expressing an objection to an unauthorized act may result in ratification, depending on the length of time that elapses between the time the principal learns of the unauthorized act and the time the principal manifests an objection. It is a question of fact in the particular circumstances whether the lapse in time is sufficient to constitute ratification.

g. Receipt or retention of benefits. A person may ratify an act under subsection (2)(b) by receiving or retaining benefits it generates if the person has knowledge of material facts . . . and no independent claim to the benefit. If a principal retains a benefit, and additionally, manifests dissent to the agent's act, the third party has a choice. The third party may elect to treat the principal's retention of the benefit as a ratification or may rescind the transaction. . . .

§4.02. Effect of Ratification

(1) Subject to the exceptions stated in subsection (2), ratification retroactively creates the effects of actual authority.

(2) Ratification is not effective:

(a) in favor of a person who causes it by misrepresentation or other conduct that would make a contract voidable;

(b) in favor of an agent against a principal when the principal ratifies to avoid a loss; or

(c) to diminish the rights or other interests of persons, not parties to the transaction, that were acquired in the subject matter prior to the ratification.

Comment

. . . .

b. Impact and irrevocability. Ratification has an immediate effect on legal relations between the principal and agent, the principal and the third party, and the agent and the third party. Ratification recasts those legal relations as they would have been had the agent acted with actual authority. Legal consequences thus "relate back" to the time the agent acted. . . .

Moreover, with the exception stated in subsection (2)(b), ratification extinguishes claims that the principal would otherwise have against the agent by exonerating the agent. . . .

c. Ratification induced by fraud or by conduct that would make a contract voidable. The exception stated in subsection (2)(a) reflects the general principle that a person who acquires rights through misrepresentation, or through the exercise of duress or undue influence, may not enforce them against the person whose assent was thereby affected or impaired. See Restatement, Second, Contracts §§164, 175 & 177. . . .

d. Principal ratifies to avoid a loss. [U]nder subsection (2)(a), ratification is not effective on behalf of one who induces it by conduct that would make a contract voidable. The same general principle underlies subsection (2)(b). In situations governed by this rule, an agent's unauthorized act has placed the principal in a position in which the principal must take affirmative steps to avoid loss. The principal's action is operative as to the principal's legal relations with third parties but, as to legal relations between the principal and the agent, does not exonerate the agent or constitute consent to the agent's actions. . . .

§4.06. Knowledge Requisite to Ratification

A person is not bound by a ratification made without knowledge of material facts involved in the original act when the person was unaware of such lack of knowledge.

Comment

. . . .

b. Effect of lack of knowledge. A person who has ratified is not bound by the ratification if it was made without knowledge of material facts about the act of the agent or other actor. . . . The burden of establishing that a ratification was made with knowledge is on the party attempting to establish that ratification occurred. . . .

c. Material facts. Not all facts are material for purposes of this doctrine. The point of materiality in this context is the relevance of the fact to the principal's consent to have legal relations affected by the agent's act. . . .

d. Risk of lack of knowledge. Ratification is the consequence of a choice freely made by the principal. The principal may choose to ratify the action of an agent or other actor without knowing material facts. A factfinder may conclude that a principal has made such a choice when the principal is shown to have had knowledge of facts that would have led a reasonable person to investigate further, but the principal ratified without further investigation. . . .

CHAPTER 6. CONTRACTS AND OTHER TRANSACTIONS WITH THIRD PARTIES

Topic 1. Parties to Contracts

§6.01. Agent for Disclosed Principal

When an agent acting with actual or apparent authority makes a contract on behalf of a disclosed principal,

(1) the principal and the third party are parties to the contract; and

(2) the agent is not a party to the contract unless the agent and third party agree otherwise.

Comment

a. Scope . . . . A principal is disclosed when the third party has notice that an agent is acting for a principal and has notice of the principal's identity. . . .

b. Bases and consequences of contractual liability when agent acts on behalf of disclosed principal . . . . An agent has power to make contracts on behalf of the agent's principal when the agent acts with actual or apparent authority. This power is consistent with the bargain principle in contemporary contract law under which "the formation of a contract requires a bargain in which there is a manifestation of mutual assent to the exchange and a consideration." Restatement, Second, Contracts §17(1). An agent enters into a contract on behalf of the agent's principal by manifesting assent to an exchange that constitutes valid consideration. The third party manifests assent to the exchange to the agent, having notice that the agent acts on behalf of a particular principal. . . .

A principal may also be subject to liability as a consequence of an agent's promise, unsupported by consideration, that should reasonably be expected to induce action or forbearance on the part of a third party. See Restatement, Second, Contracts §90(1). . . .

Through ratification, a person may become a party to a contract purportedly made on that person's behalf by another who acted without actual or apparent authority. . . .

c. Contract made on behalf of a disclosed principal. If an agent makes a contract in the name of a principal or a description in the contract is sufficient to identify the principal, the principal is a disclosed principal and is a party to the contract. . . .

Additionally, a principal may be disclosed even though the contract does not name or identify the principal; it is sufficient that the third party has notice of the principal's identity. . . . Unless the contract explicitly excludes the principal as a party, parol evidence is admissible to identify a principal and to subject the principal to liability on a contract made by an agent. . . .

§6.02. Agent for Unidentified Principal

When an agent acting with actual or apparent authority makes a contract on behalf of an unidentified principal,

(1) the principal and the third party are parties to the contract; and

(2) the agent is a party to the contract unless the agent and the third party agree otherwise.

Comment

a. Scope. . . . A principal is unidentified when the third person has notice that the agent acts on behalf of a principal but does not have notice of the principal's identity. . . .

b. Bases of contractual liability when agent acts on behalf of unidentified principal. . . . An agent has power to make contracts on behalf of an unidentified principal when the agent acts with actual or apparent authority, just as an agent acting with actual or apparent authority has power to make contracts on behalf of a disclosed principal. . . .

. . . . [A]n agent who makes a contract on behalf of an unidentified principal becomes a party to the contract unless the third party and the agent agree otherwise. When a third party has notice that an agent deals on behalf of a principal but does not have notice of the principal's identity,. . . . a third party will be unable to assess the principal's reputation, assets, and other indicia of creditworthiness and ability to perform duties under the contract. . . .

An unidentified principal becomes a party to a contract made by an agent who acts with actual or apparent authority, unless the agent and the third party agree that the principal shall not become a party. . . . Although a third party who contracts with an agent for an unidentified principal may rely on the agent's liability as a party to a contract, the principal becomes a party because the agent acts on the principal's behalf and because ordinarily a third party would wish to have the liability of the person on whose behalf the agent contracts.

Through ratification, a person may become a party to a contract purportedly made on that person's behalf by another who acted without actual or apparent authority. See §4.02.

c. Contract made on behalf of unidentified principal. A principal is unidentified when the third party does not have notice of the principal's identity at the time the agent enters into a contract on the principal's behalf. . . . Regardless of the source of notice of the principal's identity, once the third party has such notice, the third party is in a position to assess the principal's reliability. . . .

A person who wishes to act as an undisclosed or unidentified principal to a contract may provide instructions to an agent prohibiting disclosure of the principal's existence or identity in the agent's dealings with third parties on the principal's behalf. If the agent then reveals the principal's identity contrary to those instructions, or the third party otherwise learns the principal's identity, the principal nevertheless will be bound by the contract if the agent acted with actual or apparent authority in making it. . . .

If an agent makes a contract in the agent's name despite instructions from the principal to contract only in the principal's name, the principal is a party to the contract unless by its terms the contract excludes the principal as a party. . . .

§6.03. Agent for Undisclosed Principal

When an agent acting with actual authority makes a contract on behalf of an undisclosed principal,

(1) unless excluded by the contract, the principal is a party to the contract;

(2) the agent and the third party are parties to the contract; and

(3) the principal, if a party to the contract, and the third party have the same rights, liabilities, and defenses against each other as if the principal made the contract personally. . . .

Comment

. . . .

b. Rationales for contractual liability. . . . . [W]hen an agent acts on behalf of an undisclosed principal, the . . . . third party's manifestation of assent is made to the agent to whom the third party expects to render performance and from whom the third party expects to receive performance. In contrast, when an agent makes a contract on behalf of a disclosed principal, the third party has notice of the principal's existence and identity. . . . When an agent makes a contract on behalf of an unidentified principal, the third party has notice that the agent acts on behalf of a principal but does not have notice of the principal's identity. . . . In both cases, the third party manifests assent to an agent with notice that the agent represents another person who will be a party to the contract.

. . . . If an agent acts with actual authority in making a contract on an undisclosed principal's behalf, the basis for treating the principal as a party to the contract is that the agent acted reasonably on the basis of the principal's manifestation of assent to the agent. See §§2.01 and 2.02. The principal's liability on the contract is thus consistent with the agent's reasonable understanding of the principal's wishes. The principal has rights under the contract because the agent acted on the principal's behalf in making the contract. A third party, however, may exclude an undisclosed principal as a party to a contract by explicitly so providing in a contract. . . .

c. Contract made on behalf of undisclosed principal . . . . Whether an agent acts on behalf of an undisclosed principal is a question of fact. Parol evidence is admissible to prove that an agent entered into a contract on behalf of an undisclosed principal, although the contract is evidenced by a writing or record that does not mention the principal. Parol evidence is not admissible to show that the agent is not subject to liability. The writing or record evidencing the contract between the agent and the third party would be contradicted by parol evidence admitted to show that it was intended that the agent would not be a party to the contract.

An undisclosed principal only becomes a party to a contract when an agent acts on the principal's behalf in making the contract. Thus, an undisclosed principal does not become a party to a contract when the agent does not intend to act for the principal. . . .

A principal is undisclosed if, at the time a contract is made, the third party with whom the agent deals has no notice that the agent is acting on behalf of a principal. It is a question of fact whether the third party has received sufficient notice that the contract is made with an agent who represents a principal and sufficient notice of that principal's identity. The third party is not subject to a duty to discover the principal's existence or identity; the responsibility is the agent's if the agent wishes to avoid personal liability on the contract. However, a third party may have sufficient notice of the principal's existence or identity from sources apart from the agent. . . .

As a party to a contract made by an agent, an undisclosed principal may assert defenses available to a party that would not be available to an assignee of the contract. . . .

d. Circumstances that affect rights or liabilities of undisclosed principal; contract excluding undisclosed principal as party. An undisclosed principal does not become a party to a contract if the contract excludes the principal. An explicit exclusion limits the third party's manifestation of assent to be bound. . . .

Illustration

5. A enters into a stock-purchase agreement with T Corporation. The agreement contains a representation made by A that A acts solely for A's account and that no other person will have any interest in the securities that A will acquire from T Corporation. The agreement excludes P, A's undisclosed principal, from rights or obligations under the agreement.

.... If an agent falsely represents that the agent does not act on behalf of a principal, the third party may avoid a contract made with the agent. ... A third party may avoid a contract made by an agent acting for an undisclosed principal if the agent or the principal knows or has reason to know that the third party would not have dealt with the principal as a party to the contract. ...

e. Position of agent as party to contract. .... If sued on the contract, the agent may assert all defenses arising from the transaction and defenses personal to the agent. ...

Restatement (Second) of Conflict of Laws (1971 (revised 1988))

EDITORS' NOTE

In the United States, contract law is, for the most part, state law. There are federal treaties, statutes, and regulations that can supersede state contract law in particular transactions or disputes. But, the American common law of contracts and the statutory scheme that most significantly overlaps for purposes of most of this Supplement's users (the Uniform Commercial Code, as enacted in one or more particular states) are both creatures of state law.

When all parties to a particular transaction reside in the same state at all relevant times, all aspects of the transaction occurred or were to occur in that same state, and any dispute arising out of the transaction is being litigated or otherwise resolved in that same state, idiosyncratic state common or statutory law ought not pose a particular challenge for the parties, their counsel, or a court or other tribunal hearing the parties' dispute. On the other hand, when the parties reside in more than one state, the transaction takes place across state borders or in yet another state beside the ones in which the parties reside, or the dispute arising out of the transaction is pending in yet another state, the choice of one state's law to govern the transaction, dispute, or both, can have significant implications.

One of the most common standard-form and negotiated contract terms is one choosing which jurisdiction's laws will govern a contract and any dispute that arises from it. Because of the ubiquity of these choice-of-law clauses in standard-form and negotiated contracts, and because the bulk of common and statutory law governing contracts and contract disputes is state law, understanding the law governing contracts requires some awareness of the law governing conflict of laws.

The first Restatement of Conflict of Laws, published in 1934, was the third restatement completed by the American Law Institute (ALI), following the first Restatements of Contracts (1932) and Agency (1933). Harvard Law School Professor Joseph Beale served as the principal reporter for the first Restatement of Conflict of Laws. Professors Herbert Goodrich (University of Pennsylvania School of Law) and Austin Scott (Harvard Law School) also made substantial contributions.

Published in 1971, the Restatement (Second) of Conflict of Laws was seventeen years in the making and marked a significant departure in approach from the first Restatement.[1] Professor Willis Reese (Columbia University School of Law) served as the principal reporter for the Restatement (Second), with the then-venerable Professor Austin W. Scott as associate reporter. Perhaps coincidentally, perhaps not, seventeen years following the Restatement (Second)'s publication, the ALI published a compilation of revisions in 1988, including a revised version of Section 187, reproduced below.

The Restatement (Second) of Conflict of Laws devotes thirty-six sections to topics related to contracts, some of which have been superseded by treaty, statute, or more recent restatement elsewhere. This Supplement reproduces only the three sections addressing general principles of contract validity, rights, and obligations (§§186-188), as well as two sections that set forth general principles and limitations that apply across all substantive areas of the law the Restatement (Second) addresses (§§6 and 9). The bulk of the provisions in the contracts chapter deal with particular types of contracts (e.g., contracts to transfer interests in land, life insurance contracts, suretyship contract, negotiable instruments, arbitration agreements) or particular issues (e.g., capacity to contract, illegality, contract interpretation, assignability). The provisions relating to particular issues (§§198-213 & 221) tend to follow the general principles of §§186-188, with only occasional minor variations. The provisions relating to particular types of contracts (§§189-197 & 214-219) are more idiosyncratic. In the inaugural appearance of excerpts from this Restatement in this Supplement, the editors elected to focus on the forest, rather than the trees. However, if these issues pique your interest, there is much more detail to explore in the remainder of Chapter 8 of the Restatement (Second) of Conflict of Laws.

The ALI recently undertook a Restatement (Third) of Conflict of Laws. The first preliminary draft of a small fraction of the project's anticipated scope appeared in late 2015 and it is unlikely the project will be complete until the 2020s. You can follow its progress at https://www.ali.org/projects/show/conflict-laws/.

The following provisions are copyright 1971 by the American Law Institute. Reprinted with permission. All rights reserved.

---

1. Then-ALI Director Herbert Wechsler, a long-time professor at Columbia Law School who had played an integral role in the Nuremberg war crime trials after World War II and served as Chief Reporter for the Model Penal Code prior to his 1963 appointment as ALI Director, wrote that the Restatement (Second) represented "far more than a current version of the old" – indeed, "a fresh treatment of the subject." He continued:

> It is a treatment that takes full account of the enormous change in dominant judicial thought respecting conflicts problems that has taken place in relatively recent years. The essence of that change has been the jettisoning of a multiplicity of rigid rules in favor of standards of greater flexibility, according sensitivity in judgment to important values that were formerly ignored. Such a transformation in the corpus of the law reduces certitude as well as certainty, posing a special problem in the process of restatement. Its solution lies in candid recognition that black-letter formulations often must consist of open-ended standards, gaining further content from reasoned elaboration in the comments and specific instances of application given there or in the notes of the Reporter. That technique is not unique to Conflicts but the situation here has called for its employment quite pervasively throughout these volumes. The result presents a striking contrast to the first Restatement in which dogma was so thoroughly enshrined.

Restatement (Second) of Conflict of Laws vii (1971).

CHAPTER 1.   INTRODUCTION

§6.   Choice-of-Law Principles

(1) A court, subject to constitutional restrictions, will follow a statutory directive of its own state on choice of law.

(2) When there is no such directive, the factors relevant to the choice of the applicable rule of law include

    (a) the needs of the interstate and international systems,

    (b) the relevant policies of the forum,

    (c) the relevant policies of other interested states and the relative interests of those states in the determination of the particular issue,

    (d) the protection of justified expectations,

    (e) the basic policies underlying the particular field of law,

    (f) certainty, predictability and uniformity of result, and

    (g) ease in the determination and application of the law to be applied.

Comment

. . . .

c. Rationale. Legislatures usually legislate, and courts usually adjudicate, only with the local situation in mind. They rarely give thought to the extent to which the laws they enact, and the common law rules they enunciate, should apply to out-of-state facts. When there are no adequate directives in the statute or in the case law, the court will take account of the factors listed in [§6(2)] in determining the state whose local law will be applied to determine the issue at hand. It is not suggested that this list of factors is exclusive. Undoubtedly, a court will on occasion give consideration to other factors in deciding a question of choice of law. Also it is not suggested that the factors mentioned are listed in the order of their relative importance. Varying weight will be given to a particular factor, or to a group of factors, in different areas of choice of law. So, for example, . . . the policies in favor of protecting the justified expectations of the parties and of effectuating the basic policy underlying the particular field of law come to the fore in the rule that, subject to certain limitations, the parties can choose the law to govern their contract (see §187). . . .

At least some of the factors mentioned in this Subsection will point in different directions in all but the simplest case. Hence any rule of choice of law, like any other common law rule, represents an accommodation of conflicting values. Those chapters in the Restatement of this Subject which are concerned with choice of law state the rules which the courts have evolved in accommodation of the factors listed in this Subsection. In certain areas, as in parts of Property (Chapter 9), such rules are sufficiently precise to permit them to be applied in the decision of a case without explicit reference to the factors which underlie them. In other areas, such as . . . Contracts (Chapter 8), the difficulties and complexities involved have as yet prevented the courts from formulating a precise rule, or series of rules, which provide a satisfactory accommodation of the underlying factors in all of the situations which may arise. All that can presently be done in these areas is to state a general principle, such as application of the local law "of the state of most significant relationship", which provides some clue to the correct approach but does not furnish precise answers. . . . [T]he courts must look in each case to the underlying factors themselves in order to arrive at a decision which will best accommodate them. . . .

d. Needs of the interstate and international systems. Probably the most important function of choice-of-law rules is to make the interstate and international systems work well. Choice-of-law rules, among other things, should seek to further harmonious relations between states and to facilitate commercial intercourse between them. In formulating rules of choice of law, a state should have regard for the needs and policies of other states and of the community of states. Rules of choice of law formulated with regard for such needs and policies are likely to commend themselves to other states and to be adopted by these states. Adoption of the same choice-of-law rules by many states will further the needs of the interstate and international systems and likewise the values of certainty, predictability and uniformity of result.

e. Relevant policies of the state of the forum. Two situations should be distinguished. One is where the state of the forum has no interest in the case apart from the fact that it is the place of the trial of the action. Here the only relevant policies of the state of the forum will be embodied in its rules relating to trial administration. . . . The second situation is where the state of the forum has an interest in the case apart from the fact that it is the place of trial. In this latter situation, relevant policies of the state of the forum may be embodied in rules that do not relate to trial administration.

The problem dealt with in this Comment arises in the common situation where a statute or common law rule of the forum was formulated solely with the intrastate situation in mind or, at least, where there is no evidence to suggest that the statute or rule was intended to have extraterritorial application. If the legislature or court (in the case of a common law rule) did have intentions with respect to the range of application of a statute or common law rule and these intentions can be ascertained, the rule of Subsection (1) is applicable. If not, the court will interpret the statute or rule in the light of the factors stated in Subsection (2).

Every rule of law, whether embodied in a statute or in a common law rule, was designed to achieve one or more purposes. A court should have regard for these purposes in determining whether to apply its own rule or the rule of another state in the decision of a particular issue. If the purposes sought to be achieved by a local statute or common law rule would be furthered by its application to out-of-state facts, this is a weighty reason why such application should be made. On the other hand, the court is under no compulsion to apply the statute or rule to such out-of-state facts since the originating legislature or court had no ascertainable intentions on the subject. The court must decide for itself whether the purposes sought to be achieved by a local statute or rule should be furthered at the expense of the other choice-of-law factors mentioned in this Subsection.

f. Relevant policies of other interested states. In determining a question of choice of law, the forum should give consideration not only to its own relevant policies (see Comment *e*) but also to the relevant policies of all other interested states. The forum should seek to reach a result that will achieve the best possible accommodation of these policies. The forum should also appraise the relative interests of the states involved in the determination of the particular issue. In general, it is fitting that the state whose interests are most deeply affected should have its local law applied. . . .

The content of the relevant local law rule of a state may be significant in determining whether this state is the state with the dominant interest. So, for example, application of a state's statute or common law rule which would absolve the defendant from liability could hardly be justified on the basis of this state's interest in the welfare of the injured plaintiff.

g. Protection of justified expectations. This is an important value in all fields of the law, including choice of law. Generally speaking, it would be unfair and improper to hold a person liable under the local law of one state when he had justifiably molded his conduct to conform to the requirements of another state. Also, it is in part because of this factor that the parties are free within broad limits to choose the law to govern the validity of their contract (see §187). . . .

h. Basic policies underlying particular field of law. This factor is of particular importance in situations where the policies of the interested states are largely the same but where there are nevertheless minor differences between their relevant local law rules. In such instances, there is good reason for the court to apply the local law of that state which will best achieve the basic policy, or policies, underlying the particular field of law involved. . . .

i. Predictability and uniformity of result. These are important values in all areas of the law. To the extent that they are attained in choice of law, forum shopping will be discouraged. These values can, however, be purchased at too great a price. In a rapidly developing area, such as choice of law, it is often more important that good rules be developed than that predictability and uniformity of result should be assured through continued adherence to existing rules. Predictability and uniformity of result are of particular importance in areas where the parties are likely to give advance thought to the legal consequences of their transactions. It is partly on account of these factors that the parties are permitted within broad limits to choose the law that will determine the validity and effect of their contract (see §187) . . . .

§9.   Limitations on Choice of Law

A court may not apply the local law of its own state to determine a particular issue unless such application of this law would be reasonable in the light of the relationship of the state and of other states to the person, thing or occurrence involved.

Comment

. . . .

d. Basic criterion. A state has jurisdiction to apply its local law to determine a particular issue if the issue is within the reasonable scope of the state's regulatory power. A state should not improperly impinge upon the interests of other states by applying its local law to determine an issue with which it has no sufficient concern. . . .

e. Meaning of "local law". The term, "local law," as used in this Section, includes both a state's decisional and statutory law, exclusive of its rules of Conflict of Laws. . . .

g. Application of the local law of another state. . . . A court may not apply the local law of another state to determine a particular issue unless application of this law would be reasonable in the light of the relationship of this state and of other states to the person, thing or occurrence involved as to the particular issue. . . .

CHAPTER 8.   CONTRACTS

Topic 1.   Validity of Contracts and Rights Created Thereby

TITLE A.   GENERAL PRINCIPLES

§186.   Applicable Law

Issues in contract are determined by the law chosen by the parties in accordance with the rule of §187 and otherwise by the law selected in accordance with the rule of §188.

Comment

a. Scope of section. The rule of this Section states a principle applicable to all contracts and to all issues in contract. . . .

b. Reference is to "local law" of selected state. The reference, in the absence of a contrary indication of intention (see §187, Comment *b*), is to the "local law" of the state of the applicable law and not to that state's . . . choice-of-law rules . . . .

Values of certainty of result and of ease of application dictate that the forum should apply the local law of the selected state . . . . There is no basis for supposing that fairness requires the forum to apply the choice-of-law rules of the selected state. . . .

. . . [I]n judging a state's interest in the application of one of its local law rules, the forum should concern itself with the question whether the courts of that state would have applied this rule in the decision of the case. The fact that these courts would have applied this rule may indicate that an important interest of that state would be served if the rule were applied by the forum. Conversely, the fact that these courts would not have applied this rule may indicate that no important interest of that state would be infringed if the rule were not applied by the forum . . . .

Illustration

1. In state X, A and B enter into a contract which is to be performed in state Y. B, who is domiciled in Y, brings suit against A in state Z for breach of contract. If the Z court determines that Y is the state of most significant relationship, the Z court will apply Y local law. In determining whether Y is the state of most significant relationship, the Z court may consider whether the Y courts would have applied their own local law or the local law of another state in deciding the particular issue. . . .

§187. Law of the State Chosen by the Parties

(1) The law of the state chosen by the parties to govern their contractual rights and duties will be applied if the particular issue is one which the parties could have resolved by an explicit provision in their agreement directed to that issue.

(2) The law of the state chosen by the parties to govern their contractual rights and duties will be applied, even if the particular issue is one which the parties could not have resolved by an explicit provision in their agreement directed to that issue, unless either

(a) the chosen state has no substantial relationship to the parties or the transaction and there is no other reasonable basis for the parties' choice, or

(b) application of the law of the chosen state would be contrary to a fundamental policy of a state which has a materially greater interest than the chosen state in the determination of the particular issue and which, under the rule of §188, would be the state of the applicable law in the absence of an effective choice of law by the parties. . . .

Comment

a. Scope of section. The rule of this Section is applicable only in situations where it is established to the satisfaction of the forum that the parties have chosen the state of the applicable law. When the parties have made such a choice, they will usually refer expressly to the state of the chosen law in their contract, and this is the best way of insuring that their desires will be given effect. . . .

. . . [T]he rule of this Section is inapplicable unless it can be established that the parties have chosen the state of the applicable law. It does not suffice to demonstrate that the parties, if they had thought about the matter, would have wished to have the law of a particular state applied. . . .

b. *Impropriety or mistake.* A choice-of-law provision, like any other contractual provision, will not be given effect if the consent of one of the parties to its inclusion in the contract was obtained by improper means, such as by misrepresentation, duress, or undue influence, or by mistake. Whether such consent was in fact obtained by improper means or by mistake will be determined by the forum in accordance with its own legal principles. A factor which the forum may consider is whether the choice-of-law provision is contained in an "adhesion" contract, namely one that is drafted unilaterally by the dominant party and then presented on a "take-it-or-leave-it" basis to the weaker party who has no real opportunity to bargain about its terms. Such contracts are usually prepared in printed form, and frequently at least some of their provisions are in extremely small print. Common examples are tickets of various kinds and insurance policies. Choice-of-law provisions contained in such contracts are usually respected. Nevertheless, the forum will scrutinize such contracts with care and will refuse to apply any choice-of-law provision they may contain if to do so would result in substantial injustice to the adherent. . . .

c. *Issues the parties could have determined by explicit agreement directed to particular issue.* . . . The parties, generally speaking, have power to determine the terms of their contractual engagements. They may spell out these terms in the contract. In the alternative, they may incorporate into the contract by reference extrinsic material which may, among other things, be the provisions of some foreign law. . . . [M]ost rules of contract law are designed to fill gaps in a contract which the parties could themselves have filled with express provisions. This is generally true, for example, of rules relating to construction, to conditions precedent and subsequent, to sufficiency of performance and to excuse for nonperformance, including questions of frustration and impossibility. As to all such matters, the forum will apply the provisions of the chosen law. . . .

d. *Issues the parties could not have determined by explicit agreement directed to particular issue.* The rule of [§187(2)] applies. . . . when it is sought to have the chosen law determine issues which the parties could not have determined by explicit agreement directed to the particular issue. Examples of such questions are those involving capacity, formalities and substantial validity. A person cannot vest himself with contractual capacity by stating in the contract that he has such capacity. He cannot dispense with formal requirements, such as that of a writing, by agreeing with the other party that the contract shall be binding without them. Nor can he by a similar device avoid issues of substantial validity, such as whether the contract is illegal. Usually, however, the local law of the state chosen by the parties will be applied to regulate matters of this sort. . . .

Permitting the parties . . . to choose the applicable law is not, of course, tantamount to giving them complete freedom to contract as they will. Their power to choose the applicable law is subject to the two qualifications set forth in this Subsection (see Comments *f-g*). . . .

f. *Requirement of reasonable basis for parties' choice.* The forum will not apply the chosen law to determine issues the parties could not have determined by explicit agreement directed to the particular issue if the parties had no reasonable basis for choosing this law. . . .

When the state of the chosen law has some substantial relationship to the parties or the contract, the parties will be held to have had a reasonable basis for their choice. This will be the case, for example, when this state is that where performance by one of the parties is to take place or where one of the parties is domiciled or has his principal place of business. The same will also be the case when this state is the place of contracting except, perhaps, in the unusual situation where this place is wholly fortuitous and bears no real relation either to the contract or to the parties. These situations are mentioned only for purposes of example. There are undoubtedly still other situations where the state of the chosen law will have a sufficiently close relationship to the parties and the contract to make the parties' choice reasonable.

The parties to a multistate contract may have a reasonable basis for choosing a state with which the contract has no substantial relationship. For example, when contracting in countries whose legal systems are strange to them as well as relatively immature, the parties should be able to choose a law on the ground that they know it well and that it is sufficiently developed. For only in this way can they be sure of knowing accurately the extent of their rights and duties under the contract. So parties to a contract for the transportation of goods by sea between two countries with relatively undeveloped legal systems should be permitted to submit their contract to some well-known and highly elaborated commercial law.

g. When application of chosen law would be contrary to fundamental policy of state of otherwise applicable law. Fulfillment of the parties' expectations is not the only value in contract law; regard must also be had for state interest and for state regulation. The chosen law should not be applied without regard for the interests of the state . . . of the [otherwise] applicable law. The forum will not refrain from applying the chosen law merely because this would lead to a different result than would be obtained under the local law of the state of the otherwise applicable law. Application of the chosen law will be refused only (1) to protect a fundamental policy of the state which, under the rule of §188, would be the state of the otherwise applicable law, provided (2) that this state has a materially greater interest than the state of the chosen law in the determination of the particular issue. . . .

No detailed statement can be made of the situations where a "fundamental" policy of the state of the otherwise applicable law will be found to exist. An important consideration is the extent to which the significant contacts are grouped in this state. . . . The more closely the state of the chosen law is related to the contract and the parties, the more fundamental must be the policy of the state of the otherwise applicable law to justify denying effect to the choice-of-law provision.

To be "fundamental," a policy must in any event be a substantial one. . . . [A] fundamental policy may be embodied in a statute which makes one or more kinds of contracts illegal or which is designed to protect a person against the oppressive use of superior bargaining power. . . .

§188. Law Governing in Absence of Effective Choice by the Parties

(1) The rights and duties of the parties with respect to an issue in contract are determined by the local law of the state which, with respect to that issue, has the most significant relationship to the transaction and the parties. . . .

(2) In the absence of an effective choice of law by the parties (see §187), the contacts to be taken into account . . . to determine the law applicable to an issue include:

(a) the place of contracting,

(b) the place of negotiation of the contract,

(c) the place of performance,

(d) the location of the subject matter of the contract, and

(e) the domicil, residence, nationality, place of incorporation and place of business of the parties.

These contacts are to be evaluated according to their relative importance with respect to the particular issue.

(3) If the place of negotiating the contract and the place of performance are in the same state, the local law of this state will usually be applied. . . .

Comment

a. Scope of section. The rule of this Section applies in all situations where there has not been an effective choice of the applicable law by the parties (see §187). . . .

b. Rationale. The principles stated in §6 underlie all rules of choice of law and are used in evaluating the significance of a relationship, with respect to the particular issue, to the potentially interested states, the transaction and the parties. The factors listed in Subsection (2) of the rule of §6 can be divided into five groups. One group is concerned with the fact that in multistate cases it is essential that the rules of decision promote mutually harmonious and beneficial relationships in the interdependent community, federal or international. The second group focuses upon the purposes, policies, aims and objectives of each of the competing local law rules urged to govern and upon the concern of the potentially interested states in having their rules applied. The factors in this second group are at times referred to as "state interests" or as appertaining to an "interested state." The third group involves the needs of the parties, namely the protection of their justified expectations and certainty and predictability of result. The fourth group is directed to implementation of the basic policy underlying the particular field of law, such as torts or contracts, and the fifth group is concerned with the needs of judicial administration, namely with ease in the determination and application of the law to be applied.

The factors listed in Subsection (2) of the rule of §6 vary somewhat in importance from field to field and from issue to issue. Thus, the protection of the justified expectations of the parties is of considerable importance in contracts whereas it is of relatively little importance in torts. . . . In the torts area, it is the rare case where the parties give advance thought to the law that may be applied to determine the legal consequences of their actions. On the other hand, parties enter into contracts with forethought and are likely to consult a lawyer before doing so. Sometimes, they will intend that their rights and obligations under the contract should be determined by the local law of a particular state. In this event, the local law of this state will be applied, subject to the qualifications stated in the rule of §187. In situations where the parties did not give advance thought to the question of which should be the state of the applicable law, or where their intentions in this regard cannot be ascertained, it may at least be said, subject perhaps to rare exceptions, that they expected that the provisions of the contract would be binding upon them.

. . . [P]rotecting the expectations of the parties gives importance in turn to the values of certainty, predictability and uniformity of result. For unless these values are attained, the expectations of the parties are likely to be disappointed.

Protection of the justified expectations of the parties by choice-of-law rules in the field of contracts is supported both by those factors in Subsection (2) of §6 which are directed to the furtherance of the needs of the parties and by those factors which are directed to implementation of the basic policy underlying the particular field of law. Protection of the justified expectations of the parties is the basic policy underlying the field of contracts.

Protection of the justified expectations of the parties is a factor which varies somewhat in importance from issue to issue. . . . Parties entering a contract will expect at the very least, subject perhaps to rare exceptions, that the provisions of the contract will be binding upon them. Their expectations should not be disappointed by application of the local law rule of a state which would strike down the contract or a provision thereof unless the value of protecting the expectations of the parties is substantially outweighed in the particular case by the interest of the state with the invalidating rule in having this rule applied. The extent of the interest of a state in having its rule applied should be determined in the light of the purpose sought to be achieved by the rule and by the relation of the transaction and the parties to that state (see Comment c).

Protection of justified expectations plays a less significant role in the choice-of-law process with respect to issues that involve the nature of the obligations imposed by a contract upon the parties rather than the validity of the contract or of some provision thereof. By and large, it is for the parties themselves to determine the nature of their contractual obligations. They can spell out these obligations in the contract or, as a short-hand device, they can provide that these obligations shall be determined by the local law of a given state (see §187, Comment c). If the parties do neither of these two things with respect to an issue involving the nature of their obligations, as, for example, the time of performance, the resulting gap in their contract must be filled by application of the relevant rule of contract law of a particular state. All states have gap-filling rules of this sort, and indeed such rules comprise the major content of contract law. What is important for present purposes is that a gap in a contract usually results from the fact that the parties never gave thought to the issue involved. In such a situation, the expectations of the parties with respect to that issue are unlikely to be disappointed by application of the gap-filling rule of one state rather than of the rule of another state. Hence with respect to issues of this sort, protection of the justified expectations of the parties is unlikely to play so significant a role in the choice-of-law process. As a result, greater emphasis in fashioning choice-of-law rules in this area must be given to the other choice-of-law principles mentioned in the rule of §6.

c. Purpose of contract rule. The purpose sought to be achieved by the contract rules of the potentially interested states, and the relation of these states to the transaction and the parties, are important factors to be considered in determining the state of most significant relationship. This is because the interest of a state in having its contract rule applied in the determination of a particular issue will depend upon the purpose sought to be achieved by that rule and upon the relation of the state to the transaction and the parties. So the state where a party to the contract is domiciled has an obvious interest in the application of its contract rule designed to protect that party against the unfair use of superior bargaining power. And a state where a contract provides that a given business practice is to be pursued has an obvious interest in the application of its rule designed to regulate or to deter that business practice. . . .

Whether an invalidating rule should be applied will depend, among other things, upon whether the interest of the state in having its rule applied to strike down the contract outweighs in the particular case the value of protecting the justified expectations of the parties and upon whether some other state has a greater interest in the application of its own rule. . . .

e. Important contacts in determining state of most significant relationship. In the absence of an effective choice of law by the parties (see §187), the forum . . . should give consideration to the relevant policies of all potentially interested states and the relative interests of those states in the decision of the particular issue. The states which are most likely to be interested are those which have one or more of the following contacts with the transaction or the parties. Some of these contacts also figure prominently in the formulation of the applicable rules of choice of law.

The place of contracting. As used in th[is] Restatement . . . , the place of contracting is the place where occurred the last act necessary, under the forum's rules of offer and acceptance, to give the contract binding effect, assuming, hypothetically, that the local law of the state where the act occurred rendered the contract binding.

Standing alone, the place of contracting is a relatively insignificant contact. To be sure, in the absence of an effective choice of law by the parties, issues involving the validity of a contract will, in perhaps the majority of situations, be determined in accordance with the local law of the state of contracting. In such situations, however, this state will be the state of the applicable law for reasons additional to the fact that it happens to be the place where occurred the last act necessary to give the contract binding effect. The place of contracting, in other words, rarely stands alone and, almost invariably, is but one of several contacts in the state. Usually, this state will be the state where the parties conducted the negotiations which preceded the making of the contract. Likewise, this state will often be the state of the parties' common domicil as well. By way of contrast, the place of contracting will have little significance, if any, when it is purely fortuitous and bears no relation to the parties and the contract, such as when a letter of acceptance is mailed in a railroad station in the course of an interstate trip.

The place of negotiation. The place where the parties negotiate and agree on the terms of their contract is a significant contact. Such a state has an obvious interest in the conduct of the negotiations and in the agreement reached. This contact is of less importance when there is no one single place of negotiation and agreement, as, for example, when the parties do not meet but rather conduct their negotiations from separate states by mail or telephone.

The place of performance. The state where performance is to occur under a contract has an obvious interest in the nature of the performance and in the party who is to perform. . . . When both parties are to perform in the state, this state will have so close a relationship to the transaction and the parties that it will often be the state of the applicable law even with respect to issues that do not relate strictly to performance. . . .

On the other hand, the place of performance can bear little weight in the choice of the applicable law when (1) at the time of contracting it is either uncertain or unknown, or when (2) performance by a party is to be divided more or less equally among two or more states with different local law rules on the particular issue. . . .

Situs of the subject matter of the contract. When the contract deals with a specific physical thing, such as land or a chattel, or affords protection against a localized risk, such as the dishonesty of an employee in a fixed place of employment, the location of the thing or of the risk is significant. . . . The state where the thing or the risk is located will have a natural interest in transactions affecting it. Also the parties will regard the location of the thing or of the risk as important. Indeed, when the thing or the risk is the principal subject of the contract, it can often be assumed that the parties, to the extent that they thought about the matter at all, would expect that the local law of the state where the thing or risk was located would be applied to determine many of the issues arising under the contract.

Domicil, residence, nationality, place of incorporation, and place of business of the parties. These are all places of enduring relationship to the parties. Their significance depends largely upon the issue involved and upon the extent to which they are grouped with other contacts. So, for example, when a person has capacity to bind himself to the particular contract under the local law of the state of his domicil, there may be little reason to strike down the contract because that person lacked capacity under the local law of the state of contracting or of performance. . . . The fact that one of the parties is domiciled or does business in a particular state assumes greater importance when combined with other contacts, such as that this state is the place of contracting or of performance or the place where the other party to the contract is domiciled or does business. . . . At least with respect to most issues, a corporation's principal place of business is a more important contact than the place of incorporation, and this is particularly true in situations where the corporation does little, or no, business in the latter state. . . .

f. When place of negotiation and place of performance are in the same state. When the place of negotiation and the place of performance are in the same state, the local law of this state will usually be applied to govern issues arising under the contract, except as stated in §§189-199 and 203. A state having these contacts will usually be the state that has the greatest interest in the determination of issues arising under the contract. The local law of this state should be applied except when the principles stated in §6 require application of some other law. . . .

Restatement of Employment Law (2015)

EDITORS' NOTE

The Restatement of Employment Law, the American Law Institute's most recently-completed Restatement or Principles project excerpted in this Supplement, was published in 2015. First proposed in 2000, and then begun in earnest in 2006, by Chief Reporter Professor Samuel Estreicher (New York University School of Law), later joined by Professors Matthew Bodie (St. Louis University School of Law), Michael Harper (Boston University School of Law), and Stewart Schwab (Cornell Law School), the Restatement's stated purpose was to clarify and simplify the common law areas of employment law that govern issues not addressed by federal and state employment statutes.

Employment law exists at the intersections of common law and extensive federal and state statutory and regulatory law and, within the realm of common law, at the intersections of agency, contracts, torts, intellectual property, privacy, and unfair competition. Not surprisingly, therefore, the Restatement of Employment Law extends beyond contract law topics, tackling when an employment relationship exists, as contrasted with dealings between two "independent businesses" or "independent contractors," and the non-employee status of volunteers and controlling owners of employers (Chapter 1), employer tort liability for physical harm to employees (Chapter 4), wrongful discharge (Chapter 5), and defamation, wrongful interference, and misrepresentation (Chapter 6), employee privacy and autonomy (Chapter 7), employee's duties of loyalty and confidentiality and intellectual property rights (portions of Chapter 8), and remedies for breaches of various non-contractual duties (portions of Chapter 9).

At the same time, however, the Restatement of Employment Law covers a variety of contract law topics related to employment such as the duration, modification, and termination of employment contracts (Chapter 2), including the application of promissory estoppel as a limit on an employer's ability to terminate (§2.02(b)) and the role of the implied duty of good faith in employment relationships (§2.07);

employee compensation and benefits (Chapter 3), arising out of an employment contract or a quasi-contractual employment relationship; restrictive covenants in employment agreements (§§8.06 to 8.08); and employee remedies against employers and employer remedies against employees for breaching the employment agreement (§§9.01 to 9.04 & 9.07 to 9.08). Many of these provisions, as well as numerous comments and a select few illustrations, are reproduced below in edited form.

Employment agreements and legal and equitable claims arising out of employment relationships provide a number of cases, notes, and problems in the editors' casebook, Problems in Contract Law, as they do in other contracts casebooks. That said, our purpose here is not to try to cover the waterfront of an upper-level employment law course or even fully explore "just" the contractual issues arising between employers and those who are, were, might be, or might have been their employees. Consequently, in this inaugural appearance of the Restatement of Employment Law in this Supplement, we have selected from among the contract-related provisions and their accompanying comments and illustrations, rather than including them all. We welcome your feedback if you feel that we have been inappropriately underinclusive.

The following provisions are copyright © 2015 by the American Law Institute. Reprinted with permission. All rights reserved.

CHAPTER 2.   EMPLOYMENT CONTRACTS: TERMINATION

§2.01. Default Rule of an At-Will Employment Relationship
§2.02. Agreements and Binding Employer Promises or Statements Providing for Terms Other Than At-Will Employment
§2.03. Agreements for a Definite or Indefinite Term
§2.04. Cause for Termination of Employment Agreements
§2.05. Binding Employer Policy Statements
§2.06. Modification or Revocation of Binding Employer Policy Statements
§2.07. Implied Duty of Good Faith and Fair Dealing

CHAPTER 3.   EMPLOYMENT CONTRACTS: COMPENSATION AND BENEFITS

§3.01. Right to Earned Compensation
§3.02. Bonuses and Other Incentive Compensation
§3.03. Benefits
§3.04. Modification of Compensation or Benefits
§3.05. Implied Duty of Good Faith and Fair Dealing

CHAPTER 8.   EMPLOYEE OBLIGATIONS AND RESTRICTIVE COVENANTS

§8.06. Enforcement of Restrictive Covenants in Employment Agreements
§8.07. Protectable Interests for Restrictive Covenants
§8.08. Modification of Unreasonable Restrictive Covenant

CHAPTER 9.   REMEDIES

Part 1.   Claims Against Employers

A.   CONTRACT

Part 2.   Claims Against Employees

CHAPTER 2.   EMPLOYMENT CONTRACTS: TERMINATION

§2.01.   Default Rule of an At-Will Employment Relationship

Either party may terminate an employment relationship with or without cause unless the right to do so is limited by a statute, other law or public policy, or an agreement between the parties, a binding employer promise, or a binding employer policy statement (§2.02).

Comment

. . . .

b. Rebuttable presumption of at-will employment. . . . The high courts in 49 states and the District of Columbia recognize as the default rule the principle that employment is presumptively an at-will relationship. (The sole exception is Montana, which by statute requires "good cause" for an employer's termination of a non-probationary employee.)

The at-will presumption states a default rule that applies when the agreement between the parties or other binding employer promise or employer policy statement under §2.02 does not provide for a definite term or contain a limit on the employer's power to terminate the relationship. The default rule is also subject to contrary statute, law, or public policy. . . .

d. Statutory provision. The at-will default rule . . . does not supersede controlling legislation or other law. Virtually all legislation regulating the employment relationship restricts to some extent the kinds of adverse employment decisions employers may make. Many statutes, for example, bar employers from taking adverse employment actions against employees because the employees exercise a right under those laws by filing a claim or participating in investigatory and enforcement proceedings authorized by the law.

Section 2.01 should be read in a manner consistent with such statutory restrictions. . . .

   e. Other law or public policy. . . . [A] well-established public policy may supply a basis for limiting the employer's power to terminate an at-will employment relationship. . . . Some jurisdictions have recognized nonstatutory sources of public policy such as decisional law and certain established principles of professional or occupational responsibility. . . . Section 2.01 should be read to be consistent with such public-policy limitations. . . .

§2.02. Agreements and Binding Employer Promises or Statements Providing for Terms Other Than At-Will Employment

The employment relationship is not terminable at will by an employer if:

   (a) an agreement between the employer and the employee provides for (i) a definite term of employment, or (ii) an indefinite term of employment and requires cause (defined in §2.04) to terminate the employment (§2.03); or

   (b) a promise by the employer to limit termination of employment reasonably induces detrimental reliance by the employee . . . ; or

   (c) a binding policy statement made by the employer limits termination of employment (§2.05); or

   (d) the implied duty of good faith and fair dealing applicable to all employment relationships (§2.07) limits termination of employment; or

   (e) other established principles recognized in the general law of contracts limit termination of employment. . . .

Comment

   . . . .

   c. Promissory estoppel. Section 2.02(b) makes clear that an employer's promise that *reasonably* induces detrimental reliance by employees, or individuals about to become employees, is enforceable under the well-established doctrine of promissory estoppel under §90 of the Restatement Second, Contracts. The promise must be definite enough to reasonably induce the action taken in reliance on the promise and must in fact induce such reliance. . . . If the conditions for promissory estoppel are present, then a promise may be enforceable even though an agreement itself would not be enforceable for lack of a written document. . . .

§2.03. Agreements for a Definite or Indefinite Term

   (a) An employer must have cause (§2.04) for terminating:

      (1) an unexpired agreement for a definite term of employment; or

      (2) an agreement for an indefinite term of employment requiring cause for termination.

(b) In the absence of an employee's express agreement providing otherwise, the employee is under no reciprocal obligation to have cause to terminate the employment relationship.

Comment

. . . .

b. Agreements . . . . [A]greements between employers and their employees. . . . can provide for a definite term of employment whereby earlier termination of the agreement absent cause is a breach of contract (§2.03(a)(1)), or for an indefinite term yet require cause for termination such that termination without cause is a breach (§2.03(a)(2)), or for an indefinite term yet containing no limitation on termination (§2.01) except perhaps notice or a stipulated payment by the employer . . . .

d. Consideration or bargained-for exchange. . . . The general contract requirement of consideration or bargained-for exchange does not require identical or parallel consideration from both parties to the agreement. An employee's promise to work for the employer at stated terms is ordinarily sufficient to support a number of promises by the employer, including, for example, a promise to provide the employment on the stated terms and a promise not to terminate the relationship before the contract term ends except for cause.

e. Unilateral contracts. Some jurisdictions use a form of "unilateral contract" analysis to hold enforceable unilaterally promulgated employer statements that are provided to employees who then continue working after receiving those statements. Even in the majority of jurisdictions not relying on such analysis, certain employer policy statements (discussed in §2.05) may give rise to binding obligations even in the absence of consideration or bargained-for exchange or a showing that the employee detrimentally relied on the statements. . . .

f. Mutuality. Mutuality of obligation is not required for employment agreements to be enforceable. Even if an employer agrees to a "cause" limit on the authority to discharge or impose other discipline and, as is typical, the employee does not agree to eschew the prerogative to quit the job at any time, with or without cause, the employment agreement is nevertheless enforceable. . . . At the same time, the parties can. . . . require the employee to give advance notice of an intention to quit employment if the employee wishes to receive severance pay or other benefits that are not vested in the circumstances. . . .

h. Indefinite-term agreements. Agreements that limit the employer's power to terminate the employment relationship can override the presumption of at-will employment even if the employment term is indefinite. This Section thus departs from decisions holding that contracts for indefinite employment should always be treated as contracts terminable at will or as tantamount to such contracts unless the employee can meet special proof burdens to defeat the at-will presumption. Whether the parties contracted for indefinite employment with limits on the employer's power to terminate is normally a question for the trier of fact. . . .

§2.04. Cause for Termination of Employment Agreements

Unless otherwise provided for in the agreement:

(a) An employer has cause for early termination of an agreement for a definite term of employment if the employee has materially breached the agreement, including by persistent neglect of duties; by engaging in misconduct or other malfeasance, including gross negligence; or by being unable to perform the duties of the position due to a long-term disability.

(b) In addition to the grounds stated in subsection (a), an employer has a ground for terminating an agreement for an indefinite term of employment requiring cause for termination when a significant change in the employer's economic circumstances means that the employer no longer has a business need for the employee's services.

Comment

. . . .

d. Factual cause. When the parties agree to a definite term of employment or for an indefinite term with a cause limitation on power to terminate, the reasonable assumption is that the parties intend any cause requirement to be undisputed or proven employee material breach, misconduct or malfeasance, or inability to perform the work due to long-term disability; and do not intend also to permit termination based on the employer's reasonable, good-faith but erroneous belief that there was cause for termination. . . .

e. Procedural dimension. The cause required to terminate an agreement under this Section also may have a procedural dimension. When the agreement specifies termination procedures, those terms control. . . . Even where the agreement is silent on termination procedures, the fact that the parties have provided a cause limitation on the employer's power to terminate normally requires the employer to give reasons for the dismissal. The cause limitation also requires the employer to apply the grounds for termination in a regular and even-handed manner. . . .

§2.05. Binding Employer Policy Statements

Policy statements by an employer in documents such as employee manuals, personnel handbooks, and employment policy directives that are provided or made accessible to employees, whether by physical or electronic means, and that, reasonably read in context, establish limits on the employer's power to terminate the employment relationship, are binding on the employer until modified or revoked (as provided in §2.06).

Comment

a. Scope and cross-references. As a general matter, employers of any size will make agreements (whether for a definite or indefinite term) that structure an employment relationship only with their higher-level employees. When an employer is dealing with a large number of similarly situated employees, the employer is likely to communicate the terms of the employment relationship through unilateral statements in documents such as employee manuals, personnel handbooks, and employment policy directives that are provided, or made accessible, to employees. Such statements, reasonably read in context, may limit the employer's power to terminate the employment relationship at will or may provide for other undertakings that are to apply uniformly to all similarly situated employees without further negotiation with individual employees. Under certain circumstances, such statements may give rise to an employment agreement under traditional contract principles. See §2.03. In other situations, such statements may reasonably induce detrimental reliance under the promissory-estoppel doctrine. See §2.02(b). But even if the elements of an enforceable agreement or promise are not present, these unilateral policy statements can bind the employer until properly modified or revoked. . . .

Unilateral employer statements may also establish, or purport to establish, employees' obligations to the employer. Statements filling out the duties expected of employees are generally enforceable only by the employer's power to terminate employment or administer discipline and do not provide an independent basis for imposing liability on the employee. . . .

b. Rationale. Some courts have tried to fit this class of unilateral employer statements into a conventional contract-law framework, reasoning that employees "accept" or "rely on" these unilateral employer "offers" by continuing to provide services after the statements are disseminated. This has proved to be a conceptually awkward fit. Employees are rarely made aware, and even more rarely make themselves aware, of the content of such statements when they first accept employment, or later when statements are changed. That is particularly true when the employer does not provide the statements directly to employees but only to supervisors. Employees may only be able to read the statements in a personnel office or in summaries forwarded to the employee's paper or electronic-mail inbox. Such factual circumstances make it difficult to analogize this class of unilateral employer statements to unilateral-contract offers under the Restatement Second, Contracts §45, Comment *a*.

Beyond that difficulty, traditional principles of consideration and bargained-for exchange rarely, if ever, apply when the employer's unilateral statements are not made in response to a prospective employee's expressed concerns or an employee's threat to resign. For similar reasons reasonable detrimental reliance by employees on such statements under the promissory-estoppel doctrine will be rare. Moreover, many jurisdictions adopting the unilateral-contract approach do not follow traditional contract analysis by permitting employers to unilaterally modify or rescind promises contained in handbooks or personnel manuals even when there is no consideration for the change and the employee does not consent to the change other than by continuing to work under the new terms.

Against that background, other courts, and this Restatement, rest the binding effect of unilateral employer statements on general estoppel principles. Employers make certain unilateral statements about personnel policy to govern the operational decisions of their supervisors and managers. Employers do so to serve their own interests in advancing productivity, improving employee morale, or achieving some other organizational objective. Absent contrary language in the statement, the employer's purpose in promulgating a unilateral policy statement is to have it govern operational decisions while the statement is in effect but not to bind the employer to continued adherence after changing the policy and giving reasonable notice to employees of the change. The courts reach this result in a number of ways: adjusting the unilateral-contract analysis to imply employees' "consent" to a new unilateral contract from the fact that employees continue to work under the new terms; allowing unilateral modification where employers have expressly reserved their right to change their unilateral policy statements; or invoking something akin to promissory-estoppel principles even in the absence of employee reliance or by conclusively presuming such reliance.

To avoid these analytical contortions, §2.05 provides a general rule that unilateral employer policy statements that are not enforceable agreements or promises under §2.02 may still be enforceable but can be modified only on a prospective basis. . . .

c. Reasonably read in context . . . . It is often a question for the trier of fact whether a particular statement or set of statements, reasonably read in context, constitutes a binding policy statement. Several factors should inform this inquiry. First, the presence of a prominent disclaimer in the text of the statement may indicate that it is a hortatory pronouncement rather than a statement intended to govern the employer's operational personnel decisions. Any such disclaimer should be viewed, of course, in the context of the entire statement, other employer policies, and the employer's course of conduct. Second, the mode of dissemination may be relevant. Dissemination of a statement limited to supervisors, with no or limited access to the employees, suggests it is intended only as guidance to supervisors in exercising their discretion rather than as a rule or policy governing the workplace. Third, a workplace culture relying on bilateral agreements with employees may reduce the significance of unilateral employer statements. Other factors may also be relevant to determining whether a unilateral statement binds the employer. . . .

§2.06. Modification or Revocation of Binding Employer Policy Statements

(a) An employer may prospectively modify or revoke its binding policy statements if it provides reasonable advance notice of, or reasonably makes accessible, the modified statement or revocation to the affected employees.

(b) Modifications and revocations apply to all employees hired, and all employees who continue working, after the notice is given and the modification or revocation becomes effective.

(c) Modifications and revocations cannot adversely affect vested or accrued employee rights that may have been created by the statement, an agreement based on the statement (covered by §2.03), or reasonable detrimental reliance on a promise in the statement (covered by §2.02, Comment *c*).

Comment

. . . .

b. The special case of vested or accrued employee rights. An employer cannot by unilateral action modify or rescind employees' enforceable contractual rights. The terms "vested" or "accrued" are often used to indicate employee rights that cannot be reduced, taken away, or otherwise adversely changed absent the employee's consent, supported by consideration. . . . In appropriate circumstances, the employer's unilateral policy statement itself may have created vested or accrued employee rights, which, under this Section, cannot be unilaterally modified or rescinded. Factors relevant to determining whether an employer's policy statement creates a vested or accrued employee right include the statement's text, the employer's other policies, the employer's course of conduct, and custom or usage in the particular industry or occupation. . . .

c. Modification or revocation. This Section provides that, in general, undertakings in an employer's policy statements are binding on the employer only from the date of distribution or a later-stated "effective date" until they are properly modified or revoked. Employment terminations that occur while the original statement is in place are governed by that statement; terminations that occur after modification takes effect are governed by the modified statement. . . .

d. Reasonable advance notice. This Section requires employers to provide or make accessible reasonable advance notice of a modification to or revocation of a binding unilateral employer statement. Ordinarily, the reasonableness standard is met when the notice is given in the same or substantially the same way the original statement was provided or made accessible. The ultimate question is whether the employer provided notice that was reasonably calculated to alert employees to any modification or rescission of material terms in prior policy statements.

e. Effectiveness of modification or revocation. A substantial number of courts have held that an employee who continues to work for the employer after receiving proper notice of a modification or revocation of a unilateral employer statement that makes a personnel policy less advantageous to the employees than the original statement are deemed to have "accepted" the change. A smaller number of courts have held that a changed personnel policy covers only those incumbent employees who have expressly agreed to the change. For these jurisdictions, it is not enough that an employee continues to work for the employer after receiving notice of the policy change.

This Restatement adopts the first position and rejects the second. A requirement that a modification or revocation of a unilateral employer statement can be made effective for incumbent employees only by a bilateral agreement is inconsistent with the basis for treating such statements as binding employer policy statements. That basis recognizes that the statements are self-imposed limitations on the employer's authority binding as a matter of equitable estoppel rather than contract principles of consideration, bargained-for exchange, or even promissory estoppel. Requiring employees expressly to agree to changes in employer statements would be unworkable for companies with large workforces and would lead to inconsistent treatment among similarly situated employees. . . .

§2.07. Implied Duty of Good Faith and Fair Dealing

(a) Each party to an employment relationship, including at-will employment, owes a nonwaivable duty of good faith and fair dealing to each other party, which includes a party's obligation not to hinder the other party's performance under, or to deprive the other party of the benefit of, their contractual relationship (§3.05(a)).

(b) The implied duty of good faith and fair dealing applies to at-will employment relationships in manner consistent with the essential nature of such an at-will relationship.

(c) In any employment relationship, including at-will employment, the employer's implied duty of good faith and fair dealing includes the duty not to terminate or seek to terminate the employment relationship for the purpose of:

(1) preventing the vesting or accrual of an employee right or benefit; or

(2) retaliating against the employee for performing the employee's obligations under the employment contract or law.

Comment

a. Scope and cross-references. This Section recognizes in the employment context the rule of contract law set forth in §205 of the Restatement Second, Contracts. There is no principled reason to exclude employment contracts from that rule. By entering into an employment relationship, each party to the relationship undertakes a duty to cooperate with the other party in realizing the common purpose of their contractual relationship.

b. Consistency with at-will contracts. As in all contracts, the implied duty of good faith and fair dealing serves as a supplementary aid in implementing the parties' reasonable expectations and should not be read as a means of overriding the basic terms of, or otherwise undermining the essential nature of, their contractual relationship. Jurisdictions that recognize the implied duty in the employment setting [] also recognize that the duty applies to at-will employment in a manner consistent with the essential nature of such an at-will relationship – namely, except to the extent provided by law or public policy, either party may terminate the relationship with or without cause. . . .

e. Nonwaivable duty. The implied duty of good faith and fair dealing is read into every contract as a matter of law, and in that sense is not subject to modification or waiver by the parties' agreement. . . .

CHAPTER 3.   EMPLOYMENT CONTRACTS: COMPENSATION AND BENEFITS

§3.01. Right to Earned Compensation

(a) Whether the employment relationship is terminable at will or terminable only for cause, employees have a right to be paid the wages, salary, commissions, and other forms of compensation they have earned.

(b) Whether compensation has been earned is determined by the agreement on compensation between the employer and employee or any relevant binding employer promise or binding employer policy statement on compensation.

(c) Employees have a right to be timely paid the wages, salary, and other compensation they have earned. If there is a bona fide dispute as to whether all of the compensation the employee claims has been earned, the employee has a right to be timely paid any part of the claimed compensation that is not in dispute.

Comment

a. Scope and cross-references. The overarching principle of this Chapter is that employers have an obligation to pay, and employees have the right to receive, earned remuneration for their services. ... This principle applies whether employment is terminable at will or requires cause. ...

Employees also have a right to be paid the compensation they have earned on a timely basis, usually in conformity with the employer's normal payroll practices. Section 3.01(c) makes clear that even if there is a bona fide dispute over whether all of the compensation the employee claims has been earned, the employee has a right to be timely paid any part of the earned compensation that is not disputed.

As a general matter, whether employees have earned particular compensation, or are entitled to particular benefits, depends on the terms of the agreement between the employer and employee and any relevant binding employer promises inducing detrimental reliance (termed "binding employer promises") (see §2.02(b), Comment *c*) or binding employer policy statements (see §§2.02(c) and 2.05). ...

Even if no agreement, binding employer promise, or binding employer policy statement covers the compensation dispute, principles of quantum meruit may apply. These equitable principles are invoked, when needed, to prevent unjust enrichment. ...

At all times, applicable statutes control, sometimes displacing and sometimes supplementing the relevant common-law principles stated here. The most common type of legislation is state wage-payment laws, which are often premised on an enforceable agreement covering the item of compensation in question. If there is no such agreement, typically the wage-payment law does not apply. ...

§3.02. Bonuses and Other Incentive Compensation

(a) When an agreement on incentive compensation between the employer and the employee or any relevant binding employer promise or binding employer policy statement on incentive compensation so provides, employees have a right to be paid the bonuses and other items of incentive compensation they have earned. Absent such an agreement or binding employer promise or binding employer policy statement, incentive compensation awards are in the employer's discretion.

(b) Whether incentive compensation has been earned is determined by the agreement on incentive compensation between the employer and employee or any binding employer promise or binding policy statement.

(c) Employees have a right to be timely paid the bonuses and other incentive compensation they have earned. If there is a bona fide dispute as to whether the employee earned all of the incentive compensation the employee claimed, the employee has the right to be timely paid any part of the claimed incentive compensation that is not in dispute.

Comment

. . . .

b. Incentive compensation. Bonuses and other forms of incentive compensation are usually paid in addition to base pay and are contingent on the occurrence of one or more events or conditions (such as the employee's hours or the employer's sales or profits).

c. Compensation vs. discretionary award. Employers award bonuses and other types of incentive compensation to motivate their employees. Whether bonuses are a form of compensation that employees have a right to receive or awards that the employer [m]akes in its discretion depends on what the applicable agreement and any binding employer promise or binding employer policy statement provides. Important factors include (1) whether the documents establishing the bonus expressly state that it is a discretionary award; (2) whether the criteria for receiving the bonus are keyed to objective measures of employee conduct (such as remaining with the employer for a particular period of time) or performance (such as achieving certain sales objectives) rather than purely subjective assessments by the employer; and (3) the parties' course of dealing. . . .

d. Bonuses to motivate continued service or other employee conduct. Sometimes employers provide bonuses not so much to motivate exemplary employee performance as to ensure that employees will continue working for the employer during some period of corporate change. Such "stay bonuses" normally constitute earned compensation once the conditions of the bonus are satisfied. . . .

§3.03. Benefits

(a) Employees have a right to receive the retirement benefits (including pensions), healthcare benefits, or other benefits provided in the agreement between the employer and employee or in any relevant binding employer promise or binding employer policy statement.

(b) An employer has an obligation to provide promised benefits to employees on a timely basis. If there is a bona fide dispute as to whether the stated conditions for providing the benefits have been satisfied, an employer has an obligation to provide any benefits that are not in dispute.

Comment

. . . .

c. Benefit plans. Employers provide employees with benefits to motivate employees. In addition, tax advantages and economies of scale allow employers to provide benefits desired by employees at substantially lower costs than the employees would pay for comparable benefits on the open market. To derive these economies of scale, the employer establishes plans that cover a relatively large number of employees and provide common terms (including a common administration) for them.

d. Unilateral employer policy statements. In the benefits context, employers are likely to set the plan terms through unilateral policy statements rather than bilateral agreements with employees. Employers generally intend these statements to establish binding commitments while the terms are in effect (see §§2.05-2.06). . . .

§3.04. Modification of Compensation or Benefits

(a) Except as provided in (c) below, an employer may prospectively modify or revoke any prior binding employer promise or binding employer policy statement on compensation by providing reasonable notice of the modification or revocation to the affected employees.

(b) Such modifications and revocations apply to all employees hired, and all employees who continue working, after notice is given and the modification or revocation become effective.

(c) Such modifications and revocations cannot, absent agreement with the affected employees:

(1) adversely affect rights under any agreement between the employer and the employee (including any collective-bargaining agreement) (§2.03); or

(2) adversely affect any vested or accrued employee rights that may have been created by a binding employer policy statement (§2.05), or by reasonable detrimental reliance on a binding employer promise (§2.02, Comment *c*).

Comment

a. Scope and cross-references. This Section applies the principles stated in §2.06 to compensation arrangements. . . .

§3.05. Implied Duty of Good Faith and Fair Dealing

(a) Each party to an employment relationship, including at-will employment, owes a nonwaivable duty of good faith and fair dealing to the other party, which includes a party's obligation not to hinder the other party's performance under, or to deprive the other party of the benefit of, their contractual relationship (§2.07). The duty applies whether the relationship is terminable at will (as set forth in subsection (b)) or only for cause.

(b) The implied duty of good faith and fair dealing applies to at-will employment relationships in manner consistent with the essential nature of such an at-will relationship.

(c) The employer's duty of good faith and fair dealing includes the duty not to terminate or seek to terminate the employment relationship or effect other adverse employment action for the purpose of:

(1) preventing the vesting or accrual of an employee right or benefit; or

(2) retaliating against the employee for refusing to consent to a change in earned compensation or benefits.

Comment

a. Scope and cross-references. This Section applies to compensation and employee benefits the principles governing the implied covenant of good faith and fair dealing (§2.07), which in many jurisdictions is included in every contract.

b. Opportunistic firings or other adverse action. The implied duty of good faith and fair dealing not only promotes basic notions of fairness but also enables the parties to enter into certain relationships where performance is not simultaneous – where, for example, the employee renders services but the employer's obligation to pay for those services does not ripen until certain conditions subsequent have been satisfied. . . .

c. Employer retaliation. As stated in §3.04(c), employers cannot by unilateral action modify employees' accrued or vested rights. The implied duty of good faith and fair dealing also prevents the employer from taking adverse action against employees who refuse to agree to an adverse change in the compensation or benefits they are owed. Employers can try to obtain the employees' consent to such changes, but making such consent a condition of continued employment or subjecting the employee to adverse employment action for refusing to consent breaches the implied duty. Thus, in order to protect the employees' right to refuse unilateral adverse changes in the employee's earned compensation, the scope of proscribed employer action is broader here than under §2.07, which is limited to termination and constructive termination. . . .

CHAPTER 8. EMPLOYEE OBLIGATIONS AND RESTRICTIVE COVENANTS

§8.06. Enforcement of Restrictive Covenants in Employment Agreements

Except as otherwise provided by other law or applicable professional rules, a covenant in an agreement between an employer and a former employee restricting the former employee's working activities is enforceable only if it is reasonably tailored in scope, geography, and time to further a protectable interest of the employer, as defined in §8.07, unless:

(a) the employer discharges the employee on a basis that makes enforcement of the covenant inequitable;

(b) the employer acted in bad faith in requiring or invoking the covenant;

(c) the employer materially breached the underlying employment agreement; or

(d) in the geographic region covered by the restriction, a great public need for the special skills and services of the former employee outweighs any legitimate interest of the employer in enforcing the covenant.

Comment

a. Scope and cross-references. Contractual restrictions on former employees' working activities ("restrictive covenants") involve several competing interests. On the one hand, these provisions enable employers to protect customer relationships, investments in an employee's reputation, and other legitimate interests under §8.07. On the other hand, restrictive covenants inhibit the freedom of employees to leave their employers and move to other employment where the employees may be more productive; and they frustrate the public interest in promoting competition. Courts balance these competing interests by enforcing restrictive covenants only if they are reasonably tailored to protect the legitimate employer interests identified in §8.07. Some states prohibit by statute the enforcement of noncompetition clauses in employment contexts not related to the sale of a business, but these states generally will enforce restrictive covenants more limited than noncompetition clauses if they are reasonably tailored to protect a legitimate interest of the employer. . . .

b. Types of restrictive covenants . . . . Different types of restrictive covenants may be necessary to protect different types of employer interests, and courts should examine the asserted business justification for each specific limitation. The same general inquiry, however, applies to all restrictive covenants – namely, a court should determine whether the employer has a protectable interest, and whether the restrictive covenant is reasonably tailored to furthering that interest. . . .

c. Reasonably tailored. . . . To be reasonably tailored, the covenant should be no more restrictive in duration, scope of activities, or geography than necessary to protect the legitimate interest at stake. Whether limitations are reasonable will vary depending on the circumstances of the case, including industry practices and the nature of the interest justifying the restrictive covenant. When confronted with a blanket contractual restriction on all competition – even if the restriction otherwise is of reasonable duration and geographical scope – courts will inquire whether the employer's legitimate interest could not be equally well served by a narrower restriction. . . . Regardless of the nature of an employer's interest, the employer may not restrict employees from working in any market in which the employer does not do business.

The inquiry into the reasonableness of geographic, temporal, and scope-of-business limitations in restrictive covenants is context-sensitive and depends heavily on the nature of the legitimate interests at stake. Identical limitations will be reasonable to protect some interests but not others. A provision compensating the former employee during the term of the restrictive covenant (sometimes called "garden leave") may be a factor in favor of finding the restriction reasonable.

Illustrations

. . . .

6. Salesperson E agrees that, after he leaves X's employment, he will not compete with X in any state in which X services its customers. X services customers

in 36 states, but E dealt with customers in only three states while working for X. The noncompetition agreement is not reasonably tailored to protect X from losing customer relationships that E developed with X's assistance. A narrower agreement, such as one prohibiting E from soliciting the customers whom E had serviced while working for X, would be sufficient to protect X's interest.

7. E, a vice president of computer-data-storage company X, agrees not to compete with X anywhere in the world for six months. Both X and its competitors serve customers worldwide, and E has had extensive access to X's trade secrets, which apply worldwide. Because E's trade secrets have worldwide utility, the worldwide restriction is reasonably tailored to further a protectable interest of X. . . .

e. Restrictive covenants agreed to after the start of the employment relationship. The majority rule is that continuing employment of an at-will employee is sufficient consideration to support the enforcement of an otherwise valid restrictive covenant. However, a significant minority of jurisdictions require "new" or "additional" consideration. . . .

f. Terminated employees. Reasonable restrictive covenants are generally enforceable against employees who have been discharged for cause. An opposite rule would have the perverse consequence of providing an incentive for an employee who wants relief from the restrictions of a reasonable covenant to perform badly and thus trigger a for-cause termination.

In contrast, restrictive covenants are generally unenforceable against employees who are terminated without cause or who quit employment for cause attributable to the employer. . . . An opposite rule would have the perverse consequence of enabling an employer to terminate rather than retain an employee who is performing satisfactorily and then restrict the discharged employee's ability to secure new employment. By the same token, an employer should not be able to obtain enforcement of a restrictive covenant when the employer acts in bad faith, such as by securing the employee's execution of the covenant after planning to discharge the employee. . . .

g. Employer's material breach of employment agreement. If the employer materially breaches the employment agreement, it cannot enforce an otherwise valid restrictive covenant contained in the agreement. . . .

h. Professionals. Laws and regulations governing various professions may limit the enforceability of some restrictive covenants. For example, a noncompetition agreement is generally not enforceable against an attorney because the rules governing the legal profession provide that the right of clients to have an attorney of their choice outweighs the protectable interests of employers under §8.07. Enforceability of reasonable restrictive covenants against doctors, accountants, or other professionals may vary by jurisdiction because the rules regulating those professions and the availability of these professionals to serve public needs may vary. . . .

i. Public interest. Courts may, in unusual circumstances, invalidate a restrictive covenant as against the public interest, even if the covenant satisfies all of the other requirements of this Section – for example, where the particular geographic market has only a very small number of persons or firms to provide an important good or service. Most often, this rationale is used to invalidate a restrictive covenant that would prevent a medical professional from practicing in a small town or rural area where there are few practitioners or too few with a specific specialty. . . .

§8.07. Protectable Interests for Restrictive Covenants

(a) A restrictive covenant is enforceable only if the employer can demonstrate that the covenant furthers a legitimate interest of the employer.

(b) An employer has a legitimate interest in protecting, by means of a reasonably tailored restrictive covenant with its employee, the employer's:

(1) trade secrets ... and other protectable confidential information that does not meet the definition of trade secret;

(2) customer relationships;

(3) investment in the employee's reputation in the market; or

(4) purchase of a business owned by the employee.

Comment

. . . .

b. Confidential information. An employer's interest in protecting its trade secrets and other confidential information can justify a reasonable restrictive covenant. . . . [M]ost nonpublic information in which an employer has a protectable interest will be protectable as a trade secret. . . . However, an employer may occasionally seek protection through contract of additional non-trade-secret information, often termed "confidential" or "proprietary," which is similarly nonpublic. . . .

The determination of whether information is protectable as confidential or proprietary is inherently fact-specific, as it often turns on the language of the covenant at issue, the nature of the information to be protected, and the degree to which disclosure would unfairly benefit a competitor. Courts will generally protect nonpublic commercial information that provides a clear economic advantage to the employer by virtue of its confidentiality, provided that the restrictive covenant is otherwise reasonable under §8.06 and the information has been treated as confidential by the employer. . . . An employer cannot protect as confidential any information in which it does not have a protectable interest, such as information that has entered the public domain and information that would be considered part of the general experience, knowledge, training, and skills that an employee acquires in the course of employment. . . .

c. Customer relationships. An employer often makes significant investments to foster relationships between its customers and its sales force and other employees. An employer has a legitimate interest in taking reasonable measures to protect that investment by barring employees from appropriating customer relationships that the employer created and fostered by investing its resources. Because a covenant prohibiting former employees from soliciting customers with whom they dealt while employed will ordinarily fully protect this legitimate interest, a broader restriction barring all competition by former employees ordinarily is not enforceable. The length of time that employees worked for their employer is often relevant in determining the reasonableness of a restriction claimed to be necessary to preserve the former employer's customer relationships. . . .

e. Sale of business. When selling a business, the owner commonly agrees not to compete with the purchaser of the business for a period and often becomes an employee of the purchaser as well. While the basic enforceability test of §8.06

applies to these restrictive covenants as well – the covenant must be reasonably tailored in scope, geography, and time to further a protectable interest of the employer – the policy considerations that counsel narrow tailoring are less compelling. First, the employee/business-seller usually has considerable ability to negotiate appropriate terms, compared to most employees. Second, a promise not to compete is typically necessary to adequately protect the employer/buyer's interest because the employee/business-seller is so integral to the business being sold that a lesser promise such as one simply not to solicit customers or reveal confidential information would not adequately protect the buyer's investment. In fact, the sale of a business's goodwill is often difficult to accomplish effectively unless the seller agrees not to compete with the buyer. Finally, the seller is compensated for his restricted employment with proceeds from the sale, which should be higher with the noncompetition agreement.

f. Insufficient employer interests. An employer may have many economic reasons to attempt to restrict what its employees can do after termination of their employment. However, unless the employer can demonstrate a protectable interest under this Section, these reasons, standing alone, will not support an otherwise reasonable restrictive covenant because they are not sufficiently weighty to justify the social and individual costs inherent in restrictions on competition. For example, an interest in recouping investments in the training of employees may justify repayment obligations but would not justify a restriction on competition. Similarly, the desire of an employer to retain its talented, trained, or experienced employees is not an interest that can legitimately support a restrictive covenant. Finally, an employer's understandable wish to prevent competition by former employees is not, by itself, a protectable interest under this Section.

§8.08. Modification of Unreasonable Restrictive Covenants

A court may delete or modify provisions in an overbroad restrictive covenant in an employment agreement and then enforce the covenant as modified unless the agreement does not allow for modification or the employer lacked a reasonable and good-faith basis for believing the covenant was enforceable. Lack of a reasonable and good-faith basis for believing a covenant was enforceable may be manifested by its gross overbreadth alone, or by overbreadth coupled with other evidence that the employer sought to do more than protect its legitimate interests.

Comment

a. Scope and cross-references. Although unreasonable restrictive covenants should never be enforced as written, a court may modify an overly broad restrictive covenant into one that is reasonably tailored to the employer's protectable interest under §8.07, and may thereafter enforce the modified covenant. Such modification, sometimes called "blue penciling," lies within the sound discretion of the court but that discretion should be exercised with care so as not to create an incentive for employers to draft overbroad restrictive covenants that in some instances will be taken by employees at face value as enforceable. On the other hand, a rule that forbids judicial modification and leaves courts with only a binary "enforce or reject" choice can also lead over time to a legal regime that provides employers with an incentive to draft overly broad covenants that employees will similarly regard as enforceable, due to judicial unwillingness to completely reject a covenant that is partially valid. . . . The best approach, reflected in this Section, is for courts to refuse to modify an overly broad restrictive covenant when the employer lacked a reasonable good-faith belief that the covenant was enforceable. In some cases, lack of good faith can be shown by the covenant itself being so clearly overbroad that no reasonable employer would have believed it was reasonably tailored to protect the employer's legitimate interests. Other cases might require additional evidence of bad faith. Once overbreadth has been shown, the employer has the burden of demonstrating good faith in order to justify a modification.

b. Overbreadth. To be enforceable, a restrictive covenant must be . . . reasonable in scope at the time of contracting and at the time of enforcement. A restrictive covenant that is . . . objectively unreasonable at the time of contracting is unenforceable. Also, a change in circumstances between time of contracting and time of enforcement may in some cases so erode the employer's protectable interest as to render the covenant unenforceable.

CHAPTER 9. REMEDIES

Part 1. *Claims Against Employers*

A. CONTRACT

§9.01. Damages — Employer Termination in Breach of an Agreement for a Definite or Indefinite Term of Employment or of a Binding Employer Promise Limiting Termination of Employment

(a) An employer who lacks cause for terminating the employment of an employee with an unexpired agreement for a definite term (§§2.03-2.04) is subject to liability to the discharged employee for:

(1) all compensation that the employee would have received under the remaining term of the agreement, less mitigation of losses (such as the compensation earned and that reasonably could have been earned from comparable alternative employment during the remaining term);

(2) reasonably foreseeable consequential damages; and

(3) the expenses of reasonable efforts (whether or not successful) to mitigate losses.

(b) An employer who lacks cause for terminating the employment of an employee with an agreement for an indefinite term requiring cause for termination (§§2.03-2.04) is subject to liability to the discharged employee for:

(1) all compensation that the employee would have received under that agreement, less mitigation of losses (such as the compensation earned and that reasonably could have been earned from comparable alternative employment);

(2) reasonably foreseeable consequential damages; and

(3) the expenses of reasonable efforts (whether or not successful) to mitigate losses.

(c) The employer and employee may specify in the agreement a reasonable amount to be paid by the employer for termination with or without cause in lieu of the measure of damages stated in (a) and (b).

(d) An employer who breaches a promise that limits the employer's right to terminate employment and that induces reasonable and detrimental reliance by the employee (§2.02, Comment c) is subject to liability to the discharged employee for:

(1) damages (including reasonably foreseeable consequential damages) caused by the employee's reasonable reliance on that promise;

(2) less mitigation of losses (such as the compensation earned and that reasonably could have been earned from comparable alternative employment during the period covered by the promise); and

(3) the expenses of reasonable efforts (whether or not successful) to mitigate losses.

§9.02.　Damages — Employer Termination in Breach of a Binding Policy Statement Limiting Termination of Employment

An employer who breaches a binding employer policy statement that limits termination of employment (§2.05) is subject to liability to the discharged employee for:

(a) all compensation the employee would have received under that policy statement, less mitigation of losses (such as the compensation the employee earned and could have obtained by reasonable efforts in comparable alternative employment, during the period of time covered by the policy statement (§2.06));

(b) reasonably foreseeable consequential damages; and

(c) the expenses of reasonable efforts (whether successful or not) to mitigate losses.

§9.03.　Damages — Employer Breach Other Than Termination of Employment

An employer who, other than by terminating employment, breaches the terms of an agreement (§2.03), a binding employer promise (§2.02, Comment c), or a binding employer policy statement (§2.05), including one providing for compensation or benefits, is subject to liability for damages for lost compensation or benefits, any reasonably foreseeable consequential damages, and the expenses of reasonable efforts (whether or not successful) to mitigate damages, less any damages that could have been avoided with reasonable effort.

§9.04. Injunctive Relief—Employer Breach

(a) Except as otherwise provided by law, an employer's agreement, promise, or statement that it will hire or continue to employ an employee or job applicant will not be specifically enforced.

(b) An employee may obtain injunctive relief to enforce any other term of an employment agreement (§2.03), binding employer promise (§2.02, Comment *c*), or binding employer policy statement (§2.05) if the employee satisfies the traditional requirements for equitable relief.

Part 2.   Claims Against Employees

§9.07. Damages—Employee Breach of Agreement

(a) An employee who breaches any obligation that the employment agreement clearly states is a basis for damages liability is subject to liability for that breach of contract. The employer may recover damages for foreseeable economic loss that the employer could not have reasonably avoided, including any reasonably foreseeable consequential damages and the expenses of reasonable efforts to mitigate damages.

(b) Economic loss under subsection (a) does not include lost profits caused by the employee's breach unless the agreement expressly provides for such recovery or the employee knew or should have known that the employee would be held responsible for lost profits caused by the employee's breach. . . .

§9.08. Injunctive Relief—Employee Breach of Agreement

(a) An employer may not obtain specific performance of the employee's promise to work.

(b) An employer may obtain injunctive relief to enforce any other obligation expressly stated in the employment agreement if the employer satisfies the traditional requirements for obtaining equitable relief.

Restatement (Third) of Restitution and Unjust Enrichment (2011)

EDITORS' NOTE

For centuries, restitution has been, and remains, a rich field of private law in Great Britain and the Commonwealth countries, peacefully flourishing alongside the fields of contract, tort, and property, and producing both substantive and remedial rules. To be sure, like many species of flora that grow alongside fields of other flora, there has been cross-pollination, and issues that once could be classified as distinctively restitutionary in nature have bred hybrids with characteristics of both restitution and, say, contract. Nonetheless, restitution remains robust in common-law systems outside the United States and is taught as a distinctive, core subject at most of the leading common-law law schools (and law faculties) outside the United States.

In the United States, particularly since the mid-twentieth century, restitution has largely lost its distinctiveness in the case law and mainstream legal commentary as anything other than a remedy or set of remedies available in the event of some breach of promise, duty, or right in contract, tort, or property. This, despite the yeoman efforts of a number of eminent and dedicated legal scholars, including Professors Warren A. Seavey and Austin Wakeman Scott (both of Harvard Law School), who served as co-Reporters for the American Law Institute's first Restatement of Restitution, published in 1937, and Professor George E. Palmer (of the University of Michigan Law School), whose 1978 four-volume treatise, now known as Palmer on Restitution, was described shortly after its publication as "the first comprehensive, extended treatment of th[e] elusive and profound subject" of restitution in sixty-five years,[1] and remains forty years after its own publication the definitive American treatise on the subject.

The product of more than a decade of work by its Reporter, Professor Andrew Kull (then of Boston University School of Law, and now of the University of Texas

---

1. Maurice J. Holland, Book Review, 54 Ind. L.J. 313 (1979) (reviewing George E. Palmer, Law of Restitution (1978)).

School of Law), the Restatement (Third) of Restitution and Unjust Enrichment, published in 2011 "brings clarity and light to an area of law long shrouded in fogs that linger from an earlier era of the legal system," "makes an important body of law once again accessible to lawyers and judges," and "should be on every litigator's bookshelf, and a broad set of transactional lawyers and legal academics would also do well to become familiar with it."[2]

The Restatement (Third) lays out, in an economical seventy sections (which nonetheless occupy more than 1,400 pages, with comments, illustrations, and reporter's notes), a set of general principles; restitutionary causes of action for avoidable transfers, unrequested intervention, contract-related claims, tortious wrongs, interference with donative intent, and benefits conferred by third parties; remedial rules; and defenses. Many of these provisions are obviously beyond the scope of the first-year contracts course, which is this Supplement's focus; some less obviously so, the more one reads, but sometimes editorial necessity takes precedence.

What we reproduce here, in addition to some of the general principles needed to understand what follows, are the sections that most clearly overlap with the common law of and equity related to contracts and contractual relations – whether or not that overlap is apparent from the topics emphasized in the casebook or other course materials this Supplement may be accompanying. This being the Restatement (Third) of Restitution and Unjust Enrichment's inaugural appearance in this Supplement, we welcome your feedback.

The following provisions are copyright © 2011 by the American Law Institute. Reprinted with permission. All rights reserved.

PART I.   INTRODUCTION

CHAPTER 1.   GENERAL PRINCIPLES

§1.   Restitution and Unjust Enrichment

---

2. Douglas Laycock, Restoring Restitution to the Canon, 110 Mich. L. Rev. 929 (2012) (reviewing the Restatement (Third) of Restitution and Unjust Enrichment (2011)). Laycock continues:

> [H]ardly anyone who graduated from law school in the last forty years has taken a restitution course, and at least by 1989 (probably a good bit earlier), there was no restitution casebook in print. When a lawyer or judge encounters a restitution problem today, there is a substantial risk that she will view it as an isolated problem, only dimly aware that there is a large body of law on restitution and unjust enrichment and that arguments about her particular problem can be tested and refined in light of larger principles.
>
> Before this new Restatement, she might also have found it hard to investigate either that larger body of law or her particular problem within it. Contemporary lawyers do not find the other available reference books very user friendly. The first Restatement of the Law of Restitution, and Palmer's four-volume treatise, each give substantial weight to the historic division between law and equity and to the historic scope of quasi-contract. Quasi-contract, the nineteenth-century name for the common law's response to cases of what we would now call unjust enrichment, was rooted in fictional pleadings and the forms of action. The first Restatement speaks as of 1937; Palmer's treatise was published in 1978, but it feels much older. Both suffer from rather weak intermediate levels of organization, so it can be hard for new users to find what they are looking for.
>
> Treatises on remedies give modern and accessible treatment of restitutionary remedies, but they are little help on restitutionary causes of action. And the treatment of restitutionary remedies in the Restatement (Third) is clearer, more systematic, and more precise than in any of the remedies treatises.
>
> The Restatement (Third) is written in plain English for lawyers in the twenty-first century. None of its rules are stated in terms of quasi-contract or the forms of action, and almost none are stated in terms of common law or equity. There is a clear explanation of restitution's separate roots both at law and in equity, correcting the common misconception that restitution is necessarily equitable. . . .

Id. at 930-31 (footnotes and emphases omitted).

PART I.   INTRODUCTION

CHAPTER 1.   GENERAL PRINCIPLES

§1. Restitution and Unjust Enrichment

A person who is unjustly enriched at the expense of another is subject to liability in restitution.

Comment

a. Liability in restitution. Liability in restitution derives from the receipt of a benefit whose retention without payment would result in the unjust enrichment of the defendant at the expense of the claimant. While the paradigm case of unjust enrichment is one in which the benefit on one side of the transaction corresponds to an observable loss on the other, . . . "at the expense of another" can also mean "in violation of the other's legally protected rights," without the need to show that the claimant has suffered a loss. . . . The usual consequence of a liability in restitution is that the defendant must restore the benefit in question or its traceable product, or else pay money in the amount necessary to eliminate unjust enrichment. . . .

b. Unjust Enrichment. The law of restitution is predominantly the law of unjust enrichment, but "unjust enrichment" is a term of art. The substantive part of the law of restitution is concerned with identifying those forms of enrichment that the law treats as "unjust" for purposes of imposing liability.

. . . . Equity and good conscience might see an unjust enrichment in the performance of a valid but unequal bargain, or in the legally protected refusal to perform an equal one (as where the statute of limitations bars enforcement of a valid debt). Beyond these merely legal instances, moreover, "unjust enrichment" (in the natural and nontechnical sense of the words) might seem to be a pervasive fact of human experience – given any prior standard (such as equality or merit) by which people's relative entitlements might be measured.

The concern of restitution is . . . with a narrower set of circumstances giving rise to what might more appropriately be called *unjustified enrichment*. Compared to the open-ended implications of the term "unjust enrichment," instances of unjustified enrichment are both predictable and objectively determined, because the justification in question is not moral but legal. Unjustified enrichment is enrichment that lacks an adequate legal basis; it results from a transaction that the law treats as ineffective to work a conclusive alteration in ownership rights. Broadly speaking, an ineffective transaction for these purposes is one that is *nonconsensual*. Such a transaction may occur when the claimant's consent to the transaction is impaired for some reason (chapter 2); or when the claimant confers unrequested benefits without obtaining the recipient's agreement to pay for them (chapter 3); or when an attempted contractual exchange miscarries after partial performance (chapter 4). . . .

d. Benefits conferred. Restitution is the law of nonconsensual and non-bargained benefits in the same way that torts is the law of nonconsensual and nonlicensed harms. Both subjects deal with the consequences of transactions in which the parties have not specified for themselves what the consequences of their interaction should be. The law of torts identifies those circumstances in which a person is liable for injury inflicted, measuring liability by the extent of the harm; the law of restitution identifies those circumstances in which a person is liable for benefits received, measuring liability by the extent of the benefit.

. . . . [T]he benefit that is the basis of a restitution claim may take any form, direct or indirect. It may consist of services as well as property. A saved expenditure or a discharged obligation is no less beneficial to the recipient than a direct transfer. . . .

Restitution may strip a wrongdoer of all profits gained in a transaction with the claimant . . . , but principles of unjust enrichment will not support the imposition of a liability that leaves an innocent recipient worse off, apart from costs of litigation, than if the transaction with the claimant had never taken place. . . .

§2. Limiting Principles

(1) The fact that a recipient has obtained a benefit without paying for it does not of itself establish that the recipient has been unjustly enriched.

(2) A valid contract defines the obligations of the parties as to matters within its scope, displacing to that extent any inquiry into unjust enrichment.

(3) There is no liability in restitution for an unrequested benefit voluntarily conferred, unless the circumstances of the transaction justify the claimant's intervention in the absence of contract.

(4) Liability in restitution may not subject an innocent recipient to a forced exchange: in other words, an obligation to pay for a benefit that the recipient should have been free to refuse.

Comment

. . . .

b. Enrichment without liability. Receipt of a benefit at the expense of another is a necessary but not a sufficient condition of liability in restitution, because a person who receives a benefit is not necessarily obligated to pay for it. A valid gift is not a source of unjust enrichment (unlike a gift induced by mistake, fraud, or undue influence, see §11, 13, 15). Outside the context of gratuitous transfers, the fact that a benefit is retained, enjoyed, and profitably exploited by the recipient, all without compensation, does not necessarily mean that the recipient has been unjustly enriched.

It is a fact of common experience that a person may benefit from the effort and expenditure of others without incurring a legal obligation to pay. To be the subject of a claim in restitution, the benefit conferred must be something in which the claimant has a legally protected interest, and it must be acquired or retained in a manner that the law regards as unjustified. . . .

d. Benefits voluntarily conferred. Instead of proposing a bargain, the restitution claimant first confers a benefit, then seeks payment for its value. When this manner of proceeding is unacceptable – as it usually is, if the claimant neglects an opportunity to contract – a claim based on unjust enrichment will be denied.

The limitation of §2(3) is traditionally expressed by denying restitution to a claimant characterized as "officious," an "intermeddler," or a "volunteer." This section states the same rule, substituting a functional explanation for the familiar epithets. Because contract is strongly preferred over restitution as a basis for private obligations . . . , restitution is not usually available to a claimant who has neglected a suitable opportunity to make a contract beforehand.

There are cases in which a claimant may indeed recover compensation for unrequested benefits intentionally conferred – because the claimant's intervention was justified under the circumstances, and because a liability in restitution will not prejudice the recipient. . . .

e. Forced exchange. At some points within this Restatement, the protection of the recipient . . . is reinforced by the statement that the recipient may not be subjected to a "forced exchange." The usual context of this observation is one in which the claimant has conferred a nonreturnable benefit (such as services, articles for consumption, or improvements to property). Although such a benefit has a market value, it may be something that the recipient would not have chosen to purchase at that price or at all. With rare exceptions . . . , the law of restitution does not oblige a recipient to pay for a benefit he had the right (but not the opportunity) to refuse. . . .

Proof that a forced exchange is in the recipient's interest, or that the transaction is economically efficient, does not justify the claimant's failure to obtain the recipient's agreement to pay. . . . By contrast, there is no problem of forced exchange so long as liability for unrequested benefits is limited to the amount of a cash outlay that the recipient (but for the claimant's expenditure) would have been compelled to bear in any event. . . .

§3. Wrongful Gain

A person is not permitted to profit by his own wrong.

Comment

a. General principles and scope; relation to other sections. The present section . . . identifies an outlook and an objective, not a cause of action. Working rules that authorize a claim to restitution of wrongful gain appear in other sections of this Restatement, describing more precisely the nature of the wrongdoing in a particular case. . . .

Liability to disgorge profits is ordinarily limited to cases of what this Restatement calls "conscious wrongdoing," because the disincentives that are the object of a disgorgement remedy are not required in dealing either with innocent recipients . . . . The degree of culpable awareness necessary to establish a liability to disgorge profits varies with the context. . . .

Breach of an enforceable contract is not a source of unjust enrichment or wrongful gain, except in the special case of profitable and opportunistic breach (§39). . . .

b. Restitution as an alternative to damages. With few exceptions, a claimant entitled to a disgorgement remedy in restitution might instead recover compensation for the injury caused by the defendant's [wrongdoing]. Restitution becomes significant when it affords remedial or procedural advantages by comparison with an action for damages. . . .

c. Recovery exceeding the claimant's loss. When the defendant has acted in conscious disregard of the claimant's rights, the whole of the resulting gain is treated as unjust enrichment, even though the defendant's gain may exceed both (i) the measurable injury to the claimant, and (ii) the reasonable value of a license authorizing the defendant's conduct. Restitution from a conscious wrongdoer may therefore yield a recovery that is profitable to the claimant – a result that is generally not permitted when the restitution claim is against an innocent recipient . . . .

Restitution requires full disgorgement of profit by a conscious wrongdoer, not just because of the moral judgment implicit in the rule of this section, but because any lesser liability would provide an inadequate incentive to lawful behavior. If A anticipates (accurately) that unauthorized interference with B's entitlement may yield profits exceeding any damages B could prove, A has a dangerous incentive to take without asking – since the nonconsensual transaction promises to be more profitable than the forgone negotiation with B. The objective of that part of the law of restitution summarized by the rule of §3 is to frustrate any such calculation. . . .

d. Protected interests defined by other law. The law of restitution and unjust enrichment requires the surrender of benefits wrongfully obtained, but it does not tell us whether the defendant's conduct is wrongful in a particular case. As a practical matter, therefore, the contours of the claim in restitution to recover benefits wrongfully obtained will be determined by principles of law outside the scope of this Restatement. . . .

PART II.   LIABILITY IN RESTITUTION

CHAPTER 2.   TRANSFERS SUBJECT TO AVOIDANCE

Topic 1.   Benefits Conferred by Mistake

§5.   Invalidating Mistake

(1) A transfer induced by invalidating mistake is subject to rescission and restitution. The transferee is liable in restitution as necessary to avoid unjust enrichment. . . .

(2) An invalidating mistake may be a misapprehension of either fact or law. There is invalidating mistake only when

    (a) but for the mistake the transaction in question would not have taken place; and

    (b) the claimant does not bear the risk of the mistake.

(3) A claimant bears the risk of a mistake when

    (a) the risk is allocated to the claimant by agreement of the parties;

    (b) the claimant has consciously assumed the risk by deciding to act in the face of a recognized uncertainty; or

(c) allocation to the claimant of the risk in question accords with the common understanding of the transaction concerned.

(4) A claimant does not bear the risk of a mistake merely because the mistake results from the claimant's negligence.

Comment

. . . .

b. When the claimant bears the risk of mistake. The definition of "invalidating mistake" combines a test of causation with a test of risk allocation. A transfer induced by a misapprehension of fact or law is subject to avoidance unless, in the circumstances of the transaction, the claimant bears the risk of the mistake in question. Section 5(3) identifies three reasons why the claimant might bear the risk of a mistake inducing a transfer. Compare Restatement Second, Contracts § 154.

(1) Risk allocated by agreement. A party's assumption of the risk of mistake is most easily seen when it is effected by agreement, express or implied. Compare Illustrations 1 and 2. . . .

Illustrations

1. A's life is insured with B Company for $50,000. C is the named beneficiary. The body of a shipwreck victim is officially identified as that of A. Neither B nor C doubts the accuracy of the identification. On receipt of formal proof of A's death, B pays C $50,000. A is later discovered alive. The risk that A is still alive has not been allocated by agreement of the parties; nor has B chosen to act in conscious ignorance with respect to its liability under the policy. B's payment is the result of an invalidating mistake as defined in this section; B has a claim in restitution. . . .

2. Same facts as Illustration 1, except that B agrees to pay $15,000 now, to be retained by C in any event, and the balance of $35,000 in two years' time if A has not subsequently reappeared. Shortly after B's initial payment to C, A is discovered alive. The terms of the transaction constitute an express allocation between the parties of the risk that payment under the policy is not in fact due. B's payment of $15,000 to C is not the result of an invalidating mistake as defined in this section. . . .

(2) Conscious ignorance. A claimant may also assume the risk of a potentially invalidating mistake by a unilateral decision to act in conscious ignorance of relevant circumstances. The usual setting of such a transaction is the claimant's decision to satisfy a doubtful claim, in the face of a recognized uncertainty as to the underlying liability. . . .

. . . . A person who acts carelessly or on the basis of imperfect information does not thereby bear the associated risk of mistake. . . . "Assumption of risk" involves a conscious choice made by the claimant; it is not a penalty for carelessness to be levied by the court. . . .

Illustrations

4. A's life is insured with B Company for $50,000. C is the named beneficiary. A disappears without explanation and is absent for many years. C claims payment of the death benefit. Recognizing that A's death has not been positively established, B decides to pay the claim in view of (i) the perceived likelihood that A is in fact dead, and (ii) the small amount of the policy as compared to the anticipated cost of further investigation and litigation. Shortly after B's payment to C, A is discovered

alive. Because B determined to act in conscious ignorance of the relevant circumstances, B assumed the risk that payment to C was not in fact due. B's payment to C is not the result of an invalidating mistake as defined in this section. . . .

(3) Risk assigned as a matter of law. In some instances – notably where a claimant's "mistake" involves a misprediction or an error in judgment – a shared understanding about who bears certain risks in particular transactions dictates the legal conclusion that the claimant bears the risk of mistake, whether or not any risk was consciously assumed. . . .

Outside the common examples of misprediction and error of judgment, a court will rarely conclude that a risk of mistake is assigned to the claimant by common understanding. A rule that every mistaken transfer was made at the risk of the transferor would eradicate the law of restitution for mistake. A rule that the claimant bore the risk of negligent mistake would contradict the basic principles underlying this part of the law of restitution, eliminating many of its most significant examples. . . .

c. Error in judgment compared. Faulty prediction will not support a claim in restitution, and invalidating mistake is to be distinguished from the error in judgment that is visible in hindsight. Subsequent information may reveal a course of action to have been "mistaken," in the sense that someone made a poor choice; but the mistake that consists merely in the failure to identify a preferable course of action will not invalidate either an agreement or a transfer.

. . . . [T]he mistake that will potentially invalidate a transfer is one that to some degree frustrates or obstructs the normal exercise of judgment by the transferor. The result of such a mistake is a transaction that in some material respect is unintended, as opposed to one that is merely ill advised.

d. Mutual and unilateral mistake. The distinction drawn in the law of contracts between mutual and unilateral mistake has no direct application to the law of restitution. . . .

e. Causation; materiality. A transfer made under the influence of a mistake gives rise to a claim in restitution only if the mistake induces the transfer. See §5(2)(a). But causation is rarely an issue in restitution for mistake. In almost all cases . . . causation is obvious if the mistake is established. . . . Causation becomes an issue when – although the claimant was concededly mistaken about relevant circumstances – it is disputed whether it was the claimant's mistake or rather some collateral motive that induced the transfer in question. . . .

. . . [T]the distinction between a "material mistake" and a mistake of lesser significance is an idea drawn from contract law that has no direct application to a claim in restitution. . . . To take the simplest case of restitution for mistake: If the plaintiff has overpaid a debt as the result of mistake as defined in this section, the plaintiff has a claim in restitution without regard either to the amount of the overpayment or to the particular grounds of the plaintiff's misapprehension. Either factor would be irrelevant to the question of the defendant's unjust enrichment. . . .

f. Negligence. Mistake is often the result of negligence. As a general rule, neither the claimant's level of care nor the reasonableness of the claimant's conduct is relevant to the viability of a claim in restitution. . . . [T]he role of restitution for mistake is to protect property against inadvertent dispossession. A claim in restitution is not affected by the claimant's negligence, because rights of ownership are not dependent on the owner's degree of care. . . .

g. Mistake of fact and mistake of law. The present section rejects any distinction between mistake of fact and mistake of law, adopting a conclusion reached long ago by the better-reasoned American decisions. . . . If a benefit is conferred by mistake, in circumstances that would otherwise support a claim in restitution, neither the unjustified enrichment of the recipient nor the unintentional dispossession of the transferor is affected by a determination that the mistake was one of fact, one of law, or an amalgam of the two.

§12. Mistake in Expression

If an instrument is intended to transfer an interest in property or to embody an obligation pursuant to a valid agreement, and

(a) by a mistake as to its contents or legal effect, the instrument fails to reflect the terms of the agreement; and

(b) performance or enforcement on the terms of the instrument has resulted or would result in the unjust enrichment of one party at the expense of another; then the person disadvantaged by the mistake has a claim in restitution as necessary to prevent the unjust enrichment of the other.

Comment

. . . .

b. Relation to contract law. The rule stated in this section overlaps with the doctrine of reformation in the law of contracts. . . . The rationale in contract is that reformation gives effect to the real agreement of the parties; the rationale in restitution is that reformation avoids the unjust enrichment of one party at the expense of the other. . . .

e. Mutual mistake. A mistake in expression justifying relief under this section need not be "mutual," nor does restitution depend on attributing the mistake to one person rather than another. . . .

The relevant mistake in such cases consists in the assumption that an instrument correctly reflects the terms of the transaction as agreed, when in fact it does not. The circumstance that potentially justifies a claim in restitution is the fact of a divergence between the terms of the instrument and the terms of the agreement . . . .

Topic 2. Defective Consent or Authority

§13. Fraud and Misrepresentation

(1) A transfer induced by fraud or material misrepresentation is subject to rescission and restitution. The transferee is liable in restitution as necessary to avoid unjust enrichment.

(2) A transfer induced by fraud is void if the transferor had neither knowledge of, nor reasonable opportunity to learn, the character of the resulting transfer or its essential terms. Otherwise the transferee obtains voidable title.

Comment

. . . .

b. Relation to contract law. Because most transfers are made pursuant to contract, rules that determine when such a transfer is subject to rescission for fraudulent inducement necessarily coincide with rules that determine when the agreement itself is subject to avoidance. . . .

Where contract is concerned with the effectiveness of an agreement, the focus of restitution is on the effectiveness of any resulting transfer. Although many issues of fraudulent inducement are simultaneously a question of contract and of restitution, the overlap between the subjects at this point is not complete. Avoidance of a wholly executory contract, whether the reason is fraud or something else, presents no issue of restitution. Reversal of a completed exchange – whatever the basis of invalidity – is squarely within the province of restitution, while it is explained only awkwardly as a liability in contract. . . .

c. Law of misrepresentation; causation; materiality. . . . A transfer is not subject to invalidation for misrepresentation, fraudulent or otherwise, unless the misrepresentation induced the transfer. Subject to this test of causation, a transfer induced by fraud is subject to rescission without regard to materiality; whereas a transfer induced by innocent misrepresentation is subject to rescission only if the misrepresentation was material.

Cases in which the claimant confers benefits as the result of another's innocent (but material) misrepresentation will usually be characterized as cases of mistake. The distinction makes no difference to the analysis or to the outcome. . . .

e. No requirement of injury or enrichment. Rescission of a transfer induced by fraud or material misrepresentation requires no showing either that the transferor has suffered economic injury (the requirement in tort) or that the transferee has realized a benefit at the transferor's expense (the standard condition of unjust enrichment). . . . Restitution via rescission . . . protects the claimant against an involuntary dispossession. If the defendant has induced a transfer by fraud, it is no answer to show that the transaction did the claimant no harm, or that it resulted in no gain to the defendant. . . .

By contrast, a claimant who seeks restitution of unjust enrichment realized as a result of fraud or material misrepresentation – instead of, or in addition to, restitution via rescission – must establish the amount of the defendant's unjust enrichment as in every other case. . . .

§14. Duress

(1) Duress is coercion that is wrongful as a matter of law.

(2) A transfer induced by duress is subject to rescission and restitution. The transferee is liable in restitution as necessary to avoid unjust enrichment.

(3) If the effect of duress is tantamount to physical compulsion, a transfer induced by duress is void. If not, a transfer induced by duress conveys voidable title.

Comment

. . . .

b. The problem of definition. Duress is frequently defined as a threat that overcomes a person's free will or destroys a person's "apparent consent." Such a definition underscores the element that duress has in common with the other transactional defects addressed in this Topic, all of which make a transfer subject to rescission on grounds related to the validity of the transferor's consent to the transaction. . . .

. . . . Ultimately the idea of duress turns on a distinction, not between voluntary and coerced transactions, but between permissible and impermissible forms of coercion. . . . The characteristics of wrongful coercion are not reducible to a single formula, but it is possible to collect instructive examples that share certain characteristics. See Comment *g*.

c. Void and voidable transfers. . . . A transfer induced by duress that is "tantamount to physical compulsion" is altogether void, while a transfer induced by some lesser degree of impermissible coercion is merely voidable. . . .

Meaningful threats of immediate physical harm (inducing the proverbial transfer "at gunpoint") are the obvious example of duress that is tantamount to physical compulsion; most instances of impermissible coercion do not rise to that level. See comment *g*. The distinction in a marginal case must be drawn by the court.

d. Restitution to the extent of unjust enrichment. In a contractual context, the issue of duress determines whether an agreement is valid or invalid: there is ordinarily no question of partial enforceability. In the law of restitution, by contrast, . . . [t]here is a claim . . . only to the extent that a transfer induced by duress results in unjust enrichment: §14(2) is drafted accordingly. The use of bad means to coerce payment of a just debt may be illegal, but it does not present a problem in unjust enrichment. . . .

e. Payment pursuant to compromise. Payment of an unliquidated obligation, or payment of a claim as to which there is some recognized uncertainty or dispute between the parties, is either expressly or by implication a payment pursuant to compromise. If the parties agree to settle a disputed claim, the payor cannot disavow the settlement and recover the payment in restitution, merely on a showing that the payment exceeded the true amount of the original liability. The same relationship is presented when payment is made pursuant to modification of a preexisting contract, and the payor later asserts that payment was made under duress. In such cases, if the settlement or the modification was valid as a contract, a payment in accordance therewith finds an adequate legal basis in the parties' agreement; and the payor has no claim in restitution by the rules of this section.

A claim that payment in such circumstances was induced by duress is necessarily analyzed in two stages. The first inquiry, governed by contract principles, examines the validity of the parties' accord or modification in light of the assertion that it was induced by duress. . . . If the agreement of accord or modification is valid and enforceable as a contract, the restitution claim fails, regardless of the true state of the original obligation. If the accord or modification is subject to avoidance by reason of duress, the claimant has a claim in restitution to the extent permitted by this section. . . .

g. *Impermissible coercion.* A general distinction between the lawful and the unlawful forms of coercion is notoriously difficult to state. . . .

. . . . The purpose of the present Comment is [] to identify certain recurring circumstances in which a threat or refusal inducing a transfer is predictably characterized as duress. Such an enumeration of instances obviously does not purport to be comprehensive.

A threat or refusal that is independently illegal or tortious constitutes duress. This initial category of wrongful pressure includes the obvious cases in which a transfer is procured by a criminal assault . . . . Because the tort of conversion is one of strict liability, the unauthorized detention of another's property constitutes duress even when the party who refuses to release the property acts in good faith. . . .

Lawful coercion becomes impermissible when employed to support a bad-faith demand: one that the party asserting it knows (or should know) to be unjustified. Some instances of this form of duress involve the commencement or threat of civil litigation. . . .

Coercive means are frequently held to constitute duress, notwithstanding that they may be both legally authorized and employed in good faith, when they induce an overpayment of a subsisting, liquidated claim. The pattern of decisions in such cases is explained in part by observing that a payment of money not due . . . gives rise to prima facie unjust enrichment and a claim in restitution to recover the excess. The obviousness of the unjust enrichment in such circumstances, and the ease of fashioning the remedy, make these cases attractive ones for relief. . . .

. . . . The doctrine of voluntary payment bars a claim in restitution where the payor has elected to satisfy a doubtful claim in the face of a recognized uncertainty as to the underlying liability, because a payor who chooses to proceed in such circumstances has assumed the risk of overpayment. . . . [A] party's assumption of the risk is valid only if it is voluntary. The inference of assumption of risk is accordingly excluded if it appears that an overpayment was induced by duress.

. . . [C]oercion . . . that [] induces an overpayment is [not duress] where the only pressure exerted on the payor is the threat or commencement of civil litigation. . . . On the other hand, if the threat inducing the payment involves substantial prejudice to the interests of the payor, beyond the mere prospect of having to defend a lawsuit, a payment in excess of the underlying obligation will be recoverable in restitution, notwithstanding that the demand was asserted in good faith. . . .

In a final set of cases, the characteristic feature of duress is that the stronger party exploits the other's vulnerability in a manner that passes the bounds of legitimate self-interest. Legitimate self-interest (and lawful coercion) encompasses the usual freedom to deal with another on one's own terms or not at all. So long as the stronger party is not responsible for the other's vulnerability, driving a hard bargain does not constitute duress. But the exploitation of a superior bargaining position will predictably be found wrongful when the stronger party seeks additional leverage by exploiting a vulnerability to which the weaker party (in dealing with the stronger) is not properly subject.

.... Duress may be found in threats to breach a contract, when the performing party seeks to exploit the necessitous circumstances that the threatened breach would create.... Threats to exercise what would normally be a legal right may constitute duress when employed to achieve an advantage unrelated to the interests that the legal right is supposed to protect.... A similar judgment about improper bargaining leverage underlies decisions that find duress in a threat of litigation to gain an objective unrelated to the matter in suit....

h. Duress through civil litigation. The threat or commencement of litigation to enforce a demand is an important example of lawful coercion. Subject to limited exceptions, a good-faith threat of legal process, though evidently coercive, must be permissible; so that a transfer induced thereby is not subject to rescission for duress....

The generally privileged status of coercion by litigation is subject to important exceptions. The threat or instigation of legal proceedings in pursuit of a claim known to be unjustified is wrongful prima facie; such acts constitute duress, and a transfer induced thereby is voidable.... Civil process may also constitute impermissible coercion when – despite the legitimacy of the claim being advanced in court – the burden of litigation is imposed or threatened in order to obtain an advantage unrelated to the matter in suit....

j. [R]atification. ....A voidable transfer induced by duress may be ratified by the act or acquiescence of the transferor, once the improper pressure has been removed.

§15. Undue Influence

(1) Undue influence is excessive and unfair persuasion, sufficient to overcome the free will of the transferor, between parties who occupy either a confidential relation or a relation of dominance on one side and subservience on the other.

(2) A transfer induced by undue influence is subject to rescission and restitution. The transferee is liable in restitution as necessary to avoid unjust enrichment.

Comment

a. General principles and scope; relation to other sections. ....A transfer procured by undue influence may reflect the transferor's misunderstanding of relevant circumstances, but there is no need to establish misrepresentation. It is the result of persuasion that the law regards as excessive, but such persuasion need not reach the level of wrongful coercion. Undue influence presumes an unusual susceptibility on the part of the transferor, but the doctrine will protect persons of full legal capacity. ...

b. The necessary relation of the parties. The test of undue influence is not the abuse of a confidential or other preexisting relation between the parties, but the fact of overreaching and overpersuasion by which a transferor is made subject to the will of another. . . . Undue influence may thus take place between persons who stand in no particular relation to each other, outside the context of the transaction in question. In fact, however, it is a rare case that finds undue influence without finding abuse of a [dominant-subservient] relation between the parties. . . .

. . . . The doctrine of undue influence has no application to any transaction that is the product of arm's-length negotiation. (Such transactions are policed by the doctrines of fraud, duress, and incapacity.) Rather, the rule of the present section protects a limited class of susceptible persons from being taken advantage of in their dealings with those in whom they have placed a special confidence, or to whom they are otherwise subservient.

The confidential relation that is the characteristic setting of undue influence may be of two kinds. The first comprises specific relations that are characterized as fiduciary as a matter of law. These include the relations of principal and agent, trustee and beneficiary, guardian and ward, and attorney and client. The second type of confidential relation arises between persons whose relationship may or may not be fiduciary in a legal sense . . . . This second category of confidential relation includes relations between parent and child . . . ; between spouses; between siblings; between relatives generally, especially between dominant younger relatives and dependent elderly ones; between fiancs; between religious adherent and spiritual adviser; between physician and patient; between investor and financial counselor; and between close friends and neighbors. A confidential relation need not fall within any of these recurring patterns. Rather it exists whenever it can be established as a fact that one party dealt with another on a basis of special trust and confidence; or that one party was in fact subservient to the other's dominant influence. Judicial definitions of "confidential relation" often include a requirement of dominance and subservience, so that the alternatives just stated become aspects of a single test.

A judicial finding that a challenged transfer took place between parties in a confidential relation, or in a relationship of dominance and subservience. . . . will in many cases give rise to a presumption that the transfer was the result of undue influence, shifting the burden of proof on the issue to the party asserting the transfer's validity. . . .

The proposition that the alleged undue influence was exerted between parties in a confidential relation, or in a relation marked by dominance and subservience, serves as a threshold test of the claim. If the relation of the parties cannot be so characterized, the case is not one of undue influence . . . .

d. Undue influence by a third party. The undue influence that invalidates a transfer may be exerted by a third party. . . .

§16.   Incapacity of Transferor

(1) A transfer by a person lacking requisite legal capacity is subject to rescission and restitution unless ratified. The transferee is liable in restitution as necessary to avoid unjust enrichment.

(2) Except as otherwise provided by statute:
    (a) A transfer by a minor confers voidable title.
    (b) When a transfer is challenged on the ground of mental capacity:
        (i) if at the time of the transfer the transferor's incapacity has been adjudicated and is continuing, the transfer is void;
        (ii) if the transferor's incapacity is only adjudicated thereafter, the transfer confers voidable title. . . .
(3) If the transferee has dealt with the transferor in good faith on reasonable terms, then notwithstanding the transferor's incapacity
    (a) rescission and restitution leaves the transferor liable in restitution for benefits received in the transaction, as provided in §§33 and 54; and
    (b) the court may qualify or deny the right to rescission to avoid an inequitable result (§54(6)).

Comment

a. General principles and scope; relation to other sections. . . . When a transfer occurs as part of an exchange transaction, the rules of this section overlap substantially with the corresponding rules of contract law. See Restatement Second, Contracts §§12-16. Both the test of incapacity, and the rules relating to such collateral matters as disaffirmance and ratification, will be the same whether the case arises in restitution or in contract. But the characteristic applications of the two bodies of law are to different stages of the exchange transaction. Where lack of capacity is interposed as a defense to a party's obligation under a wholly executory contract, the case presents no issue of restitution. Conversely, where a party seeks to rescind an executed conveyance on the ground of incapacity, the enforceability of a purported contractual obligation is no longer directly relevant.

The present section is concerned with restitution in favor of an incapacitated *transferor.* . . . By contrast, the rules stated in §33 describe a restitution claim against an incapacitated *transferee.* Such a claim is ordinarily asserted by a person who has conferred a benefit, pursuant to contract, on a recipient whose undertaking to pay for that benefit is revealed to be unenforceable by reason of incapacity.

Many factual settings present both issues at once, making it necessary to read the two sections together. An incapacitated transferor who disaffirms an exchange transaction in which there has been any degree of reciprocal performance has a claim in restitution under the rules of this section, subject to a counterclaim under the rules of §33. See §16(3)(a) and Comment *f.* Other cases of incapacity present an issue of restitution on one side only. If an incapacitated transferor seeks to set aside a gratuitous transfer, the restitution claim is wholly within the scope of this section. By contrast, if the restitution claimant has provided goods or services on credit to a recipient who lacked the requisite capacity to contract, the claim is wholly within the scope of §33. . . .

c. Disaffirmance and ratification. The right to disaffirm a transfer on grounds of minority or mental incompetence is often described as "personal" to the incapacitated transferor, meaning that it may not be exercised by the other party to the transaction. . . .

Transfers that are voidable because of the incapacity of the transferor are subject to ratification, either by the transferor (once the incapacity is removed) or by the transferor's representative. Failure to disaffirm a transfer within a reasonable time after the incapacity has been removed – typically, after a minor transferor has reached the age of majority – is ordinarily treated as a ratification. . . .

d. Restitution for incapacity; void and voidable transfers. Section 16(1) states a general rule of rescission and restitution by reason of a transferor's lack of legal capacity . . . . Lack of capacity is a sufficient basis for rescission, notwithstanding the absence of other transactional defects. Where incapacity is established, in other words, it is not a requirement of restitution that the transfer be the product of fraud or undue influence, nor that the transfer be disadvantageous to the incapacitated transferor.

. . . [A] transfer by an incapacitated party gives rise to a claim in restitution against the transferee. Restitution in such circumstances usually involves the recovery of money paid, or the recovery *in specie* of other property transferred. . . . Where the claimant has conferred services or other nonreturnable benefits pursuant to a contract that is subsequently disaffirmed, restitution is of the money value of the benefits conferred. . . .

Illustrations

3. A, a minor, agrees to purchase Blackacre from B for $10,000, making a down payment of $2500 cash. While still a minor, A disaffirms the transaction. Upon A's tender of a reconveyance of Blackacre, A is entitled to recover $2500 plus interest from B. . . .

5. Nephew, a minor, contracts to work in Uncle's Turkish bathhouse for $200 a week. After three years, Nephew resigns his position and disaffirms the employment contract. The reasonable value of Nephew's services is $500 a week. Nephew has a claim in restitution against Uncle for $500 a week, less the wages already paid.

Section 16(2) sets forth the usual rules for determining whether a transfer by someone who lacks legal capacity is void or voidable. The distinction is relevant to cases in which the property in question has been subsequently transferred by the immediate transferee to a third party who might qualify as a bona fide purchaser. . . . If the initial transfer is altogether void, a subsequent purchaser for value and without notice acquires no title. . . .

e. Unjust enrichment as a result of rescission. . . . A transfer by an incapacitated person that is only voidable, not void, is not necessarily one that the law endeavors to suppress. Unlike most transfers subject to rescission, a transfer by an incapacitated person may be part of a transaction that is fair, reasonable, and ultimately beneficial to the transferor. . . .

. . . . Incapacity serves a protective rather than a prohibitory function, as seen from the fact that it ordinarily renders a transaction voidable at the election of the incapacitated party. Yet a rule that protects certain classes of contracting parties by permitting them to disaffirm a completed transfer imposes significant hardships on innocent parties with whom they deal. Moreover, unless both parties are made fully liable in restitution for benefits received, rescission of the transaction after full or partial performance may easily result in the unjust enrichment of the incapacitated party at the expense of the other, contradicting to that extent the basic principles of restitutionary liability. . . .

American law has traditionally shown greater indulgence toward minority than toward other forms of incapacity. In some jurisdictions it may still be the law that a minor may avoid an executed purchase and recover the price paid, without any obligation of counter-restitution beyond restoration of that part of the purchased property (if any) remaining in the minor's possession. If by contrast an adult transferor lacks mental capacity – and such incapacity has not previously been adjudicated – the same transaction may not even be subject to rescission if the court finds that it was made on reasonable terms. The position of this Restatement is that the remedy of rescission and restitution for incapacity (with the corollary obligation of counter-restitution by the claimant) is in principle the same, whatever the nature of the incapacity; that avoidance for incapacity is justified only to the extent that it serves a legitimate protective function; and that rescission must not result in unjust enrichment of the incapacitated claimant, at the expense of a person who has dealt with the claimant in good faith on reasonable terms. . . .

. . . . [A] person who supplies "necessaries" on reasonable terms to a person known to be mentally incapacitated, or to a minor, will not be liable to restore the price paid if the transaction is subsequently disaffirmed. . . .

f. Liability in restitution of the rescinding transferor. . . . The standard requirement of restoration as a condition of rescission significantly limits the power of avoidance, since its practical effect is to foreclose rescission if the party seeking avoidance is unable to restore the benefits received (or their value) in the disaffirmed transaction. Applied without qualification to incapacitated transferors, the rule would substantially undercut the protection intended to be afforded by doctrines of legal capacity. The rule of §16(3)(a). . . . applies only in cases where the transferee has dealt with the transferor in good faith on reasonable terms, thereby excluding all those transactions against which the incapacitated person most clearly requires protection. The claimant's obligation is restitutionary, not contractual: it is accordingly measured by the actual value of what was received, not by the contract price. . . . Section 33(3) supplies a further safeguard, because it authorizes a court to limit the restitutionary liability of an incapacitated transferee whenever such liability would impermissibly undermine the protective policy underlying the rule of incapacity. . . .

g. Further limitations on the power of avoidance. . . . [C]ourts have employed a variety of means to limit directly the power of avoidance for incapacity. The oldest of the rules under this heading protects a contracting party who has supplied an incapacitated person with "necessaries." To the same end, statutes in some jurisdictions validate other obligations of incapacitated persons, such as minors' debts for education loans. Alternatively, avoidance may be limited on an ad hoc basis by finding that a transferor has effectively ratified the transaction in question; or that a transferee's change of position creates an estoppel. Instead of repeating the limiting rules devised for particular circumstances, §16(3)(b) refers to the general rule that the remedy of rescission and restitution may be qualified or denied to avoid an inequitable result . . . .

§17. Lack of Authority

A transfer by an agent, trustee, or other fiduciary outside the scope of the transferor's authority, or otherwise in breach of the transferor's duty to the principal or beneficiary, is subject to rescission and restitution. The transferee is liable in restitution to the principal or beneficiary as necessary to avoid unjust enrichment.

Comment

. . . .

b. *Lack of authority; apparent authority.* As agents and trustees, the transferors in cases addressed by §17 have authority to make some dispositions of the claimant's property but not others. The determination that a particular transfer has been made without proper authority depends on legal rules outside the scope of this Restatement. . . .

. . . . A transferee from a purported agent or trustee having neither actual nor apparent authority is liable in restitution. A transferee from an agent or trustee having apparent but not actual authority is protected against prejudice from the transaction in question . . . .

The defendant in a restitution case within §17 is frequently without fault. Innocence or lack of notice on the part of the defendant (in the present context, "apparent authority" on the part of the agent or trustee) is not by itself a defense to unjust enrichment . . . .

CHAPTER 3.   UNREQUESTED INTERVENTION

Topic 1.   Emergency Intervention

§20. Protection of Another's Life or Health

(1) A person who performs, supplies, or obtains professional services required for the protection of another's life or health is entitled to restitution from the other as necessary to prevent unjust enrichment, if the circumstances justify the decision to intervene without request.

(2) Unjust enrichment under this section is measured by a reasonable charge for the services in question.

Comment

a. *General principles and scope; relation to other sections.* The claim for emergency medical services rendered in the absence of contract is one of restitution's paradigms. Its significance lies . . . in the clarity with which it reflects the general principles that justify a claim to compensation for nonbargained benefits voluntarily conferred. An emergency that threatens life or health offers the ultimate justification for conferring a benefit in the absence of contract, if need be, asserting a claim for payment only after services have been rendered. Under ordinary circumstances, this reversal of the normal sequence of an exchange transaction is not tolerated: a transferor or provider who neglects a suitable opportunity to bargain with the recipient ahead of time will be deemed to have acted gratuitously. See §2(3). The significance of the medical emergency is not only that the provider is amply justified in proceeding without first making a contract, but that the benefit to the recipient is unmistakable, even if its measurement is sometimes debated. . . .

The present section authorizes a claim in respect of "professional services," whether the claim is asserted by the provider directly, by an institution or municipality that causes the services to be provided, or by a third party who pays for the services. . . .

b. Professional services. Emergency assistance rendered by a nonprofessional, however valuable, does not give rise to a claim in restitution under existing law. The result is that professional providers of medical assistance are routinely given an enforceable claim to compensation; while the nonprofessional rescuer or good Samaritan enjoys only such rewards as others may choose to bestow. . . .

Practical concerns are often advanced to account for this difference in treatment. It is one thing to encourage professional intervention in emergencies, another to create financial incentives for would-be rescuers who might better remain on the sidelines. The problem of valuation is even more of an obstacle. Services of physicians, hospitals, and ambulance drivers are readily valued, while emergency rescue by a bystander is literally priceless. The fact that it is impossible to assign a value to the rescue of human life explains why the rule of §20 is limited to professional services while the rule of §21 (protection of another's property) is not. Unsolicited intervention to protect a person's stray livestock or unmoored sailboat can be valued with relative ease, because it usually takes the form of services (by stables and dockyards) for which there is a market. The same difficulty explains the traditional refusal in admiralty to make any award in respect of "pure life salvage," in circumstances where salvage of property would be readily compensated.

. . . . The law does not require that every benefit be paid for. See §2(1). A heroic rescue may confer a benefit of inestimable value, but it is likely to be purely altruistic in origin. The imposition of restitutionary liability in such circumstances – a principle that would become visible only when the claim was resisted – transforms an act of self-sacrifice into a contentious exchange of values. The law avoids these unedifying consequences by presuming that an emergency rescue is a gratuitous act. The heroic bystander receives nothing; the heroic professional receives a "reasonable and customary charge" for professional services, but nothing extra for heroism. . . .

§21. Preservation of Another's Property

(1) A person who takes effective action to protect another's property from threatened harm is entitled to restitution from the other as necessary to prevent

unjust enrichment, if the circumstances justify the decision to intervene without request. Unrequested intervention is justified only when it is reasonable to assume the owner would wish the action performed.

(2) Unjust enrichment under this section is measured by the loss avoided or by a reasonable charge for the services provided, whichever is less.

Comment

a. General principles and scope. The word "property" is used in this section in a broad sense. While a typical claim within §21 involves services provided in an emergency to protect real property or chattels, a case in which the claimant has intervened to protect intangibles, or to protect the defendant (and thus the defendant's assets) from a threatened liability, is likewise within the scope of this section. . . .

c. Gratuitous services. There is no claim in restitution for services, however valuable, that the provider has rendered without intent to charge. The relevant state of mind of the claimant is a question of fact. . . .

d. Valuation and refusal. As is true of noncontractual transfers generally, one party's intervention to protect another's property in the absence of agreement may confer a benefit that is less than the price the same services would command if rendered pursuant to contract. The benefit conferred under such circumstances is necessarily limited to the value of the property preserved. It may be further limited by individual factors that permit the court to determine the degree to which unrequested services have actually been of value to a particular defendant. . . .

. . . . There is no claim under this section for services rendered to an owner who was entitled to refuse them and attempted to do so. . . .

Topic 2.   *Performance Rendered to a Third Person*

§25.   Uncompensated Performance Under Contract with Third Person

(1) If the claimant renders to a third person a contractual performance for which the claimant does not receive the promised compensation, and the effect of the claimant's uncompensated performance is to confer a benefit on the defendant, the claimant is entitled to restitution from the defendant as necessary to prevent unjust enrichment.

(2) There is unjust enrichment for purposes of subsection (1) only if the following three conditions are met:

(a) Liability in restitution may not subject the defendant to a forced exchange (§2(4)). This condition is likely to be satisfied if the benefit realized by the defendant

(i) is one for which the defendant has expressed a willingness to pay,

(ii) saves the defendant an otherwise necessary expense, or

(iii) is realized by the defendant in money.

(b) Absent liability in restitution, the claimant will not be compensated for the performance in question, and the defendant will retain the benefit of the claimant's performance free of any liability to pay for it.

(c) Liability in restitution will not subject the defendant to an obligation from which it was understood by the parties that the defendant would be free.

(3) Restitution by the rule of this section may be qualified or denied if recovery would conflict with a system of priorities, established by other law, ordering claims against the third person, the defendant, or the assets of either.

Comment

a. General principles and scope. Most transactions for which restitution may be available by the rule of this section fall within one of two common (though nonexclusive) patterns. In a first set of cases, A is a subcontractor, B is a property owner, and C (now unavailable) is the general contractor with whom both parties have dealt. In a second, A has performed work benefiting B's property under a contract with C, who is typically a tenant or a family member of B; C had an interest in seeing the work performed but no authority to bind B to pay for it. In either setting, the exit or insolvency of C leaves A without compensation for work that was performed as requested. If a further consequence of the interrupted transaction is that B stands to obtain a valuable benefit without paying for it, the outcome may be one that the law will characterize as unjust enrichment. . . .

b. Threshold limits to the claim. . . . Section 25 takes as a starting point the proposition, inherited from Restatement of Restitution §110 (1937), that when A confers a benefit on B as the performance of A's contract with C, C's failure to render the performance promised to A does not necessarily mean that B has been enriched at A's expense; nor does it mean that any enrichment of B is necessarily unjust. The limited circumstances in which B might be unjustly enriched by A's performance are identified by two principal tests. The first is that restitution to A not subject B to what this Restatement calls a forced exchange (§2(4)). Circumstances in which this requirement are likely to be met are indicated by §25(2)(a)(i)-(iii). The second fundamental requirement of unjust enrichment in these circumstances is that B must stand to obtain a valuable benefit at A's expense without paying anyone for it (§25(2)(b)). There is accordingly no unjust enrichment if B has paid the contract price to C; nor if B has paid in full (to C and to others, following C's default) the price originally fixed by contract for the work to which A has made an uncompensated contribution. . . .

. . . [R]estitution will be denied where the imposition of a liability in restitution would overturn an existing allocation of risk or limitation of liability previously established by contract. There is accordingly no claim in restitution when B has already paid the contract price for the benefits received, even if the contract price is less than the cost or value of the performance in question. Nor is there restitution under this section if the imposition of liability would alter the basis of the underlying transaction, subjecting B to an obligation from which the parties understood that B would be free. . . .

. . . . If the claimant is an unpaid subcontractor, in an ideal case for recovery it might be shown that the defendant has received the very performance that he specifically requested and agreed to pay for. . . . [T]here is in principle no forced exchange to the extent that the defendant's liability in restitution is congruent with his own bargain. . . .

Different issues characterize those cases in which the defendant has not requested the performance in question, as where the claimant improves the landlord's property under contract with a tenant. Because the benefits conferred in cases of this kind are generally nonreturnable – typically consisting of services and improvements to realty – a claim under this section confronts restitution's fundamental reluctance to require a defendant to pay money, at a price set by someone else, for goods and services he had no adequate opportunity to select or to refuse. . . .

. . . . [T]he innocent defendant's liability in restitution must not leave him in a worse position than if the underlying transaction had not taken place[]. . . .

d. Measure of recovery. . . . A successful claimant under this section recovers the amount of the benefit conferred on the defendant or the claimant's cost of performance, whichever is less. Because the claimant's recovery is based on the defendant's enrichment, and not on the claimant's contract with an absent third person, the claimant necessarily bears the risk that fluctuations in value, whatever their origin, will cause the value placed in the hands of the defendant to be less than the cost of performance. . . .

CHAPTER 4.   RESTITUTION AND CONTRACT

Topic 1.   *Restitution to a Performing Party with no Claim on the Contract*

§31. Unenforceability

(1) A person who renders performance under an agreement that cannot be enforced against the recipient by reason of
  (a) indefiniteness, or
  (b) the failure to satisfy an extrinsic requirement of enforceability such as the Statute of Frauds,
has a claim in restitution against the recipient as necessary to prevent unjust enrichment. There is no unjust enrichment if the claimant receives the counter-performance specified by the parties' unenforceable agreement.

(2) There is no claim under this section if enforcement of the agreement is barred by the applicable statute of limitations, nor in any other case in which the allowance of restitution would defeat the policy of the law that makes the agreement unenforceable. Restitution is appropriate except to the extent that forfeiture is an intended or acceptable consequence of unenforceability.

Comment

a. General principles and scope; unenforceable agreements; relation to other sections.
Treatises on contract and restitution employ the term "unenforceable contract"
to indicate particular grounds of unenforceability: either the court's inability to
determine an appropriate remedy (usually as a consequence of indefiniteness),
or the failure of the contract in question to satisfy an extrinsic condition of
enforceability such as the Statute of Frauds. The present section describes the
restitution claim asserted by a performing party whose contract is unenforceable for one of these reasons. . . .

b. The effect of performance. . . . Under many circumstances, full or even
partial performance of an agreement that would have been unenforceable
under the Statute of Frauds [prior to performance] will render the agreement
enforceable by the performing party according to its terms. The scope of this
"performance exception" is determined by the contract law of each jurisdiction,
but it is a rule to which principles of unjust enrichment visibly contribute.
Where the contract remains unenforceable notwithstanding the claimant's
performance, relief (if any) takes the form of the restitution claim described in
this section. . . .

Different rules govern the availability of restitution in connection with
agreements that are merely "unenforceable" (§31) and agreements that are
unenforceable because they are "illegal" (§32). The distinction may usually be
drawn by inquiring whether the contract at issue is one for which the law merely
establishes special evidentiary requirements, or whether the underlying transaction is one that the law actually condemns. Lying somewhere astride these
familiar classifications are cases in which the claimant has violated a statute
whose objectives might be regarded as both procedural and substantive: for
example, a statute providing that a contract for auto repairs is unenforceable
unless preceded by a written estimate. Cases arising under such statutes are
classified within the present section, but their disposition – unless the restitution
claim is foreclosed by the statute in question – requires a balancing of competing
objectives more commonly associated with problems of illegal contracts. . . .

The availability of restitution is not affected by the statutory language used to
state a rule of unenforceability, so long as the statute is not interpreted to
prohibit a claim in restitution as well as a claim on the contract itself. Subject to
the limitations described in subsection (2), therefore, a claim under this section
is not foreclosed by statutory language to the effect that "no action shall be
brought" on a contract of a particular description, or describing such a contract
as "void."

c. Restitution and reliance. This section describes a liability based on the unjust
enrichment of the recipient of the claimant's contractual performance. The
language of restitution is sometimes employed to veil what could be more
candidly described as enforcement based on reliance. These are cases awarding
compensation for losses incurred in performing (or preparing to perform) an
unenforceable contract, notwithstanding the absence of benefit to the defendant as a result of the plaintiff's expenditure. A straightforward account of such
outcomes describes them in terms of promissory liability (circumventing unacceptable consequences of the Statute of Frauds), not as restitution based on
unjust enrichment. . . .

f. Statute of Frauds. Restitution is the traditional recourse of persons who have performed contracts that are unenforceable (notwithstanding such performance) for lack of a signed writing satisfying the Statute of Frauds. The important classes of contracts for these purposes are agreements respecting an interest in real property . . . and agreements not to be performed within a year of their making. . . . Unwritten contracts for the sale of personal property are not a significant source of restitution claims, because U.C.C. §2-201(3)(c) makes them enforceable to the extent of partial performance by either buyer or seller. Unwritten leases of personal property are likewise enforceable to the extent of performance. U.C.C. §2A-201(4)(c). . . .

h. Other laws requiring a writing. Besides the common provisions of the Statute of Frauds, the laws of most U.S. jurisdictions contain a variety of additional statutes or regulations . . . providing that agreements governing particular types of transaction are unenforceable unless evidenced by a signed writing. One important example, responding to a longstanding problem at common law, is a statute denying enforceability to an oral contract to make (or not to revoke) a will. More recent enactments within this category pursue regulatory objectives associated with consumer protection. Approximately half the states require a signed memorandum as a condition to enforcing an agreement to pay a commission to a real estate broker. Other transactions commonly made subject to a writing requirement include agreements governing payment for home improvements, auto repairs, or lawyers' services. A wide variety of other transactions may be subject to similar requirements in particular jurisdictions.

A party's uncompensated performance of an oral agreement made unenforceable by any such provision gives rise to the prima facie claim in restitution described in subsection (1). By comparison with the claimant whose oral contract is within the traditional Statute of Frauds, however, the claimant whose contract is made unenforceable by a modern regulatory statute is much more likely to encounter the objection that restitution is either prohibited by the statute in question or inimical to the policy behind it. Some modern legislation within this category may be fairly construed to prohibit not only enforcement of the unwritten contract but also restitution for benefits conferred thereunder. More often, a court will have to decide whether the allowance of restitution would weaken the protection intended to be afforded by a statute or regulation that (by its terms) prohibits only enforcement. The same question is posed in converse form by asking whether the forfeiture that results if restitution is denied is an intended or acceptable consequence of unenforceability. See subsection (2). . . .

. . . . Because unconvincing or doubtful allegations of oral contracts do not prevail in the face of the Statute of Frauds (or analogous writing requirements), the restitution claims that will effectively test the policy of the statute are necessarily those in which both the formation of the agreement and the benefit to the recipient from the claimant's performance can be clearly established. Because the benefit conferred in such a case is something that the recipient requested and promised to pay for, the recipient's enrichment is manifest. Because the policy behind a rule of unenforceability is ordinarily intended as a shield and not a sword, the denial of restitution in such circumstances works the kind of forfeiture that equity is said to abhor. . . .

i. Measure of recovery. Restitution based on performance of an unenforceable contract is likely to yield a smaller recovery than damages for breach. For reasons applicable to contract remedies generally, a recovery measured by benefit conferred is often less than the contractual expectation (which would give the claimant the full benefit of the bargain); it will often be less than damages measured by the claimant's expenditures in reliance (which would reimburse expenditures not resulting in measurable benefit). See Restatement Second, Contracts §344, Comment *a*. Restitution by the rule of this section is measured by the value of the claimant's performance to the recipient, not by what was promised in exchange, nor by what the claimant's performance cost the claimant. . . .

Nevertheless, the terms of the unenforceable contract will influence and may even determine the measure of recovery in restitution. . . .

If the parties have specified a price for a performance that has no definitive market value – as in most cases of personal services – the value to the recipient of claimant's performance may properly be determined, for restitution purposes, by what the recipient has offered to pay. The effect of restitution in such a case may be indistinguishable from a partial enforcement, since it awards the contract price so far as the claimant has performed. Restitution remains easily distinguishable from contract damages, even if the price term is accepted as the measure of enrichment, because it affords no remedy in respect of the executory portion of the contract. . . .

In the rare case in which the claimant might prove that a requested performance had a market value in excess of the promised compensation, recovery in restitution will be limited by the contract price (§50(2)(b)). . . .

§32. Illegality

A person who renders performance under an agreement that is illegal or otherwise unenforceable for reasons of public policy may obtain restitution from the recipient in accordance with the following rules:

(1) Restitution will be allowed, whether or not necessary to prevent unjust enrichment, if restitution is required by the policy of the underlying prohibition.

(2) Restitution will also be allowed, as necessary to prevent unjust enrichment, if the allowance of restitution will not defeat or frustrate the policy of the underlying prohibition. There is no unjust enrichment if the claimant receives the counter-performance specified by the parties' unenforceable agreement.

(3) Restitution will be denied, notwithstanding the enrichment of the defendant at the claimant's expense, if a claim under subsection (2) is foreclosed by the claimant's inequitable conduct. . . .

Comment

. . . .

b. Synopsis. . . . In the context of an illegal contract – as in all of the transactional settings addressed by §§31-36 – contractual performance by a party who does not receive (and cannot compel) the promised counterperformance will frequently result in the unjust enrichment of the recipient and a prima facie entitlement to restitution. The availability of the unjust enrichment claim is qualified in this setting, however, because ordinary considerations of justice between the parties may yield to one of two countervailing considerations.

The first involves a comparison of competing policy objectives: the policy against unjust enrichment, on the one hand, and the policy that prohibits the underlying transaction, on the other. To the extent they are incompatible, private claims based on unjust enrichment yield to public policy objectives. . . .

. . . . [Second, a] court may deny restitution . . . if the court concludes that the claimant's inequitable conduct . . . precludes the assertion of a claim based on unjust enrichment. Equitable disqualification . . . is frequently interposed to claims based on the performance of illegal contracts, because the claimant's role in the underlying transaction frequently (though by no means necessarily) involves conduct that the court may view as grounds for forfeiture of the claim.

c. The primacy of statutory purpose. The statute or regulation by which the parties' underlying transaction is prohibited may expressly decide the issue addressed by §32. For example, a statute that prohibits employment at less than a minimum wage and (as one remedy for violation) grants the employee a cause of action for any wage deficiency confers an entitlement to restitution on the protected party to an illegal contract. Conversely, a regulation providing that an unlicensed provider "shall have no action to recover compensation for services performed" in contravention of the licensing requirement will usually be interpreted to preclude not only a suit on the illegal contract but also a claim in restitution to recover the value of performance. . . .

Cases within §32(1) are those in which – although not specifically directed by statute – restitution is clearly required by the policy of the statute that makes the underlying contract illegal. If the demands of policy require a forfeiture, restitution need not depend on unjust enrichment . . . . Even where unjust enrichment is palpable, it need not necessarily be the basis of the defendant's liability . . . .

The more characteristic and difficult cases within §32 are those described in subsection (2). Here the basic question may be simply stated: would restitution to the claimant be incompatible with the underlying prohibition? But gauging the effect on underlying policy of a decision either to allow restitution or to require a forfeiture – the determination implicitly required by subsection (2) – involves a complex assessment of interrelated factors. These include the nature of the illegality; the strength of the prohibition; the extent of the claimant's culpability; whether illegal conduct was central or merely tangential to the performance in question; the deterrent effect, if any, of a decision one way or the other; the cost and difficulty of the adjudications necessitated by alternative legal rules; and the extent to which a remedy in restitution would tend to carry out (or, conversely, to frustrate) a transaction that the law has in some way sought to suppress.

Policy implications must then be weighed against considerations of private justice. Significant negative consequences for deterrence will justify the court in denying relief, even in the face of substantial unjust enrichment. By contrast, marginal or speculative consequences for deterrence will not justify the court in imposing forfeiture as a punitive remedy that the legislature has failed to specify.

Most of the doubtful cases for restitution involve an underlying illegality that is *malum prohibitum* or regulatory in nature. Restitution in such cases may be either granted or withheld, depending on the court's evaluation of the competing factors just discussed. . . . Cases of "regulatory illegality" are further discussed . . . in Comment *e*. . . .

d. Equitable disqualification. Subsection (3) describes a different reason for the denial of restitution in this context, independent of the policy calculations implicated by subsection (2). This is the rule, described in §63 as an affirmative defense to restitution generally, that a party guilty of inequitable conduct in the underlying transaction may on that account be denied a claim based on unjust enrichment. The outcome will still be described in many jurisdictions as an application of the equitable doctrine of "unclean hands." Described without metaphor, it is a rule of equitable disqualification or forfeiture that is frequently asserted as defense to liability for benefits received pursuant to illegal contracts. . . .

Cases in this category are readily distinguishable from those considered under subsection (2), because here the availability or denial of restitution has no significant consequences for the policy objectives addressed by the underlying prohibition. The potential availability of a claim in restitution between thieves who have fallen out, or between bribe-giver and duplicitous bribe-taker, will not – on any realistic appraisal – affect the decision to enter into the transaction, or undermine the deterrent effect of the criminal penalties to which both claimant and defendant are subject in any event. The reasons for denying restitution in such cases are of a different order. They rest on a longstanding judgment – susceptible of various explanations – that such a plaintiff has forfeited his ordinary claim on the resources of the court. The specific claim that is forfeit is the right to complain of unjust enrichment arising out of the transaction in which the claimant's conduct is condemned. . . .

Effective analysis requires a distinction between those cases in which restitution may be denied on account of the claimant's moral turpitude, on the one hand, and the more common cases of regulatory illegality, on the other. Statements to the effect that restitution is presumptively unavailable between parties to an illegal contract, or that the court will leave such parties as it finds them, derive most of their authority from cases in the former category. The same statements are neither true, nor a helpful guide to decision, about the cases of regulatory illegality governed by subsection (2). See Comment *e*.

The range of misconduct for which claimants have historically been subject to equitable disqualification is both vast and intricately qualified, because the judicial power to bar a claim on equitable grounds is essentially exercised ad hoc. The present scope of this barrier to restitution appears to be narrowing somewhat, as courts become less inclined to enforce a moral judgment with civil penalties, or to add an extra-statutory penalty – in the form of forfeiture of a restitution claim – for conduct that the law already punishes by other means. The kinds of wrongdoing to which the penalty applies may evidently be redefined by changing social attitudes. For example, a claim in restitution between unmarried cohabitants that would formerly have been barred by §32(3) or §63 is now explicitly cognizable by the rule of §28.

Equitable disqualification remains the predictable outcome when the underlying transaction is both *malum in se* and subject to criminal penalties. . . . An equally characteristic application of §32(3) denies relief to a wrongdoer whose claim against the defendant results from the miscarriage of a scheme to defraud third parties. . . . Mitigating factors have the same potential relevance to the availability of restitution in this context that they have to the claimant's criminal responsibility. A claimant who was induced to wrongdoing by entrapment or duress may be allowed to recover, notwithstanding the nature of the transaction in which the claim originates, because such a claimant lacks the degree of culpability that would justify forfeiture under §32(3). . . . On the other hand, the mere fact that one of the parties to a prohibited transaction can complain of being defrauded by the other will not necessarily relieve the claimant from the bar of §32(3). . . .

The issue of the claimant's relative culpability is often addressed, in cases such as these, by debating whether or not the parties are really "*in pari delicto*." Fault would not be "equal" if one party bears responsibility for the other's wrongdoing, or if the claimant's illegal conduct has to some extent been "purged" – for instance, by an attempt to withdraw from the illegal scheme. Factors such as these have an obvious and indisputable relevance to the court's evaluation of culpability in a particular case, and they will visibly influence the court's judgment on the question of equitable disqualification; yet the considerations relevant to a particular case, and the weight to be assigned to them, cannot be specified by rule. This Restatement does not attempt to define the requirements either of equity or of public policy. . . .

e. Regulatory violations; licensing requirements. The most frequent disputes within the present section involve a claim for the value of services rendered in a transaction that is intrinsically unobjectionable, but that fails in some respect to comply with applicable regulatory requirements. Standard examples include the formation of a contract (otherwise legitimate) on terms that vary from those required by law; or the performance of services by a provider who lacks a required license. The contrast in either case is to a transaction that the law condemns under any and all circumstances, such as an agreement to commit a crime. Where the illegality of the underlying transaction consists in a failure to satisfy regulatory requirements, the fact of noncompliance – with rare exceptions – will not be evidence of the moral turpitude or inequitable conduct that forecloses a claim in restitution by the rule of §32(3). Restitution is accordingly available in regulatory cases, by the rule of this Restatement, unless the court concludes that the allowance of restitution would defeat the policy of the regulation in question. That conclusion is an appropriate inference only when judicial respect for the regulatory scheme reasonably requires forfeiture as a penalty for noncompliance.

Conversely, restitution is properly denied if the possibility of a recovery for benefits conferred would constitute an unacceptable incentive to engage in the prohibited transaction; if it would circumvent a necessary mechanism of enforcement; or if restitution would compensate the claimant for a transaction that the law condemns as intrinsically harmful. . . .

In most cases of regulatory illegality, the issue of *restitution* will usually be reached only after the prior question of *enforceability* has been resolved against the claimant. Modern American decisions do not automatically deny enforcement to a contract that fails to comply with applicable regulations. Rather, the issue of enforceability (if left open by the regulations in question) is weighed in the context of both policy objectives and remedial consequences, taking into account the nature of the violation and the effect of the potential penalty. Enforceability is evidently a matter of contract law, but the decision is one to which principles of restitution and unjust enrichment contribute in two visible respects. First, the court will be aware that refusing any remedy to a plaintiff who has rendered a valuable performance will result in the unjust enrichment of the defendant. Pursuing regulatory objectives by a rule of forfeiture comes at a cost in terms of justice between the parties. Second, a court can in many circumstances impose a qualified penalty on the performing party (by denying enforcement), while avoiding a total forfeiture (by allowing restitution). Such an approach splits the difference in any case in which the claimant's contractual entitlement (were it enforceable) exceeds the measure of recovery in restitution. . . .

The recurrent question in this context is the propriety of supplementing the penalties expressly announced by statute or regulation with a judge-made rule of forfeiture. Denial of a potential claim in restitution – to the extent that risk is recognized by the potential claimant – presumably adds something to the deterrent effect of the regulation. It does not follow, however, that a rule of forfeiture (or any other judge-created penalty) should be imposed to Supplement the existing consequences of noncompliance, merely because of its presumed deterrent effect. Forfeiture as a judge-created sanction is particularly to be avoided when it exacts a penalty disproportionate to the infraction, transferred as a private windfall to a party who has suffered no injury. . . .

The decision whether or not to employ forfeiture as a tool of regulatory enforcement parallels the decision to be made in certain cases within §31, where the failure to comply with formal requirements makes a contract unenforceable but not necessarily illegal. See §31, Comment h. . . .

f. Illegality as a sword. In litigation between the parties to an illegal transaction, the illegality may be asserted defensively, by the recipient of performance, who seeks to avoid liability on the contract; or offensively, by the performing party, who repudiates the transaction and seeks to recover the performance or its value. The usual setting of the second sort of restitution claim is a suit to recover a prepayment. So long as the defendant's obligation of performance remains executory, restitution is ordinarily available – provided that the claimant is not disqualified by the rule of §32(3). The effect of restitution in such a case is simultaneously to frustrate a prohibited transaction and to prevent an unjust enrichment. . . . By contrast, where the defendant's obligation has already been performed, it is the *allowance* of the claim in restitution (rather than its refusal) that will result in forfeiture, penalizing the defendant rather than the claimant. In this setting, moreover, the claimant will rarely be able to demonstrate that the alternative to restitution is the unjust enrichment of the defendant.

If the prohibited transaction has been completed on both sides, restitution will nevertheless be available in cases governed by §32(1), because the remedy in such cases is independent of unjust enrichment. . . . Where by contrast the claim to reverse a completed exchange depends on a showing of unjust enrichment – a requirement of any claim brought under §32(2) – restitution will typically be denied. . . .

§33. Incapacity of Recipient

(1) A person who renders performance under an agreement that is unenforceable by reason of the other party's legal incapacity has a claim in restitution against the recipient as necessary to prevent unjust enrichment. There is no unjust enrichment if the claimant receives the counterperformance specified by the parties' unenforceable agreement.

(2) Restitution under this section is available only to a person who has dealt with the recipient in good faith on reasonable terms.

(3) Notwithstanding the unjust enrichment of the recipient, restitution may be limited or denied if it would be inconsistent with the protection that the doctrine of incapacity is intended to afford in the circumstances of the case.

Comment

a. General principles and scope; relation to §16. Issues of contractual incapacity are ordinarily raised as a defense to liability on an executory obligation. . . .

Rules governing the enforceability of an executory contract are not part of the law of restitution. By contrast, a restitution issue is presented whenever there has been performance on either side of a contract that is determined to be unenforceable because of the incapacity of either of the parties. Performance may have been rendered by the incapacitated party, by the other party, or by both. When an incapacitated party repudiates a contract on the basis of incapacity, a claim to recover property transferred or the value of a performance already rendered is governed by §16. Section 33 describes the converse claim in restitution: the claim to recover the value of a contractual performance rendered to a party who is excused, by reason of incapacity, from rendering the promised counterperformance – or who is permitted to reclaim it under §16.

Where there has been performance on both sides, the parties' dispute involves both restitution claims at once. For example, a case might begin with a claim by an incapacitated buyer seeking to avoid the contract and to recover a price already paid. This claim by the incapacitated buyer (a claim in restitution within §16) will be met by the claim of the seller under this section to recover the property previously transferred or its value. The obligation of the incapacitated party to restore what was received is described (both in §16 and by the present section) as part of the substantive liability in unjust enrichment involved in such a case. The same mutual restoration is often described as a requirement or condition of the rescission remedy. See §16, Comments *a* and *f*. . . .

In other cases the incapacitated party appears solely as a defendant: a recipient of performance who is excused, by incapacity, from the obligation to make the promised exchange. The most characteristic dispute within the present section arises when a person obtains goods or services on credit, then successfully resists – on grounds of incapacity – the contractual obligation to pay for them. The performing party's recourse in such circumstances is not an action on the contract but a claim in restitution. Recovery in restitution may be less than recovery in contract, because the contract of an incapacitated person does not conclusively establish the measure of the benefit conferred. . . .

b. Legal persons or entities having limited capacity to contract; unauthorized agents. The present section states a unified rule to describe the restitutionary liability of the incapacitated recipient of performance under a contract that is unenforceable for that reason, whatever the nature of the recipient's incapacity. . . .

The restitution claim of a person who has rendered performance to a principal, pursuant to contract with an unauthorized agent, bears a close analogy to the rule of this section. A rule that was specifically formulated to describe the principal's liability in such a case would be the converse of the rule stated in §17, just as §33 is the converse of §16. . . . Other instances may be resolved on grounds of apparent authority and ratification . . . .

c. Incapacity and unjust enrichment. The rule stated in this section reflects two essential premises. The first is that the doctrine of incapacity, in all of its applications, serves primarily a protective function. Infants, the mentally incompetent, and (in the case of municipal corporations) taxpayers are protected by the rules of incapacity against certain risks that persons of full legal capacity are free to assume. The protection so afforded is potentially costly. Legal incapacity is legal disability, and a person who lacks the capacity to undertake a legally binding obligation is foreclosed from participating in transactions that may be advantageous or even vitally necessary. Significant costs are imposed on the other party to the transaction, whenever a person who has dealt in good faith with an incapacitated counterparty is required to forfeit an otherwise valid legal entitlement. It follows that the contours of legal responsibility in these cases are determined, not by measuring "capacity to contract" against some *a priori* standard, but by weighing at each point the value of the protection secured against the cost of securing it.

The second premise underlying the rule of this section is that the dictates of equity and good conscience are independent of the capacity to contract. Neither the restitution claim asserted by a given plaintiff, nor the wider legal interest in avoiding unjust enrichment, is in any way diminished because the benefit in question was conferred on a person, natural or artificial, lacking full legal capacity. The consequence, as expressed by the former Restatement of this subject, is that "Incapacity to enter into a contract or to incur liability in tort is not in itself a defense in an action for restitution." Restatement of Restitution §139 (1937). . . .

d. Liability in contract distinguished from liability in restitution; measure of benefit. Liability to honor a promise, on the one hand, and liability to restore or pay for a benefit received, on the other, are distinct grounds of legal responsibility that sometimes yield congruent results. Because the incapacitated person's contractual undertaking is *ex hypothesi* invalid, such a party can be under no liability to accept or pay for a contractual performance that remains executory; nor will a liability in respect of benefits already received be imposed (or measured) by the terms of an invalid contract. . . . On the other hand, where the contract price of the benefit conferred is the same as the value of the benefit as determined by the court, the recipient's liability in restitution – while distinguishable in concept – may be identical in extent to a liability on the invalid contract. . . .

Because the value of a contractual performance is not definitively established by a contract that is unenforceable by reason of incapacity, the principal obstacle to a restitution claim under this section is the familiar problem of measuring benefit to the recipient. . . . As in other restitution contexts, the problem of valuation may be alleviated or avoided altogether where the benefit conferred takes the form of money or of property returnable *in specie*. . . . Where the recipient retains undiminished the whole of the benefit conferred, there is usually no hardship in requiring the recipient to restore it – even if liability in restitution is indistinguishable in effect from a liability on the unenforceable contract. . . . Where the extent of the recipient's enrichment is debatable, or where the benefit conferred has been dissipated in whole or part, the protective policy embodied in the recipient's incapacity to contract may justify a narrower measure of benefit than would be appropriate in the case of a recipient who lacked the same claim to special protection. . . .

Liability under this section does not require that a benefit conferred on an incapacitated recipient consist of "necessaries." The familiar notion that an infant's contract is enforceable if for necessaries – like the proposition of the older common law, that an infant's contract was enforceable if and only if the contract was beneficial to the infant – expresses a restitution idea, imperfectly assimilated to the language of contract: namely, that the liability of the infant in such cases is not really in contract (on the promise) but rather in unjust enrichment (for benefits received). There is liability for necessaries, in other words, because necessaries are presumptively beneficial. Accepting the premise, however, that liability in such cases is based not on contract but on unjust enrichment – so that there is no liability in excess of benefit received – the classification of certain benefits as "necessaries" is rendered superfluous, because it is subsumed within the basic inquiry into measure of enrichment.

Illustrations

2. Tenant, a minor, leases an apartment from Landlord for a term of one year. The lease calls for rent at $1000 per month. Tenant occupies the apartment for four months, paying a total of three months' rent, then moves out and repudiates the lease. Landlord is unable to relet the apartment and sues for $9000 unpaid rent. Tenant has no liability with respect to the remaining eight months of the lease term. Tenant is liable in restitution for the reasonable rental value of the apartment for his period of occupancy, which the court finds to be $900 per month. Because Tenant has already paid $3000, Landlord is entitled to restitution of $600. . . .

5. Widow contracts with Funeral Director for customary services in connection with the death of her husband at a price of $5000. The services, performed as requested, have a reasonable value of $6000; Director's cost of performance is $5500. Widow neglects to pay the bill; she is thereafter declared incompetent, and a Guardian appointed. On suit by Director to obtain payment, Guardian defends on the ground of incapacity. Director dealt with Widow in good faith on reasonable terms. Assuming Widow's incapacity at the time the contract was made (with the result that Director's services were not "validly requested"), and without in-

quiring whether funeral services for one's spouse constitute "necessaries" under local law, Director has a claim in restitution to recover $5000 from Widow. . . .

7. Owner buys a home for $100,000, obtaining a first mortgage loan of $80,000 from Bank. Several years' payments on the loan reduce the principal balance to $60,000; the appraised value of the property is now $150,000. It transpires at this point that Owner, at the time of the transaction, was an adjudicated incompetent subject to guardianship. Owner's guardian repudiates the loan agreement, the note, and the mortgage, all of which are void under local law by reason of Owner's incapacity. The court finds that the terms of the mortgage loan were fair and reasonable. Bank is entitled to restitution of the outstanding balance of the loan; judgment in favor of Bank will be secured by an equitable lien on the property. The court will structure the judgment and lien so that Owner's liability in restitution is no more onerous to Owner (or to Owner's successors) than were the terms of the original note and mortgage. . . .

9. Minor purchases a used car having a fair market value of $4500. The terms of sale call for a down payment of $400, followed by 24 monthly payments of $200. Two months later, when Minor has paid Seller a total of $800, the car is damaged in an uninsured accident. Minor tenders the car (fair market value now $1500), repudiates the obligation to pay for it, and asks for his money back. The parties now sue each other in restitution. . . . If the court finds that Seller has dealt with Minor in good faith on reasonable terms, rescission of the transaction on the ground of Minor's incapacity leaves Minor liable to Seller for benefits received (§16(3)). Minor's liability may be qualified, however, to respect the protective function of the doctrine of incapacity (§33(3)). If liability in restitution measured by the initial value of the car ($4500) would deprive Minor of the protection intended by local law against the consequences of his own imprudence, the court may assess the benefit conferred on Minor at such lower figure as it finds sufficient to eliminate Minor's unjust enrichment under the circumstances of the transaction. On the facts supposed, a court might attempt to achieve substantial justice by assessing the benefit to Minor at that portion of the price already paid. That result is reached by cancellation of Minor's executory payment obligation, while denying in other respects each party's restitution claim against the other. . . .

f. Good faith. Good faith under this section requires that the claimant have dealt fairly and reasonably with the incapacitated party. It is inconsistent with overreaching. . . . On the other hand, good faith does not always require that the claimant be without notice of the other party's lack of capacity. It is usually consistent with good faith to deal on reasonable terms with minors and the mentally incompetent; though if one contracting party is aware that the other is an adjudicated incompetent, subject to guardianship, it would normally be appropriate to contract with the guardian on behalf of the ward. . . .

g. No restitution if incapacitated party has performed. The claim described in this section protects those who have rendered a contractual performance to incapacitated persons without receiving (or being able to enforce) the promised counterperformance. An incapacitated person who has made the promised return for benefits received has not been unjustly enriched. . . .

h. Liability of third parties. In certain circumstances, the claimant's performance of an unenforceable contract with an incapacitated party will result in the unjust enrichment of a party with whom the claimant has not dealt. The rule of this section authorizes a claim in restitution against the third-party recipient of performance, subject to applicable defenses. . . .

§34. Mistake or Supervening Change of Circumstances

(1) A person who renders performance under a contract that is subject to avoidance by reason of mistake or supervening change of circumstances has a claim in restitution to recover the performance or its value, as necessary to prevent unjust enrichment. If the case is one in which the requirements of §54 can be met, the remedy of rescission and restitution permits the reversal of the transaction without the need to demonstrate unjust enrichment.

(2) For purposes of subsection (1):

(a) the value of a nonreturnable contractual performance is measured by reference to the recipient's contractual expectations; and

(b) the recipient's liability in restitution may be reduced to allow for loss incurred in reliance on the contract.

Comment

a. General principles and scope; relation to Restatement Second, Contracts. Contract law – applying the related tests of mistake, impossibility, impracticability, and frustration – permits the avoidance of an obligation on which the parties ostensibly agreed but for which (as a result of their failure to apprehend or anticipate relevant circumstances) they did not actually bargain. To the extent the obligation in question remains executory, the issue between the parties is limited to the enforceability of the challenged agreement. Such a question is purely a matter of contract law. If the obligation has been partially or wholly performed, the same challenge to the transaction presents what is simultaneously a question of contract and a question of restitution.

Claims within the rule of this section take two principal forms. In the case of a partially completed exchange, the party disadvantaged by the sequence of performance stands in the same position as one who has rendered performance under an agreement that is subsequently revealed to be unenforceable for some other reason. Compare §§31-33. The claimant has conferred a benefit at the request of the defendant, without obtaining the promised exchange; enforcement of the contract is unavailable, in this case because the parties' agreement has been set aside on the ground of mistake. The claimant's recourse is a claim in restitution measured by the defendant's net enrichment. See Comments *c* and *d*. The second type of restitution claim seeks to unwind a completed transaction. Although the contract has been fully performed according to its terms, the disadvantaged party asserts that the resulting exchange, in its actual realization, finds no adequate basis in contract because it is not what the parties had in mind. See Comments *e* and *f*.

From the standpoint of contract law, the central issue in these cases is to identify the deficiencies in the parties' bargain – a failure to perceive or to anticipate relevant circumstances – that will justify avoidance of the transaction. Where the disparity between anticipation and realization is sufficiently pronounced, and where the risk of the realized disparity has not been contractually assigned, a court may conclude that the exchange with which the parties are confronted is not the one they contemplated in making their contract. Conversely, a court that refuses to set aside the transaction has concluded that the outcome with which the parties are confronted, however unexpected, is within the risks that their contract has explicitly or implicitly assigned.

The possibility of restitution under this section depends on the existence of contract doctrines that permit the foregoing distinctions. While the provisions of §5 ("Invalidating Mistake") indicate a common starting point, a fuller statement of the rules according to which a particular contract either is or is not subject to avoidance on grounds of mistake or supervening circumstances is outside the scope of this Restatement. . . .

b. Extent of performance. Confronted with a disparity between anticipation and realization that interrupts a contractual performance – or that leads one party to argue that a completed performance should be unwound – a court will ordinarily ask whether the risks associated with the disparity in question have been allocated by the parties, expressly or by implication; and whether the contractual exchange of values (executory, completed, or somewhere in between) is fairly comprehended within the parties' agreement.

The relevant aspect of contract doctrine (frequently called "mistake in basic assumptions") and the associated analytical method (usually explained in terms of risk allocation) are accordingly the same, whether they are deployed defensively (to resist enforcement of the contract) or affirmatively (to unwind a completed transaction). Yet the contract defense and the affirmative restitution claim are not available on equal terms. Given an equivalent disparity between anticipation and realization, in every setting where the facts permit the comparison, a court will more readily deny enforcement to an executory agreement than order restitution of the same values once they have been exchanged. To put the matter another way: across a broad range of cases involving "mistake in basic assumptions," the predictable outcome is the denial of relief to the moving party. . . .

The paradoxical conclusion – that the legal validity of a contractual exchange may depend on the extent to which it has been performed – is partly explained by reference to the extra costs of unwinding any completed transaction. And yet courts will indeed unwind completed transactions in other circumstances, where the alternative to intervention is an exchange that a court views as extracontractual – meaning that the transaction, as revealed in performance, is outside the scope of the parties' agreement. See Comments *e* and *f.* . . . Evidently courts will intervene to allocate or reassign some unanticipated risks more readily than others. The task of drawing the necessary distinctions is a notoriously difficult problem of contract law that is outside the scope of this Restatement.

c. The partially completed exchange. Interruption of a partially completed exchange by supervening circumstances, or by the discovery of a mistake in the parties' basic assumptions, does not necessarily lead to restitution by the rule of this section. A court may conclude that circumstances as newly revealed justify termination by the disadvantaged party, and the discharge of both parties' obligations of further performance, without finding that their interrupted, partial performance has given rise to any unjust enrichment. That conclusion might follow from a finding that the value of partial performance on either side is approximately in balance – whether by happenstance, or because the interrupted transaction comprises "agreed equivalents" of performance on either side (Restatement Second, Contracts §240). . . . More fundamentally, interrupted performance results in no unjust enrichment – even when the sequence of performance is obviously unbalanced – if the agreement, whether expressly or by implication, allocates the risk of interruption to the party whose performance is the more advanced. . . .

Restitution is accordingly available when the court determines, not merely that a supervening event or discovery has discharged the parties' remaining obligations of performance, but that the contract in its entirety is subject to avoidance. From this determination it follows that benefits conferred by way of partial performance have no basis in a valid agreement, with the result that net enrichment on one side or the other is unjustified. Once these determinations have been made as a matter of contract law, the party whose performance is more advanced has a claim in restitution as necessary to prevent the unjust enrichment of the other. The restitution claimant will be the performing party, in any case where performance was to precede payment . . . ; where payment outruns performance, the claimant will be the paying party. . . .

d. Measure of benefit from interrupted performance; allocation of loss. Restitution by the rule of this section allows a recovery to the extent of the defendant's unjust enrichment. Measuring the benefit to the defendant of an interrupted performance presents characteristic difficulties, however, whenever the claimant's performance is something other than the payment of money. The same circumstances that have disrupted the parties' bargain are likely to limit the value to the defendant of the claimant's interrupted performance.

Liability is measured by the benefit to the recipient, not by the claimant's cost of performance. . . . Benefits conferred at the recipient's request are valued in restitution, prima facie, at the price fixed by a valid contract . . . , but a contract valid at its inception does not necessarily establish an agreed-on price for a partial performance – particularly when performance has been interrupted by an unforeseen discovery or turn of events. Typically, an interrupted performance may saddle the recipient with costs of completion exceeding a ratable portion of the original contract price. One consequence of the rule stated in §34(2)(a) is that the recipient's liability in restitution for part performance may not exceed the contract price for the whole, minus the cost to complete. . . . Similarly, §34(2)(b) provides that the recipient's liability in restitution for the claimant's part performance may be reduced by the recipient's expenditures in reliance on the interrupted transaction. . . .

The effect of both provisions is to allocate to the restitution claimant the losses flowing from the disruption of the parties' bargain, although in most cases of interrupted performance the parties will be equally free from fault. By deducting losses from the recovery in restitution, the law assigns them to the restitution claimant; this makes the incidence of losses from supervening circumstances a function of the contractual sequence of performance. Because the sequence of performance (or performance versus payment) is ordinarily a subject of conscious bargaining, the incidence of residual losses of this kind may legitimately be regarded as a function of the parties' agreement. . . .

Personal services of an agent confer a benefit on the principal, measured by contract price or reasonable value, that is independent of the ultimate profitability of the principal's business venture. . . . By contrast, where the claimant's contractual undertaking involves the maintenance or improvement of the defendant's physical property, and the property is destroyed in the course of performance – the parties' obligations being discharged in consequence – it is intuitively much more difficult to see that the defendant has realized any benefit from the claimant's interrupted performance. . . . Decisions in such cases tend to apportion losses between the parties. The interesting question is how to justify such an outcome, given the absence from the common law of any acknowledged principle of apportioning losses between casualty victims.

The traditional approach purports to achieve this result on a theory of restitution, by finding that some part of the claimant's wasted expenditure conferred a benefit on the defendant; but such an analysis requires a tendentious definition of "enrichment" that is foreign to the rest of the law of this subject. Decisions in these cases may be more candidly explained – without reference to any element of putative enrichment – as authority for the court's power to apportion losses in a limited set of cases. . . .

e. Unwinding a completed transaction. Rescission and restitution . . . , even of a fully completed exchange, is a basic remedial response if the underlying contract has been induced by fraud. Courts are much less likely to unwind an executed contract as a remedy for mistake. The question, simply put, is whether the exchange that has taken place is sufficiently grounded in the parties' bargain to be confirmed as legally effective. In addressing this question, many risks of variation that were not the subject of explicit negotiation will be found to have been allocated by implication, or will be assigned as a matter of law, to the disadvantaged party. See §5, Comment *b*.

Rescission of a completed exchange is a remedy for mistake when real property is involved, because the uniqueness of the subject matter may leave no other effective avenue of relief. See Comment *f*. By contrast, in those instances of mistake that involve what is commonly called "mistake as to value," the typical judicial response is to deny relief to the moving party. So long as an agreement has been freely negotiated, in other words, contract law generally assumes that buyers bear the risk of having paid too much, while sellers bear the risk of having accepted too little. Barriers to relief become nearly insuperable once the exchange has been fully performed. . . .

There are occasional cases, nevertheless, in which a court will order rescission and restitution as a remedy for mistake as to value. A rule that will identify these exceptional cases cannot be found merely in the quality of the parties' mistake. It is true in all these cases that the interests being exchanged have been valued by the parties on a basis that proves to have been fundamentally erroneous, constituting "a basic assumption on which the contract was made." See Restatement Second, Contracts §152(1). But the same can be usually said of those cases of mistake as to value, incomparably more numerous, in which restitution is denied.

Cases that do allow rescission and restitution on grounds of mistake most often involve a claimant who has paid for something that (unknown to the parties) never existed, no longer exists, or does not belong to the seller. . . . An occasional case presents the converse situation, in which the claimant has surrendered something that proves to be significantly more valuable than the parties supposed. . . . Either version yields a contract case that is ostensibly concerned with "mutual mistake in formation," but that closely resembles a restitution case of "mistake in performance" – yielding a relatively straightforward claim based on mistaken payment . . . or mistake in conferring benefits other than money . . . .

. . . [A] court will occasionally order rescission and restitution as a remedy for mistake as to value, but only in those cases where the effect of the remedy closely resembles restitution of a mistaken performance – typically an over-payment, or a payment where no payment was actually due. Where by contrast the effect of rescission and restitution would be the repricing or reallocation of risks over which the parties have explicitly or implicitly bargained – however mistakenly – the remedy will be denied. . . . The distinction to be drawn resembles the determination by which certain contingencies, and not others, are held to be within the scope of an agreement of compromise and settlement – notwithstanding its unqualified terms. . . .

Restitution in this context does not depend on whether the mistake in question is "mutual" or "unilateral." An exchange that corresponds to the understanding of one party but not the other can claim no more than a tenuous basis in the parties' agreement. The distinction is of practical significance, however, because a party who is not himself mistaken, and who is unaware that the other is acting under a mistake, will be protected in his reliance on the other's expressions of assent. The consequence is that restitution for unilateral mistake in basic assumptions will be available only when the defendant had reason to know of the claimant's mistake (see §17 . . .); or when the defendant has taken no action in reliance on the parties' apparent bargain. . . . Con-versely, knowledge by one party of the other's mistake as to value is not grounds for avoidance when the mistaken party bears the risk of the mistake in question. See §5(3) and §17. . . .

f. Mistake in real property transactions. The rule of this section is frequently applied to unwind transactions in real property. An initial set of cases involves mistakes relating to the existence, identity, or relevant characteristics (other than acreage) of the interest purportedly conveyed. . . .

Restitution in this context may be a means to avoid unjust enrichment . . . . Elsewhere its function is simply to reverse an exchange as to which the parties failed, by reason of mistake, to reach a valid agreement. The remedy of re-scission and restitution is available in such cases without the need to demon-strate enrichment. . . .

Mistakes about acreage lead to unjust enrichment and a claim in restitution when they result in the conveyance of more or less land than contemplated by the parties' agreement. The degree to which the parties will be held to have contemplated a potential variation in quantity (beyond the ordinary margin of "more or less") depends on the basis on which the sale is negotiated. Where the sale is "by the acre," a mistake as to acreage resembles other cases of mistake in performance: to the extent the vendor conveys either more or less land than the quantity by which the price has been fixed, there is unjustified enrichment (on one side or the other) by the benchmark of the parties' agreement. Where by contrast the sale is "by the tract" or "in gross," the parties will be considered to have accepted, within reasonable limits, the risk of quantity variation; so that a mistake about acreage, where the sale is in gross, must be analyzed instead by the standards of mistake in basic assumptions.

The traditional distinction between these two types of land contract – though sometimes difficult to apply in practice – has significant remedial implications.

When the sale is by the acre, as previously noted, mistake in acreage will support a claim in restitution as soon as it exceeds *de minimis* limits. Moreover, such a contract specifies a unit price that the court may readily employ to rectify the transaction, directing either an increase or an abatement of the price to be paid. Relief for mistake in sales by the acre thus resembles restitution for other kinds of contractual mistake in performance – such as payment of too much money, or delivery of too many goods – in that it is not subject to any test of "materiality," apart from the natural inertia of litigation. See §5, Comment *e*.

When land is sold in gross, by contrast, the contract itself yields no such benchmark. A party seeking restitution must first persuade the court that the magnitude of the discrepancy exceeds any variation within the contemplation of the parties, thus making the contract subject to avoidance for "mistake in basic assumptions." Even if this showing can be made, courts in many jurisdictions will refuse to adjust the price when the sale is in gross, on the ground that such a remedy enforces a contract the parties did not make. The result is that when restitution is granted in such cases, the claimant may be limited to the remedy of rescission.

The specificity of real property – its indivisibility for many purposes, and the unavailability of substitutes – frequently obstructs the formulation of a remedy in restitution. Rectification of a mistaken exchange by adjusting the quantity conveyed or the price paid may involve, if not an impossibility, a significant hardship to one of the parties. Rescission of the transaction may be impossible (as when rights of third parties intervene) or threaten hardship of a different kind. Frequently, therefore, the remedy devised by the court in a case of mistaken acreage presents the parties with one or more alternatives. A typical decree provides that the exchange may be either rectified or rescinded, with the election between the two remedies being given to the party whose interests most clearly require protection.

Principles of restitution constitute only one element in the formulation of such decrees, which seek simultaneously to prevent unjust enrichment; to place the parties' transaction on a contractual basis, so far as possible; and to allocate and minimize the losses to which their mistake may expose them. Where principles of contract and unjust enrichment are inadequate to the task, courts will adjust the parties' rights directly. See Restatement Second, Contracts §158, Comment *c*. . . .

§36. Restitution to a Party in Default

(1) A performing party whose material breach prevents a recovery on the contract has a claim in restitution against the recipient of performance, as necessary to prevent unjust enrichment.

(2) Enrichment from receipt of an incomplete or defective contractual performance is measured by comparison to the recipient's position had the contract been fully performed. The claimant has the burden of establishing the fact and amount of any net benefit conferred.

(3) A claim under this section may be displaced by a valid agreement of the parties establishing their rights and remedies in the event of default.

(4) If the claimant's default involves fraud or other inequitable conduct, restitution may on that account be denied (§63).

Comment

a. General principles and scope; relation to contract law. Standard contract remedies do not impose forfeiture as a punishment for default. Expectation damages reflect the injured party's net entitlement, subtracting what was received from what had been promised; the consequence is that the defaulting party normally receives credit (against a liability for breach) for the value of an incomplete or defective performance, measured at the contract rate. Yet if circumstances are such that it is the defaulting party (rather than the recipient of the defective performance) who appears as plaintiff, contract law affords no claim by which the same value may be reached. The absence of any claim on the contract for the value of a defaulted performance results from the contractual theory of conditions, according to which – either expressly or by implication – substantial performance by each party is a precondition of the other's obligation to perform. Where a defective performance confers a net benefit, and the parties have not validly contracted for forfeiture in the event of breach, one consequence of the theory of conditions may be the unjust and extracontractual enrichment of the recipient at the expense of the party in default.

Contract law affords the party in default no direct recourse, but it mitigates this untoward result by a number of ancillary doctrines whose common effect is to reduce the frequency with which a party in default must resort to an action "off the contract" on a restitution theory. Among them are the doctrine of substantial performance, allowing an action for damages by a party who would otherwise be barred by default or failure of condition; rules of severability, permitting a court to find that the performing party has an enforceable claim for a part performance; and judicial hostility toward contractual forfeitures, stemming not only from notions of equity but from a realistic skepticism about the likelihood that Draconian penalties have been intentionally negotiated. The theory and application of all such rules are technically matters of contract law, outside the scope of this Restatement; although the context is one in which rules of contract and restitution may be effectively congruent.

For purposes of organization, however, the rule of the present section applies exclusively to cases not governed by contract. In other words, this section applies to cases in which (i) the performing party has no enforceable rights under the contract, whether by a rule of substantial performance, of severability, or otherwise; and (ii) the claim based on unjust enrichment is not displaced by a valid contractual provision imposing forfeiture or liquidated damages. Where a remedy to the party in default is neither conferred nor foreclosed by valid terms of the agreement, restitution authorizes a claim as necessary to avoid unjust enrichment. The principal task confronting the restitution claimant is to establish that an incomplete or defective performance has in fact conferred a net benefit on the recipient, taking into account the various costs to which the defendant has been subjected in the wake of the claimant's default.

Except where the party in default has engaged in fraud or inequitable conduct (see Comment *b*), a claimant under this section is not generally viewed as a wrongdoer. The most important constraints on the availability of relief under this section relate, therefore, not to the quality of the claimant's conduct, but to the nature of the benefit conferred and the position of the recipient in light of the claimant's breach. The ultimate question is whether the court may order a remedy in restitution that does not prejudice the defendant, in light of the defendant's protected expectations under the defaulted contract. Factors relevant to this determination are common to other areas of restitution. Thus a party whose (partial) contractual performance involved the payment of money will more readily recover by the rule of this section than one whose defaulted performance consisted of nonreturnable services or improvements to real property. See Comments *d*, *e*, and *f*.

A restitution claim based on a contractual performance starts with certain inherent advantages, because the benefit in question may be shown – in some cases at least – to be something that the recipient both requested and offered to pay for. Conversely, a claim based on a *defective* performance may encounter the objection that restitution would subject the defendant to a forced exchange (§2(4)). A defendant who is obliged to pay the court-determined value of the claimant's nonconforming performance – if a significant purpose of the agreement was to obtain something else – is denied the fundamental right to choose the performance he will pay for. Restitution in such a case might leave the defendant worse off than if the transaction had not taken place at all – an outcome that is not authorized against an innocent recipient. . . .

b. Willful or deliberate default. Courts in many jurisdictions continue to state that restitution is unavailable to a party whose contractual default is willful or deliberate. The quality of the breach in a particular case manifestly determines the claimant's equitable posture in seeking restitution. The claimant's conduct may be culpable or excusable; it may reflect opportunism or merely inadequate resources; it may manifest a conscious disregard of the defendant's legal entitlement, on the one hand, or simple inadvertence, on the other. The court's sense of the claimant's relative equitable position will in many instances determine the success or failure of the claim.

It is potentially misleading, however, to describe willful or deliberate default as an absolute bar to the claim under this section. In the large and significant class of cases where the claimant's defaulted obligation is to pay money, the breach of contract – the failure to pay a debt when due – is most often the result of a conscious election. Even a debtor who faces financial hardship normally has a choice to pay one creditor rather than another. It can be difficult to explain why breach in such instances should not be qualified as "willful" or "deliberate"; yet the same instances include some of the foremost illustrations of cases in which modern American law authorizes restitution to the party in default. See Comment *d*.

Although restitution is undeniably available in some cases of deliberate default, there remain many circumstances in which the quality of the claimant's breach will effectively bar the claim. The significance of "deliberateness" in this context lies in the extraordinary costs that will frequently be imposed by an election to discontinue a contractual performance already under way. Assuming a simple choice between performance and breach, the election to perform yields a straightforward claim to the price specified by contract, securing contractual expectations on both sides; while the election to default, and then to pursue a claim in restitution, draws the litigants and the court into a complex, extracontractual evaluation of both benefit conferred and injury inflicted. The remedial inefficiency of the latter course is obvious, as is the risk that the innocent party will incur substantial uncompensated costs in consequence of the claimant's election to breach. Judicial awareness of these factors accounts for the traditional rule that denies restitution whenever default is "willful or deliberate." The omission of this condition from §36 must not be taken to imply that such factors have somehow become irrelevant.

As already noted, the present section forgoes an inquiry into "willfulness" in order to accommodate numerous decisions allowing restitution to claimants whose contractual default was evidently the result of conscious choice. At the same time, the recipient of the defaulted performance is protected against prejudice by overlapping safeguards:

(1) There is liability in restitution only to the extent of a net benefit conferred, and the claimant bears the burden of demonstrating that a net benefit exists. Where the net enrichment of the defendant remains doubtful, the claim in restitution must fail. . . . See Comment c.

(2) A liability in restitution will not impose a forced exchange–requiring the defendant to pay for something which, under the circumstances, the defendant should have been free to refuse (§2(4)). See Comment f. . . .

(3) If the party in default has engaged in fraud or inequitable conduct, a claim under §36 may be barred, notwithstanding the existence of net enrichment by some measures. . . .

c. Amount of recovery; burden of proof. There is a claim in restitution in respect of defaulted contractual performance only if and to the extent the claimant can prove that the benefit thereby conferred, net of losses attributable to claimant's default, results in the enrichment of the defendant. Requiring the claimant to carry the burden of proof on the key issue of net enrichment does not mean that the claimant must produce evidence within the knowledge of the defendant. It does mean that if the net enrichment of the defendant cannot be clearly established, restitution will be denied.

Net enrichment is measured by reference to the defendant's contractual expectation. Because the award is net of damages caused by claimant's default, the particular items entering into the account reflect the standard calculation of damages in the relevant transactional setting: lost profits in one case, cost of cure or completion in another. The uniform test is to compare the defendant's actual position with the position the defendant would have occupied in the absence of breach. See Illustration 1. Given the difficulty in many circumstances of quantifying the injury to the defendant from the claimant's breach, the appropriate reduction may be liberally estimated. The object is to insure that the nonbreaching defendant will under no circumstance be left with a net loss from the transaction; and a party who has elected not to perform the contract cannot insist on a nice calculation of extracontractual benefits conferred. . . .

When properly applied, a contractual provision for liquidated damages serves the same function, protecting the innocent party against loss when injury is difficult to quantify. Rules governing the enforceability of liquidated damages are a matter of contract law, but the enforcement of such a provision may properly decide the scope of restitution in the present context. See Illustration 3.

When the claimant seeks restitution of the value of a nonreturnable performance, it may be necessary to choose between alternative measures of the benefit conferred. To the extent the claimant's breach of contract includes an element of fault, the equities of the claim under §36 will tend to favor the application of the most restrictive test among . . . . either (i) a ratable portion of the contract price, (ii) the market value of the benefit conferred, or (iii) the resulting addition to the defendant's wealth, whichever is least. . . .

Illustrations

1. Owner and Builder contract for specified work at a price of $235,000. Builder abandons the job after part performance, and Owner has the work completed by a third party. Builder sues Owner seeking damages for breach of contract or, in the alternative, restitution by the rule of this section. The jury finds that Builder committed a material breach; that the value of labor and materials furnished by Builder is $200,000, for which Owner has paid $150,000; that Owner has been obliged to spend a further $100,000 to have the work completed according to contract specifications; and that the value of the completed work is $260,000. Because Owner was entitled to have the work done for $235,000 (and has spent $250,000), Owner has not been unjustly enriched by Builder's part performance (§36(2)). Builder has no claim in restitution. . . .

3. Mechanic contracts with Owner on January 1 for the restoration of Owner's 1931 Duesenberg roadster. The price of the work is $50,000, payable on completion; the job is to be completed by June 30; Owner may terminate the contract for lack of timely performance; Mechanic will pay liquidated damages of $100 for each day that the work remains unfinished after June 30. Mechanic performs only part of the work specified. On October 1, Owner regains possession of the vehicle by legal process, then has the work completed elsewhere at a cost of $25,000 and a further delay of three months. Mechanic sues Owner in restitution, offering to prove that his uncompensated work on the car had a reasonable value of $25,000. The provision of the parties' agreement fixing damages of $100 for each day of delay is valid and enforceable by the contract law of the jurisdiction. Calculating on the basis of 180 days' delay, there is no net enrichment of Owner (and Mechanic has no claim in restitution) except to the extent that the value of Mechanic's uncompensated labor and materials exceeds $18,000. . . .

5. Architect undertakes to prepare plans for Owner's building for a fee of eight percent of the cost of construction. The parties' agreement stipulates that the total cost of the building shall not exceed $1 million. Architect spends 250 hours preparing plans for a building that would cost at least $2 million to construct. The reasonable value of Architect's services is $200 per hour. Owner makes no use of the plans and refuses to pay for them. Architect's services have not resulted in Owner's enrichment, and Architect has no claim in restitution.

d. Benefit conferred in money. . . . Occasionally a buyer of goods or services who has paid the full price in advance will repudiate the exchange and seek to recover that portion of the payment that exceeds the seller's contractual expectation. Such a claim cannot be brought within the literal terms of §36 because the claimant is not in default. But the present section governs the case *a fortiori*, since a party who has fully performed must have at least the rights of a party in default. . . .

Illustration

12. Member reserves a place on a "wilderness tour" of Alaska, organized by Society and operated by Carrier. Terms and conditions set forth in Society's brochure specify that each reservation must be accompanied by a nonrefundable $500 deposit, and that the balance of $4500 per person must be paid not later than 30 days before the scheduled departure, on penalty of cancellation. Member instead pays the full price of $5000 six months in advance, then changes his mind and attempts to cancel the reservation 60 days before the tour is to begin. Society refuses to refund any part of the payment. On suit for restitution, Member establishes that Society made no payment to Carrier in respect of his reservation, and that the tour operated at full capacity, as the place he paid for was resold to someone on a waiting list. Interpreting the parties' agreement, the court concludes that Society made no promise, express or implied, to make any refunds in respect of a canceled reservation; but also that the parties agreed to no forfeiture or liquidated damages beyond the $500 deposit that was stated to be nonrefundable. . . . Member can recover $4500 from Society by the rule of this section.

e. Benefit conferred in goods or services. . . . A party in default under a contract to render personal services is ordinarily entitled to restitution by the rule of this section unless the nature of the default indicates fraud or inequitable conduct. Even if the claimant has been guilty of conscious wrongdoing, the tendency of more recent decisions – where the facts permit – is to distinguish periods of faithful and disloyal service, awarding the value of services performed during the former but not the latter. . . .

Claims in respect of legal services make up an important subcategory of cases within this section. One reason is practical: lawyers' contingent-fee arrangements account for a large proportion of transactions in which the performance of personal services substantially outruns the payment of compensation. Another reason for the salience of cases involving lawyers is the particular gravity attached to the lawyer's breach of an obligation to a client. From the perspective of professional responsibility, the question is whether the character of the lawyer's default is such as to make it appropriate that the lawyer forfeit some or all of the lawyer's claim to compensation. See Restatement Third, The Law Governing Lawyers §37. Within the terms of the present section, the question is whether the lawyer's breach of duty involves fraud or inequitable conduct: professional and fiduciary obligations to the client increase the likelihood that a lawyer's default may be of this character. Absent such a bar, even a lawyer discharged for cause may recover for the value of services rendered, provided that those services have conferred a net benefit on the client. By contrast, restitution will uniformly be denied to a lawyer who abandons a representation without justification. . . .

Illustrations

. . . .

14. A is employed by B Co. as regional manager, receiving a monthly salary plus a commission on B's sales in A's region. The commission is calculated and paid quarterly in arrears. On April 15, B discovers that A has been engaged since February 15 in organizing a new company to compete with B. B immediately discharges A and refuses to pay him further compensation. A sues B to recover commissions on sales from January 1 to April 15. The court determines that (i) A

was in breach of his duty of loyalty to B on February 15 and thereafter, but (ii) A continued to perform valuable services for B until the date of his discharge. A has a claim in restitution for the commissions otherwise payable in respect of sales prior to February 15. A's restitution claim in respect of services performed after that date is precluded by A's inequitable conduct toward B.

15. Attorney represents Client in litigation on a contingent-fee basis. Becoming dissatisfied with Attorney's handling of the matter, Client discharges Attorney and retains another lawyer to take over the representation. When substitute counsel obtains a favorable settlement, Attorney sues Client to recover a fee. Attorney's remedy depends on whether his discharge was with or without cause. Because public policy demands that a client be free to discharge an attorney, there is no breach of contract by Client in either event. If Attorney was discharged without cause, Attorney is entitled to restitution as if he had been performing under an unenforceable contract (§31): he recovers the reasonable value of his interrupted services in quantum meruit. . . . If Attorney was discharged with cause, his claim to a fee is. . . . limited to the net benefit, if any, conferred on Client by Attorney's interrupted services. (If Client has been obliged to pay the same contingent fee to substitute counsel, the services of an attorney previously discharged for cause are not a source of benefit to Client.) If Attorney's performance prior to discharge for cause involved professional misconduct, the claim in restitution may be denied on that account (§36(4)). . . .

f. Improvements to property. The peculiar difficulties associated with restitution in respect of improvements to property are largely the same, whether they arise in the present context or in that of mistaken improvements . . . . Where restitution is sought by a party in default under a contract, there is a greater likelihood that the improvement (or something like it) is one the defendant both wanted and expressed a willingness to pay for. So long as the defendant's contractual expectations may be respected, restitution encounters no particular obstacle. . . . On the other hand, improvements by a party in default may be the result of bad faith; while the improver who was merely mistaken is at most guilty of carelessness. Fundamental principles of restitution preclude any recovery by a party who has deliberately and fraudulently promised one thing and delivered another. . . .

If the law imposes a liability to pay for nonconforming improvements, it requires the defendant to pay for something different from what was promised under the contract. The propriety of doing so depends not only on the claimant's equitable position but on the position of the defendant if restitution is allowed. Resolution of such a controversy inevitably turns on the court's sense of what justice requires, and the potentially relevant factors are too numerous to be specified by rule. Along the range of possible outcomes, the extreme positions are occupied by contract remedies: on the one hand, finding substantial performance by the builder and measuring damages by diminution of value, possibly nil; on the other, finding breach by the builder and measuring damages by the cost of demolition and replacement. Restitution affords a set of intermediate possibilities, for cases in which the equities of the parties are more closely balanced.

. . . . [R]estitution in respect of nonconforming improvements may not exceed the defendant's net enrichment as a result of the claimant's defaulted performance. . . . [T]he defendant may not be left worse off than if the transaction had not taken place. Where the nonconformity relates to an aspect of performance about which the parties have specifically bargained, so that the defendant has chosen one thing and been given another, restitution is limited not only by the difficulty of measuring net enrichment but by the need to protect the defendant against a forced exchange. . . .

Illustrations

. . . .

20. Builder agrees to install a swimming pool in Owner's backyard. Pools of this type are normally eight feet deep, a depth that is adequate for diving and meets all building code requirements. Such a pool costs $25,000. Owner informs Builder that, for reasons of personal preference, he wants a pool nine feet deep. Builder agrees to construct a nine-foot pool at a cost of $30,000, payable $10,000 in advance and the balance on completion. Builder's foreman misreads the order, and the completed pool is only eight feet deep. Owner refuses to pay the balance of the price. Builder sues Owner in restitution, seeking the $25,000 price of an eight-foot pool less $10,000 already paid. Builder establishes by expert testimony that the eight-foot pool is fully as suitable as a nine-foot pool for all uses to which Owner or anyone else will put it. The difference in depth makes no difference to the appraised value of Owner's property, to which the completed pool has added $15,000. Owner can prove no quantifiable damages as a result of Builder's breach. Because the depth of the pool is an element of Builder's performance for which Owner specifically bargained, however, restitution by the rule of this section (measured by the usual price or market value of Builder's labor and materials) would subject Owner to an unacceptable forced exchange, imposing the very bargain that Owner had rejected. . . . Treating the eight-foot pool as a mistaken improvement yields a recovery of $5000 in restitution ($15,000 added value less $10,000 already paid).

Topic 2. *Alternative Remedies for Breach of an Enforceable Contract*

§37. Rescission for Material Breach

(1) Except as provided in subsection (2), a plaintiff who is entitled to a remedy for the defendant's material breach or repudiation may choose rescission as an alternative to enforcement if the further requirements of §54 can be met.

(2) Rescission as a remedy for breach of contract is not available against a defendant whose defaulted obligation is exclusively an obligation to pay money.

Comment

a. General principles and scope; relation to other sections. . . . The plaintiff entitled to a remedy for material breach or repudiation potentially chooses between damages, specific performance, and rescission, electing the remedy that promises the most favorable recovery at the lowest cost.

Rescission is one of the principal asset-based remedies in restitution, and breach of contract is only one of the problems to which it is a possible response. (In addition to its role as a remedy for material breach, rescission may be an obvious choice when there has been performance under a contract that is subject to avoidance for fraud, mistake, or similar grounds of invalidity.) . . .

Rescission remains a relatively uncommon remedy for breach of contract. A plaintiff whose contract is advantageous will normally seek a remedy that secures the benefit of the bargain. See Restatement Second, Contracts §344, Comments *a* and *b*. For those plaintiffs who would prefer [it], access to the rescission remedy is subject to a number of important restrictions:

(1) Rescission is a remedial option only when the defendant has repudiated the contract or committed a material breach by nonperformance. See Comment *c*.

(2) Rescission is not available against a defendant whose defaulted obligation is exclusively to pay money (§37(2)). In consequence, rescission as an alternative remedy is available to the prepaying buyer but not to the credit seller. . . .

(3) Rescission ostensibly requires each party to return to the other whatever has been received by way of performance . . . , but the practical impossibility of a perfect two-way restoration – and the need to decide in every case how much leeway to permit – means that the availability of rescission depends to an important degree on judicial discretion. . . . The underlying test, once this discretion is acknowledged, is whether "the interests of justice are served by allowing the claimant to reverse the challenged transaction instead of enforcing it". . . .

b. Rescission in practice. In theory, and sometimes in practice, rescission pursuant to §37 permits a plaintiff who has paid in advance for a defaulted performance to recover an amount exceeding compensatory damages. . . . Such outcomes are rare, because a prepaid seller will almost never forfeit a profit that might be earned, at the seller's option, by performing the contract or simply by releasing the buyer. . . . The simple rule is that a plaintiff who seeks only the return of a prepaid price will not (for reasons of both fairness and economy) be put to the burden of proving damages from the defendant's breach. There is no comparable windfall to the plaintiff if the sequence of performance is reversed, because rescission is not available as a remedy for payment default. . . .

Ordinarily, the reason to elect rescission is the relative certainty of the remedy compared with the difficulty (and expense) of proving damages or obtaining specific performance. Plaintiffs in these cases forgo the benefit of a (presumably advantageous) bargain because the anticipated recovery from rescission, net of the cost of obtaining it, is higher. . . .

c. The quality of defendant's breach. Any breach of contract that results in quantifiable injury gives the plaintiff a remedy in damages, but the remedy of rescission is available only in cases of significant default. Short of a repudiation, the defendant's breach must be "material," "substantial," "essential," or "vital"; it must "go to the root" of the defendant's obligation, or be "tantamount to a repudiation." To replace this familiar catalogue of adjectives, both Restatements of Contracts employ the expression "total breach." See Restatement of Contracts §313(1) (1932); Restatement Second, Contracts §§236(1), 243, 253 & 373. . . . [T]he expression "total breach" is easily misconstrued. In particular, it is *not* a requirement of "total breach" by the Restatement definition that the defendant have failed to render *any part* of the promised contractual performance. The present Restatement employs the term "material breach" to designate what both Restatements of Contracts call "total breach," only because its meaning is more readily understood.

Of course the real test is not verbal but functional. The effect of rescission, at a minimum, is to deprive the defendant of the benefit of the bargain. To the extent of the defendant's expense in the course of partial performance, rescission imposes on the defendant an additional loss. If the defendant repudiates the contract, or commits a breach by nonperformance of equivalent gravity, these consequences are presumably justifiable. On the other hand, if the defendant's breach is relatively minor in the context of the overall undertaking, and if the injury to the plaintiff is appropriately remedied by an award of damages, the same consequences of rescission might impose an unacceptable and punitive forfeiture. If the plaintiff (having suffered a loss of $5) could threaten to impose a loss of $100 on the defendant by seeking rescission instead of $5 damages, the availability of rescission would become a source of costly opportunism. The requirement of repudiation or material breach is a safeguard against this misuse of a remedy that is intended as a shield and not a sword. . . .

d. Requirement of mutual restoration. Traditional contract law allows a plaintiff to elect "rescission and restitution" only when it is within the power of the court to put *both* plaintiff and defendant in the positions they occupied before the contract was made. Rescission is mutual: a plaintiff seeking to be restored to the status quo ante must likewise restore to the defendant whatever the plaintiff has received in the transaction. See §54(2). Strictly interpreted, the requirement of a perfect two-way restoration would preclude rescission whenever the nature of the defendant's performance made it incapable of being returned, or when other factors (such as a decline in the value of the defendant's performance due to its own defects) prevent full restoration without the fault of the plaintiff. To preserve the availability of the remedy in a proper case, and to avoid hardship to the plaintiff, the requirement of counter-restitution by the plaintiff is sometimes relaxed. . . . In the context of breach of contract, the most familiar adjustment is that a plaintiff may be allowed to recover a prepaid price without deduction (or with only limited deduction) for certain nonreturnable benefits. . . .

Returning the parties to the status quo ante may require that the restoration of performance be supplemented by a mutual accounting for the costs and benefits of temporary ownership, or by compensation for incidental or reliance loss. . . .

Illustrations

. . . .

14. Owner contracts with Builder for the construction of a swimming pool in Owner's backyard, paying the total price of $10,000 on completion of the work. Shortly afterwards the pool begins to leak; repeated attempts at repair are unsuccessful, and the pool eventually breaks in half. Owner sues Builder for breach of contract and arranges to have a different pool (both larger and more elaborate) built by someone else. Recovery of expectation damages would require proof of the cost to replace the defective pool with a pool meeting the original specifications that was properly constructed. Because that work will not be performed, its cost may be difficult to establish. If Owner elects to rescind, Owner may recover the $10,000 paid plus the cost of removing the defective pool (§54(2)(c)).

e. Executed conveyance of real property. Rescission and restitution will be qualified or denied if the remedy would cause disruption or prejudice outweighing its advantages . . . . A limitation in these terms is frequently advanced to explain the refusal to rescind an executed conveyance of real property on grounds of material breach – whether relief is sought by the vendor (for purchaser's failure to pay the price or breach of a collateral undertaking), or by the purchaser (for vendor's failure to convey conforming title). . . .

The potentially negative attitude toward rescission in this context is subject to a notable exception. If the plaintiff has conveyed real property to the defendant in exchange for a promise of support, rescission is readily available as a remedy for material breach. . . .

Illustrations

. . . .

17. Mother conveys Blackacre to Son and Daughter-in-Law, in exchange for the couple's promise to allow her to reside on the property for the rest of her life and to provide for her support. The contract is honored for several years, and Son makes valuable improvements to Blackacre. Relations between the parties become acrimonious; Son and Daughter-in-Law evict Mother and repudiate their obligation to support her. Mother is entitled to rescission under §37, reacquiring title to Blackacre by cancellation of the deed. Relief in favor of Mother is subject to her obligation to account for net benefits received prior to the interruption of performance, including the value of improvements . . . .

The foregoing discussion, it should be remembered, refers to limitations on rescission as a remedy for breach of contract. Rescission of an executed conveyance of real property is readily available if the underlying transaction is defective in its inception, for reasons such as fraud or undue influence. . . . In the same way, rescission of an executed conveyance for title defects is more likely to be available when the problem may be characterized as one of mistake rather than breach. . . .

§38. Performance-Based Damages

(1) As an alternative to damages based on the expectation interest (Restatement Second, Contracts §347), a plaintiff who is entitled to a remedy for material breach or repudiation may recover damages measured by the cost or value of the plaintiff's performance.

(2) Performance-based damages are measured by

(a) uncompensated expenditures made in reasonable reliance on the contract, including expenditures made in preparation for performance or in performance, less any loss the defendant can prove with reasonable certainty the plaintiff would have suffered had the contract been performed (Restatement Second, Contracts §349); or

(b) the market value of the plaintiff's uncompensated contractual performance, not exceeding the price of such performance as determined by reference to the parties' agreement.

(3) A plaintiff whose damages are measured by the rules of subsection (2) may also recover for any other loss, including incidental or consequential loss, caused by the breach.

Comment

a. General principles and scope; relation to Restatement Second, Contracts. The remedy described in the present section is one of the two principal devices sometimes referred to as "restitution for breach of contract," the other being rescission (§37). . . . Though called "restitution" it is simply an award of damages. It is distinguished from ordinary contract damages, measured by the plaintiff's expectation interest, because it permits a plaintiff who cannot prove expectation to recover damages calculated on an alternative basis.

Damages of this kind have traditionally been associated with the idea of "restitution" because they tend to "restore": they restore the plaintiff to the precontractual position, or they restore to the plaintiff either the cost or the value of the plaintiff's uncompensated performance. Cost of performance is the measure more frequently employed: the plaintiff recovers damages measured by unreimbursed expenditure in reliance on the contract, subject to provable expectation as a cap. Less often, the basis of the performance-based damage calculation is the value of the plaintiff's uncompensated performance, not exceeding the price of such performance at the contract rate. Damages measured by expenditure are commonly called "reliance damages." Damages measured by the value of performance go by various names, including both "restitution" and "reliance" as well as "quantum meruit." Conceptual and terminological confusion has obscured the fact that the measures of cost and value are – for the most part – parallel versions of a single alternative damage remedy. See Comment *b*.

. . . . The rule of the present section offers a remedial alternative in cases where the plaintiff cannot establish expectation damages – either because of difficulties of proof, or because contractual expectancy is provable but negative. Performance-based damages yield a partial recovery in such cases, though they do not permit a complete escape from an unfavorable bargain: a plaintiff who was obligated to perform at a loss may not characterize losses from performance as damages from breach. (A plaintiff whose performance of a losing contract is interrupted by the defendant's breach does avoid the further losses that the plaintiff would have incurred in completing performance. See Comment *d*.) By contrast, a plaintiff who is entitled to rescission as a remedy for material breach will sometimes escape entirely the consequences of an unfavorable bargain. See §37 . . . .

The usual application of the rule of §38 . . . is either to a case in which the plaintiff's contractual expectation cannot be established at all, or to a case in which – although the plaintiff's expectancy cannot be known with certainty – it can be shown to lie somewhere within an upper limit. In either case, an alternative damage calculation by the rule of §38 protects the plaintiff's expectancy so far as the evidence permits, based on a rebuttable presumption that the plaintiff was neither performing at a loss nor selling at less than market value. More specifically, the presumption is that the plaintiff's earnings from performance would have been at least sufficient to defray the plaintiff's reliance expenditures; alternatively, that the plaintiff's unknown expectancy would have been at least equal to the market value of the plaintiff's performance. Either presumption may be rebutted by the defendant, on proof that the plaintiff's contractual expectancy was something less than the damages sought by this alternative measure.

Frequently – most obviously, where the remedy for the defendant's breach is the recovery of money paid to the defendant – there is no meaningful distinction between the cost and value of the plaintiff's performance. In other cases, the plaintiff's choice between cost and value as the basis of the alternative damage calculation (that is, between subsections (2)(a) and (2)(b)) is determined by which yields the larger recovery – or merely by which is the more easily measured. See Comment b.

This account of performance-based damages differs substantially from the description of the same remedies in the first and second Restatements of Contracts, but the present revision – outside one narrow field – will not alter the results of cases. Its purpose is rather to provide a simplified and rationalized explanation of some straightforward contract remedies that have become needlessly difficult to describe. Because this Restatement recognizes the terms of the contract as a limit on any damage recovery, it modifies the prior treatment of those few cases – prominent in theory, but rare in practice – in which a plaintiff seeks "restitution" to escape the consequences of an unfavorable bargain. See Comment c. Apart from its treatment of "losing contracts," however, the simpler rule of the present section yields the same outcomes as Restatement Second, Contracts §§349 and 373.

. . . [D]amages by the alternative measures here described are available when the effect of the defendant's breach or repudiation is to discharge the plaintiff's remaining duties of performance – making the award of damages a full reckoning of the parties' contractual obligations. . . .

b. Cost or value; "reliance damages"; special damages. A plaintiff who cannot prove expectation damages – because a benefit of the bargain cannot be established with sufficient certainty – may prove and recover, as an alternative measure of damages, either the cost or the value of the plaintiff's uncompensated performance. See Comment a. Damages so measured are a second-best remedy. They omit any element of profit: a plaintiff who could show lost profit from performance would prove and recover ordinary expectation damages. A recovery based on cost will be reduced (or eliminated altogether) if the defendant can prove that the plaintiff would have suffered a loss had the contract been performed. A recovery based on value will be limited to the contract rate for the performance in question – when such a rate may be determined – even if this is insufficient to allow the plaintiff to recoup the cost of performance.

Where the rule of this section covers damages measured by expenditure (§38 (2)(a)), it describes the remedy commonly known as "reliance damages." Comments and Illustrations explaining an award of damages based on reliance expenditures are set forth in Restatement Second, Contracts §349, and are not repeated here. The existing rule permitting damages measured by expenditure is incorporated here as subsection (2)(a), to situate it in the broader context of performance-based damages for breach.

A plaintiff with a choice will ordinarily base the alternative damage claim on reliance expenditures, rather than on the value of performance. This is because expenditures are generally easier to prove, and because expenditure in the course of partial performance (often involving preparations for performance, or the costs of "incidental reliance") typically exceeds the value of the performance actually rendered. . . . The distinction between cost and value is ignored in many cases, where the two characterizations of the alternative damage claim are effectively interchangeable. . . .

Less familiar than cases of "reliance damages," only because they are far less numerous, are cases in which it is easier to establish the market value of a contractual performance than to measure the plaintiff's expenditures in performance. Section 38(2)(b) allows a plaintiff to recover damages equal to that market value, so long as the parties' agreement does not establish a lower price for the performance in question. . . .

Damages under this section may include consequential or special damages for loss caused by the defendant's breach . . . .

c. Contract terms respected. Performance-based damages by the rule of this section are a substitute for damages based on expectancy, and they are limited by expectancy at most points where expectancy can be established. Breach of contract does not make the defendant a guarantor of the profitability of the plaintiff's bargain; damages compensate loss attributable to the breach, not loss attributable to an unfavorable exchange. Performance-based damages, like expectation damages, respect the price terms and the risk allocations established by the parties' agreement.

Damages measured by the cost of the plaintiff's performance are reduced to the extent the defendant can prove that the plaintiff would have suffered a loss had the contract been performed. In this regard the rule of §38(2)(a) is identical to Restatement Second, Contracts §349. . . . The fact that "reliance damages" are reduced by anticipated losses, while a recovery based on rescission is not, may determine the plaintiff's choice between the two. . . .

When performance-based damages are measured by the value of a performance rather than its cost, the damage calculation is also limited by the price term of the contract, but the limit is imposed differently. In determining damages by the rule of §38(2)(b), the value of a plaintiff's performance may not exceed the contract rate (if there is one) fixed by the parties' agreement. . . .

. . . . The plaintiff who seeks to recover unreimbursed expenditures is required to deduct any loss that would have been incurred upon full performance of the contract. By contrast, the plaintiff who seeks the value of a partial performance is limited to recovery at the contract rate for what has been done, but is not charged with the further loss that would have been incurred had performance been completed. The result is that damages under §38(2)(a) are limited by contractual expectancy, while damages under §38(2)(b) are limited by the contract rate but not necessarily by expectancy. See Comment d. . . .

d. Losing contracts. When a party who cannot prove expectation damages seeks instead to recover unreimbursed expenditures in reliance on the contract, it is an accepted rule that the award of damages may not shift to the defendant losses that the plaintiff would have realized on full performance. . . . When the plaintiff who has been performing at a loss seeks damages measured by the value of performance, some authorities allow a recovery "off the contract," unlimited by the contract price; but this Restatement rejects that outcome. By capping the damage calculation at the contract rate (where such a rate may be determined), §38(2)(b) prevents these plaintiffs as well from electing performance-based damages as a means of escape from an unfavorable bargain.

The contrary rule, allowing damages measured by the value of performance unlimited by the contract price, permits the injured party to reallocate or re-value risks that it is the function of contract to price and to assign. Such an outcome is contrary to fundamental objectives of contract law and inconsistent with the other remedies for breach of contract, all of which take the parties' agreement as the benchmark by which the plaintiff's remedies are measured.

.... In summary, the fact that the defendant has committed a material breach does not mean that the contract is to be disregarded, allowing the plaintiff to seek restitution as if there had never been a contract between the parties. Such precisely is the legal response where the contract was never valid to begin with, as in a case of rescission for fraud. It is not and has never been the remedy for breach of a valid and enforceable contract.

Accepting the contract price as a limit in a losing-contract case does not mean that expectation and performance-based damages are invariably the same. Because the plaintiff performing at a loss is allowed to cease performance (and terminate any remaining obligation) in response to the defendant's breach or repudiation, the plaintiff avoids the further loss that would have been sustained in completing performance. In other words, the loss that would have been realized by the plaintiff in completing performance of the contract is not subtracted from the plaintiff's recovery for partial performance. ... The result is explained by viewing the defendant's breach or repudiation as a gratuitous release of the plaintiff's further obligations under the contract. A defendant who wishes to be paid for releasing the plaintiff from an onerous obligation – a plausible resolution on the facts of some losing-contract cases – must negotiate with the plaintiff to settle the contract by agreement. If the rule were otherwise ..., the defendant would be in the position of imposing a unilateral modification or novation, on the terms most favorable to himself; and of doing so, moreover, by breach rather than by negotiation.

e. Consequential harms. Decisions authorizing "restitution" in excess of the contract price to parties who have been performing at a loss are found disproportionately in cases of long-term contracts for construction or manufacture that have been interrupted in the course of performance. Breach in such circumstances is particularly likely to subject the injured party to consequential harm; yet the plaintiff may face formidable difficulties in establishing the fact and amount of the resulting loss, if proof of damages must be made with rigorous specificity. If in such a setting the court perceives that the defendant has obtained a performance that was unexpectedly costly to the plaintiff – and if the evidence moreover suggests that the plaintiff's cost overruns may have their source in the defendant's breach – a judgment that the defendant is liable for the market value of the plaintiff's performance, although nominally explained on a theory of unjust enrichment, makes the plaintiff whole while avoiding the difficulties of proving the various elements of consequential or special damages. The practice in some jurisdictions of awarding damages in construction cases on a "total cost" basis relies on similar assumptions to achieve a similar result.

Because it prohibits a recovery in excess of the contract price for the work done, §38 forecloses this use of a performance-based damage award; but plaintiffs may obtain the same compensation if they can prove the necessary elements of special damages. A jurisdiction that adopts the position of this

Restatement should ensure that evidentiary requirements for proof of special damages caused by the defendant's breach are not unduly restrictive. . . .

§39.   Profit from Opportunistic Breach

(1) If a deliberate breach of contract results in profit to the defaulting promisor and the available damage remedy affords inadequate protection to the promisee's contractual entitlement, the promisee has a claim to restitution of the profit realized by the promisor as a result of the breach. Restitution by the rule of this section is an alternative to a remedy in damages.

(2) A case in which damages afford inadequate protection to the promisee's contractual entitlement is ordinarily one in which damages will not permit the promisee to acquire a full equivalent to the promised performance in a substitute transaction.

(3) Breach of contract is profitable when it results in gains to the defendant (net of potential liability in damages) greater than the defendant would have realized from performance of the contract. Profits from breach include saved expenditure and consequential gains that the defendant would not have realized but for the breach. . . .

Comment

a. General principles and scope; relation to other sections. In exceptional cases, a party's profitable breach of contract may be a source of unjust enrichment at the expense of the other contracting party. The law of restitution treats such cases in the same way that it treats other instances of intentional and profitable interference with another person's legally protected interests, authorizing a claim by the injured party to the measurable benefit realized as a result of the defendant's wrong. The claim described in this section is accordingly an instance of restitution for benefits wrongfully obtained (§3). . . .

The rule of this section has been placed in Chapter 4 . . . in order to group together, for clarity of exposition, the divergent themes of restitution in a contractual context. But §39 differs from the other sections of the present Chapter in fundamental respects. . . . Unlike §§31-36, the present section recognizes a claim in unjust enrichment as an alternative remedy for breach, potentially available to an injured party who might otherwise enforce the contract by an action for damages or specific performance. Unlike §§37-38, which describe contract remedies that are independent of unjust enrichment, a primary object of §39 is to prevent the unjust enrichment of the defendant at the expense of the plaintiff. Like the other rules of restitution for benefits wrongfully obtained, §39 describes a *disgorgement* remedy: a claimant under this section may recover the defendant's profits from breach, even if they exceed the provable loss to the claimant from the defendant's defaulted performance. Restitution exceeding the claimant's loss is authorized nowhere else in Chapter 4. . . .

Judged by the usual presumptions of contract law, a recovery for breach that exceeds the plaintiff's provable damages is anomalous on its face. A breach of contract – whatever the actor's state of mind – is not usually treated in law as a wrong to the injured party of a sort comparable to a tort or breach of equitable duty. There is substantial truth, though not of course the whole story, in the Holmesian paradox according to which the legal obligation imposed by contract lies in a choice between performance and payment of damages. But the observation is most accurate where it matters least: in those transactional contexts where damages can be calculated with relative confidence as a full equivalent of performance. . . .

Compared to other forms of legal entitlement, contract rights may often be easier to value in money; but they would be vulnerable to the same risks of underenforcement if the exclusive remedy for breach were an action for money damages. Where a party's contractual entitlement would be inadequately protected by the legal remedy of damages for breach, a court will often reinforce the protection given to the claimant by an order of injunction or specific performance. Restitution affords comparable protection after the fact, awarding the gains from a profitable breach of a contract that the defendant can no longer be required to perform.

The restitution claim described in this section is infrequently available, because a breach of contract that satisfies the cumulative tests of §39 is rare. See Comment *f*. At the same time, the cases in which such a remedy is appropriate are generally uncontroversial and in some instances even well known. The innovation of the present section consists, not in proposing that defendants in such cases be liable to disgorge profits derived from a deliberate breach, but in stating a rule to generalize these commonly accepted outcomes.

There are cases of unintentional breach of contract, outside the scope of this section, in which the measure of recovery applied in this section may furnish an appropriate measure of contract damages. See Comment *g*.

b. Opportunistic breach. The common rationale of every instance in which restitution allows a recovery of profits from wrongdoing, in the contractual context or any other, is the reinforcement of an entitlement that would be inadequately protected if liability for interference were limited to provable damages. Cases in which restitution reaches the profits from a breach of contract are those in which the promisee's contractual position is vulnerable to abuse. Vulnerability in this context stems from the difficulty that the promisee may face in recovering, as compensatory damages, a full equivalent of the performance for which the promisee has bargained. A promisor who was permitted to exploit the shortcomings of the promisee's damage remedy could accept the price of the promised performance, then deliver something less than what was promised. Such an outcome results in unjust enrichment as between the parties. The mere possibility of such an outcome undermines the stability of any contractual exchange in which one party's performance may be neither easily compelled nor easily valued.

A promisor who recognizes this possibility and attempts to profit by it commits what is here called an "opportunistic breach." The label suggests the reasons why a breach of this character is condemned, but there is no requirement under this section that the claimant prove the motivation of the breaching party.

In countering this form of opportunism, the rule of §39 reinforces the contractual position of the vulnerable party and condemns a form of conscious advantage-taking that is the equivalent, in the contractual context, of an intentional and profitable tort. A restitution claim in response to a profitable tort typically operates to protect property from deliberate interference: standard examples include the claim to profits from trespass or infringement. . . . The rule of §39 extends an analogous protection to contract rights, where what the wrongdoer seeks to acquire is not "property" but the modification or release of his own contractual obligation. . . . Confronted with a situation . . . in which the appropriate course of action would be to negotiate regarding legal entitlements, the wrongdoer takes without asking. The opportunistic calculation . . . is that the wrongdoer's anticipated liability in damages is less than the anticipated cost of the entitlement, were it to be purchased from the claimant in a voluntary transaction. Restitution (through the disgorgement remedy) seeks to defeat this calculation, reducing the likelihood that the conscious disregard of another's entitlement can be more advantageous than its negotiated acquisition. See §3, Comment c.

The broader function of disgorgement . . . is not merely to frustrate conscious wrongdoers but to reinforce the stability of the contract itself, enhancing the ability of the parties to negotiate for a contractual performance that may not be easily valued in money. The result is to expand the range of transactions for which parties may effectively bargain. . . .

c. Adequacy of a remedy in damages. If the promisee's contractual entitlement is adequately protected by a judgment for money damages, there is no claim to restitution by the rule of this section. . . . The adequacy of a damage remedy in particular circumstances is a determination for the court, applying its governing law to its own understanding of the case before it; but §39(2) provides the standard baseline of the inquiry.

In contract cases, questions about the adequacy of legal remedies traditionally arise when the plaintiff asks the court to prevent a threatened breach by injunction or specific performance. Disgorgement yields a remedial equivalent after the fact, returning the breaching party to the same position that (enforced) adherence to the contract would have produced. One way to examine the adequacy of a damage remedy in disgorgement cases is therefore to conduct a hypothetical test for the availability of specific relief. If a court with the benefit of hindsight would have granted a remedy by injunction or specific performance, restitution by the rule of this section is appropriate after the fact.

Important parallels between specific performance and disgorgement make this a helpful test, but it cannot be an exclusive one. Disgorgement will be appropriate in many cases where specific performance would not have been available, because specific performance is often denied for reasons having nothing to do with the adequacy of the damage remedy. Most importantly, specific performance may appear impractical, or too difficult to enforce; or the cost of performance to the defendant may not match its benefits to the plaintiff. These considerations do not apply to the disgorgement remedy. Disgorgement is a monetary remedy enforceable only against the defendant's property, not by attempting to coerce the defendant's conduct, and the value of the judgment is the same for each side.

Disgorgement is also an after-the-fact remedy, so that the problems of litigation delay that often make specific performance impractical do not affect disgorgement. If the promisee seeks to solve timing problems by requesting preliminary relief without a full trial, the sharp restriction on the defendant's procedural rights and the resulting risk of error offer substantial reasons for caution – so much so that holdings on the adequacy of legal remedies at the preliminary relief stage are fundamentally different from holdings on the adequacy of legal remedies at the final judgment stage. Disgorgement is awarded at final judgment after full procedural rights; it is not subject to the reasons for withholding preliminary relief. . . .

d. When disgorgement is available. The cases in which the law allows disgorgement for breach of contract are susceptible of various particularized explanations; the purpose of §39 is to frame a rule that will identify them all. It has been suggested, for example, that a contractual entitlement to acquire real property may sufficiently resemble *ownership* of the property (by the doctrine of equitable conversion or otherwise) that it is natural to treat a breach of the sales contract as an interference with the property right – thereby justifying recourse to the restitution claim that would be available in a case of interference with real property. . . . In cases of this kind, where specific performance is routinely available, it has long been assumed that damages are inadequate to protect the contractual entitlement of the promisee. Restitution gives the protection after the fact that specific performance would have given ahead of time.

In other contexts as well, contract rights may resemble noncontractual entitlements that are routinely protected against interference by a disgorgement remedy in restitution. Thus a promise not to disclose or utilize confidential information is the usual form by which trade secrets are protected; allowing restitution for breach of the contract is equivalent to restitution for misappropriation of the trade secret. . . . Again, if one party's contractual obligation to another has a fiduciary or confidential character, disgorgement for breach of the contract might be justified by observing that it resembles a liability to account for profits derived from a breach of fiduciary duty. . . .

In a further set of cases, the nature of the underlying transaction makes it fair to surmise that the plaintiff has (in effect) paid the defendant in advance for a performance that the defendant has failed to render. If the circumstances of the transaction are such that the plaintiff can obtain neither rescission nor a meaningful remedy in damages, restitution by the rule of §39 yields a monetary substitute for the performance the plaintiff paid for and should have received. . . .

In a final set of transactions, the existence of an explicit negative covenant points to the limited nature of rights granted to the paying party under the contract. The purpose of the limitation may be to enable the promisee to sell the rights reserved at an additional price to be negotiated in the future . . . or simply to protect the promisee against potential injuries that are difficult to quantify . . . . If the remedy for breach were limited to provable damages in either case, the defaulting promisor would obtain the benefit of rights that were neither bargained nor paid for; while the promisee would be manifestly unable to purchase a substitute for the promised performance with the damage award. . . .

e. Measure of recovery. The purpose of the disgorgement remedy for breach of contract is to eliminate the possibility that an intentional and opportunistic breach will be more profitable to the performing party than negotiation with the party to whom performance is owed. For this reason, "profit realized . . . as a result of the breach" includes the gains that motivated the promisor's decision to breach the contract. If the defendant's liability in restitution were limited to the amount that might have been paid to obtain the necessary contractual modification in a voluntary transaction, there would be inadequate incentive to bargain over the entitlement in question. . . .

While the rule of this section is intended to make breach unprofitable, it does not seek to punish a breach of contract by requiring forfeiture of the defendant's profit from the transaction as a whole. . . .

f. The exceptional nature of the claim. Of the available remedies for breach of contract, the disgorgement claim described in §39 is the least frequently encountered. The cumulative requirements of §39 will exclude the great majority of contractual defaults.

By itself, the requirement that the breach be *profitable* eliminates most instances of breach. The basic calculation of compensatory damages makes it highly unlikely, in any transaction for which there are market-based substitutes, that the gain to the defendant as a result of default will exceed the injury to the plaintiff from the same cause. The defendant's potential liability for incidental and consequential damages, over and above the cost of a substitute performance, limits the occurrence of profitable breaches almost to the vanishing point. . . .

The scope of the present rule is further restricted by the requirement that breach be deliberate – thereby excluding cases in which breach results from the defendant's inadvertence, negligence, or unsuccessful attempt at performance. . . .

Even when breach is both profitable and deliberate . . . there is no opportunism and no claim under this section if a damage remedy affords adequate protection to the promisee's contractual entitlement . . . .

h. Efficient breach. Modern American contract scholarship devotes considerable attention to a hypothetical case in which breach of contract is "efficient." The scenario most often debated involves a seller who is offered a higher price for goods or services that he has sold but not yet delivered to the buyer. The seller – it is suggested – ought to breach the contract whenever the anticipated profits from resale at the higher price would be more than sufficient to pay the buyer's damages, thereby leaving some parties better off and nobody worse off. An efficient breach of contract by this definition is easy to hypothesize but difficult to find in real life. In a market context, gain to one party is normally offset or exceeded by loss to the other; while the test of efficiency will not be met unless the injured party is fully indemnified against the cost of resolving the resulting dispute. American practice regarding the allocation of litigation expense makes satisfaction of the latter condition especially unlikely. . . .

The rationale of the disgorgement liability in restitution, in a contractual context or any other, is inherently at odds with the idea of efficient breach in its usual connotation. Given the pervasive risk of undercompensation by standard damage measures, not to mention the deadweight loss from the cost of litigation, the law of restitution strongly favors voluntary over involuntary transactions in the adjustment of conflicts over any form of legal entitlement. A voluntary transaction in the present context requires a negotiated release or modification of the existing obligation. The obligor who elects instead to take without asking – calculating that his anticipated liability for breach is less than the price he would have to pay to purchase the rights in question, and leaving the obligee to the chance of a recovery in damages – engages in precisely the conduct that the law of restitution normally condemns.

Whether the promisor's decision to modify or withhold a given performance infringes the contract rights of the promisee is a preliminary question of contract law and interpretation. If it does, the promisor's liability in restitution follows from the same principles as restitution for other instances of conscious and profitable interference with legally protected rights. . . . The rule of §39 does not automatically punish every "efficient breach" with a disgorgement remedy, because it applies only when a remedy in damages is inadequate to protect the promisee's entitlement. . . .

i. Equitable limitations. If a contract is one that a court would decline to enforce by specific performance or injunction on the ground that such relief would impose undue hardship or would otherwise be inequitable to the defaulting party, disgorgement by the rule of §39 will be inappropriate for the same reasons, notwithstanding the fact that the breach is both profitable and deliberate.

One important case in which equitable limitations preclude disgorgement involves the uncontroversial version of "efficient breach." Where contractual performance would be manifestly wasteful – imposing unexpected costs on the performing party that yield no corresponding (or bargained-for) benefit to the recipient – a court will refuse specific performance on the ground of disproportionate hardship. Under such circumstances, it is the party who insists on specific performance who is behaving opportunistically. . . .

Even if a promised performance is fully within the scope of the parties' bargain, specific enforcement may be denied for policy reasons that would make it anomalous to order disgorgement after the fact. . . . By contrast, some of the most frequent reasons for the unavailability of specific performance – either the burden of supervision, or the sheer difficulty of obtaining timely relief – have no application to a remedy via disgorgement after the fact. Unlike the all-or-nothing remedy of specific performance, moreover, a claim to disgorgement of profits under §39 permits some shaping of the remedy to accord with the equities between the parties . . . .

Principles of the Law of Software Contracts (2010)

EDITORS' NOTE

Software is ubiquitous. Not only does it enable our desktop and notebook computers – the kinds of devices that would have come to mind at the turn of the twenty-first century – to perform the many functions they perform; software also controls, or at the very least facilitates, some or all of the key functions of our smart phones, electronic readers, smart thermostats, smart appliances, fitness trackers, industrial robots, automobiles, airplanes (with apologies to my brother-in-law who is a commercial pilot), and myriad other goods. Software also plays in integral role in the provision of all manner of professional and personal services.

Contracts concerning computer software have presented difficult legal issues for many years. Although software is often bought and sold like goods, software contracts do not fit easily into the sale of goods rubric of Uniform Commercial Code Article 2.

As discussed in more detail in the Comment: Uniform Computer Information Transactions Act later in this Supplement, the American Law Institute (ALI) and the National Conference of Commissioners on Uniform State Laws (NCCUSL)[1] undertook in the 1990s to address special issues concerning software contracts by developing a new UCC Article 2B. That effort failed because of fundamental disagreements about the substance of important rules. NCCUSL (now known as the Uniform Law Commission, or ULC) then carried forward the project on its own and, in 1999, promulgated UCITA, providing a comprehensive (and controversial) set of rules for licensing computer information. To date, only Maryland and Virginia have enacted UCITA, and the ULC has ceased promoting additional enactments.

In the mid-2000s, in the wake of its split with the ULC on Article 2B and well aware of UCITA's underwhelming performance, the ALI began to develop the Principles of the Law of Software Contracts. Reporter Robert Hillman (Cornell Law School) and Associate Reporter Maureen O'Rourke (Boston University School of Law) produced a set of black-letter provisions, comments, and illustrations that read

---

1. NCCUSL is now known as the Uniform Law Commission (ULC).

very much like a Restatement, but were termed Principles because the ALI felt they were somewhat ahead of the common law or a model statute.[2]

Approved in 2009 and published in 2010, the Principles sought to weave the currently divergent threads of law governing software contracts into a coherent whole that would guide parties in drafting, performing, and enforcing software contracts, assist courts and other arbiters in resolving disputes involving software contracts, and, perhaps, inform future legislation addressing software contracts.

The Principles have provoked a significant amount of discussion in the academic literature;[3] but, to date, only one U.S. court has cited to them in a published opinion[4] and your editors are unaware of any state or federal legislation or regulations that the Principles have influenced. That said, they serve to frame interesting discussions about how the law of software contracts may yet develop, as well as the difficulty of guiding the development of a body of law in an ever-changing technological environment in which most disputes end up being settled or otherwise resolved out of court.

The following provisions are copyright © 2010 by the American Law Institute. Reprinted with permission. All rights reserved.

CHAPTER 1. DEFINITIONS, SCOPE, AND GENERAL TERMS

Topic 1. Definitions

Topic 2. Scope

Topic 3. General Terms

2. In the assessment of then-ALI Director Lance Liebman, a professor at Harvard Law School for more than twenty years before joining the Columbia Law School faculty as dean in 1991, the Principles represent

> a work in the best tradition of the ALI. It enunciates legal principles on issues posed by new technology. It addresses matters that often come to state and federal judges without adequate guidance from state contract or commercial law or from federal intellectual property law. And it draws by convincing analogy on traditional legal doctrine that history has tested for efficiency and fairness. As Professor Hillman and Dean O'Rourke say in their introduction, this fast-changing legal subject is not ready for a Restatement of common-law rules and is probably also not ready for a federal or state statute. Rather, these ALI Principles can give guidance to lawyers, persons in the software business or who rely on software, and eventually common-law judges and legislators.

Principles of the Law of Software Contracts ix-x (2010).

3. See, e.g., Symposium, The Principles of the Law of Software Contracts: A Phoenix Rising from the Ashes of Article 2B and UCITA, 84 Tulane L. Rev. 1517 (2010); Florencia Marotta-Wurgler, Will Increased Disclosure Help? Evaluating the Recommendations of the ALI's "Principles of the Law of Software Contracts," 78 U. Chi. L. Rev. 165 (2011); Juliet M. Moringiello & William L. Reynolds, From Lord Coke to Internet Privacy: The Past, Present, and Future of Electronic Contracting, 72 Md. L. Rev. 452 (2013); see also Spencer Gottlieb, Note, Installation Failure: How the Predominant Purpose Test Has Perpetuated Software's Uncertain Legal Status Under the Uniform Commercial Code, 113 Mich. L. Rev. 739 (2015) (advocating the use of the Principles' scope provisions, rather than the traditional "predominant purpose" test, to determine the law governing a transaction including software).

4. Conwell v. Gray Loon Outdoor Mktg. Group, Inc., 906 N.E.2d 805, 811 (Ind. 2009).

CHAPTER 1. DEFINITIONS, SCOPE, AND GENERAL TERMS

Topic 1. Definitions

§1.01. Definitions

As used in these Principles

(a) Access Agreement

An "access agreement" is an agreement that authorizes the user of software to access the provider's software via a data-transmission system, such as the Internet, or via a private network or another intermediary now known or hereafter developed.

(b) Agreement

An "agreement" is the bargain of the parties in fact as found in their language or other circumstances, including course of performance, course of dealing, or usage of trade.

(c) Computer

A "computer" is an electronic device that processes information and follows instructions to accomplish a result.

(d) Consumer Agreement

A "consumer agreement" is an agreement for the transfer of software or access to software primarily for personal, family, or household purposes.

(e) Contract

A "contract" is the total legal obligation that results from the parties' agreement, these Principles, and any other applicable law.

(f) Digital Content

"Digital content" consists of "digital art" or a "digital database."

(1) "Digital art" is literary and artistic information stored electronically, such as music, photographs, motion pictures, books, newspapers, and other images and sounds.

(2) A "digital database" is a compilation of facts arranged in a systematic manner and stored electronically. A digital database does not include digital art.

(g) Digital-Content Player

A "digital-content player" consists of software that renders digital content visible, audible, or otherwise perceivable.

(h) Electronic

"Electronic" means technology having electrical, digital, magnetic, wireless, optical, electromagnetic, or similar capabilities.

(i) Record

A "record" is information that is inscribed on a tangible medium or that is stored in an electronic or other medium and is retrievable in perceivable form.

(j) Software

(1) "Software" consists of statements or instructions that are executed by a computer to produce a certain result.

(2) Software does not include digital content, but does include a digital-content player.

(k) Standard Form and Standard Term

(1) A "standard form" is a record regularly used to embody terms of agreements of the same type.

(2) A "standard term" is a term appearing in a standard form and relating to a particular matter.

(l) Standard-Form Transfer of Generally Available Software

A "standard-form transfer of generally available software" is a transfer using a standard form of

(1) a small number of copies of software to an end user; or

(2) the right to access software to a small number of end users

if the software is generally available to the public under substantially the same standard terms.

(m) Transfer

A "transfer" is a conveyance of rights in software or an authorization to access software, including by way of sale, license, lease, or access agreement.

(n) Transferor and Transferee

(1) Except where otherwise provided, a "transferor" is a party who, pursuant to an agreement with the transferee, has transferred or has agreed to transfer software.

(2) Except where otherwise provided, a "transferee" is party who, pursuant to an agreement with the transferor, has received or has agreed to receive rights in or access to software.

Topic 2. Scope

§1.06. Scope; Generally

(a) These Principles apply to agreements for the transfer of software for a consideration. Software agreements include agreements to sell, lease, license, access, or otherwise transfer or share software.

(b) These Principles do not apply to

(1) the transfer of any disk, CD–ROM, or other tangible medium that stores the software, or

(2) the transfer of a security interest in software.

§1.07. Scope; Embedded Software

(a) Subject to §1.06, these Principles apply to agreements for the transfer of software embedded in goods if a reasonable transferor would believe the transferee's predominant purpose for engaging in the transfer is to obtain the software.

(b) These Principles apply to agreements for the transfer of embedded software upgrades and replacements of embedded software only if these Principles applied to the transfer of the embedded software being upgraded or replaced.

§1.08. Scope; Mixed Transfers Including Non-Embedded Software

(a) For purposes of this section,
  (1) "goods" include any embedded software, and
  (2) A "mixed transfer" constitutes a single transaction that consists of the transfer of non-embedded software and any combination of goods, digital content, and services.

(b) Subject to §1.06, in the case of an agreement for a mixed transfer, these Principles apply to the transfer of the non-embedded software unless the transfer also includes digital content or services and a reasonable transferor would believe the transferee's predominant purpose for engaging in the transfer is to obtain the digital content or services.

Topic 3. General Terms

§1.09. Enforcement of Terms under Federal Intellectual Property Law

A term of an agreement is unenforceable if it
  (a) conflicts with a mandatory rule of federal intellectual property law; or
  (b) conflicts impermissibly with the purposes and policies of federal intellectual property law; or
  (c) would constitute federal intellectual property misuse in an infringement proceeding.

§1.10. Public Policy

A term of an agreement is unenforceable if the interest in enforcement of the term is clearly outweighed in the circumstances by a public policy against its enforcement.

§1.11. Unconscionability

(a) If the court as a matter of law finds the agreement or any term of the agreement to have been unconscionable at the time it was made, the court may refuse to enforce the agreement, or it may enforce the remainder of the agreement without the unconscionable term, or it may so limit the application of any unconscionable term to avoid any unconscionable result.

(b) When it is claimed or appears to the court that the agreement or any term thereof may be unconscionable, the parties shall be afforded a reasonable opportunity to present evidence as to its commercial setting, purpose, and effect to aid the court in making the determination.

§1.12. Relation to Outside Law

These Principles should be considered in the context of other applicable law.

§1.13. Choice of Law in Standard–Form Transfers of Generally Available Software

(a) The parties to a standard-form transfer of generally available software may by agreement select the law of a domestic or foreign jurisdiction to govern their rights and duties with respect to an issue in contract if their transaction bears a reasonable relationship to the selected jurisdiction. However, if application of the selected law to an issue would lead to a result that is repugnant to public policy as expressed in the law of the jurisdiction that would otherwise govern under subsection (b), then the law of the jurisdiction chosen by subsection (b) governs with respect to that issue.

(b) In the absence of an enforceable agreement on choice of law, the rights and duties of the parties to a standard-form transfer of generally available software with respect to an issue in contract are determined

(1) in the case of a consumer agreement, by the law of the jurisdiction where the consumer is located; and

(2) in all other cases, by the law of the jurisdiction where the transferor is located.

(c) For purposes of subsection (b):

(1) an individual is located at the individual's principal residence.

(2) an organization that has only one place of business is located at its place of business.

(3) an organization that has more than one place of business is located at its chief executive office.

(4) an organization that does not have a physical place of business is located at its place of incorporation or primary registration.

§1.14. Forum-Selection Clauses

The parties may by agreement choose an exclusive forum unless the choice is unfair or unreasonable. A forum choice may be unfair or unreasonable if:

(a) the forum is unreasonably inconvenient for a party;

(b) the agreement as to the forum was obtained by misrepresentation, duress, the abuse of economic power, or other unconscionable means;

(c) the forum does not have power under its domestic law to entertain the action or to award remedies otherwise available; or

(d) enforcement of the forum-selection clause would be repugnant to public policy as expressed in the law of the forum in which suit is brought.

CHAPTER 2. FORMATION AND ENFORCEMENT

Topic 1. Formation, Generally

§2.01. Formation, Generally

(a) Subject to §2.02, a contract may be formed in any manner sufficient to show an agreement, including by offer and acceptance and by conduct.

(b) A contract may be formed under subsection (a) even though

(1) one or more terms are left open, if there is a reasonably certain basis for granting an appropriate remedy in the event of a breach; or

(2) the parties' records are different. In such a case, the terms of the contract are

    (A) terms, whether in a record or not, to which both parties agree;

    (B) terms that appear in the records of both parties; and

    (C) terms supplied by these Principles or other law.

Topic 2.   *Standard-Form Transfers of Generally Available Software; Enforcement of the Standard Form*

§2.02.   Standard-Form Transfers of Generally Available Software; Enforcement of the Standard Form

(a) This Section applies to standard-form transfers of generally available software as defined in §1.01(1).

(b) A transferee adopts a standard form as a contract when a reasonable transferor would believe the transferee intends to be bound to the form.

(c) A transferee will be deemed to have adopted a standard form as a contract if

(1) the standard form is reasonably accessible electronically prior to initiation of the transfer at issue;

(2) upon initiating the transfer, the transferee has reasonable notice of and access to the standard form before payment or, if there is no payment, before completion of the transfer;

(3) in the case of an electronic transfer of software, the transferee signifies agreement at the end of or adjacent to the electronic standard form, or in the case of a standard form printed on or attached to packaged software or separately wrapped from the software, the transferee does not exercise the opportunity to return the software unopened for a full refund within a reasonable time after the transfer; and

(4) the transferee can store and reproduce the standard form if presented electronically.

(d) Subject to §1.10 (public policy), §1.11 (unconscionability), and other invalidating defenses supplied by these Principles or outside law, a standard term is enforceable if reasonably comprehensible.

(e) If a transferee asserts that it did not adopt a standard form as a contract under subsection (b) or asserts a failure of the transferor to comply with subsection (c) or (d), the transferor has the burden of production and persuasion on the issue of compliance with the subsections.

Topic 3.   *Contract Modification*

§2.03.   Contract Modification

(a) Subject to subsection (c), an agreement modifying a contract is enforceable without consideration and may be formed in any manner sufficient to show an agreement, including by offer and acceptance and by conduct.

(b) In the case of an electronic transfer of software, a transferee will be deemed to have agreed to a modification if the transferee receives reasonable electronic notice of the modification and the transferee signifies agreement to the modification electronically at the end of or adjacent to the electronic notice.

(c) An agreement modifying a contract is not enforceable if

(1) A party agrees to the modification as a result of fraud, duress, or another invalidating cause, or

(2) The contract being modified is in a record that includes a no-oral-modification or other clause excluding modification except by an authenticated record, and the modification is oral or unauthenticated by the party contesting the modification, unless the other party has reasonably relied on a waiver of the no-oral-modification or other clause.

(d) Subject to subsection (a) through (c), the parties may agree in their contract to procedures for unmodifying it. However, in the case of a standard-form transfer of generally available software, mere notice of a material modification sent by one party is insufficient to prove agreement by the other party, even if the original contract authorizes this manner of modifying the contract.

CHAPTER 3.   PERFORMANCE

Topic 1.   Indemnification and Warranties

§3.01.   Implied Indemnification Against Infringement

(a) Except as provided in (d) or as excluded or modified under (e), a transferor that deals in software of the kind transferred or holds itself out by occupation as having knowledge or skill peculiar to the software, and that receives money or a right to payment of a monetary obligation in exchange for the software, must indemnify and hold the transferee harmless against any claim of a third party based on infringement of an intellectual property or like right which right exists at the time of transfer and is based on the laws of the United States or a State thereof. The transferor must pay those costs and damages incurred by the transferee that are specifically attributable to such claim or those costs and damages agreed to in a monetary settlement of such claim.

(b) If a court enjoins the transferee's use of the software or holds the software infringing or otherwise in violation of a like right under subsection (a), the transferor may be liable for damages under §4.05 and must at its own expense and on reasonable notice from the transferee of its desire for a remedy provide the transferee with one of the following remedies as the transferor chooses:

(1) procure for the transferee at no cost to the transferee the continued right to use the software under the terms of the applicable agreement;

(2) replace or modify the software with noninfringing software of substantially equivalent functionality; or

(3) cancel the applicable agreement and refund to the transferee the fees actually paid by the transferee for the infringing components of the software. If the infringement renders the software substantially unusable, the transferor must refund the entire fee. In either case, the transferor must also reimburse

the transferee for incidental expenses incurred in replacing the software, but the transferor may deduct from the amounts due to the transferee under this Section a reasonable allowance for the period of time the transferee used the software.

(c) The indemnification law of the state whose law applies to the agreement under §1.13 or under otherwise applicable law applies to the duty of indemnification of subsection (a).

(d) Unless otherwise agreed, a transferor has no obligations under subsections (a) and (b) if

(1) the transferee uses or modifies the software in a manner not permitted by the terms of the agreement where such use or modification gives rise to the claim; or

(2) the infringement arises from the transferor's compliance with (i) transferee-provided detailed functional specifications; and (ii) a transferee-provided method or process for implementation of those specifications, unless the transferor knows of potential infringement or a claim of infringement at the time of transfer and does not notify the transferee that compliance with the specifications and method or process may result in an infringement.

(e) Indemnification under subsection (a) and the duties of subsection (b) may be excluded or modified

(1) if the exclusion or modification is in a record, is conspicuous, and uses language that gives the transferee reasonable notice of the modification or notice that the transferor has no obligation to indemnify the transferee; or

(2) by course of performance, course of dealing, or usage of trade.

§3.02. Express Quality Warranties

(a) In this Section "transferee" includes both an "immediate transferee" that enters an agreement with the transferor and a "remote transferee" that receives the software or access to the software in the normal chain of distribution.

(b) Except as provided in subsection (d), the transferor creates an express warranty to the transferee as follows:

(1) An affirmation of fact or promise made by the transferor to the transferee, including by advertising or by a record packaged with or accompanying the software, that relates to the software and on which a reasonable transferee could rely creates an express warranty that the software will conform to the affirmation of fact or promise.

(2) Any description of the software made by the transferor to the transferee on which a reasonable transferee could rely creates an express warranty that the software will conform to the description.

(3) Any demonstration of software shown by the transferor to the transferee on which a reasonable transferee could rely creates an express warranty that the software will conform to the demonstration.

(c) A transferor can create an express warranty without using formal words, such as "warrant" or "guarantee," or without intending to create an express warranty. However, a mere opinion or commendation of the software does not create an express warranty.

(d) A distributor or dealer that merely transfers software covered by a warranty in a record made by another party, which warranty identifies the maker of the record as the warrantor, is not liable for breach of the warranty. The distributor or dealer is liable for any express warranties of its own or if it adopts the maker's warranty.

§3.03. Implied Warranty of Merchantability

(a) Unless excluded or modified, a transferor that deals in software of the kind transferred or that holds itself out by occupation as having knowledge or skill peculiar to the software warrants to the transferee that the software is merchantable.

(b) Merchantable software at minimum must
   (1) pass without objection in the trade under the contract description; and
   (2) be fit for the ordinary purposes for which such software is used; and
   (3) be adequately packaged and labeled.

§3.04. Implied Warranty of Fitness for a Particular Purpose

(a) Unless excluded or modified, if a transferor at the time of contracting has reason to know any particular purpose for which the transferee requires the software and the transferee relies on the transferor's skill or judgment to select, develop, or furnish the software, the transferor warrants that the software is fit for the transferee's purpose.

(b) Unless excluded or modified, if an agreement requires a transferor to provide or select a system of hardware and software and the transferor at the time of contracting has reason to know that the transferee is relying on the skill or judgment of the transferor to select the components of the system, the transferor warrants that the software provided or selected will function together with the hardware as a system.

§3.05. Other Implied Quality Warranties

(a) Unless modified or excluded, implied warranties may arise from course of dealing or usage of trade.

(b) A transferor that receives money or a right to payment of a monetary obligation in exchange for the software warrants to any party in the normal chain of distribution that the software contains no material hidden defects of which the transferor was aware at the time of the transfer. This warranty may not be excluded. In addition, this warranty does not displace an action for misrepresentation or its remedies.

§3.06. Disclaimer of Express and Implied Quality Warranties

(a) A statement intending to exclude or modify an express quality warranty is unenforceable if a reasonable transferee would not expect the exclusion or modification.

(b) Unless the circumstances suggest otherwise, all implied quality warranties other than the warranty of no material hidden defects (§3.05(b)) are excluded by language in a record communicated to the transferee such as "as is," "with all faults," or other language that a reasonable transferee would believe excludes all implied quality warranties.

(c) The implied warranty of merchantability is excluded if the exclusion is in a record communicated to the transferee, is conspicuous, and mentions "merchantability."

(d) The implied warranty of fitness for a particular purpose is excluded if the exclusion is in a record communicated to the transferee, is conspicuous, and mentions "fitness for a particular purpose."

(e) If before entering an agreement a transferee has tested the software as fully as desired or unreasonably has refused to test it, there are no implied quality warranties with regard to defects that a test should have or would have revealed.

(f) An implied quality warranty other than the warranty of no material hidden defects (§3.05(b)) may be excluded or modified by course performance, course of dealing, or usage of trade.

(g) Remedies for breach of quality warranties may be limited in accordance with §4.01 of these Principles.

§3.07.   Third-Party Beneficiaries of Warranty

(a) A transferor's warranty extends to any person for whose benefit the transferor intends to supply the software if the person uses the software in a manner contemplated or that should have been contemplated by the transferor.

(b) A transferor's warranty to a consumer extends to the consumer's immediate family, household members, or guests if the transferor reasonably should expect such persons to use the software.

(c) Except as provided in (b), a contractual term that excludes or limits the third parties to which a warranty extends is enforceable.

(d) An exclusion or modification of a warranty that is effective against the transferee is also effective against third parties to which the warranty extends under this Section.

Topic 2.   *Parol Evidence Rule and Interpretation*

§3.08.   Integration, Ambiguity, and Parol Evidence

(a) A full integration constitutes a record or records intended by the parties as a complete and exclusive statement of the terms of an agreement. A partial integration constitutes a record or records intended by the parties as the complete and exclusive statement of one or more terms of an agreement.

(b) The court should determine whether a record is fully integrated, partially integrated, or not integrated prior to applying subsections (e) and (f). In making this determination, the court should consider all credible and relevant extrinsic evidence, including evidence of agreements and negotiations prior to or contemporaneous with the adoption of the record.

(c) If the transfer is a standard-form transfer of generally available software, a term in a record indicating that the record is fully integrated or partially integrated should be probative but not conclusive on the issue.

(d) The court should determine whether a term in a record is ambiguous prior to applying subsections (e) and (f). In making this determination, the court should consider all credible and relevant extrinsic evidence, including evidence of agreements and negotiations prior to or contemporaneous with the adoption of the record. If a term or terms is ambiguous, extrinsic evidence is admissible to prove the meaning of the term or terms.

(e) Unambiguous terms set forth in a fully integrated record may not be contradicted by evidence of any prior agreement or of a contemporaneous oral agreement, but may be explained by evidence of a course of performance, course of dealing, or usage of trade.

(f) Unambiguous terms set forth in a partially integrated record may not be contradicted by evidence of prior or contemporaneous oral conflicting terms, but may be explained by evidence of course of performance, course of dealing, usage of trade, or consistent additional terms.

(g) Notwithstanding subsections (e) and (f),
  (1) evidence is admissible to prove
    (A) illegality, fraud, duress, mistake, or other invalidating causes; and
    (B) independent agreements; and
  (2) evidence of course of performance, course of dealing, and usage of trade is admissible to Supplement a record.

§3.09. General Principles of Interpretation

(a) Words or conduct should be interpreted in accordance with the meaning intended by both parties. Subject to §3.10, if the parties disagree over that meaning, words or conduct should be interpreted reasonably in light of all of the circumstances.

(b) In determining a reasonable interpretation of the words or conduct, significant factors include:
  (1) each party's purpose or purposes in making the contract;
  (2) any course of performance, course of dealing, or usage of trade; and
  (3) the language of the entire agreement.

§3.10. Whose Meaning Prevails

(a) If the parties disagree over the meaning of words or conduct, the meaning intended by one of them should be enforced if at the time the parties made the agreement that party did not know or have reason to know any different meaning intended by the other party, and the other party knew or had reason to know the meaning intended by the first party.

(b) The parties have not made an enforceable agreement if
  (1) the parties disagree over the meaning of a fundamental term or terms;

(2) the term or terms are ambiguous; and

(3) neither party knew or should have known of the other's meaning.

(c) In all other cases of disagreement as to the meaning of a term or terms, §3.09 applies.

Topic 3.   Breach

§3.11.   Breach and Material Breach

(a) A breach occurs if a party without legal excuse fails to perform an obligation as required by the agreement.

(b) An uncured breach, whether or not material, entitles the aggrieved party to remedies.

(c) In determining whether a breach is material, significant factors include:

(1) the terms of the agreement;

(2) usage of trade, course of dealing, and course of performance;

(3) the extent to which the aggrieved party will be deprived of the benefit reasonably expected;

(4) the extent to which the aggrieved party can be adequately compensated for the part of the benefit deprived;

(5) the degree of harm or likely harm to the aggrieved party; and

(6) the extent to which the behavior of the party failing to perform or to offer to perform departs from standards of good faith and fair dealing.

(d) Notwithstanding subsection (c) or any provision to the contrary in the agreement, a material breach occurs if:

(1) the transferor breaches the warranty of §3.05(b);

(2) an exclusive or limited remedy fails of its essential purpose under §4.01; or

(3) the transferor breaches the agreement by failing to comply with §4.03.

(e) The cumulative effect of nonmaterial breaches may be material.

§3.12.   Cure of Breach

(a) Unless otherwise agreed, a party in breach of contract may, on seasonable notice to the aggrieved party and at its own expense, cure the breach by making a conforming performance if:

(1) the time for performance has not yet expired and the conforming performance occurs within the time for performance; or

(2) the breaching party had reasonable grounds to believe the non-conforming performance would be acceptable with or without money allowance and provides a conforming performance within a further reasonable time after performance was due; or

(3) the breaching party seasonably notifies the aggrieved party of its intent to cure and promptly provides a conforming performance before the aggrieved party cancels under §4.04.

(b) If a breaching party fails to cure a material breach, the aggrieved party's obligation to perform any remaining duties is suspended except with respect to restrictions on the use of the software. The aggrieved party also may cancel under §4.04.

(c) A party may not cancel or refuse to perform because of a breach that has been seasonably cured under subsection (a).

(d) The cumulative effect of repeated attempts to cure may be a material breach.

CHAPTER 4.   REMEDIES

Topic 1.   Agreements with Respect to Remedy

§4.01.   Contractual Modification or Limitation of Remedy

(a) Subject to the provisions of subsections (b) and (c) of this Section, §4.02 (liquidation and limitation of damages), §4.03(e) (unauthorized automated disablement), and except for damages for breach of the warranty of §3.05(b) (no material hidden defects),

(1) the agreement may provide for remedies in addition to or in substitution for those provided in these Principles and may limit or alter the measure of damages recoverable under these Principles, as by limiting the transferee's remedy to return of the software and repayment of the price or to repair and replacement of nonconforming software; and

(2) resort to a remedy as provided is optional unless the remedy is expressly agreed to be exclusive, in which case it is the sole remedy.

(b) If circumstances cause an exclusive or limited remedy to fail of its essential purpose, the aggrieved party may recover a remedy as provided in these Principles or applicable outside law.

(c) Subject to the provisions of §4.03(e) (unauthorized automated disablement), and except for damages for breach of the warranty of §3.05(b) (no material hidden defects), consequential damages may be limited or excluded unless the limitation or exclusion is unconscionable at the time of contracting or operates in an unconscionable way. This rule applies even if circumstances cause an exclusive or limited remedy to fail of its essential purpose under subsection (b). Limitation of consequential damages for injury to the person in the case of consumer software is prima facie unconscionable but limitation of damages where the loss is commercial is not.

§4.02.   Liquidation and Limitation of Damages

(a) Damages for breach by either party may be liquidated in the agreement but only at an amount that is reasonable in light of the anticipated or actual harm caused by the breach, the difficulties of proof of loss, and the inconvenience or nonfeasibility of otherwise obtaining an adequate remedy. Section 4.01 determines the enforceability of a term that limits but does not liquidate damages.

(b) If a term liquidating damages is unenforceable under this Section, the aggrieved party may recover a remedy as provided in these Principles, except as limited by other terms of the agreement.

§4.03. Use of Automated Disablement to Impair Use

(a) "Automated disablement" means the use of electronic means to disable or materially impair the functionality of software.

(b) A transferor may not use automated disablement if the process results in the loss of: (i) rights granted in the agreement unless the transferee has materially breached and such rights do not survive the material breach; or (ii) the use of other software or digital content.

(c) Notwithstanding anything to the contrary in the agreement, a transferor may not use automated disablement as a remedy for breach if the agreement is a standard-form transfer of generally available software or if the transaction is a consumer agreement.

(d) Subject to subsection (c), if the transferor has a right to cancel under §4.04, it may do so using automated disablement only if such authorization is provided for in the agreement and under the following circumstances:

(1) the term authorizing automated disablement is conspicuous;

(2) the transferor provides timely notice of the breach and its intent to use automated disablement and provides the transferee with a reasonable opportunity to cure the breach and the transferee has not so cured; and

(3) the transferor has obtained a court order permitting it to use automated disablement.

(e) A transferee may recover direct, incidental, and consequential damages caused by use of automated disablement in violation of this Section notwithstanding any agreement to the contrary.

(f) Obligations of the transferor and rights of the transferee under this Section may not be waived.

Topic 2.   Remedies in the Absence of Agreement

§4.04. Cancellation

(a) An aggrieved party may cancel a contract on a material breach of the whole contract if the breach has not been cured under §3.12 or waived.

(b) Cancellation is not effective unless the canceling party gives reasonable notice of cancellation to the party in breach.

(c) Except as otherwise provided in the agreement, upon effective cancellation by the transferor:

(1) of an access contract, any rights of access are discontinued; and

(2) all rights of the transferee in the software provided under the agreement terminate and the transferee must destroy any physical copies of the software or seasonably return them to the transferor, delete all electronic copies on its systems, and refuse delivery of any physical copies.

(d) Except as otherwise provided in the agreement, upon cancellation by either party, all executory obligations of both parties are discharged except those based on a previous breach or performance or those that the parties agreed would survive termination or cancellation.

(e) A cancellation is ineffective if it fails to meet the standard of subsection (a) or the requirements of subsection (b).

§4.05. Expectation Damages

Unless otherwise agreed, damages under these Principles should put the aggrieved party in as good a position as if the other party had fully performed. Damages for lost expectancy include direct, incidental, and consequential damages, less expenses saved in consequence of the breach.

§4.06. Specific Performance

(a) Specific performance may be decreed when the software to be transferred is unique, or in other proper circumstances. Specific performance is not available if it would require the performance of personal services or if an award of damages would be adequate to protect the expectation interest of the transferee.

(b) The decree for specific performance may include such terms and conditions as to payment of the price, damages, confidentiality, and rights in the software as the court may deem just.

(c) An aggrieved transferor who does not cancel may be entitled to a decree requiring adherence to the terms of the agreement as against a breaching transferee, but not if the decree would require the performance of personal services or if an award of damages would be adequate to protect the expectation interest of the transferor.

Uniform Commercial Code (2016 Official Text)

EDITORS' NOTE

History of the UCC[1]

As the United States developed a national market economy during the nineteenth century, the number of business transactions across state lines increased dramatically. Many of these transactions were cumbersome, however, because of differences among the states on commercial subjects, such as negotiable instruments, sales, and warehousing. Recognizing these problems, a number of business lawyers suggested the need for greater uniformity among the states in commercial law.

In 1889, the legislature of New York, the leading commercial state at that time, passed a statute providing for the appointment of commissioners who were authorized to solicit the appointment of commissioners from other states to prepare uniform state laws. In 1892, the first meeting of the National Conference of Commissioners on Uniform State Laws (NCCUSL)[2] was held in connection with the annual meeting of the American Bar Association. At first, NCCUSL concentrated on technical questions, such as standardized forms for acknowledgment of instruments, but it soon ventured into more substantive areas.

By the early part of the twentieth century, NCCUSL had promulgated uniform acts on several commercial subjects: negotiable instruments, sales, warehouse receipts, bills of lading, and trust receipts, to name just a few. Adopted in many states, these acts advanced the cause of uniformity.

---

1. For more discussion of the history, nature, and scope of the UCC, see Robert Braucher & Robert A. Riegert, Introduction to Commercial Transactions 19-31 (1977), Robert A. Stein, Forming a More Perfect Union: A History of the Uniform Law Commission (2013), Nathan M. Crystal, Codification and the Rise of the Restatement Movement, 54 Wash. L. Rev. 239 (1979), Allen R. Kamp, Uptown Act: A History of the Uniform Commercial Code, 1940-49, 51 SMU L. Rev. 275 (1998), and Allen R. Kamp, Downtown Code: A History of the Uniform Commercial Code, 1949-1954, 49 Buff. L. Rev. 359 (2001).

2. NCCUSL is now the Uniform Law Commission or ULC.

By 1940, it was apparent that many of the uniform acts adopted early in the century required revision. At its fiftieth annual meeting, NCCUSL's president William A. Schnader called for the creation of a uniform commercial code. The Conference quickly adopted his suggestion, subject to obtaining funding. In 1944, NCCUSL combined forces with the American Law Institute (ALI) to sponsor the project, with Professor Karl Llewellyn of Columbia Law School as Chief Reporter.

After a lengthy process, involving circulation of drafts among advisors, business groups, and others, NCCUSL and the ALI issued an official text of the proposed Uniform Commercial Code (UCC) in 1951. Pennsylvania became the first state to adopt the UCC, in 1953. The project received a major setback in 1956, when the New York Law Revision Commission, after a three-year study yielding six published volumes, advised the New York Legislature that the UCC was "not satisfactory in its present form."

The New York study caused NCCUSL and the ALI to reexamine the UCC. In 1958, they issued a revised UCC. New York adopted this revised UCC in 1962, and other states quickly followed suit. By 1968, the UCC was in force in all jurisdictions except Louisiana, which has only enacted certain articles (not including Article 2). In 1961, the ALI and NCCUSL created a Permanent Editorial Board for the Uniform Commercial Code to monitor developments in commercial law and propose revisions of the UCC.

Nature and Scope of the UCC

Although titled a commercial code, the name is something of a misnomer. The UCC governs consumer transactions as well as transactions among commercial entities. It is also not as comprehensive as the uninitiated might assume. Transactions involving real property, insurance, intellectual property, and personal services are generally outside the UCC's scope. In addition, many aspects of transactions within the UCC's scope are regulated by other bodies of law – sometimes in conjunction with the UCC, sometimes superseding it. For example, UCC Article 8 deals with title in and transfer of investment securities, such as corporate stock, but most of the law regulating transactions in investment securities lies outside the UCC. Moreover, common law and equitable principles govern transactions within the UCC's scope unless the UCC specifically displaces them. See UCC §1-103(b).

Rather than a comprehensive code of commercial law, the UCC instead is a collection of articles governing various types of commercial transactions. Article 1 covers a number of general matters, including definitions, which apply to any transaction that falls within the scope of another article. (Thus, if you have a transaction within Article 2's scope, you must also refer to Article 1 to understand the entirety of UCC law governing that transaction.) Article 2, which is the principal part of the UCC addressed in most Contracts courses, governs sale of goods. Article 2A, built on the framework of Article 2, governs leases of goods.

For several years the ALI and NCCUSL worked on a proposed Article 2B, dealing with computer information transactions. After much controversy over the provisions, the ALI and NCCUSL decided that such rules should not be proposed as part of the UCC. Instead, the project was transformed into a separate Uniform Computer Information Transactions Act (UCITA), which NCCUSL adopted in 1999. We include additional discussion of and selected provisions from UCITA in the Materials on Electronic Contracting in this Supplement. The ALI went a different route, eventually promulgating in 2010 its Principles of the Law of Software Contracts, which we also discuss further and excerpt in this Supplement.

Article 3 governs commercial paper: checks, promissory notes, and drafts. Article 4 governs the processing of such instruments through the banking system. Article 4A governs fund transfers (a.k.a. wire transfers). Article 5 governs the rights and liabilities of parties to letters of credit. Article 6 establishes rules governing bulk sales – transactions in which a business sells all or substantially all its inventory to a single buyer outside the ordinary course of the seller's business. (On the ULC's recommendation, most states have repealed Article 6 in recent years.) Article 7 governs documents of title, such as bills of lading issued by carriers of goods or warehouse receipts issued by companies that are involved in storing someone else's goods. Article 8 governs the ownership and transfer of investment securities. Finally, Article 9 governs security interests in personal property, tangible and intangible, including certain personal property in which an interest arises under real property law.

Unlike the Restatements, which have only persuasive weight, the UCC – once a state enacts it – is a statute and has the force of law. It is important to be aware that each state's enacted version of the UCC varies to some degree from the Official Text. Because those variations are idiosyncratic, and because we assume this Supplement's users are interested in the law of more than one state, we present the Official Text promulgated by the ALI and the ULC, rather than trying to present each variation in each state or choosing one state's enacted version of the UCC. Both Uniform Laws Annotated and the UCC Reporting Service provide regularly-updated catalogues of state-by-state variations.

Each section of the complete Official Text of the Code is accompanied by an Official Comment, which includes references to prior law, discussion of the purposes of the section, and definitional cross-references. Some states have enacted the comments, giving them the force of law, most states have not. In states that have not enacted the comments, court opinions frequently have given the comments substantial weight. See Joseph M. Perillo, Contracts 17 (7th ed. 2014); see, e.g., Carlund Corp. v. Crown Center Redevelopment, 849 S.W.2d 647, 650 (Mo. Ct. App. 1993); B & W Glass, Inc. v. Weather Shield Mfg., Inc., 829 P.2d 809, 816 (Wyo. 1992) (treating comments as persuasive authority).

Focus on Articles 1 and 2

This part of the Supplement includes the text of most of Articles 1 and 2 of the Code, along with a few provisions from Articles 2A, 3, and 9. One or more Official Comments for some significant sections are included as well.

Article 1 was comprehensively revised in 2001 and amendments to Article 2 were promulgated in 2003. As of June 1, 2017, Revised Article 1 had been adopted in all 50 states and the District of Columbia, and it will take effect in the final adopting state – Missouri – on August 28, 2017.[3] Thus, this Supplement includes only Revised Article 1. For those who are more familiar with former Article 1 or who are reading a

---

3. See www.uniformlaws.org (last visited June 1, 2017).

court opinion discussing or applying former Article 1, we discuss specific changes to Article 1 below and provide a guide to help identify where comparable sections of former Article 1 are now located in Revised Article 1.

From the beginning the amendments to Article 2 appeared destined to have trouble gaining acceptance by the states and that proved correct. The drafting process for the Article 2 amendments began in 1988 and was not completed until 2003, some fifteen years later. The length of the drafting process reflects the substantial opposition to the various proposals. For a discussion of those difficulties, see Richard E. Speidel, Introduction to Symposium on Proposed Revised Article 2, 54 SMU L. Rev. 787 (2001). Opposition was based on a number of factors, including a dispute about the degree to which revised Article 2 would protect consumers, the potential application of Article 2 to computer software or information transactions, and a general sense among commercial sellers and buyers that Article 2 did not need major changes. Id. at 791-93. Eventually, the ALI and NCCUSL abandoned the idea of comprehensively revising Article 2, opting instead to promulgate a set of amendments to existing sections and a handful of new sections. By fall 2010, no state had adopted any of the Article 2 amendments–although in 2005 Oklahoma did amend two sections of its Article 2, capturing the essence of one of the 2003 amendments. Ultimately, the ULC and ALI voted in 2011 to withdraw the proposed amendments to Article 2 (and Article 2A).[4] This Supplement includes unamended Article 2.

Notable Changes to Article 1

Revised Article 1 contains few significant substantive changes from former Article 1; most of the revision involved relocating provisions and stylistic or technical updates. As originally proposed, revised §1-301 would have departed significantly from former Article 1 by allowing parties to a nonconsumer transaction to choose applicable law from a state having no relationship to the parties or the transaction – a proposal that caused substantial controversy. See William J. Woodward, Jr., Contractual Choice of Law: Legislative Choice in an Era of Party Autonomy, 54 SMU L. Rev. 697 (2001). None of the first nineteen states to enact Revised Article 1 adopted the original version of §1-301. See Keith A. Rowley, The Often Imitated, But Not Yet Duplicated, Revised Uniform Commercial Code Article 1, 38 UCC L.J. 195 (2006). In the face of such opposition, the ULC and the ALI subsequently decided to revert to the choice of law rules embodied in former §1-105 (which were consistent with the Restatement (Second) of Conflict of Laws). Thus, the Official Text version of §1-301 is – and the versions of §1-301 enacted in all 50 states and the District of Columbia are – substantively identical to former §1-105.

---

4. See Recommendation of the Permanent Editorial Board for the Uniform Commercial Code to Withdraw the 2003 Amendments to UCC Articles 2 and 2A from the Official Text of the Uniform Commercial Code, reproduced at 65 Consumer Fin. L.Q. Rep. 150 (2011). The PEB's recommendation and report of the ULC Executive Committee's vote to withdraw the 2003 amendments was distributed to ALI members in advance of the 2011 ALI Annual Meeting, where the ALI membership voted to withdraw its support as well. See 88th Annual Meeting Updates, available at http://2011am.ali.org/updates.cfm (last visited June 1, 2017).

The most notable change in Revised Article 1 involves the duty of good faith. Previously, the UCC offered two definitions of "good faith": former §1-201(19) provided a general definition applicable to all parties throughout the UCC that "good faith" meant simply "honesty in fact," while Article 2 defined "good faith" for merchants buying or selling goods to mean both "honesty in fact" and "the observance of reasonable commercial standards of fair dealing in the trade," §2-103(1)(b). Revised Article 1 defines "good faith" in §1-201(b)(20) to require both honesty in fact and the observance of reasonable commercial standards of fair dealing. This unitary definition ostensibly applies to all parties – merchants and nonmerchants alike – but its effect on the obligations of nonmerchants remains unclear. See Robyn L. Meadows, Russell A. Hakes, Stephen L. Sepinuck, The Uniform Commercial Code Survey: Introduction, 59 Bus. Law. 1553 (2004); Keith A. Rowley, One for All, But None for (All of) One: Part 2 of 2, Nev. Law., Aug. 2004, at 28. The states enacting Revised Article 1 have been divided (unevenly) on whether to adopt the new unitary definition of good faith or to retain the bifurcated definition of "good faith" from former Article 1 and §2-103(1)(b).[4] Whether courts will apply the same or different *de facto* good faith standards for merchants and nonmerchants in one of the *de jure* unitary definition jurisdictions remains to be seen.

Article 1 Correlation Guide

Topic	Former Article 1	Revised Article 1
Liberal construction to promote uniformity	§1-102(1), (2)	§1-103(a)
Variation by agreement of non-mandatory provisions	§1-102(3), (4)	§1-302
Supplementation by principles of common law and equity	§1-103	§1-103(b)
Choice of law provisions	§1-105	§1-301
Remedies administered to achieve compensation	§1-106	§1-305
Ability to waive claim after breach	§1-107	§1-306
Definition of good faith	§§1-201(19) & 2-103(1)(b)	§1-201(b)(20)
Definitions of notice and knowledge	§1-201(25)-(27)	§1-202
Lease distinguished from sale with security interest	§1-201(37)	§1-203
Duty of good faith	§1-203	§1-304

4. As of June 1, 2017, thirty-eight enacting states and the District of Columbia have adopted the revised definition of "good faith" requiring all parties to all UCC transactions (except those Article 5 governs) to act honestly in fact and observe commercially reasonable standards of fair dealing, see, e.g., Del. Code Ann., tit. 6, §1-201(b)(20) (2006); Tex. Bus. & Com. Code Ann. §1.201(b)(20) (Vernon 2009); the other twelve enacting states maintain the former definition of "good faith," requiring only honesty in fact except from merchants in transactions within the scope of Article 2, see, e.g., Ala. Code §§7-1-201(b)(20) & 7-2-103(1)(b) (2006); Haw. Rev. Stat. Ann. §§490:1-201(b) & 490:2-103(1)(b) (West 2008).

Topic	Former Article 1	Revised Article 1
Meaning of reasonable time	§1-204	§1-205
Meaning and effect of usage of trade, course of dealing, course of performance	§§1-205 & 2-208	§1-303
Option to accelerate payment at will	§1-208	§1-309

ARTICLE 1. GENERAL PROVISIONS

Part 1. General Provisions

Part 2. General Definitions and Principles of Interpretation

Part 3. Territorial Applicability and General Rules

ARTICLE 2. SALES

Part 1. Short Title, General Construction and Subject Matter

ARTICLE 2A.   LEASES

Part 1.   General Provisions

ARTICLE 1. GENERAL PROVISIONS

Part 1. General Provisions

§1-102. Scope of Article

This article applies to a transaction to the extent that it is governed by another article of [the Uniform Commercial Code].

§1-103. Construction of [Uniform Commercial Code] to Promote Its Purposes and Policies; Applicability of Supplemental Principles of Law

(a) [The Uniform Commercial Code] must be liberally construed and applied to promote its underlying purposes and policies, which are:

(1) to simplify, clarify, and modernize the law governing commercial transactions;

(2) to permit the continued expansion of commercial practices through custom, usage, and agreement of the parties; and

(3) to make uniform the law among the various jurisdictions.

(b) Unless displaced by the particular provisions of [the Uniform Commercial Code], the principles of law and equity, including the law merchant and the law relative to capacity to contract, principal and agent, estoppel, fraud, misrepresentation, duress, coercion, mistake, bankruptcy, and other validating or invalidating cause Supplement its provisions.

Official Comments

. . . .

2. **Applicability of supplemental principles of law.** Subsection (b) states the basic relationship of the Uniform Commercial Code to supplemental bodies of law. The Uniform Commercial Code was drafted against the backdrop of existing bodies of law, including the common law and equity, and relies on those bodies of law to Supplement it provisions in many important ways. At the same time, the Uniform Commercial Code is the primary source of commercial law rules in areas that it governs, and its rules represent choices made by its drafters and the enacting legislatures about the appropriate policies to be furthered in the transactions it covers. Therefore, while principles of common law and equity may *supplement* provisions of the Uniform Commercial Code, they may not be used to *supplant* its provisions, or the purposes and policies those provisions reflect, unless a specific provision of the Uniform Commercial Code provides otherwise. In the absence of such a provision, the Uniform Commercial Code preempts principles of common law and equity that are inconsistent with either its provisions or its purposes and policies. . . .

3. **Application of subsection (b) to statutes.** The primary focus of Section 1-103 is on the relationship between the Uniform Commercial Code and

principles of common law and equity as developed by the courts. State law, however, increasingly is statutory. Not only are there a growing number of state statutes addressing specific issues that come within the scope of the Uniform Commercial Code, but in some States many general principles of common law and equity have been codified. When the other law relating to a matter within the scope of the Uniform Commercial Code is a statute, the principles of subsection (b) remain relevant to the court's analysis of the relationship between that statute and the Uniform Commercial Code, but other principles of statutory interpretation that specifically address the interrelationship between statutes will be relevant as well. In some situations, the principles of subsection (b) still will be determinative. For example, the mere fact that an equitable principle is stated in statutory form rather than in judicial decisions should not change the court's analysis of whether the principle can be used to Supplement the Uniform Commercial Code – under subsection (b), equitable principles may Supplement provisions of the Uniform Commercial Code only if they are consistent with the purposes and policies of the Uniform Commercial Code as well as its text. In other situations, however, other interpretive principles addressing the interrelationship between statutes may lead the court to conclude that the other statute is controlling, even though it conflicts with the Uniform Commercial Code. This, for example, would be the result in a situation where the other statute was specifically intended to provide additional protection to a class of individuals engaging in transactions covered by the Uniform Commercial Code.

4. **Listing not exclusive.** The list of sources of supplemental law in subsection (b) is intended to be merely illustrative of the other law that may Supplement the Uniform Commercial Code, and is not exclusive. No listing could be exhaustive. Further, the fact that a particular section of the Uniform Commercial Code makes express reference to other law is not intended to suggest the negation of the general application of the principles of subsection (b). Note also that the word "bankruptcy" in subsection (b), continuing the use of that word from former Section 1-103, should be understood not as a specific reference to federal bankruptcy law but, rather as a reference to general principles of insolvency, whether under federal or state law.

§1-108.   Relation to Electronic Signatures in Global and National Commerce Act

This article modifies, limits, and supersedes the federal Electronic Signatures in Global and National Commerce Act, 15 U.S.C. Section 7001 et seq., except that nothing in this article modifies, limits, or supersedes Section 7001(c) of that Act or authorizes electronic delivery of any of the notices described in Section 7003(b) of that Act.

Official Comments

1. The federal Electronic Signatures in Global and National Commerce Act, 15 U.S.C. Section 7001 et seq. became effective in 2000. Section 102(a) of that

Act provides that a State statute may modify, limit, or supersede the provisions of section 101 of that Act with respect to state law if such statute, inter alia, specifies the alternative procedures or requirements for the use or acceptance (or both) of electronic records or electronic signatures to establish the legal effect, validity, or enforceability of contracts or other records, and (i) such alternative procedures or requirements are consistent with Titles I and II of that Act, (ii) such alternative procedures or requirements do not require, or accord greater legal status or effect to, the implementation or application of a specific technology or technical specification for performing the functions of creating, storing, generating, receiving, communicating, or authenticating electronic records or electronic signatures; and (iii) if enacted or adopted after the date of the enactment of that Act, makes specific reference to that Act. [Other sections of] Article 1 fulfill[] the first two of those three criteria; this Section fulfills the third criterion listed above.

2. . . . Article 1 does not modify, limit, or supersede Section 101(c) of the Electronic Signatures in Global and National Commerce Act (requiring affirmative consent from a consumer to electronic delivery of transactional disclosures that are required by state law to be in writing); nor does it authorize electronic delivery of any of the notices described in Section 103(b) of that Act.

Part 2.　General Definitions and Principles of Interpretation

§1-201.　General Definitions

(a) Unless the context otherwise requires, words or phrases defined in this section, or in the additional definitions contained in other articles of [the Uniform Commercial Code] that apply to particular articles or parts thereof, have the meanings stated.

(b) Subject to definitions contained in other articles of [the Uniform Commercial Code] that apply to particular articles or parts thereof:

(1) "Action", in the sense of a judicial proceeding, includes recoupment, counterclaim, set-off, suit in equity, and any other proceeding in which rights are determined.

(2) "Aggrieved party" means a party entitled to pursue a remedy.

(3) "Agreement", as distinguished from "contract", means the bargain of the parties in fact, as found in their language or inferred from other circumstances, including course of performance, course of dealing, or usage of trade as provided in Section 1-303.

(4) "Bank" means a person engaged in the business of banking and includes a savings bank, savings and loan association, credit union, and trust company.

(5) "Bearer" means a person in possession of a negotiable instrument, document of title, or certificated security that is payable to bearer or indorsed in blank.

(6) "Bill of lading" means a document evidencing the receipt of goods for shipment issued by a person engaged in the business of transporting or forwarding goods.

(7) "Branch" includes a separately incorporated foreign branch of a bank.

(8) "Burden of establishing" a fact means the burden of persuading the trier of fact that the existence of the fact is more probable than its nonexistence.

(9) "Buyer in ordinary course of business" means a person that buys goods in good faith, without knowledge that the sale violates the rights of another person in the goods, and in the ordinary course from a person, other than a pawnbroker, in the business of selling goods of that kind. A person buys goods in the ordinary course if the sale to the person comports with the usual or customary practices in the kind of business in which the seller is engaged or with the seller's own usual or customary practices. A person that sells oil, gas, or other minerals at the wellhead or minehead is a person in the business of selling goods of that kind. A buyer in ordinary course of business may buy for cash, by exchange of other property, or on secured or unsecured credit, and may acquire goods or documents of title under a preexisting contract for sale. Only a buyer that takes possession of the goods or has a right to recover the goods from the seller under Article 2 may be a buyer in ordinary course of business. "Buyer in ordinary course of business" does not include a person that acquires goods in a transfer in bulk or as security for or in total or partial satisfaction of a money debt.

(10) "Conspicuous", with reference to a term, means so written, displayed, or presented that a reasonable person against which it is to operate ought to have noticed it. Whether a term is "conspicuous" or not is a decision for the court. Conspicuous terms include the following:

(A) a heading in capitals equal to or greater in size than the surrounding text, or in contrasting type, font, or color to the surrounding text of the same or lesser size; and

(B) language in the body of a record or display in larger type than the surrounding text, or in contrasting type, font, or color to the surrounding text of the same size, or set off from surrounding text of the same size by symbols or other marks that call attention to the language.

(11) "Consumer" means an individual who enters into a transaction primarily for personal, family, or household purposes.

(12) "Contract", as distinguished from "agreement", means the total legal obligation that results from the parties' agreement as determined by [the Uniform Commercial Code] as supplemented by any other applicable laws.

(13) "Creditor" includes a general creditor, a secured creditor, a lien creditor, and any representative of creditors, including an assignee for the benefit of creditors, a trustee in bankruptcy, a receiver in equity, and an executor or administrator of an insolvent debtor's or assignor's estate.

(14) "Defendant" includes a person in the position of defendant in a counterclaim, cross-claim, or third-party claim.

(15) "Delivery", with respect to an instrument, document of title, or chattel paper, means voluntary transfer of possession.

(16) "Document of title" includes bill of lading, dock warrant, dock receipt, warehouse receipt or order for the delivery of goods, and also any other document which in the regular course of business or financing is treated as adequately evidencing that the person in possession of it is entitled to receive, hold, and dispose of the document and the goods it covers. To be a document of title, a document must purport to be issued by or addressed to a bailee and purport to cover goods in the bailee's possession which are either identified or are fungible portions of an identified mass.

(17) "Fault" means a default, breach, or wrongful act or omission.

(18) "Fungible goods" means:

(A) goods of which any unit, by nature or usage of trade, is the equivalent of any other like unit; or

(B) goods that by agreement are treated as equivalent.

(19) "Genuine" means free of forgery or counterfeiting.

(20) "Good faith," except as otherwise provided in Article 5, means honesty in fact and the observance of reasonable commercial standards of fair dealing.

(21) "Holder" means:

(A) the person in possession of a negotiable instrument that is payable either to bearer or to an identified person that is the person in possession; or

(B) the person in possession of a document of title if the goods are deliverable either to bearer or to the order of the person in possession.

(22) "Insolvency proceeding" includes an assignment for the benefit of creditors or other proceeding intended to liquidate or rehabilitate the estate of the person involved.

(23) "Insolvent" means:

(A) having generally ceased to pay debts in the ordinary course of business other than as a result of bona fide dispute;

(B) being unable to pay debts as they become due; or

(C) being insolvent within the meaning of federal bankruptcy law.

(24) "Money" means a medium of exchange currently authorized or adopted by a domestic or foreign government. The term includes a monetary unit of account established by an intergovernmental organization or by agreement between two or more countries.

(25) "Organization" means a person other than an individual.

(26) "Party", as distinguished from "third party", means a person that has engaged in a transaction or made an agreement subject to [the Uniform Commercial Code].

(27) "Person" means an individual, corporation, business trust, estate, trust, partnership, limited liability company, association, joint venture, government, governmental subdivision, agency, or instrumentality, public corporation, or any other legal or commercial entity.

(28) "Present value" means the amount as of a date certain of one or more sums payable in the future, discounted to the date certain by use of either an interest rate specified by the parties if that rate is not manifestly unreasonable at the time the transaction is entered into or, if an interest rate is not so specified, a commercially reasonable rate that takes into account the facts and circumstances at the time the transaction is entered into.

(29) "Purchase" means taking by sale, lease, discount, negotiation, mortgage, pledge, lien, security interest, issue or reissue, gift, or any other voluntary transaction creating an interest in property.

(30) "Purchaser" means a person that takes by purchase.

(31) "Record" means information that is inscribed on a tangible medium or that is stored in an electronic or other medium and is retrievable in perceivable form.

(32) "Remedy" means any remedial right to which an aggrieved party is entitled with or without resort to a tribunal.

(33) "Representative" means a person empowered to act for another, including an agent, an officer of a corporation or association, and a trustee, executor, or administrator of an estate.

(34) "Right" includes remedy.

(35) "Security interest" means an interest in personal property or fixtures which secures payment or performance of an obligation. "Security interest" includes any interest of a consignor and a buyer of accounts, chattel paper, a payment intangible, or a promissory note in a transaction that is subject to Article 9. "Security interest" does not include the special property interest of a buyer of goods on identification of those goods to a contract for sale under Section 2-401, but a buyer may also acquire a "security interest" by complying with Article 9. Except as otherwise provided in Section 2-505, the right of a seller or lessor of goods under Article 2 or 2A to retain or acquire possession of the goods is not a "security interest", but a seller or lessor may also acquire a "security interest" by complying with Article 9. The retention or reservation of title by a seller of goods notwithstanding shipment or delivery to the buyer under Section 2-401 is limited in effect to a reservation of a "security interest." Whether a transaction in the form of a lease creates a "security interest" is determined pursuant to Section 1-203.

(36) "Send" in connection with a writing, record, or notice means:

(A) to deposit in the mail or deliver for transmission by any other usual means of communication with postage or cost of transmission provided for and properly addressed and, in the case of an instrument, to an address specified thereon or otherwise agreed, or if there be none to any address reasonable under the circumstances; or

(B) in any other way to cause to be received any record or notice within the time it would have arrived if properly sent.

(37) "Signed" includes using any symbol executed or adopted with present intention to adopt or accept a writing.

(38) "State" means a State of the United States, the District of Columbia, Puerto Rico, the United States Virgin Islands, or any territory or insular possession subject to the jurisdiction of the United States.

(39) "Surety" includes a guarantor or other secondary obligor.

(40) "Term" means a portion of an agreement that relates to a particular matter.

(41) "Unauthorized signature" means a signature made without actual, implied, or apparent authority. The term includes a forgery.

(42) "Warehouse receipt" means a receipt issued by a person engaged in the business of storing goods for hire.

(43) "Writing" includes printing, typewriting, or any other intentional reduction to tangible form. "Written" has a corresponding meaning.

§1-202.   Notice; Knowledge

(a) Subject to subsection (f), a person has "notice" of a fact if the person:

(1) has actual knowledge of it;

(2) has received a notice or notification of it; or

(3) from all the facts and circumstances known to the person at the time in question, has reason to know that it exists.

(b) "Knowledge" means actual knowledge. "Knows" has a corresponding meaning.

(c) "Discover", "learn", or words of similar import refer to knowledge rather than to reason to know.

(d) A person "notifies" or "gives" a notice or notification to another person by taking such steps as may be reasonably required to inform the other person in ordinary course, whether or not the other person actually comes to know of it.

(e) Subject to subsection (f), a person "receives" a notice or notification when:

(1) it comes to that person's attention; or

(2) it is duly delivered in a form reasonable under the circumstances at the place of business through which the contract was made or at another location held out by that person as the place for receipt of such communications.

(f) Notice, knowledge, or a notice or notification received by an organization is effective for a particular transaction from the time it is brought to the attention of the individual conducting that transaction and, in any event, from the time it would have been brought to the individual's attention if the organization had exercised due diligence. An organization exercises due diligence if it maintains reasonable routines for communicating significant information to the person conducting the transaction and there is reasonable compliance with the routines. Due diligence does not require an individual acting for the organization to communicate information unless the communication is part of the individual's regular duties or the individual has reason to know of the transaction and that the transaction would be materially affected by the information.

§1-203. Lease Distinguished from Security Interest

(a) Whether a transaction in the form of a lease creates a lease or security interest is determined by the facts of each case.

(b) A transaction in the form of a lease creates a security interest if the consideration that the lessee is to pay the lessor for the right to possession and use of the goods is an obligation for the term of the lease and is not subject to termination by the lessee, and:

(1) the original term of the lease is equal to or greater than the remaining economic life of the goods;

(2) the lessee is bound to renew the lease for the remaining economic life of the goods or is bound to become the owner of the goods;

(3) the lessee has an option to renew the lease for the remaining economic life of the goods for no additional consideration or for nominal additional consideration upon compliance with the lease agreement; or

(4) the lessee has an option to become the owner of the goods for no additional consideration or for nominal additional consideration upon compliance with the lease agreement.

(c) A transaction in the form of a lease does not create a security interest merely because:

(1) the present value of the consideration the lessee is obligated to pay the lessor for the right to possession and use of the goods is substantially equal to or is greater than the fair market value of the goods at the time the lease is entered into;

(2) the lessee assumes risk of loss of the goods;

(3) the lessee agrees to pay, with respect to the goods, taxes, insurance, filing, recording, or registration fees, or service or maintenance costs;

(4) the lessee has an option to renew the lease or to become the owner of the goods;

(5) the lessee has an option to renew the lease for a fixed rent that is equal to or greater than the reasonably predictable fair market rent for the use of the goods for the term of the renewal at the time the option is to be performed; or

(6) the lessee has an option to become the owner of the goods for a fixed price that is equal to or greater than the reasonably predictable fair market value of the goods at the time the option is to be performed.

(d) Additional consideration is nominal if it is less than the lessee's reasonably predictable cost of performing under the lease agreement if the option is not exercised. Additional consideration is not nominal if:

(1) when the option to renew the lease is granted to the lessee, the rent is stated to be the fair market rent for the use of the goods for the term of the renewal determined at the time the option is to be performed; or

(2) when the option to become the owner of the goods is granted to the lessee, the price is stated to be the fair market value of the goods determined at the time the option is to be performed.

(e) The "remaining economic life of the goods" and "reasonably predictable" fair market rent, fair market value, or cost of performing under the lease agreement must be determined with reference to the facts and circumstances at the time the transaction is entered into.

Official Comments

. . . .

1. An interest in personal property or fixtures which secures payment or performance of an obligation is a "security interest." See Section 1-201[(b)(35)]. Security interests are sometimes created by transactions in the form of leases. Because it can be difficult to distinguish leases that create security interests from those that do not, this section provides rules that govern the determination of whether a transaction in the form of a lease creates a security interest.

2. . . . . If a transaction creates a lease and not a security interest, the lessee's interest in the goods is limited to its leasehold estate; the residual interest in the goods belongs to the lessor. This has significant implications to the lessee's creditors. . . .

Lease is defined in Article 2A as a transfer of the right to possession and use of goods for a term, in return for consideration. Section 2A-103(1)(j). The definition continues by stating that the retention or creation of a security interest is not a lease. Thus, the task of sharpening the line between true leases and security interests disguised as leases continues to be a function of this Article.

This section begins where Section 1-201[(b)](35) leaves off. It draws a sharper line between leases and security interests disguised as leases to create greater certainty in commercial transactions. . . .

. . . . Whether a transaction creates a lease or a security interest [is] determined by the facts of each case. Subsection (b) further provides that a transaction creates a security interest if the lessee has an obligation to continue paying consideration for the term of the lease, if the obligation is not terminable by the lessee . . . and if one of four additional tests is met. . . . All of these tests focus on economics, not the intent of the parties. . . .

The focus on economics is reinforced by subsection (c). It states that a transaction does not create a security interest merely because the transaction has certain characteristics listed therein. . . .

The relationship of subsection (b) to subsection (c) deserves to be explored. The fixed price purchase option provides a useful example. A fixed price purchase option in a lease does not of itself create a security interest. This is particularly true if the fixed price is equal to or greater than the reasonably predictable fair market value of the goods at the time the option is to be performed. A security interest is created only if the option price is nominal and the conditions stated in the introduction to the second paragraph of this subsection are met. There is a set of purchase options whose fixed price is less than fair market value but greater than nominal that must be determined on the facts of each case to ascertain whether the transaction in which the option is included creates a lease or a security interest. . . .

§1-204. Value

Except as otherwise provided in Articles 3, 4, [and] 5, [and 6], a person gives value for rights if the person acquires them:

(1) in return for a binding commitment to extend credit or for the extension of immediately available credit, whether or not drawn upon and whether or not a charge-back is provided for in the event of difficulties in collection;

(2) as security for, or in total or partial satisfaction of, a preexisting claim;

(3) by accepting delivery under a preexisting contract for purchase; or

(4) in return for any consideration sufficient to support a simple contract.

§1-205. Reasonable Time; Seasonableness

(a) Whether a time for taking an action required by [the Uniform Commercial Code] is reasonable depends on the nature, purpose, and circumstances of the action.

(b) An action is taken seasonably if it is taken at or within the time agreed or, if no time is agreed, at or within a reasonable time.

§1-206. Presumptions

Whenever [the Uniform Commercial Code] creates a "presumption" with respect to a fact, or provides that a fact is "presumed," the trier of fact must find the existence of the fact unless and until evidence is introduced that supports a finding of its nonexistence.

Part 3.   Territorial Applicability and General Rules

§1-301.   Territorial Applicability; Parties' Power to Choose Applicable Law

(a) Except as otherwise provided in this section, when a transaction bears a reasonable relation to this state and also to another state or nation the parties may agree that the law either of this state or of such other state or nation shall govern their rights and duties.

(b) In the absence of an agreement effective under subsection (a), and except as provided in subsection (c), [the Uniform Commercial Code] applies to transactions bearing an appropriate relation to this state.

(c) If one of the following provisions of [the Uniform Commercial Code] specifies the applicable law, that provision governs and a contrary agreement is effective only to the extent permitted by the law so specified:

(1) Section 2-402;

(2) Sections 2A-105 and 2A-106;

(3) Section 4-102;

(4) Section 4A-507;

(5) Section 5-116;

[(6) Section 6-103;]

(7) Section 8-110;

(8) Sections 9-301 through 9-307.

Official Comments

Source: Former Section 1-105.

Changes from former law: This section is substantively identical to former Section 1-105. Changes in language are stylistic only.

1. Subsection (a) states affirmatively the right of the parties to a multi-state transaction or a transaction involving foreign trade to choose their own law. That right is subject to the firm rules stated in the sections listed in subsection (c), and is limited to jurisdictions to which the transaction bears a "reasonable relation." In general, the test of "reasonable relation" is similar to that laid down by the Supreme Court in Seeman v. Philadelphia Warehouse Co., 274 U.S. 403, 47 S. Ct. 626, 71 L. Ed. 1123 (1927). Ordinarily the law chosen must be that of a jurisdiction where a significant enough portion of the making or performance of the contract is to occur or occurs. But an agreement as to choice of law may sometimes take effect as a shorthand expression of the intent of the parties as to matters governed by their agreement, even though the transaction has no significant contact with the jurisdiction chosen.

2. Where there is no agreement as to the governing law, the Act is applicable to any transaction having an "appropriate" relation to any state which enacts it. Of course, the Act applies to any transaction which takes place in its entirety in a state which has enacted the Act. But the mere fact that suit is brought in a state does not make it appropriate to apply the substantive law of that state. Cases where a relation to the enacting state is not "appropriate" include, for example,

those where the parties have clearly contracted on the basis of some other law, as where the law of the place of contracting and the law of the place of contemplated performance are the same and are contrary to the law under the Code.

3. Where a transaction has significant contacts with a state which has enacted the Act and also with other jurisdictions, the question what relation is "appropriate" is left to judicial decision. In deciding that question, the court is not strictly bound by precedents established in other contexts. Thus a conflict-of-laws decision refusing to apply a purely local statute or rule of law to a particular multi-state transaction may not be valid precedent for refusal to apply the Code in an analogous situation. Application of the Code in such circumstances may be justified by its comprehensiveness, by the policy of uniformity, and by the fact that it is in large part a reformulation and restatement of the law merchant and of the understanding of a business community which transcends state and even national boundaries. Compare Global Commerce Corp. v. Clark-Babbitt Industries, Inc., 239 F.2d 716, 719 (2d Cir. 1956). In particular, where a transaction is governed in large part by the Code, application of another law to some detail of performance because of an accident of geography may violate the commercial understanding of the parties. . . .

6. This section is subject to Section 1-102, which states the scope of Article 1. As that section indicates, the rules of Article 1, including this section, apply to a transaction to the extent that transaction is governed by one of the other Articles of the Uniform Commercial Code.

§1-302. Variation by Agreement

(a) Except as otherwise provided in subsection (b) or elsewhere in [the Uniform Commercial Code], the effect of provisions of [the Uniform Commercial Code] may be varied by agreement.

(b) The obligations of good faith, diligence, reasonableness, and care prescribed by [the Uniform Commercial Code] may not be disclaimed by agreement. The parties, by agreement, may determine the standards by which the performance of those obligations is to be measured if those standards are not manifestly unreasonable. Whenever [the Uniform Commercial Code] requires an action to be taken within a reasonable time, a time that is not manifestly unreasonable may be fixed by agreement.

(c) The presence in certain provisions of [the Uniform Commercial Code] of the phrase "unless otherwise agreed", or words of similar import, does not imply that the effect of other provisions may not be varied by agreement under this section.

§1-303. Course of Performance, Course of Dealing, and Usage of Trade

(a) A "course of performance" is a sequence of conduct between the parties to a particular transaction that exists if:

(1) the agreement of the parties with respect to the transaction involves repeated occasions for performance by a party; and

(2) the other party, with knowledge of the nature of the performance and opportunity for objection to it, accepts the performance or acquiesces in it without objection.

(b) A "course of dealing" is a sequence of conduct concerning previous transactions between the parties to a particular transaction that is fairly to be regarded as establishing a common basis of understanding for interpreting their expressions and other conduct.

(c) A "usage of trade" is any practice or method of dealing having such regularity of observance in a place, vocation, or trade as to justify an expectation that it will be observed with respect to the transaction in question. The existence and scope of such a usage must be proved as facts. If it is established that such a usage is embodied in a trade code or similar record, the interpretation of the record is a question of law.

(d) A course of performance or course of dealing between the parties or usage of trade in the vocation or trade in which they are engaged or of which they are or should be aware is relevant in ascertaining the meaning of the parties' agreement, may give particular meaning to specific terms of the agreement, and may Supplement or qualify the terms of the agreement. A usage of trade applicable in the place in which part of the performance under the agreement is to occur may be so utilized as to that part of the performance.

(e) Except as otherwise provided in subsection (f), the express terms of an agreement and any applicable course of performance, course of dealing, or usage of trade must be construed whenever reasonable as consistent with each other. If such a construction is unreasonable:

(1) express terms prevail over course of performance, course of dealing, and usage of trade;

(2) course of performance prevails over course of dealing and usage of trade; and

(3) course of dealing prevails over usage of trade.

(f) Subject to Section 2-209, a course of performance is relevant to show a waiver or modification of any term inconsistent with the course of performance.

(g) Evidence of a relevant usage of trade offered by one party is not admissible unless that party has given the other party notice that the court finds sufficient to prevent unfair surprise to the other party.

Official Comments

. . . .

1. The Uniform Commercial Code rejects both the "lay-dictionary" and the "conveyancer's" reading of a commercial agreement. Instead the meaning of the agreement of the parties is to be determined by the language used by them and by their action, read and interpreted in the light of commercial practices and other surrounding circumstances. The measure and background for interpretation are set by the commercial context, which may explain and Supplement even the language of a formal or final writing.

2. "Course of dealing," as defined in subsection (b), is restricted, literally, to a sequence of conduct between the parties previous to the agreement. A sequence of conduct after or under the agreement, however, is a "course of

performance." "Course of dealing" may enter the agreement either by explicit provisions of the agreement or by tacit recognition.

3. The Uniform Commercial Code deals with "usage of trade" as a factor in reaching the commercial meaning of the agreement that the parties have made. The language used is to be interpreted as meaning what it may fairly be expected to mean to parties involved in the particular commercial transaction in a given locality or in a given vocation or trade. By adopting in this context the term "usage of trade," the Uniform Commercial Code expresses its intent to reject those cases which see evidence of "custom" as representing an effort to displace or negate "established rules of law." A distinction is to be drawn between mandatory rules of law such as the Statute of Frauds provisions of Article 2 on Sales whose very office is to control and restrict the actions of the parties, and which cannot be abrogated by agreement, or by a usage of trade, and those rules of law (such as those in Part 3 of Article 2 on Sales) which fill in points which the parties have not considered and in fact agreed upon. The latter rules hold "unless otherwise agreed" but yield to the contrary agreement of the parties. Part of the agreement of the parties to which such rules yield is to be sought for in the usages of trade which furnish the background and give particular meaning to the language used, and are the framework of common understanding controlling any general rules of law which hold only when there is no such understanding.

4. A usage of trade under subsection (c) must have the "regularity of observance" specified. The ancient English tests for "custom" are abandoned in this connection. Therefore, it is not required that a usage of trade be "ancient or immemorial," "universal," or the like. Under the requirement of subsection (c) full recognition is thus available for new usages and for usages currently observed by the great majority of decent dealers, even though dissidents ready to cut corners do not agree. There is room also for proper recognition of usage agreed upon by merchants in trade codes.

5. The policies of the Uniform Commercial Code . . . carry forward the policy underlying the ancient requirement that a custom or usage must be "reasonable." However, the emphasis is shifted. The very fact of commercial acceptance makes out a *prima facie* case that the usage is reasonable, and the burden is no longer on the usage to establish itself as being reasonable. . . .

6. Subsection (d), giving the prescribed effect to usages of which the parties "are or should be aware," reinforces the provision of subsection (c) requiring not universality but only the described "regularity of observance" of the practice or method. This subsection also reinforces the point of subsection (c) that such usages may be either general to trade or particular to a special branch of trade.

7. Although the definition of "agreement" in Section 1-201 includes the elements of course of performance, course of dealing, and usage of trade, the fact that express reference is made in some sections to those elements is not to be construed as carrying a contrary intent or implication elsewhere. Compare Section 1-302(c). . . .

§1-304. Obligation of Good Faith

Every contract or duty within [the Uniform Commercial Code] imposes an obligation of good faith in its performance and enforcement.

Official Comments

. . . .

1. This section sets forth a basic principle running throughout the Uniform Commercial Code. The principle is that in commercial transactions good faith is required in the performance and enforcement of all agreements or duties. While this duty is explicitly stated in some provisions of the Uniform Commercial Code, the applicability of the duty is broader than merely these situations and applies generally, as stated in this section, to the performance or enforcement of every contract or duty within this Act. . . . This section does not support an independent cause of action for failure to perform or enforce in good faith. Rather, this section means that a failure to perform or enforce, in good faith, a specific duty or obligation under the contract, constitutes a breach of that contract or makes unavailable, under the particular circumstances, a remedial right or power. This distinction makes it clear that the doctrine of good faith merely directs a court towards interpreting contracts within the commercial context in which they are created, performed, and enforced, and does not create a separate duty of fairness and reasonableness which can be independently breached.

2. "Performance and enforcement" of contracts and duties within the Uniform Commercial Code include the exercise of rights created by the Uniform Commercial Code.

§1-305. Remedies to Be Liberally Administered

(a) The remedies provided by [the Uniform Commercial Code] must be liberally administered to the end that the aggrieved party may be put in as good a position as if the other party had fully performed but neither consequential or special damages nor penal damages may be had except as specifically provided in [the Uniform Commercial Code] or by other rule of law.

(b) Any right or obligation declared by [the Uniform Commercial Code] is enforceable by action unless the provision declaring it specifies a different and limited effect.

§1-306. Waiver or Renunciation of Claim or Right After Breach

A claim or right arising out of an alleged breach may be discharged in whole or in part without consideration by agreement of the aggrieved party in an authenticated record.

§1-308. Performance or Acceptance Under Reservation of Rights

(a) A party that with explicit reservation of rights performs or promises performance or assents to performance in a manner demanded or offered by the other party does not thereby prejudice the rights reserved. Such words as "without prejudice," "under protest," or the like are sufficient.

(b) Subsection (a) does not apply to an accord and satisfaction.

§1-309. Option to Accelerate at Will

A term providing that one party or that party's successor in interest may accelerate payment or performance or require collateral or additional collateral "at will" or when the party "deems itself insecure," or words of similar import, means that the party has power to do so only if that party in good faith believes that the prospect of payment or performance is impaired. The burden of establishing lack of good faith is on the party against which the power has been exercised.

ARTICLE 2. SALES

Part 1. Short Title, General Construction and Subject Matter

§2-102. Scope; Certain Security and Other Transactions Excluded from This Article

Unless the context otherwise requires, this Article applies to transactions in goods; it does not apply to any transaction which although in the form of an unconditional contract to sell or present sale is intended to operate only as a security transaction nor does this Article impair or repeal any statute regulating sales to consumers, farmers or other specified classes of buyers.

§2-103. Definitions and Index of Definitions

(1) In this Article unless the context otherwise requires:

(a) "Buyer" means a person who buys or contracts to buy goods.

(b) [Reserved.] ["Good faith" in the case of a merchant means honesty in fact and the observance of reasonable commercial standards of fair dealing in the trade.]

(c) "Receipt" of goods means taking physical possession of them.

(d) "Seller" means a person who sells or contracts to sell goods.

(2) Other definitions applying to this Article or to specified Parts thereof, and the sections in which they appear are:

"Acceptance." Section 2-606.

"Banker's credit." Section 2-325.
"Between merchants." Section 2-104.
"Cancellation." Section 2-106(4).
"Commercial unit." Section 2-105.
"Confirmed credit." Section 2-325.
"Conforming to contract." Section 2-106.
"Contract for sale." Section 2-106.
"Cover." Section 2-712.
"Entrusting." Section 2-403.
"Financing agency." Section 2-104.
"Future goods." Section 2-105.
"Goods." Section 2-105.
"Identification." Section 2-501.
"Installment contract." Section 2-612.
"Letter of Credit." Section 2-325.
"Lot." Section 2-105.
"Merchant." Section 2-104.
"Overseas." Section 2-323.
"Person in position of seller." Section 2-707.
"Present sale." Section 2-106.
"Sale." Section 2-106.
"Sale on approval." Section 2-326.
"Sale or return." Section 2-326.
"Termination." Section 2-106.
(3) The following definitions in other Articles apply to this Article:
"Check." Section 3-104.
"Consignee." Section 7-102.
"Consignor." Section 7-102.
"Consumer goods." Section 9-102.
"Dishonor." Section 3-502.
"Draft." Section 3-104.
(4) In addition Article 1 contains general definitions and principles of construction and interpretation applicable throughout this Article.

§2-104. Definitions: "Merchant"; "Between Merchants"; "Financing Agency"

(1) "Merchant" means a person who deals in goods of the kind or otherwise by his occupation holds himself out as having knowledge or skill peculiar to the practices or goods involved in the transaction or to whom such knowledge or skill may be attributed by his employment of an agent or broker or other intermediary who by his occupation holds himself out as having such knowledge or skill.

(2) "Financing agency" means a bank, finance company or other person who in the ordinary course of business makes advances against goods or documents of title or who by arrangement with either the seller or the buyer intervenes in ordinary course to make or collect payment due or claimed under the contract for sale, as by purchasing or paying the seller's draft or making advances against it or

by merely taking it for collection whether or not documents of title accompany the draft. . . .

(3) "Between merchants" means in any transaction with respect to which both parties are chargeable with the knowledge or skill of merchants.

Official Comment

. . . .

1. This Article assumes that transactions between professionals in a given field require special and clear rules which may not apply to a casual or inexperienced seller or buyer. It thus adopts a policy of expressly stating rules applicable "between merchants" and "as against a merchant" wherever they are needed instead of making them depend upon the circumstances of each case as in the statutes cited above. This section lays the foundation of this policy by defining those who are to be regarded as professionals or "merchants" and by stating when a transaction is deemed to be "between merchants".

2. The term "merchant" as defined here roots in the "law merchant" concept of a professional in business. The professional status under the definition may be based upon specialized knowledge as to the goods, specialized knowledge as to business practices, or specialized knowledge as to both and which kind of specialized knowledge may be sufficient to establish the merchant status is indicated by the nature of the provisions.

The special provisions as to merchants appear only in this Article and they are of three kinds. Sections 2-201(2), 2-205, 2-207 and 2-209 dealing with the statute of frauds, firm offers, confirmatory memoranda and modification rest on normal business practices which are or ought to be typical of and familiar to any person in business. For purposes of these sections almost every person in business would, therefore, be deemed to be a "merchant" under the language "who . . . by his occupation holds himself out as having knowledge or skill peculiar to the practices . . . involved in the transaction . . ." since the practices involved in the transaction are non-specialized business practices such as answering mail. In this type of provision, banks or even universities, for example, well may be "merchants." But even these sections only apply to a merchant in his mercantile capacity; a lawyer or bank president buying fishing tackle for his own use is not a merchant.

On the other hand, in Section 2-314 on the warranty of merchantability, such warranty is implied only "if the seller is a merchant with respect to goods of that kind." Obviously this qualification restricts the implied warranty to a much smaller group than everyone who is engaged in business and requires a professional status as to particular kinds of goods. The exception in Section 2-402(2) for retention of possession by a merchant-seller falls in the same class; as does Section 2-403(2) on entrusting of possession to a merchant "who deals in goods of that kind".

A third group of sections includes . . . 2-327(1)(c), 2-603 and 2-605, dealing with responsibilities of merchant buyers to follow seller's instructions, etc.; 2-509 on risk of loss, and 2-609 on adequate assurance of performance.

This group of sections applies to persons who are merchants under either the "practices" or the "goods" aspect of the definition of merchant.

3. The "or to whom such knowledge or skill may be attributed by his employment of an agent or broker . . ." clause of the definition of merchant means that even persons such as universities, for example, can come within the definition of merchant if they have regular purchasing departments or business personnel who are familiar with business practices and who are equipped to take any action required. . . .

Definitional Cross References:
"Bank." Section 1-201.
"Buyer." Section 2-103.
"Contract for sale." Section 2-106.
"Document of title." Section 1-201.
"Draft." Section 3-104.
"Goods." Section 2-105.
"Person." Section 1-201.
"Purchase." Section 1-201.
"Seller." Section 2-103.

§2-105. Definitions: Transferability; "Goods"; "Future" Goods; "Lot"; "Commercial Unit"

(1) "Goods" means all things (including specially manufactured goods) which are movable at the time of identification to the contract for sale other than the money in which the price is to be paid, investment securities (Article 8) and things in action. "Goods" also includes the unborn young of animals and growing crops and other identified things attached to realty as described in the section on goods to be severed from realty (Section 2-107).

(2) Goods must be both existing and identified before any interest in them can pass. Goods which are not both existing and identified are "future" goods. A purported present sale of future goods or of any interest therein operates as a contract to sell.

(3) There may be a sale of a part interest in existing identified goods.

(4) An undivided share in an identified bulk of fungible goods is sufficiently identified to be sold although the quantity of the bulk is not determined. Any agreed proportion of such a bulk or any quantity thereof agreed upon by number, weight or other measure may to the extent of the seller's interest in the bulk be sold to the buyer who then becomes an owner in common.

(5) "Lot" means a parcel or a single article which is the subject matter of a separate sale or delivery, whether or not it is sufficient to perform the contract.

(6) "Commercial unit" means such a unit of goods as by commercial usage is a single whole for purposes of sale and division of which materially impairs its character or value on the market or in use. A commercial unit may be a single article (as a machine) or a set of articles (as a suite of furniture or an assortment of sizes) or a quantity (as a bale, gross, or carload) or any other unit treated in use or in the relevant market as a single whole.

Official Comment

. . . .

1. . . . . Growing crops are included within the definition of goods since they are frequently intended for sale. . . . The young of animals are also included expressly in this defintion since they, too, are frequently intended for sale and may be contracted for before birth. The period of gestation of domestic animals is such that the provisions of the section on identification can apply as in the case of crops to be planted. The reason of this definition also leads to the inclusion of a wool crop or the like as "goods" subject to identification under this Article.

The exclusion of "money in which the price is to be paid" from the definition of goods does not mean that foreign currency which is included in the definition of money may not be the subject matter of a sales transaction. Goods is intended to cover the sale of money when money is being treated as a commodity but not to include it when money is the medium of payment. . . .

§2-106.   Definitions: "Contract"; "Agreement"; "Contract for Sale"; "Sale"; "Present Sale"; "Conforming" to Contract; "Termination"; "Cancellation"

(1) In this Article unless the context otherwise requires "contract" and "agreement" are limited to those relating to the present or future sale of goods. "Contract for sale" includes both a present sale of goods and a contract to sell goods at a future time. A "sale" consists in the passing of title from the seller to the buyer for a price (Section 2-401). A "present sale" means a sale which is accomplished by the making of the contract.

(2) Goods or conduct including any part of a performance are "conforming" or conform to the contract when they are in accordance with the obligations under the contract.

(3) "Termination" occurs when either party pursuant to a power created by agreement or law puts an end to the contract otherwise than for its breach. On "termination" all obligations which are still executory on both sides are discharged but any right based on prior breach or performance survives.

(4) "Cancellation" occurs when either party puts an end to the contract for breach by the other and its effect is the same as that of "termination" except that the cancelling party also retains any remedy for breach of the whole contract or any unperformed balance.

§2-107.   Goods to Be Severed From Realty; Recording

(1) A contract for the sale of minerals or the like (including oil and gas) or a structure or its materials to be removed from realty is a contract for the sale of goods within this Article if they are to be severed by the seller but until severance a purported present sale thereof which is not effective as a transfer of an interest in land is effective only as a contract to sell.

(2) A contract for the sale apart from the land of growing crops and other things attached to realty and capable of severance without material harm thereto but not described in subsection (1) or of timber to be cut is a contract for the sale of goods within this Article whether the subject matter is to be severed by the buyer or by the seller even though it forms part of the realty at the time of contracting, and the parties can by identification effect a present sale before severance.

(3) The provisions of this section are subject to any third party rights provided by the law relating to realty records, and the contract for sale may be executed and recorded as a document transferring an interest in land and shall then constitute notice to third parties of the buyer's rights under the contract for sale.

Official Comment

. . . .

1. Subsection (1) . . . applies only if the minerals or structures "are to be severed by the seller." If the buyer is to sever, such transactions are considered contracts affecting land and all problems of the Statute of Frauds and of the recording of land rights apply to them. . . .

Part 2.   Form, Formation and Readjustment of Contract

§2-201.   Formal Requirements; Statute of Frauds

(1) Except as otherwise provided in this section a contract for the sale of goods for the price of $500 or more is not enforceable by way of action or defense unless there is some writing sufficient to indicate that a contract for sale has been made between the parties and signed by the party against whom enforcement is sought or by his authorized agent or broker. A writing is not insufficient because it omits or incorrectly states a term agreed upon but the contract is not enforceable under this paragraph beyond the quantity of goods shown in such writing.

(2) Between merchants if within a reasonable time a writing in confirmation of the contract and sufficient against the sender is received and the party receiving it has reason to know its contents, it satisfies the requirements of subsection (1) against such party unless written notice of objection to its contents is given within 10 days after it is received.

(3) A contract which does not satisfy the requirements of subsection (1) but which is valid in other respects is enforceable

(a) if the goods are to be specially manufactured for the buyer and are not suitable for sale to others in the ordinary course of the seller's business and the seller, before notice of repudiation is received and under circumstances which reasonably indicate that the goods are for the buyer, has made either a substantial beginning of their manufacture or commitments for their procurement; or

(b) if the party against whom enforcement is sought admits in his pleading, testimony or otherwise in court that a contract for sale was made, but the contract is not enforceable under this provision beyond the quantity of goods admitted; or

(c) with respect to goods for which payment has been made and accepted or which have been received and accepted (Sec. 2-606).

Official Comment

. . . .

1. The required writing need not contain all the material terms of the contract and such material terms as are stated need not be precisely stated. All that is required is that the writing afford a basis for believing that the offered oral evidence rests on a real transaction. It may be written in lead pencil on a scratch pad. It need not indicate which party is the buyer and which the seller. The only term which must appear is the quantity term which need not be accurately stated but recovery is limited to the amount stated. The price, time and place of payment or delivery, the general quality of the goods, or any particular warranties may all be omitted.

Special emphasis must be placed on the permissibility of omitting the price term in view of the insistence of some courts on the express inclusion of this term even where the parties have contracted on the basis of a published price list. In many valid contracts for sale the parties do not mention the price in express terms, the buyer being bound to pay and the seller to accept a reasonable price which the trier of the fact may well be trusted to determine. Again, frequently the price is not mentioned since the parties have based their agreement on a price list or catalogue known to both of them and this list serves as an efficient safeguard against perjury. Finally, "market" prices and valuations that are current in the vicinity constitute a similar check. Thus if the price is not stated in the memorandum it can normally be supplied without danger of fraud. Of course if the "price" consists of goods rather than money the quantity of goods must be stated.

Only three definite and invariable requirements as to the memorandum are made by this subsection. First, it must evidence a contract for the sale of goods; second, it must be "signed," a word which includes any authentication which identifies the party to be charged; and third, it must specify a quantity.

2. "Partial performance" as a substitute for the required memorandum can validate the contract only for the goods which have been accepted or for which payment has been made and accepted.

Receipt and acceptance either of goods or of the price constitutes an unambiguous overt admission by both parties that a contract actually exists. If the court can make a just apportionment, therefore, the agreed price of any goods actually delivered can be recovered without a writing or, if the price has been paid, the seller can be forced to deliver an apportionable part of the goods. The overt actions of the parties make admissible evidence of the other terms of the contract necessary to a just apportionment. This is true even though the actions of the parties are not in themselves inconsistent with a different transaction such as a consignment for resale or a mere loan of money.

Part performance by the buyer requires the delivery of something by him that is accepted by the seller as such performance. Thus, part payment may be made by money or check, accepted by the seller. If the agreed price consists of goods or services, then they must also have been delivered and accepted.

3. Between merchants, failure to answer a written confirmation of a contract within ten days of receipt is tantamount to a writing under subsection (2) and is sufficient against both parties under subsection (1). The only effect, however, is to take away from the party who fails to answer the defense of the Statute of Frauds; the burden of persuading the trier of fact that a contract was in fact made orally prior to the written confirmation is unaffected. Compare the effect of a failure to reply under Section 2-207.

4. Failure to satisfy the requirements of this section does not render the contract void for all purposes, but merely prevents it from being judicially enforced in favor of a party to the contract. For example, a buyer who takes possession of goods as provided in an oral contract which the seller has not meanwhile repudiated, is not a trespasser. Nor would the Statute of Frauds provisions of this section be a defense to a third person who wrongfully induces a party to refuse to perform an oral contract, even though the injured party cannot maintain an action for damages against the party so refusing to perform.

5. The requirement of "signing" is discussed in . . . Section 1-201.

6. It is not necessary that the writing be delivered to anybody. It need not be signed or authenticated by both parties but it is, of course, not sufficient against one who has not signed it. Prior to a dispute no one can determine which party's signing of the memorandum may be necessary but from the time of contracting each party should be aware that to him it is signing by the other which is important.

7. If the making of a contract is admitted in court, either in a written pleading, by stipulation or by oral statement before the court, no additional writing is necessary for protection against fraud. Under this section it is no longer possible to admit the contract in court and still treat the Statute as a defense. However, the contract is not thus conclusively established. The admission so made by a party is itself evidential against him of the truth of the facts so admitted and of nothing more; as against the other party, it is not evidential at all. . . .

Definitional Cross References:
    "Action." Section 1-201.
    "Between merchants." Section 2-104.
    "Buyer." Section 2-103.
    "Contract." Section 1-201.
    "Contract for sale." Section 2-106.
    "Goods." Section 2-105.
    "Notice." Section 1-201.
    "Party." Section 1-201.
    "Reasonable time." Section 1-204.
    "Sale." Section 2-106.
    "Seller." Section 2-103.

§2-202.   Final Written Expression: Parol or Extrinsic Evidence

Terms with respect to which the confirmatory memoranda of the parties agree or which are otherwise set forth in a writing intended by the parties as a final expression of their agreement with respect to such terms as are included therein may not be contradicted by evidence of any prior agreement or of a contemporaneous oral agreement but may be explained or supplemented

(a) by course of performance, course of dealing, or usage of trade (Section 1-303); and

(b) by evidence of consistent additional terms unless the court finds the writing to have been intended also as a complete and exclusive statement of the terms of the agreement.

Official Comment

. . . .

1. This section definitely rejects:

(a) Any assumption that because a writing has been worked out which is final on some matters, it is to be taken as including all the matters agreed upon;

(b) The premise that the language used has the meaning attributable to such language by rules of construction existing in the law rather than the meaning which arises out of the commercial context in which it was used; and

(c) The requirement that a condition precedent to the admissibility of the type of evidence specified in paragraph (a) is an original determination by the court that the language used is ambiguous.

2. Paragraph (a) makes admissible evidence of course of dealing, usage of trade and course of performance to explain or Supplement the terms of any writing stating the agreement of the parties in order that the true understanding of the parties as to the agreement may be reached. Such writings are to be read on the assumption that the course of prior dealings between the parties and the usages of trade were taken for granted when the document was phrased. Unless carefully negated they have become an element of the meaning of the words used. Similarly, the course of actual performance by the parties is considered the best indication of what they intended the writing to mean.

3. Under paragraph (b) consistent additional terms, not reduced to writing, may be proved unless the court finds that the writing was intended by both parties as a complete and exclusive statement of all the terms. If the additional terms are such that, if agreed upon, they would certainly have been included in the document in the view of the court, then evidence of their alleged making must be kept from the trier of fact. . . .

Definitional Cross References:

"Agreed" and "agreement." Section 1-201.

"Course of dealing." Section 1-303.

"Course of performance." Section 1-303.

"Party." Section 1-201.
"Term." Section 1-201.
"Usage of trade." Section 1-303.
"Written" and "writing." Section 1-201.

§2-203. Seals Inoperative

The affixing of a seal to a writing evidencing a contract for sale or an offer to buy or sell goods does not constitute the writing a sealed instrument and the law with respect to sealed instruments does not apply to such a contract or offer.

§2-204. Formation in General

(1) A contract for sale of goods may be made in any manner sufficient to show agreement, including conduct by both parties which recognizes the existence of such a contract.

(2) An agreement sufficient to constitute a contract for sale may be found even though the moment of its making is undetermined.

(3) Even though one or more terms are left open a contract for sale does not fail for indefiniteness if the parties have intended to make a contract and there is a reasonably certain basis for giving an appropriate remedy.

Official Comment

. . . .

Subsection (1) . . . recogniz[es] any manner of expression of agreement, oral, written or otherwise. The legal effect of such an agreement is, of course, qualified by other provisions of this Article.

Under subsection (1) appropriate conduct by the parties may be sufficient to establish an agreement. Subsection (2) is directed primarily to the situation where the interchanged correspondence does not disclose the exact point at which the deal was closed, but the actions of the parties indicate that a binding obligation has been undertaken.

Subsection (3) states the principle as to "open terms" underlying later sections of the Article. If the parties intend to enter into a binding agreement, this subsection recognizes that agreement as valid in law, despite missing terms, if there is any reasonably certain basis for granting a remedy. The test is not certainty as to what the parties were to do nor as to the exact amount of damages due the plaintiff. Nor is the fact that one or more terms are left to be agreed upon enough of itself to defeat an otherwise adequate agreement. Rather, commercial standards on the point of "indefiniteness" are intended to be applied, this Act making provision elsewhere for missing terms needed for performance, open price, remedies and the like.

The more terms the parties leave open, the less likely it is that they have intended to conclude a binding agreement, but their actions may be frequently conclusive on the matter despite the omissions. . . .

Definitional Cross References:
"Agreement." Section 1-201.
"Contract." Section 1-201.
"Contract for sale." Section 2-106.
"Goods." Section 2-105.
"Party." Section 1-201.
"Remedy." Section 1-201.
"Term." Section 1-201.

§2-205. Firm Offers

An offer by a merchant to buy or sell goods in a signed writing which by its terms gives assurance that it will be held open is not revocable, for lack of consideration, during the time stated or if no time is stated for a reasonable time, but in no event may such period of irrevocability exceed three months; but any such term of assurance on a form supplied by the offeree must be separately signed by the offeror.

Official Comment

. . . .

1. This section is intended to modify the former rule which required that "firm offers" be sustained by consideration in order to bind, and to require instead that they must merely be characterized as such and expressed in signed writings.

2. The primary purpose of this section is to give effect to the deliberate intention of a merchant to make a current firm offer binding. The deliberation is shown in the case of an individualized document by the merchant's signature to the offer, and in the case of an offer included on a form supplied by the other party to the transaction by the separate signing of the particular clause which contains the offer. "Signed" here also includes authentication but the reasonableness of the authentication herein allowed must be determined in the light of the purpose of the section. The circumstances surrounding the signing may justify something less than a formal signature or initialing but typically the kind of authentication involved here would consist of a minimum of initialing of the clause involved. A handwritten memorandum on the writer's letterhead purporting in its terms to "confirm" a firm offer already made would be enough to satisfy this section, although not subscribed, since under the circumstances it could not be considered a memorandum of mere negotiation and it would adequately show its own authenticity. Similarly, an authorized telegram will suffice, and this is true even though the original draft contained only a typewritten signature. However, despite settled courses of dealing or usages of the trade whereby firm offers are made by oral communication and relied upon without more evidence, such offers remain revocable under this Article since authentication by a writing is the essence of this section.

3. This section is intended to apply to current "firm" offers and not to long term options, and an outside time limit of three months during which such offers remain irrevocable has been set. The three month period during which firm offers remain irrevocable under this section need not be stated by days or by date. If the offer states that it is "guaranteed" or "firm" until the happening of a contingency which will occur within the three month period, it will remain irrevocable until that event. A promise made for a longer period will operate under this section to bind the offeror only for the first three months of the period but may of course be renewed. If supported by consideration it may continue for as long as the parties specify. This section deals only with the offer which is not supported by consideration.

4. Protection is afforded against the inadvertent signing of a firm offer when contained in a form prepared by the offeree by requiring that such a clause be separately authenticated. If the offer clause is called to the offeror's attention and he separately authenticates it, he will be bound; Section 2-302 may operate, however, to prevent an unconscionable result which otherwise would flow from other terms appearing in the form.

5. Safeguards are provided to offer relief in the case of material mistake by virtue of the requirement of good faith and the general law of mistake. . . .

Definitional Cross References:
  "Goods." Section 2-105.
  "Merchant." Section 2-104.
  "Signed." Section 1-201.
  "Writing." Section 1-201.

§2-206. Offer and Acceptance in Formation of Contract

(1) Unless otherwise unambiguously indicated by the language or circumstances
    (a) an offer to make a contract shall be construed as inviting acceptance in any manner and by any medium reasonable in the circumstances;
    (b) an order or other offer to buy goods for prompt or current shipment shall be construed as inviting acceptance either by a prompt promise to ship or by the prompt or current shipment of conforming or non-conforming goods, but such a shipment of non-conforming goods does not constitute an acceptance if the seller seasonably notifies the buyer that the shipment is offered only as an accommodation to the buyer.
(2) Where the beginning of a requested performance is a reasonable mode of acceptance an offeror who is not notified of acceptance within a reasonable time may treat the offer as having lapsed before acceptance.

Official Comment

. . . .

1. Any reasonable manner of acceptance is intended to be regarded as available unless the offeror has made quite clear that it will not be acceptable. Former technical rules as to acceptance, such as requiring that telegraphic

offers be accepted by telegraphed acceptance, etc., are rejected and a criterion that the acceptance be "in any manner and by any medium reasonable under the circumstances," is substituted. This section is intended to remain flexible and its applicability to be enlarged as new media of communication develop or as the more time-saving present day media come into general use.

2. Either shipment or a prompt promise to ship is made a proper means of acceptance of an offer looking to current shipment. In accordance with ordinary commercial understanding the section interprets an order looking to current shipment as allowing acceptance either by actual shipment or by a prompt promise to ship and rejects the artificial theory that only a single mode of acceptance is normally envisaged by an offer. . . .

3. The beginning of performance by an offeree can be effective as acceptance so as to bind the offeror only if followed within a reasonable time by notice to the offeror. Such a beginning of performance must unambiguously express the offeree's intention to engage himself. For the protection of both parties it is essential that notice follow in due course to constitute acceptance. Nothing in this section however bars the possibility that under the common law performance begun may have an intermediate effect of temporarily barring revocation of the offer, or at the offeror's option, final effect in constituting acceptance.

4. Subsection (1)(b) deals with the situation where a shipment made following an order is shown by a notification of shipment to be referable to that order but has a defect. Such a non-conforming shipment is normally to be understood as intended to close the bargain, even though it proves to have been at the same time a breach. However, the seller by stating that the shipment is non-conforming and is offered only as an accommodation to the buyer keeps the shipment or notification from operating as an acceptance.

Definitional Cross References:
"Buyer." Section 2-103.
"Conforming." Section 2-106.
"Contract." Section 1-201.
"Goods." Section 2-105.
"Notifies." Section 1-20[2].
"Reasonable time." Section 1-20[5].

§2-207. Additional Terms in Acceptance or Confirmation

(1) A definite and seasonable expression of acceptance or a written confirmation which is sent within a reasonable time operates as an acceptance even though it states terms additional to or different from those offered or agreed upon, unless acceptance is expressly made conditional on assent to the additional or different terms.

(2) The additional terms are to be construed as proposals for addition to the contract. Between merchants such terms become part of the contract unless:

    (a) the offer expressly limits acceptance to the terms of the offer;

    (b) they materially alter it; or

(c) notification of objection to them has already been given or is given within a reasonable time after notice of them is received.

(3) Conduct by both parties which recognizes the existence of a contract is sufficient to establish a contract for sale although the writings of the parties do not otherwise establish a contract. In such case the terms of the particular contract consist of those terms on which the writings of the parties agree, together with any supplementary terms incorporated under any other provisions of this Act.

Official Comment

. . . .

1. This section is intended to deal with two typical situations. The one is the written confirmation, where an agreement has been reached either orally or by informal correspondence between the parties and is followed by one or both of the parties sending formal memoranda embodying the terms so far as agreed upon and adding terms not discussed. The other situation is offer and acceptance, in which a wire or letter expressed and intended as an acceptance or the closing of an agreement adds further minor suggestions or proposals such as "ship by Tuesday," "rush," "ship draft against bill of lading inspection allowed," or the like. A frequent example of the second situation is the exchange of printed purchase order and acceptance (sometimes called "acknowledgment") forms. Because the forms are oriented to the thinking of the respective drafting parties, the terms contained in them often do not correspond. Often the seller's form contains terms different from or additional to those set forth in the buyer's form. Nevertheless, the parties proceed with the transaction.

2. Under this Article a proposed deal which in commercial understanding has in fact been closed is recognized as a contract. Therefore, any additional matter contained in the confirmation or in the acceptance falls within subsection (2) and must be regarded as a proposal for an added term unless the acceptance is made conditional on the acceptance of the additional or different terms.

3. Whether or not additional or different terms will become part of the agreement depends upon the provisions of subsection (2). If they are such as materially to alter the original bargain, they will not be included unless expressly agreed to by the other party. If, however, they are terms which would not so change the bargain they will be incorporated unless notice of objection to them has already been given or is given within a reasonable time.

4. Examples of typical clauses which would normally "materially alter" the contract and so result in surprise or hardship if incorporated without express awareness by the other party are: a clause negating such standard warranties as that of merchantability or fitness for a particular purpose in circumstances in which either warranty normally attaches; a clause requiring a guaranty of 90% or 100% deliveries in a case such as a contract by cannery, where the usage of the trade allows greater quantity leeways; a clause reserving to the seller the power to cancel upon the buyer's failure to meet any invoice when due; a clause

requiring that complaints be made in a time materially shorter than customary or reasonable.

5. Examples of clauses which involve no element of unreasonable surprise and which therefore are to be incorporated in the contract unless notice of objection is seasonably given are: a clause setting forth and perhaps enlarging slightly upon the seller's exemption due to supervening causes beyond his control, similar to those covered by the provision of this Article on merchant's excuse by failure of presupposed conditions or a clause fixing in advance any reasonable formula of proration under such circumstances; a clause fixing a reasonable time for complaints within customary limits, or in the case of a purchase for sub-sale, providing for inspection by the sub-purchaser; a clause providing for interest on overdue invoices or fixing the seller's standard credit terms where they are within the range of trade practice and do not limit any credit bargained for; a clause limiting the right of rejection for defects which fall within the customary trade tolerances for acceptance "with adjustment" or otherwise limiting remedy in a reasonable manner (see Sections 2-718 and 2-719).

6. If no answer is received within a reasonable time after additional terms are proposed, it is both fair and commercially sound to assume that their inclusion has been assented to. Where clauses on confirming forms sent by both parties conflict each party must be assumed to object to a clause of the other conflicting with one on the confirmation sent by himself. As a result the requirement that there be notice of objection which is found in subsection (2) is satisfied and the conflicting terms do not become a part of the contract. The contract then consists of the terms originally expressly agreed to, terms on which the confirmations agree, and terms supplied by this Act, including subsection (2). The written confirmation is also subject to Section 2-201. Under that section a failure to respond permits enforcement of a prior oral agreement; under this section a failure to respond permits additional terms to become part of the agreement.

7. In many cases, as where goods are shipped, accepted and paid for before any dispute arises, there is no question whether a contract has been made. In such cases, where the writings of the parties do not establish a contract, it is not necessary to determine which act or document constituted the offer and which the acceptance. See Section 2-204. The only question is what terms are included in the contract, and subsection (3) furnishes the governing rule. . . .

Definitional Cross References:
   "Between merchants." Section 2-104.
   "Contract." Section 1-201.
   "Notification." Section 1-20[2].
   "Reasonable time." Section 1-20[5].
   "Seasonably." Section 1-204.
   "Send." Section 1-201.
   "Term." Section 1-201.
   "Written." Section 1-201.

§2-209. Modification, Rescission and Waiver

(1) An agreement modifying a contract within this Article needs no consideration to be binding.

(2) A signed agreement which excludes modification or rescission except by a signed writing cannot be otherwise modified or rescinded, but except as between merchants such a requirement on a form supplied by the merchant must be separately signed by the other party.

(3) The requirements of the statute of frauds section of this Article (Section 2-201) must be satisfied if the contract as modified is within its provisions.

(4) Although an attempt at modification or rescission does not satisfy the requirements of subsection (2) or (3) it can operate as a waiver.

(5) A party who has made a waiver affecting an executory portion of the contract may retract the waiver by reasonable notification received by the other party that strict performance will be required of any term waived, unless the retraction would be unjust in view of a material change of position in reliance on the waiver.

Official Comment

. . . .

2. Subsection (1) provides that an agreement modifying a sales contract needs no consideration to be binding.

However, modifications made thereunder must meet the test of good faith imposed by this Act. The effective use of bad faith to escape performance on the original contract terms is barred, and the extortion of a "modification" without legitimate commercial reason is ineffective as a violation of the duty of good faith. Nor can a mere technical consideration support a modification made in bad faith.

The test of "good faith" between merchants or as against merchants includes "observance of reasonable commercial standards of fair dealing in the trade" (Section 2-103), and may in some situations require an objectively demonstrable reason for seeking a modification. But such matters as a market shift which makes performance come to involve a loss may provide such a reason even though there is no such unforeseen difficulty as would make out a legal excuse from performance under Sections 2-615 and 2-616.

3. Subsections (2) and (3) are intended to protect against false allegations of oral modifications. "Modification or rescission" includes abandonment or other change by mutual consent, contrary to the decision in Green v. Doniger, 300 N.Y. 238, 90 N.E.2d 56 (1949); it does not include unilateral "termination" or "cancellation" as defined in Section 2-106.

The Statute of Frauds provisions of this Article are expressly applied to modifications by subsection (3). Under those provisions the "delivery and acceptance" test is limited to the goods which have been accepted, that is, to the past. "Modification" for the future cannot therefore be conjured up by oral testimony if the price involved is $500.00 or more since such modification must be shown at least by an authenticated memo. And since a memo is limited in its effect to the quantity of goods set forth in it there is safeguard against oral evidence.

Subsection (2) permits the parties in effect to make their own Statute of Frauds as regards any future modification of the contract by giving effect to a clause in a signed agreement which expressly requires any modification to be by signed writing. But note that if a consumer is to be held to such a clause on a form supplied by a merchant it must be separately signed.

4. Subsection (4) is intended, despite the provisions of subsections (2) and (3), to prevent contractual provisions excluding modification except by a signed writing from limiting in other respects the legal effect of the parties' actual later conduct. The effect of such conduct as a waiver is further regulated in subsection (5). . . .

Definitional Cross References:
"Agreement." Section 1-201.
"Between merchants." Section 2-104.
"Contract." Section 1-201.
"Notification." Section 1-20[2].
"Signed." Section 1-201.
"Term." Section 1-201.
"Writing." Section 1-201.

§2-210. Delegation of Performance; Assignment of Rights

(1) A party may perform his duty through a delegate unless otherwise agreed or unless the other party has a substantial interest in having his original promisor perform or control the acts required by the contract. No delegation of performance relieves the party delegating of any duty to perform or any liability for breach.

(2) Except as otherwise provided in Section 9-406, unless otherwise agreed, all rights of either seller or buyer can be assigned except where the assignment would materially change the duty of the other party, or increase materially the burden or risk imposed on him by his contract, or impair materially his chance of obtaining return performance. A right to damages for breach of the whole contract or a right arising out of the assignor's due performance of his entire obligation can be assigned despite agreement otherwise.

(3) The creation, attachment, perfection, or enforcement of a security interest in the seller's interest under a contract is not a transfer that materially changes the duty of or increases materially the burden or risk imposed on the buyer or impairs materially the buyer's chance of obtaining return performance within the purview of subsection (2) unless, and then only to the extent that, enforcement actually results in a delegation of material performance of the seller. Even in that event, the creation, attachment, perfection, and enforcement of the security interest remain effective, but (i) the seller is liable to the buyer for damages caused by the delegation to the extent that the damages could not reasonably be prevented by the buyer, and (ii) a court having jurisdiction may grant other appropriate relief, including cancellation of the contract for sale or an injunction against enforcement of the security interest or consummation of the enforcement.

(4) Unless the circumstances indicate the contrary a prohibition of assignment of "the contract" is to be construed as barring only the delegation to the assignee of the assignor's performance.

(5) An assignment of "the contract" or of "all my rights under the contract" or an assignment in similar general terms is an assignment of rights and unless the language or the circumstances (as in an assignment for security) indicate the contrary, it is delegation of performance of the duties of the assignor and its acceptance by the assignee constitutes a promise by him to perform those duties. This promise is enforceable by either the assignor or the other party to the original contract.

(6) The other party may treat any assignment which delegates performance as creating reasonable grounds for insecurity and may without prejudice to his rights against the assignor demand assurances from the assignee (Section 2-609).

Official Comment

. . . .

2. Delegation of performance, either in conjunction with an assignment or otherwise, is provided for by subsection (1) where no substantial reason can be shown as to why the delegated performance will not be as satisfactory as personal performance.

3. Under subsection (2) rights which are no longer executory such as a right to damages for breach may be assigned although the agreement prohibits assignment. In such cases no question of delegation of any performance is involved. Subsection (2) is subject to Section 9-406, which makes rights to payment for goods sold ("accounts"), whether or not earned, freely alienable notwithstanding a contrary agreement or rule of law.

4. The nature of the contract or the circumstances of the case, however, may bar assignment of the contract even where delegation of performance is not involved. This Article and this section are intended to clarify this problem, particularly in cases dealing with output requirement and exclusive dealing contracts. In the first place the section on requirements and exclusive dealing removes from the construction of the original contract most of the "personal discretion" element by substituting the reasonably objective standard of good faith operation of the plant or business to be supplied. Secondly, the section on insecurity and assurances, which is specifically referred to in subsection (6) of this section, frees the other party from the doubts and uncertainty which may afflict him under an assignment of the character in question by permitting him to demand adequate assurance of due performance without which he may suspend his own performance. Subsection (6) is not in any way intended to limit the effect of the section on insecurity and assurances and the word "performance" includes the giving of orders under a requirements contract. Of course, in any case where a material personal discretion is sought to be transferred, effective assignment is barred by subsection (2).

5. Subsection (5) lays down a general rule of construction distinguishing between a normal commercial assignment, which substitutes the assignee for the assignor both as to rights and duties, and a financing assignment in which only the assignor's rights are transferred.

This Article takes no position on the possibility of extending some recognition or power to the original parties to work out normal commercial readjustments of the contract in the case of financing assignments even after the original obligor has been notified of the assignment. This question is dealt with in the Article on Secured Transactions (Article 9).

6. Subsection (6) recognizes that the non-assigning original party has a stake in the reliability of the person with whom he has closed the original contract, and is, therefore, entitled to due assurance that any delegated performance will be properly forthcoming.

7. This section is not intended as a complete statement of the law of delegation and assignment but is limited to clarifying a few points doubtful under the case law. Particularly, neither this section nor this Article touches directly on such questions as the need or effect of notice of the assignment, the rights of successive assignees, or any question of the form of an assignment, either as between the parties or as against any third parties. Some of these questions are dealt with in Article 9. . . .

Definitional Cross References:
"Agreement." Section 1-201.
"Buyer." Section 2-103.
"Contract." Section 1-201.
"Party." Section 1-201.
"Rights." Section 1-201.
"Seller." Section 2-103.
"Term." Section 1-201.

Part 3. General Obligation and Construction of Contract

§2-301. General Obligations of Parties

The obligation of the seller is to transfer and deliver and that of the buyer is to accept and pay in accordance with the contract.

§2-302. Unconscionable Contract or Clause

(1) If the court as a matter of law finds the contract or any clause of the contract to have been unconscionable at the time it was made the court may refuse to enforce the contract, or it may enforce the remainder of the contract without the unconscionable clause, or it may so limit the application of any unconscionable clause as to avoid any unconscionable result.

(2) When it is claimed or appears to the court that the contract or any clause thereof may be unconscionable the parties shall be afforded a reasonable opportunity to present evidence as to its commercial setting, purpose and effect to aid the court in making the determination.

Official Comment

. . . .

1. This section is intended to make it possible for the courts to police explicitly against the contracts or clauses which they find to be unconscionable. In the past such policing has been accomplished by adverse construction of language, by manipulation of the rules of offer and acceptance or by determinations that the clause is contrary to public policy or to the dominant purpose of the contract. This section is intended to allow the court to pass directly on the unconscionability of the contract or particular clause therein and to make a conclusion of law as to its unconscionability. The basic test is whether, in the light of the general commercial background and the commercial needs of the particular trade or case, the clauses involved are so one-sided as to be unconscionable under the circumstances existing at the time of the making of the contract. Subsection (2) makes it clear that it is proper for the court to hear evidence upon these questions. The principle is one of the prevention of oppression and unfair surprise (Cf. Campbell Soup Co. v. Wentz, 172 F.2d 80, 3d Cir. 1948) and not of disturbance of allocation of risks because of superior bargaining power. The underlying basis of this section is illustrated by the results in cases such as the following:

Kansas City Wholesale Grocery Co. v. Weber Packing Corporation, 93 Utah 414, 73 P.2d 1272 (1937), where a clause limiting time for complaints was held inapplicable to latent defects in a shipment of catsup which could be discovered only by microscopic analysis; Hardy v. General Motors Acceptance Corporation, 38 Ga. App. 463, 144 S.E. 327 (1928), holding that a disclaimer of warranty clause applied only to express warranties, thus letting in a fair implied warranty; Andrews Bros. v. Singer & Co. (1934 CA) 1 K.B. 17, holding that where a car with substantial mileage was delivered instead of a "new" car, a disclaimer of warranties, including those "implied," left unaffected an "express obligation" on the description, even though the Sale of Goods Act called such an implied warranty; New Prague Flouring Mill Co. v. G.A. Spears, 194 Iowa 417, 189 N.W. 815 (1922), holding that a clause permitting the seller, upon the buyer's failure to supply shipping instructions, to cancel, ship, or allow delivery date to be indefinitely postponed 30 days at a time by the inaction, does not indefinitely postpone the date of measuring damages for the buyer's breach, to the seller's advantage; and Kansas Flour Mills Co. v. Dirks, 100 Kan. 376, 164 P. 273 (1917), where under a similar clause in a rising market the court permitted the buyer to measure his damages for non-delivery at the end of only one 30 day postponement; Green v. Arcos, Ltd. (1931 CA) 47 T.L.R. 336, where a blanket clause prohibiting rejection of shipments by the buyer was restricted to apply to shipments where discrepancies represented merely mercantile variations; Meyer v. Packard Cleveland Motor Co., 106 Ohio St. 328, 140 N.E. 118 (1922), in which the court held that a "waiver" of all agreements not specified did not preclude implied warranty of fitness of a rebuilt dump truck for ordinary use as a dump truck; Austin Co. v. J. H. Tillman Co., 104 Or. 541, 209 P. 131 (1922), where a clause limiting the buyer's remedy to return was held to be applicable only if the seller had delivered a machine needed for a construction job which reasonably met the contract description; Bekkevold v.

Potts, 173 Minn. 87, 216 N.W. 790, 59 A.L.R. 1164 (1927), refusing to allow warranty of fitness for purpose imposed by law to be negated by clause excluding all warranties "made" by the seller; Robert A. Munroe & Co. v. Meyer (1930) 2 K.B. 312, holding that the warranty of description overrides a clause reading "with all faults and defects" where adulterated meat not up to the contract description was delivered.

2. Under this section the court, in its discretion, may refuse to enforce the contract as a whole if it is permeated by the unconscionability, or it may strike any single clause or group of clauses which are so tainted or which are contrary to the essential purpose of the agreement, or it may simply limit unconscionable clauses so as to avoid unconscionable results.

3. The present section is addressed to the court, and the decision is to be made by it. The commercial evidence referred to in subsection (2) is for the court's consideration, not the jury's. Only the agreement which results from the court's action on these matters is to be submitted to the general triers of the facts. . . .

§2-304. Price Payable in Money, Goods, Realty, or Otherwise

(1) The price can be made payable in money or otherwise. If it is payable in whole or in part in goods each party is a seller of the goods which he is to transfer.

(2) Even though all or part of the price is payable in an interest in realty the transfer of the goods and the seller's obligations with reference to them are subject to this Article, but not the transfer of the interest in realty or the transferor's obligations in connection therewith.

Official Comment

. . . .

2. Under subsection (1) the provisions of this Article are applicable to transactions where the "price" of goods is payable in something other than money. This does not mean, however, that this whole Article applies automatically and in its entirety simply because an agreed transfer of title to goods is not a gift. The basic purposes and reasons of the Article must always be considered in determining the applicability of any of its provisions.

3. Subsection (2) lays down the general principle that when goods are to be exchanged for realty, the provisions of this Article apply only to those aspects of the transaction which concern the transfer of title to goods but do not affect the transfer of the realty since the detailed regulation of various particular contracts which fall outside the scope of this Article is left to the courts and other legislation. However, the complexities of these situations may be such that each must be analyzed in the light of the underlying reasons in order to determine the applicable principles. . . .

Definitional Cross References:
"Goods." Section 2-105.
"Money." Section 1-201.
"Party." Section 1-201.
"Seller." Section 2-103.

§2-305. Open Price Term

(1) The parties if they so intend can conclude a contract for sale even though the price is not settled. In such a case the price is a reasonable price at the time for delivery if

(a) nothing is said as to price; or

(b) the price is left to be agreed by the parties and they fail to agree; or

(c) the price is to be fixed in terms of some agreed market or other standard as set or recorded by a third person or agency and it is not so set or recorded.

(2) A price to be fixed by the seller or by the buyer means a price for him to fix in good faith.

(3) When a price left to be fixed otherwise than by agreement of the parties fails to be fixed through fault of one party the other may at his option treat the contract as cancelled or himself fix a reasonable price.

(4) Where, however, the parties intend not to be bound unless the price be fixed or agreed and it is not fixed or agreed there is no contract. In such a case the buyer must return any goods already received or if unable so to do must pay their reasonable value at the time of delivery and the seller must return any portion of the price paid on account.

Official Comment

. . . .

1. This section applies when the price term is left open on the making of an agreement which is nevertheless intended by the parties to be a binding agreement. This Article rejects in these instances the formula that "an agreement to agree is unenforceable" if the case falls within subsection (1) of this section, and rejects also defeating such agreements on the ground of "indefiniteness." Instead this Article recognizes the dominant intention of the parties to have the deal continue to be binding upon both. As to future performance, since this Article recognizes remedies such as cover (Section 2-712), resale (Section 2-706) and specific performance (Section 2-716) which go beyond any mere arithmetic as between contract price and market price, there is usually a "reasonably certain basis for granting an appropriate remedy for breach" so that the contract need not fail for indefiniteness.

2. Under some circumstances the postponement of agreement on price will mean that no deal has really been concluded, and this is made express in the preamble of subsection (1) ("The parties *if they so intend*") and in subsection (4). Whether or not this is so is, in most cases, a question to be determined by the trier of fact.

3. Subsection (2), dealing with the situation where the price is to be fixed by one party rejects the uncommercial idea that an agreement that the seller may

fix the price means that he may fix any price he may wish by the express qualification that the price so fixed must be fixed in good faith. Good faith includes observance of reasonable commercial standards of fair dealing in the trade if the party is a merchant (Section 2-103). But in the normal case a "posted price" or a future seller's or buyer's "given price," "price in effect," "market price," or the like satisfies the good faith requirement.

4. The section recognizes that there may be cases in which a particular person's judgment is not chosen merely as a barometer or index of a fair price but is an essential condition to the parties' intent to make any contract at all. For example, the case where a known and trusted expert is to "value" a particular painting for which there is no market standard differs sharply from the situation where a named expert is to determine the grade of cotton, and the difference would support a finding that in the one the parties did not intend to make a binding agreement if that expert were unavailable whereas in the other they did so intend. Other circumstances would of course affect the validity of such a finding.

5. Under subsection (3), wrongful interference by one party with any agreed machinery for price fixing in the contract may be treated by the other party as a repudiation justifying cancellation, or merely as a failure to take cooperative action thus shifting to the aggrieved party the reasonable leeway in fixing the price.

6. Throughout the entire section, the purpose is to give effect to the agreement which has been made. That effect, however, is always conditioned by the requirement of good faith action which is made an inherent part of all contracts within this Act (Section 1-203). . . .

Definitional Cross References:
"Agreement." Section 1-201.
"Burden of establishing." Section 1-201.
"Buyer." Section 2-103.
"Cancellation." Section 2-106.
"Contract." Section 1-201.
"Contract for sale." Section 2-106.
"Fault." Section 1-201.
"Goods." Section 2-105.
"Party." Section 1-201.
"Receipt of goods." Section 2-103.
"Seller." Section 2-103.
"Term." Section 1-201.

§2-306. Output, Requirements and Exclusive Dealings

(1) A term which measures the quantity by the output of the seller or the requirements of the buyer means such actual output or requirements as may occur in good faith, except that no quantity unreasonably disproportionate to any stated estimate or in the absence of a stated estimate to any normal or otherwise comparable prior output or requirements may be tendered or demanded.

(2) A lawful agreement by either the seller or the buyer for exclusive dealing in the kind of goods concerned imposes unless otherwise agreed an obligation by the seller to use best efforts to supply the goods and by the buyer to use best efforts to promote their sale.

Official Comment

. . . .

1. Subsection (1) of this section, in regard to output and requirements, . . . requires the reading of commercial background and intent into the language of any agreement and demands good faith in the performance of that agreement. It applies to such contracts of nonproducing establishments such as dealers or distributors as well as to manufacturing concerns.

2. Under this Article, a contract for output or requirements is not too indefinite since it is held to mean the actual good faith output or requirements of the particular party. Nor does such a contract lack mutuality of obligation since, under this section, the party who will determine quantity is required to operate his plant or conduct his business in good faith and according to commercial standards of fair dealing in the trade so that his output or requirements will approximate a reasonably foreseeable figure. Reasonable elasticity in the requirements is expressly envisaged by this section and good faith variations from prior requirements are permitted even when the variation may be such as to result in discontinuance. A shut-down by a requirements buyer for lack of orders might be permissible when a shut-down merely to curtail losses would not. The essential test is whether the party is acting in good faith. Similarly, a sudden expansion of the plant by which requirements are to be measured would not be included within the scope of the contract as made but normal expansion undertaken in good faith would be within the scope of this section. One of the factors in an expansion situation would be whether the market price had risen greatly in a case in which the requirements contract contained a fixed price. Reasonable variation of an extreme sort is exemplified in Southwest Natural Gas Co. v. Oklahoma Portland Cement Co., 102 F.2d 630 ([10th Cir.] 1939). This Article takes no position as to whether a requirements contract is a provable claim in bankruptcy.

3. If an estimate of output or requirements is included in the agreement, no quantity unreasonably disproportionate to it may be tendered or demanded. Any minimum or maximum set by the agreement shows a clear limit on the intended elasticity. In similar fashion, the agreed estimate is to be regarded as a center around which the parties intend the variation to occur.

4. When an enterprise is sold, the question may arise whether the buyer is bound by an existing output or requirements contract. That question is outside the scope of this Article, and is to be determined on other principles of law. Assuming that the contract continues, the output or requirements in the hands of the new owner continue to be measured by the actual good faith output or requirements under the normal operation of the enterprise prior to sale. The sale itself is not grounds for sudden expansion or decrease.

5. Subsection (2), on exclusive dealing, makes explicit the commercial rule embodied in this Act under which the parties to such contracts are held to have impliedly, even when not expressly, bound themselves to use reasonable diligence as well as good faith in their performance of the contract. Under such contracts the exclusive agent is required, although no express commitment has been made, to use reasonable effort and due diligence in the expansion of the market or the promotion of the product, as the case may be. The principal is expected under such a contract to refrain from supplying any other dealer or agent within the exclusive territory. An exclusive dealing agreement brings into play all of the good faith aspects of the output and requirement problems of subsection (1). It also raises questions of insecurity and right to adequate assurance under this Article. . . .

Definitional Cross References:
"Agreement." Section 1-201.
"Buyer." Section 2-103.
"Contract for sale." Section 2-106.
"Good faith." Section 1-201.
"Goods." Section 2-105.
"Party." Section 1-201.
"Term." Section 1-203.
"Seller." Section 2-101.

§2-307. Delivery in Single Lot or Several Lots

Unless otherwise agreed all goods called for by a contract for sale must be tendered in a single delivery and payment is due only on such tender but where the circumstances give either party the right to make or demand delivery in lots the price if it can be apportioned may be demanded for each lot.

§2-308. Absence of Specified Place for Delivery

Unless otherwise agreed
(a) the place for delivery of goods is the seller's place of business or if he has none his residence; but
(b) in a contract for sale of identified goods which to the knowledge of the parties at the time of contracting are in some other place, that place is the place for their delivery; and
(c) documents of title may be delivered through customary banking channels.

§2-309. Absence of Specific Time Provisions; Notice of Termination

(1) The time for shipment or delivery or any other action under a contract if not provided in this Article or agreed upon shall be a reasonable time.

(2) Where the contract provides for successive performances but is indefinite in duration it is valid for a reasonable time but unless otherwise agreed may be terminated at any time by either party.

(3) Termination of a contract by one party except on the happening of an agreed event requires that reasonable notification be received by the other party and an agreement dispensing with notification is invalid if its operation would be unconscionable.

Official Comment

. . . .

1. Subsection (1) requires that all actions taken under a sales contract must be taken within a reasonable time where no time has been agreed upon. The reasonable time under this provision turns on the criteria as to "reasonable time" and on good faith and commercial standards set forth in Sections 1-20[5] and [1-304]. It thus depends upon what constitutes acceptable commercial conduct in view of the nature, purpose and circumstances of the action to be taken. Agreement as to a definite time, however, may be found in a term implied from the contractual circumstances, usage of trade or course of dealing or performance as well as in an express term. Such cases fall outside of this subsection since in them the time for action is "agreed" by usage.

2. The time for payment, where not agreed upon, is related to the time for delivery; the particular problems which arise in connection with determining the appropriate time of payment and the time for any inspection before payment which is both allowed by law and demanded by the buyer are covered in Section 2-513.

3. The facts in regard to shipment and delivery differ so widely as to make detailed provision for them in the text of this Article impracticable. The applicable principles, however, make it clear that surprise is to be avoided, good faith judgment is to be protected, and notice or negotiation to reduce the uncertainty to certainty is to be favored.

4. When the time for delivery is left open, unreasonably early offers of or demands for delivery are intended to be read under this Article as expressions of desire or intention, requesting the assent or acquiescence of the other party, not as final positions which may amount without more to breach or to create breach by the other side. See Sections 2-207 and 2-609.

5. The obligation of good faith under this Act requires reasonable notification before a contract may be treated as breached because a reasonable time for delivery or demand has expired. This operates both in the case of a contract originally indefinite as to time and of one subsequently made indefinite by waiver.

When both parties let an originally reasonable time go by in silence, the course of conduct under the contract may be viewed as enlarging the reasonable time for tender or demand of performance. The contract may be terminated by abandonment.

6. Parties to a contract are not required in giving reasonable notification to fix, at peril of breach, a time which is in fact reasonable in the unforeseeable judgment of a later trier of fact. Effective communication of a proposed time limit calls for a response, so that failure to reply will make out acquiescence.

Where objection is made, however, or if the demand is merely for information as to when goods will be delivered or will be ordered out, demand for assurances on the ground of insecurity may be made under this Article pending further negotiations. Only when a party insists on undue delay or on rejection of the other party's reasonable proposal is there a question of flat breach under the present section.

7. Subsection (2) applies a commercially reasonable view to resolve the conflict which has arisen in the cases as to contracts of indefinite duration. The "reasonable time" of duration appropriate to a given arrangement is limited by the circumstances. When the arrangement has been carried on by the parties over the years, the "reasonable time" can continue indefinitely and the contract will not terminate until notice.

8. Subsection (3) recognizes that the application of principles of good faith and sound commercial practice normally call for such notification of the termination of a going contract relationship as will give the other party reasonable time to seek a substitute arrangement. An agreement dispensing with notification or limiting the time for the seeking of a substitute arrangement is, of course, valid under this subsection unless the results of putting it into operation would be the creation of an unconscionable state of affairs.

9. Justifiable cancellation for breach is a remedy for breach and is not the kind of termination covered by the present subsection.

10. The requirement of notification is dispensed with where the contract provides for termination on the happening of an "agreed event." "Event" is a term chosen here to contrast with "option" or the like. . . .

Definitional Cross References:
"Agreement." Section 1-201.
"Contract." Section 1-201.
"Notification." Section 1-20[2].
"Party." Section 1-201.
"Reasonable time." Section 1-20[5].
"Termination." Section 2-106.

§2-310. Open Time for Payment . . . ; Authority to Ship Under Reservation

Unless otherwise agreed

(a) payment is due at the time and place at which the buyer is to receive the goods even though the place of shipment is the place of delivery; and

(b) if the seller is authorized to send the goods he may ship them under reservation, and may tender the documents of title, but the buyer may inspect the goods after their arrival before payment is due unless such inspection is inconsistent with the terms of the contract (Section 2-513); and

(c) if delivery is authorized and made by way of documents of title otherwise than by subsection (b) then payment is due at the time and place at which the buyer is to receive the documents regardless of where the goods are to be received. . . .

Official Comment

. . . .

1. Paragraph (a) provides that payment is due at the time and place "the buyer is to receive the goods" rather than at the point of delivery except in documentary shipment cases (paragraph (c)). This grants an opportunity for the exercise by the buyer of his preliminary right to inspection before paying even though under the delivery term the risk of loss may have previously passed to him or the running of the credit period has already started.

2. Paragraph (b) while providing for inspection by the buyer before he pays, protects the seller. He is not required to give up possession of the goods until he has received payment, where no credit has been contemplated by the parties. . . . In the absence of a credit term, the seller is permitted to ship under reservation and if he does payment is then due where and when the buyer is to receive the documents.

3. Unless otherwise agreed, the place for the receipt of the documents and payment is the buyer's city but the time for payment is only after arrival of the goods, since under paragraph (b), and Sections 2-512 and 2-513 the buyer is under no duty to pay prior to inspection.

4. Where the mode of shipment is such that goods must be unloaded immediately upon arrival, too rapidly to permit adequate inspection before receipt, the seller must be guided by the provisions of this Article on inspection which provide that if the seller wishes to demand payment before inspection, he must put an appropriate term into the contract. Even requiring payment against documents will not of itself have this desired result if the documents are to be held until the arrival of the goods. But under (b) and (c) if the terms are C.I.F., C.O.D., or cash against documents payment may be due before inspection. . . .

Definitional Cross References:
  "Buyer." Section 2-103.
  "Delivery." Section 1-201.
  "Document of title." Section 1-201.
  "Goods." Section 2-105.
  "Receipt of goods." Section 2-103.
  "Seller." Section 2-103.
  "Send." Section 1-201.
  "Term." Section 1-201.

§2-311. Options and Cooperation Respecting Performance

(1) An agreement for sale which is otherwise sufficiently definite (subsection (3) of Section 2-204) to be a contract is not made invalid by the fact that it leaves particulars of performance to be specified by one of the parties. Any such specification must be made in good faith and within limits set by commercial reasonableness.

(2) Unless otherwise agreed specifications relating to assortment of the goods are at the buyer's option and except as otherwise provided in subsections (1)(c)

and (3) of Section 2-319 specifications or arrangements relating to shipment are at the seller's option.

(3) Where such specification would materially affect the other party's performance but is not seasonably made or where one party's cooperation is necessary to the agreed performance of the other but is not seasonably forthcoming, the other party in addition to all other remedies

    (a) is excused for any resulting delay in his own performance; and

    (b) may also either proceed to perform in any reasonable manner or after the time for a material part of his own performance treat the failure to specify or to cooperate as a breach by failure to deliver or accept the goods.

§2-312. Warranty of Title and Against Infringement; Buyer's Obligation Against Infringement

(1) Subject to subsection (2) there is in a contract for sale a warranty by the seller that

    (a) the title conveyed shall be good, and its transfer rightful; and

    (b) the goods shall be delivered free from any security interest or other lien or encumbrance of which the buyer at the time of contracting has no knowledge.

(2) A warranty under subsection (1) will be excluded or modified only by specific language or by circumstances which give the buyer reason to know that the person selling does not claim title in himself or that he is purporting to sell only such right or title as he or a third person may have.

(3) Unless otherwise agreed a seller who is a merchant regularly dealing in goods of the kind warrants that the goods shall be delivered free of the rightful claim of any third person by way of infringement or the like but a buyer who furnishes specifications to the seller must hold the seller harmless against any such claim which arises out of compliance with the specifications.

Official Comment

. . . .

1. Subsection (1) makes provision for a buyer's basic needs in respect to a title which he in good faith expects to acquire by his purchase, namely, that he receive a good, clean title transferred to him also in a rightful manner so that he will not be exposed to a lawsuit in order to protect it.

The warranty extends to a buyer whether or not the seller was in possession of the goods at the time the sale or contract to sell was made. . . .

The "knowledge" referred to in subsection 1(b) is actual knowledge as distinct from notice. . . .

3. When the goods are part of the seller's normal stock and are sold in his normal course of business, it is his duty to see that no claim of infringement of a patent or trademark by a third party will mar the buyer's title. A sale by a person other than a dealer, however, raises no implication in its circumstances of such a warranty. Nor is there such an implication when the buyer orders

goods to be assembled, prepared or manufactured on his own specifications. . . .

6. The warranty of subsection (1) is not designated as an "implied" warranty, and hence is not subject to Section 2-316(3). Disclaimer of the warranty of title is governed instead by subsection (2), which requires either specific language or the described circumstances. . . .

Definitional Cross References:
"Buyer." Section 2-103.
"Contract for sale." Section 2-106.
"Goods." Section 2-105.
"Person." Section 1-201.
"Right." Section 1-201.
"Seller." Section 2-103.

§2-313. Express Warranties by Affirmation, Promise, Description, Sample

(1) Express warranties by the seller are created as follows:

(a) Any affirmation of fact or promise made by the seller to the buyer which relates to the goods and becomes part of the basis of the bargain creates an express warranty that the goods shall conform to the affirmation or promise.

(b) Any description of the goods which is made part of the basis of the bargain creates an express warranty that the goods shall conform to the description.

(c) Any sample or model which is made part of the basis of the bargain creates an express warranty that the whole of the goods shall conform to the sample or model.

(2) It is not necessary to the creation of an express warranty that the seller use formal words such as "warrant" or "guarantee" or that he have a specific intention to make a warranty, but an affirmation merely of the value of the goods or a statement purporting to be merely the seller's opinion or commendation of the goods does not create a warranty.

Official Comment

. . . .

1. "Express" warranties rest on "dickered" aspects of the individual bargain, and go so clearly to the essence of that bargain that words of disclaimer in a form are repugnant to the basic dickered terms. "Implied" warranties rest so clearly on a common factual situation or set of conditions that no particular language or action is necessary to evidence them and they will arise in such a situation unless unmistakably negated. . . .

2. Although this section is limited in its scope and direct purpose to warranties made by the seller to the buyer as part of a contract for sale, the

warranty sections of this Article are not designed in any way to disturb those lines of case law growth which have recognized that warranties need not be confined either to sales contracts or to the direct parties to such a contract. They may arise in other appropriate circumstances such as in the case of bailments for hire, whether such bailment is itself the main contract or is merely a supplying of containers under a contract for the sale of their contents. The provisions of Section 2-318 on third party beneficiaries expressly recognize this case law development within one particular area. Beyond that, the matter is left to the case law with the intention that the policies of this Act may offer useful guidance in dealing with further cases as they arise.

3. The present section deals with affirmations of fact by the seller, descriptions of the goods or exhibitions of samples, exactly as any other part of a negotiation which ends in a contract is dealt with. No specific intention to make a warranty is necessary if any of these factors is made part of the basis of the bargain. In actual practice affirmations of fact made by the seller about the goods during a bargain are regarded as part of the description of those goods; hence no particular reliance on such statements need be shown in order to weave them into the fabric of the agreement. Rather, any fact which is to take such affirmations, once made, out of the agreement requires clear affirmative proof. The issue normally is one of fact.

4. In view of the principle that the whole purpose of the law of warranty is to determine what it is that the seller has in essence agreed to sell, the policy is adopted of those cases which refuse except in unusual circumstances to recognize a material deletion of the seller's obligation. Thus, a contract is normally a contract for a sale of something describable and described. A clause generally disclaiming "all warranties, express or implied" cannot reduce the seller's obligation with respect to such description and therefore cannot be given literal effect under Section 2-316.

This is not intended to mean that the parties, if they consciously desire, cannot make their own bargain as they wish. But in determining what they have agreed upon good faith is a factor and consideration should be given to the fact that the probability is small that a real price is intended to be exchanged for a pseudo-obligation.

5. Paragraph (1)(b) makes specific some of the principles set forth above when a description of the goods is given by the seller.

A description need not be by words. Technical specifications, blueprints and the like can afford more exact description than mere language and if made part of the basis of the bargain goods must conform with them. Past deliveries may set the description of quality, either expressly or impliedly by course of dealing. Of course, all descriptions by merchants must be read against the applicable trade usages with the general rules as to merchantability resolving any doubts.

6. The basic situation as to statements affecting the true essence of the bargain is no different when a sample or model is involved in the transaction. This section includes both a "sample" actually drawn from the bulk of goods which is the subject matter of the sale, and a "model" which is offered for inspection when the subject matter is not at hand and which has not been drawn from the bulk of the goods.

Although the underlying principles are unchanged, the facts are often ambiguous when something is shown as illustrative, rather than as a straight sample. In general, the presumption is that any sample or model just as any affirmation of fact is intended to become a basis of the bargain. But there is no escape from the question of fact. When the seller exhibits a sample purporting to be drawn from an existing bulk, good faith of course requires that the sample be fairly drawn. But in mercantile experience the mere exhibition of a "sample" does not of itself show whether it is merely intended to "suggest" or to "be" the character of the subject-matter of the contract. The question is whether the seller has so acted with reference to the sample as to make him responsible that the whole shall have at least the values shown by it. The circumstances aid in answering this question. If the sample has been drawn from an existing bulk, it must be regarded as describing values of the goods contracted for unless it is accompanied by an unmistakable denial of such responsibility. If, on the other hand, a model of merchandise not on hand is offered, the mercantile presumption that it has become a literal description of the subject matter is not so strong, and particularly so if modification on the buyer's initiative impairs any feature of the model.

7. The precise time when words of description or affirmation are made or samples are shown is not material. The sole question is whether the language or samples or models are fairly to be regarded as part of the contract. If language is used after the closing of the deal (as when the buyer when taking delivery asks and receives an additional assurance), the warranty becomes a modification, and need not be supported by consideration if it is otherwise reasonable and in order (Section 2-209).

8. Concerning affirmations of value or a seller's opinion or commendation under subsection (2), the basic question remains the same: What statements of the seller have in the circumstances and in objective judgment become part of the basis of the bargain? As indicated above, all of the statements of the seller do so unless good reason is shown to the contrary. The provisions of subsection (2) are included, however, since common experience discloses that some statements or predictions cannot fairly be viewed as entering into the bargain. Even as to false statements of value, however, the possibility is left open that a remedy may be provided by the law relating to fraud or misrepresentation. . . .

Definitional Cross References:
"Buyer." Section 2-103.
"Conforming." Section 2-106.
"Goods." Section 2-105.
"Seller." Section 2-103.

§2-314. Implied Warranty: Merchantability; Usage of Trade

(1) Unless excluded or modified (Section 2-316), a warranty that the goods shall be merchantable is implied in a contract for their sale if the seller is a merchant with respect to goods of that kind. Under this section the serving for value of food or drink to be consumed either on the premises or elsewhere is a sale.

(2) Goods to be merchantable must be at least such as

    (a) pass without objection in the trade under the contract description; and

    (b) in the case of fungible goods, are of fair average quality within the description; and

    (c) are fit for the ordinary purposes for which such goods are used; and

    (d) run, within the variations permitted by the agreement, of even kind, quality and quantity within each unit and among all units involved; and

    (e) are adequately contained, packaged, and labeled as the agreement may require; and

    (f) conform to the promises or affirmations of fact made on the container or label if any.

(3) Unless excluded or modified (Section 2-316) other implied warranties may arise from course of dealing or usage of trade.

Official Comment

. . . .

1. The seller's obligation applies to present sales as well as to contracts to sell subject to the effects of any examination of specific goods. (Subsection (2) of Section 2-316.) Also, the warranty of merchantability applies to sales for use as well as to sales for resale.

2. The question when the warranty is imposed turns basically on the meaning of the terms of the agreement as recognized in the trade. Goods delivered under an agreement made by a merchant in a given line of trade must be of a quality comparable to that generally acceptable in that line of trade under the description or other designation of the goods used in the agreement. The responsibility imposed rests on any merchant-seller. . . .

3. A specific designation of goods by the buyer does not exclude the seller's obligation that they be fit for the general purposes appropriate to such goods. A contract for the sale of second-hand goods, however, involves only such obligation as is appropriate to such goods for that is their contract description. A person making an isolated sale of goods is not a "merchant" within the meaning of the full scope of this section and, thus, no warranty of merchantability would apply. His knowledge of any defects not apparent on inspection would, however, without need for express agreement and in keeping with the underlying reason of the present section and the provisions on good faith, impose an obligation that known material but hidden defects be fully disclosed.

4. Although a seller may not be a "merchant" as to the goods in question, if he states generally that they are "guaranteed" the provisions of this section may furnish a guide to the content of the resulting express warranty. This has particular significance in the case of second-hand sales, and has further significance in limiting the effect of fine-print disclaimer clauses where their effect would be inconsistent with large-print assertions of "guarantee."

5. The second sentence of subsection (1) covers the warranty with respect to food and drink. Serving food or drink for value is a sale, whether to be consumed on the premises or elsewhere. Cases to the contrary are rejected. The principal warranty is that stated in subsections (1) and (2)(c) of this section.

6. Subsection (2) does not purport to exhaust the meaning of "merchantable" nor to negate any of its attributes not specifically mentioned in the text of

the statute, but arising by usage of trade or through case law. The language used is "must be at least such as . . . ," and the intention is to leave open other possible attributes of merchantability.

7. Paragraphs (a) and (b) of subsection (2) are to be read together. Both refer, as indicated above, to the standards of that line of the trade which fits the transaction and the seller's business. "Fair average" is a term directly appropriate to agricultural bulk products and means goods centering around the middle belt of quality, not the least or the worst that can be understood in the particular trade by the designation, but such as can pass "without objection." Of course a fair percentage of the least is permissible but the goods are not "fair average" if they are all of the least or worst quality possible under the description. In cases of doubt as to what quality is intended, the price at which a merchant closes a contract is an excellent index of the nature and scope of his obligation under the present section.

8. Fitness for the ordinary purposes for which goods of the type are used is a fundamental concept of the present section and is covered in paragraph (c). As stated above, merchantability is also a part of the obligation owing to the purchaser for use. Correspondingly, protection, under this aspect of the warranty, of the person buying for resale to the ultimate consumer is equally necessary, and merchantable goods must therefore be "honestly" resalable in the normal course of business because they are what they purport to be.

9. Paragraph (d) on evenness of kind, quality and quantity follows case law. But precautionary language has been added as a reminder of the frequent usages of trade which permit substantial variations both with and without an allowance or an obligation to replace the varying units.

10. Paragraph (e) applies only where the nature of the goods and of the transaction require a certain type of container, package or label. Paragraph (f) applies, on the other hand, wherever there is a label or container on which representations are made, even though the original contract, either by express terms or usage of trade, may not have required either the labeling or the representation. This follows from the general obligation of good faith which requires that a buyer should not be placed in the position of reselling or using goods delivered under false representations appearing on the package or container. No problem of extra consideration arises in this connection since, under this Article, an obligation is imposed by the original contract not to deliver mislabeled articles, and the obligation is imposed where mercantile good faith so requires and without reference to the doctrine of consideration.

11. Exclusion or modification of the warranty of merchantability, or of any part of it, is dealt with in the section to which the text of the present section makes explicit precautionary references. That section must be read with particular reference to its subsection (4) on limitation of remedies. The warranty of merchantability, wherever it is normal, is so commonly taken for granted that its exclusion from the contract is a matter threatening surprise and therefore requiring special precaution.

12. Subsection (3) is to make explicit that usage of trade and course of dealing can create warranties and that they are implied rather than express warranties and thus subject to exclusion or modification under Section 2-316. A typical instance would be the obligation to provide pedigree papers to evidence conformity of the animal to the contract in the case of a pedigreed dog or blooded bull.

13. In an action based on breach of warranty, it is of course necessary to show not only the existence of the warranty but the fact that the warranty was broken and that the breach of the warranty was the proximate cause of the loss sustained. In such an action an affirmative showing by the seller that the loss resulted from some action or event following his own delivery of the goods can operate as a defense. Equally, evidence indicating that the seller exercised care in the manufacture, processing or selection of the goods is relevant to the issue of whether the warranty was in fact broken. Action by the buyer following an examination of the goods which ought to have indicated the defect complained of can be shown as matter bearing on whether the breach itself was the cause of the injury. . . .

Definitional Cross References:
   "Agreement." Section 1-201.
   "Contract." Section 1-201.
   "Contract for sale." Section 2-106.
   "Goods." Section 2-105.
   "Merchant." Section 2-104.
   "Seller." Section 2-103.

§2-315.   Implied Warranty: Fitness for Particular Purpose

Where the seller at the time of contracting has reason to know any particular purpose for which the goods are required and that the buyer is relying on the seller's skill or judgment to select or furnish suitable goods, there is unless excluded or modified under the next section an implied warranty that the goods shall be fit for such purpose.

Official Comment

. . . .

1. Whether or not this warranty arises in any individual case is basically a question of fact to be determined by the circumstances of the contracting. Under this section the buyer need not bring home to the seller actual knowledge of the particular purpose for which the goods are intended or of his reliance on the seller's skill and judgment, if the circumstances are such that the seller has reason to realize the purpose intended or that the reliance exists. The buyer, of course, must actually be relying on the seller.

2. A "particular purpose" differs from the ordinary purpose for which the goods are used in that it envisages a specific use by the buyer which is peculiar to the nature of his business whereas the ordinary purposes for which goods are used are those envisaged in the concept of merchantability and go to uses which are customarily made of the goods in question. For example, shoes are generally used for the purpose of walking upon ordinary ground, but a seller may know that a particular pair was selected to be used for climbing mountains.

A contract may of course include both a warranty of merchantability and one of fitness for a particular purpose.

The provisions of this Article on the cumulation and conflict of express and implied warranties must be considered on the question of inconsistency between or among warranties. In such a case any question of fact as to which warranty was intended by the parties to apply must be resolved in favor of the warranty of fitness for particular purpose as against all other warranties except where the buyer has taken upon himself the responsibility of furnishing the technical specifications.

3. In connection with the warranty of fitness for a particular purpose the provisions of this Article on the allocation or division of risks are particularly applicable in any transaction in which the purpose for which the goods are to be used combines requirements both as to the quality of the goods themselves and compliance with certain laws or regulations. How the risks are divided is a question of fact to be determined, where not expressly contained in the agreement, from the circumstances of contracting, usage of trade, course of performance and the like, matters which may constitute the "otherwise agreement" of the parties by which they may divide the risk or burden.

4. The absence from this section of the language used in the Uniform Sales Act in referring to the seller, "whether he be the grower or manufacturer or not," is not intended to impose any requirement that the seller be a grower or manufacturer. Although normally the warranty will arise only where the seller is a merchant with the appropriate "skill or judgment," it can arise as to non-merchants where this is justified by the particular circumstances.

5. The elimination of the "patent or other trade name" exception constitutes the major extension of the warranty of fitness which has been made by the cases and continued in this Article. Under the present section the existence of a patent or other trade name and the designation of the article by that name, or indeed in any other definite manner, is only one of the facts to be considered on the question of whether the buyer actually relied on the seller, but it is not of itself decisive of the issue. If the buyer himself is insisting on a particular brand he is not relying on the seller's skill and judgment and so no warranty results. But the mere fact that the article purchased has a particular patent or trade name is not sufficient to indicate nonreliance if the article has been recommended by the seller as adequate for the buyer's purposes.

6. The specific reference forward in the present section to the following section on exclusion or modification of warranties is to call attention to the possibility of eliminating the warranty in any given case. However it must be noted that under the following section the warranty of fitness for a particular purpose must be excluded or modified by a conspicuous writing. . . .

Definitional Cross References:
"Buyer." Section 2-103.
"Goods." Section 2-105.
"Seller." Section 2-103.

§2-316.   Exclusion or Modification of Warranties

(1) Words or conduct relevant to the creation of an express warranty and words or conduct tending to negate or limit warranty shall be construed wherever reasonable as consistent with each other; but subject to the provisions of this Article on parol or extrinsic evidence (Section 2-202) negation or limitation is inoperative to the extent that such construction is unreasonable.

(2) Subject to subsection (3), to exclude or modify the implied warranty of merchantability or any part of it the language must mention merchantability and in case of a writing must be conspicuous, and to exclude or modify any implied warranty of fitness the exclusion must be by a writing and conspicuous. Language to exclude all implied warranties of fitness is sufficient if it states, for example, that "There are no warranties which extend beyond the description on the face hereof."

(3) Notwithstanding subsection (2)

(a) unless the circumstances indicate otherwise, all implied warranties are excluded by expressions like "as is," "with all faults" or other language which in common understanding calls the buyer's attention to the exclusion of warranties and makes plain that there is no implied warranty; and

(b) when the buyer before entering into the contract has examined the goods or the sample or model as fully as he desired or has refused to examine the goods there is no implied warranty with regard to defects which an examination ought in the circumstances to have revealed to him; and

(c) an implied warranty can also be excluded or modified by course of dealing or course of performance or usage of trade.

(4) Remedies for breach of warranty can be limited in accordance with the provisions of this Article on liquidation or limitation of damages and on contractual modification of remedy (Sections 2-718 and 2-719).

Official Comment

. . . .

1. This section is designed principally to deal with those frequent clauses in sales contracts which seek to exclude "all warranties, express or implied." It seeks to protect a buyer from unexpected and unbargained language of disclaimer by denying effect to such language when inconsistent with language of express warranty and permitting the exclusion of implied warranties only by conspicuous language or other circumstances which protect the buyer from surprise.

2. The seller is protected under this Article against false allegations of oral warranties by its provisions on parol and extrinsic evidence and against unauthorized representations by the customary "lack of authority" clauses. This Article treats the limitation or avoidance of consequential damages as a matter of limiting remedies for breach, separate from the matter of creation of liability under a warranty. If no warranty exists, there is of course no problem of limiting remedies for breach of warranty. Under subsection (4) the question of limitation of remedy is governed by the sections referred to rather than by this section.

3. Disclaimer of the implied warranty of merchantability is permitted under subsection (2), but with the safeguard that such disclaimers must mention merchantability and in case of a writing must be conspicuous.

4. Unlike the implied warranty of merchantability, implied warranties of fitness for a particular purpose may be excluded by general language, but only if it is in writing and conspicuous.

5. Subsection (2) presupposes that the implied warranty in question exists unless excluded or modified. Whether or not language of disclaimer satisfies the requirements of this section, such language may be relevant under other sections to the question whether the warranty was ever in fact created. Thus, unless the provisions of this Article on parol and extrinsic evidence prevent, oral language of disclaimer may raise issues of fact as to whether reliance by the buyer occurred and whether the seller had "reason to know" under the section on implied warranty of fitness for a particular purpose.

6. The exceptions to the general rule set forth in paragraphs (a), (b) and (c) of subsection (3) are common factual situations in which the circumstances surrounding the transaction are in themselves sufficient to call the buyer's attention to the fact that no implied warranties are made or that a certain implied warranty is being excluded.

7. Paragraph (a) of subsection (3) deals with general terms such as "as is," "as they stand," "with all faults," and the like. Such terms in ordinary commercial usage are understood to mean that the buyer takes the entire risk as to the quality of the goods involved. The terms covered by paragraph (a) are in fact merely a particularization of paragraph (c) which provides for exclusion or modification of implied warranties by usage of trade.

8. Under paragraph (b) of subsection (3) warranties may be excluded or modified by the circumstances where the buyer examines the goods or a sample or model of them before entering into the contract. "Examination" as used in this paragraph is not synonymous with inspection before acceptance or at any other time after the contract has been made. It goes rather to the nature of the responsibility assumed by the seller at the time of the making of the contract. Of course if the buyer discovers the defect and uses the goods anyway, or if he unreasonably fails to examine the goods before he uses them, resulting injuries may be found to result from his own action rather than proximately from a breach of warranty. See Sections 2-314 and 2-715 and comments thereto.

In order to bring the transaction within the scope of "refused to examine" in paragraph (b), it is not sufficient that the goods are available for inspection. There must in addition be a demand by the seller that the buyer examine the goods fully. The seller by the demand puts the buyer on notice that he is assuming the risk of defects which the examination ought to reveal. The language "refused to examine" in this paragraph is intended to make clear the necessity for such demand.

Application of the doctrine of "caveat emptor" in all cases where the buyer examines the goods regardless of statements made by the seller is, however, rejected by this Article. Thus, if the offer of examination is accompanied by words as to their merchantability or specific attributes and the buyer indicates clearly that he is relying on those words rather than on his examination, they give rise to an "express" warranty. In such cases the question is one of fact as to whether a warranty of merchantability has been expressly incorporated in the agreement. Disclaimer of such an express warranty is governed by subsection (1) of the present section.

The particular buyer's skill and the normal method of examining goods in the circumstances determine what defects are excluded by the examination. A failure to notice defects which are obvious cannot excuse the buyer. However, an examination under circumstances which do not permit chemical or other testing of the goods would not exclude defects which could be ascertained only by such testing. Nor can latent defects be excluded by a simple examination. A professional buyer examining a product in his field will be held to have assumed the risk as to all defects which a professional in the field ought to observe, while a nonprofessional buyer will be held to have assumed the risk only for such defects as a layman might be expected to observe.

9. The situation in which the buyer gives precise and complete specifications to the seller is not explicitly covered in this section, but this is a frequent circumstance by which the implied warranties may be excluded. The warranty of fitness for a particular purpose would not normally arise since in such a situation there is usually no reliance on the seller by the buyer. The warranty of merchantability in such a transaction, however, must be considered in connection with the next section on the cumulation and conflict of warranties. Under paragraph (c) of that section in case of such an inconsistency the implied warranty of merchantability is displaced by the express warranty that the goods will comply with the specifications. Thus, where the buyer gives detailed specifications as to the goods, neither of the implied warranties as to quality will normally apply to the transaction unless consistent with the specifications. . . .

Definitional Cross References:
"Agreement." Section 1-201.
"Buyer." Section 2-103.
"Contract." Section 1-201.
"Course of dealing." Section 1-205.
"Goods." Section 2-105.
"Remedy." Section 1-201.
"Seller." Section 2-103.
"Usage of trade." Section 1-205.

§2-317.   Cumulation and Conflict of Warranties Express or Implied

Warranties whether express or implied shall be construed as consistent with each other and as cumulative, but if such construction is unreasonable the intention of the parties shall determine which warranty is dominant. In ascertaining that intention the following rules apply:

(a) Exact or technical specifications displace an inconsistent sample or model or general language of description.

(b) A sample from an existing bulk displaces inconsistent general language of description.

(c) Express warranties displace inconsistent implied warranties other than an implied warranty of fitness for a particular purpose.

§2-318. Third Party Beneficiaries of Warranties Express or Implied

Note: *If this Act is introduced in the Congress of the United States this section should be omitted. (States to select one alternative.)*

ALTERNATIVE A

A seller's warranty whether express or implied extends to any natural person who is in the family or household of his buyer or who is a guest in his home if it is reasonable to expect that such person may use, consume or be affected by the goods and who is injured in person by breach of the warranty. A seller may not exclude or limit the operation of this section.

ALTERNATIVE B

A seller's warranty whether express or implied extends to any natural person who may reasonably be expected to use, consume or be affected by the goods and who is injured in person by breach of the warranty. A seller may not exclude or limit the operation of this section.

ALTERNATIVE C

A seller's warranty whether express or implied extends to any person who may reasonably be expected to use, consume or be affected by the goods and who is injured by breach of the warranty. A seller may not exclude or limit the operation of this section with respect to injury to the person of an individual to whom the warranty extends.

Official Comment

. . . .

1. The last sentence of this section does not mean that a seller is precluded from excluding or disclaiming a warranty which might otherwise arise in connection with the sale provided such exclusion or modification is permitted by Section 2-316. Nor does that sentence preclude the seller from limiting the remedies of his own buyer and of any beneficiaries, in any manner provided in Sections 2-718 or 2-719. To the extent that the contract of sale contains provisions under which warranties are excluded or modified, or remedies for breach are limited, such provisions are equally operative against beneficiaries of warranties under this section. What this last sentence forbids is exclusion of liability by the seller to the persons to whom the warranties which he has made to his buyer would extend under this section.

2. The purpose of this section is to give certain beneficiaries the benefit of the same warranty which the buyer received in the contract of sale, thereby freeing any such beneficiaries from any technical rules as to "privity." It seeks

to accomplish this purpose without any derogation of any right or remedy resting on negligence. . . . Implicit in the section is that any beneficiary of a warranty may bring a direct action for breach of warranty against the seller whose warranty extends to him. . . .

Definitional Cross References:
"Buyer." Section 2-103.
"Goods." Section 2-105.
"Seller." Section 2-103.

§2-319. F.O.B. and F.A.S. Terms

(1) Unless otherwise agreed the term F.O.B. (which means "free on board") at a named place, even though used only in connection with the stated price, is a delivery term under which

(a) when the term is F.O.B. the place of shipment, the seller must at that place ship the goods in the manner provided in this Article (Section 2-504) and bear the expense and risk of putting them into the possession of the carrier; or

(b) when the term is F.O.B. the place of destination, the seller must at his own expense and risk transport the goods to that place and there tender delivery of them in the manner provided in this Article (Section 2-503);

(c) when under either (a) or (b) the term is also F.O.B. vessel, car or other vehicle, the seller must in addition at his own expense and risk load the goods on board. If the term is F.O.B. vessel the buyer must name the vessel . . . .

(2) Unless otherwise agreed the term F.A.S. vessel (which means "free alongside") at a named port, even though used only in connection with the stated price, is a delivery term under which the seller must

(a) at his own expense and risk deliver the goods alongside the vessel in the manner usual in that port or on a dock designated and provided by the buyer; and

(b) obtain and tender a receipt for the goods in exchange for which the carrier is under a duty to issue a bill of lading.

(3) Unless otherwise agreed in any case falling within subsection (1)(a) or (c) or subsection (2) the buyer must seasonably give any needed instructions for making delivery, including when the term is F.A.S. or F.O.B. the loading berth of the vessel and in an appropriate case its name and sailing date. The seller may treat the failure of needed instructions as a failure of cooperation under this Article (Section 2-311). He may also at his option move the goods in any reasonable manner preparatory to delivery or shipment.

(4) Under the term F.O.B. vessel or F.A.S. unless otherwise agreed the buyer must make payment against tender of the required documents and the seller may not tender nor the buyer demand delivery of the goods in substitution for the documents.

§2-320. C.I.F. and C. & F. Terms

(1) The term C.I.F. means that the price includes in a lump sum the cost of the goods and the insurance and freight to the named destination. The term

C. & F. or C.F. means that the price so includes cost and freight to the named destination.

(2) Unless otherwise agreed and even though used only in connection with the stated price and destination, the term C.I.F. destination or its equivalent requires the seller at his own expense and risk to

(a) put the goods into the possession of a carrier at the port for shipment and obtain a negotiable bill or bills of lading covering the entire transportation to the named destination; and

(b) load the goods and obtain a receipt from the carrier (which may be contained in the bill of lading) showing that the freight has been paid or provided for; and

(c) obtain a policy or certificate of insurance, including any war risk insurance, of a kind and on terms then current at the port of shipment in the usual amount, in the currency of the contract, shown to cover the same goods covered by the bill of lading and providing for payment of loss to the order of the buyer or for the account of whom it may concern; but the seller may add to the price the amount of the premium for any such war risk insurance; and

(d) prepare an invoice of the goods and procure any other documents required to effect shipment or to comply with the contract; and

(e) forward and tender with commercial promptness all the documents in due form and with any indorsement necessary to perfect the buyer's rights.

(3) Unless otherwise agreed the term C. & F. or its equivalent has the same effect and imposes upon the seller the same obligations and risks as a C.I.F. term except the obligation as to insurance.

(4) Under the term C.I.F. or C. & F. unless otherwise agreed the buyer must make payment against tender of the required documents and the seller may not tender nor the buyer demand delivery of the goods in substitution for the documents.

§2-326. Sale on Approval and Sale or Return; Rights of Creditors

(1) Unless otherwise agreed, if delivered goods may be returned by the buyer even though they conform to the contract, the transaction is

(a) a "sale on approval" if the goods are delivered primarily for use, and

(b) a "sale or return" if the goods are delivered primarily for resale.

(2) Goods held on approval are not subject to the claims of the buyer's creditors until acceptance; goods held on sale or return are subject to such claims while in the buyer's possession.

(3) Any "or return" term of a contract for sale is to be treated as a separate contract for sale within the statute of frauds section of this Article (Section 2-201) and as contradicting the sale aspect of the contract within the provisions of this Article on parol or extrinsic evidence (Section 2-202).

§2-327. Special Incidents of Sale on Approval and Sale or Return

(1) Under a sale on approval unless otherwise agreed

(a) although the goods are identified to the contract the risk of loss and the title do not pass to the buyer until acceptance; and

(b) use of the goods consistent with the purpose of trial is not acceptance but failure seasonably to notify the seller of election to return the goods is acceptance, and if the goods conform to the contract acceptance of any part is acceptance of the whole; and

(c) after due notification of election to return, the return is at the seller's risk and expense but a merchant buyer must follow any reasonable instructions.

(2) Under a sale or return unless otherwise agreed

(a) the option to return extends to the whole or any commercial unit of the goods while in substantially their original condition, but must be exercised seasonably; and

(b) the return is at the buyer's risk and expense.

§2-328.   Sale by Auction

(1) In a sale by auction if goods are put up in lots each lot is the subject of a separate sale.

(2) A sale by auction is complete when the auctioneer so announces by the fall of the hammer or in other customary manner. Where a bid is made while the hammer is falling in acceptance of a prior bid the auctioneer may in his discretion reopen the bidding or declare the goods sold under the bid on which the hammer was falling.

(3) Such a sale is with reserve unless the goods are in explicit terms put up without reserve. In an auction with reserve the auctioneer may withdraw the goods at any time until he announces completion of the sale. In an auction without reserve, after the auctioneer calls for bids on an article or lot, that article or lot cannot be withdrawn unless no bid is made within a reasonable time. In either case a bidder may retract his bid until the auctioneer's announcement of completion of the sale, but a bidder's retraction does not revive any previous bid.

(4) If the auctioneer knowingly receives a bid on the seller's behalf or the seller makes or procures such a bid, and notice has not been given that liberty for such bidding is reserved, the buyer may at his option avoid the sale or take the goods at the price of the last good faith bid prior to the completion of the sale. This subsection shall not apply to any bid at a forced sale.

Part 4.   Title, Creditors and Good Faith Purchasers

§2-401.   Passing of Title; Reservation for Security; Limited Application of This Section

Each provision of this Article with regard to the rights, obligations and remedies of the seller, the buyer, purchasers or other third parties applies irrespective of title to the goods except where the provision refers to such title. Insofar as situations are not covered by the other provisions of this Article and matters concerning title become material the following rules apply:

(1) Title to goods cannot pass under a contract for sale prior to their identification to the contract (Section 2-501), and unless otherwise explicitly agreed the buyer acquires by their identification a special property as limited by this Act. Any retention or reservation by the seller of the title (property) in goods shipped or delivered to the buyer is limited in effect to a reservation of a security interest. Subject to these provisions and to the provisions of the Article on Secured Transactions (Article 9), title to goods passes from the seller to the buyer in any manner and on any conditions explicitly agreed on by the parties.

(2) Unless otherwise explicitly agreed title passes to the buyer at the time and place at which the seller completes his performance with reference to the physical delivery of the goods, despite any reservation of a security interest and even though a document of title is to be delivered at a different time or place; and in particular and despite any reservation of a security interest by the bill of lading

(a) if the contract requires or authorizes the seller to send the goods to the buyer but does not require him to deliver them at destination, title passes to the buyer at the time and place of shipment; but

(b) if the contract requires delivery at destination, title passes on tender there.

(3) Unless otherwise explicitly agreed where delivery is to be made without moving the goods,

(a) if the seller is to deliver a document of title, title passes at the time when and the place where he delivers such documents; or

(b) if the goods are at the time of contracting already identified and no documents are to be delivered, title passes at the time and place of contracting.

(4) A rejection or other refusal by the buyer to receive or retain the goods, whether or not justified, or a justified revocation of acceptance revests title to the goods in the seller. Such revesting occurs by operation of law and is not a "sale."

§2-402. Rights of Seller's Creditors Against Sold Goods

(1) Except as provided in subsections (2) and (3), rights of unsecured creditors of the seller with respect to goods which have been identified to a contract for sale are subject to the buyer's rights to recover the goods under this Article (Sections 2-502 and 2-716).

(2) A creditor of the seller may treat a sale or an identification of goods to a contract for sale as void if as against him a retention of possession by the seller is fraudulent under any rule of law of the state where the goods are situated, except that retention of possession in good faith and current course of trade by a merchant-seller for a commercially reasonable time after a sale or identification is not fraudulent.

(3) Nothing in this Article shall be deemed to impair the rights of creditors of the seller

(a) under the provisions of the Article on Secured Transactions (Article 9); or

(b) where identification to the contract or delivery is made not in current course of trade but in satisfaction of or as security for a pre-existing claim for money, security or the like and is made under circumstances which under any rule of law of the state where the goods are situated would apart from this Article constitute the transaction a fraudulent transfer or voidable preference.

§2-403. Power to Transfer; Good Faith Purchase of Goods; "Entrusting"

(1) A purchaser of goods acquires all title which his transferor had or had power to transfer except that a purchaser of a limited interest acquires rights only to the extent of the interest purchased. A person with voidable title has power to transfer a good title to a good faith purchaser for value. When goods have been delivered under a transaction of purchase the purchaser has such power even though

(a) the transferor was deceived as to the identity of the purchaser, or

(b) the delivery was in exchange for a check which is later dishonored, or

(c) it was agreed that the transaction was to be a "cash sale," or

(d) the delivery was procured through fraud punishable as larcenous under the criminal law.

(2) Any entrusting of possession of goods to a merchant who deals in goods of that kind gives him power to transfer all rights of the entruster to a buyer in ordinary course of business.

(3) "Entrusting" includes any delivery and any acquiescence in retention of possession regardless of any condition expressed between the parties to the delivery or acquiescence and regardless of whether the procurement of the entrusting or the possessor's disposition of the goods have been such as to be larcenous under the criminal law.

(4) The rights of other purchasers of goods and of lien creditors are governed by the Articles on Secured Transactions (Article 9), [Bulk Transfers (Article 6)] and Documents of Title (Article 7).

Part 5. Performance

§2-501. Insurable Interest in Goods; Manner of Identification of Goods

(1) The buyer obtains a special property and an insurable interest in goods by identification of existing goods as goods to which the contract refers even though the goods so identified are non-conforming and he has an option to return or reject them. Such identification can be made at any time and in any manner explicitly agreed to by the parties. In the absence of explicit agreement identification occurs

(a) when the contract is made if it is for the sale of goods already existing and identified;

(b) if the contract is for the sale of future goods other than those described in paragraph (c), when goods are shipped, marked or otherwise designated by the seller as goods to which the contract refers;

(c) when the crops are planted or otherwise become growing crops or the young are conceived if the contract is for the sale of unborn young to be born within twelve months after contracting or for the sale of crops to be harvested within twelve months or the next normal harvest season after contracting whichever is longer.

(2) The seller retains an insurable interest in goods so long as title to or any security interest in the goods remains in him and where the identification is by the seller alone he may until default or insolvency or notification to the buyer that the identification is final substitute other goods for those identified.

(3) Nothing in this section impairs any insurable interest recognized under any other statute or rule of law.

§2-502. Buyer's Right to Goods on Seller's Repudiation, Failure to Deliver, or Insolvency

(1) Subject to subsections (2) and (3) and even though the goods have not been shipped a buyer who has paid a part or all of the price of goods in which he has a special property under the provisions of the immediately preceding section may on making and keeping good a tender of any unpaid portion of their price recover them from the seller if:

(a) in the case of goods bought for personal, family, or household purposes, the seller repudiates or fails to deliver as required by the contract; or

(b) in all cases, the seller becomes insolvent within ten days after receipt of the first installment on their price.

(2) The buyer's right to recover the goods under subsection (1)(a) vests upon acquisition of a special property, even if the seller had not then repudiated or failed to deliver.

(3) If the identification creating his special property has been made by the buyer he acquires the right to recover the goods only if they conform to the contract for sale.

§2-503. Manner of Seller's Tender of Delivery

(1) Tender of delivery requires that the seller put and hold conforming goods at the buyer's disposition and give the buyer any notification reasonably necessary to enable him to take delivery. The manner, time and place for tender are determined by the agreement and this Article, and in particular

(a) tender must be at a reasonable hour, and if it is of goods they must be kept available for the period reasonably necessary to enable the buyer to take possession; but

(b) unless otherwise agreed the buyer must furnish facilities reasonably suited to the receipt of the goods.

(2) Where the case is within the next section respecting shipment tender requires that the seller comply with its provisions.

(3) Where the seller is required to deliver at a particular destination tender requires that he comply with subsection (1) and also in any appropriate case tender documents as described in subsections (4) and (5) of this section.

(4) Where goods are in the possession of a bailee and are to be delivered without being moved

(a) tender requires that the seller either tender a negotiable document of title covering such goods or procure acknowledgment by the bailee of the buyer's right to possession of the goods; but

(b) tender to the buyer of a non-negotiable document of title or of a written direction to the bailee to deliver is sufficient tender unless the buyer seasonably objects, and receipt by the bailee of notification of the buyer's rights fixes those rights as against the bailee and all third persons; but risk of loss of the goods and of any failure by the bailee to honor the non-negotiable document of title or to obey the direction remains on the seller until the buyer has had a reasonable time to present the document or direction, and a refusal by the bailee to honor the document or to obey the direction defeats the tender.

(5) Where the contract requires the seller to deliver documents

(a) he must tender all such documents in correct form, except as provided in this Article with respect to bills of lading in a set (subsection (2) of Section 2-323); and

(b) tender through customary banking channels is sufficient and dishonor of a draft accompanying the documents constitutes non-acceptance or rejection.

Official Comment

. . . .

1. The major general rules governing the manner of proper or due tender of delivery are gathered in this section. The term "tender" is used in this Article in two different senses. In one sense it refers to "due tender" which contemplates an offer coupled with a present ability to fulfill all the conditions resting on the tendering party and must be followed by actual performance if the other party shows himself ready to proceed. Unless the context unmistakably indicates otherwise this is the meaning of "tender" in this Article and the occasional addition of the word "due" is only for clarity and emphasis. At other times it is used to refer to an offer of goods or documents under a contract as if in fulfillment of its conditions even though there is a defect when measured against the contract obligation. Used in either sense, however, "tender" connotes such performance by the tendering party as puts the other party in default if he fails to proceed in some manner.

2. . . . Subsection (1) of the present section proceeds to set forth two primary requirements of tender: first, that the seller "put and hold conforming goods at the buyer's disposition" and, second, that he "give the buyer any notice reasonably necessary to enable him to take delivery."

In cases in which payment is due and demanded upon delivery the "buyer's disposition" is qualified by the seller's right to retain control of the goods until payment by the provision of this Article on delivery on condition. However, where the seller is demanding payment on delivery he must first allow the buyer to inspect the goods in order to avoid impairing his tender unless the contract for sale is on C.I.F., C.O.D., cash against documents or similar terms negating the privilege of inspection before payment.

In the case of contracts involving documents the seller can "put and hold conforming goods at the buyer's disposition" under subsection (1) by tendering documents which give the buyer complete control of the goods under the provisions of Article 7 on due negotiation.

3. Under paragraph (a) of subsection (1) usage of the trade and the circumstances of the particular case determine what is a reasonable hour for tender and what constitutes a reasonable period of holding the goods available.

4. The buyer must furnish reasonable facilities for the receipt of the goods tendered by the seller under subsection (1), paragraph (b). This obligation of the buyer is no part of the seller's tender.

5. For the purposes of subsections (2) and (3) there is omitted from this Article the rule under prior uniform legislation that a term requiring the seller to pay the freight or cost of transportation to the buyer is equivalent to an agreement by the seller to deliver to the buyer or at an agreed destination. This omission is with the specific intention of negating the rule, for under this Article the "shipment" contract is regarded as the normal one and the "destination" contract as the variant type. The seller is not obligated to deliver at a named destination and bear the concurrent risk of loss until arrival, unless he has specifically agreed so to deliver or the commercial understanding of the terms used by the parties contemplates such delivery.

6. Paragraph (a) of subsection (4) continues the rule of the prior uniform legislation as to acknowledgment by the bailee. Paragraph (b) of subsection (4) adopts the rule that between the buyer and the seller the risk of loss remains on the seller during a period reasonable for securing acknowledgment of the transfer from the bailee, while as against all other parties the buyer's rights are fixed as of the time the bailee receives notice of the transfer.

7. Under subsection (5) documents are never "required" except where there is an express contract term or it is plainly implicit in the peculiar circumstances of the case or in a usage of trade. Documents may, of course, be "authorized" although not required, but such cases are not within the scope of this subsection. When documents are required, there are three main requirements of this subsection: (1) "All": each required document is essential to a proper tender; (2) "Such": the documents must be the ones actually required by the contract in terms of source and substance; (3) "Correct form": All documents must be in correct form.

When a prescribed document cannot be procured, a question of fact arises under the provision of this Article on substituted performance as to whether the agreed manner of delivery is actually commercially impracticable and whether the substitute is commercially reasonable. . . .

Definitional Cross References:
"Agreement." Section 1-201.
"Bill of lading." Section 1-201.
"Buyer." Section 2-103.
"Conforming." Section 2-106.
"Contract." Section 1-201.
"Delivery." Section 1-201.
"Dishonor." Section 3-508.
"Document of title." Section 1-201.
"Draft." Section 3-104.
"Goods." Section 2-105.

"Notification." Section 1-20[2].
"Reasonable time." Section 1-20[5].
"Receipt" of goods. Section 2-103.
"Rights." Section 1-201.
"Seasonably." Section 1-20[5].
"Seller." Section 2-103.
"Written." Section 1-201.

§2-504. Shipment by Seller

Where the seller is required or authorized to send the goods to the buyer and the contract does not require him to deliver them at a particular destination, then unless otherwise agreed he must

(a) put the goods in the possession of such a carrier and make such a contract for their transportation as may be reasonable having regard to the nature of the goods and other circumstances of the case; and

(b) obtain and promptly deliver or tender in due form any document necessary to enable the buyer to obtain possession of the goods or otherwise required by the agreement or by usage of trade; and

(c) promptly notify the buyer of the shipment.

Failure to notify the buyer under paragraph (c) or to make a proper contract under paragraph (a) is a ground for rejection only if material delay or loss ensues.

Official Comment

. . . .

1. The section is limited to "shipment" contracts as contrasted with "destination" contracts or contracts for delivery at the place where the goods are located. The general principles embodied in this section cover the special cases of F.O.B. point of shipment contracts and C.I.F. and C. & F. contracts. Under the preceding section on manner of tender of delivery, due tender by the seller requires that he comply with the requirements of this section in appropriate cases.

2. The contract to be made with the carrier under paragraph (a) must conform to all express terms of the agreement, subject to any substitution necessary because of failure of agreed facilities as provided in the later provision on substituted performance. However, under the policies of this Article on good faith and commercial standards and on buyer's rights on improper delivery, the requirements of explicit provisions must be read in terms of their commercial and not their literal meaning. This policy is made express with respect to bills of lading in a set in the provision of this Article on form of bills of lading required in overseas shipment.

3. In the absence of agreement, the provision of this Article on options and cooperation respecting performance gives the seller the choice of any reasonable carrier, routing and other arrangements. Whether or not the shipment is at the buyer's expense the seller must see to any arrangements, reasonable in

the circumstances, such as refrigeration, watering of live stock, protection against cold, the sending along of any necessary help, selection of specialized cars and the like for paragraph (a) is intended to cover all necessary arrangements whether made by contract with the carrier or otherwise. There is, however, a proper relaxation of such requirements if the buyer is himself in a position to make the appropriate arrangements and the seller gives him reasonable notice of the need to do so. It is an improper contract under paragraph (a) for the seller to agree with the carrier to a limited valuation below the true value and thus cut off the buyer's opportunity to recover from the carrier in the event of loss, when the risk of shipment is placed on the buyer by his contract with the seller.

4. Both the language of paragraph (b) and the nature of the situation it concerns indicate that the requirement that the seller must obtain and deliver promptly to the buyer in due form any document necessary to enable him to obtain possession of the goods is intended to cumulate with the other duties of the seller such as those covered in paragraph (a). . . .

5. This Article . . . makes it the seller's duty to notify the buyer of shipment in all cases. The consequences of his failure to do so, however, are limited in that the buyer may reject on this ground only where material delay or loss ensues. . . .

6. Generally, under the final sentence of the section, rejection by the buyer is justified only when the seller's dereliction as to any of the requirements of this section in fact is followed by material delay or damage. It rests on the seller, so far as concerns matters not within the peculiar knowledge of the buyer, to establish that his error has not been followed by events which justify rejection. . . .

Definitional Cross References:
   "Agreement." Section 1-201.
   "Buyer." Section 2-103.
   "Contract." Section 1-201.
   "Delivery." Section 1-201.
   "Goods." Section 2-105.
   "Notifies." Section 1-20[2].
   "Seller." Section 2-103.
   "Send." Section 1-201.
   "Usage of trade." Section 1-[303].

§2-505. Seller's Shipment Under Reservation

(1) Where the seller has identified goods to the contract by or before shipment:
   (a) his procurement of a negotiable bill of lading to his own order or otherwise reserves in him a security interest in the goods. His procurement of the bill to the order of a financing agency or of the buyer indicates in addition only the seller's expectation of transferring that interest to the person named.
   (b) a non-negotiable bill of lading to himself or his nominee reserves possession of the goods as security but except in a case of conditional delivery

(subsection (2) of Section 2-507) a non-negotiable bill of lading naming the buyer as consignee reserves no security interest even though the seller retains possession of the bill of lading.

(2) When shipment by the seller with reservation of a security interest is in violation of the contract for sale it constitutes an improper contract for transportation within the preceding section but impairs neither the rights given to the buyer by shipment and identification of the goods to the contract nor the seller's powers as a holder of a negotiable document.

§2-507. Effect of Seller's Tender; Delivery on Condition

(1) Tender of delivery is a condition to the buyer's duty to accept the goods and, unless otherwise agreed, to his duty to pay for them. Tender entitles the seller to acceptance of the goods and to payment according to the contract.

(2) Where payment is due and demanded on the delivery to the buyer of goods or documents of title, his right as against the seller to retain or dispose of them is conditional upon his making the payment due.

§2-508. Cure by Seller of Improper Tender or Delivery; Replacement

(1) Where any tender or delivery by the seller is rejected because non-conforming and the time for performance has not yet expired, the seller may seasonably notify the buyer of his intention to cure and may then within the contract time make a conforming delivery.

(2) Where the buyer rejects a non-conforming tender which the seller had reasonable grounds to believe would be acceptable with or without money allowance the seller may if he seasonably notifies the buyer have a further reasonable time to substitute a conforming tender.

Official Comment

. . . .

1. Subsection (1) permits a seller who has made a non-conforming tender in any case to make a conforming delivery within the contract time upon seasonable notification to the buyer. It applies even where the seller has taken back the non-conforming goods and refunded the purchase price. He may still make a good tender within the contract period. The closer, however, it is to the contract date, the greater is the necessity for extreme promptness on the seller's part in notifying of his intention to cure, if such notification is to be "seasonable" under this subsection.

The rule of this subsection, moreover, is qualified by its underlying reasons. Thus if, after contracting for June delivery, a buyer later makes known to the seller his need for shipment early in the month and the seller ships accordingly, the "contract time" has been cut down by the supervening modification and the time for cure of tender must be referred to this modified time term.

2. Subsection (2) seeks to avoid injustice to the seller by reason of a surprise rejection by the buyer. However, the seller is not protected unless he had "reasonable grounds to believe" that the tender would be acceptable. Such reasonable grounds can lie in prior course of dealing, course of performance or usage of trade as well as in the particular circumstances surrounding the making of the contract. The seller is charged with commercial knowledge of any factors in a particular sales situation which require him to comply strictly with his obligations under the contract as, for example, strict conformity of documents in an overseas shipment or the sale of precision parts or chemicals for use in manufacture. Further, if the buyer gives notice either implicitly, as by a prior course of dealing involving rigorous inspections, or expressly, as by the deliberate inclusion of a "no replacement" clause in the contract, the seller is to be held to rigid compliance. If the clause appears in a "form" contract evidence that it is out of line with trade usage or the prior course of dealing and was not called to the seller's attention may be sufficient to show that the seller had reasonable grounds to believe that the tender would be acceptable.

3. The words "a further reasonable time to substitute a conforming tender" are intended as words of limitation to protect the buyer. What is a "reasonable time" depends upon the attending circumstances. Compare Section 2-511 on the comparable case of a seller's surprise demand for legal tender.

4. Existing trade usages permitting variations without rejection but with price allowance enter into the agreement itself as contractual limitations of remedy and are not covered by this section. . . .

Definitional Cross References:
"Buyer." Section 2-103.
"Conforming." Section 2-106.
"Contract." Section 1-201.
"Money." Section 1-201.
"Notifies." Section 1-20[2].
"Reasonable time." Section 1-204.
"Seasonably." Section 1-204.
"Seller." Section 2-103.

§2-509. Risk of Loss in the Absence of Breach

(1) Where the contract requires or authorizes the seller to ship the goods by carrier
    (a) if it does not require him to deliver them at a particular destination, the risk of loss passes to the buyer when the goods are duly delivered to the carrier even though the shipment is under reservation (Section 2-505); but
    (b) if it does require him to deliver them at a particular destination and the goods are there duly tendered while in the possession of the carrier, the risk of loss passes to the buyer when the goods are there duly so tendered as to enable the buyer to take delivery.

(2) Where the goods are held by a bailee to be delivered without being moved, the risk of loss passes to the buyer

(a) on his receipt of a negotiable document of title covering the goods; or

(b) on acknowledgment by the bailee of the buyer's right to possession of the goods; or

(c) after his receipt of a non-negotiable document of title or other written direction to deliver, as provided in subsection (4) (b) of Section 2-503.

(3) In any case not within subsection (1) or (2), the risk of loss passes to the buyer on his receipt of the goods if the seller is a merchant; otherwise the risk passes to the buyer on tender of delivery.

(4) The provisions of this section are subject to contrary agreement of the parties and to the provisions of this Article on sale on approval (Section 2-327) and on effect of breach on risk of loss (Section 2-510).

Official Comment

. . . .

2. The provisions of subsection (1) apply where the contract "requires or authorizes" shipment of the goods. This language is intended to be construed parallel to comparable language in the section on shipment by seller. In order that the goods be "duly delivered to the carrier" under paragraph (a) a contract must be entered into with the carrier which will satisfy the requirements of the section on shipment by the seller and the delivery must be made under circumstances which will enable the seller to take any further steps necessary to a due tender. The underlying reason of this subsection does not require that the shipment be made after contracting, but where, for example, the seller buys the goods afloat and later diverts the shipment to the buyer, he must identify the goods to the contract before the risk of loss can pass. To transfer the risk it is enough that a proper shipment and a proper identification come to apply to the same goods although, aside from special agreement, the risk will not pass retroactively to the time of shipment in such a case.

3. Whether the contract involves delivery at the seller's place of business or at the situs of the goods, a merchant seller cannot transfer risk of loss and it remains upon him until actual receipt by the buyer, even though full payment has been made and the buyer has been notified that the goods are at his disposal. Protection is afforded him, in the event of breach by the buyer, under the next section.

The underlying theory of this rule is that a merchant who is to make physical delivery at his own place continues meanwhile to control the goods and can be expected to insure his interest in them. The buyer, on the other hand, has no control of the goods and it is extremely unlikely that he will carry insurance on goods not yet in his possession.

4. Where the agreement provides for delivery of the goods as between the buyer and seller without removal from the physical possession of a bailee, the provisions on manner of tender of delivery apply on the point of transfer of risk. Due delivery of a negotiable document of title covering the goods or acknowledgment by the bailee that he holds for the buyer completes the "delivery" and passes the risk.

5. The provisions of this section are made subject by subsection (4) to the "contrary agreement" of the parties. This language is intended as the equiva-

lent of the phrase "unless otherwise agreed" used more frequently throughout this Act. "Contrary" is in no way used as a word of limitation and the buyer and seller are left free to readjust their rights and risks as declared by this section in any manner agreeable to them. Contrary agreement can also be found in the circumstances of the case, a trade usage or practice, or a course of dealing or performance. . . .

Definitional Cross References:
  "Agreement." Section 1-201.
  "Buyer." Section 2-103.
  "Contract." Section 1-201.
  "Delivery." Section 1-201.
  "Document of title." Section 1-201.
  "Goods." Section 2-105.
  "Merchant." Section 2-104.
  "Party." Section 1-201.
  "Receipt" of goods. Section 2-103.
  "Sale on approval." Section 2-326.
  "Seller." Section 2-103.

§2-510. Effect of Breach on Risk of Loss

(1) Where a tender or delivery of goods so fails to conform to the contract as to give a right of rejection the risk of their loss remains on the seller until cure or acceptance.

(2) Where the buyer rightfully revokes acceptance he may to the extent of any deficiency in his effective insurance coverage treat the risk of loss as having rested on the seller from the beginning.

(3) Where the buyer as to conforming goods already identified to the contract for sale repudiates or is otherwise in breach before risk of their loss has passed to him, the seller may to the extent of any deficiency in his effective insurance coverage treat the risk of loss as resting on the buyer for a commercially reasonable time.

Official Comment

. . . .

1. Under subsection (1) the seller by his individual action cannot shift the risk of loss to the buyer unless his action conforms with all the conditions resting on him under the contract.

2. The "cure" of defective tenders contemplated by subsection (1) applies only to those situations in which the seller makes changes in goods already tendered, such as repair, partial substitution, sorting out from an improper mixture and the like since "cure" by repossession and new tender has no effect

on the risk of loss of the goods originally tendered. The seller's privilege of cure does not shift the risk, however, until the cure is completed. . . .

3. In cases where there has been a breach of the contract, if the one in control of the goods is the aggrieved party, whatever loss or damage may prove to be uncovered by his insurance falls upon the contract breaker under subsections (2) and (3) rather than upon him. The word "effective" as applied to insurance coverage in those subsections is used to meet the case of supervening insolvency of the insurer. The "deficiency" referred to in the text means such deficiency in the insurance coverage as exists without subrogation. This section merely distributes the risk of loss as stated and is not intended to be disturbed by any subrogation of an insurer. . . .

Definitional Cross References:
"Buyer." Section 2-103.
"Conform." Section 2-106.
"Contract for sale." Section 2-106.
"Goods." Section 2-105.
"Seller." Section 2-103.

§2-511. Tender of Payment by Buyer; Payment by Check

(1) Unless otherwise agreed tender of payment is a condition to the seller's duty to tender and complete any delivery.

(2) Tender of payment is sufficient when made by any means or in any manner current in the ordinary course of business unless the seller demands payment in legal tender and gives any extension of time reasonably necessary to procure it.

(3) Subject to the provisions of this Act on the effect of an instrument on an obligation (Section 3-310), payment by check is conditional and is defeated as between the parties by dishonor of the check on due presentment.

§2-512. Payment by Buyer Before Inspection

(1) Where the contract requires payment before inspection non-conformity of goods does not excuse the buyer from so making payment unless
    (a) the non-conformity appears without inspection; or
    (b) despite tender of the required documents the circumstances would justify injunction against honor under this Act (Section 5-109(b)).

(2) Payment pursuant to subsection (1) does not constitute an acceptance of goods or impair the buyer's right to inspect or any of his remedies.

§2-513. Buyer's Right to Inspection of Goods

(1) Unless otherwise agreed and subject to subsection (3), where goods are tendered or delivered or identified to the contract for sale, the buyer has a right before payment or acceptance to inspect them at any reasonable place and time

and in any reasonable manner. When the seller is required or authorized to send the goods to the buyer, the inspection may be after their arrival.

(2) Expenses of inspection must be borne by the buyer but may be recovered from the seller if the goods do not conform and are rejected.

(3) Unless otherwise agreed and subject to the provisions of this Article on C.I.F. contracts (subsection (3) of Section 2-321), the buyer is not entitled to inspect the goods before payment of the price when the contract provides

(a) for delivery "C.O.D." or on other like terms; or

(b) for payment against documents of title, except where such payment is due only after the goods are to become available for inspection.

(4) A place or method of inspection fixed by the parties is presumed to be exclusive but unless otherwise expressly agreed it does not postpone identification or shift the place for delivery or for passing the risk of loss. If compliance becomes impossible, inspection shall be as provided in this section unless the place or method fixed was clearly intended as an indispensable condition failure of which avoids the contract.

Official Comment

. . . .

1. The buyer is entitled to inspect goods as provided in subsection (1) unless it has been otherwise agreed by the parties. The phrase "unless otherwise agreed" is intended principally to cover such situations as those outlined in subsections (3) and (4) and those in which the agreement of the parties negates inspection before tender of delivery. However, no agreement by the parties can displace the entire right of inspection except where the contract is simply for the sale of "this thing." Even in a sale of boxed goods "as is" inspection is a right of the buyer, since if the boxes prove to contain some other merchandise altogether the price can be recovered back; nor do the limitations of the provision on effect of acceptance apply in such a case.

2. The buyer's right of inspection is available to him upon tender, delivery or appropriation of the goods with notice to him. Since inspection is available to him on tender, where payment is due against delivery he may, unless otherwise agreed, make his inspection before payment of the price. It is also available to him after receipt of the goods and so may be postponed after receipt for a reasonable time. Failure to inspect before payment does not impair the right to inspect after receipt of the goods unless the case falls within subsection (4) on agreed and exclusive inspection provisions. The right to inspect goods which have been appropriated with notice to the buyer holds whether or not the sale was by sample.

3. The buyer may exercise his right of inspection at any reasonable time or place and in any reasonable manner. It is not necessary that he select the most appropriate time, place or manner to inspect or that his selection be the customary one in the trade or locality. Any reasonable time, place or manner is available to him and the reasonableness will be determined by trade usages, past practices between the parties and the other circumstances of the case.

The last sentence of subsection (1) makes it clear that the place of arrival of shipped goods is a reasonable place for their inspection.

4. Expenses of an inspection made to satisfy the buyer of the seller's performance must be assumed by the buyer in the first instance. Since the rule provides merely for an allocation of expense there is no policy to prevent the parties from providing otherwise in the agreement. Where the buyer would normally bear the expenses of the inspection but the goods are rightly rejected because of what the inspection reveals, demonstrable and reasonable costs of the inspection are part of his incidental damage caused by the seller's breach. . . .

6. Under subsection (4) an agreed place or method of inspection is generally held to be intended as exclusive. However, where compliance with such an agreed inspection term becomes impossible, the question is basically one of intention. If the parties clearly intend that the method of inspection named is to be a necessary condition without which the entire deal is to fail, the contract is at an end if that method becomes impossible. On the other hand, if the parties merely seek to indicate a convenient and reliable method but do not intend to give up the deal in the event of its failure, any reasonable method of inspection may be substituted under this Article.

Since the purpose of an agreed place of inspection is only to make sure at that point whether or not the goods will be thrown back, the "exclusive" feature of the named place is satisfied under this Article if the buyer's failure to inspect there is held to be an acceptance with the knowledge of such defects as inspection would have revealed within the section on waiver of buyer's objections by failure to particularize. Revocation of the acceptance is limited to the situations stated in the section pertaining to that subject. The reasonable time within which to give notice of defects within the section on notice of breach begins to run from the point of the "acceptance." . . .

9. "Inspection" under this section has to do with the buyer's check-up on whether the seller's performance is in accordance with a contract previously made and is not to be confused with the "examination" of the goods or of a sample or model of them at the time of contracting which may affect the warranties involved in the contract. . . .

Definitional Cross References:
    "Buyer." Section 2-103.
    "Conform." Section 2-106.
    "Contract." Section 1-201.
    "Contract for sale." Section 2-106.
    "Document of title." Section 1-201.
    "Goods." Section 2-105.
    "Party." Section 1-201.
    "Presumed." Section 1-201.
    "Reasonable time." Section 1-20[5].
    "Rights." Section 1-201.
    "Seller." Section 2-103.
    "Send." Section 1-201.
    "Term." Section 1-201.

Part 6. Breach, Repudiation and Excuse

§2-601. Buyer's Rights on Improper Delivery

Subject to the provisions of this Article on breach in installment contracts (Section 2-612) and unless otherwise agreed under the sections on contractual limitations of remedy (Section 2-718 and 2-719), if the goods or the tender of delivery fail in any respect to conform to the contract, the buyer may

    (a) reject the whole; or

    (b) accept the whole; or

    (c) accept any commercial unit or units and reject the rest.

Official Comment

. . . .

1. A buyer accepting a non-conforming tender is not penalized by the loss of any remedy otherwise open to him. This policy extends to cover and regulate the acceptance of a part of any lot improperly tendered in any case where the price can reasonably be apportioned. Partial acceptance is permitted whether the part of the goods accepted conforms or not. The only limitation on partial acceptance is that good faith and commercial reasonableness must be used to avoid undue impairment of the value of the remaining portion of the goods. This is the reason for the insistence on the "commercial unit" in paragraph (c). In this respect, the test is not only what unit has been the basis of contract, but whether the partial acceptance produces so materially adverse an effect on the remainder as to constitute bad faith.

2. Acceptance made with the knowledge of the other party is final. An original refusal to accept may be withdrawn by a later acceptance if the seller has indicated that he is holding the tender open. However, if the buyer attempts to accept, either in whole or in part, after his original rejection has caused the seller to arrange for other disposition of the goods, the buyer must answer for any ensuing damage since the next section provides that any exercise of ownership after rejection is wrongful as against the seller. Further, he is liable even though the seller may choose to treat his action as acceptance rather than conversion, since the damage flows from the misleading notice. Such arrangements for resale or other disposition of the goods by the seller must be viewed as within the normal contemplation of a buyer who has given notice of rejection. However, the buyer's attempts in good faith to dispose of defective goods where the seller has failed to give instructions within a reasonable time are not to be regarded as an acceptance. . . .

Definitional Cross References:

    "Buyer." Section 2-103.

    "Commercial unit." Section 2-105.

    "Conform." Section 2-106.

    "Contract." Section 1-201.

    "Goods." Section 2-105.

"Installment contract." Section 2-612.
"Rights." Section 1-201.

§2-602.   Manner and Effect of Rightful Rejection

(1) Rejection of goods must be within a reasonable time after their delivery or tender. It is ineffective unless the buyer seasonably notifies the seller.

(2) Subject to the provisions of the two following sections on rejected goods (Sections 2-603 and 2-604),

(a) after rejection any exercise of ownership by the buyer with respect to any commercial unit is wrongful as against the seller; and

(b) if the buyer has before rejection taken physical possession of goods in which he does not have a security interest under the provisions of this Article (subsection (3) of Section 2-711), he is under a duty after rejection to hold them with reasonable care at the seller's disposition for a time sufficient to permit the seller to remove them; but

(c) the buyer has no further obligations with regard to goods rightfully rejected.

(3) The seller's rights with respect to goods wrongfully rejected are governed by the provisions of this Article on Seller's remedies in general (Section 2-703).

Official Comment

. . . .

1. A tender or delivery of goods made pursuant to a contract of sale, even though wholly non-conforming, requires affirmative action by the buyer to avoid acceptance. Under subsection (1), therefore, the buyer is given a reasonable time to notify the seller of his rejection, but without such seasonable notification his rejection is ineffective. The sections of this Article dealing with inspection of goods must be read in connection with the buyer's reasonable time for action under this subsection. Contract provisions limiting the time for rejection fall within the rule of the section on "Time" and are effective if the time set gives the buyer a reasonable time for discovery of defects. What constitutes a due "notifying" of rejection by the buyer to the seller is defined in Section 1-201.

2. Subsection (2) lays down the normal duties of the buyer upon rejection, which flow from the relationship of the parties. Beyond his duty to hold the goods with reasonable care for the buyer's [seller's] disposition, this section continues the policy of prior uniform legislation in generally relieving the buyer from any duties with respect to them, except when the circumstances impose the limited obligation of salvage upon him under the next section.

3. The present section applies only to rightful rejection by the buyer. If the seller has made a tender which in all respects conforms to the contract, the buyer has a positive duty to accept and his failure to do so constitutes a "wrongful rejection" which gives the seller immediate remedies for breach. Subsection (3) is included here to emphasize the sharp distinction between the

rejection of an improper tender and the non-acceptance which is a breach by the buyer.

4. The provisions of this section are to be appropriately limited or modified when a negotiation is in process. . . .

Definitional Cross References:
"Buyer." Section 2-103.
"Commercial unit." Section 2-105.
"Goods." Section 2-105.
"Merchant." Section 2-104.
"Notifies." Section 1-20[2].
"Reasonable time." Section 1-20[5].
"Remedy." Section 1-201.
"Rights." Section 1-201.
"Seasonably." Section 1-20[5].
"Security interest." Section 1-201.
"Seller." Section 2-103.

§2-603. Merchant Buyer's Duties as to Rightfully Rejected Goods

(1) Subject to any security interest in the buyer (subsection (3) of Section 2-711), when the seller has no agent or place of business at the market of rejection a merchant buyer is under a duty after rejection of goods in his possession or control to follow any reasonable instructions received from the seller with respect to the goods and in the absence of such instructions to make reasonable efforts to sell them for the seller's account if they are perishable or threaten to decline in value speedily. Instructions are not reasonable if on demand indemnity for expenses is not forthcoming.

(2) When the buyer sells goods under subsection (1), he is entitled to reimbursement from the seller or out of the proceeds for reasonable expenses of caring for and selling them, and if the expenses include no selling commission then to such commission as is usual in the trade or if there is none to a reasonable sum not exceeding ten per cent on the gross proceeds.

(3) In complying with this section the buyer is held only to good faith and good faith conduct hereunder is neither acceptance nor conversion nor the basis of an action for damages.

§2-604. Buyer's Options as to Salvage of Rightfully Rejected Goods

Subject to the provisions of the immediately preceding section on perishables if the seller gives no instructions within a reasonable time after notification of rejection the buyer may store the rejected goods for the seller's account or reship them to him or re-sell them for the seller's account with reimbursement as provided in the preceding section. Such action is not acceptance or conversion.

§2-605. Waiver of Buyer's Objections by Failure to Particularize

(1) The buyer's failure to state in connection with rejection a particular defect which is ascertainable by reasonable inspection precludes him from relying on the unstated defect to justify rejection or to establish breach

(a) where the seller could have cured it if stated seasonably; or

(b) between merchants when the seller has after rejection made a request in writing for a full and final written statement of all defects on which the buyer proposes to rely.

(2) Payment against documents made without reservation of rights precludes recovery of the payment for defects apparent on the face of the documents.

Official Comment

. . . .

1. The present section rests upon a policy of permitting the buyer to give a quick and informal notice of defects in a tender without penalizing him for omissions in his statement, while at the same time protecting a seller who is reasonably misled by the buyer's failure to state curable defects.

2. Where the defect in a tender is one which could have been cured by the seller, a buyer who merely rejects the delivery without stating his objections to it is probably acting in commercial bad faith and seeking to get out of a deal which has become unprofitable. Subsection (1)(a), following the general policy of this Article which looks to preserving the deal wherever possible, therefore insists that the seller's right to correct his tender in such circumstances be protected.

3. When the time for cure is past, subsection (1)(b) makes it plain that a seller is entitled upon request to a final statement of objections upon which he can rely. What is needed is that he make clear to the buyer exactly what is being sought. A formal demand under paragraph (b) will be sufficient in the case of a merchant-buyer.

4. Subsection (2) applies to the particular case of documents the same principle which the section on effects of acceptance applies to the case of goods. The matter is dealt with in this section in terms of "waiver" of objections rather than of right to revoke acceptance, partly to avoid any confusion with the problems of acceptance of goods and partly because defects in documents which are not taken as grounds for rejection are generally minor ones. The only defects concerned in the present subsection are defects in the documents which are apparent on their face. Where payment is required against the documents they must be inspected before payment, and the payment then constitutes acceptance of the documents. Under the section dealing with this problem, such acceptance of the documents does not constitute an acceptance of the goods or impair any options or remedies of the buyer for their improper delivery. Where the documents are delivered without requiring such contemporary action as payment from the buyer, the reason of the next section on

what constitutes acceptance of goods, applies. Their acceptance by non-objection is therefore postponed until after a reasonable time for their inspection. In either situation, however, the buyer "waives" only what is apparent on the face of the documents. . . .

Definitional Cross References:
"Between merchants." Section 2-104.
"Buyer." Section 2-103.
"Seasonably." Section 1-20[5].
"Seller." Section 2-103.
"Writing" and "written." Section 1-201.

§2-606. What Constitutes Acceptance of Goods

(1) Acceptance of goods occurs when the buyer
  (a) after a reasonable opportunity to inspect the goods signifies to the seller that the goods are conforming or that he will take or retain them in spite of their non-conformity; or
  (b) fails to make an effective rejection (subsection (1) of Section 2-602), but such acceptance does not occur until the buyer has had a reasonable opportunity to inspect them; or
  (c) does any act inconsistent with the seller's ownership; but if such act is wrongful as against the seller it is an acceptance only if ratified by him.
(2) Acceptance of a part of any commercial unit is acceptance of that entire unit.

§2-607. Effect of Acceptance; Notice of Breach; Burden of Establishing Breach After Acceptance; Notice of Claim or Litigation to Person Answerable Over

(1) The buyer must pay at the contract rate for any goods accepted.
(2) Acceptance of goods by the buyer precludes rejection of the goods accepted and if made with knowledge of a non-conformity cannot be revoked because of it unless the acceptance was on the reasonable assumption that the non-conformity would be seasonably cured but acceptance does not of itself impair any other remedy provided by this Article for non-conformity.
(3) Where a tender has been accepted
  (a) the buyer must within a reasonable time after he discovers or should have discovered any breach notify the seller of breach or be barred from any remedy; and
  (b) if the claim is one for infringement or the like (subsection (3) of Section 2-312) and the buyer is sued as a result of such a breach he must so notify the seller within a reasonable time after he receives notice of the litigation or be barred from any remedy over for liability established by the litigation.
(4) The burden is on the buyer to establish any breach with respect to the goods accepted.

(5) Where the buyer is sued for breach of a warranty or other obligation for which his seller is answerable over

(a) he may give his seller written notice of the litigation. If the notice states that the seller may come in and defend and that if the seller does not do so he will be bound in any action against him by his buyer by any determination of fact common to the two litigations, then unless the seller after seasonable receipt of the notice does come in and defend he is so bound.

(b) if the claim is one for infringement or the like (subsection (3) of Section 2-312) the original seller may demand in writing that his buyer turn over to him control of the litigation including settlement or else be barred from any remedy over and if he also agrees to bear all expense and to satisfy any adverse judgment, then unless the buyer after seasonable receipt of the demand does turn over control the buyer is so barred.

(6) The provisions of subsections (3), (4) and (5) apply to any obligation of a buyer to hold the seller harmless against infringement or the like (subsection (3) of Section 2-312).

Official Comment

. . . .

1. Under subsection (1), once the buyer accepts a tender the seller acquires a right to its price on the contract terms. In cases of partial acceptance, the price of any part accepted is, if possible, to be reasonably apportioned, using the type of apportionment familiar to the courts in quantum valebat cases, to be determined in terms of "the contract rate," which is the rate determined from the bargain in fact (the agreement) after the rules and policies of this Article have been brought to bear.

2. Under subsection (2) acceptance of goods precludes their subsequent rejection. Any return of the goods thereafter must be by way of revocation of acceptance under the next section. Revocation is unavailable for a non-conformity known to the buyer at the time of acceptance, except where the buyer has accepted on the reasonable assumption that the non-conformity would be seasonably cured.

3. All other remedies of the buyer remain unimpaired under subsection (2). This is intended to include the buyer's full rights with respect to future installments despite his acceptance of any earlier non-conforming installment.

4. The time of notification is to be determined by applying commercial standards to a merchant buyer. "A reasonable time" for notification from a retail consumer is to be judged by different standards so that in his case it will be extended, for the rule of requiring notification is designed to defeat commercial bad faith, not to deprive a good faith consumer of his remedy.

The content of the notification need merely be sufficient to let the seller know that the transaction is still troublesome and must be watched. There is no reason to require that the notification which saves the buyer's rights under this section must include a clear statement of all the objections that will be relied on by the buyer, as under the section covering statements of defects upon rejection (Section 2-605). Nor is there reason for requiring the notification to be a claim for damages or of any threatened litigation or other resort to a remedy. The notification which saves the buyer's rights under this Article need only be such as informs the seller that the transaction is claimed to involve a breach, and thus opens the way for normal settlement through negotiation.

5. Under this Article various beneficiaries are given rights for injuries sustained by them because of the seller's breach of warranty. Such a beneficiary does not fall within the reason of the present section in regard to discovery of defects and the giving of notice within a reasonable time after acceptance, since he has nothing to do with acceptance. However, the reason of this section does extend to requiring the beneficiary to notify the seller that an injury has occurred. What is said above, with regard to the extended time for reasonable notification from the lay consumer after the injury is also applicable here; but even a beneficiary can be properly held to the use of good faith in notifying, once he has had time to become aware of the legal situation.

6. Subsection (4) unambiguously places the burden of proof to establish breach on the buyer after acceptance. However, this rule becomes one purely of procedure when the tender accepted was non-conforming and the buyer has given the seller notice of breach under subsection (3). For subsection (2) makes it clear that acceptance leaves unimpaired the buyer's right to be made whole, and that right can be exercised by the buyer not only by way of cross-claim for damages, but also by way of recoupment in diminution or extinction of the price.

7. Subsections (3)(b) and (5)(b) give a warrantor against infringement an opportunity to defend or compromise third-party claims or be relieved of his liability. Subsection (5)(a) codifies for all warranties the practice of voucher to defend. Compare Section 3-803. Subsection (6) makes these provisions applicable to the buyer's liability for infringement under Section 2-312.

8. All of the provisions of the present section are subject to any explicit reservation of rights. . . .

Definitional Cross References:
"Burden of establishing." Section 1-201.
"Buyer." Section 2-103.
"Conform." Section 2-106.
"Contract." Section 1-201.
"Goods." Section 2-105.
"Notifies." Section 1-20[2].
"Reasonable time." Section 1-20[5].
"Remedy." Section 1-201.
"Seasonably." Section 1-20[5].

§2-608. Revocation of Acceptance in Whole or in Part

(1) The buyer may revoke his acceptance of a lot or commercial unit whose non-conformity substantially impairs its value to him if he has accepted it

(a) on the reasonable assumption that its non-conformity would be cured and it has not been seasonably cured; or

(b) without discovery of such non-conformity if his acceptance was reasonably induced either by the difficulty of discovery before acceptance or by the seller's assurances.

(2) Revocation of acceptance must occur within a reasonable time after the buyer discovers or should have discovered the ground for it and before any substantial change in condition of the goods which is not caused by their own defects. It is not effective until the buyer notifies the seller of it.

(3) A buyer who so revokes has the same rights and duties with regard to the goods involved as if he had rejected them.

Official Comment

. . . .

2. Revocation of acceptance is possible only where the non-conformity substantially impairs the value of the goods to the buyer. For this purpose the test is not what the seller had reason to know at the time of contracting; the question is whether the non-conformity is such as will in fact cause a substantial impairment of value to the buyer though the seller had no advance knowledge as to the buyer's particular circumstances.

3. "Assurances" by the seller under paragraph (b) of subsection (1) can rest as well in the circumstances or in the contract as in explicit language used at the time of delivery. The reason for recognizing such assurances is that they induce the buyer to delay discovery. These are the only assurances involved in paragraph (b). Explicit assurances may be made either in good faith or bad faith. In either case any remedy accorded by this Article is available to the buyer under the section on remedies for fraud.

4. Subsection (2) requires notification of revocation of acceptance within a reasonable time after discovery of the grounds for such revocation. Since this remedy will be generally resorted to only after attempts at adjustment have failed, the reasonable time period should extend in most cases beyond the time in which notification of breach must be given, beyond the time for discovery of non-conformity after acceptance and beyond the time for rejection after tender. The parties may by their agreement limit the time for notification under this section, but the same sanctions and considerations apply to such agreements as are discussed in the comment on manner and effect of rightful rejection. . . .

6. . . . . [T]he buyer may not revoke his acceptance if the goods have materially deteriorated except by reason of their own defects. Worthless goods, however, need not be offered back and minor defects in the articles reoffered are to be disregarded.

7. The policy of the section allowing partial acceptance is carried over into the present section and the buyer may revoke his acceptance, in appropriate cases, as to the entire lot or any commercial unit thereof. . . .

Definitional Cross References:
"Buyer." Section 2-103.
"Commercial unit." Section 2-105.

"Conform." Section 2-106.
"Goods." Section 2-105.
"Lot." Section 2-105.
"Notifies." Section 1-20[2].
"Reasonable time." Section 1-20[5].
"Rights." Section 1-201.
"Seasonably." Section 1-20[5].
"Seller." Section 2-103.

§2-609. Right to Adequate Assurance of Performance

(1) A contract for sale imposes an obligation on each party that the other's expectation of receiving due performance will not be impaired. When reasonable grounds for insecurity arise with respect to the performance of either party the other may in writing demand adequate assurance of due performance and until he receives such assurance may if commercially reasonable suspend any performance for which he has not already received the agreed return.

(2) Between merchants the reasonableness of grounds for insecurity and the adequacy of any assurance offered shall be determined according to commercial standards.

(3) Acceptance of any improper delivery or payment does not prejudice the aggrieved party's right to demand adequate assurance of future performance.

(4) After receipt of a justified demand failure to provide within a reasonable time not exceeding thirty days such assurance of due performance as is adequate under the circumstances of the particular case is a repudiation of the contract.

Official Comment

. . . .

1. The section rests on the recognition of the fact that the essential purpose of a contract between commercial men is actual performance and they do not bargain merely for a promise, or for a promise plus the right to win a lawsuit and that a continuing sense of reliance and security that the promised performance will be forthcoming when due, is an important feature of the bargain. If either the willingness or the ability of a party to perform declines materially between the time of contracting and the time for performance, the other party is threatened with the loss of a substantial part of what he has bargained for. A seller needs protection not merely against having to deliver on credit to a shaky buyer, but also against having to procure and manufacture the goods, perhaps turning down other customers. Once he has been given reason to believe that the buyer's performance has become uncertain, it is an undue hardship to force him to continue his own performance. Similarly, a buyer who believes that the seller's deliveries have become uncertain cannot safely wait for the due date of performance when he has been buying to assure himself of materials for his current manufacturing or to replenish his stock of merchandise.

2. Three measures have been adopted to meet the needs of commercial men in such situations. First, the aggrieved party is permitted to suspend his own

performance and any preparation therefore with excuse for any resulting necessary delay, until the situation has been clarified. "Suspend performance" under this section means to hold up performance pending the outcome of the demand, and includes also the holding up of any preparatory action. . . .

Secondly, the aggrieved party is given the right to require adequate assurance that the other party's performance will be duly forthcoming. This principle is reflected in the familiar clauses permitting the seller to curtail deliveries if the buyer's credit becomes impaired, which when held within the limits of reasonableness and good faith actually express no more than the fair business meaning of any commercial contract.

Third, and finally, this section provides the means by which the aggrieved party may treat the contract as broken if his reasonable grounds for insecurity are not cleared up within a reasonable time. This is the principle underlying the law of anticipatory breach, whether by way of defective part performance or by repudiation. The present section merges these three principles of law and commercial practice into a single theory of general application to all sales agreements looking to future performance.

3. Subsection (2) of the present section requires that "reasonable" grounds and "adequate" assurance as used in subsection (1) be defined by commercial rather than legal standards. The express reference to commercial standards carries no connotation that the obligation of good faith is not equally applicable here.

Under commercial standards and in accord with commercial practice, a ground for insecurity need not arise from or be directly related to the contract in question. The law as to "dependence" or "independence" of promises within a single contract does not control the application of the present section.

Thus a buyer who falls behind in "his account" with the seller, even though the items involved have to do with separate and legally distinct contracts, impairs the seller's expectation of due performance. Again, under the same test, a buyer who requires precision parts which he intends to use immediately upon delivery, may have reasonable grounds for insecurity if he discovers that his seller is making defective deliveries of such parts to other buyers with similar needs. Thus, too, in a situation such as arose in Jay Dreher Corporation v. Delco Appliance Corporation, 93 F.2d 275 ([2d Cir.] 1937), where a manufacturer gave a dealer an exclusive franchise for the sale of his product but on two or three occasions breached the exclusive dealing clause, although there was no default in orders, deliveries or payments under the separate sales contract between the parties, the aggrieved dealer would be entitled to suspend his performance of the contract for sale under the present section and to demand assurance that the exclusive dealing contract would be lived up to. There is no need for an explicit clause tying the exclusive franchise into the contract for the sale of goods since the situation itself ties the agreements together.

The nature of the sales contract enters also into the question of reasonableness. For example, a report from an apparently trustworthy source that the seller had shipped defective goods or was planning to ship them would normally give the buyer reasonable grounds for insecurity. But when the buyer has assumed the risk of payment before inspection of the goods, as in a sales contract on C.I.F. or similar cash against documents terms, that risk is not to be evaded by a demand for assurance. Therefore no ground for insecurity would exist under this section unless the report went to a ground which would excuse payment by the buyer.

4. What constitutes "adequate" assurance of due performance is subject to the same test of factual conditions. For example, where the buyer can make use of a defective delivery, a mere promise by a seller of good repute that he is giving the matter his attention and that the defect will not be repeated, is normally sufficient. Under the same circumstances, however, a similar statement by a known corner-cutter might well be considered insufficient without the posting of a guaranty or, if so demanded by the buyer, a speedy replacement of the delivery involved. By the same token where a delivery has defects, even though easily curable, which interfere with easy use by the buyer, no verbal assurance can be deemed adequate which is not accompanied by replacement, repair, money-allowance, or other commercially reasonable cure.

A fact situation such as arose in Corn Products Refining Co. v. Fasola, 94 N.J.L. 181, 109 A. 505 (1920) offers illustration both of reasonable grounds for insecurity and "adequate" assurance. In that case a contract for the sale of oils on 30 days' credit, 2% off for payment within 10 days, provided that credit was to be extended to the buyer only if his financial responsibility was satisfactory to the seller. The buyer had been in the habit of taking advantage of the discount but at the same time that he failed to make his customary 10 day payment, the seller heard rumors, in fact false, that the buyer's financial condition was shaky. Thereupon, the seller demanded cash before shipment or security satisfactory to him. The buyer sent a good credit report from his banker, expressed willingness to make payments when due on the 30 day terms and insisted on further deliveries under the contract. Under this Article the rumors, although false, were enough to make the buyer's financial condition "unsatisfactory" to the seller under the contract clause. Moreover, the buyer's practice of taking the cash discounts is enough, apart from the contract clause, to lay a commercial foundation for suspicion when the practice is suddenly stopped. These matters, however, go only to the justification of the seller's demand for security, or his "reasonable grounds for insecurity."

The adequacy of the assurance given is not measured as in the type of "satisfaction" situation affected with intangibles, such as in personal service cases, cases involving a third party's judgment as final, or cases in which the whole contract is dependent on one party's satisfaction, as in a sale on approval. Here, the seller must exercise good faith and observe commercial standards. This Article thus approves the statement of the court in James B. Berry's Sons Co. of Illinois v. Monark Gasoline & Oil Co., Inc., 32 F.2d 74 ([8th Cir.] 1929), that the seller's satisfaction under such a clause must be based upon reason and must not be arbitrary or capricious; and rejects the purely personal "good faith" test of the Corn Products Refining Co. case, which held that in the seller's sole judgment, if for *any* reason he was dissatisfied, he was entitled to revoke the credit. In the absence of the buyer's failure to take the 2% discount as was his custom, the banker's report given in that case would have been "adequate" assurance under this Act, regardless of the language of the "satisfaction" clause. However, the seller is reasonably entitled to feel insecure at a sudden expansion of the buyer's use of a credit term, and should be entitled either to security or to a satisfactory explanation.

The entire foregoing discussion as to adequacy of assurance by way of explanation is subject to qualification when repeated occasions for the application of this section arise. This Act recognizes that repeated delinquencies must be viewed as cumulative. On the other hand, commercial sense also requires that if repeated claims for assurance are made under this section, the basis for these claims must be increasingly obvious.

5. A failure to provide adequate assurance of performance and thereby to reestablish the security of expectation, results in a breach only "by repudiation" under subsection (4). Therefore, the possibility is continued of retraction of the repudiation under the section dealing with that problem, unless the aggrieved party has acted on the breach in some manner.

The thirty day limit on the time to provide assurance is laid down to free the question of reasonable time from uncertainty in later litigation.

6. Clauses seeking to give the protected party exceedingly wide powers to cancel or readjust the contract when ground for insecurity arises must be read against the fact that good faith is a part of the obligation of the contract and not subject to modification by agreement and includes, in the case of a merchant, the reasonable observance of commercial standards of fair dealing in the trade. Such clauses can thus be effective to enlarge the protection given by the present section to a certain extent, to fix the reasonable time within which requested assurance must be given, or to define adequacy of the assurance in any commercially reasonable fashion. But any clause seeking to set up arbitrary standards for action is ineffective under this Article. . . .

Definitional Cross References:
"Aggrieved party." Section 1-201.
"Between merchants." Section 2-104.
"Contract." Section 1-201.
"Contract for sale." Section 2-106.
"Party." Section 1-201.
"Reasonable time." Section 1-20[5].
"Rights." Section 1-201.
"Writing." Section 1-201.

§2-610. Anticipatory Repudiation

When either party repudiates the contract with respect to a performance not yet due the loss of which will substantially impair the value of the contract to the other, the aggrieved party may

　　　(a) for a commercially reasonable time await performance by the repudiating party; or

　　　(b) resort to any remedy for breach (Section 2-703 or Section 2-711), even though he has notified the repudiating party that he would await the latter's performance and has urged retraction; and

　　　(c) in either case suspend his own performance or proceed in accordance with the provisions of this Article on the seller's right to identify goods to the contract notwithstanding breach or to salvage unfinished goods (Section 2-704).

Official Comment

. . . .

1. . . . [A]nticipatory repudiation centers upon an overt communication of intention or an action which renders performance impossible or demonstrates a clear determination not to continue with performance.

Under the present section when such a repudiation substantially impairs the value of the contract, the aggrieved party may at any time resort to his remedies for breach, or he may suspend his own performance while he negotiates with, or awaits performance by, the other party. But if he awaits performance beyond a commercially reasonable time he cannot recover resulting damages which he should have avoided.

2. It is not necessary for repudiation that performance be made literally and utterly impossible. Repudiation can result from action which reasonably indicates a rejection of the continuing obligation. And, a repudiation automatically results under the preceding section on insecurity when a party fails to provide adequate assurance of due future performance within thirty days after a justifiable demand therefore has been made. Under the language of this section, a demand by one or both parties for more than the contract calls for in the way of counter-performance is not in itself a repudiation nor does it invalidate a plain expression of desire for future performance. However, when under a fair reading it amounts to a statement of intention not to perform except on conditions which go beyond the contract, it becomes a repudiation.

3. The test chosen to justify an aggrieved party's action under this section is the same as that in the section on breach in installment contracts — namely the substantial value of the contract. The most useful test of substantial value is to determine whether material inconvenience or injustice will result if the aggrieved party is forced to wait and receive an ultimate tender minus the part or aspect repudiated.

4. After repudiation, the aggrieved party may immediately resort to any remedy he chooses provided he moves in good faith (see Section 1-203). Inaction and silence by the aggrieved party may leave the matter open but it cannot be regarded as misleading the repudiating party. Therefore the aggrieved party is left free to proceed at any time with his options under this section, unless he has taken some positive action which in good faith requires notification to the other party before the remedy is pursued. . . .

Definitional Cross References:
"Aggrieved party." Section 1-201.
"Contract." Section 1-201.
"Party." Section 1-201.
"Remedy." Section 1-201.

§2-611.   Retraction of Anticipatory Repudiation

(1) Until the repudiating party's next performance is due he can retract his repudiation unless the aggrieved party has since the repudiation cancelled or

materially changed his position or otherwise indicated that he considers the repudiation final.

(2) Retraction may be by any method which clearly indicates to the aggrieved party that the repudiating party intends to perform, but must include any assurance justifiably demanded under the provisions of this Article (Section 2-609).

(3) Retraction reinstates the repudiating party's rights under the contract with due excuse and allowance to the aggrieved party for any delay occasioned by the repudiation.

§2-612. "Installment Contract"; Breach

(1) An "installment contract" is one which requires or authorizes the delivery of goods in separate lots to be separately accepted, even though the contract contains a clause "each delivery is a separate contract" or its equivalent.

(2) The buyer may reject any installment which is non-conforming if the non-conformity substantially impairs the value of that installment and cannot be cured or if the non-conformity is a defect in the required documents; but if the non-conformity does not fall within subsection (3) and the seller gives adequate assurance of its cure the buyer must accept that installment.

(3) Whenever non-conformity or default with respect to one or more installments substantially impairs the value of the whole contract there is a breach of the whole. But the aggrieved party reinstates the contract if he accepts a non-conforming installment without seasonably notifying of cancellation or if he brings an action with respect only to past installments or demands performance as to future installments.

§2-613. Casualty to Identified Goods

Where the contract requires for its performance goods identified when the contract is made, and the goods suffer casualty without fault of either party before the risk of loss passes to the buyer, or in a proper case under a "no arrival, no sale" term (Section 2-324) then

(a) if the loss is total the contract is avoided; and

(b) if the loss is partial or the goods have so deteriorated as no longer to conform to the contract the buyer may nevertheless demand inspection and at his option either treat the contract as avoided or accept the goods with due allowance from the contract price for the deterioration or the deficiency in quantity but without further right against the seller.

§2-614. Substituted Performance

(1) Where without fault of either party the agreed berthing, loading, or unloading facilities fail or an agreed type of carrier becomes unavailable or the agreed manner of delivery otherwise becomes commercially impracticable but a commercially reasonable substitute is available, such substitute performance must be tendered and accepted.

(2) If the agreed means or manner of payment fails because of domestic or foreign governmental regulation, the seller may withhold or stop delivery unless the buyer provides a means or manner of payment which is commercially a substantial equivalent. If delivery has already been taken, payment by the means or in the manner provided by the regulation discharges the buyer's obligation unless the regulation is discriminatory, oppressive or predatory.

§2-615.   Excuse by Failure of Presupposed Conditions

Except so far as a seller may have assumed a greater obligation and subject to the preceding section on substituted performance:

(a) Delay in delivery or non-delivery in whole or in part by a seller who complies with paragraphs (b) and (c) is not a breach of his duty under a contract for sale if performance as agreed has been made impracticable by the occurrence of a contingency the non-occurrence of which was a basic assumption on which the contract was made or by compliance in good faith with any applicable foreign or domestic governmental regulation or order whether or not it later proves to be invalid.

(b) Where the causes mentioned in paragraph (a) affect only a part of the seller's capacity to perform, he must allocate production and deliveries among his customers but may at his option include regular customers not then under contract as well as his own requirements for further manufacture. He may so allocate in any manner which is fair and reasonable.

(c) The seller must notify the buyer seasonably that there will be delay or non-delivery and, when allocation is required under paragraph (b), of the estimated quota thus made available for the buyer.

Official Comment

. . . .

1. This section excuses a seller from timely delivery of goods contracted for, where his performance has become commercially impracticable because of unforeseen supervening circumstances not within the contemplation of the parties at the time of contracting. The destruction of specific goods and the problem of the use of substituted performance on points other than delay or quantity, treated elsewhere in this Article, must be distinguished from the matter covered by this section.

2. The present section deliberately refrains from any effort at an exhaustive expression of contingencies and is to be interpreted in all cases sought to be brought within its scope in terms of its underlying reason and purpose.

3. The first test for excuse under this Article in terms of basic assumption is a familiar one. The additional test of commercial impracticability (as contrasted with "impossibility," "frustration of performance" or "frustration of the venture") has been adopted in order to call attention to the commercial character of the criterion chosen by this Article.

4. Increased cost alone does not excuse performance unless the rise in cost is due to some unforeseen contingency which alters the essential nature of the performance. Neither is a rise or a collapse in the market in itself a justification, for that is exactly the type of business risk which business contracts made at fixed prices are intended to cover. But a severe shortage of raw materials or of supplies due to a contingency such as war, embargo, local crop failure, unforeseen shutdown of major sources of supply or the like, which either causes a marked increase in cost or altogether prevents the seller from securing supplies necessary to his performance, is within the contemplation of this section. . . .

5. Where a particular source of supply is exclusive under the agreement and fails through casualty, the present section applies rather than the provision on destruction or deterioration of specific goods. The same holds true where a particular source of supply is shown by the circumstances to have been contemplated or assumed by the parties at the time of contracting. (See Davis Co. v. Hoffmann-LaRoche Chemical Works, 178 App. Div. 855, 166 N.Y.S. 179 (1917) and International Paper Co. v. Rockefeller, 161 App. Div. 180, 146 N.Y.S. 371 (1914).) There is no excuse under this section, however, unless the seller has employed all due measures to assure himself that his source will not fail. (See Canadian Industrial Alcohol Co., Ltd. v. Dunbar Molasses Co., 258 N.Y. 194, 179 N.E. 383, 80 A.L.R. 1173 (1932) and Washington Mfg. Co. v. Midland Lumber Co., 113 Wash. 593, 194 P. 777 (1921).)

In the case of failure of production by an agreed source for causes beyond the seller's control, the seller should, if possible, be excused since production by an agreed source is without more a basic assumption of the contract. Such excuse should not result in relieving the defaulting supplier from liability nor in dropping into the seller's lap an unearned bonus of damages over. The flexible adjustment machinery of this Article provides the solution under the provision on the obligation of good faith. A condition to his making good the claim of excuse is the turning over to the buyer of his rights against the defaulting source of supply to the extent of the buyer's contract in relation to which excuse is being claimed.

6. In situations in which neither sense nor justice is served by either answer when the issue is posed in flat terms of "excuse" or "no excuse," adjustment under the various provisions of this Article is necessary, especially the sections on good faith, on insecurity and assurance and on the reading of all provisions in the light of their purposes, and the general policy of this Act to use equitable principles in furtherance of commercial standards and good faith.

7. The failure of conditions which go to convenience or collateral values rather than to the commercial practicability of the main performance does not amount to a complete excuse. However, good faith and the reason of the present section and of the preceding one may properly be held to justify and even to require any needed delay involved in a good faith inquiry seeking a readjustment of the contract terms to meet the new conditions.

8. The provisions of this section are made subject to assumption of greater liability by agreement and such agreement is to be found not only in the expressed terms of the contract but in the circumstances surrounding the contracting, in trade usage and the like. Thus the exemptions of this section do not apply when the contingency in question is sufficiently foreshadowed at the

time of contracting to be included among the business risks which are fairly to be regarded as part of the dickered terms, either consciously or as a matter of reasonable, commercial interpretation from the circumstances. (See Madeirense Do Brasil, S. A. v. Stulman-Emrick Lumber Co., 147 F.2d 399 ([2d Cir.] 1945).) The exemption otherwise present through usage of trade under the present section may also be expressly negated by the language of the agreement. Generally, express agreements as to exemptions designed to enlarge upon or supplant the provisions of this section are to be read in the light of mercantile sense and reason, for this section itself sets up the commercial standard for normal and reasonable interpretation and provides a minimum beyond which agreement may not go.

Agreement can also be made in regard to the consequences of exemption as laid down in paragraphs (b) and (c) and the next section on procedure on notice claiming excuse.

9. The case of a farmer who has contracted to sell crops to be grown on designated land may be regarded as falling either within the section on casualty to identified goods or this section, and he may be excused, when there is a failure of the specific crop, either on the basis of the destruction of identified goods or because of the failure of a basic assumption of the contract.

Exemption of the buyer in the case of a "requirements" contract is covered by the "Output and Requirements" section both as to assumption and allocation of the relevant risks. But when a contract by a manufacturer to buy fuel or raw material makes no specific reference to a particular venture and no such reference may be drawn from the circumstances, commercial understanding views it as a general deal in the general market and not conditioned on any assumption of the continuing operation of the buyer's plant. Even when notice is given by the buyer that the supplies are needed to fill a specific contract of a normal commercial kind, commercial understanding does not see such a supply contract as conditioned on the continuance of the buyer's further contract for outlet. On the other hand, where the buyer's contract is in reasonable commercial understanding conditioned on a definite and specific venture or assumption as, for instance, a war procurement subcontract known to be based on a prime contract which is subject to termination, or a supply contract for a particular construction venture, the reason of the present section may well apply and entitle the buyer to the exemption.

10. Following its basic policy of using commercial practicability as a test for excuse, this section recognizes as of equal significance either a foreign or domestic regulation and disregards any technical distinctions between "law," "regulation," "order" and the like. Nor does it make the present action of the seller depend upon the eventual judicial determination of the legality of the particular governmental action. The seller's good faith belief in the validity of the regulation is the test under this Article and the best evidence of his good faith is the general commercial acceptance of the regulation. However, governmental interference cannot excuse unless it truly "supervenes" in such a manner as to be beyond the seller's assumption of risk. And any action by the party claiming excuse which causes or colludes in inducing the governmental action preventing his performance would be in breach of good faith and would destroy his exemption.

11. An excused seller must fulfill his contract to the extent which the supervening contingency permits, and if the situation is such that his customers are generally affected he must take account of all in supplying one. Subsections (a) and (b), therefore, explicitly permit in any proration a fair and reasonable attention to the needs of regular customers who are probably relying on spot orders for supplies. Customers at different stages of the manufacturing process may be fairly treated by including the seller's manufacturing requirements. A fortiori, the seller may also take account of contracts later in date than the one in question. The fact that such spot orders may be closed at an advanced price causes no difficulty, since any allocation which exceeds normal past requirements will not be reasonable. However, good faith requires, when prices have advanced, that the seller exercise real care in making his allocations, and in case of doubt his contract customers should be favored and supplies prorated evenly among them regardless of price. Save for the extra care thus required by changes in the market, this section seeks to leave every reasonable business leeway to the seller. . . .

Definitional Cross References:
"Between merchants." Section 2-104.
"Buyer." Section 2-103.
"Contract." Section 1-201.
"Contract for sale." Section 2-106.
"Good faith." Section 1-201.
"Merchant." Section 2-104.
"Notifies." Section 1-20[2].
"Seasonably." Section 1-20[5].
"Seller." Section 2-103.

§2-616. Procedure on Notice Claiming Excuse

(1) Where the buyer receives notification of a material or indefinite delay or an allocation justified under the preceding section he may by written notification to the seller as to any delivery concerned, and where the prospective deficiency substantially impairs the value of the whole contract under the provisions of this Article relating to breach of installment contracts (Section 2-612), then also as to the whole,

(a) terminate and thereby discharge any unexecuted portion of the contract; or

(b) modify the contract by agreeing to take his available quota in substitution.

(2) If after receipt of such notification from the seller the buyer fails so to modify the contract within a reasonable time not exceeding thirty days the contract lapses with respect to any deliveries affected.

(3) The provisions of this section may not be negated by agreement except in so far as the seller has assumed a greater obligation under the preceding section.

Part 7.   Remedies

§2-702.   Seller's Remedies on Discovery of Buyer's Insolvency

(1) Where the seller discovers the buyer to be insolvent he may refuse delivery except for cash including payment for all goods theretofore delivered under the contract, and stop delivery under this Article (Section 2-705).

(2) Where the seller discovers that the buyer has received goods on credit while insolvent he may reclaim the goods upon demand made within ten days after the receipt, but if misrepresentation of solvency has been made to the particular seller in writing within three months before delivery the ten day limitation does not apply. Except as provided in this subsection the seller may not base a right to reclaim goods on the buyer's fraudulent or innocent misrepresentation of solvency or of intent to pay.

(3) The seller's right to reclaim under subsection (2) is subject to the rights of a buyer in ordinary course or other good faith purchaser under this Article (Section 2-403). Successful reclamation of goods excludes all other remedies with respect to them.

§2-703.   Seller's Remedies in General

Where the buyer wrongfully rejects or revokes acceptance of goods or fails to make a payment due on or before delivery or repudiates with respect to a part or the whole, then with respect to any goods directly affected and, if the breach is of the whole contract (Section 2-612), then also with respect to the whole undelivered balance, the aggrieved seller may

(a) withhold delivery of such goods;

(b) stop delivery by any bailee as hereafter provided (Section 2-705);

(c) proceed under the next section respecting goods still unidentified to the contract;

(d) resell and recover damages as hereafter provided (Section 2-706);

(e) recover damages for non-acceptance (Section 2-708) or in a proper case the price (Section 2-709);

(f) cancel.

§2-704.   Seller's Right to Identify Goods to the Contract Notwithstanding Breach or to Salvage Unfinished Goods

(1) An aggrieved seller under the preceding section may

(a) identify to the contract conforming goods not already identified if at the time he learned of the breach they are in his possession or control;

(b) treat as the subject of resale goods which have demonstrably been intended for the particular contract even though those goods are unfinished.

(2) Where the goods are unfinished an aggrieved seller may in the exercise of reasonable commercial judgment for the purposes of avoiding loss and of effective

realization either complete the manufacture and wholly identify the goods to the contract or cease manufacture and resell for scrap or salvage value or proceed in any other reasonable manner.

§2-705. Seller's Stoppage of Delivery in Transit or Otherwise

(1) The seller may stop delivery of goods in the possession of a carrier or other bailee when he discovers the buyer to be insolvent (Section 2-702) and may stop delivery of carload, truckload, planeload or larger shipments of express or freight when the buyer repudiates or fails to make a payment due before delivery or if for any other reason the seller has a right to withhold or reclaim the goods.

(2) As against such buyer the seller may stop delivery until

(a) receipt of the goods by the buyer; or

(b) acknowledgment to the buyer by any bailee of the goods except a carrier that the bailee holds the goods for the buyer; or

(c) such acknowledgment to the buyer by a carrier by reshipment or as warehouseman; or

(d) negotiation to the buyer of any negotiable document of title covering the goods.

(3)(a) To stop delivery the seller must so notify as to enable the bailee by reasonable diligence to prevent delivery of the goods.

(b) After such notification the bailee must hold and deliver the goods according to the directions of the seller but the seller is liable to the bailee for any ensuing charges or damages.

(c) If a negotiable document of title has been issued for goods the bailee is not obliged to obey a notification to stop until surrender of the document.

(d) A carrier who has issued a non-negotiable bill of lading is not obliged to obey a notification to stop received from a person other than the consignor.

§2-706. Seller's Resale Including Contract for Resale

(1) Under the conditions stated in Section 2-703 on seller's remedies, the seller may resell the goods concerned or the undelivered balance thereof. Where the resale is made in good faith and in a commercially reasonable manner the seller may recover the difference between the resale price and the contract price together with any incidental damages allowed under the provisions of this Article (Section 2-710), but less expenses saved in consequence of the buyer's breach.

(2) Except as otherwise provided in subsection (3) or unless otherwise agreed resale may be at public or private sale including sale by way of one or more contracts to sell or of identification to an existing contract of the seller. Sale may be as a unit or in parcels and at any time and place and on any terms but every aspect of the sale including the method, manner, time, place and terms must be commercially reasonable. The resale must be reasonably identified as referring to the broken contract, but it is not necessary that the goods be in existence or that any or all of them have been identified to the contract before the breach.

(3) Where the resale is at private sale the seller must give the buyer reasonable notification of his intention to resell.

(4) Where the resale is at public sale

(a) only identified goods can be sold except where there is a recognized market for a public sale of futures in goods of the kind; and

(b) it must be made at a usual place or market for public sale if one is reasonably available and except in the case of goods which are perishable or threaten to decline in value speedily the seller must give the buyer reasonable notice of the time and place of the resale; and

(c) if the goods are not to be within the view of those attending the sale the notification of sale must state the place where the goods are located and provide for their reasonable inspection by prospective bidders; and

(d) the seller may buy.

(5) A purchaser who buys in good faith at a resale takes the goods free of any rights of the original buyer even though the seller fails to comply with one or more of the requirements of this section.

(6) The seller is not accountable to the buyer for any profit made on any resale. A person in the position of a seller (Section 2-707) or a buyer who has rightfully rejected or justifiably revoked acceptance must account for any excess over the amount of his security interest, as hereinafter defined (subsection (3) of Section 2-711).

§2-708. Seller's Damages for Non-acceptance or Repudiation

(1) Subject to subsection (2) and to the provisions of this Article with respect to proof of market price (Section 2-723), the measure of damages for non-acceptance or repudiation by the buyer is the difference between the market price at the time and place for tender and the unpaid contract price together with any incidental damages provided in this Article (Section 2-710), but less expenses saved in consequence of the buyer's breach.

(2) If the measure of damages provided in subsection (1) is inadequate to put the seller in as good a position as performance would have done then the measure of damages is the profit (including reasonable overhead) which the seller would have made from full performance by the buyer, together with any incidental damages provided in this Article (Section 2-710), due allowance for costs reasonably incurred and due credit for payments or proceeds of resale.

§2-709. Action for the Price

(1) When the buyer fails to pay the price as it becomes due the seller may recover, together with any incidental damages under the next section, the price

(a) of goods accepted or of conforming goods lost or damaged within a commercially reasonable time after risk of their loss has passed to the buyer; and

(b) of goods identified to the contract if the seller is unable after reasonable effort to resell them at a reasonable price or the circumstances reasonably indicate that such effort will be unavailing.

(2) Where the seller sues for the price he must hold for the buyer any goods which have been identified to the contract and are still in his control except that if resale becomes possible he may resell them at any time prior to the collection of

the judgment. The net proceeds of any such resale must be credited to the buyer and payment of the judgment entitles him to any goods not resold.

(3) After the buyer has wrongfully rejected or revoked acceptance of the goods or has failed to make a payment due or has repudiated (Section 2-610), a seller who is held not entitled to the price under this section shall nevertheless be awarded damages for non-acceptance under the preceding section.

Official Comment

. . . .

2. The action for the price is now generally limited to those cases where resale of the goods is impracticable except where the buyer has accepted the goods or where they have been destroyed after risk of loss has passed to the buyer.

3. . . . An action for the price under subsection (1)(b) can be sustained only after a "reasonable effort to resell" the goods "at reasonable price" has actually been made or where the circumstances "reasonably indicate" that such an effort will be unavailing. . . .

5. "Goods accepted" by the buyer under subsection (1)(a) include only goods as to which there has been no justified revocation of acceptance, for such a revocation means that there has been a default by the seller which bars his rights under this section. "Goods lost or damaged" are covered by the section on risk of loss. "Goods identified to the contract" under subsection (1)(b) are covered by the section on identification and the section on identification notwithstanding breach.

6. This section is intended to be exhaustive in its enumeration of cases where an action for the price lies.

7. If the action for the price fails, the seller may nonetheless have proved a case entitling him to damages for non-acceptance. In such a situation, subsection (3) permits recovery of those damages in the same action. . . .

Definitional Cross References:
"Action." Section 1-201.
"Buyer." Section 2-103.
"Conforming." Section 2-106.
"Contract." Section 1-201.
"Goods." Section 2-105.
"Seller." Section 2-103.

§2-710. Seller's Incidental Damages

Incidental damages to an aggrieved seller include any commercially reasonable charges, expenses or commissions incurred in stopping delivery, in the transportation, care and custody of goods after the buyer's breach, in connection with return or resale of the goods or otherwise resulting from the breach.

§2-711. Buyer's Remedies in General; Buyer's Security Interest in Rejected Goods

(1) Where the seller fails to make delivery or repudiates or the buyer rightfully rejects or justifiably revokes acceptance then with respect to any goods involved, and with respect to the whole if the breach goes to the whole contract (Section 2-612), the buyer may cancel and whether or not he has done so may in addition to recovering so much of the price as has been paid

(a) "cover" and have damages under the next section as to all the goods affected whether or not they have been identified to the contract; or

(b) recover damages for non-delivery as provided in this Article (Section 2-713).

(2) Where the seller fails to deliver or repudiates the buyer may also

(a) if the goods have been identified recover them as provided in this Article (Section 2-502); or

(b) in a proper case obtain specific performance or replevy the goods as provided in this Article (Section 2-716).

(3) On rightful rejection or justifiable revocation of acceptance a buyer has a security interest in goods in his possession or control for any payments made on their price and any expenses reasonably incurred in their inspection, receipt, transportation, care and custody and may hold such goods and resell them in like manner as an aggrieved seller (Section 2-706).

§2-712. "Cover"; Buyer's Procurement of Substitute Goods

(1) After a breach within the preceding section the buyer may "cover" by making in good faith and without unreasonable delay any reasonable purchase of or contract to purchase goods in substitution for those due from the seller.

(2) The buyer may recover from the seller as damages the difference between the cost of cover and the contract price together with any incidental or consequential damages as hereinafter defined (Section 2-715), but less expenses saved in consequence of the seller's breach.

(3) Failure of the buyer to effect cover within this Section does not bar him from any other remedy.

Official Comment

. . . .

1. This section provides the buyer with a remedy aimed at enabling him to obtain the goods he needs thus meeting his essential need. This remedy is the buyer's equivalent of the seller's right to resell.

2. The definition of "cover" under subsection (1) envisages a series of contracts or sales, as well as a single contract or sale; goods not identical with those involved but commercially usable as reasonable substitutes under the circumstances of the particular case; and contracts on credit or delivery terms differing from the contract in breach, but again reasonable under the circumstances. The test of proper cover is whether at the time and place the buyer acted in good faith and in

a reasonable manner, and it is immaterial that hindsight may later prove that the method of cover used was not the cheapest or most effective.

The requirement that the buyer must cover "without unreasonable delay" is not intended to limit the time necessary for him to look around and decide as to how he may best effect cover. The test here is similar to that generally used in this Article as to reasonable time and seasonable action.

3. Subsection (3) expresses the policy that cover is not a mandatory remedy for the buyer. The buyer is always free to choose between cover and damages for non-delivery under the next section.

However, this subsection must be read in conjunction with the section which limits the recovery of consequential damages to such as could not have been obviated by cover. Moreover, the operation of the section on specific performance of contracts for "unique" goods must be considered in this connection for availability of the goods to the particular buyer for his particular needs is the test for that remedy and inability to cover is made an express condition to the right of the buyer to replevy the goods. . . .

Definitional Cross References:
"Buyer." Section 2-103.
"Contract." Section 1-201.
"Good faith." Section [1-201].
"Goods." Section 2-105.
"Purchase." Section 1-201.
"Remedy." Section 1-201.
"Seller." Section 2-103.

§2-713. Buyer's Damages for Non-delivery or Repudiation

(1) Subject to the provisions of this Article with respect to proof of market price (Section 2-723), the measure of damages for non-delivery or repudiation by the seller is the difference between the market price at the time when the buyer learned of the breach and the contract price together with any incidental and consequential damages provided in this Article (Section 2-715), but less expenses saved in consequence of the seller's breach.

(2) Market price is to be determined as of the place for tender or, in cases of rejection after arrival or revocation of acceptance, as of the place of arrival.

Official Comment

. . . .

1. . . . . [T]his section uses as a yardstick the market in which the buyer would have obtained cover had he sought that relief. So the place for measuring damages is the place of tender (or the place of arrival if the goods are rejected or their acceptance is revoked after reaching their destination) and the crucial time is the time at which the buyer learns of the breach.

2. The market or current price to be used in comparison with the contract price under this section is the price for goods of the same kind and in the same branch of trade.

3. When the current market price under this section is difficult to prove the section on determination and proof of market price is available to permit a showing of a comparable market price or, where no market price is available, evidence of spot sale prices is proper. Where the unavailability of a market price is caused by a scarcity of goods of the type involved, a good case is normally made for specific performance under this Article. Such scarcity conditions, moreover, indicate that the price has risen and under the section providing for liberal administration of remedies, opinion evidence as to the value of the goods would be admissible in the absence of a market price and a liberal construction of allowable consequential damages should also result.

4. This section carries forward the standard rule that the buyer must deduct from his damages any expenses saved as a result of the breach.

5. The present section provides a remedy which is completely alternative to cover under the preceding section and applies only when and to the extent that the buyer has not covered. . . .

Definitional Cross References:
"Buyer." Section 2-103.
"Contract." Section 1-201.
"Seller." Section 2-103.

§2-714.   Buyer's Damages for Breach in Regard to Accepted Goods

(1) Where the buyer has accepted goods and given notification (subsection (3) of Section 2-607) he may recover as damages for any non-conformity of tender the loss resulting in the ordinary course of events from the seller's breach as determined in any manner which is reasonable.

(2) The measure of damages for breach of warranty is the difference at the time and place of acceptance between the value of the goods accepted and the value they would have had if they had been as warranted, unless special circumstances show proximate damages of a different amount.

(3) In a proper case any incidental and consequential damages under the next section may also be recovered.

Official Comment

. . . .

1. This section deals with the remedies available to the buyer after the goods have been accepted and the time for revocation of acceptance has gone by. . . .

The section on deduction of damages from price provides an additional remedy for a buyer who still owes part of the purchase price, and frequently the two remedies will be available concurrently. The buyer's failure to notify of his claim under the section on effects of acceptance, however, operates to bar his remedies under either that section or the present section.

2. The "non-conformity" referred to in subsection (1) includes not only breaches of warranties but also any failure of the seller to perform according to his obligations under the contract. In the case of such non-conformity, the buyer is permitted to recover for his loss "in any manner which is reasonable."

3. Subsection (2) describes the usual, standard and reasonable method of ascertaining damages in the case of breach of warranty but it is not intended as an exclusive measure. It departs from the measure of damages for non-delivery in utilizing the place of acceptance rather than the place of tender. In some cases the two may coincide, as where the buyer signifies his acceptance upon the tender. If, however, the non-conformity is such as would justify revocation of acceptance, the time and place of acceptance under this section is determined as of the buyer's decision not to revoke. . . .

Definitional Cross References:
   "Buyer." Section 2-103.
   "Conform." Section 2-106.
   "Goods." Section [2-105].
   "Notification." Section 1-20[2].
   "Seller." Section 2-103.

§2-715.   Buyer's Incidental and Consequential Damages

(1) Incidental damages resulting from the seller's breach include expenses reasonably incurred in inspection, receipt, transportation and care and custody of goods rightfully rejected, any commercially reasonable charges, expenses or commissions in connection with effecting cover and any other reasonable expense incident to the delay or other breach.

(2) Consequential damages resulting from the seller's breach include

   (a) any loss resulting from general or particular requirements and needs of which the seller at the time of contracting had reason to know and which could not reasonably be prevented by cover or otherwise; and

   (b) injury to person or property proximately resulting from any breach of warranty.

Official Comment

. . . .

1. Subsection (1) is intended to provide reimbursement for the buyer who incurs reasonable expenses in connection with the handling of rightfully rejected goods or goods whose acceptance may be justifiably revoked, or in connection with effecting cover where the breach of the contract lies in non-conformity or non-delivery of the goods. The incidental damages listed are not intended to be exhaustive but are merely illustrative of the typical kinds of incidental damage.

2. Subsection (2) operates to allow the buyer, in an appropriate case, any consequential damages which are the result of the seller's breach. The "tacit agreement" test for the recovery of consequential damages is rejected. Although the older rule at common law which made the seller liable for all consequential damages of which he had "reason to know" in advance is followed, the liberality of that rule is modified by refusing to permit recovery unless the buyer could not reasonably have prevented the loss by cover or otherwise. Subparagraph (2) carries forward the provisions of the prior uniform statutory provision as to consequential damages resulting from breach of warranty, but modifies the rule by requiring first that the buyer attempt to minimize his damages in good faith, either by cover or otherwise.

3. In the absence of excuse under the section on merchant's excuse by failure of presupposed conditions, the seller is liable for consequential damages in all cases where he had reason to know of the buyer's general or particular requirements at the time of contracting. It is not necessary that there be a conscious acceptance of an insurer's liability on the seller's part, nor is his obligation for consequential damages limited to cases in which he fails to use due effort in good faith.

Particular needs of the buyer must generally be made known to the seller while general needs must rarely be made known to charge the seller with knowledge.

Any seller who does not wish to take the risk of consequential damages has available the section on contractual limitation of remedy.

4. The burden of proving the extent of loss incurred by way of consequential damage is on the buyer, but the section on liberal administration of remedies rejects any doctrine of certainty which requires almost mathematical precision in the proof of loss. Loss may be determined in any manner which is reasonable under the circumstances.

5. Subsection (2)(b) states the usual rule as to breach of warranty, allowing recovery for injuries "proximately" resulting from the breach. Where the injury involved follows the use of goods without discovery of the defect causing the damage, the question of "proximate" cause turns on whether it was reasonable for the buyer to use the goods without such inspection as would have revealed the defects. If it was not reasonable for him to do so, or if he did in fact discover the defect prior to his use, the injury would not proximately result from the breach of warranty.

6. In the case of sale of wares to one in the business of reselling them, resale is one of the requirements of which the seller has reason to know within the meaning of subsection (2)(a). . . .

Definitional Cross References:
  "Cover." Section 2-712.
  "Goods." Section [2-105].
  "Person." Section 1-201.
  "Receipt" of goods. Section 2-103.
  "Seller." Section 2-103.

§2-716. Buyer's Right to Specific Performance or Replevin

(1) Specific performance may be decreed where the goods are unique or in other proper circumstances.

(2) The decree for specific performance may include such terms and conditions as to payment of the price, damages, or other relief as the court may deem just.

(3) The buyer has a right of replevin for goods identified to the contract if after reasonable effort he is unable to effect cover for such goods or the circumstances reasonably indicate that such effort will be unavailing or if the goods have been shipped under reservation and satisfaction of the security interest in them has been made or tendered. In the case of goods bought for personal, family, or household purposes, the buyer's right of replevin vests upon acquisition of a special property, even if the seller had not then repudiated or failed to deliver.

Official Comment

. . . .

1. . . . [W]ithout intending to impair in any way the exercise of the court's sound discretion in the matter, this Article seeks to further a more liberal attitude than some courts have shown in connection with the specific performance of contracts of sale.

2. In view of this Article's emphasis on the commercial feasibility of replacement, a new concept of what are "unique" goods is introduced under this section. Specific performance is no longer limited to goods which are already specific or ascertained at the time of contracting. The test of uniqueness under this section must be made in terms of the total situation which characterizes the contract. Output and requirements contracts involving a particular or peculiarly available source or market present today the typical commercial specific performance situation, as contrasted with contracts for the sale of heirlooms or priceless works of art which were usually involved in the older cases. However, uniqueness is not the sole basis of the remedy under this section for the relief may also be granted "in other proper circumstances" and inability to cover is strong evidence of "other proper circumstances". . . .

4. This section is intended to give the buyer rights to the goods comparable to the seller's rights to the price. . . .

Definitional Cross References:
  "Buyer." Section 2-103.
  "Goods." Section [2-105].
  "Rights." Section 1-201.

§2-717. Deduction of Damages from the Price

The buyer on notifying the seller of his intention to do so may deduct all or any part of the damages resulting from any breach of the contract from any part of the price still due under the same contract.

§2-718. Liquidation or Limitation of Damages; Deposits

(1) Damages for breach by either party may be liquidated in the agreement but only at an amount which is reasonable in the light of the anticipated or actual harm caused by the breach, the difficulties of proof of loss, and the inconvenience or nonfeasibility of otherwise obtaining an adequate remedy. A term fixing unreasonably large liquidated damages is void as a penalty.

(2) Where the seller justifiably withholds delivery of goods because of the buyer's breach, the buyer is entitled to restitution of any amount by which the sum of his payments exceeds

(a) the amount to which the seller is entitled by virtue of terms liquidating the seller's damages in accordance with subsection (1), or

(b) in the absence of such terms, twenty per cent of the value of the total performance for which the buyer is obligated under the contract or $500, whichever is smaller.

(3) The buyer's right to restitution under subsection (2) is subject to offset to the extent that the seller establishes

(a) a right to recover damages under the provisions of this Article other than subsection (1), and

(b) the amount or value of any benefits received by the buyer directly or indirectly by reason of the contract.

(4) Where a seller has received payment in goods their reasonable value or the proceeds of their resale shall be treated as payments for the purposes of subsection (2); but if the seller has notice of the buyer's breach before reselling goods received in part performance, his resale is subject to the conditions laid down in this Article on resale by an aggrieved seller (Section 2-706).

Official Comment

. . . .

1. Under subsection (1) liquidated damage clauses are allowed where the amount involved is reasonable in the light of the circumstances of the case. The subsection sets forth explicitly the elements to be considered in determining the reasonableness of a liquidated damage clause. A term fixing unreasonably large liquidated damages is expressly made void as a penalty. An unreasonably small amount would be subject to similar criticism and might be stricken under the section on unconscionable contracts or clauses.

2. Subsection (2) refuses to recognize a forfeiture unless the amount of the payment so forfeited represents a reasonable liquidation of damages as determined under subsection (1). A special exception is made in the case of small amounts (20% of the price or $500, whichever is smaller) deposited as security. No distinction is made between cases in which the payment is to be applied on the price and those in which it is intended as security for performance. Subsection (2) is applicable to any deposit or down or part payment. In the case of a deposit or turn in of goods resold before the breach, the amount actually received on the resale is to be viewed as the deposit rather than the amount allowed the buyer for the trade in. However, if the seller knows of the breach

prior to the resale of the goods turned in, he must make reasonable efforts to realize their true value, and this is assured by requiring him to comply with the conditions laid down in the section on resale by an aggrieved seller. . . .

Definitional Cross References:
"Aggrieved party." Section 1-201.
"Agreement." Section 1-201.
"Buyer." Section 2-103.
"Goods." Section 2-105.
"Notice." Section 1-20[2].
"Party." Section 1-201.
"Remedy." Section 1-201.
"Seller." Section 2-103.
"Term." Section 1-201.

§2-719. Contractual Modification or Limitation of Remedy

(1) Subject to the provisions of subsections (2) and (3) of this section and of the preceding section on liquidation and limitation of damages,

(a) the agreement may provide for remedies in addition to or in substitution for those provided in this Article and may limit or alter the measure of damages recoverable under this Article, as by limiting the buyer's remedies to return of the goods and repayment of the price or to repair and replacement of non-conforming goods or parts; and

(b) resort to a remedy as provided is optional unless the remedy is expressly agreed to be exclusive, in which case it is the sole remedy.

(2) Where circumstances cause an exclusive or limited remedy to fail of its essential purpose, remedy may be had as provided in this Act.

(3) Consequential damages may be limited or excluded unless the limitation or exclusion is unconscionable. Limitation of consequential damages for injury to the person in the case of consumer goods is prima facie unconscionable but limitation of damages where the loss is commercial is not.

Official Comment

. . . .

1. Under this section parties are left free to shape their remedies to their particular requirements and reasonable agreements limiting or modifying remedies are to be given effect.

However, it is of the very essence of a sales contract that at least minimum adequate remedies be available. If the parties intend to conclude a contract for sale within this Article they must accept the legal consequence that there be at least a fair quantum of remedy for breach of the obligations or duties outlined in the contract. Thus any clause purporting to modify or limit the remedial provisions of this Article in an unconscionable manner is subject to deletion and in that event the remedies made available by this Article are applicable as if the stricken clause had never existed. Similarly, under subsection (2), where an apparently fair and reasonable clause because of circumstances fails in its purpose or operates to deprive either party of the substantial value of the bargain, it must give way to the general remedy provisions of this Article.

2. Subsection (1)(b) creates a presumption that clauses prescribing remedies are cumulative rather than exclusive. If the parties intend the term to describe the sole remedy under the contract, this must be clearly expressed.

3. Subsection (3) recognizes the validity of clauses limiting or excluding consequential damages but makes it clear that they may not operate in an unconscionable manner. . . .

Definitional Cross References:
"Agreement." Section 1-201.
"Buyer." Section 2-103.
"Conforming." Section 2-106.
"Contract." Section 1-201.
"Goods." Section 2-105.
"Remedy." Section 1-201.
"Seller." Section 2-103.

§2-721. Remedies for Fraud

Remedies for material misrepresentation or fraud include all remedies available under this Article for non-fraudulent breach. Neither rescission or a claim for rescission of the contract for sale nor rejection or return of the goods shall bar or be deemed inconsistent with a claim for damages or other remedy.

§2-723. Proof of Market Price; Time and Place

(1) If an action based on anticipatory repudiation comes to trial before the time for performance with respect to some or all of the goods, any damages based on market price (Section 2-708 or Section 2-713) shall be determined according to the price of such goods prevailing at the time when the aggrieved party learned of the repudiation.

(2) If evidence of a price prevailing at the times or places described in this Article is not readily available the price prevailing within any reasonable time before or after the time described or at any other place which in commercial judgment or under usage of trade would serve as a reasonable substitute for the one described may be used, making any proper allowance for the cost of transporting the goods to or from such other place.

(3) Evidence of a relevant price prevailing at a time or place other than the one described in this Article offered by one party is not admissible unless and until he has given the other party such notice as the court finds sufficient to prevent unfair surprise.

§2-725.   Statute of Limitations in Contracts for Sale

(1) An action for breach of any contract for sale must be commenced within four years after the cause of action has accrued. By the original agreement the parties may reduce the period of limitation to not less than one year but may not extend it.

(2) A cause of action accrues when the breach occurs, regardless of the aggrieved party's lack of knowledge of the breach. A breach of warranty occurs when tender of delivery is made, except that where a warranty explicitly extends to future performance of the goods and discovery of the breach must await the time of such performance the cause of action accrues when the breach is or should have been discovered.

(3) Where an action commenced within the time limited by subsection (1) is so terminated as to leave available a remedy by another action for the same breach such other action may be commenced after the expiration of the time limited and within six months after the termination of the first action unless the termination resulted from voluntary discontinuance or from dismissal for failure or neglect to prosecute.

(4) This section does not alter the law on tolling of the statute of limitations. . . .

Official Comment

. . . . To introduce a uniform statute of limitations for sales contracts, . . . [t]his Article takes sales contracts out of the general laws limiting the time for commencing contractual actions and selects a four year period as the most appropriate to modern business practice. This is within the normal commercial record keeping period.

Subsection (1) permits the parties to reduce the period of limitation. The minimum period is set at one year. The parties may not, however, extend the statutory period.

Subsection (2), providing that the cause of action accrues when the breach occurs, states an exception where the warranty extends to future performance.

Subsection (3) states the saving provision included in many state statutes and permits an additional short period for bringing new actions, where suits begun within the four year period have been terminated so as to leave a remedy still available for the same breach.

Subsection (4) makes it clear that this Article does not purport to alter or modify in any respect the law on tolling of the Statute of Limitations as it now prevails in the various jurisdictions.

Definitional Cross References:

"Action." Section 1-201.
"Aggrieved party." Section 1-201.
"Agreement." Section 1-201.
"Contract for sale." Section 2-106.
"Goods." Section 2-105.
"Party." Section 1-201.
"Remedy." Section 1-201.
"Term." Section 1-201.
"Termination." Section 2-106.

ARTICLE 2A.   LEASES

Part 1.   General Provisions

§2A-102.   Scope

This Article applies to any transaction, regardless of form, that creates a lease.

Official Comment

. . . . Since lease is defined as a transfer of an interest in goods (Section 2A-103(1)(j)) and goods is defined to include fixtures (Section 2A-103(1)(h)), application is limited to the extent the transaction relates to goods, including fixtures. Further, since the definition of lease does not include a sale (Section 2-106(1)) or retention or creation of a security interest (Section 1-201[(b)(35)]), application is further limited; sales and security interests are governed by other Articles of this Act.

Finally, in recognition of the diversity of the transactions to be governed, the sophistication of many of the parties to these transactions, and the common law tradition as it applies to the bailment for hire or lease, freedom of contract has been preserved. . . . Thus, despite the extensive regulatory scheme established by this Article, the parties to a lease will be able to create private rules to govern their transaction. Sections 2A-103(4) and 1-[302]. However, there are special rules in this Article governing consumer leases, as well as other state and federal statutes, that may further limit freedom of contract with respect to consumer leases.

A court may apply this Article by analogy to any transaction, regardless of form, that creates a lease of personal property other than goods, taking into account the expressed intentions of the parties to the transaction and any differences between a lease of goods and a lease of other property. . . .

Further, parties to a transaction creating a lease of personal property other than goods, or a bailment of personal property may provide by agreement that this Article applies. Upholding the parties' choice is consistent with the spirit of this Article. . . .

§2A-103.   Definitions and Index of Definitions

(1) In this Article unless the context otherwise requires: . . .

(e) "Consumer lease" means a lease that a lessor regularly engaged in the business of leasing or selling makes to a lessee who is an individual and who takes under the lease primarily for a personal, family, or household purpose [, if the total payments to be made under the lease contract, excluding payments for options to renew or buy, do not exceed $_____]. . . .

(g) "Finance lease" means a lease with respect to which:

(i) the lessor does not select, manufacture, or supply the goods;

(ii) the lessor acquires the goods or the right to possession and use of the goods in connection with the lease; and

(iii) one of the following occurs:

(A) the lessee receives a copy of the contract by which the lessor acquired the goods or the right to possession and use of the goods before signing the lease contract;

(B) the lessee's approval of the contract by which the lessor acquired the goods or the right to possession and use of the goods is a condition to effectiveness of the lease contract;

(C) the lessee, before signing the lease contract, receives an accurate and complete statement designating the promises and warranties, and any disclaimers of warranties, limitations or modifications of remedies, or liquidated damages, including those of a third party, such as the manufacturer of the goods, provided to the lessor by the person supplying the goods in connection with or as part of the contract by which the lessor acquired the goods or the right to possession and use of the goods; or

(D) if the lease is not a consumer lease, the lessor, before the lessee signs the lease contract, informs the lessee in writing (a) of the identity of the person supplying the goods to the lessor, unless the lessee has selected that person and directed the lessor to acquire the goods or the right to possession and use of the goods from that person, (b) that the lessee is entitled under this Article to the promises and warranties, including those of any third party, provided to the lessor by the person supplying the goods in connection with or as part of the contract by which the lessor acquired the goods or the right to possession and use of the goods, and (c) that the lessee may communicate with the person supplying the goods to the lessor and receive an accurate and complete statement of those promises and warranties, including any disclaimers and limitations of them or of remedies.

(h) "Goods" means all things that are movable at the time of identification to the lease contract, or are fixtures (Section 2A-309), but the term does not include money, documents, instruments, accounts, chattel paper, general intangibles, or minerals or the like, including oil and gas, before extraction. The term also includes the unborn young of animals. . . .

(j) "Lease" means a transfer of the right to possession and use of goods for a term in return for consideration, but a sale, including a sale on approval or a sale or return, or retention or creation of a security interest is not a lease. Unless the context clearly indicates otherwise, the term includes a sublease.

(k) "Lease agreement" means the bargain, with respect to the lease, of the lessor and the lessee in fact as found in their language or by implication from other circumstances including course of dealing or usage of trade or course of performance as provided in this Article. Unless the context clearly indicates otherwise, the term includes a sublease agreement.

(l) "Lease contract" means the total legal obligation that results from the lease agreement as affected by this Article and any other applicable rules of law. Unless the context clearly indicates otherwise, the term includes a sublease contract. . . .

(n) "Lessee" means a person who acquires the right to possession and use of goods under a lease. Unless the context clearly indicates otherwise, the term includes a sublessee. . . .

(p) "Lessor" means a person who transfers the right to possession and use of goods under a lease. Unless the context clearly indicates otherwise, the term includes a sublessor. . . .

(w) "Sublease" means a lease of goods the right to possession and use of which was acquired by the lessor as a lessee under an existing lease.

(x) "Supplier" means a person from whom a lessor buys or leases goods to be leased under a finance lease.

(y) "Supply contract" means a contract under which a lessor buys or leases goods to be leased.

(z) "Termination" occurs when either party pursuant to a power created by agreement or law puts an end to the lease contract otherwise than for default. . . .

(3) The following definitions in other Articles apply to this Article:

"Account." Section 9-102(a)(2). . . .

"Chattel paper." Section 9-102(a)(11).

"Consumer goods." Section 9-102(a)(23).

"Document." Section 9-102(a)(30).

"Entrusting." Section 2-403(3).

"General intangible." Section 9-102(a)(42).

"Instrument." Section 9-102(a)(47).

"Merchant." Section 2-104(1). . . .

"Receipt." Section 2-103(1)(c).

"Sale." Section 2-106(1).

"Sale on approval." Section 2-326.

"Sale or return." Section 2-326.

"Seller." Section 2-103(1)(d).

(4) In addition, Article 1 contains general definitions and principles of construction and interpretation applicable throughout this Article.

§2A-108. Unconscionability

(1) If the court as a matter of law finds a lease contract or any clause of a lease contract to have been unconscionable at the time it was made the court may refuse to enforce the lease contract, or it may enforce the remainder of the lease contract without the unconscionable clause, or it may so limit the application of any unconscionable clause as to avoid any unconscionable result.

(2) With respect to a consumer lease, if the court as a matter of law finds that a lease contract or any clause of a lease contract has been induced by unconscionable conduct or that unconscionable conduct has occurred in the collection of a claim arising from a lease contract, the court may grant appropriate relief.

(3) Before making a finding of unconscionability under subsection (1) or (2), the court, on its own motion or that of a party, shall afford the parties a reasonable opportunity to present evidence as to the setting, purpose, and effect of the lease contract or clause thereof, or of the conduct.

(4) In an action in which the lessee claims unconscionability with respect to a consumer lease:

(a) If the court finds unconscionability under subsection (1) or (2), the court shall award reasonable attorney's fees to the lessee.

(b) If the court does not find unconscionability and the lessee claiming unconscionability has brought or maintained an action he [or she] knew to be groundless, the court shall award reasonable attorney's fees to the party against whom the claim is made.

(c) In determining attorney's fees, the amount of the recovery on behalf of the claimant under subsections (1) and (2) is not controlling.

§2A-109.   Option to Accelerate at Will

(1) A term providing that one party or his [or her] successor in interest may accelerate payment or performance or require collateral or additional collateral "at will" or "when he [or she] deems himself [or herself] insecure" or in words of similar import must be construed to mean that he [or she] has power to do so only if he [or she] in good faith believes that the prospect of payment or performance is impaired.

(2) With respect to a consumer lease, the burden of establishing good faith under subsection (1) is on the party who exercised the power; otherwise the burden of establishing lack of good faith is on the party against whom the power has been exercised.

Part 2.   Formation and Construction of Lease Contract

§2A-201.   Statute of Frauds

(1) A lease contract is not enforceable by way of action or defense unless:

(a) the total payments to be made under the lease contract, excluding payments for options to renew or buy, are less than $1,000; or

(b) there is a writing, signed by the party against whom enforcement is sought or by that party's authorized agent, sufficient to indicate that a lease contract has been made between the parties and to describe the goods leased and the lease term.

(2) Any description of leased goods or of the lease term is sufficient and satisfies subsection (1)(b), whether or not it is specific, if it reasonably identifies what is described.

(3) A writing is not insufficient because it omits or incorrectly states a term agreed upon, but the lease contract is not enforceable under subsection (1)(b) beyond the lease term and the quantity of goods shown in the writing.

(4) A lease contract that does not satisfy the requirements of subsection (1), but which is valid in other respects, is enforceable:

(a) if the goods are to be specially manufactured or obtained for the lessee and are not suitable for lease or sale to others in the ordinary course of the lessor's business, and the lessor, before notice of repudiation is received and under circumstances that reasonably indicate that the goods are for the lessee, has made either a substantial beginning of their manufacture or commitments for their procurement;

(b) if the party against whom enforcement is sought admits in that party's pleading, testimony or otherwise in court that a lease contract was made, but the lease contract is not enforceable under this provision beyond the quantity of goods admitted; or

(c) with respect to goods that have been received and accepted by the lessee.

(5) The lease term under a lease contract referred to in subsection (4) is:

(a) if there is a writing signed by the party against whom enforcement is sought or by that party's authorized agent specifying the lease term, the term so specified;

(b) if the party against whom enforcement is sought admits in that party's pleading, testimony, or otherwise in court a lease term, the term so admitted; or

(c) a reasonable lease term.

§2A-209. Lessee Under Finance Lease as Beneficiary of Supply Contract

(1) The benefit of a supplier's promises to the lessor under the supply contract and of all warranties, whether express or implied, including those of any third party provided in connection with or as part of the supply contract, extends to the lessee to the extent of the lessee's leasehold interest under a finance lease related to the supply contract, but is subject to the terms of the warranty and of the supply contract and all defenses or claims arising therefrom.

(2) The extension of the benefit of a supplier's promises and of warranties to the lessee [] does not: (i) modify the rights and obligations of the parties to the supply contract, whether arising therefrom or otherwise, or(ii) impose any duty or liability under the supply contract on the lessee.

(3) Any modification or rescission of the supply contract by the supplier and the lessor is effective between the supplier and the lessee unless, before the modification or rescission, the supplier has received notice that the lessee has entered into a finance lease related to the supply contract. If the modification or rescission is effective between the supplier and the lessee, the lessor is deemed to have assumed, in addition to the obligations of the lessor to the lessee under the lease contract, promises of the supplier to the lessor and warranties that were so modified or rescinded as they existed and were available to the lessee before modification or rescission.

(4) In addition to the extension of the benefit of the supplier's promises and of warranties to the lessee under subsection (1), the lessee retains all rights that the lessee may have against the supplier which arise from an agreement between the lessee and the supplier or under other law.

§2A-211. Warranties Against Interference and Against Infringement; Lessee's Obligation Against Infringement

(1) There is in a lease contract a warranty that for the lease term no person holds a claim to or interest in the goods that arose from an act or omission of the lessor, other than a claim by way of infringement or the like, which will interfere with the lessee's enjoyment of its leasehold interest.

(2) Except in a finance lease there is in a lease contract by a lessor who is a merchant regularly dealing in goods of the kind a warranty that the goods are delivered free of the rightful claim of any person by way of infringement or the like.

(3) A lessee who furnishes specifications to a lessor or a supplier shall hold the lessor and the supplier harmless against any claim by way of infringement or the like that arises out of compliance with the specifications.

§2A-219. Risk of Loss

(1) Except in the case of a finance lease, risk of loss is retained by the lessor and does not pass to the lessee. In the case of a finance lease, risk of loss passes to the lessee.

(2) Subject to the provisions of this Article on the effect of default on risk of loss (Section 2A-220), if risk of loss is to pass to the lessee and the time of passage is not stated, the following rules apply:

(a) If the lease contract requires or authorizes the goods to be shipped by carrier

(i) and it does not require delivery at a particular destination, the risk of loss passes to the lessee when the goods are duly delivered to the carrier; but

(ii) if it does require delivery at a particular destination and the goods are there duly tendered while in the possession of the carrier, the risk of loss passes to the lessee when the goods are there duly so tendered as to enable the lessee to take delivery.

(b) If the goods are held by a bailee to be delivered without being moved, the risk of loss passes to the lessee on acknowledgment by the bailee of the lessee's right to possession of the goods.

(c) In any case not within subsection (a) or (b), the risk of loss passes to the lessee on the lessee's receipt of the goods if the lessor, or, in the case of a finance lease, the supplier, is a merchant; otherwise the risk passes to the lessee on tender of delivery.

§2A-220. Effect of Default on Risk of Loss

(1) Where risk of loss is to pass to the lessee and the time of passage is not stated:

(a) If a tender or delivery of goods so fails to conform to the lease contract as to give a right of rejection, the risk of their loss remains with the lessor, or, in the case of a finance lease, the supplier, until cure or acceptance.

(b) If the lessee rightfully revokes acceptance, he [or she], to the extent of any deficiency in his [or her] effective insurance coverage, may treat the risk of loss as having remained with the lessor from the beginning.

(2) Whether or not risk of loss is to pass to the lessee, if the lessee as to conforming goods already identified to a lease contract repudiates or is otherwise in default under the lease contract, the lessor, or, in the case of a finance lease, the supplier, to the extent of any deficiency in his [or her] effective insurance coverage may treat the risk of loss as resting on the lessee for a commercially reasonable time.

Part 3.   Effect of Lease Contract

§2A-302.   Title to and Possession of Goods

Except as otherwise provided in this Article, each provision of this Article applies whether the lessor or a third party has title to the goods, and whether the lessor, the lessee, or a third party has possession of the goods, notwithstanding any statute or rule of law that possession or the absence of possession is fraudulent.

Part 4.   Performance of Lease Contract

§2A-407.   Irrevocable Promises: Finance Leases

(1) In the case of a finance lease that is not a consumer lease the lessee's promises under the lease contract become irrevocable and independent upon the lessee's acceptance of the goods.

(2) A promise that has become irrevocable and independent under subsection (1):

(a) is effective and enforceable between the parties, and by or against third parties including assignees of the parties; and

(b) is not subject to cancellation, termination, modification, repudiation, excuse, or substitution without the consent of the party to whom the promise runs.

(3) This section does not affect the validity under any other law of a covenant in any lease contract making the lessee's promises irrevocable and independent upon the lessee's acceptance of the goods.

Official Comment

. . . .

1. . . . . . This section is self-executing; no special provision need be added to the contract. This section makes covenants in a finance lease irrevocable and

independent due to the function of the finance lessor in a three party relationship: the lessee is looking to the supplier to perform the essential covenants and warranties. Section 2A-209. Thus, upon the lessee's acceptance of the goods the lessee's promises to the lessor under the lease contract become irrevocable and independent. The provisions of this section remain subject to the obligation of good faith (Sections 2A-103(4) and 1-[304]), and the lessee's revocation of acceptance (Section 2A-517).

2. The section requires the lessee to perform even if the lessor's performance after the lessee's acceptance is not in accordance with the lease contract; the lessee may, however, have and pursue a cause of action against the lessor, *e.g.*, breach of certain limited warranties (Sections 2A-210 and 2A-211(1)). This is appropriate because the benefit of the supplier's promises and warranties to the lessor under the supply contract and, in some cases, the warranty of a manufacturer who is not the supplier, is extended to the lessee under the finance lease. Section 2A-209. Despite this balance, this section excludes a finance lease that is a consumer lease. That a consumer be obligated to pay notwithstanding defective goods or the like is a principle that is not tenable under case law (Unico v. Owen, 50 N.J. 101, 232 A.2d 405 (1967)), state statute (Unif. Consumer Credit Code §§3.403-.405, 7A U.L.A. 126-31 (1974)), or federal statute (15 U.S.C. §1666i (1982)). . . .

6. This section does not address whether a "hell or high water" clause, *i.e.*, a clause that is to the effect of this section, is enforceable if [expressly] included in a finance lease that is a consumer lease or a lease that is not a finance lease. That issue will continue to be determined by the facts of each case and other law which this section does not affect. Sections 2A-104, 2A-103(4), 9-403 and 9-404. However, with respect to finance leases that are not consumer leases courts have enforced "hell or high water" clauses. *In re O.P.M. Leasing Servs.*, 21 Bankr. 993, 1006 (Bankr. S.D.N.Y. 1982).

7. Subsection (2) further provides that a promise that has become irrevocable and independent under subsection (1) is enforceable not only between the parties but also against third parties. Thus, the finance lease can be transferred or assigned without disturbing enforceability. Further, subsection (2) also provides that the promise cannot, among other things, be cancelled or terminated without the consent of the lessor. . . .

Definitional Cross References:
"Cancellation." Section 2A-103(1)(b).
"Consumer lease." Section 2A-103(1)(e).
"Finance lease." Section 2A-103(1)(g).
"Goods." Section 2A-103(1)(h).
"Lease contract." Section 2A-103(1)(l).
"Lessee." Section 2A-103(1)(n).
"Party." Section 1-201[(b)(26)].
"Termination." Section 2A-103(1)(z).

ARTICLE 3.   NEGOTIABLE INSTRUMENTS

Part 1.   General Provisions and Definitions

§3-104.   Negotiable Instrument

(a) Except as provided in subsections (c) and (d), "negotiable instrument" means an unconditional promise or order to pay a fixed amount of money, with or without interest or other charges described in the promise or order, if it:

   (1) is payable to bearer or to order at the time it is issued or first comes into possession of a holder;

   (2) is payable on demand or at a definite time; and

   (3) does not state any other undertaking or instruction by the person promising or ordering payment to do any act in addition to the payment of money, but the promise or order may contain (i) an undertaking or power to give, maintain, or protect collateral to secure payment, (ii) an authorization or power to the holder to confess judgment or realize on or dispose of collateral, or (iii) a waiver of the benefit of any law intended for the advantage or protection of an obligor.

(b) "Instrument" means a negotiable instrument.

(c) An order that meets all of the requirements of subsection (a), except paragraph (1), and otherwise falls within the definition of "check" in subsection (f) is a negotiable instrument and a check.

(d) A promise or order other than a check is not an instrument if, at the time it is issued or first comes into possession of a holder, it contains a conspicuous statement, however expressed, to the effect that the promise or order is not negotiable or is not an instrument governed by this Article.

(e) An instrument is a "note" if it is a promise and is a "draft" if it is an order. If an instrument falls within the definition of both "note" and "draft," a person entitled to enforce the instrument may treat it as either.

(f) "Check" means (i) a draft, other than a documentary draft, payable on demand and drawn on a bank or (ii) a cashier's check or teller's check. An instrument may be a check even though it is described on its face by another term, such as "money order."

(g) "Cashier's check" means a draft with respect to which the drawer and drawee are the same bank or branches of the same bank.

(h) "Teller's check" means a draft drawn by a bank (i) on another bank, or (ii) payable at or through a bank.

(i) "Traveler's check" means an instrument that (i) is payable on demand, (ii) is drawn on or payable at or through a bank, (iii) is designated by the term "traveler's check" or by a substantially similar term, and (iv) requires, as a condition to payment, a countersignature by a person whose specimen signature appears on the instrument.

(j) "Certificate of deposit" means an instrument containing an acknowledgment by a bank that a sum of money has been received by the bank and a promise by the bank to repay the sum of money. A certificate of deposit is a note of the bank.

Part 3. Enforcement of Instruments

§3-302. Holder in Due Course

(a) Subject to subsection (c) and Section 3-106(d), "holder in due course" means the holder of an instrument if:

(1) the instrument when issued or negotiated to the holder does not bear such apparent evidence of forgery or alteration or is not otherwise so irregular or incomplete as to call into question its authenticity; and

(2) the holder took the instrument

(i) for value,

(ii) in good faith,

(iii) without notice that the instrument is overdue or has been dishonored or that there is an uncured default with respect to payment of another instrument issued as part of the same series,

(iv) without notice that the instrument contains an unauthorized signature or has been altered,

(v) without notice of any claim to the instrument described in Section 3-306, and

(vi) without notice that any party has a defense or claim in recoupment described in Section 3-305(a).

(b) Notice of discharge of a party, other than discharge in an insolvency proceeding, is not notice of a defense under subsection (a), but discharge is effective against a person who became a holder in due course with notice of the discharge. Public filing or recording of a document does not of itself constitute notice of a defense, claim in recoupment, or claim to the instrument.

(c) Except to the extent a transferor or predecessor in interest has rights as a holder in due course, a person does not acquire rights of a holder in due course of an instrument taken

(i) by legal process or by purchase in an execution, bankruptcy, or creditor's sale or similar proceeding,

(ii) by purchase as part of a bulk transaction not in ordinary course of business of the transferor, or

(iii) as the successor in interest to an estate or other organization.

(d) If, under Section 3-303(a)(1), the promise of performance that is the consideration for an instrument has been partially performed, the holder may assert rights as a holder in due course of the instrument only to the fraction of the amount payable under the instrument equal to the value of the partial performance divided by the value of the promised performance.

(e) If (i) the person entitled to enforce an instrument has only a security interest in the instrument and (ii) the person obliged to pay the instrument has a defense, claim in recoupment, or claim to the instrument that may be asserted against the person who granted the security interest, the person entitled to enforce the instrument may assert rights as a holder in due course only to an amount payable under the instrument which, at the time of enforcement of the instrument, does not exceed the amount of the unpaid obligation secured.

(f) To be effective, notice must be received at a time and in a manner that gives a reasonable opportunity to act on it.

(g) This section is subject to any law limiting status as a holder in due course in particular classes of transactions.

§3-303. Value and Consideration

(a) An instrument is issued or transferred for value if:

(1) the instrument is issued or transferred for a promise of performance, to the extent the promise has been performed;

(2) the transferee acquires a security interest or other lien in the instrument other than a lien obtained by judicial proceeding;

(3) the instrument is issued or transferred as payment of, or as security for, an antecedent claim against any person, whether or not the claim is due;

(4) the instrument is issued or transferred in exchange for a negotiable instrument; or

(5) the instrument is issued or transferred in exchange for the incurring of an irrevocable obligation to a third party by the person taking the instrument.

(b) "Consideration" means any consideration sufficient to support a simple contract. The drawer or maker of an instrument has a defense if the instrument is issued without consideration. If an instrument is issued for a promise of performance, the issuer has a defense to the extent performance of the promise is due and the promise has not been performed. If an instrument is issued for value as stated in subsection (a), the instrument is also issued for consideration.

§3-305. Defenses and Claims in Recoupment; Claims in Consumer Transactions

(a) Except as otherwise provided in this section, the right to enforce the obligation of a party to pay an instrument is subject to the following:

(1) a defense of the obligor based on (i) infancy of the obligor to the extent it is a defense to a simple contract, (ii) duress, lack of legal capacity, or illegality of the transaction which, under other law, nullifies the obligation of the obligor, (iii) fraud that induced the obligor to sign the instrument with neither knowledge nor reasonable opportunity to learn of its character or its essential terms, or (iv) discharge of the obligor in insolvency proceedings;

(2) a defense of the obligor stated in another section of this Article or a defense of the obligor that would be available if the person entitled to enforce the instrument were enforcing a right to payment under a simple contract; and

(3) a claim in recoupment of the obligor against the original payee of the instrument if the claim arose from the transaction that gave rise to the instrument; but the claim of the obligor may be asserted against a transferee of the instrument only to reduce the amount owing on the instrument at the time the action is brought.

(b) The right of a holder in due course to enforce the obligation of a party to pay the instrument is subject to defenses of the obligor stated in subsection (a)(1), but is not subject to defenses of the obligor stated in subsection (a)(2) or claims in recoupment stated in subsection (a)(3) against a person other than the holder.

(c) Except as stated in subsection (d), in an action to enforce the obligation of a party to pay the instrument, the obligor may not assert against the person entitled to enforce the instrument a defense, claim in recoupment, or claim to the instrument (Section 3-306) of another person, but the other person's claim to the instrument may be asserted by the obligor if the other person is joined in the action and personally asserts the claim against the person entitled to enforce the instrument. An obligor is not obliged to pay the instrument if the person seeking enforcement of the instrument does not have rights of a holder in due course and the obligor proves that the instrument is a lost or stolen instrument.

(d) In an action to enforce the obligation of an accommodation party to pay an instrument, the accommodation party may assert against the person entitled to enforce the instrument any defense or claim in recoupment under subsection (a) that the accommodated party could assert against the person entitled to enforce the instrument, except the defenses of discharge in insolvency proceedings, infancy, and lack of legal capacity.

(e) In a consumer transaction, if law other than this article requires that an instrument include a statement to the effect that the rights of a holder or transferee are subject to a claim or defense that the issuer could assert against the original payee, and the instrument does not include such a statement:

(1) the instrument has the same effect as if the instrument included such a statement;

(2) the issuer may assert against the holder or transferee all claims and defenses that would have been available if the instrument included such a statement; and

(3) the extent to which claims may be asserted against the holder or transferee is determined as if the instrument included such a statement.

(f) This section is subject to law other than this article that establishes a different rule for consumer transactions.

§3-306. Claims to an Instrument

A person taking an instrument, other than a person having rights of a holder in due course, is subject to a claim of a property or possessory right in the instrument or its proceeds, including a claim to rescind a negotiation and to recover the instrument or its proceeds. A person having rights of a holder in due course takes free of the claim to the instrument.

§3-311. Accord and Satisfaction by Use of Instrument

(a) If a person against whom a claim is asserted proves that (i) that person in good faith tendered an instrument to the claimant as full satisfaction of the claim, (ii) the amount of the claim was unliquidated or subject to a bona fide dispute, and (iii) the claimant obtained payment of the instrument, the following subsections apply.

(b) Unless subsection (c) applies, the claim is discharged if the person against whom the claim is asserted proves that the instrument or an accompanying written communication contained a conspicuous statement to the effect that the instrument was tendered as full satisfaction of the claim.

(c) Subject to subsection (d), a claim is not discharged under subsection (b) if either of the following applies:

(1) The claimant, if an organization, proves that

(i) within a reasonable time before the tender, the claimant sent a conspicuous statement to the person against whom the claim is asserted that communications concerning disputed debts, including an instrument tendered as full satisfaction of a debt, are to be sent to a designated person, office, or place, and

(ii) the instrument or accompanying communication was not received by that designated person, office, or place.

(2) The claimant, whether or not an organization, proves that within 90 days after payment of the instrument, the claimant tendered repayment of the amount of the instrument to the person against whom the claim is asserted.

This paragraph does not apply if the claimant is an organization that sent a statement complying with paragraph (1)(i).

(d) A claim is discharged if the person against whom the claim is asserted proves that within a reasonable time before collection of the instrument was initiated, the claimant, or an agent of the claimant having direct responsibility with respect to the disputed obligation, knew that the instrument was tendered in full satisfaction of the claim.

ARTICLE 9.   SECURED TRANSACTIONS

Part 1.   General Provisions

§9-102.   Definitions and Index of Definitions

(a) [**Article 9 definitions.**] In this article:
. . . .

(2) "Account", except as used in "account for", means a right to payment of a monetary obligation, whether or not earned by performance, (i) for property that has been or is to be sold, leased, licensed, assigned, or otherwise disposed of, (ii) for services rendered or to be rendered, (iii) for a policy of insurance issued or to be issued, (iv) for a secondary obligation incurred or to be incurred, (v) for energy provided or to be provided, (vi) for the use or hire of a vessel under a charter or other contract, (vii) arising out of the use of a credit or charge card or information contained on or for use with the card, or (viii) as winnings in a lottery or other game of chance operated or sponsored by a State, governmental unit of a State, or person licensed or authorized to operate the game by a State or governmental unit of a State. The term includes health-care-insurance receivables. The term does not include (i) rights to payment evidenced by chattel paper or an instrument, (ii) commercial tort claims, (iii) deposit accounts, (iv) investment property, (v) letter-of-credit rights or letters of credit, or (vi) rights to payment for money or funds advanced or sold, other

than rights arising out of the use of a credit or charge card or information contained on or for use with the card.

(3) "Account debtor" means a person obligated on an account, chattel paper, or general intangible. The term does not include persons obligated to pay a negotiable instrument, even if the instrument constitutes part of chattel paper. . . .

(7) "Authenticate" means:

(A) to sign; or

(B) with present intent to adopt or accept a record, to attach to or logically associate with the record an electronic sound, symbol, or process.

(8) "Bank" means an organization that is engaged in the business of banking. The term includes savings banks, savings and loan associations, credit unions, and trust companies. . . .

(11) "Chattel paper" means a record or records that evidence both a monetary obligation and a security interest in specific goods, a security interest in specific goods and software used in the goods, a security interest in specific goods and license of software used in the goods, a lease of specific goods, or a lease of specific goods and license of software used in the goods. In this paragraph, "monetary obligation" means a monetary obligation secured by the goods or owed under a lease of the goods and includes a monetary obligation with respect to software used in the goods. The term does not include (i) charters or other contracts involving the use or hire of a vessel or (ii) records that evidence a right to payment arising out of the use of a credit or charge card or information contained on or for use with the card. If a transaction is evidenced by records that include an instrument or series of instruments, the group of records taken together constitutes chattel paper.

(12) "Collateral" means the property subject to a security interest or agricultural lien. The term includes:

(A) proceeds to which a security interest attaches;

(B) accounts, chattel paper, payment intangibles, and promissory notes that have been sold; and

(C) goods that are the subject of a consignment.

(13) "Commercial tort claim" means a claim arising in tort with respect to which:

(A) the claimant is an organization; or

(B) the claimant is an individual and the claim:

(i) arose in the course of the claimant's business or profession; and

(ii) does not include damages arising out of personal injury to or the death of an individual.

(14) "Commodity account" means an account maintained by a commodity intermediary in which a commodity contract is carried for a commodity customer.

(15) "Commodity contract" means a commodity futures contract, an option on a commodity futures contract, a commodity option, or another contract if the contract or option is:

(A) traded on or subject to the rules of a board of trade that has been designated as a contract market for such a contract pursuant to federal commodities laws; or

(B) traded on a foreign commodity board of trade, exchange, or market, and is carried on the books of a commodity intermediary for a commodity customer.

(16) "Commodity customer" means a person for which a commodity intermediary carries a commodity contract on its books.

(17) "Commodity intermediary" means a person that:

(A) is registered as a futures commission merchant under federal commodities law; or

(B) in the ordinary course of its business provides clearance or settlement services for a board of trade that has been designated as a contract market pursuant to federal commodities law. . . .

(19) "Consignee" means a merchant to which goods are delivered in a consignment.

(20) "Consignment" means a transaction, regardless of its form, in which a person delivers goods to a merchant for the purpose of sale and:

(A) the merchant:

(i) deals in goods of that kind under a name other than the name of the person making delivery;

(ii) is not an auctioneer; and

(iii) is not generally known by its creditors to be substantially engaged in selling the goods of others;

(B) with respect to each delivery, the aggregate value of the goods is $1,000 or more at the time of delivery;

(C) the goods are not consumer goods immediately before delivery; and

(D) the transaction does not create a security interest that secures an obligation.

(21) "Consignor" means a person that delivers goods to a consignee in a consignment. . . .

(23) "Consumer goods" means goods that are used or bought for use primarily for personal, family, or household purposes. . . .

(26) "Consumer transaction" means a transaction in which (i) an individual incurs an obligation primarily for personal, family, or household purposes, (ii) a security interest secures the obligation, and (iii) the collateral is held or acquired primarily for personal, family, or household purposes. . . .

(28) "Debtor" means:

(A) a person having an interest, other than a security interest or other lien, in the collateral, whether or not the person is an obligor;

(B) a seller of accounts, chattel paper, payment intangibles, or promissory notes; or

(C) a consignee.

(29) "Deposit account" means a demand, time, savings, passbook, or similar account maintained with a bank. The term does not include investment property or accounts evidenced by an instrument.

(30) "Document" means a document of title or a receipt of the type described in Section 7-201(2).

(31) "Electronic chattel paper" means chattel paper evidenced by a record or records consisting of information stored in an electronic medium. . . .

(33) "Equipment" means goods other than inventory, farm products, or consumer goods.

(34) "Farm products" means goods, other than standing timber, with respect to which the debtor is engaged in a farming operation and which are:

(A) crops grown, growing, or to be grown, including:

(i) crops produced on trees, vines, and bushes; and

(ii) aquatic goods produced in aquacultural operations;

(B) livestock, born or unborn, including aquatic goods produced in aquacultural operations;

(C) supplies used or produced in a farming operation; or

(D) products of crops or livestock in their unmanufactured states.

(35) "Farming operation" means raising, cultivating, propagating, fattening, grazing, or any other farming, livestock, or aquacultural operation. . . .

(41) "Fixtures" means goods that have become so related to particular real property that an interest in them arises under real property law.

(42) "General intangible" means any personal property, including things in action, other than accounts, chattel paper, commercial tort claims, deposit accounts, documents, goods, instruments, investment property, letter-of-credit rights, letters of credit, money, and oil, gas, or other minerals before extraction. The term includes payment intangibles and software. . . .

(44) "Goods" means all things that are movable when a security interest attaches. The term includes (i) fixtures, (ii) standing timber that is to be cut and removed under a conveyance or contract for sale, (iii) the unborn young of animals, (iv) crops grown, growing, or to be grown, even if the crops are produced on trees, vines, or bushes, and (v) manufactured homes. The term also includes a computer program embedded in goods and any supporting information provided in connection with a transaction relating to the program if (i) the program is associated with the goods in such a manner that it customarily is considered part of the goods, or (ii) by becoming the owner of the goods, a person acquires a right to use the program in connection with the goods. The term does not include a computer program embedded in goods that consist solely of the medium in which the program is embedded. The term also does not include accounts, chattel paper, commercial tort claims, deposit accounts, documents, general intangibles, instruments, investment property, letter-of-credit rights, letters of credit, money, or oil, gas, or other minerals before extraction. . . .

(46) "Health-care-insurance receivable" means an interest in or claim under a policy of insurance which is a right to payment of a monetary obligation for health-care goods or services provided or to be provided.

(47) "Instrument" means a negotiable instrument or any other writing that evidences a right to the payment of a monetary obligation, is not itself a security agreement or lease, and is of a type that in ordinary course of business is transferred by delivery with any necessary indorsement or assignment. The term does not include (i) investment property, (ii) letters of credit, or (iii) writings that evidence a right to payment arising out of the use of a credit or charge card or information contained on or for use with the card.

(48) "Inventory" means goods, other than farm products, which:

(A) are leased by a person as lessor;

(B) are held by a person for sale or lease or to be furnished under a contract of service;

(C) are furnished by a person under a contract of service; or

(D) consist of raw materials, work in process, or materials used or consumed in a business.

(49) "Investment property" means a security, whether certificated or
uncertificated, security entitlement, securities account, commodity contract, or
commodity account. . . .

(51) "Letter-of-credit right" means a right to payment or performance under
a letter of credit, whether or not the beneficiary has demanded or is at the time
entitled to demand payment or performance. The term does not include the
right of a beneficiary to demand payment or performance under a letter of
credit. . . .

(53) "Manufactured home" means a structure, transportable in one or more
sections, which, in the traveling mode, is eight body feet or more in width or 40
body feet or more in length, or, when erected on site, is 320 or more square
feet, and which is built on a permanent chassis and designed to be used as a
dwelling with or without a permanent foundation when connected to the required utilities, and includes the plumbing, heating, air-conditioning, and
electrical systems contained therein. The term includes any structure that meets
all of the requirements of this paragraph except the size requirements and with
respect to which the manufacturer voluntarily files a certification required by
the United States Secretary of Housing and Urban Development and complies
with the standards established under Title 42 of the United States Code. . . .

(59) "Obligor" means a person that, with respect to an obligation secured by
a security interest in or an agricultural lien on the collateral, (i) owes payment
or other performance of the obligation, (ii) has provided property other than
the collateral to secure payment or other performance of the obligation, or (iii)
is otherwise accountable in whole or in part for payment or other performance
of the obligation. The term does not include issuers or nominated persons
under a letter of credit. . . .

(61) "Payment intangible" means a general intangible under which the account debtor's principal obligation is a monetary obligation. . . .

(64) "Proceeds", except as used in Section 9-609(b), means the following
property:

(A) whatever is acquired upon the sale, lease, license, exchange, or other
disposition of collateral;

(B) whatever is collected on, or distributed on account of, collateral;

(C) rights arising out of collateral;

(D) to the extent of the value of collateral, claims arising out of the loss,
nonconformity, or interference with the use of, defects or infringement of
rights in, or damage to, the collateral; or

(E) to the extent of the value of collateral and to the extent payable to the
debtor or the secured party, insurance payable by reason of the loss or
nonconformity of, defects or infringement of rights in, or damage to, the
collateral.

(65) "Promissory note" means an instrument that evidences a promise to pay
a monetary obligation, does not evidence an order to pay, and does not contain
an acknowledgment by a bank that the bank has received for deposit a sum of
money or funds. . . .

(70) "Record", except as used in "for record", "of record", "record or legal
title", and "record owner", means information that is inscribed on a tangible

medium or which is stored in an electronic or other medium and is retrievable in perceivable form. . . .

(73) "Secured party" means:

(A) a person in whose favor a security interest is created or provided for under a security agreement, whether or not any obligation to be secured is outstanding;

(B) a person that holds an agricultural lien;

(C) a consignor;

(D) a person to which accounts, chattel paper, payment intangibles, or promissory notes have been sold;

(E) a trustee, indenture trustee, agent, collateral agent, or other representative in whose favor a security interest or agricultural lien is created or provided for; or

(F) a person that holds a security interest arising under Section 2-401, 2-505, 2-711(3), 2A-508(5), 4-210, or 5-118.

(74) "Security agreement" means an agreement that creates or provides for a security interest. . . .

(76) "Software" means a computer program and any supporting information provided in connection with a transaction relating to the program. The term does not include a computer program that is included in the definition of goods. . . .

(79) "Tangible chattel paper" means chattel paper evidenced by a record or records consisting of information that is inscribed on a tangible medium. . . .

(b) **[Definitions in other articles.]** The following definitions in other articles apply to this article: . . .

"Beneficiary" Section 5-102. . . .

"Contract for sale" Section 2-106. . . .

"Holder in due course" Section 3-302. . . .

"Issuer" (with respect to a letter of credit or letter-of-credit right) Section 5-102. . . .

"Lease" Section 2A-103. . . .

"Letter of credit" Section 5-102.

"Merchant" Section 2-104.

"Negotiable instrument" Section 3-104.

"Nominated person" Section 5-102.

"Note" Section 3-104. . . .

"Sale" Section 2-106.

"Securities account" Section 8-501.

"Securities intermediary" Section 8-102.

"Security" Section 8-102. . . .

"Security entitlement" Section 8-102. . . .

(c) **[Article 1 definitions and principles.]** Article 1 contains general definitions and principles of construction and interpretation applicable throughout this article.

§9-109. Scope

(a) **[General scope of article.]** Except as otherwise provided in subsections (c) and (d), this article applies to:

(1) a transaction, regardless of its form, that creates a security interest in personal property or fixtures by contract;

(2) an agricultural lien;

(3) a sale of accounts, chattel paper, payment intangibles, or promissory notes;

(4) a consignment;

(5) a security interest arising under Sections 2-401, 2-505, 2-711(3), or 2A-508(5), as provided in Section 9-110; and

(6) a security interest arising under Sections 4-210 or 5-118.

(b) **[Security interest in secured obligation.]** The application of this article to a security interest in a secured obligation is not affected by the fact that the obligation is itself secured by a transaction or interest to which this article does not apply.

(c) **[Extent to which article does not apply.]** This article does not apply to the extent that:

(1) a statute, regulation, or treaty of the United States preempts this article;

(2) another statute of this State expressly governs the creation, perfection, priority, or enforcement of a security interest created by this State or a governmental unit of this State;

(3) a statute of another State, a foreign country, or a governmental unit of another State or a foreign country, other than a statute generally applicable to security interests, expressly governs creation, perfection, priority, or enforcement of a security interest created by the State, country, or governmental unit; or

(4) the rights of a transferee beneficiary or nominated person under a letter of credit are independent and superior under Section 5-114.

(d) **[Inapplicability of article.]** This article does not apply to:

(1) a landlord's lien, other than an agricultural lien;

(2) a lien, other than an agricultural lien, given by statute or other rule of law for services or materials, but Section 9-333 applies with respect to priority of the lien;

(3) an assignment of a claim for wages, salary, or other compensation of an employee;

(4) a sale of accounts, chattel paper, payment intangibles, or promissory notes as part of a sale of the business out of which they arose;

(5) an assignment of accounts, chattel paper, payment intangibles, or promissory notes which is for the purpose of collection only;

(6) an assignment of a right to payment under a contract to an assignee that is also obligated to perform under the contract;

(7) an assignment of a single account, payment intangible, or promissory note to an assignee in full or partial satisfaction of a preexisting indebtedness;

(8) a transfer of an interest in or an assignment of a claim under a policy of insurance, other than an assignment by or to a health-care provider of a health-care-insurance receivable and any subsequent assignment of the right to payment, but Sections 9-315 and 9-322 apply with respect to proceeds and priorities in proceeds;

(9) an assignment of a right represented by a judgment, other than a judgment taken on a right to payment that was collateral;

(10) a right of recoupment or set-off, but:

(A) Section 9-340 applies with respect to the effectiveness of rights of recoupment or set-off against deposit accounts; and

(B) Section 9-404 applies with respect to defenses or claims of an account debtor;

(11) the creation or transfer of an interest in or lien on real property, including a lease or rents thereunder, except to the extent that provision is made for:

(A) liens on real property in Sections 9-203 and 9-308;

(B) fixtures in Section 9-334;

(C) fixture filings in Sections 9-501, 9-502, 9-512, 9-516, and 9-519; and

(D) security agreements covering personal and real property in Section 9-604;

(12) an assignment of a claim arising in tort, other than a commercial tort claim, but Sections 9-315 and 9-322 apply with respect to proceeds and priorities in proceeds; or

(13) an assignment of a deposit account in a consumer transaction, but Sections 9-315 and 9-322 apply with respect to proceeds and priorities in proceeds.

§9-110. Security Interests Arising Under Article 2 or 2A

A security interest arising under Section 2-401, 2-505, 2-711(3), or 2A-508(5) is subject to this article. However, until the debtor obtains possession of the goods:

(1) the security interest is enforceable, even if Section 9-203(b)(3) has not been satisfied;

(2) filing is not required to perfect the security interest;

(3) the rights of the secured party after default by the debtor are governed by Article 2 or 2A; and

(4) the security interest has priority over a conflicting security interest created by the debtor.

Part 4. Rights of Third Parties

§9-403. Agreement Not to Assert Defenses Against Assignee

(a) ["**Value.**"] In this section, "value" has the meaning provided in Section 3-303(a).

(b) [**Agreement not to assert claim or defense.**] Except as otherwise provided in this section, an agreement between an account debtor and an assignor not to assert against an assignee any claim or defense that the account debtor may have against the assignor is enforceable by an assignee that takes an assignment:

(1) for value;

(2) in good faith;

(3) without notice of a claim of a property or possessory right to the property assigned; and

(4) without notice of a defense or claim in recoupment of the type that may be asserted against a person entitled to enforce a negotiable instrument under Section 3-305(a).

(c) **[When subsection (b) not applicable.]** Subsection (b) does not apply to defenses of a type that may be asserted against a holder in due course of a negotiable instrument under Section 3-305(b).

(d) **[Omission of required statement in consumer transaction.]** In a consumer transaction, if a record evidences the account debtor's obligation, law other than this article requires that the record include a statement to the effect that the rights of an assignee are subject to claims or defenses that the account debtor could assert against the original obligee, and the record does not include such a statement:

(1) the record has the same effect as if the record included such a statement; and

(2) the account debtor may assert against an assignee those claims and defenses that would have been available if the record included such a statement.

(e) **[Rule for individual under other law.]** This section is subject to law other than this article which establishes a different rule for an account debtor who is an individual and who incurred the obligation primarily for personal, family, or household purposes.

(f) **[Other law not displaced.]** Except as otherwise provided in subsection (d), this section does not displace law other than this article which gives effect to an agreement by an account debtor not to assert a claim or defense against an assignee.

§9-404. Rights Acquired by Assignee; Claims and Defenses Against Assignee

(a) **[Assignee's rights subject to terms, claims, and defenses; exceptions.]** Unless an account debtor has made an enforceable agreement not to assert defenses or claims, and subject to subsections (b) through (e), the rights of an assignee are subject to:

(1) all terms of the agreement between the account debtor and assignor and any defense or claim in recoupment arising from the transaction that gave rise to the contract; and

(2) any other defense or claim of the account debtor against the assignor which accrues before the account debtor receives a notification of the assignment authenticated by the assignor or the assignee.

(b) **[Account debtor's claim reduces amount owed to assignee.]** Subject to subsection (c) and except as otherwise provided in subsection (d), the claim of an account debtor against an assignor may be asserted against an assignee under subsection (a) only to reduce the amount the account debtor owes.

(c) **[Rule for individual under other law.]** This section is subject to law other than this article which establishes a different rule for an account debtor who is an individual and who incurred the obligation primarily for personal, family, or household purposes.

(d) **[Omission of required statement in consumer transaction.]** In a consumer transaction, if a record evidences the account debtor's obligation, law other than

493

this article requires that the record include a statement to the effect that the account debtor's recovery against an assignee with respect to claims and defenses against the assignor may not exceed amounts paid by the account debtor under the record, and the record does not include such a statement, the extent to which a claim of an account debtor against the assignor may be asserted against an assignee is determined as if the record included such a statement.

(e) **[Inapplicability to health-care-insurance receivable.]** This section does not apply to an assignment of a health-care-insurance receivable.

§9-405.   Modification of Assigned Contract

(a) **[Effect of modification on assignee.]** A modification of or substitution for an assigned contract is effective against an assignee if made in good faith. The assignee acquires corresponding rights under the modified or substituted contract. The assignment may provide that the modification or substitution is a breach of contract by the assignor. This subsection is subject to subsections (b) through (d).

(b) **[Applicability of subsection (a).]** Subsection (a) applies to the extent that:

(1) the right to payment or a part thereof under an assigned contract has not been fully earned by performance; or

(2) the right to payment or a part thereof has been fully earned by performance and the account debtor has not received notification of the assignment under Section 9-406(a).

(c) **[Rule for individual under other law.]** This section is subject to law other than this article which establishes a different rule for an account debtor who is an individual and who incurred the obligation primarily for personal, family, or household purposes.

(d) **[Inapplicability to health-care-insurance receivable.]** This section does not apply to an assignment of a health-care-insurance receivable.

§9-406.   Discharge of Account Debtor; Notification of Assignment; Identification and Proof of Assignment; Restrictions on Assignment of Accounts, Chattel Paper, Payment Intangibles, and Promissory Notes Ineffective

(a) **[Discharge of account debtor; effect of notification.]** Subject to subsections (b) through (i), an account debtor on an account, chattel paper, or a payment intangible may discharge its obligation by paying the assignor until, but not after, the account debtor receives a notification, authenticated by the assignor or the assignee, that the amount due or to become due has been assigned and that payment is to be made to the assignee. After receipt of the notification, the account debtor may discharge its obligation by paying the assignee and may not discharge the obligation by paying the assignor.

(b) **[When notification ineffective.]** Subject to subsection (h), notification is ineffective under subsection (a):

(1) if it does not reasonably identify the rights assigned;

(2) to the extent that an agreement between an account debtor and a seller of a payment intangible limits the account debtor's duty to pay a person other than the seller and the limitation is effective under law other than this article; or

(3) at the option of an account debtor, if the notification notifies the account debtor to make less than the full amount of any installment or other periodic payment to the assignee, even if:

    (A) only a portion of the account, chattel paper, or payment intangible has been assigned to that assignee;

    (B) a portion has been assigned to another assignee; or

    (C) the account debtor knows that the assignment to that assignee is limited.

(c) **[Proof of assignment.]** Subject to subsection (h), if requested by the account debtor, an assignee shall seasonably furnish reasonable proof that the assignment has been made. Unless the assignee complies, the account debtor may discharge its obligation by paying the assignor, even if the account debtor has received a notification under subsection (a).

(d) **[Term restricting assignment generally ineffective.]** Except as otherwise provided in subsection (e) and Sections 2A-303 and 9-407, and subject to subsection (h), a term in an agreement between an account debtor and an assignor or in a promissory note is ineffective to the extent that it:

(1) prohibits, restricts, or requires the consent of the account debtor or person obligated on the promissory note to the assignment or transfer of, or the creation, attachment, perfection, or enforcement of a security interest in, the account, chattel paper, payment intangible, or promissory note; or

(2) provides that the assignment or transfer or the creation, attachment, perfection, or enforcement of the security interest may give rise to a default, breach, right of recoupment, claim, defense, termination, right of termination, or remedy under the account, chattel paper, payment intangible, or promissory note.

(e) **[Inapplicability of subsection (d) to certain sales.]** Subsection (d) does not apply to the sale of a payment intangible or promissory note, other than a sale pursuant to a disposition under Section 9-610 or as acceptance of collateral under Section 9-620.

(f) **[Legal restrictions on assignment generally ineffective.]** Except as otherwise provided in Sections 2A-303 and 9-407 and subject to subsections (h) and (i), a rule of law, statute, or regulation that prohibits, restricts, or requires the consent of a government, governmental body or official, or account debtor to the assignment or transfer of, or creation of a security interest in, an account or chattel paper is ineffective to the extent that the rule of law, statute, or regulation:

(1) prohibits, restricts, or requires the consent of the government, governmental body or official, or account debtor to the assignment or transfer of, or the creation, attachment, perfection, or enforcement of a security interest in the account or chattel paper; or

(2) provides that the assignment or transfer or the creation, attachment, perfection, or enforcement of the security interest may give rise to a default, breach, right of recoupment, claim, defense, termination, right of termination, or remedy under the account or chattel paper.

(g) **[Subsection (b)(3) not waivable.]** Subject to subsection (h), an account debtor may not waive or vary its option under subsection (b)(3).

(h) **[Rule for individual under other law.]** This section is subject to law other than this article which establishes a different rule for an account debtor who is an individual and who incurred the obligation primarily for personal, family, or household purposes.

(i) **[Inapplicability to health-care-insurance receivable.]** This section does not apply to an assignment of a health-care-insurance receivable.

(j) **[Section prevails over specified inconsistent law.]** This section prevails over any inconsistent provisions of the following statutes, rules, and regulations:

[List here any statutes, rules, and regulations containing provisions inconsistent with this section.]

Legislative Note: States that amend statutes, rules, and regulations to remove provisions inconsistent with this section need not enact subsection (j).

U.N. Convention on Contracts for the International Sale of Goods (1980)

EDITORS' NOTE

The United Nations Commission on International Trade Law (UNCITRAL)[1] promulgated the United Nations Convention on Contracts for the International Sale of Goods (CISG) in 1980.[2] UNCITRAL was itself the outgrowth of earlier efforts to unify international trade law, particularly the 1964 Hague Convention Relating to a Uniform Law on the International Sale of Goods.[3]

The United States ratified the CISG on December 11, 1986, and the CISG took effect in the U.S. and ten other countries (Argentina, China, Egypt, France, Hungary, Italy, Lesotho, Syria, Yugoslavia, and Zambia) on January 1, 1988.[4] The CISG was the product of almost two decades of work by UNCITRAL.

The CISG is the international counterpart to UCC Article 2. Generally speaking, in assessing the contractual rights and duties of a North Carolina manufacturer selling goods to a retailer in Frankfort, Kentucky, we begin with UCC Article 2; but, if the same manufacturer sells the same goods to a retailer in Frankfurt, Germany, then we begin with the CISG.

Many of the United States' largest trading partners, including Brazil, Canada, the People's Republic of China, Mexico, France, Germany, Italy, Japan, the Republic of

---

1. The United Nations established UNCITRAL in 1966 as a permanent body responsible for promoting "the progressive harmonization and unification of the law of international trade." GA Res. 2205 (XXI), 21 UN GAOR Supp. No. 16 at 99, UN Doc A/6316 (1967).

2. United Nations Convention on Contracts for the International Sale of Goods, Apr. 11, 1980, U.N. Doc. A/CONF.97/18 (1980).

3. For more discussion of developments up to and including the Hague Convention, see John Honnold, The Uniform Law for the International Sale of Goods: The Hague Convention of 1964, 30 L. & Contemp. Probs. 326 (1965). For more discussion of the CISG's evolution, see John O. Honnold, Uniform Law for International Sales Under the 1980 United Nations Convention 5-12 (3d ed. 1999).

4. See Daniel Barstow Magraw & Reed R. Kathrein, The Convention for the International Sale of Goods: A Handbook of Basic Materials 67-69 (2d ed. 1990).

Korea, and the Netherlands, are parties to the CISG.[5] The United Kingdom, India, and most of the OPEC member countries are not parties to the CISG.

Subject to several exceptions, the CISG governs contracts for the sale of goods between parties each of whose relevant place of business is in a different "Contracting State" (a country or its legal equivalent that has acceded, accepted, approved, or ratified the CISG or been deemed the successor to a country that had previously done so). Article 1(1)(a).[6] The threshold factor is the location of each party's relevant places of business – rather than the parties' nationality or legal residence. If a party has multiple places of business, the place of business that has the "closest relationship to the contract and its performance" controls. Article 10(a). If a party has no place of business, then the party's "habitual residence" controls. Article 10(b).

Even if both parties have their relevant places of business in different Contracting States, the CISG does not apply if the parties do not know or have reason to know that their relevant places of business are in different countries, Article 1(2); if the purchase is primarily for personal, family, or household purposes, Article 2(a); to purchases by auction, Article 2(b); to purchases of intangible personal property, including securities, negotiable instruments, and money, Article 2(d); to purchases of ships, vessels, hovercraft, aircraft, or electricity, Article 2(e)-(f); or to contracts in which the seller's primary obligation is to provide services, Article 3(2), including contracts for goods in which the buyer supplies all or a substantial part of the materials the seller needs to manufacture or produce the goods, Article 3(1).

Although the CISG and UCC Article 2 share much common ground, the CISG does not address defenses against enforcement of the contract, such as duress, fraud, mistake, and unconscionability (compare CISG Article 4(a) with UCC §§ 1-103(b) & 2-302), the effect of a transaction on title in or ownership of the goods (compare CISG Article 4(b) with UCC § 2-401), or a seller's liability for death or personal injury caused by goods (compare CISG Article 5 with UCC §§ 2-318 & 2-715).[7] Moreover,

---

5. As of June 1, 2017, eighty-five countries had acceded, accepted, approved, ratified, or succeeded to the CISG: Albania, Argentina, Armenia, Australia, Austria, Azerbaijan, Bahrain, Belarus, Belgium, Benin, Bosnia and Herzegovina, Brazil, Bulgaria, Burundi, Canada, Chile, China, Colombia, Congo, Croatia, Cuba, Cyprus, Czech Republic, Denmark, Dominican Republic, Ecuador, Egypt, El Salvador, Estonia, Finland, France, Gabon, Georgia, Germany, Greece, Guinea, Guyana, Honduras, Hungary, Iceland, Iraq, Israel, Italy, Japan, Kyrgyzstan, Latvia, Lebanon, Lesotho, Liberia, Lithuania, Luxembourg, Macedonia, Madagascar, Mauritania, Mexico, Moldova, Mongolia, Montenegro, Netherlands, New Zealand, Norway, Paraguay, Peru, Poland, Republic of (South) Korea, Romania, Russian Federation, Saint Vincent and the Grenadines, San Marino, Serbia, Singapore, Slovakia, Slovenia, Spain, Sweden, Switzerland, Syrian Arab Republic, Turkey, Uganda, Ukraine, United States, Uruguay, Uzbekistan, Vietnam, and Zambia. Two other countries, Ghana and Venezuela, were among the earliest signatories to the CISG, but have not taken the required action to bring the treaty into effect under their national law. UNCITRAL's website (http://www.uncitral.org/uncitral/en/uncitral_texts/sale_goods/1980CISG_status.html) provides a regularly updated list of countries that have become parties to the CISG.

6. Article 1(1)(b) further provides that the CISG applies when "the rules of private international law lead to the application of the law of a Contracting State," but this provision is not effective with respect to a buyer or seller whose place of business is in the United States because the United States has declared, pursuant to Article 95 of the Convention, that it is not bound by Article 1(1)(b). So, unless a real-life transaction or dispute, a professor's hypothetical, or an exam question involves parties whose relevant places of business are in two different Contracting States, neither of which is the United States, Article 1(1)(b) will be of little consequence.

7. Because of these and other "gaps" in the CISG, other bodies of law must be consulted when such issues arise. The UNIDROIT Principles of International Commercial Contracts, reprinted and discussed in the next section of this Supplement, deal with many such issues and were designed to Supplement the CISG.

the CISG and UCC Article 2 take decidedly different approaches with respect to important concepts such as contract formation and terms in the absence of complete agreement on terms – a.k.a. the "battle of the forms" (compare CISG Article 19 with UCC § 2-201); a statute of frauds (compare CISG Article 11 with UCC § 2-201); a parol evidence rule (compare CISG Article 11 with UCC § 2-202); and a buyer's ability to reject goods that fail in any respect to conform to the contract – a.k.a. the "perfect tender rule" – and avoid the contract if the seller fails to timely cure a nonconformity that does not amount to a fundamental breach (compare UCC §§ 2-601 & 2-711 with CISG Articles 49 & 25).

The CISG expressly allows the parties to agree that the CISG will not apply to their transaction or "derogate from or vary the effect of [most] of its provisions." Article 6. If a buyer and seller with places of business in different Contracting States agree to a sales contract that is silent about the CISG's applicability, the CISG applies. Moreover, the leading U.S. case on CISG Article 6 makes clear that simply choosing the law of a jurisdiction (e.g., California law or British Columbia law) does not avoid the CISG if the CISG is part of the law of the chosen jurisdiction. See Asante Technologies, Inc. v. PMC-Sierra, Inc., 164 F. Supp. 2d 1142 (N.D. Cal. 2001). Thus, it is important for lawyers to determine whether the CISG applies in the absence of a contrary agreement, to evaluate the CISG's substantive provisions to decide whether a sales agreement should exclude the CISG entirely or modify any of those provisions, and to effectively opt out if doing so is in the client's best interest.

For useful comparisons of the CISG's provisions with those of UCC Article 2, accompanied by expert analysis, see Henry Deeb Gabriel, Contracts for the Sale of Goods: A Comparison of U.S. and International Law (2d ed. 2009), and Clayton P. Gillette & Steven D. Walt, Sales Law: Domestic and International (3d ed. 2016). See generally William S. Dodge, Teaching the CISG in Contracts, 50 J. Leg. Ed. 72 (2000); Keith A. Rowley, The Convention on the International Sale of Goods, in Howard O. Hunter, Modern Law of Contracts ch. 23 (3d ed. rev. 2007); Symposium, Celebrating the 25th Anniversary of the United Nations Convention on Contracts for the International Sale of Goods, 25 J.L. & Com. 1 (2005); and Letter of Submittal of the CISG from the State Department to President Reagan, dated August 30, 1983, reprinted in 3A Uniform Laws Annotated App. IV (2002). For an interesting recent discussion of how U.S. attorneys and the clients they represent have received the CISG in practice, see John F. Coyle, The Role of the CISG in U.S. Contract Practice: An Empirical Study, 38 U. Pa. J. Int'l L. 195 (2016).

The CISG has been in force for nearly 30 years and the number of reported decisions applying the Convention, within the United States and in foreign states, has steadily grown. Pace University's Institute for International Commercial Law maintains a global database devoted to the CISG, providing access to thousands of case opinions, arbitral decisions, and case synopses in English, as well as many other primary and secondary materials related to the CISG.[8]

---

8. Pace Law's Albert H. Kritzer CISG Database can be found at: http://www.iicl.law.pace.edu/cisg/cisg (last visited June 1, 2017).

9. The Article titles listed in this table have been prepared by the editors and are not part of the Convention. We include them as a finding tool. The titles do not have any authoritative value.

U.N. Convention on Contracts for the International Sale of Goods (1980)

THE STATES PARTIES TO THIS CONVENTION,

BEARING IN MIND the broad objectives in the resolutions adopted by the sixth special session of the General Assembly of the United Nations on the establishment of a New International Economic Order,

CONSIDERING that the development of international trade on the basis of equality and mutual benefit is an important element in promoting friendly relations among States,

BEING OF THE OPINION that the adoption of uniform rules which govern contracts for the international sale of goods and take into account the different social, economic and legal systems would contribute to the removal of legal barriers in international trade and promote the development of international trade,

HAVE AGREED as follows:

PART I. SPHERE OF APPLICATION AND GENERAL PROVISIONS

Chapter I. Sphere of Application

Article 1

(1) This Convention applies to contracts of sale of goods between parties whose places of business are in different States:

(a) when the States are Contracting States; or

(b) when the rules of private international law lead to the application of the law of a Contracting State.[10]

(2) The fact that the parties have their places of business in different States is to be disregarded whenever this fact does not appear either from the contract or from any dealings between, or from information disclosed by, the parties at any time before or at the conclusion of the contract.

(3) Neither the nationality of the parties nor the civil or commercial character of the parties or of the contract is to be taken into consideration in determining the application of this Convention.

Article 2

This Convention does not apply to sales:

(a) of goods bought for personal, family or household use, unless the seller, at any time before or at the conclusion of the contract, neither knew nor ought to have known that the goods were bought for any such use;

(b) by auction;

(c) on execution or otherwise by authority of law;

(d) of stocks, shares, investment securities, negotiable instruments or money;

(e) of ships, vessels, hovercraft or aircraft;

(f) of electricity

---

10. As discussed in the Editors' Note, Article 1(1)(b) does not bind the United States. See supra note 6.

Article 3

(1) Contracts for the supply of goods to be manufactured or produced are to be considered sales unless the party who orders the goods undertakes to supply a substantial part of the materials necessary for such manufacture or production.

(2) This Convention does not apply to contracts in which the preponderant part of the obligations of the party who furnishes the goods consists in the supply of labour or other services.

Article 4

This Convention governs only the formation of the contract of sale and the rights and obligations of the seller and the buyer arising from such a contract. In particular, except as otherwise expressly provided in this Convention, it is not concerned with:

(a) the validity of the contract or of any of its provisions or of any usage;

(b) the effect which the contract may have on the property in the goods sold.

Article 5

This Convention does not apply to the liability of the seller for death or personal injury caused by the goods to any person.

Article 6

The parties may exclude the application of this Convention or, subject to article 12, derogate from or vary the effect of any of its provisions.

Chapter II. General Provisions

Article 7

(1) In the interpretation of this Convention, regard is to be had to its international character and to the need to promote uniformity in its application and the observance of good faith in international trade.

(2) Questions concerning matters governed by this Convention which are not expressly settled in it are to be settled in conformity with the general principles on which it is based or, in the absence of such principles, in conformity with the law applicable by virtue of the rules of private international law.

Article 8

(1) For the purposes of this Convention statements made by and other conduct of a party are to be interpreted according to his intent where the other party knew or could not have been unaware what that intent was.

(2) If the preceding paragraph is not applicable, statements made by and other conduct of a party are to be interpreted according to the understanding that a reasonable person of the same kind as the other party would have had in the same circumstances.

(3) In determining the intent of a party or the understanding a reasonable person would have had, due consideration is to be given to all relevant

circumstances of the case including the negotiations, any practices which the parties have established between themselves, usages and any subsequent conduct of the parties.

Article 9

(1) The parties are bound by any usage to which they have agreed and by any practices which they have established between themselves.

(2) The parties are considered, unless otherwise agreed, to have impliedly made applicable to their contract or its formation a usage of which the parties knew or ought to have known and which in international trade is widely known to, and regularly observed by, parties to contracts of the type involved in the particular trade concerned.

Article 10

For the purposes of this Convention:

(a) if a party has more than one place of business, the place of business is that which has the closest relationship to the contract and its performance, having regard to the circumstances known to or contemplated by the parties at any time before or at the conclusion of the contract;

(b) if a party does not have a place of business, reference is to be made to his habitual residence.

Article 11

A contract of sale need not be concluded in or evidenced by writing and is not subject to any other requirement as to form. It may be proved by any means, including witnesses.

Article 12

Any provision of article 11, article 29 or Part II of this Convention that allows a contract of sale or its modification or termination by agreement or any offer, acceptance or other indication of intention to be made in any form other than in writing does not apply where any party has his place of business in a Contracting State which has made a declaration under article 96 of this Convention. The parties may not derogate from or vary the effect of this article.

Article 13

For the purposes of this Convention "writing" includes telegram and telex.

PART II. FORMATION OF THE CONTRACT

Article 14

(1) A proposal for concluding a contract addressed to one or more specific persons constitutes an offer if it is sufficiently definite and indicates the intention

of the offeror to be bound in case of acceptance. A proposal is sufficiently definite if it indicates the goods and expressly or implicitly fixes or makes provision for determining the quantity and the price.

(2) A proposal other than one addressed to one or more specific persons is to be considered merely as an invitation to make offers, unless the contrary is clearly indicated by the person making the proposal.

Article 15

(1) An offer becomes effective when it reaches the offeree.

(2) An offer, even if it is irrevocable, may be withdrawn if the withdrawal reaches the offeree before or at the same time as the offer.

Article 16

(1) Until a contract is concluded an offer may be revoked if the revocation reaches the offeree before he has dispatched an acceptance.

(2) However, an offer cannot be revoked:

(a) if it indicates, whether by stating a fixed time for acceptance or otherwise, that it is irrevocable; or

(b) if it was reasonable for the offeree to rely on the offer as being irrevocable and the offeree has acted in reliance on the offer.

Article 17

An offer, even if it is irrevocable, is terminated when a rejection reaches the offeror.

Article 18

(1) A statement made by or other conduct of the offeree indicating assent to an offer is an acceptance. Silence or inactivity does not in itself amount to acceptance.

(2) An acceptance of an offer becomes effective at the moment the indication of assent reaches the offeror. An acceptance is not effective if the indication of assent does not reach the offeror within the time he has fixed or, if no time is fixed, within a reasonable time, due account being taken of the circumstances of the transaction, including the rapidity of the means of communication employed by the offeror. An oral offer must be accepted immediately unless the circumstances indicate otherwise.

(3) However, if, by virtue of the offer or as a result of practices which the parties have established between themselves or of usage, the offeree may indicate assent by performing an act, such as one relating to the dispatch of the goods or payment of the price, without notice to the offeror, the acceptance is effective at the moment the act is performed, provided that the act is performed within the period of time laid down in the preceding paragraph.

Article 19

(1) A reply to an offer which purports to be an acceptance but contains additions, limitations or other modifications is a rejection of the offer and constitutes a counter-offer.

(2) However, a reply to an offer which purports to be an acceptance but contains additional or different terms which do not materially alter the terms of

the offer constitutes an acceptance, unless the offeror, without undue delay, objects orally to the discrepancy or dispatches a notice to that effect. If he does not so object, the terms of the contract are the terms of the offer with the modifications contained in the acceptance.

(3) Additional or different terms relating, among other things, to the price, payment, quality and quantity of the goods, place and time of delivery, extent of one party's liability to the other or the settlement of disputes are considered to alter the terms of the offer materially.

Article 20

(1) A period of time for acceptance fixed by the offeror in a telegram or a letter begins to run from the moment the telegram is handed in for dispatch or from the date shown on the letter or, if no such date is shown, from the date shown on the envelope. A period of time for acceptance fixed by the offeror by telephone, telex or other means of instantaneous communication, begins to run from the moment that the offer reaches the offeree.

(2) Official holidays or non-business days occurring during the period for acceptance are included in calculating the period. However, if a notice of acceptance cannot be delivered at the address of the offeror on the last day of the period because that day falls on an official holiday or a non-business day at the place of business of the offeror, the period is extended until the first business day which follows.

Article 21

(1) A late acceptance is nevertheless effective as an acceptance if without delay the offeror orally so informs the offeree or dispatches a notice to that effect.

(2) If a letter or other writing containing a late acceptance shows that it has been sent in such circumstances that if its transmission had been normal it would have reached the offeror in due time, the late acceptance is effective as an acceptance unless, without delay, the offeror orally informs the offeree that he considers his offer as having lapsed or dispatches a notice to that effect.

Article 22

An acceptance may be withdrawn if the withdrawal reaches the offeror before or at the same time as the acceptance would have become effective.

Article 23

A contract is concluded at the moment when an acceptance of an offer becomes effective in accordance with the provisions of this Convention.

Article 24

For the purposes of this Part of the Convention, an offer, declaration of acceptance or any other indication of intention "reaches" the addressee when it is made orally to him or delivered by any other means to him personally, to his place of business or mailing address or, if he does not have a place of business or mailing address, to his habitual residence.

PART III. SALE OF GOODS

Chapter I. General Provisions

Article 25

A breach of contract committed by one of the parties is fundamental if it results in such detriment to the other party as substantially to deprive him of what he is entitled to expect under the contract, unless the party in breach did not foresee and a reasonable person of the same kind in the same circumstances would not have foreseen such a result.

Article 26

A declaration of avoidance of the contract is effective only if made by notice to the other party.

Article 27

Unless otherwise expressly provided in this Part of the Convention, if any notice, request or other communication is given or made by a party in accordance with this Part and by means appropriate in the circumstances, a delay or error in the transmission of the communication or its failure to arrive does not deprive that party of the right to rely on the communication.

Article 28

If, in accordance with the provisions of this Convention, one party is entitled to require performance of any obligation by the other party, a court is not bound to enter a judgement for specific performance unless the court would do so under its own law in respect of similar contracts of sale not governed by this Convention.

Article 29

(1) A contract may be modified or terminated by the mere agreement of the parties.

(2) A contract in writing which contains a provision requiring any modification or termination by agreement to be in writing may not be otherwise modified or terminated by agreement. However, a party may be precluded by his conduct from asserting such a provision to the extent that the other party has relied on that conduct.

Chapter II. Obligations of the Seller

Article 30

The seller must deliver the goods, hand over any documents relating to them and transfer the property in the goods, as required by the contract and this Convention.

Section I. Delivery of the Goods and Handing Over of Documents

Article 31

If the seller is not bound to deliver the goods at any other particular place, his obligation to deliver consists:

(a) if the contract of sale involves carriage of the goods — in handing the goods over to the first carrier for transmission to the buyer;

(b) if, in cases not within the preceding subparagraph, the contract relates to specific goods, or unidentified goods to be drawn from a specific stock or to be manufactured or produced, and at the time of the conclusion of the contract the parties knew that the goods were at, or were to be manufactured or produced at, a particular place — in placing the goods at the buyer's disposal at that place;

(c) in other cases — in placing the goods at the buyer's disposal at the place where the seller had his place of business at the time of the conclusion of the contract.

Article 32

(1) If the seller, in accordance with the contract or this Convention, hands the goods over to a carrier and if the goods are not clearly identified to the contract by markings on the goods, by shipping documents or otherwise, the seller must give the buyer notice of the consignment specifying the goods.

(2) If the seller is bound to arrange for carriage of the goods, he must make such contracts as are necessary for carriage to the place fixed by means of transportation appropriate in the circumstances and according to the usual terms for such transportation.

(3) If the seller is not bound to effect insurance in respect of the carriage of the goods, he must, at the buyer's request, provide him with all available information necessary to enable him to effect such insurance.

Article 33

The seller must deliver the goods:

(a) if a date is fixed by or determinable from the contract, on that date;

(b) if a period of time is fixed by or determinable from the contract, at any time within that period unless circumstances indicate that the buyer is to choose a date; or

(c) in any other case, within a reasonable time after the conclusion of the contract.

Article 34

If the seller is bound to hand over documents relating to the goods, he must hand them over at the time and place and in the form required by the contract. If the seller has handed over documents before that time, he may, up to that time, cure any lack of conformity in the documents, if the exercise of this right does not cause the buyer unreasonable inconvenience or unreasonable expense. However, the buyer retains any right to claim damages as provided for in this Convention.

Section II. Conformity of the Goods and Third-Party Claims

Article 35

(1) The seller must deliver goods which are of the quantity, quality and description required by the contract and which are contained or packaged in the manner required by the contract.

(2) Except where the parties have agreed otherwise, the goods do not conform with the contract unless they:

(a) are fit for the purposes for which goods of the same description would ordinarily be used;

(b) are fit for any particular purpose expressly or impliedly made known to the seller at the time of the conclusion of the contract, except where the circumstances show that the buyer did not rely, or that it was unreasonable for him to rely, on the seller's skill and judgment;

(c) possess the qualities of goods which the seller has held out to the buyer as a sample or model;

(d) are contained or packaged in the manner usual for such goods or, where there is no such manner, in a manner adequate to preserve and protect the goods.

(3) The seller is not liable under subparagraphs (a) to (d) of the preceding paragraph for any lack of conformity of the goods if, at the time of the conclusion of the contract, the buyer knew or could not have been unaware of such lack of conformity.

Article 36

(1) The seller is liable in accordance with the contract and this Convention for any lack of conformity which exists at the time when the risk passes to the buyer, even though the lack of conformity becomes apparent only after that time.

(2) The seller is also liable for any lack of conformity which occurs after the time indicated in the preceding paragraph and which is due to a breach of any of his obligations, including a breach of any guarantee that for a period of time the goods will remain fit for their ordinary purpose or for some particular purpose or will retain specified qualities or characteristics.

Article 37

If the seller has delivered goods before the date for delivery, he may, up to that date, deliver any missing part or make up any deficiency in the quantity of the goods delivered, or deliver goods in replacement of any non-conforming goods delivered or remedy any lack of conformity in the goods delivered, provided that the exercise of this right does not cause the buyer unreasonable inconvenience or unreasonable expense. However, the buyer retains any right to claim damages as provided for in this Convention.

Article 38

(1) The buyer must examine the goods, or cause them to be examined, within as short a period as is practicable in the circumstances.

(2) If the contract involves carriage of the goods, examination may be deferred until after the goods have arrived at their destination.

(3) If the goods are redirected in transit or redispatched by the buyer without a reasonable opportunity for examination by him and at the time of the conclusion of the contract the seller knew or ought to have known of the possibility of such redirection or redispatch, examination may be deferred until after the goods have arrived at the new destination.

Article 39

(1) The buyer loses the right to rely on a lack of conformity of the goods if he does not give notice to the seller specifying the nature of the lack of conformity within a reasonable time after he has discovered it or ought to have discovered it.

(2) In any event, the buyer loses the right to rely on a lack of conformity of the goods if he does not give the seller notice thereof at the latest within a period of two years from the date on which the goods were actually handed over to the buyer, unless this time limit is inconsistent with a contractual period of guarantee.

Article 40

The seller is not entitled to rely on the provisions of articles 38 and 39 if the lack of conformity relates to facts of which he knew or could not have been unaware and which he did not disclose to the buyer.

Article 41

The seller must deliver goods which are free from any right or claim of a third party, unless the buyer agreed to take the goods subject to that right or claim. However, if such right or claim is based on industrial property or other intellectual property, the seller's obligation is governed by article 42.

Article 42

(1) The seller must deliver goods which are free from any right or claim of a third party based on industrial property or other intellectual property, of which at the time of the conclusion of the contract the seller knew or could not have been unaware, provided that the right or claim is based on industrial property or other intellectual property:

(a) under the law of the State where the goods will be resold or otherwise used, if it was contemplated by the parties at the time of the conclusion of the contract that the goods would be resold or otherwise used in that State; or

(b) in any other case, under the law of the State where the buyer has his place of business.

(2) The obligation of the seller under the preceding paragraph does not extend to cases where:

(a) at the time of the conclusion of the contract the buyer knew or could not have been unaware of the right or claim; or

(b) the right or claim results from the seller's compliance with technical drawings, designs, formulae or other such specifications furnished by the buyer.

Article 43

(1) The buyer loses the right to rely on the provisions of article 41 or article 42 if he does not give notice to the seller specifying the nature of the right or claim of the third party within a reasonable time after he has become aware or ought to have become aware of the right or claim.

(2) The seller is not entitled to rely on the provisions of the preceding paragraph if he knew of the right or claim of the third party and the nature of it.

Article 44

Notwithstanding the provisions of paragraph (1) of article 39 and paragraph (1) of article 43, the buyer may reduce the price in accordance with article 50 or claim damages, except for loss of profit, if he has a reasonable excuse for his failure to give the required notice.

Section III. Remedies for Breach of Contract by the Seller

Article 45

(1) If the seller fails to perform any of his obligations under the contract or this Convention, the buyer may:

(a) exercise the rights provided in articles 46 to 52;

(b) claim damages as provided in articles 74 to 77.

(2) The buyer is not deprived of any right he may have to claim damages by exercising his right to other remedies.

(3) No period of grace may be granted to the seller by a court or arbitral tribunal when the buyer resorts to a remedy for breach of contract.

Article 46

(1) The buyer may require performance by the seller of his obligations unless the buyer has resorted to a remedy which is inconsistent with this requirement.

(2) If the goods do not conform with the contract, the buyer may require delivery of substitute goods only if the lack of conformity constitutes a fundamental breach of contract and a request for substitute goods is made either in conjunction with notice given under article 39 or within a reasonable time thereafter.

(3) If the goods do not conform with the contract, the buyer may require the seller to remedy the lack of conformity by repair, unless this is unreasonable having regard to all the circumstances. A request for repair must be made either in conjunction with notice given under article 39 or within a reasonable time thereafter.

Article 47

(1) The buyer may fix an additional period of time of reasonable length for performance by the seller of his obligations.

(2) Unless the buyer has received notice from the seller that he will not perform within the period so fixed, the buyer may not, during that period, resort to any

remedy for breach of contract. However, the buyer is not deprived thereby of any right he may have to claim damages for delay in performance.

Article 48

(1) Subject to article 49, the seller may, even after the date for delivery, remedy at his own expense any failure to perform his obligations, if he can do so without unreasonable delay and without causing the buyer unreasonable inconvenience or uncertainty of reimbursement by the seller of expenses advanced by the buyer. However, the buyer retains any right to claim damages as provided for in this Convention.

(2) If the seller requests the buyer to make known whether he will accept performance and the buyer does not comply with the request within a reasonable time, the seller may perform within the time indicated in his request. The buyer may not, during that period of time, resort to any remedy which is inconsistent with performance by the seller.

(3) A notice by the seller that he will perform within a specified period of time is assumed to include a request, under the preceding paragraph, that the buyer make known his decision.

(4) A request or notice by the seller under paragraph (2) or (3) of this article is not effective unless received by the buyer.

Article 49

(1) The buyer may declare the contract avoided:

(a) if the failure by the seller to perform any of his obligations under the contract or this Convention amounts to a fundamental breach of contract; or

(b) in case of non-delivery, if the seller does not deliver the goods within the additional period of time fixed by the buyer in accordance with paragraph (1) of article 47 or declares that he will not deliver within the period so fixed.

(2) However, in cases where the seller has delivered the goods, the buyer loses the right to declare the contract avoided unless he does so:

(a) in respect of late delivery, within a reasonable time after he has become aware that delivery has been made:

(b) in respect of any breach other than late delivery, within a reasonable time:

(i) after he knew or ought to have known of the breach;

(ii) after the expiration of any additional period of time fixed by the buyer in accordance with paragraph (1) of article 47, or after the seller has declared that he will not perform his obligations within such an additional period; or

(iii) after the expiration of any additional period of time indicated by the seller in accordance with paragraph (2) of article 48, or after the buyer has declared that he will not accept performance.

Article 50

If the goods do not conform with the contract and whether or not the price has already been paid, the buyer may reduce the price in the same proportion as the value that the goods actually delivered had at the time of the delivery bears to the value that conforming goods would have had at that time. However, if the seller remedies any failure to perform his obligations in accordance with article 37 or article 48 or if the buyer refuses to accept performance by the seller in accordance with those articles, the buyer may not reduce the price.

Article 51

(1) If the seller delivers only a part of the goods or if only a part of the goods delivered is in conformity with the contract, articles 46 to 50 apply in respect of the part which is missing or which does not conform.

(2) The buyer may declare the contract avoided in its entirety only if the failure to make delivery completely or in conformity with the contract amounts to a fundamental breach of the contract.

Article 52

(1) If the seller delivers the goods before the date fixed, the buyer may take delivery or refuse to take delivery.

(2) If the seller delivers a quantity of goods greater than that provided for in the contract, the buyer may take delivery or refuse to take delivery of the excess quantity. If the buyer takes delivery of all or part of the excess quantity, he must pay for it at the contract rate.

Chapter III. Obligations of the Buyer

Article 53

The buyer must pay the price for the goods and take delivery of them as required by the contract and this Convention.

Section I. Payment of the Price

Article 54

The buyer's obligation to pay the price includes taking such steps and complying with such formalities as may be required under the contract or any laws and regulations to enable payment to be made.

Article 55

Where a contract has been validly concluded but does not expressly or implicitly fix or make provision for determining the price, the parties are considered, in the absence of any indication to the contrary, to have impliedly made reference to the price generally charged at the time of the conclusion of the contract for such goods sold under comparable circumstances in the trade concerned.

Article 56

If the price is fixed according to the weight of the goods, in case of doubt it is to be determined by the net weight.

Article 57

(1) If the buyer is not bound to pay the price at any other particular place, he must pay it to the seller:

(a) at the seller's place of business; or

(b) if the payment is to be made against the handing over of the goods or of documents, at the place where the handing over takes place.

(2) The seller must bear any increase in the expenses incidental to payment which is caused by a change in his place of business subsequent to the conclusion of the contract.

Article 58

(1) If the buyer is not bound to pay the price at any other specific time, he must pay it when the seller places either the goods or documents controlling their disposition at the buyer's disposal in accordance with the contract and this Convention. The seller may make such payment a condition for handing over the goods or documents.

(2) If the contract involves carriage of the goods, the seller may dispatch the goods on terms whereby the goods, or documents controlling their disposition, will not be handed over to the buyer except against payment of the price.

(3) The buyer is not bound to pay the price until he has had an opportunity to examine the goods, unless the procedures for delivery or payment agreed upon by the parties are inconsistent with his having such an opportunity.

Article 59

The buyer must pay the price on the date fixed by or determinable from the contract and this Convention without the need for any request or compliance with any formality on the part of the seller.

Section II. Taking Delivery

Article 60

The buyer's obligation to take delivery consists:

(a) in doing all the acts which could reasonably be expected of him in order to enable the seller to make delivery; and

(b) in taking over the goods.

Section III. Remedies for Breach of Contract by the Buyer

Article 61

(1) If the buyer fails to perform any of his obligations under the contract or this Convention, the seller may:

(a) exercise the rights provided in articles 62 to 65;

(b) claim damages as provided in articles 74 to 77.

(2) The seller is not deprived of any right he may have to claim damages by exercising his right to other remedies.

(3) No period of grace may be granted to the buyer by a court or arbitral tribunal when the seller resorts to a remedy for breach of contract.

Article 62

The seller may require the buyer to pay the price, take delivery or perform his other obligations, unless the seller has resorted to a remedy which is inconsistent with this requirement.

Article 63

(1) The seller may fix an additional period of time of reasonable length for performance by the buyer of his obligations.

(2) Unless the seller has received notice from the buyer that he will not perform within the period so fixed, the seller may not, during that period, resort to any remedy for breach of contract. However, the seller is not deprived thereby of any right he may have to claim damages for delay in performance.

Article 64

(1) The seller may declare the contract avoided:

(a) if the failure by the buyer to perform any of his obligations under the contract or this Convention amounts to a fundamental breach of contract; or

(b) if the buyer does not, within the additional period of time fixed by the seller in accordance with paragraph (1) of article 63, perform his obligation to pay the price or take delivery of the goods, or declares that he will not do so within the period so fixed.

(2) However, in cases where the buyer has paid the price, the seller loses the right to declare the contract avoided unless he does so:

(a) in respect of late performance by the buyer, before the seller has become aware that performance has been rendered; or

(b) in respect of any breach other than late performance by the buyer, within a reasonable time:

(i) after the seller knew or ought to have known of the breach; or

(ii) after the expiration of any additional period of time fixed by the seller in accordance with paragraph (1) of article 63, or after the buyer has declared that he will not perform his obligations within such an additional period.

Article 65

(1) If under the contract the buyer is to specify the form, measurement or other features of the goods and he fails to make such specification either on the date agreed upon or within a reasonable time after receipt of a request from the seller, the seller may, without prejudice to any other rights he may have, make the specification himself in accordance with the requirements of the buyer that may be known to him.

(2) If the seller makes the specification himself, he must inform the buyer of the details thereof and must fix a reasonable time within which the buyer may make a different specification. If, after receipt of such a communication, the buyer fails to do so within the time so fixed, the specification made by the seller is binding.

Chapter IV. Passing of Risk

Article 66

Loss of or damage to the goods after the risk has passed to the buyer does not discharge him from his obligation to pay the price, unless the loss or damage is due to an act or omission of the seller.

Article 67

(1) If the contract of sale involves carriage of the goods and the seller is not bound to hand them over at a particular place, the risk passes to the buyer when the goods are handed over to the first carrier for transmission to the buyer in accordance with the contract of sale. If the seller is bound to hand the goods over to a carrier at a particular place, the risk does not pass to the buyer until the goods are handed over to the carrier at that place. The fact that the seller is authorized to retain documents controlling the disposition of the goods does not affect the passage of the risk.

(2) Nevertheless, the risk does not pass to the buyer until the goods are clearly identified to the contract, whether by markings on the goods, by shipping documents, by notice given to the buyer or otherwise.

Article 68

The risk in respect of goods sold in transit passes to the buyer from the time of the conclusion of the contract. However, if the circumstances so indicate, the risk is assumed by the buyer from the time the goods were handed over to the carrier who issued the documents embodying the contract of carriage. Nevertheless, if at the time of the conclusion of the contract of sale the seller knew or ought to have known that the goods had been lost or damaged and did not disclose this to the buyer, the loss or damage is at the risk of the seller.

Article 69

(1) In cases not within articles 67 and 68, the risk passes to the buyer when he takes over the goods or, if he does not do so in due time, from the time when the goods are placed at his disposal and he commits a breach of contract by failing to take delivery.

(2) However, if the buyer is bound to take over the goods at a place other than a place of business of the seller, the risk passes when delivery is due and the buyer is aware of the fact that the goods are placed at his disposal at that place.

(3) If the contract relates to goods not then identified, the goods are considered not to be placed at the disposal of the buyer until they are clearly identified to the contract.

Article 70

If the seller has committed a fundamental breach of contract, articles 67, 68, and 69 do not impair the remedies available to the buyer on account of the breach.

Chapter V. Provisions Common to the Obligations of the Seller and of the Buyer

Section I. Anticipatory Breach and Instalment Contracts

Article 71

(1) A party may suspend the performance of his obligations if, after the conclusion of the contract, it becomes apparent that the other party will not perform a substantial part of his obligations as a result of:

    (a) a serious deficiency in his ability to perform or in his creditworthiness; or

    (b) his conduct in preparing to perform or in performing the contract.

(2) If the seller has already dispatched the goods before the grounds described in the preceding paragraph become evident, he may prevent the handing over of the goods to the buyer even though the buyer holds a document which entitles him to obtain them. The present paragraph relates only to the rights in the goods as between the buyer and the seller.

(3) A party suspending performance, whether before or after dispatch of the goods, must immediately give notice of the suspension to the other party and must continue with performance if the other party provides adequate assurance of his performance.

Article 72

(1) If prior to the date for performance of the contract it is clear that one of the parties will commit a fundamental breach of contract, the other party may declare the contract avoided.

(2) If time allows, the party intending to declare the contract avoided must give reasonable notice to the other party in order to permit him to provide adequate assurance of his performance.

(3) The requirements of the preceding paragraph do not apply if the other party has declared that he will not perform his obligations.

Article 73

(1) In the case of a contract for delivery of goods by instalments, if the failure of one party to perform any of his obligations in respect of any instalment constitutes a fundamental breach of contract with respect to that instalment, the other party may declare the contract avoided with respect to that instalment.

(2) If one party's failure to perform any of his obligations in respect of any instalment gives the other party good grounds to conclude that a fundamental breach of contract will occur with respect to future instalments, he may declare the contract avoided for the future, provided that he does so within a reasonable time.

(3) A buyer who declares the contract avoided in respect of any delivery may, at the same time, declare it avoided in respect of deliveries already made or of future deliveries if, by reason of their interdependence, those deliveries could not be used for the purpose contemplated by the parties at the time of the conclusion of the contract.

Section II. Damages

Article 74

Damages for breach of contract by one party consist of a sum equal to the loss, including loss of profit, suffered by the other party as a consequence of the breach. Such damages may not exceed the loss which the party in breach foresaw or ought to have foreseen at the time of the conclusion of the contract, in the light of the facts and matters of which he then knew or ought to have known, as a possible consequence of the breach of contract.

Article 75

If the contract is avoided and if, in a reasonable manner and within a reasonable time after avoidance, the buyer has bought goods in replacement or the seller has resold the goods, the party claiming damages may recover the difference between the contract price and the price in the substitute transaction as well as any further damages recoverable under article 74.

Article 76

(1) If the contract is avoided and there is a current price for the goods, the party claiming damages may, if he has not made a purchase or resale under article 75, recover the difference between the price fixed by the contract and the current price at the time of avoidance as well as any further damages recoverable under article 74. If, however, the party claiming damages has avoided the contract after taking over the goods, the current price at the time of such taking over shall be applied instead of the current price at the time of avoidance.

(2) For the purposes of the preceding paragraph, the current price is the price prevailing at the place where delivery of the goods should have been made or, if there is no current price at that place, the price at such other place serves as a reasonable substitute, making due allowance for differences in the cost of transporting the goods.

Article 77

A party who relies on a breach of contract must take such measures as are reasonable in the circumstances to mitigate the loss, including loss of profit, resulting from the breach. If he fails to take such measures, the party in breach may claim a reduction in the damages in the amount by which the loss should have been mitigated.

Section III. Interest

Article 78

If a party fails to pay the price or any other sum that is in arrears, the other party is entitled to interest on it, without prejudice to any claim for damages recoverable under article 74.

Section IV. Exemptions

Article 79

(1) A party is not liable for a failure to perform any of his obligations if he proves that the failure was due to an impediment beyond his control and that he could not reasonably be expected to have taken the impediment into account at the time of the conclusion of the contract or to have avoided or overcome it or its consequences.

(2) If the party's failure is due to the failure by a third person whom he has engaged to perform the whole or a part of the contract, that party is exempt from liability only if:

(a) he is exempt under the preceding paragraph; and

(b) the person whom he has so engaged would be so exempt if the provisions of that paragraph were applied to him.

(3) The exemption provided by this article has effect for the period during which the impediment exists.

(4) The party who fails to perform must give notice to the other party of the impediment and its effect on his ability to perform. If the notice is not received by the other party within a reasonable time after the party who fails to perform knew or ought to have known of the impediment, he is liable for damages resulting from such non-receipt.

(5) Nothing in this article prevents either party from exercising any right other than to claim damages under this Convention.

Article 80

A party may not rely on a failure of the other party to perform, to the extent that such failure was caused by the first party's act or omission.

Section V. Effects of Avoidance

Article 81

(1) Avoidance of the contract releases both parties from their obligations under it, subject to any damages which may be due. Avoidance does not affect any provision of the contract for the settlement of disputes or any other provision of the contract governing the rights and obligations of the parties consequent upon the avoidance of the contract.

(2) A party who has performed the contract either wholly or in part may claim restitution from the other party of whatever the first party has supplied or paid under the contract. If both parties are bound to make restitution, they must do so concurrently.

Article 82

(1) The buyer loses the right to declare the contract avoided or to require the seller to deliver substitute goods if it is impossible for him to make restitution of the goods substantially in the condition in which he received them.

(2) The preceding paragraph does not apply:

(a) if the impossibility of making restitution of the goods or of making restitution of the goods substantially in the condition in which the buyer received them is not due to his act or omission;

(b) if the goods or part of the goods have perished or deteriorated as a result of the examination provided for in article 38; or

(c) if the goods or part of the goods have been sold in the normal course of business or have been consumed or transformed by the buyer in the course of normal use before he discovered or ought to have discovered the lack of conformity.

Article 83

A buyer who has lost the right to declare the contract avoided or to require the seller to deliver substitute goods in accordance with article 82 retains all other remedies under the contract and this Convention.

Article 84

(1) If the seller is bound to refund the price, he must also pay interest on it, from the date on which the price was paid.

(2) The buyer must account to the seller for all benefits which he has derived from the goods or part of them:

(a) if he must make restitution of the goods or part of them; or

(b) if it is impossible for him to make restitution of all or part of the goods or to make restitution of all or part of the goods substantially in the condition in which he received them, but he has nevertheless declared the contract avoided or required the seller to deliver substitute goods.

Section VI. Preservation of the Goods

Article 85

If the buyer is in delay in taking delivery of the goods or, where payment of the price and delivery of the goods are to be made concurrently, if he fails to pay the price, and the seller is either in possession of the goods or otherwise able to control their disposition, the seller must take such steps as are reasonable in the circumstances to preserve them. He is entitled to retain them until he has been reimbursed his reasonable expenses by the buyer.

Article 86

(1) If the buyer has received the goods and intends to exercise any right under the contract or this Convention to reject them, he must take such steps to preserve them as are reasonable in the circumstances. He is entitled to retain them until he has been reimbursed his reasonable expenses by the seller.

(2) If the goods dispatched to the buyer have been placed at his disposal at their destination and he exercises the right to reject them, he must take possession of them on behalf of the seller, provided that this can be done without payment of the price and without unreasonable inconvenience or unreasonable expense. This

provision does not apply if the seller or a person authorized to take charge of the goods on his behalf is present at the destination. If the buyer takes possession of the goods under this paragraph, his rights and obligations are governed by the preceding paragraph.

Article 87

A party who is bound to take steps to preserve the goods may deposit them in a warehouse of a third person at the expense of the other party provided that the expense incurred is not unreasonable.

Article 88

(1) A party who is bound to preserve the goods in accordance with article 85 or 86 may sell them by any appropriate means if there has been an unreasonable delay by the other party in taking possession of the goods or in taking them back or in paying the price or the cost of preservation, provided that reasonable notice of the intention to sell has been given to the other party.

(2) If the goods are subject to rapid deterioration or their preservation would involve unreasonable expense, a party who is bound to preserve the goods in accordance with article 85 or 86 must take reasonable measures to sell them. To the extent possible he must give notice to the other party of this intention to sell.

(3) A party selling the goods has the right to retain out of the proceeds of sale an amount equal to the reasonable expenses of preserving the goods and of selling them. He must account to the other party for the balance.

PART IV. FINAL PROVISIONS

Article 92

(1) A Contracting State may declare at the time of signature, ratification, acceptance, approval or accession that it will not be bound by Part II of this Convention or that it will not be bound by Part III of this Convention.

(2) A Contracting State which makes a declaration in accordance with the preceding paragraph in respect of Part II or Part III of this Convention is not to be considered a Contracting State within paragraph (1) of article 1 of this Convention in respect of matters governed by the Part to which the declaration applies.

Article 94

(1) Two or more Contracting States which have the same or closely related legal rules on matters governed by this Convention may at any time declare that the Convention is not to apply to contracts of sale or to their formation where the parties have their places of business in those States. Such declarations may be made jointly or by reciprocal unilateral declarations.

(2) A Contracting State which has the same or closely related legal rules on matters governed by this Convention as one or more non-Contracting States may

at any time declare that the Convention is not to apply to contracts of sale or to their formation where the parties have their places of business in those States.

(3) If a State which is the object of a declaration under the preceding paragraph subsequently becomes a Contracting State, the declaration made will, as from the date on which the Convention enters into force in respect of the new Contracting State, have the effect of a declaration made under paragraph (1), provided that the new Contracting State joins in such declaration or makes a reciprocal unilateral declaration.

Article 95

Any State may declare at the time of the deposit of its instrument of ratification, acceptance, approval or accession that it will not be bound by subparagraph (1)(b) of article 1 of this Convention.

Article 96

A Contracting State whose legislation requires contracts of sale to be concluded in or evidenced by writing may at any time make a declaration in accordance with article 12 that any provision of article 11, article 29, or Part II of this Convention, that allows a contract of sale or its modification or termination by agreement or any offer, acceptance, or other indication of intention to be made in any form other than in writing, does not apply where any party has his place of business in that State.

UNIDROIT Principles of International Commercial Contracts (2016)

EDITORS' NOTE

The International Institute for the Unification of Private Law (UNIDROIT) has been working since the 1920s to promote harmonization and modernization of rules governing international transactions. In 1994, after more than a decade of work, the Institute published the Principles of International Commercial Contracts. UNIDROIT published new editions of the Principles in 2004, 2010, and 2016, with additional chapters, revisions of some provisions, and updated text to adapt to the growth in electronic contracting and to better address special issues raised by long-term contracts and contracts with one or more open terms. The black letter of the 2016 UNIDROIT Principles, adopted by the UNIDROIT Governing Council at its 95th Session, held in Rome, Italy, May 18-20, 2016, is reproduced following this introductory note.[1]

The UNIDROIT Principles, like the Restatement (Second) of Contracts and other Restatements of the Law, several of which are excerpted in this Supplement, have been prepared by a respected private organization, but do not have the force of law. But a striking difference exists: while the Restatements are based on common law, the UNIDROIT Principles represent a blend of legal traditions, drawing heavily on both the civil law and the common law. As a result, a common law lawyer reading the principles will find much that is familiar, only to be jarred by an encounter with a foreign concept. See E. Allan Farnsworth, An International Restatement: The UNIDROIT Principles of International Commercial Contracts, 26 U. Balt. L. Rev. 1 (1997).

At the inception, commentators identified a number of functions that the UNIDROIT Principles could play in international commercial transactions. First, the UNIDROIT Principles may be an important resource for drafters of international

---

1. Reproduced by kind permission of UNIDROIT. The voluminous comments and illustrations are an integral part of the UNIDROIT Principles. The full-text 2016 Principles with comments and illustrations is available for download at http://www.unidroit.org/english/principles/contracts/principles2016/principles2016-e.pdf (last visited June 1, 2017).

commercial contracts. Parties to such contracts often include a "choice of law" provision to avoid uncertainty about the law that governs a cross-border transaction. Because parties in different countries may be reluctant to agree to apply the law of the country of the other party to the contract, the UNIDROIT Principles may provide a neutral source of law for incorporation in the contract. Second, the Principles can play a significant role in dispute resolution. If the parties expressly incorporated the UNIDROIT Principles into their contract, the Principles will provide the rules of decision (except to the extent that they differ from some mandatory legal rule); if the contract is silent on choice of law, or if it has a general choice of law provision ("*lex mercatoria*," "general commercial law," or similar provision), the dispute resolution body – whether an arbitral panel or a court – could turn to the UNIDROIT Principles to resolve the dispute. In those cases in which the CISG applies because the contracting parties have places of business in states that are parties to the Convention, the UNIDROIT Principles can Supplement the CISG when the latter does not deal definitively with a particular issue. Finally, the UNIDROIT Principles have the potential to be an influential source for law reform. By drawing on what the drafters consider the best rules of the civil and common law, they have provided a set of standards to which legislatures in various countries can turn when considering modernization of their law. See Joseph M. Perillo, UNIDROIT Principles of International Commercial Contracts: The Black Letter Text and a Review, 63 Fordham L. Rev. 281, 283-284 (1994). See generally Michael J. Bonell, UNIDROIT Symposium: Soft Law and Party Autonomy: The Case of the UNIDROIT Principles, 51 Loy. L. Rev. 229 (2005); Symposium: The UNIDROIT Principles of International Commercial Contracts, 69 Tul. L. Rev. 1121 (1995).

The UNIDROIT Principles have been cited by many arbitral tribunals and several courts, received substantial attention from scholars, and have even had influence on states engaged in reform of commercial law. See Sandeep Gopalan, New Trends in the Making of International Commercial Law, 23 J.L. & Com. 117, 159-164 (2004) (citing positive effect of the UNIDROIT Principles in arbitral proceedings and noting they have influenced law reform in Russia, Estonia, and Lithuania); Fabrizio Marrella, International Commercial Arbitration: Choice of Law in Third-Millennium Arbitrations: The Relevance of the UNIDROIT Principles of International Commercial Contracts, 36 Vand. J. Transnat'l L. 1137 (2003) (stating that the UNIDROIT Principles have played a positive role in international commercial arbitration). A database on the UNIDROIT Principles, as well as the CISG, has been established by the Rome-based Centre for Comparative and Foreign Law Studies and allows access to arbitral and court decisions which cite the UNIDROIT Principles.[2]

Another project that has paralleled the emergence of the UNIDROIT Principles has been the work of the Commission on European Contract Law in preparing the Principles of European Contract Law (PECL).[3] The Commission on European Contract Law is an independent body of experts from each Member State of the European Union that began its work in 1982.[4] The Principles of European Contract Law are stated in the form of articles with a detailed commentary explaining the

---

2. See http://www.unilex.info (last visited June 1, 2017).

3. The text of PECL can be found at http://www.trans-lex.org/400200/_/pecl/ (last visited June 1, 2017).

4 An introduction to the PECL reflects the Commission's hope that the PECL will play an important role in the possible development of a code of common European contract law. See Ole Lando, The Common Core of European Private Law and the Principles of European Contract Law, 21 Hastings Int'l & Comp. L. Rev. 809 (1998).

purpose and operation of each article, along with notes that explain how each article relates to the various national laws. While there was some reciprocal influence during the drafting of the UNIDROIT Principles and the PECL, one important difference between the two publications is that the former applies only to commercial transactions while the latter also applies to consumer contracts. See Sandeep Gopalan, New Trends in the Making of International Commercial Law, *supra* at 164-67. Ultimately, the future impact of the PECL remains uncertain. See generally Michael J. Bonell, The CISG, European Contract Law and the Development of a World Contract Law, 56 Am. J. Comp. L. 1 (2008).

PREAMBLE

CHAPTER 1: GENERAL PROVISIONS

CHAPTER 2: FORMATION AND AUTHORITY OF AGENTS

Section 1: Formation

CHAPTER 8: SET-OFF

CHAPTER 9: ASSIGNMENT OF RIGHTS, TRANSFER OF
OBLIGATIONS, ASSIGNMENT OF CONTRACTS

Section 1: Assignment of Rights

Section 2: Transfer of Obligations

Section 3: Assignment of Contracts

CHAPTER 10: LIMITATION PERIODS

PREAMBLE

(Purpose of the Principles)

These Principles set forth general rules for international commercial contracts.

They shall be applied when the parties have agreed that their contract be governed by them.*

They may be applied when the parties have agreed that their contract be governed by general principles of law, the *lex mercatoria* or the like.

---

* Parties wishing to provide that their agreement be governed by the Principles might use one of the *Model Clauses for the Use of the UNIDROIT Principles of International Commercial Contracts* (see http://www. unidroit.org/instruments/commercial-contracts/upicc-model-clauses).

They may be applied when the parties have not chosen any law to govern their contract.

They may be used to interpret or Supplement international uniform law instruments.

They may be used to interpret or Supplement domestic law.

They may serve as a model for national and international legislators.

CHAPTER 1: GENERAL PROVISIONS

Article 1.1   Freedom of Contract

The parties are free to enter into a contract and to determine its content.

Article 1.2   No Form Required

Nothing in these Principles requires a contract, statement or any other act to be made in or evidenced by a particular form. It may be proved by any means, including witnesses.

Article 1.3   Binding Character of Contract

A contract validly entered into is binding upon the parties. It can only be modified or terminated in accordance with its terms or by agreement or as otherwise provided in these Principles.

Article 1.4   Mandatory Rules

Nothing in these Principles shall restrict the application of mandatory rules, whether of national, international or supranational origin, which are applicable in accordance with the relevant rules of private international law.

Article 1.5   Exclusion or Modification by the Parties

The parties may exclude the application of these Principles or derogate from or vary the effect of any of their provisions, except as otherwise provided in the Principles.

Article 1.6   Interpretation and Supplementation of the Principles

(1) In the interpretation of these Principles, regard is to be had to their international character and to their purposes including the need to promote uniformity in their application.

(2) Issues within the scope of these Principles but not expressly settled by them are as far as possible to be settled in accordance with their underlying general principles.

Article 1.7   Good Faith and Fair Dealing

(1) Each party must act in accordance with good faith and fair dealing in international trade.

(2) The parties may not exclude or limit this duty.

Article 1.8   Inconsistent Behaviour

A party cannot act inconsistently with an understanding it has caused the other party to have and upon which that other party reasonably has acted in reliance to its detriment.

Article 1.9   Usages and Practices

(1) The parties are bound by any usage to which they have agreed and by any practices which they have established between themselves.

(2) The parties are bound by a usage that is widely known to and regularly observed in international trade by parties in the particular trade concerned except where the application of such a usage would be unreasonable.

Article 1.10   Notice

(1) Where notice is required it may be given by any means appropriate to the circumstances.

(2) A notice is effective when it reaches the person to whom it is given.

(3) For the purpose of paragraph (2) a notice "reaches" a person when given to that person orally or delivered at that person's place of business or mailing address.

(4) For the purpose of this Article "notice" includes a declaration, demand, request or any other communication of intention.

Article 1.11   Definitions

In these Principles
  - "court" includes an arbitral tribunal;
  - where a party has more than one place of business the relevant "place of business" is that which has the closest relationship to the contract and its performance, having regard to the circumstances known to or contemplated by the parties at any time before or at the conclusion of the contract;
  - "long-term contract" refers to a contract which is to be performed over a period of time and which normally involves, to a varying degree, complexity of the transaction and an ongoing relationship between the parties;
  - "obligor" refers to the party who is to perform an obligation and "obligee" refers to the party who is entitled to performance of that obligation.
  - "writing" means any mode of communication that preserves a record of the information contained therein and is capable of being reproduced in tangible form.

Article 1.12   Computation of Time Set by Parties

(1) Official holidays or non-business days occurring during a period set by parties for an act to be performed are included in calculating the period.

(2) However, if the last day of the period is an official holiday or a non-business day at the place of business of the party to perform the act, the period is extended until the first business day which follows, unless the circumstances indicate otherwise.

(3) The relevant time zone is that of the place of business of the party setting the time, unless the circumstances indicate otherwise.

CHAPTER 2: FORMATION AND AUTHORITY OF AGENTS

Section 1: Formation

Article 2.1.1 Manner of Formation

A contract may be concluded either by the acceptance of an offer or by conduct of the parties that is sufficient to show agreement.

Article 2.1.2 Definition of Offer

A proposal for concluding a contract constitutes an offer if it is sufficiently definite and indicates the intention of the offeror to be bound in case of acceptance.

Article 2.1.3 Withdrawal of Offer

(1) An offer becomes effective when it reaches the offeree.

(2) An offer, even if it is irrevocable, may be withdrawn if the withdrawal reaches the offeree before or at the same time as the offer.

Article 2.1.4 Revocation of Offer

(1) Until a contract is concluded an offer may be revoked if the revocation reaches the offeree before it has dispatched an acceptance.

(2) However, an offer cannot be revoked

(a) if it indicates, whether by stating a fixed time for acceptance or otherwise, that it is irrevocable; or

(b) if it was reasonable for the offeree to rely on the offer as being irrevocable and the offeree has acted in reliance on the offer.

Article 2.1.5 Rejection of Offer

An offer is terminated when a rejection reaches the offeror.

Article 2.1.6 Mode of Acceptance

(1) A statement made by or other conduct of the offeree indicating assent to an offer is an acceptance. Silence or inactivity does not in itself amount to acceptance.

(2) An acceptance of an offer becomes effective when the indication of assent reaches the offeror.

(3) However, if, by virtue of the offer or as a result of practices which the parties have established between themselves or of usage, the offeree may indicate assent by performing an act without notice to the offeror, the acceptance is effective when the act is performed.

Article 2.1.7 Time of Acceptance

An offer must be accepted within the time the offeror has fixed or, if no time is fixed, within a reasonable time having regard to the circumstances, including the rapidity of the means of communication employed by the offeror. An oral offer must be accepted immediately unless the circumstances indicate otherwise.

Article 2.1.8   Acceptance Within a Fixed Period of Time

A period of acceptance fixed by the offeror begins to run from the time that the offer is dispatched. A time indicated in the offer is deemed to be the time of dispatch unless the circumstances indicate otherwise.

Article 2.1.9   Late Acceptance. Delay in Transmission

(1) A late acceptance is nevertheless effective as an acceptance if without undue delay the offeror so informs the offeree or gives notice to that effect.

(2) If a communication containing a late acceptance shows that it has been sent in such circumstances that if its transmission had been normal it would have reached the offeror in due time, the late acceptance is effective as an acceptance unless, without undue delay, the offeror informs the offeree that it considers the offer as having lapsed.

Article 2.1.10   Withdrawal of Acceptance

An acceptance may be withdrawn if the withdrawal reaches the offeror before or at the same time as the acceptance would have become effective.

Article 2.1.11   Modified Acceptance

(1) A reply to an offer which purports to be an acceptance but contains additions, limitations or other modifications is a rejection of the offer and constitutes a counter-offer.

(2) However, a reply to an offer which purports to be an acceptance but contains additional or different terms which do not materially alter the terms of the offer constitutes an acceptance, unless the offeror, without undue delay, objects to the discrepancy. If the offeror does not object, the terms of the contract are the terms of the offer with the modifications contained in the acceptance.

Article 2.1.12   Writings in Confirmation

If a writing which is sent within a reasonable time after the conclusion of the contract and which purports to be a confirmation of the contract contains additional or different terms, such terms become part of the contract, unless they materially alter the contract or the recipient, without undue delay, objects to the discrepancy.

Article 2.1.13   Conclusion of Contract Dependent on Agreement on Specific Matters or in a Particular Form

Where in the course of negotiations one of the parties insists that the contract is not concluded until there is agreement on specific matters or in a particular form, no contract is concluded before agreement is reached on those matters or in that form.

Article 2.1.14   Contract with Terms Deliberately Left Open

(1) If the parties intend to conclude a contract, the fact that they intentionally leave a term to be agreed upon in further negotiations or to be

determined by one of the parties or by a third person does not prevent a contract from coming into existence.

(2) The existence of the contract is not affected by the fact that subsequently

(a) the parties reach no agreement on the term;

(b) the party who is to determine the term does not do so; or

(c) the third person does not determine the term, provided that there is an alternative means of rendering the term definite that is reasonable in the circumstances, having regard to the intention of the parties.

Article 2.1.15   Negotiations in Bad Faith

(1) A party is free to negotiate and is not liable for failure to reach an agreement.

(2) However, a party who negotiates or breaks off negotiations in bad faith is liable for the losses caused to the other party.

(3) It is bad faith, in particular, for a party to enter into or continue negotiations when intending not to reach an agreement with the other party.

Article 2.1.16   Duty of Confidentiality

Where information is given as confidential by one party in the course of negotiations, the other party is under a duty not to disclose that information or to use it improperly for its own purposes, whether or not a contract is subsequently concluded. Where appropriate, the remedy for breach of that duty may include compensation based on the benefit received by the other party.

Article 2.1.17   Merger Clauses

A contract in writing which contains a clause indicating that the writing completely embodies the terms on which the parties have agreed cannot be contradicted or supplemented by evidence of prior statements or agreements. However, such statements or agreements may be used to interpret the writing.

Article 2.1.18   Modification in a Particular Form

A contract in writing which contains a clause requiring any modification or termination by agreement to be in a particular form may not be otherwise modified or terminated. However, a party may be precluded by its conduct from asserting such a clause to the extent that the other party has reasonably acted in reliance on that conduct.

Article 2.1.19   Contracting Under Standard Terms

(1) Where one party or both parties use standard terms in concluding a contract, the general rules on formation apply, subject to Articles 2.1.20-2.1.22.

(2) Standard terms are provisions which are prepared in advance for general and repeated use by one party and which are actually used without negotiation with the other party.

Article 2.1.20   Surprising Terms

(1) No term contained in standard terms which is of such a character that the other party could not reasonably have expected it, is effective unless it has been expressly accepted by that party.

(2) In determining whether a term is of such a character regard shall be had to its content, language and presentation.

Article 2.1.21   Conflict Between Standard Terms and Non-Standard Terms

In case of conflict between a standard term and a term which is not a standard term the latter prevails.

Article 2.1.22   Battle of Forms

Where both parties use standard terms and reach agreement except on those terms, a contract is concluded on the basis of the agreed terms and of any standard terms which are common in substance unless one party clearly indicates in advance, or later and without undue delay informs the other party, that it does not intend to be bound by such a contract.

Section 2: Authority of Agents

Article 2.2.1   Scope of the Section

(1) This Section governs the authority of a person ("the agent"), to affect the legal relations of another person ("the principal"), by or with respect to a contract with a third party, whether the agent acts in its own name or in that of the principal.

(2) It governs only the relations between the principal or the agent on the one hand, and the third party on the other.

(3) It does not govern an agent's authority conferred by law or the authority of an agent appointed by a public or judicial authority.

Article 2.2.2   Establishment and Scope of the Authority of the Agent

(1) The principal's grant of authority to an agent may be express or implied.

(2) The agent has authority to perform all acts necessary in the circumstances to achieve the purposes for which the authority was granted.

Article 2.2.3   Agency Disclosed

(1) Where an agent acts within the scope of its authority and the third party knew or ought to have known that the agent was acting as an agent, the acts of the agent shall directly affect the legal relations between the principal and the third party and no legal relation is created between the agent and the third party.

(2) However, the acts of the agent shall affect only the relations between the agent and the third party, where the agent with the consent of the principal undertakes to become the party to the contract.

Article 2.2.4   Agency Undisclosed

(1) Where an agent acts within the scope of its authority and the third party neither knew nor ought to have known that the agent was acting as an agent, the acts of the agent shall affect only the relations between the agent and the third party.

(2) However, where such an agent, when contracting with the third party on behalf of a business, represents itself to be the owner of that business, the third party, upon discovery of the real owner of the business, may exercise also against the latter the rights it has against the agent.

Article 2.2.5   Agent Acting Without or Exceeding
Its Authority

(1) Where an agent acts without authority or exceeds its authority, its acts do not affect the legal relations between the principal and the third party.

(2) However, where the principal causes the third party reasonably to believe that the agent has authority to act on behalf of the principal and that the agent is acting within the scope of that authority, the principal may not invoke against the third party the lack of authority of the agent.

Article 2.2.6   Liability of Agent Acting Without or
Exceeding Its Authority

(1) An agent that acts without authority or exceeds its authority is, failing ratification by the principal, liable for damages that will place the third party in the same position as if the agent had acted with authority and not exceeded its authority.

(2) However, the agent is not liable if the third party knew or ought to have known that the agent had no authority or was exceeding its authority.

Article 2.2.7   Conflict of Interests

(1) If a contract concluded by an agent involves the agent in a conflict of interests with the principal of which the third party knew or ought to have known, the principal may avoid the contract. The right to avoid is subject to Articles 3.2.9 and 3.2.11 to 3.2.15.

(2) However, the principal may not avoid the contract
  (a) if the principal had consented to, or knew or ought to have known of, the agent's involvement in the conflict of interests; or
  (b) if the agent had disclosed the conflict of interests to the principal and the latter had not objected within a reasonable time.

Article 2.2.8   Sub-Agency

An agent has implied authority to appoint a sub-agent to perform acts which it is not reasonable to expect the agent to perform itself. The rules of this Section apply to the sub-agency.

Article 2.2.9   Ratification

(1) An act by an agent that acts without authority or exceeds its authority may be ratified by the principal. On ratification the act produces the same effects as if it had initially been carried out with authority.

(2) The third party may by notice to the principal specify a reasonable period of time for ratification. If the principal does not ratify within that period of time it can no longer do so.

(3) If, at the time of the agent's act, the third party neither knew nor ought to have known of the lack of authority, it may, at any time before ratification, by notice to the principal indicate its refusal to become bound by a ratification.

Article 2.2.10   Termination of Authority

(1) Termination of authority is not effective in relation to the third party unless the third party knew or ought to have known of it.

(2) Notwithstanding the termination of its authority, an agent remains authorised to perform the acts that are necessary to prevent harm to the principal's interests.

CHAPTER 3. VALIDITY

Section 1: General Provisions

Article 3.1.1   Matters Not Covered

This Chapter does not deal with lack of capacity.

Article 3.1.2   Validity of Mere Agreement

A contract is concluded, modified or terminated by the mere agreement of the parties, without any further requirement.

Article 3.1.3   Initial Impossibility

(1) The mere fact that at the time of the conclusion of the contract the performance of the obligation assumed was impossible does not affect the validity of the contract.

(2) The mere fact that at the time of the conclusion of the contract a party was not entitled to dispose of the assets to which the contract relates does not affect the validity of the contract.

Article 3.1.4   Mandatory Character of the Provisions

The provisions on fraud, threat, gross disparity and illegality contained in this Chapter are mandatory.

Section 2: Grounds for Avoidance

Article 3.2.1   Definition of Mistake

Mistake is an erroneous assumption relating to facts or to law existing when the contract was concluded.

Article 3.2.2 Relevant Mistake

(1) A party may only avoid the contract for mistake if, when the contract was concluded, the mistake was of such importance that a reasonable person in the same situation as the party in error would only have concluded the contract on materially different terms or would not have concluded it at all if the true state of affairs had been known, and

(a) the other party made the same mistake, or caused the mistake, or knew or ought to have known of the mistake and it was contrary to reasonable commercial standards of fair dealing to leave the mistaken party in error; or

(b) the other party had not at the time of avoidance reasonably acted in reliance on the contract.

(2) However, a party may not avoid the contract if

(a) it was grossly negligent in committing the mistake; or

(b) the mistake relates to a matter in regard to which the risk of mistake was assumed or, having regard to the circumstances, should be borne by the mistaken party.

Article 3.2.3 Error in Expression or Transmission

An error occurring in the expression or transmission of a declaration is considered to be a mistake of the person from whom the declaration emanated.

Article 3.2.4 Remedies for Non-Performance

A party is not entitled to avoid the contract on the ground of mistake if the circumstances on which that party relies afford, or could have afforded, a remedy for non-performance.

Article 3.2.5 Fraud

A party may avoid the contract when it has been led to conclude the contract by the other party's fraudulent representation, including language or practices, or fraudulent non-disclosure of circumstances which, according to reasonable commercial standards of fair dealing, the latter party should have disclosed.

Article 3.2.6 Threat

A party may avoid the contract when it has been led to conclude the contract by the other party's unjustified threat which, having regard to the circumstances, is so imminent and serious as to leave the first party no reasonable alternative. In particular, a threat is unjustified if the act or omission with which a party has been threatened is wrongful in itself, or it is wrongful to use it as a means to obtain the conclusion of the contract.

Article 3.2.7 Gross Disparity

(1) A party may avoid the contract or an individual term of it if, at the time of the conclusion of the contract, the contract or term unjustifiably gave the other party an excessive advantage. Regard is to be had, among other factors, to

(a) the fact that the other party has taken unfair advantage of the first party's dependence, economic distress or urgent needs, or of its improvidence, ignorance, inexperience or lack of bargaining skill, and

(b) the nature and purpose of the contract.

(2) Upon the request of the party entitled to avoidance, a court may adapt the contract or term in order to make it accord with reasonable commercial standards of fair dealing.

(3) A court may also adapt the contract or term upon the request of the party receiving notice of avoidance, provided that that party informs the other party of its request promptly after receiving such notice and before the other party has reasonably acted in reliance on it. Article 3.2.10(2) applies accordingly.

Article 3.2.8   Third Persons

(1) Where fraud, threat, gross disparity or a party's mistake is imputable to, or is known or ought to be known by, a third person for whose acts the other party is responsible, the contract may be avoided under the same conditions as if the behaviour or knowledge had been that of the party itself.

(2) Where fraud, threat or gross disparity is imputable to a third person for whose acts the other party is not responsible, the contract may be avoided if that party knew or ought to have known of the fraud, threat or disparity, or has not at the time of avoidance reasonably acted in reliance on the contract.

Article 3.2.9   Confirmation

If the party entitled to avoid the contract expressly or impliedly confirms the contract after the period of time for giving notice of avoidance has begun to run, avoidance of the contract is excluded.

Article 3.2.10   Loss of Right to Avoid

(1) If a party is entitled to avoid the contract for mistake but the other party declares itself willing to perform or performs the contract as it was understood by the party entitled to avoidance, the contract is considered to have been concluded as the latter party understood it. The other party must make such a declaration or render such performance promptly after having been informed of the manner in which the party entitled to avoidance had understood the contract and before that party has reasonably acted in reliance on a notice of avoidance.

(2) After such a declaration or performance the right to avoidance is lost and any earlier notice of avoidance is ineffective.

Article 3.2.11   Notice of Avoidance

The right of a party to avoid the contract is exercised by notice to the other party.

Article 3.2.12   Time Limits

(1) Notice of avoidance shall be given within a reasonable time, having regard to the circumstances, after the avoiding party knew or could not have been unaware of the relevant facts or became capable of acting freely.

(2) Where an individual term of the contract may be avoided by a party under Article 3.2.7, the period of time for giving notice of avoidance begins to run when that term is asserted by the other party.

Article 3.2.13   Partial Avoidance

Where a ground of avoidance affects only individual terms of the contract, the effect of avoidance is limited to those terms unless, having regard to the circumstances, it is unreasonable to uphold the remaining contract.

Article 3.2.14   Retroactive Effect of Avoidance

Avoidance takes effect retroactively.

Article 3.2.15   Restitution

(1) On avoidance either party may claim restitution of whatever it has supplied under the contract, or the part of it avoided, provided that the party concurrently makes restitution of whatever it has received under the contract, or the part of it avoided.

(2) If restitution in kind is not possible or appropriate, an allowance has to be made in money whenever reasonable.

(3) The recipient of the performance does not have to make an allowance in money if the impossibility to make restitution in kind is attributable to the other party.

(4) Compensation may be claimed for expenses reasonably required to pre-serve or maintain the performance received.

Article 3.2.16   Damages

Irrespective of whether or not the contract has been avoided, the party who knew or ought to have known of the ground for avoidance is liable for damages so as to put the other party in the same position in which it would have been if it had not concluded the contract.

Article 3.2.17   Unilateral Declarations

The provisions of this Chapter apply with appropriate adaptations to any communication of intention addressed by one party to the other.

Section 3: Illegality

Article 3.3.1   Contracts Infringing Mandatory Rules

(1) Where a contract infringes a mandatory rule, whether of national, inter-national or supranational origin, applicable under Article 1.4 of these Principles, the effects of that infringement upon the contract are the effects, if any, expressly prescribed by that mandatory rule.

(2) Where the mandatory rule does not expressly prescribe the effects of an infringement upon a contract, the parties have the right to exercise such remedies under the contract as in the circumstances are reasonable.

(3) In determining what is reasonable regard is to be had in particular to:

(a) the purpose of the rule which has been infringed;

(b) the category of persons for whose protection the rule exists;

(c) any sanction that may be imposed under the rule infringed;

(d) the seriousness of the infringement;

(e) whether one or both parties knew or ought to have known of the infringement;

(f) whether the performance of the contract necessitates the infringement; and

(g) the parties' reasonable expectations.

Article 3.3.2   Restitution

(1) Where there has been performance under a contract infringing a mandatory rule under Article 3.3.1, restitution may be granted where this would be reasonable in the circumstances.

(2) In determining what is reasonable, regard is to be had, with the appropriate adaptations, to the criteria referred to in Article 3.3.1(3).

(3) If restitution is granted, the rules set out in Article 3.2.15 apply with appropriate adaptations.

CHAPTER 4: INTERPRETATION

Article 4.1   Intention of the Parties

(1) A contract shall be interpreted according to the common intention of the parties.

(2) If such an intention cannot be established, the contract shall be interpreted according to the meaning that reasonable persons of the same kind as the parties would give to it in the same circumstances.

Article 4.2   Interpretation of Statements and Other Conduct

(1) The statements and other conduct of a party shall be interpreted according to that party's intention if the other party knew or could not have been unaware of that intention.

(2) If the preceding paragraph is not applicable, such statements and other conduct shall be interpreted according to the meaning that a reasonable person of the same kind as the other party would give to it in the same circumstances.

Article 4.3   Relevant Circumstances

In applying Articles 4.1 and 4.2, regard shall be had to all the circumstances, including

(a) preliminary negotiations between the parties;

(b) practices which the parties have established between themselves;

(c) the conduct of the parties subsequent to the conclusion of the contract;

(d) the nature and purpose of the contract;

(e) the meaning commonly given to terms and expressions in the trade concerned;

(f) usages.

Article 4.4   Reference to Contract or Statement as a Whole

Terms and expressions shall be interpreted in the light of the whole contract or statement in which they appear.

Article 4.5   All Terms to Be Given Effect

Contract terms shall be interpreted so as to give effect to all the terms rather than to deprive some of them of effect.

Article 4.6   Contra Proferentem Rule

If contract terms supplied by one party are unclear, an interpretation against that party is preferred.

Article 4.7   Linguistic Discrepancies

Where a contract is drawn up in two or more language versions which are equally authoritative there is, in case of discrepancy between the versions, a preference for the interpretation according to a version in which the contract was originally drawn up.

Article 4.8   Supplying an Omitted Term

(1) Where the parties to a contract have not agreed with respect to a term which is important for a determination of their rights and duties, a term which is appropriate in the circumstances shall be supplied.

(2) In determining what is an appropriate term regard shall be had, among other factors, to

(a) the intention of the parties;

(b) the nature and purpose of the contract;

(c) good faith and fair dealing;

(d) reasonableness.

CHAPTER 5: CONTENT, THIRD PARTY RIGHTS AND CONDITIONS

Section 1: Content

Article 5.1.1   Express and Implied Obligations

The contractual obligations of the parties may be express or implied.

Article 5.1.2   Implied Obligations

Implied obligations stem from
(a) the nature and purpose of the contract;
(b) practices established between the parties and usages;
(c) good faith and fair dealing;
(d) reasonableness.

Article 5.1.3   Co-operation Between the Parties

Each party shall cooperate with the other party when such co-operation may reasonably be expected for the performance of that party's obligations.

Article 5.1.4   Duty to Achieve a Specific Result. Duty of Best Efforts

(1) To the extent that an obligation of a party involves a duty to achieve a specific result, that party is bound to achieve that result.

(2) To the extent that an obligation of a party involves a duty of best efforts in the performance of an activity, that party is bound to make such efforts as would be made by a reasonable person of the same kind in the same circumstances.

Article 5.1.5   Determination of Kind of Duty Involved

In determining the extent to which an obligation of a party involves a duty of best efforts in the performance of an activity or a duty to achieve a specific result, regard shall be had, among other factors, to
(a) the way in which the obligation is expressed in the contract;
(b) the contractual price and other terms of the contract;
(c) the degree of risk normally involved in achieving the expected result;
(d) the ability of the other party to influence the performance of the obligation.

Article 5.1.6   Determination of Quality of Performance

Where the quality of performance is neither fixed by, nor determinable from, the contract a party is bound to render a performance of a quality that is reasonable and not less than average in the circumstances.

Article 5.1.7   Price Determination

(1) Where a contract does not fix or make provision for determining the price, the parties are considered, in the absence of any indication to the contrary, to have made reference to the price generally charged at the time of the conclusion of the contract for such performance in comparable circumstances in the trade concerned or, if no such price is available, to a reasonable price.

(2) Where the price is to be determined by one party and that determination is manifestly unreasonable, a reasonable price shall be substituted notwithstanding any contract term to the contrary.

(3) Where the price is to be fixed by one party or a third person, and that party or third person does not do so, the price shall be a reasonable price.

(4) Where the price is to be fixed by reference to factors which do not exist or have ceased to exist or to be accessible, the nearest equivalent factor shall be treated as a substitute.

Article 5.1.8   Termination of a Contract for an Indefinite Period

A contract for an indefinite period may be terminated by either party by giving notice a reasonable time in advance. As to the effects of termination in general, and as to restitution, the provisions in Articles 7.3.5 and 7.3.7 apply.

Article 5.1.9   Release by Agreement

(1) An obligee may release its right by agreement with the obligor.

(2) An offer to release a right gratuitously shall be deemed accepted if the obligor does not reject the offer without delay after having become aware of it.

Section 2: Third Party Rights

Article 5.2.1   Contracts in Favour of Third Parties

(1) The parties (the "promisor" and the "promisee") may confer by express or implied agreement a right on a third party (the "beneficiary").

(2) The existence and content of the beneficiary's right against the promisor are determined by the agreement of the parties and are subject to any conditions or other limitations under the agreement.

Article 5.2.2   Third Party Identifiable

The beneficiary must be identifiable with adequate certainty by the contract but need not be in existence at the time the contract is made.

Article 5.2.3   Exclusion and Limitation Clauses

The conferment of rights in the beneficiary includes the right to invoke a clause in the contract which excludes or limits the liability of the beneficiary.

Article 5.2.4   Defences

The promisor may assert against the beneficiary all defences which the promisor could assert against the promisee.

Article 5.2.5   Revocation

The parties may modify or revoke the rights conferred by the contract on the beneficiary until the beneficiary has accepted them or reasonably acted in reliance on them.

Article 5.2.6   Renunciation

The beneficiary may renounce a right conferred on it.

Section 3: Conditions

Article 5.3.1 Types of Condition

A contract or a contractual obligation may be made conditional upon the occurrence of a future uncertain event, so that the contract or the contractual obligation only takes effect if the event occurs (suspensive condition) or comes to an end if the event occurs (resolutive condition).

Article 5.3.2 Effect of Conditions

Unless the parties otherwise agree:
(a) the relevant contract or contractual obligation takes effect upon fulfilment of a suspensive condition;
(b) the relevant contract or contractual obligation comes to an end upon fulfillment of a resolutive condition.

Article 5.3.3 Interference with Conditions

(1) If fulfilment of a condition is prevented by a party, contrary to the duty of good faith and fair dealing or the duty of co-operation, that party may not rely on the non-fulfilment of the condition.
(2) If fulfilment of a condition is brought about by a party, contrary to the duty of good faith and fair dealing or the duty of co-operation, that party may not rely on the fulfilment of the condition.

Article 5.3.4 Duty to Preserve Rights

Pending fulfilment of a condition, a party may not, contrary to the duty to act in accordance with good faith and fair dealing, act so as to prejudice the other party's rights in case of fulfilment of the condition.

Article 5.3.5 Restitution in Case of Fulfilment of a Resolutive Condition

(1) On fulfilment of a resolutive condition, the rules on restitution set out in Articles 7.3.6 and 7.3.7 apply with appropriate adaptations.
(2) If the parties have agreed that the resolutive condition is to operate retroactively, the rules on restitution set out in Article 3.2.15 apply with appropriate adaptations.

CHAPTER 6: PERFORMANCE

Section 1: Performance in General

Article 6.1.1 Time of Performance

A party must perform its obligations:
(a) if a time is fixed by or determinable from the contract, at that time;
(b) if a period of time is fixed by or determinable from the contract, at any time within that period unless circumstances indicate that the other party is to choose a time;

(c) in any other case, within a reasonable time after the conclusion of the contract.

Article 6.1.2   Performance at One Time or in Instalments

In cases under Article 6.1.1(b) or (c), a party must perform its obligations at one time if that performance can be rendered at one time and the circumstances do not indicate otherwise.

Article 6.1.3   Partial Performance

(1) The obligee may reject an offer to perform in part at the time performance is due, whether or not such offer is coupled with an assurance as to the balance of the performance, unless the obligee has no legitimate interest in so doing.

(2) Additional expenses caused to the obligee by partial performance are to be borne by the obligor without prejudice to any other remedy.

Article 6.1.4   Order of Performance

(1) To the extent that the performances of the parties can be rendered simultaneously, the parties are bound to render them simultaneously unless the circumstances indicate otherwise.

(2) To the extent that the performance of only one party requires a period of time, that party is bound to render its performance first, unless the circumstances indicate otherwise.

Article 6.1.5   Earlier Performance

(1) The obligee may reject an earlier performance unless it has no legitimate interest in so doing.

(2) Acceptance by a party of an earlier performance does not affect the time for the performance of its own obligations if that time has been fixed irrespective of the performance of the other party's obligations.

(3) Additional expenses caused to the obligee by earlier performance are to be borne by the obligor, without prejudice to any other remedy.

Article 6.1.6   Place of Performance

(1) If the place of performance is neither fixed by, nor determinable from, the contract, a party is to perform:

   (a) a monetary obligation, at the obligee's place of business;

   (b) any other obligation, at its own place of business.

(2) A party must bear any increase in the expenses incidental to performance which is caused by a change in its place of business subsequent to the conclusion of the contract.

Article 6.1.7   Payment by Cheque or Other Instrument

(1) Payment may be made in any form used in the ordinary course of business at the place for payment.

(2) However, an obligee who accepts, either by virtue of paragraph (1) or voluntarily, a cheque, any other order to pay or a promise to pay, is presumed to do so only on condition that it will be honoured.

Article 6.1.8   Payment by Funds Transfer

(1) Unless the obligee has indicated a particular account, payment may be made by a transfer to any of the financial institutions in which the obligee has made it known that it has an account.

(2) In case of payment by a transfer the obligation of the obligor is discharged when the transfer to the obligee's financial institution becomes effective.

Article 6.1.9   Currency of Payment

(1) If a monetary obligation is expressed in a currency other than that of the place for payment, it may be paid by the obligor in the currency of the place for payment unless

(a) that currency is not freely convertible; or

(b) the parties have agreed that payment should be made only in the currency in which the monetary obligation is expressed.

(2) If it is impossible for the obligor to make payment in the currency in which the monetary obligation is expressed, the obligee may require payment in the currency of the place for payment, even in the case referred to in paragraph (1)(b).

(3) Payment in the currency of the place for payment is to be made according to the applicable rate of exchange prevailing there when payment is due.

(4) However, if the obligor has not paid at the time when payment is due, the obligee may require payment according to the applicable rate of exchange prevailing either when payment is due or at the time of actual payment.

Article 6.1.10   Currency Not Expressed

Where a monetary obligation is not expressed in a particular currency, payment must be made in the currency of the place where payment is to be made.

Article 6.1.11   Costs of Performance

Each party shall bear the costs of performance of its obligations.

Article 6.1.12   Imputation of Payments

(1) An obligor owing several monetary obligations to the same obligee may specify at the time of payment the debt to which it intends the payment to be applied. However, the payment discharges first any expenses, then interest due and finally the principal.

(2) If the obligor makes no such specification, the obligee may, within a reasonable time after payment, declare to the obligor the obligation to which it imputes the payment, provided that the obligation is due and undisputed.

(3) In the absence of imputation under paragraphs (1) or (2), payment is imputed to that obligation which satisfies one of the following criteria in the order indicated:

    (a) an obligation which is due or which is the first to fall due;

    (b) the obligation for which the obligee has least security;

    (c) the obligation which is the most burdensome for the obligor;

    (d) the obligation which has arisen first.

If none of the preceding criteria applies, payment is imputed to all the obligations proportionally.

Article 6.1.13   Imputation of Non-Monetary Obligations

Article 6.1.12 applies with appropriate adaptations to the imputation of performance of non-monetary obligations.

Article 6.1.14   Application for Public Permission

Where the law of a State requires a public permission affecting the validity of the contract or its performance and neither that law nor the circumstances indicate otherwise

    (a) if only one party has its place of business in that State, that party shall take the measures necessary to obtain the permission;

    (b) in any other case the party whose performance requires permission shall take the necessary measures.

Article 6.1.15   Procedure in Applying for Permission

(1) The party required to take the measures necessary to obtain the permission shall do so without undue delay and shall bear any expenses incurred.

(2) That party shall whenever appropriate give the other party notice of the grant or refusal of such permission without undue delay.

Article 6.1.16   Permission Neither Granted Nor Refused

(1) If, notwithstanding the fact that the party responsible has taken all measures required, permission is neither granted nor refused within an agreed period or, where no period has been agreed, within a reasonable time from the conclusion of the contract, either party is entitled to terminate the contract.

(2) Where the permission affects some terms only, paragraph (1) does not apply if, having regard to the circumstances, it is reasonable to uphold the remaining contract even if the permission is refused.

Article 6.1.17   Permission Refused

(1) The refusal of a permission affecting the validity of the contract renders the contract void. If the refusal affects the validity of some terms only, only such terms are void if, having regard to the circumstances, it is reasonable to uphold the remaining contract.

(2) Where the refusal of a permission renders the performance of the contract impossible in whole or in part, the rules on non-performance apply.

Section 2: Hardship

Article 6.2.1   Contract to Be Observed

Where the performance of a contract becomes more onerous for one of the parties, that party is nevertheless bound to perform its obligations subject to the following provisions on hardship.

Article 6.2.2   Definition of Hardship

There is hardship where the occurrence of events fundamentally alters the equilibrium of the contract either because the cost of a party's performance has increased or because the value of the performance a party receives has diminished, and

> (a) the events occur or become known to the disadvantaged party after the conclusion of the contract;
> (b) the events could not reasonably have been taken into account by the disadvantaged party at the time of the conclusion of the contract;
> (c) the events are beyond the control of the disadvantaged party; and
> (d) the risk of the events was not assumed by the disadvantaged party.

Article 6.2.3   Effects of Hardship

(1) In case of hardship the disadvantaged party is entitled to request renegotiations. The request shall be made without undue delay and shall indicate the grounds on which it is based.

(2) The request for renegotiation does not in itself entitle the disadvantaged party to withhold performance.

(3) Upon failure to reach agreement within a reasonable time either party may resort to the court.

(4) If the court finds hardship it may, if reasonable,

> (a) terminate the contract at a date and on terms to be fixed, or
> (b) adapt the contract with a view to restoring its equilibrium.

CHAPTER 7: NON-PERFORMANCE

Section 1: Non-Performance in General

Article 7.1.1   Non-Performance Defined

Non-performance is failure by a party to perform any of its obligations under the contract, including defective performance or late performance.

Article 7.1.2   Interference by the Other Party

A party may not rely on the non-performance of the other party to the extent that such non-performance was caused by the first party's act or omission or by another event for which the first party bears the risk.

Article 7.1.3 Withholding Performance

(1) Where the parties are to perform simultaneously, either party may withhold performance until the other party tenders its performance.

(2) Where the parties are to perform consecutively, the party that is to perform later may withhold its performance until the first party has performed.

Article 7.1.4 Cure by Non-Performing Party

(1) The non-performing party may, at its own expense, cure any nonperformance, provided that

    (a) without undue delay, it gives notice indicating the proposed manner and timing of the cure;

    (b) cure is appropriate in the circumstances;

    (c) the aggrieved party has no legitimate interest in refusing cure; and

    (d) cure is effected promptly.

(2) The right to cure is not precluded by notice of termination.

(3) Upon effective notice of cure, rights of the aggrieved party that are inconsistent with the non-performing party's performance are suspended until the time for cure has expired.

(4) The aggrieved party may withhold performance pending cure.

(5) Notwithstanding cure, the aggrieved party retains the right to claim damages for delay as well as for any harm caused or not prevented by the cure.

Article 7.1.5 Additional Period for Performance

(1) In a case of non-performance the aggrieved party may by notice to the other party allow an additional period of time for performance.

(2) During the additional period the aggrieved party may withhold performance of its own reciprocal obligations and may claim damages but may not resort to any other remedy. If it receives notice from the other party that the latter will not perform within that period, or if upon expiry of that period due performance has not been made, the aggrieved party may resort to any of the remedies that may be available under this Chapter.

(3) Where in a case of delay in performance which is not fundamental the aggrieved party has given notice allowing an additional period of time of reasonable length, it may terminate the contract at the end of that period. If the additional period allowed is not of reasonable length it shall be extended to a reasonable length. The aggrieved party may in its notice provide that if the other party fails to perform within the period allowed by the notice the contract shall automatically terminate.

(4) Paragraph (3) does not apply where the obligation which has not been performed is only a minor part of the contractual obligation of the non-performing party.

Article 7.1.6 Exemption Clauses

A clause which limits or excludes one party's liability for non-performance or which permits one party to render performance substantially different from what the other party reasonably expected may not be invoked if it would be grossly unfair to do so, having regard to the purpose of the contract.

Article 7.1.7   Force Majeure

(1) Non-performance by a party is excused if that party proves that the nonper-formance was due to an impediment beyond its control and that it could not rea-sonably be expected to have taken the impediment into account at the time of the conclusion of the contract or to have avoided or overcome it or its consequences.

(2) When the impediment is only temporary, the excuse shall have effect for such period as is reasonable having regard to the effect of the impediment on the performance of the contract.

(3) The party who fails to perform must give notice to the other party of the impediment and its effect on its ability to perform. If the notice is not received by the other party within a reasonable time after the party who fails to perform knew or ought to have known of the impediment, it is liable for damages resulting from such non-receipt.

(4) Nothing in this Article prevents a party from exercising a right to terminate the contract or to withhold performance or request interest on money due.

Section 2: Right to Performance

Article 7.2.1   Performance of Monetary Obligation

Where a party who is obliged to pay money does not do so, the other party may require payment.

Article 7.2.2   Performance of Non-Monetary Obligation

Where a party who owes an obligation other than one to pay money does not perform, the other party may require performance, unless

(a) performance is impossible in law or in fact;

(b) performance or, where relevant, enforcement is unreasonably burden-some or expensive;

(c) the party entitled to performance may reasonably obtain performance from another source;

(d) performance is of an exclusively personal character; or

(e) the party entitled to performance does not require performance within a reasonable time after it has, or ought to have, become aware of the non-performance.

Article 7.2.3   Repair and Replacement of Defective Performance

The right to performance includes in appropriate cases the right to require repair, replacement, or other cure of defective performance. The provisions of Articles 7.2.1 and 7.2.2 apply accordingly.

Article 7.2.4   Judicial Penalty

(1) Where the court orders a party to perform, it may also direct that this party pay a penalty if it does not comply with the order.

(2) The penalty shall be paid to the aggrieved party unless mandatory provisions of the law of the forum provide otherwise. Payment of the penalty to the aggrieved party does not exclude any claim for damages.

Article 7.2.5   Change of Remedy

(1) An aggrieved party who has required performance of a non-monetary obligation and who has not received performance within a period fixed or otherwise within a reasonable period of time may invoke any other remedy.

(2) Where the decision of a court for performance of a non-monetary obligation cannot be enforced, the aggrieved party may invoke any other remedy.

Section 3: Termination

Article 7.3.1   Right to Terminate the Contract

(1) A party may terminate the contract where the failure of the other party to perform an obligation under the contract amounts to a fundamental non-performance.

(2) In determining whether a failure to perform an obligation amounts to a fundamental non-performance regard shall be had, in particular, to whether

   (a) the non-performance substantially deprives the aggrieved party of what it was entitled to expect under the contract unless the other party did not foresee and could not reasonably have foreseen such result;

   (b) strict compliance with the obligation which has not been performed is of essence under the contract;

   (c) the non-performance is intentional or reckless;

   (d) the non-performance gives the aggrieved party reason to believe that it cannot rely on the other party's future performance;

   (e) the non-performing party will suffer disproportionate loss as a result of the preparation or performance if the contract is terminated.

(3) In the case of delay the aggrieved party may also terminate the contract if the other party fails to perform before the time allowed it under Article 7.1.5 has expired.

Article 7.3.2   Notice of Termination

(1) The right of a party to terminate the contract is exercised by notice to the other party.

(2) If performance has been offered late or otherwise does not conform to the contract the aggrieved party will lose its right to terminate the contract unless it gives notice to the other party within a reasonable time after it has or ought to have become aware of the offer or of the non-conforming performance.

Article 7.3.3   Anticipatory Non-Performance

Where prior to the date for performance by one of the parties it is clear that there will be a fundamental non-performance by that party, the other party may terminate the contract.

Article 7.3.4   Adequate Assurance of Due Performance

A party who reasonably believes that there will be a fundamental non-performance by the other party may demand adequate assurance of due performance and may meanwhile withhold its own performance. Where this assurance is not provided within a reasonable time the party demanding it may terminate the contract.

Article 7.3.5   Effects of Termination in General

(1) Termination of the contract releases both parties from their obligation to effect and to receive future performance.

(2) Termination does not preclude a claim for damages for non-performance.

(3) Termination does not affect any provision in the contract for the settlement of disputes or any other term of the contract which is to operate even after termination.

Article 7.3.6   Restitution with Respect to Contracts to Be Performed at One Time

(1) On termination of a contract to be performed at one time either party may claim restitution of whatever it has supplied under the contract, provided that such party concurrently makes restitution of whatever it has received under the contract.

(2) If restitution in kind is not possible or appropriate, an allowance has to be made in money whenever reasonable.

(3) The recipient of the performance does not have to make an allowance in money if the impossibility to make restitution in kind is attributable to the other party.

(4) Compensation may be claimed for expenses reasonably required to preserve or maintain the performance received.

Article 7.3.7   Restitution with Respect to Long-Term Contracts

(1) On termination of a long-term contract restitution can only be claimed for the period after termination has taken effect, provided the contract is divisible.

(2) As far as restitution has to be made, the provisions of Article 7.3.6 apply.

Section 4: Damages

Article 7.4.1   Right to Damages

Any non-performance gives the aggrieved party a right to damages either exclusively or in conjunction with any other remedies except where the non-performance is excused under these Principles.

Article 7.4.2   Full Compensation

(1) The aggrieved party is entitled to full compensation for harm sustained as a result of the non-performance. Such harm includes both any loss which it suffered and any gain of which it was deprived, taking into account any gain to the aggrieved party resulting from its avoidance of cost or harm.

(2) Such harm may be non-pecuniary and includes, for instance, physical suffering or emotional distress.

Article 7.4.3   Certainty of Harm

(1) Compensation is due only for harm, including future harm, that is established with a reasonable degree of certainty.

(2) Compensation may be due for the loss of a chance in proportion to the probability of its occurrence.

(3) Where the amount of damages cannot be established with a sufficient degree of certainty, the assessment is at the discretion of the court.

Article 7.4.4   Foreseeability of Harm

The non-performing party is liable only for harm which it foresaw or could reasonably have foreseen at the time of the conclusion of the contract as being likely to result from its non-performance.

Article 7.4.5   Proof of Harm in Case of Replacement Transaction

Where the aggrieved party has terminated the contract and has made a replacement transaction within a reasonable time and in a reasonable manner it may recover the difference between the contract price and the price of the replacement transaction as well as damages for any further harm.

Article 7.4.6   Proof of Harm by Current Price

(1) Where the aggrieved party has terminated the contract and has not made a replacement transaction but there is a current price for the performance contracted for, it may recover the difference between the contract price and the price current at the time the contract is terminated as well as damages for any further harm.

(2) Current price is the price generally charged for goods delivered or services rendered in comparable circumstances at the place where the contract should have been performed or, if there is no current price at that place, the current price at such other place that appears reasonable to take as a reference.

Article 7.4.7   Harm Due in Part to Aggrieved Party

Where the harm is due in part to an act or omission of the aggrieved party or to another event for which that party bears the risk, the amount of damages shall be reduced to the extent that these factors have contributed to the harm, having regard to the conduct of each of the parties.

Article 7.4.8   Mitigation of Harm

(1) The non-performing party is not liable for harm suffered by the aggrieved party to the extent that the harm could have been reduced by the latter party's taking reasonable steps.

(2) The aggrieved party is entitled to recover any expenses reasonably incurred in attempting to reduce the harm.

Article 7.4.9   Interest for Failure to Pay Money

(1) If a party does not pay a sum of money when it falls due the aggrieved party is entitled to interest upon that sum from the time when payment is due to the time of payment whether or not the non-payment is excused.

(2) The rate of interest shall be the average bank short-term lending rate to prime borrowers prevailing for the currency of payment at the place for payment, or where no such rate exists at that place, then the same rate in the State of the currency of payment. In the absence of such a rate at either place the rate of interest shall be the appropriate rate fixed by the law of the State of the currency of payment.

(3) The aggrieved party is entitled to additional damages if the non-payment caused it a greater harm.

Article 7.4.10   Interest on Damages

Unless otherwise agreed, interest on damages for non-performance of non-monetary obligations accrues as from the time of non-performance.

Article 7.4.11   Manner of Monetary Redress

(1) Damages are to be paid in a lump sum. However, they may be payable in instalments where the nature of the harm makes this appropriate.

(2) Damages to be paid in instalments may be indexed.

Article 7.4.12   Currency in Which to Assess Damages

Damages are to be assessed either in the currency in which the monetary obligation was expressed or in the currency in which the harm was suffered, whichever is more appropriate.

Article 7.4.13   Agreed Payment for Non-Performance

(1) Where the contract provides that a party who does not perform is to pay a specified sum to the aggrieved party for such non-performance, the aggrieved party is entitled to that sum irrespective of its actual harm.

(2) However, notwithstanding any agreement to the contrary the specified sum may be reduced to a reasonable amount where it is grossly excessive in relation to the harm resulting from the non-performance and to the other circumstances.

CHAPTER 8: SET-OFF

Article 8.1   Conditions of Set-Off

(1) Where two parties owe each other money or other performances of the same kind, either of them ("the first party") may set off its obligation against that of its obligee ("the other party") if at the time of set-off,

   (a) the first party is entitled to perform its obligation;

(b) the other party's obligation is ascertained as to its existence and amount and performance is due.

(2) If the obligations of both parties arise from the same contract, the first party may also set off its obligation against an obligation of the other party which is not ascertained as to its existence or to its amount.

Article 8.2   Foreign Currency Set-Off

Where the obligations are to pay money in different currencies, the right of set-off may be exercised, provided that both currencies are freely convertible and the parties have not agreed that the first party shall pay only in a specified currency.

Article 8.3   Set-Off by Notice

The right of set-off is exercised by notice to the other party.

Article 8.4   Content of Notice

(1) The notice must specify the obligations to which it relates.

(2) If the notice does not specify the obligation against which set-off is exercised, the other party may, within a reasonable time, declare to the first party the obligation to which set-off relates. If no such declaration is made, the set-off will relate to all the obligations proportionally.

Article 8.5   Effect of Set-Off

(1) Set-off discharges the obligations.

(2) If obligations differ in amount, set-off discharges the obligations up to the amount of the lesser obligation.

(3) Set-off takes effect as from the time of notice.

CHAPTER 9: ASSIGNMENT OF RIGHTS, TRANSFER OF OBLIGATIONS, ASSIGNMENT OF CONTRACTS

Section 1: Assignment of Rights

Article 9.1.1   Definitions

"Assignment of a right" means the transfer by agreement from one person (the "assignor") to another person (the "assignee"), including transfer by way of security, of the assignor's right to payment of a monetary sum or other performance from a third person ("the obligor").

Article 9.1.2   Exclusions

This Section does not apply to transfers made under the special rules governing the transfers:

(a) of instruments such as negotiable instruments, documents of title or financial instruments, or

(b) of rights in the course of transferring a business.

Article 9.1.3   Assignability of Non-Monetary Rights

A right to non-monetary performance may be assigned only if the assignment does not render the obligation significantly more burdensome.

Article 9.1.4   Partial Assignment

(1) A right to the payment of a monetary sum may be assigned partially.

(2) A right to other performance may be assigned partially only if it is divisible, and the assignment does not render the obligation significantly more burdensome.

Article 9.1.5   Future Rights

A future right is deemed to be transferred at the time of the agreement, provided the right, when it comes into existence, can be identified as the right to which the assignment relates.

Article 9.1.6   Rights Assigned Without Individual Specification

A number of rights may be assigned without individual specification, provided such rights can be identified as rights to which the assignment relates at the time of the assignment or when they come into existence.

Article 9.1.7   Agreement Between Assignor and Assignee Sufficient

(1) A right is assigned by mere agreement between the assignor and the assignee, without notice to the obligor.

(2) The consent of the obligor is not required unless the obligation in the circumstances is of an essentially personal character.

Article 9.1.8   Obligor's Additional Costs

The obligor has a right to be compensated by the assignor or the assignee for any additional costs caused by the assignment.

Article 9.1.9   Non-Assignment Clauses

(1) The assignment of a right to the payment of a monetary sum is effective notwithstanding an agreement between the assignor and the obligor limiting or prohibiting such an assignment. However, the assignor may be liable to the obligor for breach of contract.

(2) The assignment of a right to other performance is ineffective if it is contrary to an agreement between the assignor and the obligor limiting or prohibiting the assignment. Nevertheless, the assignment is effective if the assignee, at the time of the assignment, neither knew nor ought to have known of the agreement. The assignor may then be liable to the obligor for breach of contract.

Article 9.1.10 Notice to the Obligor

(1) Until the obligor receives a notice of the assignment from either the assignor or the assignee, it is discharged by paying the assignor.

(2) After the obligor receives such a notice, it is discharged only by paying the assignee.

Article 9.1.11 Successive Assignments

If the same right has been assigned by the same assignor to two or more successive assignees, the obligor is discharged by paying according to the order in which the notices were received.

Article 9.1.12 Adequate Proof of Assignment

(1) If notice of the assignment is given by the assignee, the obligor may request the assignee to provide within a reasonable time adequate proof that the assignment has been made.

(2) Until adequate proof is provided, the obligor may withhold payment.

(3) Unless adequate proof is provided, notice is not effective.

(4) Adequate proof includes, but is not limited to, any writing emanating from the assignor and indicating that the assignment has taken place.

Article 9.1.13 Defences and Rights of Set-Off

(1) The obligor may assert against the assignee all defences that the obligor could assert against the assignor.

(2) The obligor may exercise against the assignee any right of set-off available to the obligor against the assignor up to the time notice of assignment was received.

Article 9.1.14 Rights Related to the Right Assigned

The assignment of a right transfers to the assignee:

(a) all the assignor's rights to payment or other performance under the contract in respect of the right assigned, and

(b) all rights securing performance of the right assigned.

Article 9.1.15 Undertakings of the Assignor

The assignor undertakes towards the assignee, except as otherwise disclosed to the assignee, that:

(a) the assigned right exists at the time of the assignment, unless the right is a future right;

(b) the assignor is entitled to assign the right;

(c) the right has not been previously assigned to another assignee, and it is free from any right or claim from a third party;

(d) the obligor does not have any defences;

(e) neither the obligor nor the assignor has given notice of set-off concerning the assigned right and will not give any such notice;

(f) the assignor will reimburse the assignee for any payment received from the obligor before notice of the assignment was given.

Section 2: Transfer of Obligations

Article 9.2.1   Modes of Transfer

An obligation to pay money or render other performance may be transferred from one person (the "original obligor") to another person (the "new obligor") either

(a) by an agreement between the original obligor and the new obligor subject to Article 9.2.3, or

(b) by an agreement between the obligee and the new obligor, by which the new obligor assumes the obligation.

Article 9.2.2   Exclusion

This Section does not apply to transfers of obligations made under the special rules governing transfers of obligations in the course of transferring a business.

Article 9.2.3   Requirement of Obligee's Consent to Transfer

The transfer of an obligation by an agreement between the original obligor and the new obligor requires the consent of the obligee.

Article 9.2.4   Advance Consent of Obligee

(1) The obligee may give its consent in advance.

(2) If the obligee has given its consent in advance, the transfer of the obligation becomes effective when a notice of the transfer is given to the obligee or when the obligee acknowledges it.

Article 9.2.5   Discharge of Original Obligor

(1) The obligee may discharge the original obligor.

(2) The obligee may also retain the original obligor as an obligor in case the new obligor does not perform properly.

(3) Otherwise the original obligor and the new obligor are jointly and severally liable.

Article 9.2.6   Third Party Performance

(1) Without the obligee's consent, the obligor may contract with another person that this person will perform the obligation in place of the obligor, unless the obligation in the circumstances has an essentially personal character.

(2) The obligee retains its claim against the obligor.

Article 9.2.7   Defences and Rights of Set-Off

(1) The new obligor may assert against the obligee all defences which the original obligor could assert against the obligee.

(2) The new obligor may not exercise against the obligee any right of set-off available to the original obligor against the obligee.

Article 9.2.8 Rights Related to the Obligation Transferred

(1) The obligee may assert against the new obligor all its rights to payment or other performance under the contract in respect of the obligation transferred.

(2) If the original obligor is discharged under Article 9.2.5(1), a security granted by any person other than the new obligor for the performance of the obligation is discharged, unless that other person agrees that it should continue to be available to the obligee.

(3) Discharge of the original obligor also extends to any security of the original obligor given to the obligee for the performance of the obligation, unless the security is over an asset which is transferred as part of a transaction between the original obligor and the new obligor.

Section 3: Assignment of Contracts

Article 9.3.1 Definitions

"Assignment of a contract" means the transfer by agreement from one person (the "assignor") to another person (the "assignee") of the assignor's rights and obligations arising out of a contract with another person (the "other party").

Article 9.3.2 Exclusion

This Section does not apply to the assignment of contracts made under the special rules governing transfers of contracts in the course of transferring a business.

Article 9.3.3 Requirement of Consent of the Other Party

The assignment of a contract requires the consent of the other party.

Article 9.3.4 Advance Consent of the Other Party

(1) The other party may give its consent in advance.

(2) If the other party has given its consent in advance, the assignment of the contract becomes effective when a notice of the assignment is given to the other party or when the other party acknowledges it.

Article 9.3.5 Discharge of the Assignor

(1) The other party may discharge the assignor.

(2) The other party may also retain the assignor as an obligor in case the assignee does not perform properly.

(3) Otherwise the assignor and the assignee are jointly and severally liable.

Article 9.3.6 Defences and Rights of Set-Off

(1) To the extent that the assignment of a contract involves an assignment of rights, Article 9.1.13 applies accordingly.

(2) To the extent that the assignment of a contract involves a transfer of obligations, Article 9.2.7 applies accordingly.

Article 9.3.7   Rights Transferred with the Contract

(1) To the extent that the assignment of a contract involves an assignment of rights, Article 9.1.14 applies accordingly.

(2) To the extent that the assignment of a contract involves a transfer of obligations, Article 9.2.8 applies accordingly.

CHAPTER 10: LIMITATION PERIODS

Article 10.1   Scope of the Chapter

(1) The exercise of rights governed by the Principles is barred by the expiration of a period of time, referred to as "limitation period", according to the rules of this Chapter.

(2) This Chapter does not govern the time within which one party is required under the Principles, as a condition for the acquisition or exercise of its right, to give notice to the other party or to perform any act other than the institution of legal proceedings.

Article 10.2   Limitation Periods

(1) The general limitation period is three years beginning on the day after the day the obligee knows or ought to know the facts as a result of which the obligee's right can be exercised.

(2) In any event, the maximum limitation period is ten years beginning on the day after the day the right can be exercised.

Article 10.3   Modification of Limitation Periods
by the Parties

(1) The parties may modify the limitation periods.

(2) However they may not
    (a) shorten the general limitation period to less than one year;
    (b) shorten the maximum limitation period to less than four years;
    (c) extend the maximum limitation period to more than fifteen years.

Article 10.4   New Limitation Period by
Acknowledgement

(1) Where the obligor before the expiration of the general limitation period acknowledges the right of the obligee, a new general limitation period begins on the day after the day of the acknowledgement.

(2) The maximum limitation period does not begin to run again, but may be exceeded by the beginning of a new general limitation period under Art. 10.2(1).

Article 10.5   Suspension by Judicial Proceedings

(1) The running of the limitation period is suspended

(a) when the obligee performs any act, by commencing judicial proceedings or in judicial proceedings already instituted, that is recognised by the law of the court as asserting the obligee's right against the obligor;

(b) in the case of the obligor's insolvency when the obligee has asserted its rights in the insolvency proceedings; or

(c) in the case of proceedings for dissolution of the entity which is the obligor when the obligee has asserted its rights in the dissolution proceedings.

(2) Suspension lasts until a final decision has been issued or until the proceedings have been otherwise terminated.

Article 10.6   Suspension by Arbitral Proceedings

(1) The running of the limitation period is suspended when the obligee performs any act, by commencing arbitral proceedings or in arbitral proceedings already instituted, that is recognised by the law of the arbitral tribunal as asserting the obligee's right against the obligor. In the absence of regulations for arbitral proceedings or provisions determining the exact date of the commencement of arbitral proceedings, the proceedings are deemed to commence on the date on which a request that the right in dispute should be adjudicated reaches the obligor.

(2) Suspension lasts until a binding decision has been issued or until the proceedings have been otherwise terminated.

Article 10.7   Alternative Dispute Resolution

The provisions of Articles 10.5 and 10.6 apply with appropriate modifications to other proceedings whereby the parties request a third person to assist them in their attempt to reach an amicable settlement of their dispute.

Article 10.8   Suspension in Case of Force Majeure, Death or Incapacity

(1) Where the obligee has been prevented by an impediment that is beyond its control and that it could neither avoid nor overcome, from causing a limitation period to cease to run under the preceding Articles, the general limitation period is suspended so as not to expire before one year after the relevant impediment has ceased to exist.

(2) Where the impediment consists of the incapacity or death of the obligee or obligor, suspension ceases when a representative for the incapacitated or deceased party or its estate has been appointed or a successor has inherited the respective party's position. The additional one-year period under paragraph (1) applies accordingly.

Article 10.9   Effects of Expiration of Limitation Period

(1) The expiration of the limitation period does not extinguish the right.

(2) For the expiration of the limitation period to have effect, the obligor must assert it as a defence.

(3) A right may still be relied on as a defence even though the expiration of the limitation period for that right has been asserted.

Article 10.10   Right of Set-Off

The obligee may exercise the right of set-off until the obligor has asserted the expiration of the limitation period.

Article 10.11   Restitution

Where there has been performance in order to discharge an obligation, there is no right of restitution merely because the limitation period has expired.

CHAPTER 11: PLURALITY OF OBLIGORS AND OF OBLIGEES

Section 1: Plurality of Obligors

Article 11.1.1   Definitions

When several obligors are bound by the same obligation towards an obligee:
(a) the obligations are joint and several when each obligor is bound for the whole obligation;
(b) the obligations are separate when each obligor is bound only for its share.

Article 11.1.2   Presumption of Joint and Several Obligations

When several obligors are bound by the same obligation towards an obligee, they are presumed to be jointly and severally bound, unless the circumstances indicate otherwise.

Article 11.1.3   Obligee's Rights Against Joint and Several Obligors

When obligors are jointly and severally bound, the obligee may require performance from any one of them, until full performance has been received.

Article 11.1.4   Availability of Defences and Rights of Set-Off

A joint and several obligor against whom a claim is made by the obligee may assert all the defences and rights of set-off that are personal to it or that are common to all the co-obligors, but may not assert defences or rights of set-off that are personal to one or several of the other co-obligors.

Article 11.1.5   Effect of Performance or Set-Off

Performance or set-off by a joint and several obligor or set-off by the obligee against one joint and several obligor discharges the other obligors in relation to the obligee to the extent of the performance or set-off.

Article 11.1.6   Effect of Release or Settlement

(1) Release of one joint and several obligor, or settlement with one joint and several obligor, discharges all the other obligors for the share of the released or settling obligor, unless the circumstances indicate otherwise.

(2) When the other obligors are discharged for the share of the released obligor, they no longer have a contributory claim against the released obligor under Article 11.1.10.

Article 11.1.7   Effect of Expiration or Suspension of Limitation Period

(1) Expiration of the limitation period of the obligee's rights against one joint and several obligor does not affect:
  (a) the obligations to the obligee of the other joint and several obligors; or
  (b) the rights of recourse between the joint and several obligors under Article 11.1.10.
(2) If the obligee initiates proceedings under Articles 10.5, 10.6 or 10.7 against one joint and several obligor, the running of the limitation period is also suspended against the other joint and several obligors.

Article 11.1.8   Effect of Judgment

(1) A decision by a court as to the liability to the obligee of one joint and several obligor does not affect:
  (a) the obligations to the obligee of the other joint and several obligors; or
  (b) the rights of recourse between the joint and several obligors under Article 11.1.10.
(2) However, the other joint and several obligors may rely on such a decision, except if it was based on grounds personal to the obligor concerned. In such a case, the rights of recourse between the joint and several obligors under Article 11.1.10 are affected accordingly.

Article 11.1.9   Apportionment Among Joint and Several Obligors

As among themselves, joint and several obligors are bound in equal shares, unless the circumstances indicate otherwise.

Article 11.1.10   Extent of Contributory Claim

A joint and several obligor who has performed more than its share may claim the excess from any of the other obligors to the extent of each obligor's unperformed share.

Article 11.1.11   Rights of the Obligee

(1) A joint and several obligor to whom Article 11.1.10 applies may also exercise the rights of the obligee, including all rights securing their performance, to recover the excess from all or any of the other obligors to the extent of each obligor's unperformed share.
(2) An obligee who has not received full performance retains its rights against the co-obligors to the extent of the unperformed part, with precedence over co-obligors exercising contributory claims.

Article 11.1.12   Defences in Contributory Claims

A joint and several obligor against whom a claim is made by the co-obligor who has performed the obligation:

(a) may raise any common defences and rights of set-off that were available to be asserted by the co-obligor against the obligee;

(b) may assert defences which are personal to itself;

(c) may not assert defences and rights of set-off which are personal to one or several of the other co-obligors.

Article 11.1.13   Inability to Recover

If a joint and several obligor who has performed more than that obligor's share is unable, despite all reasonable efforts, to recover contribution from another joint and several obligor, the share of the others, including the one who has performed, is increased proportionally.

Section 2:   Plurality of Obligees

Article 11.2.1   Definitions

When several obligees can claim performance of the same obligation from an obligor:

(a) the claims are separate when each obligee can only claim its share;

(b) the claims are joint and several when each obligee can claim the whole performance;

(c) the claims are joint when all obligees have to claim performance together.

Article 11.2.2   Effects of Joint and Several Claims

Full performance of an obligation in favour of one of the joint and several obligees discharges the obligor towards the other obligees.

Article 11.2.3   Availability of Defences Against Joint and Several Obligees

(1) The obligor may assert against any of the joint and several obligees all the defences and rights of set-off that are personal to its relationship to that obligee or that it can assert against all the co-obligees, but may not assert defences and rights of set-off that are personal to its relationship to one or several of the other co-obligees.

(2) The provisions of Articles 11.1.5, 11.1.6, 11.1.7 and 11.1.8 apply, with appropriate adaptations, to joint and several claims.

Article 11.2.4   Allocation Between Joint and Several Obligees

(1) As among themselves, joint and several obligees are entitled to equal shares, unless the circumstances indicate otherwise.

(2) An obligee who has received more than its share must transfer the excess to the other obligees to the extent of their respective shares.

Materials on Electronic Contracting

COMMENT: UNIFORM COMPUTER INFORMATION TRANSACTIONS ACT

Drafting History[1]

The origins of the Uniform Computer Information Transactions Act (UCITA) are intertwined with efforts to revise Uniform Commercial Code Article 2, excerpted earlier in this Supplement. The entities responsible for the systematic review of the Uniform Commercial Code, the National Conference of Commissioners on Uniform State Laws (NCCUSL)[2] and the American Law Institute (ALI), undertook revising UCC Article 2 in the late 1980s. Early in that process, a consensus emerged that a new body of uniform law was needed to address the ongoing transformation of the U.S. economy from one dominated by transactions in goods to one in which transactions in information products and services, as well as transactions in goods that were conducted utilizing information products and services, were becoming increasingly prevalent. Although courts applied UCC Article 2 provisions to answer some of the growing number of questions raised by computer- and software-related transactions, its provisions predictably did not address many information-transaction issues, and its application was likely to produce uncertain and nonuniform results.[3]

---

1. For general discussion of UCITA and its drafting history, see John A. Chanin, The Uniform Computer Information Transactions Act: A Practitioner's View, 18 John Marshall J. Comp. & Info. L. 279 (Winter 1999); Maureen A. O'Rourke, An Essay on the Challenges of Drafting a Uniform Law of Software Contracting, 10 Lewis & Clark L. Rev. 925 (2006); Carlyle C. Ring, Jr., Uniform Rules for Internet Information Transactions: An Overview of Proposed UCITA, 38 Duq. L. Rev. 319 (2000).

2. NCCUSL is now known officially as the Uniform Law Commission.

3. See, e.g., Specht v. Netscape Comm'ns Corp., 306 F.3d 17, 30 n.13 (2d Cir. 2002) (discussing application of Article 2 to software and information transactions in earlier cases); Advent Sys. Ltd. v. Unisys Corp., 925 F.2d 670 (3d Cir. 1991) (holding that computer software falls within definition of "goods" under U.C.C. Article 2); I. Lan Sys., Inc. v. Nextpoint Networks, Inc., 183 F. Supp. 2d 328 (D. Mass. 2002) (noting that earlier decisions have applied Article 2 to software licenses but expressing doubt about the correctness of that approach).

For these reasons, the ALI and NCCUSL decided to add a new article to the Uniform Commercial Code to specifically address the contract issues arising in software licensing and other computer information transactions.

Precedent existed for expanding the Uniform Commercial Code to address evolving segments of the marketplace. The ALI and NCCUSL promulgated UCC Article 2A in 1989 to address increasingly common lease transactions in goods. Prior to the promulgation of Article 2A, courts were divided on the question of whether Article 2 applied to lease transactions. Some courts held that leases were indeed "transactions in goods" under Section 2-102 and governed by Article 2 as a matter of law.[4] Courts more frequently decided that leases were not strictly subject to Article 2, but that the provisions of Article 2 could be applied by analogy to leases when appropriate.[5] The ALI and NCCUSL resolved the question by promulgating Article 2A to specifically address lease transactions. The provisions of Article 2A closely track many provisions of Article 2 with the adaptations necessary to regulate lease transactions. Article 2A, portions of which are excerpted in this Supplement, has now been adopted in the District of Columbia and every state except Louisiana.

With Articles 2 and 2A before them and arguably in need of revision, the UCC Permanent Editorial Board appointed a drafting committee in the early 1990s that began work on an article that would be designed to address the sale and licensing of intangible products. During an early phase of the process, the drafters pursued a "hub and spoke" concept for the Articles 2 and 2A revisions and the new computer information article. The essence of this proposal was that Article 2 would serve as a "hub," containing provisions relevant to all types of transactions; provisions that related specifically to a particular type of transaction would be placed in separate "spoke" articles on sales, leases, and computer information transactions. Over time, however, the "hub and spoke" concept lost support and the drafters reverted to a more traditional format, with separate committees working to revise Articles 2 and 2A and to write a new Article 2B on computer information transactions.

During the course of Article 2B's drafting, the draft proposals drew substantial criticism from academics, consumer advocates, governmental agencies, the entertainment industry, and others. At the same time, the position eventually emerged that a uniform law on computer information transfers would not properly match the framework of Articles 2 and 2A on the sales and leases of goods. Ultimately, in spring 1999, the ALI withdrew its support of proposed Article 2B.[6] Subsequently, the drafters and supporters of Article 2B tendered the proposed statute as a uniform law that would stand apart from the UCC, with the new name of the Uniform Computer Information Transactions Act, or "UCITA." NCCUSL

---

4. See, e.g., Sawyer, v. Pioneer Leasing Corp., 244 Ark. 943, 428 S.W.2d 46 (1968); Capital Assocs., Inc. v. Hudgens, 455 So. 2d 651 (Fla. Dist. Ct. App. 1984); Xerox Corp. v. Hawkes, 124 N.H. 610, 475 A.2d 7 (1984); Owens v. Patent Scaffolding Co., Div. of Harsco, 77 Misc. 2d 992, 354 N.Y.S.2d 778 (N.Y. Sup. Ct. 1974), rev'd on other grounds, 50 A.D.2d 866, 376 N.Y.S.2d 948 (1975). But, see, e.g., D&D Leasing Co. v. Gentry, 298 S.C. 342, 380 S.E.2d 342 (1989) (declining to hold that Article 2 applied to leases of goods in general).

5. See, e.g., Pac. Am. Leasing Corp. v. S.P.E. Bldg. Sys., Inc., 156 Ariz. 96, 730 P.2d 273 (Ct. App. 1986); Walter E. Heller & Co. v. Convalescent Home of the First Church of Deliverance, 49 Ill. App. 3d 213, 365 N.E.2d 1285 (1977).

6. See Letter from Michael Traynor, ALI President, to ALI membership (Feb. 4, 2003) (published in ALI Reporter, Winter 2003 at p. 3) (stating that ALI discontinued work on UCITA because of expectation that the product would not "meet the ALI's standards of legal coherence, appropriate coordination with existing legal doctrine, and fairness to all parties").

adopted UCITA in July 1999. Each state then faced the question of whether to enact the law. Ultimately, Maryland and Virginia were the only states to do so.[7] The controversy over UCITA is reflected by the fact that more states have adopted laws designed to insulate their citizens or residents from UCITA's application than have enacted UCITA.[8]

After UCITA's initial promulgation in 1999, a NCCUSL "Standby Committee" continued to study issues raised by the act's supporters and opponents. A number of recommendations for amending UCITA also resulted from the efforts of an American Bar Association (ABA) Working Group. In response to the commentary from all parties, NCCUSL approved several amendments to UCITA at its 2002 Annual Meeting. The amendments clarified a number of issues, such as the prohibition on vendors engaging in a self-help remedy for a licensee's breach by electronically disabling software and the requirement that UCITA provisions yield to applicable federal or state consumer protection laws.[9] The amendments did not lead to any additional adoptions; nor did they change the ALI's stance withholding its support of the effort.

Scope of UCITA

The scope provision of UCITA, Section 103(a), states that it applies to "computer information transactions," which Section 102(11) defines as agreements "to create, modify, transfer, or license computer information or informational rights in computer information." The definitional provisions further reveal that the Act applies to "information in electronic form which is obtained from or through the use of a computer or which is in a form capable of being processed by a computer." Section 102(10). Thus, UCITA applies to transactions that include the use of computer software, computer databases, and Internet and online information. As set out in the text and explained in the comments, Section 103(d) excludes a number of transactions from UCITA's scope, including contracts for personal services (except computer information development and support agreements); employment contracts; contracts where computer information is insignificant (de minimis); computers, televisions, VCRs, DVD players, or similar goods; financial services transactions; contracts for sound recordings and musical works; and contracts for motion pictures and broadcast or cable programming. Commentators have generally recognized that the attempt to define computer information can be particularly difficult and that the formulation in UCITA may prove to be less than ideal.[10]

Transactions that involve a mixture of computer information and other subject matter raise questions of whether all or any part of the transactions should be governed by UCITA or other law. The comments to UCITA explain that it should

---

7. The status of state enactments or pending legislation can be obtained from the ULC website, http://www.uniformlaws.org.

8. See Amelia H. Boss, Taking UCITA on the Road: What Lessons Have We Learned?, 7 Roger Williams U. L. Rev. 167, 175 n.19 (2001) (discussing opposition to UCITA and citing Iowa, West Virginia, and North Carolina as states that have adopted anti-UCITA laws – a.k.a. "UCITA bomb shelters").

9. The amendments are explained in a NCCUSL document, Draft Amendments to UCITA, 2002 NCCUSL Annual Meeting, July 26-August 2, 2002, available at the NCCUSL website (http://www.uniformlaws.org/shared/docs/computer_information_transactions/ucita_amds_am02.pdf) (last visited June 1, 2017).

10. See John A. Chanin, The Uniform Computer Information Transactions Act: A Practitioner's View, 18 John Marshall J. Comp. & Info. L. 279 (1999).

generally apply to the computer information part of a transaction, while common law or the UCC, including Article 2 (Sales) or 2A (Leases), may apply to another portion.[11] The comments take the position that there should be "no overlap between goods and computer information since computer information and informational rights are not goods."[12] The comments offer this example: "A diskette is a tangible object but the information on the diskette does not become goods simply because it is copied on tangible medium, any more than the information in a book is governed by the law of goods because the book binding and paper may be Article 2 goods." Thus, if a transaction involves goods and computer information (e.g., a computer and software), Article 2 or Article 2A applies to the aspect of the transaction pertaining to the sale or lease of goods, but UCITA applies to the computer information aspects. Adopting what is often called the "gravamen of the action" standard, the comment provides that the "law applicable to an issue depends on whether the issue pertains to goods or to computer information."[13]

Ability to Select Law

Section 115 of the 2002 version of UCITA (previously Section 113 in the 1999 version of UCITA) grants parties a broad right to vary by agreement any provision of UCITA except for a limited number of mandatory provisions, such as the obligation of good faith and the rule limiting enforceability of unconscionable terms. Comment 2 to Section 115 explains that the "fundamental policy of this Act is freedom of contract." As perhaps the ultimate manifestation of that freedom of contract theme, Section 104 in the 1999 version of the Act allowed parties to opt into or opt out of the statute. The general ability under pre-revision Section 104 to opt into or opt out of UCITA was limited by mandatory provisions—in UCITA or other law, such as certain consumer protection requirements—that cannot be avoided or varied by the agreement of the parties. Nevertheless, the "opt out" provision could lend itself to use by licensors to obtain applicable law that would be less favorable to consumers. In the 2002 amendments, Section 104 was deleted from the official version of UCITA on the ground that Section 115 effectively allows the same ability to opt in or out of UCITA provisions and that original Section 104 was redundant.[14]

Section 109 of UCITA allows the parties to choose the applicable state law, subject only to the limitation that the agreement may not avoid mandatory consumer protection rules. The comments explain that a primary motive for the section is that it allows a small company to engage in dealings with remote parties "spanning multiple jurisdictions and in circumstances that do not depend on physical location of either party or the information" without being subject to the law of all 50 States and all countries in the world.[15] The comments indicate that allowing such small companies to choose the applicable law would avoid barriers to entry.[16] Section 110 provides that "[t]he parties in their agreement may choose an exclusive judicial forum unless the choice

11. Section 103 cmt. 4.
12. Id.
13. Section 103 cmt. 4(b)(1).
14. See UCITA 2002 Annual Meeting Draft, available at http://www.uniformlaws.org/shared/docs/computer_information_transactions/ucita_final_02.pdf (last visited June 1, 2017).
15. Section 109 cmt. 2.
16. Id.

is unreasonable and unjust." Such a choice of forum, however, will not be exclusive unless the agreement expressly so provides.

Notably, contract transactions relating to computer information will also be subject to copyright or intellectual property law, which protects the rights of the creator or publisher of the information. As state law, UCITA would necessarily yield to federal copyright law on such issues. UCITA Section 105(a) recognizes the preemptive authority of federal law when there is a conflict between its provisions and federal law, such as the Copyright Act.

Contract Formation

A UCITA transaction may be the grant of a license permitting limited use of the information technology, or it may be a more general sale of the rights pertinent to the information.[17] The "license" concept departs substantially from the transfer of rights attendant to a sale or lease. UCITA's drafters noted that a license may contain a variety of rights and restrictions that limit or govern commercial use, the right to access the information, the computers on which the information can be used, the ability to share use with others, the ability to distribute copies, and the ability to modify the computer information.[18] UCITA also recognizes that some licenses will be sold by mass marketing to consumers at large, addressing this issue by creation of the concept of a "mass market license" in Sections 102(a)(44) and (45), and facilitating the use of a standard form contract as an efficient manner to handle such transactions.[19] Mass market licenses include retail transactions directed to the general public offering the license on substantially similar terms.

In addressing the mass market license, Section 209 offers limited consumer protection by providing a consumer is not bound by the contract unless he has consented to the contract after an opportunity to review during initial use or access to the information, or has the right to return, with an allowance for reasonable expense involved, if the terms of the agreement are not available until after the initial agreement has been made. The section also limits the enforceability of the terms of the standard license by denying enforcement to unconscionable terms and any terms conflicting with ones on which the parties have expressly agreed. Section 209, however, must be read together with Section 208, which specifically allows that the parties may adopt terms "after beginning performance or use if the parties had reason to know that their agreement would be represented in whole or part by a later record to be agreed on and there would not be an opportunity to review the record or a copy of it before performance or use begins."

The transformation of the proposed legislation from Article 2B to UCITA did not silence its critics.[20] Those who continued to voice concerns about UCITA included the Federal Trade Commission, consumer groups, library associations, entertainment industry groups (motion pictures, recording industry, and writers), academics,

---

17. See Section 102(a)(41) (definition of license); 102(a)(65)(B) (definition of transfer of computer information, a sale).

18. See UCITA, Prefatory Note.

19. See Holly K. Towle, Mass Market Transactions in the Uniform Computer Information Transactions Act, 38 Duq. L. Rev. 371 (2000).

20. See Amelia H. Boss, Taking UCITA on the Road: What Lessons Have We Learned?, 7 Roger Williams U. L. Rev. 167, 174-176 (2001) (discussing opposition to UCITA); Jean Braucher. The Failed Promise of the UCITA Mass-Market Concept and Its Lessons for Policing Standard Form Contracts, 7 J. Small & Emerging Bus. L. 393 (2003).

and state attorneys general. Perhaps the most frequently heard complaint was that UCITA favors software producers to the detriment of software users. The most controversial provisions in UCITA are those that allow licensors to use "shrinkwrap" or "clickwrap" agreements to establish terms governing the licensing or transfer of the computer information.[21] The shrinkwrap license includes terms that are not discovered by the licensee until after payment has been made, the wrapping on the product has been opened, and use of the information has begun. Additionally, the licensor may provide that the failure to return the product within a specified time period will mean that the licensee agrees to all of the licensor's terms in such a license. (The Hines v. Overstock.com and DeFontes v. Dell, Inc. cases in the editors' casebook, Problems in Contract Law, both raise clickwrap, shrinkwrap or later-added terms issues.) The effect of Sections 208 and 209, as indicated above, is to allow the terms to be added after the initial agreement between the parties in mass market licenses, subject to the opportunity to review before final assent and the right of return if the later added terms are rejected.[22] The "clickwrap" (or "clickthrough") concept applies to Internet transactions in which the customer must click on "I accept" options to be able to complete the transaction, thus indicating assent to the vendor's terms whether actually read or not.[23] Significantly however, the clickwrap scenario appears to present the terms of the agreement *before* the licensee gives apparent assent to the terms of the contract.[24]

UCITA makes an attempt to adapt concepts of assent from the Restatement (Second) of Contracts to the computer information context. More specifically, Section 112 builds on the basic concept that terms are proposed and then the parties to the contract must manifest assent to those terms in some meaningful way. The comments to the section cite the Restatement (Second) of Contracts §19 for the proposition that assent may be given by "written or spoken words or by other acts or by failure to act."[25] UCITA does differentiate between situations in which there is a question of manifestation of assent to a particular term as compared with a contract as a whole. Thus, as explained by the comments to Section 112, there may be occasions when UCITA or an agreement contemplates that a party will manifest assent to a particular term in a manner analogous to the initialing of a term in a paper agreement.[26] Section 112 ostensibly offers some safeguards against vendor or licensor abuse by requiring that the person manifesting assent have the opportunity to review the terms before accepting proposed terms. The complementary provision

---

21. See Brian D. McDonald, Contract Enforceability: The Uniform Computer Information Transactions Act, 16 Berkeley Tech. L.J. 461, 463 (2001) (describing criticism of the UCITA related to power given to computer information industry over consumers); Robert E. Scott, The Rise and Fall of Article 2, 62 La. L. Rev. 1009, 1049-1050 (2002) (summarizing difficulties arising in UCITA drafting process concerning its "seller-friendly" nature).

22. Sean F. Crotty, Note, The How and Why of Shrinkwrap License Validation Under the Uniform Computer Information Transactions Act, 33 Rutgers L.J. 745 (2002) (describing and defending enforceability of shrinkwrap licenses under UCITA).

23. See Jennifer Femminella, Note, Online Terms and Conditions Agreements: Bound by the Web, 17 St. John's J. Legal Comment. 87 (2003) (discussing "shrink-wrap," "click-wrap," and "web-wrap" agreements, with the latter presenting the license agreement terms on the vendor's website home page or some other site that must be visited through a "link").

24. For a general defense of shrinkwrap and similar methods of assent, see Dan Streeter, Comment, Into Contract's Undiscovered Country: A Defense of Browse-Wrap Licenses, 39 S.D. L. Rev. 1363 (2002).

25. Section 112 cmt. 2.

26. Id. cmt. 3(d).

of Section 113 (added by the 2002 amendments to UCITA), defines the "right to return" required by Section 209 when additional terms are disclosed by the vendor after the initial agreement has been made. Sections 112 and 113 are reprinted following this comment.

In the electronic contracting context, assent is typically not reflected by a "signature" in the traditional sense. Instead, UCITA envisions a "record" that is "authenticated" in some form by the parties as a manifestation of assent. Authentication may take various forms that suggest that the party should reasonably be understood as agreeing to the proposed terms. As noted above, in some cases such manifestation of assent may take the form of the failure to return computer information after being chargeable with knowledge of the terms. A person may also authenticate a record, as specified in Section 102(a)(6)(B), by executing or adopting "an electronic symbol, sound, message, or process referring to, attached to, included in, or logically associated or linked with, that record." Section 112(b) also recognizes that the manifestation of assent may be made by an "electronic agent" without need for human intervention with regard to the transaction.

Contract Terms

The recognition of the shrinkwrap approach to assent takes on even greater significance in light of the warranty provisions of UCITA. While UCITA adopts several warranties similar to those in Article 2 and adds additional warranties tailored to computer information transactions,[27] Section 406 also allows for disclaimer of all implied warranties, provided the disclaimer is conspicuous as defined by Section 102(a)(14), which generally requires that language be in a heading or contrasting type from the surrounding text. The official comment states that the test for conspicuousness of a term depends on whether "the attention of an ordinary person reasonably ought to have been called to it."[28] The specific provisions of the section, particularly in classifying a heading of the same size as surrounding text as being conspicuous, suggest that the test may be more lenient than in cases decided under UCC Section 2-316.[29] Therefore, the later-added terms in a shrinkwrap agreement, or the unread pre-assent terms in a clickwrap agreement, may well include a disclaimer of warranty liability or limitation on the remedy available for breach.

UCITA includes an unconscionability provision intended to allow courts to police against unfair contracts or behavior. The provisions of UCC Section 2-302 are repeated almost verbatim in UCITA Section 111 and the accompanying comments to Section 111 make it clear that UCITA fully embraces UCC Section 2-302 and cases decided thereunder. One innovation in the comments to Section 111, however, is a reflection that unconscionability may be used to guard against oppression that might result from automated contracting through electronic agents. Similarly, UCITA Section 116(b) (Section 114(b) of the 1999 version of UCITA) incorporates the principle that the duty of good faith inures in the performance and enforcement of all contracts in language identical to UCC Article §1-304. These

---

27. See Section 402 on express warranty, Section 403 on implied warranty of merchantability of computer program, Section 404 on implied warranty of informational content, and Section 405 on implied warranty related to licensee's purpose.

28. Section 102 cmt. 12.

29. Section 102(a)(14)(A)(i).

provisions may have particular relevance to issues of assent to or enforcement of contract terms.

UNIFORM COMPUTER INFORMATION TRANSACTIONS ACT

Section 112. Manifesting Assent

(a) **[How person manifests assent.]** A person manifests assent to a record or term if the person, acting with knowledge of, or after having an opportunity to review the record or term or a copy of it:

(1) authenticates the record or term with intent to adopt or accept it; or

(2) intentionally engages in conduct or makes statements with reason to know that the other party or its electronic agent may infer from the conduct or statement that the person assents to the record or term.

(b) **[How electronic agent manifests assent.]** An electronic agent manifests assent to a record or term if, after having an opportunity to review it, the electronic agent:

(1) authenticates the record or term; or

(2) engages in operations that in the circumstances indicate acceptance of the record or term.

(c) **[Assent to specific term.]** If this [Act] or other law requires assent to a specific term, a manifestation of assent must relate specifically to the term.

(d) **[Proof of assent.]** Conduct or operations manifesting assent may be proved in any manner, including a showing that a person or an electronic agent obtained or used the information or informational rights and that a procedure existed by which a person or an electronic agent must have engaged in the conduct or operations in order to do so. Proof of compliance with subsection (a)(2) is sufficient if there is conduct that assents and subsequent conduct that reaffirms assent by electronic means.

(e) **[Agreement for future transactions.]** The effect of this section may be modified by an agreement setting out standards applicable to future transactions between the parties.

(f) **[Online services, network access, and telecommunications services.]** Providers of online services, network access, and telecommunications services, or the operators of facilities thereof, do not manifest assent to a contractual relationship simply by their provision of those services to other parties, including, without limitation, transmission, routing, or providing connections; linking; caching; hosting; information location tools; and storage of materials, at the request or initiation of a person other than the service provider.

Comment

1. Scope of Section. This section provides standards for "manifestation of assent." Section 113 deals with the related, important concept of an "opportunity to review". In this Act, having an opportunity to review a record is a precondition to manifesting assent.

2. General Theme. The term "manifesting assent" comes from *Restatement (Second) of Contracts* §19. This section ... more fully explicates the concept. Codification establishes uniformity that is lacking in common law.

Restatement (Second) of Contracts §19(1) provides: "The manifestation of assent may be made wholly or partly by written or spoken words or by other acts or by failure to act." This section adopts that view. Conduct can convey assent as clearly as words. This rule is important in electronic commerce, where most interactions involve conduct rather than words. Subsection (b) adapts that principle to electronic agent contracting.

"Manifesting assent" has several roles: 1) a method by which a party agrees to a contract; 2) a method by which a party adopts terms of a record as the terms of a contract; and 3) if required by this Act, a means of assenting to a particular term. In most cases, the same act accomplishes the results under 1 and 2.

Manifesting assent does not require any specific formality of language or conduct. In this Act, however, to manifest assent to a record or term requires meeting three conditions:

• **First**, the person must have knowledge of the record or term or an opportunity to review it before assenting. An opportunity to review requires that the record be available in a manner that ought to call it to the attention of a reasonable person and that readily permits review. Section 113 may also require a right of return if the opportunity to review comes after a person becomes obligated to pay or begins performance.

• **Second**, having had an opportunity to review, the person must manifest assent. The person may authenticate the record or term, express assent verbally, or intentionally engage in conduct with reason to know that the conduct indicates assent. *Restatement (Second) of Contracts* §19. As in the *Restatement* this can include a failure to action if the circumstances so indicate.

• **Third**, the conduct, statement, or authentication must be attributable in law to the person. General agency law and Section 212 provide standards for attribution.

3. Manifesting Assent.

a. Assent by Statements or Authentication. A person can assent to a record or term by stating or otherwise indicating its assent or by "authenticating" the record or term. Authentication occurs if a party signs a record or does an electronic equivalent. ...

b. Assent by Conduct. Assent occurs if a person acts or fails to act having reason to know its behavior will be viewed by the other party as indicating assent. Whether this occurs depends on the circumstances. As in common law, proof of assent does not require proof of a person's subjective intent or purpose, but focuses on objective indicia, including whether there was an act or a failure to act voluntarily engaged in with reason to know that an inference of assent would be drawn. Actions objectively indicating assent are assent. This follows modern contract law doctrines of objective assent. Doctrines of mistake, fraud, and duress apply in appropriate cases.

Assent does not require that a party be able to negotiate or modify terms, but the assenting behavior must be intentional (voluntary). This same rule prevails in all other contract law. Intentional conduct is satisfied if the alternative of refusing to act exists, even if refusing leaves no alternative source for the computer information. On the other hand, conduct is not assent if it is conduct which the assenting party cannot avoid doing, such as blinking one's eyes. Courts use common sense in applying this standard in common law and will do so under this Act. Actions in a context of a mutual reservation of the right to defer agreement to a contract do not manifest assent; neither party has any reason to believe that its conduct will suggest assent to the other party. . . .

5. Proof of Assent. Many different acts can establish assent to a contract or a contract term. It is not possible to state them in a statute. In electronic commerce, one important method is by showing that a procedure existed that required an authentication or other assent in order to proceed in an automated system. This is recognized in subsection (d).

Subsection (d) also encourages use of double assent procedures as a reconfirmation showing intentional assent ("intentionally engages in conduct . . . with reason to know"). It makes clear that if the assenting party has an opportunity to confirm or deny assent before proceeding to obtain or use information, confirmation meets the requirement of subsection (a)(2). This does not alter the effectiveness of a single indication of assent. When properly set out with an opportunity to review terms and to make clear that an act such as clicking assent on-screen is assent, a single indication of assent suffices. See Caspi v. Microsoft Network, L.L.C., 323 N.J. Super. 118, 732 A.2d 528 (N.J. A.D. 1999) . . . ; Register.com, Inc. v. Verio, Inc., 126 F. Supp. 2d 238 (S.D.N.Y. 2000).

> **Illustration 1:** The registration screen for NY Online prominently states: "Please read the License. It contains important terms about your use and our obligations. If you agree to the license, indicate this by clicking the 'I agree' button. If you do not agree, click 'I decline'." The on-screen buttons are clearly identified. The underlined text is a hypertext link that, if selected, promptly displays the license. A party that indicates "I agree" assents to the license and adopts its terms. . . .

Section 113. Opportunity to Review

(a) [**Manner of availability generally.**] A person has an opportunity to review a record or term only if it is made available in a manner that ought to call it to the attention of a reasonable person and permit review.

(b) [**Manner of availability by electronic agent.**] An electronic agent has an opportunity to review a record or term only if it is made available in a manner that would enable a reasonably configured electronic agent to react to the record or term.

(c) [**When right of return required.**] If a record or term is available for review only after a person becomes obligated to pay or begins its performance, the person has an opportunity to review only if it has a right to a return if it rejects the record. However, a right to a return is not required if:

(1) the record proposes a modification of contract or provides particulars of performance under Section 305; or

(2) the primary performance is other than delivery or acceptance of a copy, the agreement is not a mass-market transaction, and the parties at the time of contracting had reason to know that a record or term would be presented after performance, use, or access to the information began.

(d) **[Right of return created.]** The right to a return under this section may arise by law or agreement.

(e) **[Agreement for future transactions.]** The effect of this section may be modified by an agreement setting out standards applicable to future transactions between the parties.

Comment

1. Scope of this Section. This section sets out the basic standards for when a party has been given an opportunity to review the terms of a record. Unless there is an opportunity to review the record, under Section 112 the party cannot manifest assent to it.

2. Opportunity to Review. A manifestation of assent to a record or term under this Act cannot occur unless there was an opportunity to review the record or term. Common law does not clearly establish this requirement, but the requirement of an opportunity to review terms reasonably made available reflects simple fairness and establishes concepts that curtail procedural aspects of unconscionability. Section 111. For a person, an opportunity to review requires that a record be made available in a manner that ought to call it to the attention of a reasonable person and permit review. See Specht v. Netscape Communications Corp., [306 F.3d 17, 28-29 n. 13 (2d Cir. 2002)]. This requirement is met if the person knows of the record or has reason to know that the record or term exists in a form and location that in the circumstances permit review of it or a copy of it. For an electronic agent, an opportunity to review exists only if the record is one to which a reasonably configured electronic agent could respond. Terms made available for review during an over-the-counter transaction or otherwise in a manner required under federal law give an opportunity to review.

a. Declining to Use the Opportunity to Review. An opportunity to review does not require that the person use that opportunity. The condition is met even if the person does not read or actually review the record. This is not changed because the party desires to complete the transaction rapidly, is under pressure to do so, or because the party has other demands on its attention, unless the one party actively manipulates circumstances to induce the other party not to review the record. Such manipulation may vitiate the alleged opportunity to review.

b. Permits Review. How a record is made available for review may differ for electronic and paper records. In both, however, a record is not available for review if access to it is so time-consuming or cumbersome, or if its presentation is so obscure or oblique, as to make it difficult to review. It must be presented in a way as to reasonably permit review. In an electronic system, a record promptly accessible through an electronic link ordinarily qualifies. Actions that comply with federal or other applicable consumer laws that require making contract terms or disclosure available, or that provide standards for doing so, satisfy this requirement.

c. Right to Return. If terms in a record are not available until after there is an initial commitment to the transaction, subsection (c) indicates that ordinarily there is no opportunity to review unless the party can return the product (or for a vendor that refuses the other party's terms, recover the product) and receive appropriate reimbursement of payments if it rejects the terms. The return right creates a situation where meaningful assent can occur. The right exists only for the first licensee. If the right to a return is created only by agreement or by an offer from the one party, rather than by law, the right must be communicated to the other person so that the person ought to become aware of it. . . .

E-SIGN ACT AND UNIFORM ELECTRONIC TRANSACTIONS ACT

EDITORS' NOTE

In 1994, Utah became the first state to enact a law regulating electronic contracting and other states soon adopted legislation, but their approaches varied widely.[1] In 1997, the National Conference of Commissioners on Uniform State Laws (NCCUSL)[2] undertook to draft a uniform state law on the subject, and approved the Uniform Electronic Transactions Act (UETA) in July 1999.[3]

Following UETA's promulgation, high tech and financial services industry interests, concerned that states were not moving quickly enough to adopt the uniform law and that inconsistencies persisted among the various state laws, urged Congress to develop federal e-commerce legislation.[4] On June 30, 2000, President Clinton signed the Electronic Signatures in Global and National Commerce Act (E-Sign Act).[5]

The relationship between UETA and the E-Sign Act is somewhat complex. With certain exceptions, the E-Sign Act preempts state laws and regulations.[6] However, Congress authorized states to supersede the E-Sign Act if they adopt the 1999 version of UETA. See E-Sign Act § 102(a)(1). A state that does not adopt UETA can opt out of the E-Sign Act if it enacts other legislation that is not inconsistent with the requirements of the E-Sign Act. See E-Sign Act § 102(a)(2). Thus, if a state has adopted UETA without amendments, that state's law, rather than the E-Sign Act, will control a transaction. If a state has not adopted any legislation, the E-Sign Act provides the governing rules. If a state has adopted some legislation on electronic

---

1. See Robert A. Wittie & Jane K. Winn, Electronic Records and Signatures under the Federal E-Sign Legislation and the UETA, 56 Bus. Law. 293, 294-95 (2000).

2. NCCUSL is now known officially as the Uniform Law Commission.

3. UETA should not be confused with the Uniform Computer Information Transactions Act (UCITA), discussed and excerpted supra, with which UETA does overlap somewhat. For a comparison of UCITA and UETA and their relative merits, see Cem Kaner, E-Commerce Provisions in the UCITA and UETA (June 17, 1999), available at http://www.badsoftware.uetaanducitauccbull.htm (last visited June 1, 2017).

4. See Wittie & Winn, *supra*, 56 Bus. Law. at 296; see also Anda Lincoln, Comment, Electronic Signature Laws and the Need for Uniformity in the Global Market, 8 J. Small & Emerging Bus. L. 67 (2004).

5. 15 U.S.C.A. §§ 7001-7031 (2017).

6. See Jean Braucher, Rent-Seeking and Risk-Fixing in the New Statutory Law of Electronic Commerce: Difficulties in Moving Consumer Protection Online, 2001 Wis. L. Rev. 527 (analyzing and comparing UETA and the E-Sign Act). See generally U.S. Const. art. VI, cl. 2.

contracting other than UETA, the validity of such legislation will depend on its consistency with the E-Sign Act.

As explained by the Official Comments to Section 7 of UETA, the fundamental premise of the Act is that the use of an electronic medium should not preclude the satisfaction of requirements for contract formation. UETA Section 7 (a) provides that: "A record or signature may not be denied legal effect or enforceability solely because it is in electronic form." Similarly, Section 7(c) provides that an electronic record satisfies any legal requirement that a record be in writing, and 7(d) states that an electronic signature will satisfy any requirement under the law for a signature. Thus, UETA does not change the substantive law of contracts, but rather provides that electronic communications may be used to satisfy any requirements for a writing or a signature.[7]

Another basic principle of UETA is that it depends on the free agreement of the parties to conduct a transaction electronically, as stated in Section 5. The test of whether the parties have reached such an agreement, however, is rather liberally construed with the goal of promoting broader application of UETA. Section 5(b) states, "Whether the parties agree to conduct a transaction by electronic means is determined from the context and surrounding circumstances, including the parties' conduct." Thus, an agreement to conduct a transaction electronically need not be explicit and it may be found in the parties' conduct. This latter point is emphasized by the Official Comment to Section 5. The full text of UETA is available online at ULC website.[8] As of June 1, 2017, 47 states and the District of Columbia had adopted UETA.[9]

The E-Sign Act has three core provisions. First, section 101(a)(1) authorizes the use of electronic signatures. The Act provides for technological innovation and diversity by a broad definition of what constitutes an electronic signature: "The term 'electronic signature' means an electronic sound, symbol, or process, attached to or logically associated with a contract or other record and executed or adopted by a person with the intent to sign the record." Section 106(5). The Act does not require businesses or consumers to use electronic signatures and it preserves other rights and obligations. See § 101(b). Second, section 101(a)(2) validates the use of electronic records of transactions and states that a contract may not be denied legal effect solely because an electronic signature or electronic record was used in its formation. The Act prohibits states from giving greater legal status to any specific technology used to make an electronic signature or record. See § 102(a)(2)(A)(ii). Finally, the Act contains various consumer protection measures. See §§ 101(c)(1) (disclosure and consent) and 101(c)(2) (preservation of consumer rights granted under other law). Some transactions are specifically exempted from the E-Sign Act. These include execution of wills, codicils, and trusts; documents affecting family matters such as divorce decrees or separation agreements; and foreclosure notices. See § 103. While the E-Sign Act authorizes use of electronic signatures and electronic recordkeeping, the extent and form that such transactions take will vary widely depending on market considerations. See Bill Zoellick, Wide Use of Electronic Signatures Awaits Market Decisions about Their Risks and Benefits, N.Y. St. B.J.,

---

7. See Valerie Watnick, The Electronic Formation of Contracts and the Common Law "Mailbox Rule," 56 Baylor L. Rev. 175, 189-90 (2004).

8. http://www.uniformlaws.org (last visited June 1, 2017).

9. See id. Only Illinois, New York, and Washington have not enacted UETA.

Nov./Dec. 2000, at 10. For further discussions of the E-Sign Act, see Holly K. Towle, E-Signatures — Basics of the U.S. Structure, 38 Hous. L. Rev. 921(2001); Scott R. Zemnick, Note, The E-Sign Act: The Means to Effectively Facilitate the Growth and Development of E-Commerce, 76 Chi.-Kent L. Rev. 1965 (2001).

The E-sign Act is reprinted immediately below, followed by most of the sections and some comments from UETA.

ELECTRONIC SIGNATURES IN GLOBAL AND NATIONAL COMMERCE ACT

PL 106-229, 114 Stat 464, June 30, 2000

An Act to facilitate the use of electronic records and signatures in interstate or foreign commerce.

Be it enacted by the Senate and House of Representatives of the United States of America in Congress assembled,

§1. Short Title

This Act may be cited as the "Electronic Signatures in Global and National Commerce Act".

TITLE I — ELECTRONIC RECORDS AND SIGNATURES IN COMMERCE

§101. GENERAL RULE OF VALIDITY. [15 USCA §7001]

(a) IN GENERAL. — Notwithstanding any statute, regulation, or other rule of law (other than this title and title II), with respect to any transaction in or affecting interstate or foreign commerce —

(1) a signature, contract, or other record relating to such transaction may not be denied legal effect, validity, or enforceability solely because it is in electronic form; and

(2) a contract relating to such transaction may not be denied legal effect, validity, or enforceability solely because an electronic signature or electronic record was used in its formation.

(b) PRESERVATION OF RIGHTS AND OBLIGATIONS. — This title does not —

(1) limit, alter, or otherwise affect any requirement imposed by a statute, regulation, or rule of law relating to the rights and obligations of persons under such statute, regulation, or rule of law other than a requirement that contracts or other records be written, signed, or in nonelectronic form; or

(2) require any person to agree to use or accept electronic records or electronic signatures, other than a governmental agency with respect to a record other than a contract to which it is a party.

(c) CONSUMER DISCLOSURES. —

(1) CONSENT TO ELECTRONIC RECORDS. — Notwithstanding subsection (a), if a statute, regulation, or other rule of law requires that information

relating to a transaction or transactions in or affecting interstate or foreign commerce be provided or made available to a consumer in writing, the use of an electronic record to provide or make available (whichever is required) such information satisfies the requirement that such information be in writing if —

(A) the consumer has affirmatively consented to such use and has not withdrawn such consent;

(B) the consumer, prior to consenting, is provided with a clear and conspicuous statement —

(i) informing the consumer of (I) any right or option of the consumer to have the record provided or made available on paper or in nonelectronic form, and (II) the right of the consumer to withdraw the consent to have the record provided or made available in an electronic form and of any conditions, consequences (which may include termination of the parties' relationship), or fees in the event of such withdrawal;

(ii) informing the consumer of whether the consent applies (I) only to the particular transaction which gave rise to the obligation to provide the record, or (II) to identified categories of records that may be provided or made available during the course of the parties' relationship;

(iii) describing the procedures the consumer must use to withdraw consent as provided in clause (i) and to update information needed to contact the consumer electronically; and

(iv) informing the consumer (I) how, after the consent, the consumer may, upon request, obtain a paper copy of an electronic record, and (II) whether any fee will be charged for such copy;

(C) the consumer —

(i) prior to consenting, is provided with a statement of the hardware and software requirements for access to and retention of the electronic records; and

(ii) consents electronically, or confirms his or her consent electronically, in a manner that reasonably demonstrates that the consumer can access information in the electronic form that will be used to provide the information that is the subject of the consent; and

(D) after the consent of a consumer in accordance with subparagraph (A), if a change in the hardware or software requirements needed to access or retain electronic records creates a material risk that the consumer will not be able to access or retain a subsequent electronic record that was the subject of the consent, the person providing the electronic record —

(i) provides the consumer with a statement of (I) the revised hardware and software requirements for access to and retention of the electronic records, and (II) the right to withdraw consent without the imposition of any fees for such withdrawal and without the imposition of any condition or consequence that was not disclosed under subparagraph (B)(i); and

(ii) again complies with subparagraph (C).

(2) OTHER RIGHTS. —

(A) PRESERVATION OF CONSUMER PROTECTIONS. — Nothing in this title affects the content or timing of any disclosure or other record required to be provided or made available to any consumer under any statute, regulation, or other rule of law.

(B) VERIFICATION OR ACKNOWLEDGMENT. — If a law that was enacted prior to this Act expressly requires a record to be provided or made available by a specified method that requires verification or acknowledgment of receipt, the record may be provided or made available electronically only if the method used provides verification or acknowledgment of receipt (whichever is required).

(3) EFFECT OF FAILURE TO OBTAIN ELECTRONIC CONSENT OR CONFIRMATION OF CONSENT. — The legal effectiveness, validity, or enforceability of any contract executed by a consumer shall not be denied solely because of the failure to obtain electronic consent or confirmation of consent by that consumer in accordance with paragraph (1)(C)(ii).

(4) PROSPECTIVE EFFECT. — Withdrawal of consent by a consumer shall not affect the legal effectiveness, validity, or enforceability of electronic records provided or made available to that consumer in accordance with paragraph (1) prior to implementation of the consumer's withdrawal of consent. A consumer's withdrawal of consent shall be effective within a reasonable period of time after receipt of the withdrawal by the provider of the record. Failure to comply with paragraph (1)(D) may, at the election of the consumer, be treated as a withdrawal of consent for purposes of this paragraph.

(5) PRIOR CONSENT. — This subsection does not apply to any records that are provided or made available to a consumer who has consented prior to the effective date of this title to receive such records in electronic form as permitted by any statute, regulation, or other rule of law.

(6) ORAL COMMUNICATIONS. — An oral communication or a recording of an oral communication shall not qualify as an electronic record for purposes of this subsection except as otherwise provided under applicable law.

(d) RETENTION OF CONTRACTS AND RECORDS. —

(1) ACCURACY AND ACCESSIBILITY. — If a statute, regulation, or other rule of law requires that a contract or other record relating to a transaction in or affecting interstate or foreign commerce be retained, that requirement is met by retaining an electronic record of the information in the contract or other record that —

(A) accurately reflects the information set forth in the contract or other record; and

(B) remains accessible to all persons who are entitled to access by statute, regulation, or rule of law, for the period required by such statute, regulation, or rule of law, in a form that is capable of being accurately reproduced for later reference, whether by transmission, printing, or otherwise.

(2) EXCEPTION. — A requirement to retain a contract or other record in accordance with paragraph (1) does not apply to any information whose sole purpose is to enable the contract or other record to be sent, communicated, or received.

(3) ORIGINALS. — If a statute, regulation, or other rule of law requires a contract or other record relating to a transaction in or affecting interstate or foreign commerce to be provided, available, or retained in its original form, or provides consequences if the contract or other record is not provided, available, or retained in its original form, that statute, regulation, or rule of law is satisfied by an electronic record that complies with paragraph (1).

(4) CHECKS. — If a statute, regulation, or other rule of law requires the retention of a check, that requirement is satisfied by retention of an electronic record of the information on the front and back of the check in accordance with paragraph (1).

(e) ACCURACY AND ABILITY TO RETAIN CONTRACTS AND OTHER RECORDS. — Notwithstanding subsection (a), if a statute, regulation, or other rule of law requires that a contract or other record relating to a transaction in or affecting interstate or foreign commerce be in writing, the legal effect, validity, or enforceability of an electronic record of such contract or other record may be denied if such electronic record is not in a form that is capable of being retained and accurately reproduced for later reference by all parties or persons who are entitled to retain the contract or other record.

(f) PROXIMITY. — Nothing in this title affects the proximity required by any statute, regulation, or other rule of law with respect to any warning, notice, disclosure, or other record required to be posted, displayed, or publicly affixed.

(g) NOTARIZATION AND ACKNOWLEDGMENT. — If a statute, regulation, or other rule of law requires a signature or record relating to a transaction in or affecting interstate or foreign commerce to be notarized, acknowledged, verified, or made under oath, that requirement is satisfied if the electronic signature of the person authorized to perform those acts, together with all other information required to be included by other applicable statute, regulation, or rule of law, is attached to or logically associated with the signature or record.

(h) ELECTRONIC AGENTS. — A contract or other record relating to a transaction in or affecting interstate or foreign commerce may not be denied legal effect, validity, or enforceability solely because its formation, creation, or delivery involved the action of one or more electronic agents so long as the action of any such electronic agent is legally attributable to the person to be bound.

(i) INSURANCE. — It is the specific intent of the Congress that this title and title II apply to the business of insurance.

(j) INSURANCE AGENTS AND BROKERS. — An insurance agent or broker acting under the direction of a party that enters into a contract by means of an electronic record or electronic signature may not be held liable for any deficiency in the electronic procedures agreed to by the parties under that contract if —

(1) the agent or broker has not engaged in negligent, reckless, or intentional tortuous conduct;

(2) the agent or broker was not involved in the development or establishment of such electronic procedures; and

(3) the agent or broker did not deviate from such procedures.

§102. EXEMPTION TO PREEMPTION. [15 USCA §7002]

(a) IN GENERAL. — A State statute, regulation, or other rule of law may modify, limit, or supersede the provisions of section 101 with respect to State law only if such statute, regulation, or rule of law —

(1) constitutes an enactment or adoption of the Uniform Electronic Transactions Act as approved and recommended for enactment in all the States by the National Conference of Commissioners on Uniform State Laws in 1999, except that any exception to the scope of such Act enacted by a State under section 3(b)(4) of such Act shall be preempted to the extent such exception is

inconsistent with this title or title II, or would not be permitted under paragraph (2)(A)(ii) of this subsection; or

(2) (A) specifies the alternative procedures or requirements for the use or acceptance (or both) of electronic records or electronic signatures to establish the legal effect, validity, or enforceability of contracts or other records, if—

(i) such alternative procedures or requirements are consistent with this title and title II; and

(ii) such alternative procedures or requirements do not require, or accord greater legal status or effect to, the implementation or application of a specific technology or technical specification for performing the functions of creating, storing, generating, receiving, communicating, or authenticating electronic records or electronic signatures; and

(B) if enacted or adopted after the date of the enactment of this Act, makes specific reference to this Act.

(b) EXCEPTIONS FOR ACTIONS BY STATES AS MARKET PARTICIPANTS. — Subsection (a)(2)(A)(ii) shall not apply to the statutes, regulations, or other rules of law governing procurement by any State, or any agency or instrumentality thereof.

(c) PREVENTION OF CIRCUMVENTION. — Subsection (a) does not permit a State to circumvent this title or title II through the imposition of nonelectronic delivery methods under section 8(b)(2) of the Uniform Electronic Transactions Act.

§103. SPECIFIC EXCEPTIONS. [15 USCA §7003]

(a) EXCEPTED REQUIREMENTS. — The provisions of section 101 shall not apply to a contract or other record to the extent it is governed by —

(1) a statute, regulation, or other rule of law governing the creation and execution of wills, codicils, or testamentary trusts;

(2) a State statute, regulation, or other rule of law governing adoption, divorce, or other matters of family law; or

(3) the Uniform Commercial Code, as in effect in any State, other than section[] 1-[306] . . . and Articles 2 and 2A.

(b) ADDITIONAL EXCEPTIONS. — The provisions of section 101 shall not apply to —

(1) court orders or notices, or official court documents (including briefs, pleadings, and other writings) required to be executed in connection with court proceedings;

(2) any notice of—

(A) the cancellation or termination of utility services (including water, heat, and power);

(B) default, acceleration, repossession, foreclosure, or eviction, or the right to cure, under a credit agreement secured by, or a rental agreement for, a primary residence of an individual;

(C) the cancellation or termination of health insurance or benefits or life insurance benefits (excluding annuities); or

(D) recall of a product, or material failure of a product, that risks endangering health or safety; or

(3) any document required to accompany any transportation or handling of hazardous materials, pesticides, or other toxic or dangerous materials.

(c) REVIEW OF EXCEPTIONS. —

(1) EVALUATION REQUIRED. — The Secretary of Commerce, acting through the Assistant Secretary for Communications and Information, shall review the operation of the exceptions in subsections (a) and (b) to evaluate, over a period of 3 years, whether such exceptions continue to be necessary for the protection of consumers. Within 3 years after the date of enactment of this Act, the Assistant Secretary shall submit a report to the Congress on the results of such evaluation.

(2) DETERMINATIONS. — If a Federal regulatory agency, with respect to matter within its jurisdiction, determines after notice and an opportunity for public comment, and publishes a finding, that one or more such exceptions are no longer necessary for the protection of consumers and eliminating such exceptions will not increase the material risk of harm to consumers, such agency may extend the application of section 101 to the exceptions identified in such finding.

§104. APPLICABILITY TO FEDERAL AND STATE GOVERNMENTS.
[15 USCA §7004]

(a) FILING AND ACCESS REQUIREMENTS. — Subject to subsection (c)(2), nothing in this title limits or supersedes any requirement by a Federal regulatory agency, self-regulatory organization, or State regulatory agency that records be filed with such agency or organization in accordance with specified standards or formats.

(b) PRESERVATION OF EXISTING RULEMAKING AUTHORITY. —

(1) USE OF AUTHORITY TO INTERPRET. — Subject to paragraph (2) and subsection (c), a Federal regulatory agency or State regulatory agency that is responsible for rulemaking under any other statute may interpret section 101 with respect to such statute through —

(A) the issuance of regulations pursuant to a statute; or

(B) to the extent such agency is authorized by statute to issue orders or guidance, the issuance of orders or guidance of general applicability that are publicly available and published (in the Federal Register in the case of an order or guidance issued by a Federal regulatory agency).

This paragraph does not grant any Federal regulatory agency or State regulatory agency authority to issue regulations, orders, or guidance pursuant to any statute that does not authorize such issuance.

(2) LIMITATIONS ON INTERPRETATION AUTHORITY. — Notwithstanding paragraph (1), a Federal regulatory agency shall not adopt any regulation, order, or guidance described in paragraph (1), and a State regulatory agency is preempted by section 101 from adopting any regulation, order, or guidance described in paragraph (1), unless —

(A) such regulation, order, or guidance is consistent with section 101;

(B) such regulation, order, or guidance does not add to the requirements of such section; and

(C) such agency finds, in connection with the issuance of such regulation, order, or guidance, that —

(i) there is a substantial justification for the regulation, order, or guidance;

(ii) the methods selected to carry out that purpose —

(I) are substantially equivalent to the requirements imposed on records that are not electronic records; and

(II) will not impose unreasonable costs on the acceptance and use of electronic records; and

(iii) the methods selected to carry out that purpose do not require, or accord greater legal status or effect to, the implementation or application of a specific technology or technical specification for performing the functions of creating, storing, generating, receiving, communicating, or authenticating electronic records or electronic signatures.

(3) PERFORMANCE STANDARDS. —

(A) ACCURACY, RECORD INTEGRITY, ACCESSIBILITY. — Notwithstanding paragraph (2)(C)(iii), a Federal regulatory agency or State regulatory agency may interpret section 101(d) to specify performance standards to assure accuracy, record integrity, and accessibility of records that are required to be retained. Such performance standards may be specified in a manner that imposes a requirement in violation of paragraph (2)(C)(iii) if the requirement (i) serves an important governmental objective; and (ii) is substantially related to the achievement of that objective. Nothing in this paragraph shall be construed to grant any Federal regulatory agency or State regulatory agency authority to require use of a particular type of software or hardware in order to comply with section 101(d).

(B) PAPER OR PRINTED FORM. — Notwithstanding subsection (c)(1), a Federal regulatory agency or State regulatory agency may interpret section 101(d) to require retention of a record in a tangible printed or paper form if —

(i) there is a compelling governmental interest relating to law enforcement or national security for imposing such requirement; and

(ii) imposing such requirement is essential to attaining such interest.

(4) EXCEPTIONS FOR ACTIONS BY GOVERNMENT AS MARKET PARTICIPANT. — Paragraph (2)(C)(iii) shall not apply to the statutes, regulations, or other rules of law governing procurement by the Federal or any State government, or any agency or instrumentality thereof.

(c) ADDITIONAL LIMITATIONS. —

(1) REIMPOSING PAPER PROHIBITED. — Nothing in subsection (b) (other than paragraph (3)(B) thereof) shall be construed to grant any Federal regulatory agency or State regulatory agency authority to impose or reimpose any requirement that a record be in a tangible printed or paper form.

(2) CONTINUING OBLIGATION UNDER GOVERNMENT PAPERWORK ELIMINATION ACT. — Nothing in subsection (a) or (b) relieves any Federal regulatory agency of its obligations under the Government Paperwork Elimination Act (title XVII of Public Law 105-277).

(d) AUTHORITY TO EXEMPT FROM CONSENT PROVISION. —

(1) IN GENERAL. — A Federal regulatory agency may, with respect to matter within its jurisdiction, by regulation or order issued after notice and an opportunity for public comment, exempt without condition a specified category or type of record from the requirements relating to consent in section 101(c) if such exemption is necessary to eliminate a substantial burden on electronic commerce and will not increase the material risk of harm to consumers.

(2) PROSPECTUSES. — Within 30 days after the date of enactment of this Act, the Securities and Exchange Commission shall issue a regulation or order

pursuant to paragraph (1) exempting from section 101(c) any records that are required to be provided in order to allow advertising, sales literature, or other information concerning a security issued by an investment company that is registered under the Investment Company Act of 1940 [15 U.S.C.A. §80a-1 et seq.], or concerning the issuer thereof, to be excluded from the definition of a prospectus under section 2(a)(10)(A) of the Securities Act of 1933 [15 U.S.C.A. §77b(a)(10)(A)].

(e) ELECTRONIC LETTERS OF AGENCY. — The Federal Communications Commission shall not hold any contract for telecommunications service or letter of agency for a preferred carrier change, that otherwise complies with the Commission's rules, to be legally ineffective, invalid, or unenforceable solely because an electronic record or electronic signature was used in its formation or authorization.

§105. STUDIES. [15 USCA §7005]

(a) DELIVERY. — Within 12 months after the date of the enactment of this Act, the Secretary of Commerce shall conduct an inquiry regarding the effectiveness of the delivery of electronic records to consumers using electronic mail as compared with delivery of written records via the United States Postal Service and private express mail services. The Secretary shall submit a report to the Congress regarding the results of such inquiry by the conclusion of such 12-month period.

(b) STUDY OF ELECTRONIC CONSENT. — Within 12 months after the date of the enactment of this Act, the Secretary of Commerce and the Federal Trade Commission shall submit a report to the Congress evaluating any benefits provided to consumers by the procedure required by section 101(c)(1)(C)(ii); any burdens imposed on electronic commerce by that provision; whether the benefits outweigh the burdens; whether the absence of the procedure required by section 101(c)(1)(C)(ii) would increase the incidence of fraud directed against consumers; and suggesting any revisions to the provision deemed appropriate by the Secretary and the Commission. In conducting this evaluation, the Secretary and the Commission shall solicit comment from the general public, consumer representatives, and electronic commerce businesses.

§106. DEFINITIONS. [15 USCA §7006]

For purposes of this title:

(1) CONSUMER. — The term "consumer" means an individual who obtains, through a transaction, products or services which are used primarily for personal, family, or household purposes, and also means the legal representative of such an individual.

(2) ELECTRONIC. — The term "electronic" means relating to technology having electrical, digital, magnetic, wireless, optical, electromagnetic, or similar capabilities.

(3) ELECTRONIC AGENT. — The term "electronic agent" means a computer program or an electronic or other automated means used independently to initiate an action or respond to electronic records or performances in whole or in part without review or action by an individual at the time of the action or response.

(4) ELECTRONIC RECORD. — The term "electronic record" means a contract or other record created, generated, sent, communicated, received, or stored by electronic means.

(5) ELECTRONIC SIGNATURE. — The term "electronic signature" means an electronic sound, symbol, or process, attached to or logically associated with a contract or other record and executed or adopted by a person with the intent to sign the record.

(6) FEDERAL REGULATORY AGENCY. — The term "Federal regulatory agency" means an agency, as that term is defined in section 552(f) of title 5, United States Code.

(7) INFORMATION. — The term "information" means data, text, images, sounds, codes, computer programs, software, databases, or the like.

(8) PERSON. — The term "person" means an individual, corporation, business trust, estate, trust, partnership, limited liability company, association, joint venture, governmental agency, public corporation, or any other legal or commercial entity.

(9) RECORD. — The term "record" means information that is inscribed on a tangible medium or that is stored in an electronic or other medium and is retrievable in perceivable form.

(10) REQUIREMENT. — The term "requirement" includes a prohibition.

(11) SELF-REGULATORY ORGANIZATION. — The term "self-regulatory organization" means an organization or entity that is not a Federal regulatory agency or a State, but that is under the supervision of a Federal regulatory agency and is authorized under Federal law to adopt and administer rules applicable to its members that are enforced by such organization or entity, by a Federal regulatory agency, or by another self-regulatory organization.

(12) STATE. — The term "State" includes the District of Columbia and the territories and possessions of the United States.

(13) TRANSACTION. — The term "transaction" means an action or set of actions relating to the conduct of business, consumer, or commercial affairs between two or more persons, including any of the following types of conduct —

(A) the sale, lease, exchange, licensing, or other disposition of (i) personal property, including goods and intangibles, (ii) services, and (iii) any combination thereof; and

(B) the sale, lease, exchange, or other disposition of any interest in real property, or any combination thereof.

§107. EFFECTIVE DATE. [15 USCA §7001 NOTE]

(a) IN GENERAL. — Except as provided in subsection (b), this title shall be effective on October 1, 2000.

(b) EXCEPTIONS. —

(1) RECORD RETENTION. —

(A) IN GENERAL. — Subject to subparagraph (B), this title shall be effective on March 1, 2001, with respect to a requirement that a record be retained imposed by —

(i) a Federal statute, regulation, or other rule of law, or

(ii) a State statute, regulation, or other rule of law administered or promulgated by a State regulatory agency.

(B) DELAYED EFFECT FOR PENDING RULEMAKINGS. — If on March 1, 2001, a Federal regulatory agency or State regulatory agency has announced, proposed, or initiated, but not completed, a rulemaking proceeding to prescribe a regulation under section 104(b)(3) with respect to a requirement described in subparagraph (A), this title shall be effective on June 1, 2001, with respect to such requirement.

(2) CERTAIN GUARANTEED AND INSURED LOANS. — With regard to any transaction involving a loan guarantee or loan guarantee commitment (as those terms are defined in section 502 of the Federal Credit Reform Act of 1990), or involving a program listed in the Federal Credit Supplement, Budget of the United States, FY 2001, this title applies only to such transactions entered into, and to any loan or mortgage made, insured, or guaranteed by the United States Government thereunder, on and after one year after the date of enactment of this Act.

(3) STUDENT LOANS. — With respect to any records that are provided or made available to a consumer pursuant to an application for a loan, or a loan made, pursuant to title IV of the Higher Education Act of 1965, section 101(c) of this Act shall not apply until the earlier of—

(A) such time as the Secretary of Education publishes revised promissory notes under section 432(m) of the Higher Education Act of 1965; or

(B) one year after the date of enactment of this Act.

Title II — Transferable Records

§201. TRANSFERABLE RECORDS. [15 USCA §7021]

(a) DEFINITIONS. — For purposes of this section:

(1) TRANSFERABLE RECORD. — The term "transferable record" means an electronic record that —

(A) would be a note under Article 3 of the Uniform Commercial Code if the electronic record were in writing;

(B) the issuer of the electronic record expressly has agreed is a transferable record; and

(C) relates to a loan secured by real property.

A transferable record may be executed using an electronic signature.

(2) OTHER DEFINITIONS. — The terms "electronic record", "electronic signature", and "person" have the same meanings provided in section 106 of this Act.

(b) CONTROL. — A person has control of a transferable record if a system employed for evidencing the transfer of interests in the transferable record reliably establishes that person as the person to which the transferable record was issued or transferred.

(c) CONDITIONS. — A system satisfies subsection (b), and a person is deemed to have control of a transferable record, if the transferable record is created, stored, and assigned in such a manner that —

(1) a single authoritative copy of the transferable record exists which is unique, identifiable, and, except as otherwise provided in paragraphs (4), (5), and (6), unalterable;

(2) the authoritative copy identifies the person asserting control as —

(A) the person to which the transferable record was issued; or

(B) if the authoritative copy indicates that the transferable record has been transferred, the person to which the transferable record was most recently transferred;

(3) the authoritative copy is communicated to and maintained by the person asserting control or its designated custodian;

(4) copies or revisions that add or change an identified assignee of the authoritative copy can be made only with the consent of the person asserting control;

(5) each copy of the authoritative copy and any copy of a copy is readily identifiable as a copy that is not the authoritative copy; and

(6) any revision of the authoritative copy is readily identifiable as authorized or unauthorized.

(d) STATUS AS HOLDER. — Except as otherwise agreed, a person having control of a transferable record is the holder, as defined in section 1-201(20) of the Uniform Commercial Code, of the transferable record and has the same rights and defenses as a holder of an equivalent record or writing under the Uniform Commercial Code, including, if the applicable statutory requirements under section 3-302(a), 9-308, or revised section 9-330 of the Uniform Commercial Code are satisfied, the rights and defenses of a holder in due course or a purchaser, respectively. Delivery, possession, and endorsement are not required to obtain or exercise any of the rights under this subsection.

(e) OBLIGOR RIGHTS. — Except as otherwise agreed, an obligor under a transferable record has the same rights and defenses as an equivalent obligor under equivalent records or writings under the Uniform Commercial Code.

(f) PROOF OF CONTROL. — If requested by a person against which enforcement is sought, the person seeking to enforce the transferable record shall provide reasonable proof that the person is in control of the transferable record. Proof may include access to the authoritative copy of the transferable record and related business records sufficient to review the terms of the transferable record and to establish the identity of the person having control of the transferable record.

(g) UCC REFERENCES. — For purposes of this subsection, all references to the Uniform Commercial Code are to the Uniform Commercial Code as in effect in the jurisdiction the law of which governs the transferable record.

§202. EFFECTIVE DATE. [15 USCA §7021 NOTE]
This title shall be effective 90 days after the date of enactment of this Act.

TITLE III — PROMOTION OF INTERNATIONAL ELECTRONIC COMMERCE

§301. PRINCIPLES GOVERNING THE USE OF ELECTRONIC SIGNATURES IN INTERNATIONAL TRANSACTIONS. [15 USCA §7031]

(a) PROMOTION OF ELECTRONIC SIGNATURES. —

(1) REQUIRED ACTIONS. — The Secretary of Commerce shall promote the acceptance and use, on an international basis, of electronic signatures in accordance with the principles specified in paragraph (2) and in a manner consistent with section 101 of this Act. The Secretary of Commerce shall take all actions necessary in a manner consistent with such principles to eliminate or reduce, to the maximum extent possible, the impediments to commerce in electronic signatures, for the purpose of facilitating the development of interstate and foreign commerce.

(2) PRINCIPLES. — The principles specified in this paragraph are the following:

(A) Remove paper-based obstacles to electronic transactions by adopting relevant principles from the Model Law on Electronic Commerce adopted in 1996 by the United Nations Commission on International Trade Law.

(B) Permit parties to a transaction to determine the appropriate authentication technologies and implementation models for their transactions, with assurance that those technologies and implementation models will be recognized and enforced.

(C) Permit parties to a transaction to have the opportunity to prove in court or other proceedings that their authentication approaches and their transactions are valid.

(D) Take a nondiscriminatory approach to electronic signatures and authentication methods from other jurisdictions.

(b) CONSULTATION. — In conducting the activities required by this section, the Secretary shall consult with users and providers of electronic signature products and services and other interested persons.

(c) DEFINITIONS. — As used in this section, the terms "electronic record" and "electronic signature" have the same meanings provided in section 106 of this Act. . . .

UNIFORM ELECTRONIC TRANSACTIONS ACT
(1999)

TABLE OF CONTENTS

PREFATORY NOTE

With the advent of electronic means of communication and information transfer, business models and methods for doing business have evolved to take advantage of the speed, efficiencies, and cost benefits of electronic technologies. These developments have occurred in the face of existing legal barriers to the legal efficacy of records and documents which exist solely in electronic media. Whether the legal requirement that information or an agreement or contract must be contained or set forth in a pen and paper writing derives from a statute of frauds affecting the enforceability of an agreement, or from a record retention statute that calls for keeping the paper record of a transaction, such legal requirements raise real barriers to the effective use of electronic media.

One striking example of electronic barriers involves so called check retention statutes in every State. A study conducted by the Federal Reserve Bank of Boston identified more than 2500 different state laws which require the retention of canceled checks by the issuers of those checks. These requirements not only impose burdens on the issuers, but also effectively restrain the ability of banks handling the checks to automate the process. Although check truncation is validated under the Uniform Commercial Code, if the bank's customer must store the canceled paper check, the bank will not be able to deal with the item through electronic transmission of the information. By establishing the equivalence of an electronic record of the information, the Uniform Electronic Transactions Act (UETA) removes these barriers without affecting the underlying legal rules and requirements.

It is important to understand that the purpose of the UETA is to remove barriers to electronic commerce by validating and effectuating electronic records and signatures. It is NOT a general contracting statute — the substantive rules of contracts remain unaffected by UETA. Nor is it a digital signature statute. To the extent that a State has a Digital Signature Law, the UETA is designed to support and compliment that statute.

A. Scope of the Act and Procedural Approach. The scope of this Act provides coverage which sets forth a clear framework for covered transactions, and also avoids unwarranted surprises for unsophisticated parties dealing in this relatively new media. The clarity and certainty of the scope of the Act have been obtained while still providing a solid legal framework that allows for the continued development of innovative technology to facilitate electronic transactions.

With regard to the general scope of the Act, the Act's "coverage is inherently limited by the definition of transaction." The Act does not apply to *all* writings and signatures, but only to electronic records and signatures relating to a transaction, defined as those interactions between people relating to business, commercial and governmental affairs. In general, there are few writing or signature requirements imposed by law on many of the "standard" transactions that had been considered for exclusion. A good example relates to trusts, where the general rule on creation of a trust imposes no formal writing requirement. Further, the writing requirements in other contexts derived from governmental filing issues. For example, real estate transactions were considered potentially troublesome because of the need to file a deed or other instrument for protection against third parties. Since the efficacy of a real estate purchase contract, or even a deed, between the parties is not affected by any sort of filing, the question was raised why these transactions should not be validated by this Act if done via an electronic medium. No sound reason was found. Filing requirements fall within Sections 17-19 on governmental records. An exclusion of all real estate transactions would be particularly unwarranted in the event that a State chose to convert to an electronic recording system, as many have for Article 9 financing statement filings under the Uniform Commercial Code.

The exclusion of specific Articles of the Uniform Commercial Code reflects the recognition that, particularly in the case of Articles 5, 8 and revised Article 9, electronic transactions were addressed in the specific contexts of those revision processes. In the context of Articles 2 and 2A the UETA provides the vehicle for assuring that such transactions may be accomplished and effected via an electronic medium. At such time as Articles 2 and 2A are revised the extent of coverage in those Articles/Acts may make application of this Act as a gap-filling law desirable. Similar considerations apply to the recently promulgated Uniform Computer Information Transactions Act ("UCITA").

The need for certainty as to the scope and applicability of this Act is critical, and makes any sort of a broad, general exception based on notions of inconsistency with existing writing and signature requirements unwise at best. The uncertainty inherent in leaving the applicability of the Act to judicial construction of this Act with other laws is unacceptable if electronic transactions are to be facilitated.

Finally, recognition that the paradigm for the Act involves two willing parties conducting a transaction electronically, makes it necessary to expressly provide that some form of acquiescence or intent on the part of a person to conduct transactions electronically is necessary before the Act can be invoked. Accordingly, Section 5 specifically provides that the Act only applies between parties that have agreed to conduct transactions electronically. In this context, the construction of the term agreement must be broad in order to assure that the Act applies whenever the circumstances show the parties intention to transact electronically, regardless of whether the intent rises to the level of a formal agreement.

B. Procedural Approach. Another fundamental premise of the Act is that it be minimalist and procedural. The general efficacy of existing law in an electronic context, so long as biases and barriers to the medium are removed, validates this approach. The Act defers to existing substantive law. Specific areas of deference to other law in this Act include: (1) the meaning and effect of "sign" under existing law, (2) the method and manner of displaying, transmitting and formatting information in Section 8, (3) rules of attribution in Section 9, and (4) the law of mistake in Section 10.

The Act's treatment of records and signatures demonstrates best the minimalist approach that has been adopted. Whether a record is attributed to a person is left to law outside this Act. Whether an electronic signature has any effect is left to the surrounding circumstances and other law. These provisions are salutary directives to assure that records and signatures will be treated in the same manner, under currently existing law, as written records and manual signatures.

The deference of the Act to other substantive law does not negate the necessity of setting forth rules and standards for using electronic media. The Act expressly validates electronic records, signatures and contracts. It provides for the use of electronic records and information for retention purposes, providing certainty in an area with great potential in cost savings and efficiency. The Act makes clear that the actions of machines ("electronic agents") programmed and used by people will bind the user of the machine, regardless of whether human review of a particular transaction has occurred. It specifies the standards for sending and receipt of electronic records, and it allows for innovation in financial services through the implementation of transferable records. In these ways the Act permits electronic transactions to be accomplished with certainty under existing substantive rules of law.

§1. Short Title

This [Act] may be cited as the Uniform Electronic Transactions Act.

§2. Definitions

In this [Act]:

(1) "Agreement" means the bargain of the parties in fact, as found in their language or inferred from other circumstances and from rules, regulations, and procedures given the effect of agreements under laws otherwise applicable to a particular transaction.

(2) "Automated transaction" means a transaction conducted or performed, in whole or in part, by electronic means or electronic records, in which the acts or records of one or both parties are not reviewed by an individual in the ordinary course in forming a contract, performing under an existing contract, or fulfilling an obligation required by the transaction.

(3) "Computer program" means a set of statements or instructions to be used directly or indirectly in an information processing system in order to bring about a certain result.

(4) "Contract" means the total legal obligation resulting from the parties' agreement as affected by this [Act] and other applicable law.

(5) "Electronic" means relating to technology having electrical, digital, magnetic, wireless, optical, electromagnetic, or similar capabilities.

(6) "Electronic agent" means a computer program or an electronic or other automated means used independently to initiate an action or respond to electronic records or performances in whole or in part, without review or action by an individual.

(7) "Electronic record" means a record created, generated, sent, communicated, received, or stored by electronic means.

(8) "Electronic signature" means an electronic sound, symbol, or process attached to or logically associated with a record and executed or adopted by a person with the intent to sign the record.

(9) "Governmental agency" means an executive, legislative, or judicial agency, department, board, commission, authority, institution, or instrumentality of the federal government or of a State or of a county, municipality, or other political subdivision of a State.

(10) "Information" means data, text, images, sounds, codes, computer programs, software, databases, or the like.

(11) "Information processing system" means an electronic system for creating, generating, sending, receiving, storing, displaying, or processing information.

(12) "Person" means an individual, corporation, business trust, estate, trust, partnership, limited liability company, association, joint venture, governmental agency, public corporation, or any other legal or commercial entity.

(13) "Record" means information that is inscribed on a tangible medium or that is stored in an electronic or other medium and is retrievable in perceivable form.

(14) "Security procedure" means a procedure employed for the purpose of verifying that an electronic signature, record, or performance is that of a specific person or for detecting changes or errors in the information in an electronic record. The term includes a procedure that requires the use of algorithms or other codes, identifying words or numbers, encryption, or callback or other acknowledgment procedures.

(15) "State" means a State of the United States, the District of Columbia, Puerto Rico, the United States Virgin Islands, or any territory or insular possession subject to the jurisdiction of the United States. The term includes an Indian tribe or band, or Alaskan native village, which is recognized by federal law or formally acknowledged by a State.

(16) "Transaction" means an action or set of actions occurring between two or more persons relating to the conduct of business, commercial, or governmental affairs.

Comment

1. "Agreement." Whether the parties have reached an agreement is determined by their express language and all surrounding circumstances. The Restatement 2d Contracts §3 provides that, "An agreement is a manifestation of mutual assent on the part of two or more persons." See also Restatement 2d Contracts, Section 2, Comment b. The Uniform Commercial Code specifically includes in the circumstances from which an agreement may be inferred "course of performance, course of dealing and usage of trade . . ." as defined in the UCC. Although the definition of agreement in this Act does not make specific reference to usage of trade and other party conduct, this definition is not intended to affect the construction of the parties' agreement under the substantive law applicable to a particular transaction. Where that law takes account of usage and conduct in informing the terms of the parties' agreement, the usage or conduct would be relevant as "other circumstances" included in the definition under this Act.

Where the law applicable to a given transaction provides that system rules and the like constitute part of the agreement of the parties, such rules will have the same effect in determining the parties['] agreement under this Act. . . . Such agreements by law properly would be included in the definition of agreement in this Act.

The parties' agreement is relevant in determining whether the provisions of this Act have been varied by agreement. In addition, the parties' agreement may establish the parameters of the parties' use of electronic records and signatures, security procedures and similar aspects of the transaction . . . . See Section 5(b) and Comments thereto.

2. "Automated Transaction." An automated transaction is a transaction performed or conducted by electronic means in which machines are used without human intervention to form contracts and perform obligations under existing contracts. Such broad coverage is necessary because of the diversity of transactions to which this Act may apply.

As with electronic agents, this definition addresses the circumstance where electronic records may result in action or performance by a party although no human review of the electronic records is anticipated. Section 14 provides specific rules to assure that where one or both parties do not review the electronic records, the resulting agreement will be effective.

The critical element in this definition is the lack of a human actor on one or both sides of a transaction. . . .

3. "Computer Program." This definition refers to the functional and operating aspects of an electronic, digital system. It relates to operating instructions used in an electronic system such as an electronic agent. . . .

4. "Electronic." The basic nature of most current technologies and the need for a recognized, single term warrants the use of "electronic" as the defined term. The definition is intended to assure that the Act will be applied broadly as new technologies develop. The term must be construed broadly in light of developing technologies in order to fulfill the purpose of this Act to validate commercial transactions regardless of the medium used by the parties. Current legal requirements for "writings" can be satisfied by almost any tangible media, whether paper, other fibers, or even stone. The purpose and applicability of this Act covers intangible media which are technologically capable of storing, transmitting and reproducing information in human perceivable form, but which lack the tangible aspect of paper, papyrus or stone.

While not all technologies listed are technically "electronic" in nature (e.g., optical fiber technology), the term "electronic" is the most descriptive term available to describe the majority of current technologies. For example, the development of biological and chemical processes for communication and storage of data, while not specifically mentioned in the definition, are included within the technical definition because such processes operate on electromagnetic impulses. However, whether a particular technology may be characterized as technically "electronic," i.e., operates on electromagnetic impulses, should not be determinative of whether records and signatures created, used and stored by means of a particular technology are covered by this Act. This Act is intended to apply to all records and signatures created, used and stored by any medium which permits the information to be retrieved in perceivable form.

5. "Electronic agent." This definition establishes that an electronic agent is a machine. As the term "electronic agent" has come to be recognized, it is limited to a tool function. The effect on the party using the agent is addressed in the operative provisions of the Act (e.g., Section 14).

An electronic agent, such as a computer program or other automated means employed by a person, is a tool of that person. As a general rule, the employer of a tool is responsible for the results obtained by the use of that tool since the tool has no independent volition of its own. However, an electronic agent, by definition, is capable within the parameters of its programming, of initiating, responding or interacting with other parties or their electronic agents once it has been activated by a party, without further attention of that party.

While this Act proceeds on the paradigm that an electronic agent is capable of performing only within the technical strictures of its preset programming, it is conceivable that, within the useful life of this Act, electronic agents may be created with the ability to act autonomously, and not just automatically. That is, through developments in artificial intelligence, a computer may be able to "learn through experience, modify the instructions in their own programs, and even devise new instructions." Allen and Widdison, "Can Computers Make Contracts?" *9 Harv. J.L. & Tech 25* (Winter, 1996). If such developments occur, courts may construe the definition of electronic agent accordingly, in order to recognize such new capabilities.

The examples involving Bookseller.com and Automaker in the Comment to the definition of Automated Transaction are equally applicable here. Bookseller acts through an electronic agent in processing an order for books. Automaker and the supplier each act through electronic agents in facilitating and effectuating the just-in-time inventory process through EDI.

6. "Electronic record." An electronic record is a subset of the broader defined term "record." It is any record created, used or stored in a medium other than paper (see definition of electronic). The defined term is also used in this Act as a limiting definition in those provisions in which it is used.

Information processing systems, computer equipment and programs, electronic data interchange, electronic mail, voice mail, facsimile, telex, telecopying, scanning, and similar technologies all qualify as electronic under this Act. Accordingly information stored on a computer hard drive or floppy disc, facsimiles, voice mail messages, messages on a telephone answering machine, audio and video tape recordings, among other records, all would be electronic records under this Act.

7. "Electronic signature." The idea of a signature is broad and not specifically defined. Whether any particular record is "signed" is a question of fact. Proof of that fact must be made under other applicable law. This Act simply assures that the signature may be accomplished through electronic means. No specific technology need be used in order to create a valid signature. One's voice on an answering machine may suffice if the requisite intention is present. Similarly, including one's name as part of an electronic mail communication also may suffice, as may the firm name on a facsimile. It also may be shown that the requisite intent was not present and accordingly the symbol, sound or process did not amount to a signature. One may use a digital signature with the requisite intention, or one may use the private key solely as an access device with no intention to sign, or otherwise accomplish a legally binding act. In any case the critical element is the intention to execute or adopt the sound or symbol or process for the purpose of signing the related record.

The definition requires that the signer execute or adopt the sound, symbol, or process with the intent to sign the record. The act of applying a sound, symbol or process to an electronic record could have differing meanings and effects. The consequence of the act and the effect of the act as a signature are determined under other applicable law. However, the essential attribute of a signature involves applying a sound, symbol or process with an intent to do a legally significant act. It is that intention that is understood in the law as a part of the word "sign", without the need for a definition.

This Act establishes, to the greatest extent possible, the equivalency of electronic signatures and manual signatures. Therefore the term "signature" has been used to connote and convey that equivalency. The purpose is to overcome unwarranted biases against electronic methods of signing and authenticating records. The term "authentication," used in other laws, often has a narrower meaning and purpose than an electronic signature as used in this Act. However, an authentication under any of those other laws constitutes an electronic signature under this Act. . . .

This definition includes as an electronic signature the standard webpage click through process. For example, when a person orders goods or services through a vendor's website, the person will be required to provide information as part of a process which will result in receipt of the goods or services. When the customer ultimately gets to the last step and clicks "I agree," the person has adopted the process and has done so with the intent to associate the person with the record of that process. The actual effect of the electronic signature will be determined from all the surrounding circumstances, however, the person adopted a process which the circumstances indicate s/he intended to have the effect of getting the goods/services and being bound to pay for them. The adoption of the process carried the intent to do a legally significant act, the hallmark of a signature.

Another important aspect of this definition lies in the necessity that the electronic signature be linked or logically associated with the record. In the paper world, it is assumed that the symbol adopted by a party is attached to or located somewhere in the same paper that is intended to be authenticated, e.g., an allonge firmly attached to a promissory note, or the classic signature at the end of a long contract. These tangible manifestations do not exist in the electronic environment, and accordingly, this definition expressly provides that the symbol must in some way be linked to, or connected with, the electronic record being signed. . . .

A digital signature using public key encryption technology would qualify as an electronic signature, as would the mere inclusion of one's name as a part of an e-mail message so long as in each case the signer executed or adopted the symbol with the intent to sign. . . .

10. "Record." This is a standard definition designed to embrace all means of communicating or storing information except human memory. It includes any method for storing or communicating information, including "writings." A record need not be indestructible or permanent, but the term does not include oral or other communications which are not stored or preserved by some means. Information that has not been retained other than through human memory does not qualify as a record. As in the case of the terms "writing" or "written," the term "record" does not establish the purposes, permitted uses or legal effect which a record may have under any particular provision of substantive law. . . .

12. "Transaction." The definition has been limited to actions between people taken in the context of business, commercial or governmental activities. The term includes all interactions between people for business, commercial, including specifically consumer, or governmental purposes. However, the term does not include unilateral or non-transactional actions. . . .

. . . . Consequently, to the extent that the execution of a will, trust, or a health care power of attorney or similar health care designation does not involve another person and is a unilateral act, it would not be covered by this Act because not occurring as a part of a transaction as defined in this Act. However, this Act *does* apply to all electronic records and signatures *related* to a transaction, and so does cover, for example, internal auditing and accounting records related to a transaction.

§3. Scope

(a) Except as otherwise provided in subsection (b), this [Act] applies to electronic records and electronic signatures relating to a transaction.

(b) This [Act] does not apply to a transaction to the extent it is governed by:

(1) a law governing the creation and execution of wills, codicils, or testamentary trusts;

(2) [The Uniform Commercial Code other than Sections 1-107 and 1-206, Article 2, and Article 2A];

(3) [the Uniform Computer Information Transactions Act]; and

(4) [other laws, if any, identified by State].

(c) This [Act] applies to an electronic record or electronic signature otherwise excluded from the application of this [Act] under subsection (b) to the extent it is governed by a law other than those specified in subsection (b).

(d) A transaction subject to this [Act] is also subject to other applicable substantive law.

Comment

1. The scope of this Act is inherently limited by the fact that it only applies to transactions related to business, commercial (including consumer) and governmental matters. Consequently, transactions with no relation to business, commercial or governmental transactions would not be subject to this Act. Unilaterally generated electronic records and signatures which are not part of a transaction also are not covered by this Act. See Section 2, Comment 12.

2. This Act affects the medium in which information, records and signatures may be presented and retained under current legal requirements. While this Act covers all electronic records and signatures which are used in a business, commercial (including consumer) or governmental transaction, the operative provisions of the Act relate to requirements for writings and signatures under other laws. Accordingly, the exclusions in subsection (b) focus on those legal rules imposing certain writing and signature requirements which will *not* be affected by this Act.

3. The exclusions listed in subsection (b) provide clarity and certainty regarding the laws which are and are not affected by this Act. This section provides that transactions subject to specific laws are unaffected by this Act and leaves the balance subject to this Act.

4. Paragraph (1) excludes wills, codicils and testamentary trusts. This exclusion is largely salutary given the unilateral context in which such records are generally created and the unlikely use of such records in a transaction as defined in this Act (i.e., actions taken by two or more persons in the context of business, commercial or governmental affairs). Paragraph (2) excludes all of the Uniform Commercial Code other than UCC Section[] 1-[306], and Articles 2 and 2A. This Act does not apply to the excluded UCC articles, whether in "current" or "revised" form. The Act does apply to UCC Articles 2 and 2A and to UCC Section[] 1-[306].

5. Articles 3, 4 and 4A of the UCC impact payment systems and have specifically been removed from the coverage of this Act. The check collection and electronic fund transfer systems governed by Articles 3, 4 and 4A involve systems and relationships involving numerous parties beyond the parties to the underlying contract. The impact of validating electronic media in such systems involves considerations beyond the scope of this Act. Articles 5, 8 and 9 have been excluded because the revision process relating to those Articles included significant consideration of electronic practices. Paragraph 4 provides for exclusion from this Act of the Uniform Computer Information Transactions Act (UCITA) because the drafting process of that Act also included significant consideration of electronic contracting provisions.

6. The very limited application of this Act to Transferable Records in Section 16 does not affect payment systems, and the section is designed to apply to a transaction only through express agreement of the parties. The exclusion of Articles 3 and 4 will not affect the Act's coverage of Transferable Records. Section 16 is designed to allow for the development of systems which will provide "control" as defined in Section 16. Such control is necessary as a substitute for the idea of possession which undergirds negotiable instrument law. The technology has yet to be developed which will allow for the possession of a unique electronic token embodying the rights associated with a negotiable promissory note. Section 16's concept of control is intended as a substitute for possession.

The provisions in Section 16 operate as free standing rules, establishing the rights of parties using Transferable Records *under this Act*. The references in Section 16 to UCC Sections 3-302, 7-501, and [9-330(d)] are designed to incorporate the substance of those provisions into this Act for the limited purposes noted in Section 16(c). Accordingly, an electronic record which is also a Transferable Record, would not be used for purposes of a transaction governed by Articles 3, 4, or 9, but would be an electronic record used for purposes of a transaction governed by Section 16. However, it is important to remember that those UCC Articles will still apply to the transferable record in their own right. Accordingly any other substantive requirements, e.g., method and manner of perfection under Article 9, must be complied with under those other laws. See Comments to Section 16.

7. This Act does apply, *in toto*, to transactions under [] Articles 2 and 2A. There is every reason to validate electronic contracting in these situations. Sale and lease transactions do not implicate broad systems beyond the parties to the underlying transaction, such as are present in check collection and electronic funds transfers. Further sales and leases generally do not have as far reaching effect on the rights of third parties beyond the contracting parties, such as exists in the secured transactions system. Finally, it is in the area of sales, licenses and leases that electronic commerce is occurring to its greatest extent today. To exclude these transactions would largely gut the purpose of this Act.

In the event that Articles 2 and 2A are revised and adopted in the future, UETA will only apply to the extent provided in those Acts.

8. An electronic record/signature may be used for purposes of more than one legal requirement, or may be covered by more than one law. Consequently, it is important to make clear, despite any apparent redundancy, in subsection (c) that an electronic record used for purposes of a law which is *not* affected by this Act under subsection (b) may nonetheless be used and validated for

purposes of other laws not excluded by subsection (b). For example, this Act does not apply to an electronic record of a check when used for purposes of a transaction governed by Article 4 of the Uniform Commercial Code, i.e., the Act does not validate so-called electronic checks. However, for purposes of check retention statutes, the same electronic record of the check is covered by this Act, so that retention of an electronic image/record of a check will satisfy such retention statutes, so long as the requirements of Section 12 are fulfilled.

In another context, subsection (c) would operate to allow this Act to apply to what would appear to be an excluded transaction under subsection (b). For example, Article 9 of the Uniform Commercial Code applies generally to any transaction that creates a security interest in personal property. However, Article 9 excludes landlord's liens. Accordingly, although this Act excludes from its application transactions subject to Article 9, this Act would apply to the creation of a landlord lien if the law otherwise applicable to landlord's liens did not provide otherwise, because the landlord's lien transaction is excluded from Article 9.

9. Additional exclusions under subparagraph (b)(4) should be limited to laws which govern electronic records and signatures which may be used in transactions as defined in Section 2(16). Records used unilaterally, or which do not relate to business, commercial (including consumer), or governmental affairs are not governed by this Act in any event, and exclusion of laws relating to such records may create unintended inferences about whether other records and signatures are covered by this Act.

It is also important that additional exclusions, if any, be incorporated under subsection (b)(4). As noted in Comment 8 above, an electronic record used in a transaction excluded under subsection (b), e.g., a check used to pay one's taxes, will nonetheless be validated for purposes of other, non-excluded laws under subsection (c), e.g., the check when used as proof of payment. It is critical that additional exclusions, if any, be incorporated into subsection (b) so that the salutary effect of subsection (c) apply to validate those records in other, non-excluded transactions. While a legislature may determine that a particular notice, such as a utility shutoff notice, be provided to a person in writing on paper, it is difficult to see why the utility should not be entitled to use electronic media for storage and evidentiary purposes. . . .

§4. Prospective Application

This [Act] applies to any electronic record or electronic signature created, generated, sent, communicated, received, or stored on or after the effective date of this [Act].

§5. Use of Electronic Records and Electronic Signatures; Variation by Agreement

(a) This [Act] does not require a record or signature to be created, generated, sent, communicated, received, stored, or otherwise processed or used by electronic means or in electronic form.

(b) This [Act] applies only to transactions between parties each of which has agreed to conduct transactions by electronic means. Whether the parties agree to conduct a transaction by electronic means is determined from the context and surrounding circumstances, including the parties' conduct.

(c) A party that agrees to conduct a transaction by electronic means may refuse to conduct other transactions by electronic means. The right granted by this subsection may not be waived by agreement.

(d) Except as otherwise provided in this [Act], the effect of any of its provisions may be varied by agreement. The presence in certain provisions of this [Act] of the words "unless otherwise agreed", or words of similar import, does not imply that the effect of other provisions may not be varied by agreement.

(e) Whether an electronic record or electronic signature has legal consequences is determined by this [Act] and other applicable law.

Comment

This section limits the applicability of this Act to transactions which parties have agreed to conduct electronically. Broad interpretation of the term agreement is necessary to assure that this Act has the widest possible application consistent with its purpose of removing barriers to electronic commerce.

1. This section makes clear that this Act is intended to facilitate the use of electronic means, but does not require the use of electronic records and signatures. This fundamental principle is set forth in subsection (a) and elaborated by subsections (b) and (c), which require an intention to conduct transactions electronically and preserve the right of a party to refuse to use electronics in any subsequent transaction.

2. The paradigm of this Act is two willing parties doing transactions electronically. It is therefore appropriate that the Act is voluntary and preserves the greatest possible party autonomy to refuse electronic transactions. The requirement that party agreement be found from all the surrounding circumstances is a limitation on the scope of this Act.

3. If this Act is to serve to facilitate electronic transactions, it must be applicable under circumstances not rising to a full fledged contract to use electronics. While absolute certainty can be accomplished by obtaining an explicit contract before relying on electronic transactions, such an explicit contract should not be necessary before one may feel safe in conducting transactions electronically. Indeed, such a requirement would itself be an unreasonable barrier to electronic commerce, at odds with the fundamental purpose of this Act. Accordingly, the requisite agreement, express or implied, must be determined from all available circumstances and evidence.

4. Subsection (b) provides that the Act applies to transactions in which the parties have agreed to conduct the transaction electronically. In this context it is essential that the parties' actions and words be broadly construed in determining whether the requisite agreement exists. Accordingly, the Act expressly provides that the party's agreement is to be found from all circumstances, including the parties' conduct. The critical element is the intent

of a party to conduct a transaction electronically. Once that intent is established, this Act applies. See Restatement 2d Contracts, Sections 2, 3, and 19.

Examples of circumstances from which it may be found that parties have reached an agreement to conduct transactions electronically include the following:

    A. Automaker and supplier enter into a Trading Partner Agreement setting forth the terms, conditions and methods for the conduct of business between them electronically.

    B. Joe gives out his business card with his business e-mail address. It may be reasonable, under the circumstances, for a recipient of the card to infer that Joe has agreed to communicate electronically for business purposes. However, in the absence of additional facts, it would not necessarily be reasonable to infer Joe's agreement to communicate electronically for purposes outside the scope of the business indicated by use of the business card.

    C. Sally may have several e-mail addresses home, main office, office of a non-profit organization on whose board Sally sits. In each case, it may be reasonable to infer that Sally is willing to communicate electronically with respect to business related to the business/purpose associated with the respective e-mail addresses. However, depending on the circumstances, it may not be reasonable to communicate with Sally for purposes other than those related to the purpose for which she maintained a particular e-mail account.

    D. Among the circumstances to be considered in finding an agreement would be the time when the assent occurred relative to the timing of the use of electronic communications. If one orders books from an on-line vendor, such as Bookseller.com, the intention to conduct that transaction and to receive any correspondence related to the transaction electronically can be inferred from the conduct. Accordingly, as to information related to that transaction it is reasonable for Bookseller to deal with the individual electronically.

The examples noted above are intended to focus the inquiry on the party's agreement to conduct a transaction electronically. Similarly, if two people are at a meeting and one tells the other to send an e-mail to confirm a transaction the requisite agreement under subsection (b) would exist. In each case, the use of a business card, statement at a meeting, or other evidence of willingness to conduct a transaction electronically must be viewed in light of all the surrounding circumstances with a view toward broad validation of electronic transactions.

5. Just as circumstances may indicate the existence of agreement, express or implied from surrounding circumstances, circumstances may also demonstrate the absence of true agreement. For example:

    A. If Automaker, Inc. were to issue a recall of automobiles via its Internet website, it would not be able to rely on this Act to validate that notice in the case of a person who never logged on to the website, or indeed, had no ability to do so, notwithstanding a clause in a paper purchase contract by which the buyer agreed to receive such notices in such a manner.

    B. Buyer executes a standard form contract in which an agreement to receive all notices electronically in set forth on page 3 in the midst of other fine print. Buyer has never communicated with Seller electronically, and has not provided any other information in the contract to suggest a willingness to deal electronically. Not only is it unlikely that any but the most formalistic of agreements may be found, but nothing in this Act prevents courts from policing such form contracts under common law doctrines relating to contract formation, unconscionability and the like.

6. Subsection (c) has been added to make clear the ability of a party to refuse to conduct a transaction electronically, even if the person has conducted transactions electronically in the past. The effectiveness of a party's refusal to conduct a transaction electronically will be determined under other applicable law in light of all surrounding circumstances. Such circumstances must include an assessment of the transaction involved.

A party's right to decline to act electronically under a specific contract, on the ground that each action under that contract amounts to a separate "transaction," must be considered in light of the purpose of the contract and the action to be taken electronically. For example, under a contract for the purchase of goods, the giving and receipt of notices electronically, as provided in the contract, should not be viewed as discreet transactions. Rather such notices amount to separate actions which are part of the "transaction" of purchase evidenced by the contract. Allowing one party to require a change of medium in the middle of the transaction evidenced by that contract is not the purpose of this subsection. Rather this subsection is intended to preserve the party's right to conduct the next purchase in a non-electronic medium.

7. Subsection (e) is an essential provision in the overall scheme of this Act. While this Act validates and effectuates electronic records and electronic signatures, the legal effect of such records and signatures is left to existing substantive law outside this Act except in very narrow circumstances. See, e.g., Section 16. Even when this Act operates to validate records and signatures in an electronic medium, it expressly preserves the substantive rules of other law applicable to such records. See, e.g., Section 11.

For example, beyond validation of records, signatures and contracts based on the medium used, Section 7 (a) and (b) should not be interpreted as establishing the legal effectiveness of any given record, signature or contract. Where a rule of law requires that the record contain minimum substantive content, the legal effect of such a record will depend on whether the record meets the substantive requirements of other applicable law.

Section 8 expressly preserves a number of legal requirements in currently existing law relating to the presentation of information in writing. Although this Act now would allow such information to be presented in an electronic record, Section 8 provides that the other substantive requirements of law must be satisfied in the electronic medium as well.

§6. Construction and Application

This [Act] must be construed and applied:
   (1) to facilitate electronic transactions consistent with other applicable law;

(2) to be consistent with reasonable practices concerning electronic transactions and with the continued expansion of those practices; and

(3) to effectuate its general purpose to make uniform the law with respect to the subject of this [Act] among States enacting it.

Comment

1. The purposes and policies of this Act are

    (a) to facilitate and promote commerce and governmental transactions by validating and authorizing the use of electronic records and electronic signatures;

    (b) to eliminate barriers to electronic commerce and governmental transactions resulting from uncertainties relating to writing and signature requirements;

    (c) to simplify, clarify and modernize the law governing commerce and governmental transactions through the use of electronic means;

    (d) to permit the continued expansion of commercial and governmental electronic practices through custom, usage and agreement of the parties;

    (e) to promote uniformity of the law among the States (and worldwide) relating to the use of electronic and similar technological means of effecting and performing commercial and governmental transactions;

    (f) to promote public confidence in the validity, integrity and reliability of electronic commerce and governmental transactions; and

    (g) to promote the development of the legal and business infrastructure necessary to implement electronic commerce and governmental transactions.

2. This Act has been drafted to permit flexible application consistent with its purpose to validate electronic transactions. The provisions of this Act validating and effectuating the employ of electronic media allow the courts to apply them to new and unforeseen technologies and practices. As time progresses, it is anticipated that what is new and unforeseen today will be commonplace tomorrow. Accordingly, this legislation is intended to set a framework for the validation of media which may be developed in the future and which demonstrate the same qualities as the electronic media contemplated and validated under this Act.

§7. Legal Recognition of Electronic Records, Electronic Signatures, and Electronic Contracts

(a) A record or signature may not be denied legal effect or enforceability solely because it is in electronic form.

(b) A contract may not be denied legal effect or enforceability solely because an electronic record was used in its formation.

(c) If a law requires a record to be in writing, an electronic record satisfies the law.

(d) If a law requires a signature, an electronic signature satisfies the law.

Comment

1. This section sets forth the fundamental premise of this Act: namely, that the medium in which a record, signature, or contract is created, presented or retained does not affect its legal significance. Subsections (a) and (b) are designed to eliminate the single element of medium as a reason to deny effect or enforceability to a record, signature, or contract. The fact that the information is set forth in an electronic, as opposed to paper, record is irrelevant.

2. Under Restatement 2d Contracts Section 8, a contract may have legal effect and yet be unenforceable. Indeed, one circumstance where a record or contract may have effect but be unenforceable is in the context of the Statute of Frauds. Though a contract may be unenforceable, the records may have collateral effects, as in the case of a buyer that insures goods purchased under a contract unenforceable under the Statute of Frauds. The insurance company may not deny a claim on the ground that the buyer is not the owner, though the buyer may have no direct remedy against seller for failure to deliver. See Restatement 2d Contracts, Section 8, Illustration 4.

While this section would validate an electronic record for purposes of a statute of frauds, if an agreement to conduct the transaction electronically cannot reasonably be found (See Section 5(b)) then a necessary predicate to the applicability of this Act would be absent and this Act would not validate the electronic record. Whether the electronic record might be valid under other law is not addressed by this Act.

3. Subsections (c) and (d) provide the positive assertion that electronic records and signatures satisfy legal requirements for writings and signatures. The provisions are limited to requirements in laws that a record be in writing or be signed. This section does not address requirements imposed by other law in addition to requirements for writings and signatures See, e.g., Section 8.

Subsections (c) and (d) are particularized applications of subsection (a). The purpose is to validate and effectuate electronic records and signatures as the equivalent of writings, subject to all of the rules applicable to the efficacy of a writing, except as such other rules are modified by the more specific provisions of this Act.

Illustration 1: A sends the following e-mail to B: "I hereby offer to buy widgets from you, delivery next Tuesday. /s/ A." B responds with the following e-mail: "I accept your offer to buy widgets for delivery next Tuesday. /s/ B." The e-mails may not be denied effect solely because they are electronic. In addition, the e-mails do qualify as records under the Statute of Frauds. However, because there is no quantity stated in either record, the parties' agreement would be unenforceable under existing UCC Section 2-201(1).

Illustration 2: A sends the following e-mail to B: "I hereby offer to buy 100 widgets for $1000, delivery next Tuesday. /s/ A." B responds with the following e-mail: "I accept your offer to purchase 100 widgets for $1000, delivery next Tuesday. /s/ B." In this case the analysis is the same as in Illustration 1 except that here the records otherwise satisfy the requirements of UCC Section 2-201(1). The transaction may not be denied legal effect solely because there is not a pen and ink "writing" or "signature".

4. Section 8 addresses additional requirements imposed by other law which may affect the legal effect or enforceability of an electronic record in a particular case. For example, in Section 8(a) the legal requirement addressed is *the provision of information* in writing. The section then sets forth the standards to be applied in determining whether the provision of information by an electronic record is the equivalent of the provision of information in writing. The requirements in Section 8 are in addition to the bare validation that occurs under this section.

5. Under the substantive law applicable to a particular transaction within this Act, the legal effect of an electronic record may be separate from the issue of whether the record contains a signature. For example, where notice must be given as part of a contractual obligation, the effectiveness of the notice will turn on whether the party provided the notice regardless of whether the notice was signed (See Section 15). An electronic record attributed to a party under Section 9 and complying with the requirements of Section 15 would suffice in that case, notwithstanding that it may not contain an electronic signature.

§8. Provision of Information in Writing; Presentation of Records

(a) If parties have agreed to conduct a transaction by electronic means and a law requires a person to provide, send, or deliver information in writing to another person, the requirement is satisfied if the information is provided, sent, or delivered, as the case may be, in an electronic record capable of retention by the recipient at the time of receipt. An electronic record is not capable of retention by the recipient if the sender or its information processing system inhibits the ability of the recipient to print or store the electronic record.

(b) If a law other than this [Act] requires a record (i) to be posted or displayed in a certain manner, (ii) to be sent, communicated, or transmitted by a specified method, or (iii) to contain information that is formatted in a certain manner, the following rules apply:

(1) The record must be posted or displayed in the manner specified in the other law.

(2) Except as otherwise provided in subsection (d)(2), the record must be sent, communicated, or transmitted by the method specified in the other law.

(3) The record must contain the information formatted in the manner specified in the other law.

(c) If a sender inhibits the ability of a recipient to store or print an electronic record, the electronic record is not enforceable against the recipient.

(d) The requirements of this section may not be varied by agreement, but:

(1) to the extent a law other than this [Act] requires information to be provided, sent, or delivered in writing but permits that requirement to be varied by agreement, the requirement under subsection (a) that the information be in the form of an electronic record capable of retention may also be varied by agreement; and

(2) a requirement under a law other than this [Act] to send, communicate, or transmit a record by [first-class mail, postage prepaid] [regular United States mail], may be varied by agreement to the extent permitted by the other law.

Comment

1. This section is a savings provision, designed to assure, consistent with the fundamental purpose of this Act, that otherwise applicable substantive law will not be overridden by this Act. The section makes clear that while the pen and ink provisions of such other law may be satisfied electronically, nothing in this Act vitiates the other requirements of such laws. The section addresses a number of issues related to disclosures and notice provisions in other laws.

2. This section is independent of the prior section. Section 7 refers to legal requirements for a writing. This section refers to legal requirements for the provision of information in writing or relating to the method or manner of presentation or delivery of information. The section addresses more specific legal requirements of other laws, provides standards for satisfying the more particular legal requirements, and defers to other law for satisfaction of requirements under those laws.

3. Under subsection (a), to meet a requirement of other law that information be provided in writing, the recipient of an electronic record of the information must be able to get to the electronic record and read it, and must have the ability to get back to the information in some way at a later date. Accordingly, the section requires that the electronic record be capable of retention for later review. . . .

6. The protective purposes of this section justify the non-waivability provided by subsection (d). However, since the requirements for sending and formatting and the like are imposed by other law, to the extent other law permits waiver of such protections, there is no justification for imposing a more severe burden in an electronic environment.

§9. Attribution and Effect of Electronic Record and Electronic Signature

(a) An electronic record or electronic signature is attributable to a person if it was the act of the person. The act of the person may be shown in any manner, including a showing of the efficacy of any security procedure applied to determine the person to which the electronic record or electronic signature was attributable.

(b) The effect of an electronic record or electronic signature attributed to a person under subsection (a) is determined from the context and surrounding circumstances at the time of its creation, execution, or adoption, including the parties' agreement, if any, and otherwise as provided by law.

Comment

1. Under subsection (a), so long as the electronic record or electronic signature resulted from a person's action it will be attributed to that person the legal effect of that attribution is addressed in subsection (b). This section does not alter existing rules of law regarding attribution. The section assures that such rules will be applied in the electronic environment. A person's actions include actions taken by human agents of the person, as well as actions taken by an electronic agent, i.e., the tool, of the person. Although the rule may appear to state the obvious, it assures that the record or signature is not ascribed to a machine, as opposed to the person operating or programing the machine.

In each of the following cases, both the electronic record and electronic signature would be attributable to a person under subsection (a):

A. The person types his/her name as part of an e-mail purchase order;

B. The person's employee, pursuant to authority, types the person's name as part of an e-mail purchase order;

C. The person's computer, programmed to order goods upon receipt of inventory information within particular parameters, issues a purchase order which includes the person's name, or other identifying information, as part of the order.

In each of the above cases, law other than this Act would ascribe both the signature and the action to the person if done in a paper medium. Subsection (a) expressly provides that the same result will occur when an electronic medium is used.

2. Nothing in this section affects the use of a signature as a device for attributing a record to a person. Indeed, a signature is often the primary method for attributing a record to a person. In the foregoing examples, once the electronic signature is attributed to the person, the electronic record would also be attributed to the person, unless the person established fraud, forgery, or other invalidating cause. However, a signature is not the only method for attribution.

3. The use of facsimile transmissions provides a number of examples of attribution using information other than a signature. A facsimile may be attributed to a person because of the information printed across the top of the page that indicates the machine from which it was sent. Similarly, the transmission may contain a letterhead which identifies the sender. Some cases have held that the letterhead actually constituted a signature because it was a symbol adopted by the sender with intent to authenticate the facsimile. However, the signature determination resulted from the necessary finding of intention in that case. Other cases have found facsimile letterheads NOT to be signatures because the requisite intention was not present. The critical point is that with or without a signature, information within the electronic record may well suffice to provide the facts resulting in attribution of an electronic record to a particular party.

In the context of attribution of records, normally the content of the record will provide the necessary information for a finding of attribution. It is also possible that an established course of dealing between parties may result in a finding of attribution Just as with a paper record, evidence of forgery or counterfeiting may be introduced to rebut the evidence of attribution.

4. Certain information may be present in an electronic environment that does not appear to attribute but which clearly links a person to a particular record. Numerical codes, personal identification numbers, public and private key combinations all serve to establish the party to whom an electronic record should be attributed. Of course security procedures will be another piece of evidence available to establish attribution.

The inclusion of a specific reference to security procedures as a means of proving attribution is salutary because of the unique importance of security procedures in the electronic environment. In certain processes, a technical and technological security procedure may be the best way to convince a trier of fact that a particular electronic record or signature was that of a particular person. In certain circumstances, the use of a security procedure to establish that the record and related signature came from the person's business might be necessary to overcome a claim that a hacker intervened. The reference to security procedures is not intended to suggest that other forms of proof of attribution should be accorded less persuasive effect. It is also important to recall that the particular strength of a given procedure does not affect the procedure's status as a security procedure, but only affects the weight to be accorded the evidence of the security procedure as tending to establish attribution.

5. This section does apply in determining the effect of a "click-through" transaction. A "click-through" transaction involves a process which, if executed with an intent to "sign," will be an electronic signature. See definition of Electronic Signature. In the context of an anonymous "click-through," issues of proof will be paramount. This section will be relevant to establish that the resulting electronic record is attributable to a particular person upon the requisite proof, including security procedures which may track the source of the click-through.

6. Once it is established that a record or signature is attributable to a particular party, the effect of a record or signature must be determined in light of the context and surrounding circumstances, including the parties' agreement, if any. Also informing the effect of any attribution will be other legal requirements considered in light of the context. Subsection (b) addresses the effect of the record or signature once attributed to a person.

§10. Effect of Change or Error

If a change or error in an electronic record occurs in a transmission between parties to a transaction, the following rules apply:

(1) If the parties have agreed to use a security procedure to detect changes or errors and one party has conformed to the procedure, but the other party has not, and the nonconforming party would have detected the change or error had that party also conformed, the conforming party may avoid the effect of the changed or erroneous electronic record.

(2) In an automated transaction involving an individual, the individual may avoid the effect of an electronic record that resulted from an error made by the individual in dealing with the electronic agent of another person if the electronic

agent did not provide an opportunity for the prevention or correction of the error and, at the time the individual learns of the error, the individual:

(A) promptly notifies the other person of the error and that the individual did not intend to be bound by the electronic record received by the other person;

(B) takes reasonable steps, including steps that conform to the other person's reasonable instructions, to return to the other person or, if instructed by the other person, to destroy the consideration received, if any, as a result of the erroneous electronic record; and

(C) has not used or received any benefit or value from the consideration, if any, received from the other person.

(3) If neither paragraph (1) nor paragraph (2) applies, the change or error has the effect provided by other law, including the law of mistake, and the parties' contract, if any.

(4) Paragraphs (2) and (3) may not be varied by agreement.

Comment

1. . . . . The section focuses on the effect of changes and errors occurring when records are exchanged between parties. In cases where changes and errors occur in contexts other than transmission, the law of mistake is expressly made applicable to resolve the conflict. . . .

2. Paragraph (1) deals with any transmission where the parties have agreed to use a security procedure to detect changes and errors. It operates against the non-conforming party, i.e., the party in the best position to have avoided the change or error, regardless of whether that person is the sender or recipient. The source of the error/change is not indicated, and so both human and machine errors/changes would be covered. With respect to errors or changes that would not be detected by the security procedure even if applied, the parties are left to the general law of mistake to resolve the dispute.

3. Paragraph (1) applies only in the situation where a security procedure would detect the error/change but one party fails to use the procedure and does not detect the error/change. In such a case, . . . the record is made avoidable at the instance of the party who took all available steps to avoid the mistake . . . .

Making the erroneous record avoidable by the conforming party is consistent with Sections 153 and 154 of the Restatement 2d Contracts because the non-conforming party was in the best position to avoid the problem, and would bear the risk of mistake. Such a case would constitute mistake by one party. The mistaken party (the conforming party) would be entitled to avoid any resulting contract under Section 153 because s/he does not have the risk of mistake and the non-conforming party had reason to know of the mistake.

4. As with paragraph (1), paragraph (2), when applicable, allows the mistaken party to avoid the effect of the erroneous electronic record. However, the subsection is limited to human error on the part of an individual when dealing with the electronic agent of the other party. In a transaction between individuals there is a greater ability to correct the error before parties have acted on it. However, when an individual makes an error while dealing with the

electronic agent of the other party, it may not be possible to correct the error before the other party has shipped or taken other action in reliance on the erroneous record. . . .

§11. Notarization and Acknowledgment

If a law requires a signature or record to be notarized, acknowledged, verified, or made under oath, the requirement is satisfied if the electronic signature of the person authorized to perform those acts, together with all other information required to be included by other applicable law, is attached to or logically associated with the signature or record.

§12. Retention of Electronic Records; Originals

(a) If a law requires that a record be retained, the requirement is satisfied by retaining an electronic record of the information in the record which:

(1) accurately reflects the information set forth in the record after it was first generated in its final form as an electronic record or otherwise; and

(2) remains accessible for later reference.

(b) A requirement to retain a record in accordance with subsection (a) does not apply to any information the sole purpose of which is to enable the record to be sent, communicated, or received.

(c) A person may satisfy subsection (a) by using the services of another person if the requirements of that subsection are satisfied.

(d) If a law requires a record to be presented or retained in its original form, or provides consequences if the record is not presented or retained in its original form, that law is satisfied by an electronic record retained in accordance with subsection (a).

(e) If a law requires retention of a check, that requirement is satisfied by retention of an electronic record of the information on the front and back of the check in accordance with subsection (a).

(f) A record retained as an electronic record in accordance with subsection (a) satisfies a law requiring a person to retain a record for evidentiary, audit, or like purposes, unless a law enacted after the effective date of this [Act] specifically prohibits the use of an electronic record for the specified purpose.

(g) This section does not preclude a governmental agency of this State from specifying additional requirements for the retention of a record subject to the agency's jurisdiction.

§13. Admissibility in Evidence

In a proceeding, evidence of a record or signature may not be excluded solely because it is in electronic form.

Comment

Like Section 7, this section prevents the nonrecognition of electronic records and signatures solely on the ground of the media in which information is presented.

Nothing in this section relieves a party from establishing the necessary foundation for the admission of an electronic record. See Uniform Rules of Evidence 1001(3), 1002, 1003 and 1004.

§14. Automated Transaction

In an automated transaction, the following rules apply:

(1) A contract may be formed by the interaction of electronic agents of the parties, even if no individual was aware of or reviewed the electronic agents' actions or the resulting terms and agreements.

(2) A contract may be formed by the interaction of an electronic agent and an individual, acting on the individual's own behalf or for another person, including by an interaction in which the individual performs actions that the individual is free to refuse to perform and which the individual knows or has reason to know will cause the electronic agent to complete the transaction or performance.

(3) The terms of the contract are determined by the substantive law applicable to it.

Comment

1. This section confirms that contracts can be formed by machines functioning as electronic agents for parties to a transaction. It negates any claim that lack of human intent, at the time of contract formation, prevents contract formation. When machines are involved, the requisite intention flows from the programming and use of the machine. As in other cases, these are salutary provisions consistent with the fundamental purpose of the Act to remove barriers to electronic transactions while leaving the substantive law, e.g., law of mistake, law of contract formation, unaffected to the greatest extent possible.

2. .... It is possible that an anonymous click-through process may simply result in no recognizable legal relationship, e.g., A goes to a person's website and acquires access without in any way identifying herself, or otherwise indicating agreement or assent to any limitation or obligation, and the owner's site grants A access. In such a case no legal relationship has been created.

On the other hand it may be possible that A's actions indicate agreement to a particular term. For example, A goes to a website and is confronted by an initial screen which advises her that the information at this site is proprietary, that A may use the information for her own personal purposes, but that, by clicking below, A agrees that any other use without the site owner's permission is prohibited. If A clicks "agree" and downloads the information and then uses the information for other, prohibited purposes, should not A be bound by the click? It seems the answer properly should be, and would be, yes.

If the owner can show that the only way A could have obtained the information was from his website, and that the process to access the subject information required that A must have clicked the "I agree" button after having the ability to see the conditions on use, A has performed actions which A was free to refuse, which A knew would cause the site to grant her access, i.e., "complete the transaction." The terms of the resulting contract will be determined under general contract principles, but will include the limitation on A's use of the information, as a condition precedent to granting her access to the information.

3. In the transaction set forth in Comment 2, the record of the transaction also will include an electronic signature. By clicking "I agree" A adopted a process with the intent to "sign," i.e., bind herself to a legal obligation, the resulting record of the transaction. If a "signed writing" were required under otherwise applicable law, this transaction would be enforceable. If a "signed writing" were not required, it may be sufficient to establish that the electronic record is attributable to A under Section 9. Attribution may be shown in any manner reasonable including showing that, of necessity, A could only have gotten the information through the process at the website.

§15. Time and Place of Sending and Receipt

(a) Unless otherwise agreed between the sender and the recipient, an electronic record is sent when it:

(1) is addressed properly or otherwise directed properly to an information processing system that the recipient has designated or uses for the purpose of receiving electronic records or information of the type sent and from which the recipient is able to retrieve the electronic record;

(2) is in a form capable of being processed by that system; and

(3) enters an information processing system outside the control of the sender or of a person that sent the electronic record on behalf of the sender or enters a region of the information processing system designated or used by the recipient which is under the control of the recipient.

(b) Unless otherwise agreed between a sender and the recipient, an electronic record is received when:

(1) it enters an information processing system that the recipient has designated or uses for the purpose of receiving electronic records or information of the type sent and from which the recipient is able to retrieve the electronic record; and

(2) it is in a form capable of being processed by that system.

(c) Subsection (b) applies even if the place the information processing system is located is different from the place the electronic record is deemed to be received under subsection (d).

(d) Unless otherwise expressly provided in the electronic record or agreed between the sender and the recipient, an electronic record is deemed to be sent from the sender's place of business and to be received at the recipient's place of business. For purposes of this subsection, the following rules apply:

(1) If the sender or recipient has more than one place of business, the place of business of that person is the place having the closest relationship to the underlying transaction.

(2) If the sender or the recipient does not have a place of business, the place of business is the sender's or recipient's residence, as the case may be.

(e) An electronic record is received under subsection (b) even if no individual is aware of its receipt.

(f) Receipt of an electronic acknowledgment from an information processing system described in subsection (b) establishes that a record was received but, by itself, does not establish that the content sent corresponds to the content received.

(g) If a person is aware that an electronic record purportedly sent under subsection (a), or purportedly received under subsection (b), was not actually sent or received, the legal effect of the sending or receipt is determined by other applicable law. Except to the extent permitted by the other law, the requirements of this subsection may not be varied by agreement.

Comment

1. This section provides default rules regarding when and from where an electronic record is sent and when and where an electronic record is received. This section does not address the efficacy of the record that is sent or received. That is, whether a record is unintelligible or unusable by a recipient is a separate issue from whether that record was sent or received. The effectiveness of an illegible record, whether it binds any party, are questions left to other law. . . .

§16. Transferable Records

(a) In this section, "transferable record" means an electronic record that:

(1) would be a note under [Article 3 of the Uniform Commercial Code] or a document under [Article 7 of the Uniform Commercial Code] if the electronic record were in writing; and

(2) the issuer of the electronic record expressly has agreed is a transferable record.

(b) A person has control of a transferable record if a system employed for evidencing the transfer of interests in the transferable record reliably establishes that person as the person to which the transferable record was issued or transferred.

(c) A system satisfies subsection (b), and a person is deemed to have control of a transferable record, if the transferable record is created, stored, and assigned in such a manner that:

(1) a single authoritative copy of the transferable record exists which is unique, identifiable, and, except as otherwise provided in paragraphs (4), (5), and (6), unalterable;

(2) the authoritative copy identifies the person asserting control as:

(A) the person to which the transferable record was issued; or

(B) if the authoritative copy indicates that the transferable record has been transferred, the person to which the transferable record was most recently transferred;

(3) the authoritative copy is communicated to and maintained by the person asserting control or its designated custodian;

(4) copies or revisions that add or change an identified assignee of the authoritative copy can be made only with the consent of the person asserting control;

(5) each copy of the authoritative copy and any copy of a copy is readily identifiable as a copy that is not the authoritative copy; and

(6) any revision of the authoritative copy is readily identifiable as authorized or unauthorized.

(d) Except as otherwise agreed, a person having control of a transferable record is the holder, as defined in [Section 1-201[(b)(21)] of the Uniform Commercial Code], of the transferable record and has the same rights and defenses as a holder of an equivalent record or writing under [the Uniform Commercial Code], including, if the applicable statutory requirements under [Section 3-302(a), 7-501, or [9-330(d)] of the Uniform Commercial Code] are satisfied, the rights and defenses of a holder in due course, a holder to which a negotiable document of title has been duly negotiated, or a purchaser, respectively. Delivery, possession, and indorsement are not required to obtain or exercise any of the rights under this subsection.

(e) Except as otherwise agreed, an obligor under a transferable record has the same rights and defenses as an equivalent obligor under equivalent records or writings under [the Uniform Commercial Code].

(f) If requested by a person against which enforcement is sought, the person seeking to enforce the transferable record shall provide reasonable proof that the person is in control of the transferable record. Proof may include access to the authoritative copy of the transferable record and related business records sufficient to review the terms of the transferable record and to establish the identity of the person having control of the transferable record.

Comment

1. Paper negotiable instruments and documents are unique in the fact that a tangible token-a piece of paper-actually embodies intangible rights and obligations. The extreme difficulty of creating a unique electronic token which embodies the singular attributes of a paper negotiable document or instrument dictates that the rules relating to negotiable documents and instruments not be simply amended to allow the use of an electronic record for the requisite paper writing. However, the desirability of establishing rules by which business parties might be able to acquire some of the benefits of negotiability in an electronic environment is recognized by the inclusion of this section on Transferable Records.

This section provides legal support for the creation, transferability and enforceability of electronic note and document equivalents, as against the issuer/obligor. The certainty created by the section provides the requisite incentive for industry to develop the systems and processes, which involve significant expenditures of time and resources, to enable the use of such electronic documents.

The importance of facilitating the development of systems which will permit electronic equivalents is a function of cost, efficiency and safety for the records. The storage cost and space needed for the billions of paper notes and documents is phenomenal. Further, natural disasters can wreak havoc on the ability to meet legal requirements for retaining, retrieving and delivering paper instruments. The development of electronic systems meeting the rigorous standards of this section will permit retention of copies which reflect the same integrity as the original. As a result storage, transmission and other costs will be reduced, while security and the ability to satisfy legal requirements governing such paper records will be enhanced.

Section 16 provides for the creation of an electronic record which may be controlled by the holder, who in turn may obtain the benefits of holder in due course and good faith purchaser status. If the benefits and efficiencies of electronic media are to be realized in this industry it is essential to establish a means by which transactions involving paper promissory notes may be accomplished completely electronically. Particularly as other aspects of such transactions are accomplished electronically, the drag on the transaction of requiring a paper note becomes evident. In addition to alleviating the logistical problems of generating, storing and retrieving paper, the mailing and transmission costs associated with such transactions will also be reduced. . . .

Comment: Commercial, Employment, and Consumer Arbitration

For years complaints have raged about the slowness and expense of judicial adjudication. Because of these concerns, critics of litigation have urged the use of alternative forms of dispute resolution, particularly arbitration. Although courts of an earlier day were extremely hostile to contracts providing for arbitration, regarding this as an attempt to oust them of their rightful jurisdiction, this attitude has given way to one that encourages arbitration as a means of relieving congested court dockets. See generally Ian R. MacNeil, American Arbitration Law: Reformation, Nationalization, Internationalization (1992); Thomas E. Carbonneau, The Revolution in Law Through Arbitration, 56 Clev. St. L. Rev. 233 (2008).

To change the restrictive common law rules dealing with arbitration, statutes providing for its use have been enacted at both the federal and state levels. In 1925 Congress enacted the United States Arbitration Act (the Federal Act), which establishes federal substantive law for arbitration of maritime matters or transactions involving interstate commerce. 9 U.S.C. §§1-16. In 1955, the National Conference of Commissioners on Uniform State Laws (NCCUSL)[1] promulgated the Uniform Arbitration Act to govern arbitration to the extent not superseded by the federal legislation. 7 U.L.A. 1 (1997). In 2000, NCCUSL produced a revised Arbitration Act. 7 U.L.A. (Supp. 2002).[2] The initial Uniform Arbitration Act or substantially similar legislation was adopted in 49 jurisdictions and, as of June 1, 2017, the revised Arbitration Act had been adopted in 19 jurisdictions. The status of adoptions can be found at the ULC website at www.uniformlaws.org.

Arbitration is now regularly used to resolve disputes arising from many employment contracts (including both unionized and individual employees), consumer transactions, securities transactions, construction agreements, and commercial contracts, both domestic and international. See Domke on Commercial Arbitration (3d ed., Larry E. Edmondson ed. 2011); Dennis R. Nolan, Labor and Employment Arbitration in a Nutshell (2d ed. 2006); Larry J. Pittman, Mandatory

---

1. NCCUSL is now known officially as the Uniform Law Commission.
2. The 2000 revision of the Uniform Arbitration Act is also available on the NCCUSL website at http://www.uniformlaws.org/shared/docs/arbitration/arbitration_final_00.pdf.

Arbitration: Due Process and Other Constitutional Concerns, 39 Cap. U. L. Rev. 853 (2011). Fundamental differences exist, however, with regard to arbitration of commercial disputes between sophisticated entities and arbitration of employment or consumer matters. This comment provides a brief overview of these various types of arbitration.

A dispute is subject to arbitration if the parties have entered into a valid contract calling for arbitration and the dispute is "arbitrable." While some types of disputes may not be subject to arbitration, the courts have greatly broadened the scope of matters subject to arbitration. See Thomas J. Stipanowich, The Third Arbitration Trilogy: *Stolt-Nielsen*, *Rent-A-Center*, *Concepcion* and the Future of American Arbitration, 22 Am. Rev. Int'l Arb. 323 (2011).

Commercial Arbitration

The following is a typical pre-dispute contractual provision calling for arbitration of a commercial matter:

> Any controversy or claim arising out of or relating to this contract, or the breach thereof, shall be settled by arbitration administered by the American Arbitration Association under its Commercial Arbitration Rules, and judgment on the award rendered by the arbitrator(s) may be entered in any court having jurisdiction thereof.

The American Arbitration Association (AAA), a private, nonprofit organization based in New York, has published rules on various types of arbitration proceedings. The AAA adopted revised Commercial Arbitration Rules and Mediation Procedures (hereinafter referred to as "CAR"), which became effective October 1, 2013. These rules, numbered R-1 to R-58, are available at the AAA's website (www.adr.org). You may recall that the arbitration agreements in the *Higgins* opinion in the authors' Problems in Contract Law casebook provided that arbitration would take place under AAA commercial arbitration rules.

If a dispute develops under a commercial contract containing an arbitration clause, a party who wishes to arbitrate the matter must file a written "demand" for arbitration with the AAA, submit a copy of the arbitration agreement, and pay its administrative fee, which is set by a schedule in accordance with the amount involved in the matter to be arbitrated. The demand, which is usually much simpler than a complaint filed in court, should state the intent to arbitrate, contain a statement of the nature of the dispute, the names and addresses of all involved parties, the amount involved, the remedy sought, and the hearing locale requested. The demand is served on the opposing party, who has an opportunity to file an answer or counterclaim. CAR R-4.

Under the CAR, the administrative fees for a case depend on the size of the claim and the payment scheduled chosen. The standard AAA fee schedule, as amended in July 2016, provides that a claim involving not more than $75,000 requires an initial filing fee of $750 and an additional final fee of $800 for all cases that proceed to an initial hearing; if the case involves $75,000 to $150,000, the initial filing fee is $1750 and the final fee is $1250. As would be expected, the fees increase on a graduated scale for even larger claims. The administrative fees do not cover arbitrator compensation or expenses.

The Commercial Arbitration Rules contemplate that cases with claims that do not exceed $75,000 will also be governed by the "Expedited Procedures" (E-1 to E-10) and larger cases with claims of at least $500,000 will be governed by the "Procedures for Large, Complex Commercial Disputes" (L-1 to L-3) published with the CAR. Moreover, the Expedited Procedures provide that a claim for $25,000 or less should be resolved by submission of documents. See CAR E-6. As part of changes made in 2013, the Commercial Arbitration Rules now provide for mediation of all claims in excess of $75,000, to be conducted while the arbitration is in progress and without delaying the arbitration process. Parties do have the ability to opt out of the mediation process. CAR R-9.

If the party receiving a demand refuses to submit to arbitration, court proceedings to compel arbitration may be necessary. The party demanding arbitration could file a court action seeking an order compelling the other party to arbitrate the dispute. On the other hand, the party resisting arbitration could file an action to "stay" the arbitration proceeding, perhaps in response to a lawsuit initiated by the other side. Federal Act §3; Uniform Act §7. In each of these cases, the court must decide whether the parties entered into a valid agreement to arbitrate.

Assuming a matter has been effectively referred to arbitration, either because both parties have voluntarily submitted to arbitration or one party has obtained a court order, the next step in the process is the selection of an arbitrator. Sometimes the agreement will designate an arbitrator or provide a method for selection. CAR R-13. If the agreement is silent on the selection of an arbitrator, rules of the AAA provide a "list method" of selection. The AAA sends a list of ten proposed arbitrators, along with their biographical statements, to each of the parties who are asked to strike unacceptable names from the list and to rank acceptable candidates in order of preference. If possible, the AAA will appoint an arbitrator in accordance with the mutual preferences of the parties; if not, the AAA will choose one. CAR R-12. Commercial arbitrators are usually not lawyers; typically, they work in the relevant industry. Normally, one arbitrator is used, although the AAA in its discretion can direct the use of three arbitrators. CAR R-16.

Once the arbitrator is selected, a hearing date will be fixed. CAR R-24. In most jurisdictions, pretrial discovery is not allowed in arbitration proceedings, although the parties could agree to it informally. The arbitrator is granted power to control and require the reasonable exchange of pre-hearing information between the parties to promote an economical resolution of the dispute. CAR R-22. The arbitrator has the power to subpoena witnesses or documents for the hearing. Federal Act §7; Uniform Act §17. In addition, under the Uniform Act, the arbitrator may allow the taking of a deposition of a witness who cannot be subpoenaed or is unable to attend. Uniform Act §17. By agreement of the parties, it is also possible for a matter to be submitted to the arbitrator in writing for decision without a hearing. CAR R-32(d). If a hearing is held, it is less formal than the typical court proceeding. In particular, the arbitrator may consider any evidence that is relevant and material, even if it does not comply with the rules of evidence. CAR R-34.

After the close of the hearing, the arbitrator is required to reach a decision within 30 days. CAR R-45. Except in labor arbitration, the arbitrator's "award" typically states only the result without any reasons. CAR R-46. (This form of award is recommended in arbitration in order to insulate the award from judicial scrutiny.) Subject to the agreement of the parties, the award may provide for any legal or equitable remedy, including specific performance. See generally Michael F.

Hoellering, Remedies in Arbitration, in Arbitration and the Law (1984) (Annual Report of General Counsel of AAA).

In many cases the award will be voluntarily honored by the losing party. While the losing party may seek judicial review, the grounds for "vacating" an award are extremely limited. An arbitration award cannot be overturned on the ground that it is contrary to the law or the evidence. The Federal Act authorizes judicial review of an arbitration award:

(1) Where the award was procured by corruption, fraud, or undue means.

(2) Where there was evident partiality or corruption in the arbitrators, or either of them.

(3) Where the arbitrators were guilty of misconduct in refusing to postpone the hearing, upon sufficient cause shown, or in refusing to hear evidence pertinent and material to the controversy; or of any other misbehavior by which the rights of any party have been prejudiced.

(4) Where the arbitrators exceeded their powers, or so imperfectly executed them that a mutual, final, and definite award upon the subject matter submitted was not made.

Federal Act §10(a). Section 23 of the Uniform Act is similar.

After an award is issued, if the agreement to arbitrate so provides, the prevailing party may seek judicial "confirmation" of the award, the effect of which is to make the award a judgment of a court. Federal Act §9; Uniform Act §25.

Employment Arbitration

One of the areas in which arbitration first found acceptance was unionized employment. Dating back to the 1950s, the courts accepted that employers and unions could enter into binding agreements requiring arbitration of disputes between employers and unions, partly as a way of avoiding extended labor disputes, though in that early period the U.S. Supreme Court held that federal statutorily based antidiscrimination claims could be brought in court notwithstanding the union's arbitration agreement. See Frederick L. Sullivan, Accepting Evolution in Workplace Justice: The Need for Congress to Mandate Arbitration, 26 W. New Eng. L. Rev. 281, 290–293 (2004). Details of the collective-bargaining arbitration process are beyond the scope of this comment.

In subsequent years, the U.S. Supreme Court has interpreted the FAA in an expansive manner that resulted in the presumptive enforceability of mandatory arbitration agreements between employers and independent (or non-unionized) employees, even in claims concerning federal antidiscrimination laws. See Circuit City Stores, Inc. v. Adams, 532 U.S. 105, 109-10 (2001) (holding that the FAA applied to all employment except a narrow class of interstate transportation workers listed in the Act). As one article described, the application of the pro-arbitration policy of the FAA to a broad range of individual employees has resulted in "a tidal wave of employment contracts containing arbitration clauses." William H. Daughtrey, Jr. & Donnie L. Kidd, Jr., Modifications Necessary for Commercial Arbitration Law to Protect Statutory Rights Against Discrimination in Employment: A Discussion and Proposals for Change, 14 Ohio St. J. on Disp. Resol. 29, 31 (1998). The percentage of employers using arbitration to resolve disputes grew from less than 4 percent in 1993 to 19 percent in 1996, and the AAA caseload of employment arbitrations grew from three million in 1997 to six million in 2002. See Elizabeth Hill, Due Process at Low Cost: An Empirical Study of Employment Arbitration Under the Auspices of the American Arbitration Association, 18 Ohio St. J. on Disp. Resol. 777, 779–780 (2003).

The expansion of the arbitration process to a broad range of employment (and, as discussed below, consumer) disputes has engendered great controversy and criticism but it remains the applicable law. See, e.g., Jean R. Sternlight, Rethinking the Constitutionality of the Supreme Court's Preference for Binding Arbitration: A Fresh Assessment of Jury Trial, Separation of Powers, and Due Process Concerns, 72 Tul. L. Rev. 1 (1997); David L. Gregory & Edward McNamara, Mandatory Labor Arbitration of Statutory Claims, and the Future of Fair Employment: 14 Penn Plaza v. Pyett, 19 Cornell J.L. & Pub. Pol'y 429 (2010). Thus, the application of the FAA's pro-arbitration policy to individual employment contracts means that employees will find it difficult to avoid enforcement of an agreement to arbitrate. For an employee who does wish to avoid arbitration, the only avenue available is to find some general grounds for invalidating a contract, such as unconscionability, that can be applied specifically to the arbitration agreement. See Susan Randall, Judicial Attitudes Toward Arbitration and the Resurgence of Unconscionability, 52 Buffalo L. Rev. 185 (2004); Jeffrey W. Stempel, Arbitration, Unconscionability, and Equilibrium: The Return of Unconscionability Analysis as a Counterweight to Arbitration Formalism, 19 Ohio St. J. on Disp. Resol. 757 (2004). As indicated by the *Comment: Mandatory Arbitration and Unconscionability*, following the *Higgins* case in the authors' casebook, the once promising avenue of unconscionability as grounds for challenging pre-dispute arbitration agreements has been significantly narrowed by recent U.S. Supreme Court decisions. See also Thomas J. Stipanowich, The Third Arbitration Trilogy: Stolt-Nielsen, Rent-A-Center, Concepcion and the Future of American Arbitration, 22 Am. Rev. Int'l Arb. 323 (2011).

Assuming that the dispute between the individual employee and the employer is ultimately submitted to arbitration, the arbitral rules that are likely to be applied are derivative of the commercial arbitration model described above rather than the form of arbitration found in collective bargaining arrangements. See Michael H. LeRoy & Peter Feuille, Reinventing the Enterprise Wheel: Court Review of Punitive Awards in Labor and Employment Arbitrations, 11 Harv. Negotiation L. Rev. 199, 212–213 (2006). In 1996, the AAA issued National Rules for the Resolution of Employment Disputes to govern arbitration in employment settings. These rules are now known as the Employment Arbitration Rules and Mediation Procedures, most recently amended effective November 1, 2009. The rules are available at the AAA website (www.adr.org).

The 1996 National Rules for the Resolution of Employment Disputes reflected the "Due Process Protocol for Mediation and Arbitration of Statutory Disputes Arising Out of the Employment Relationship" promulgated in 1995 by a special task force composed of individuals representing management, labor, employment, civil rights organizations, private administrative agencies, government, and the AAA. The Due Process Protocol was designed to promote fairness and equity in resolving workplace disputes and has been endorsed by a broad range of organizations including the AAA, the Judicial Arbitration and Mediation Services, Inc. (JAMS), and the American Bar Association Section on Labor and Employment. See Margaret M. Harding, The Limits of the Due Process Protocols, 19 Ohio St. J. on Disp. Resol. 369, 403-405 (2004). By agreeing to arbitrate only agreements that meet the requirements of the

Due Process Protocol, organizations such as AAA and JAMS are offering some procedural protection to the independent employee in arbitration.

A fundamental concern in employment arbitration is whether the employee can afford to pursue the claim. The AAA Employment Arbitration Rules distinguish between disputes arising out of employer-promulgated plans that are imposed on employees as a condition of employment and disputes arising out of individually-negotiated employment agreements. The AAA categorizes the claim when the arbitration is filed, but appeal can be made to the arbitrator. For arbitration of an employee's claim under an employer-promulgated plan, the employee's nonrefundable filing fee is capped in the amount of $200, payable in full when a claim is filed unless the plan provides that the employee pay less. The employer pays an initial fee of $1500 and other expenses of the hearing. If the case is filed by the employer against the employee, then the employer pays all of the $1700 initial fee.

For individually-negotiated employment agreements, the employee must pay filing fees according to a schedule similar to that used in commercial arbitration. A claim involving no more than $75,000 requires an initial filing fee of $750 and a final fee of $800 upon the first hearing; if the case involves $75,000 to $150,000, the initial filing fee is $1750 and a final fee of $1250. Higher fees are assessed for larger claims. In addition, other arbitral expenses are generally borne equally by both sides. The AAA also adopted Supplementary Rules for Class Action Arbitration that adjust fees based on that factor. Procedures other than AAA may require that the employee pay a larger share of the costs, and the state law in California may require that the employer pay a larger share.

Arbitration may begin either by joint submission of the parties or a demand by a single party. Employment Arbitration Rule-4. The appointment process contemplates that the parties may have agreed in advance to an arbitrator or a process for naming one, or may agree at the time the dispute arises. Alternatively, the AAA will provide a list of arbitrators and the parties will reach agreement through a process of objecting to some names and ranking the others. Employment Arbitration Rule-12.

The arbitrator has the ability to order such discovery as may appear necessary to the full exploration of the issues. Employment Arbitration Rule-9. Similarly, the parties are permitted to offer evidence deemed relevant and material to the dispute. Employment Arbitration Rule-30. The arbitrator is required to make an award in writing no later than 30 days from the date of closing of the hearing, in most cases, and the awards are made public and are deemed final and binding. The arbitrator is able to grant any remedy or relief that would have been available to the parties had the matter been heard in court, including awards of attorney's fees and costs, in accordance with applicable law. Employment Arbitration Rule-39.

Consumer Arbitration

As suggested by the *Higgins* case and the notes following it, there has been a dramatic increase in the use of mandatory arbitration agreements in a wide variety of contracts involving consumers or otherwise noncommercial parties. The AAA describes consumer transactions as those involving goods or services primarily for personal, family, or household use, including:

among other things, transactions involving: banking, credit cards, home loans and other financial services; health care services; brokerage services; home construction and improvements; insurance; communications; and the purchase and lease of motor vehicles and other personal property.

See Statement of Principles of the National Consumer Disputes Advisory Committee: Introduction, available under the "Consumer Due Process Protocol" at the AAA website: (www.adr.org). While there are a variety of fora in which a consumer arbitration procedure could be conducted, the AAA plays a leading role in this area as well. The Due Process Protocol for employment arbitration served as a model for a Consumer Due Process Protocol adopted in 1998 at the instigation of the AAA, and the latter document expands and refines many of the principles set forth in the employment protocol. The Consumer Protocol does not prohibit the use of mandatory pre-dispute arbitration clauses, but it does state that notice of mandatory arbitration should be "clear and adequate," and it preserves for consumers the right to go to the local small claims court instead of arbitration if the claim meets that court's jurisdictional requirements. The consumer protocol establishes the norms that arbitration should be held in a location that is convenient for both parties and in a reasonably prompt fashion. For a general discussion of the positive impact of the Consumer Protocol, see Christopher R. Drahozal & Samantha Zyontz, Private Regulation of Consumer Arbitration, 79 Tenn. L. Rev. 289 (2012).

Similar to the employment protocol, the consumer rules indicate that the AAA will not participate in an arbitration governed by an agreement that does not meet its standards. Unlike the employment protocol, the Consumer Protocol explicitly requires that the any alternative dispute resolution program be independent of the parties. See Margaret M. Harding, The Limits of the Due Process Protocols, 19 Ohio St. J. on Disp. Resol. 369, 405-406 (2004). The AAA Consumer Protocol provides that it applies to standardized non-negotiable contracts between businesses and consumers.

For consumer arbitrations that proceed before the AAA, the applicable rules were initially the Commercial Dispute Resolution Procedures described above, as altered by the AAA's Supplementary Procedures for Consumer-Related Disputes (numbered C-1 to C-8 and effective September 15, 2005). More recently, however, the AAA amended its procedures and renamed them the "Consumer Arbitration Rules," effective September 1, 2014. As with the commercial and employment procedures, the consumer process begins with a demand by the claimant. Consumer Arbitration Rule-2. If the parties have not agreed upon an arbitrator or a process for naming an arbitrator, the AAA simply appoints a neutral arbitrator. Consumer Arbitration Rule-16. For claims not exceeding $25,000, the expectation is that the arbitrator will decide the case based on submission of documents without a hearing. Consumer Arbitration Rule D-1. The arbitrator will normally make a written award within 14 days in a case decided on submission of documents or within 30 days of the close of the hearing. Consumer Arbitration Rule-42. The arbitrator may award any remedy that would be available in court under the applicable law. Consumer Arbitration Rule-44.

The Consumer Arbitration Rules provide that a consumer who files a complaint will pay only a $200 filing fee. The consumer does not pay a fee for a counterclaim. The business is generally required to pay a $1700 filing fee, a $500 hearing fee, if applicable, and the costs of the arbitrator. Any agreement by the consumer to pay part of the arbitrator's fees must be made post-dispute and voluntarily. The arbitrator's fee is set at $750 for a desk arbitration that is decided on submission of papers or at $1500 per day for a telephone or in-person hearing.

In theory, arbitration should offer consumers a quick and low cost process for resolving disputes. In reality, however, the agreements between consumers and businesses are rarely consensual, and businesses tend to stack the process in their favor by prohibiting consumer class actions, imposing prohibitive costs on individuals, limiting remedies, and setting up discovery rules that favor the business. See Richard M. Alderman, Pre-dispute Mandatory Arbitration in Consumer Contracts: A Call for Reform, 38 Hous. L. Rev. 1237 (2001); Mark E. Budnitz, Mandatory Arbitration: The High Cost of Mandatory Consumer Arbitration, 67 Law & Contemp. Prob. 133 (2004). On the other hand, there are studies which tend to prove that arbitration may work better for some consumers than the judicial process. See Sarah Rudolph Cole, On Babies and Bathwater: The Arbitration Fairness Act and the Supreme Court's Recent Arbitration Jurisprudence, 48 Hous. L. Rev. 457, 472–475 (2011) (citing studies which show that consumers pay lower fees, get faster results and receive greater remedies in arbitration). Given the nature of this debate, it is likely that consumers will continue to seek to avoid arbitration under the mandatory agreements typically found in consumer contracts but the courts will regularly continue to require that disputes be resolved through that process.

Notably, Section 1028 of the 2010 Dodd-Frank Wall Street Reform and Consumer Protection Act (Pub. L. No. 111–203, 124 Stat. 1376 (2010)) requires the Consumer Financial Protection Bureau (CFPB) to study the use of pre-dispute arbitration clauses in consumer financial contracts, to report to Congress on its findings, and to possibly regulate or impose conditions on pre-dispute arbitration if that would be in the public interest and for the protection of consumers. In March 2015, the CFPB released results of the second portion of its two-phase arbitration study.[3] The lengthy report was empirical in nature and did not take on the task of evaluating whether regulation of consumer pre-dispute arbitration agreements was advisable. There were some significant conclusions in the report, however. Nearly one-half of consumer credit card and checking accounts include arbitration provisions affecting millions of consumers, about 75% of consumers did not know they were subject to an arbitration agreement and others were wrong about the impact of the terms, consumers did not pursue individual claims at a very high rate but did get effective relief through class actions when available, arbitration did not reduce the costs of dispute resolution for consumers, and the wide spread prohibitions on class actions in arbitration agreements (85–100% across different types of transactions) effectively barred consumers from that form of remedy.

Subsequently, in October 2015, the CFPB outlined regulations that would prohibit contractual bans on class action litigation in consumer financial services contracts.[4] The CFPB issued proposed regulations to the same effect in May 2016.[5] The

---

3. The CFPB Report is available on its website at http://files.consumerfinance.gov/f/201503_cfpb_arbitration-study-report-to-congress-2015.pdf.

4. The proposed regulations are included in a report available on the CFPB website: http://files.consumerfinance.gov/f/201510_cfpb_small-business-review-panel-packet-explaining-theproposalunder-consideration.pdf.

5. See https://www.federalregister.gov/documents/2016/05/24/2016-10961/arbitration-agreements.

proposal received mixed reaction.[6] It remains to be seen whether the CFPB will regulate pre-dispute arbitration agreements in consumer financial contracts in a way that promotes remedial relief for perceived abuses by businesses. The prospects for the proposed regulations are complicated by the current political atmosphere and persistent efforts by some in the U.S. Congress to curtail the powers and product of the CFPB.[7]

6. See generally Jack Downing, Note, An Important Time for the Future of Class Action Waivers and the Power Struggle Between Businesses and Consumers, 81 Mo. L. Rev. 1151 (2016); Nicholas M. Engel, Comment, On Waiving Class Action Waivers: A Critique and Defense of the Consumer Financial Protection Bureau's Proposed Regulations, 89 Temp. L. Rev. 231 (2016).

7. See Ramona L. Lampley, The CFPB Proposed Arbitration Ban, the Rule, the Data, and Some Considerations for Change, Business Law Today (May 2017), available at https://www.americanbar.org/publications/blt/2017/05/07_lampley.html.

Contract Drafting: A Sample Problem

I. THE PROBLEM

Memorandum

To: File of Owens Chemical, Inc.
From: Attorney
Date: September 1, 2017

Tom Owens, owner of Owens Chemical, Inc., one of our clients, called me today. He wants me to draft a contract for his sales personnel.

The company sells cleaning chemicals to hotels, restaurants, and other businesses through commission salespeople. In the past, the company has relied on oral agreements, but for several reasons Tom has now decided to have a written contract. He wants the contract to cover several points.

First, the company treats its sales force as independent contractors for tax purposes. This is important so that the company will not be responsible for withholding Social Security and other employment taxes. His accountant has said that it would be desirable to have this arrangement reflected in writing. Second, the company has had some problems with salespeople selling outside their territories. He says that the agreement should specify that salespeople are limited to certain territories.

I asked Tom about other provisions of the agreement. He said that sales personnel are paid a commission of 6 percent of gross sales each month and are responsible for paying all of their own automobile and other expenses. The company does not provide them with retirement or other employment benefits. I asked about duration of the contract, and he said that a one-year term would be fine.

Tom also said to keep it simple. He doesn't want a 20-page agreement and doesn't want a big bill.

II. THE LAWYER'S ROLE AND ETHICAL
OBLIGATIONS IN CONTRACT DRAFTING

Contract drafting is a significant service that lawyers provide for their clients. Situations in which clients call on their lawyers to draft contracts typically fall in two categories. In the most common case, like the one involving Owens Chemical, the client asks the lawyer to draft a contract that the client will use in transactions with one or more other people. Examples of such contracts include leases of real property, contracts of purchase and sale of goods or real estate, and employment agreements.

In this first type of drafting situation, the lawyer does not have an attorney-client relationship with the other party, but only with the client for whom the lawyer drafted the contract. In fact, the lawyer may never even meet the other party to the contract. The other party may be represented by counsel, but it is often the case that this person will be unrepresented. If the lawyer does have any contact with an unrepresented party, the lawyer should be careful to make it clear that the lawyer does not represent that person. See American Bar Association, Model Rules of Professional Conduct, Rule 4.3.

In the second type of drafting situation, a lawyer may be called on to serve as an intermediary between two or more persons, all of whom will be clients. For example, a lawyer might be asked to form a corporation and to prepare various agreements (such as employment and buy/sell contracts) between the shareholders. The lawyer could, of course, refuse to represent all the parties in this transaction and instead represent only one of the parties. In that case, the other participants would need to retain independent counsel or be unrepresented. To reduce legal fees and to facilitate the transaction, the parties to a business venture may prefer that one lawyer represent all their interests. Ethically, an attorney may do so, but the attorney must proceed with caution. The lawyer must fully advise all parties of the advantages and risks of multiple representation, must obtain their informed consent in writing, must treat all clients equally, and must withdraw from representation should an actual conflict of interest develop. See Model Rule 1.7 and comment 28.

The Owens Chemical situation involves the first type of transaction. Owens Chemical wants the lawyer to draft a standard form agreement to be used to employ its sales personnel. Owens Chemical is the lawyer's client; the lawyer does not have an attorney-client relationship with the company's sales representatives. Since Owens is the client, the attorney has an ethical obligation to draft the agreement to protect her client's interests. This does not mean, however, that the attorney has no ethical obligations to the sales personnel. Under the ABA Model Rules of Professional Conduct, a lawyer "shall not counsel a client to engage, or assist a client, in conduct that the lawyer knows is criminal or fraudulent." Model Rule 1.2(d). On occasion a client may ask a lawyer to draft an agreement that would violate the criminal law, such as a price-fixing agreement.

Even if not criminal, some contractual provisions that a client might want to include would clearly be unenforceable. Some state statutes, for example, prohibit a seller of goods from disclaiming the implied warranty of merchantability in the sale of consumer goods. See, e.g., Miss. Code Ann. §75-2-316 (2014). See generally 18 Richard A. Lord, Williston on Contracts §52:87 (4th ed. 2001 & supp-2017); Peter Millspaugh & Richard Coffinberger, Sellers' Disclaimers of Implied Warranties: The

Legislatures Strike Back, 13 UCC L.J. 160 (1980). Drafting a clearly unenforceable disclaimer would be tantamount to fraud on the other person. If a client demands that a lawyer draft an agreement that includes a clearly illegal or fraudulent provision, the lawyer should refuse to do so and should withdraw from representation if necessary. Model Rule 1.16(a) (1) (lawyer must withdraw if "representation will result in violation of the rules of professional conduct or other law"). In addition, as discussed below in the comments to the model agreement, the lawyer often must consider the fair-ness of provisions being drafted. See generally Lee A. Pizzimenti, Prohibiting Lawyers from Assisting in Unconscionable Transactions: Using an Overt Tool, 72 Marq. L. Rev. 151 (1989).

III. THE DRAFTING PROCESS

How does one begin the process of contract drafting? The client will have given the lawyer some major points to include in the contract, as Mr. Owens has done for an agreement with his sales representatives. These include the following:

— independent contractor status
— definition of territory
— six percent commission
— responsibility for all expenses
— no retirement or other benefits
— one-year duration

Can the lawyer simply reduce to written form the points that the client wishes to include in the contract? Clearly not. Attorneys have a duty to represent their clients competently. Model Rule 1.1. Indeed, attorneys have been subject to professional discipline when they purported to do nothing more than act as a mere scrivener. See In re Solomon, 413 S.E.2d 808 (S.C. 1992) (rejecting "mere scrivener" defense to charge of representing conflicting interests). The lawyer's duty of competency in drafting a contract requires that the lawyer determine whether the client's expressed desires can be legally effectuated. Mr. Owens says that his company treats sales personnel as independent contractors for tax purposes, but is it proper for it to do so under federal and state tax law? The attorney or a specialist in tax law must research this point. See Horne v. Peckham, 158 Cal. Rptr. 714 (Ct. App. 1979) (in specialized area like tax law, lawyer must either refer matter to specialist or handle matter with degree of care and skill that would be exercised by specialist).

The duty of competency also means that the lawyer cannot simply focus on the provisions that the client wishes to include in the agreement. The lawyer must determine whether other matters should be covered by the agreement or at least discussed with the client for possible addition to the agreement.

Here the lawyer's duty of competency may encounter the economic realities of law practice. Owens says that he does not want a long contract; he wants to keep it simple and does not want a big bill. Yet, to adequately research and draft the agreement may require considerable time. In some cases, this may mean that the lawyer simply cannot bill the client for the actual time spent on the matter. An attorney can view this unbilled time either as an investment in good client relations or as a cost that must be incurred along with the benefits of being a professional. What the attorney must *not* do, however, is consider the obligation to prepare the agreement competently as somehow reduced because the client will not pay a full fee. It would be better to refuse the matter to begin with than to "cut corners."

How does a lawyer proceed to determine other provisions to consider including in the agreement? Experience and discussion with other lawyers can suggest some provisions that the agreement should contain. Usually, an attorney will turn to previously prepared agreements and checklists for guidance. Law offices typically maintain form files that an attorney can consult. In addition, commercial publishers offer form books of various types that normally include checklists, sample agreements, and commentary. Comprehensive sets of forms include the following:

American Jurisprudence, Legal Forms (2d ed.)
Nichols Cyclopedia of Legal Forms Annotated
Rabkin & Johnson, Current Legal Forms with Tax Analysis
West's Legal Forms

After consulting these various sources, the lawyer should be able to prepare an outline of provisions to include in the agreement, along with suggested language for a number of these terms. The lawyer is now ready to prepare a draft of the agreement.

IV. MODEL AGREEMENT WITH COMMENTS

Independent Contractor Agreement[1]

Agreement entered into this _____ day of _____, 20____, between Owens Chemical, Inc. (the "Company"), of _____, and _____ ("Contractor"). of _____.[2]

Recitals[3]

Company operates an industrial chemical business and wishes to hire Contractor as an independent contractor to sell chemicals on behalf of the Company.

Contractor is willing to perform sales services for the Company as an independent contractor.

---

1. The Agreement is titled "Independent Contractor Agreement" both for ease of identification and to bolster one of the client's major goals, to clarify the status of the sales personnel for tax purposes.

2. Contracts typically begin with an introduction that includes date, names of the parties, and the city or county in which they reside or do business. Shorthand references like "Company" and "Contractor" eliminate the need to fill in blanks. Avoid terms like "party of the first part," which are cumbersome and hard to follow.

3. Recitals are background facts and statements of the purposes of the agreement. Both may be useful should an issue of interpretation later develop. Older forms usually began the recitals with "Witnesseth." The trend in drafting is to use plain English whenever possible. Archaic language usually serves no useful purpose and should generally be eliminated. However, some "magic" phrases ("heirs and assigns," for example) have such an established meaning that it would be difficult and probably counterproductive to attempt to develop a modern equivalent.

In consideration[4] of the mutual covenants set forth below, the parties hereby agree as follows:

1. *Description of Work.*[5] Contractor shall devote contractor's[6] full time and use best efforts[7] to sell the company's products to the Company's existing and prospective customers.

2. *Territory.*[8] Absent prior approval, Contractor shall contact only customers whose principal place of business is located in the following territory: _____

In case of doubt Contractor shall notify the Company and obtain permission to contact a customer. If Contractor learns of customers in other territories who are interested in purchasing the Company's products, Contractor shall promptly notify the Company of the names of these customers.

3. *Commission.* Company shall pay Contractor a commission of six percent (6%) of gross sales.[9] Payment shall be made on the 15th of each month for sales made during the previous month.[10]

4. *Relationship of Parties.* The parties intend that this agreement will create an independent contractor-employer relationship between contractor and company. The Company is interested only in the results to be achieved, and the conduct and control of the work will lie solely with the Contractor.[11]

---

4. The consideration clause is not strictly necessary because the agreement contains mutual promises, but it is customary to include and serves as a transition to the body of the agreement.

5. The drafter should strive to have a logical order to the substantive provisions. In the Model Contract, Paragraphs 1 and 2 deal with the duties of the contractor. Paragraph 3 sets forth the compensation paid by the company. Paragraphs 4 through 6 focus on the various aspects of the independent contractor relationship. Paragraph 7 deals with termination of the relationship. Paragraph 8 is a merger clause. Agreements, particularly long ones, should include headings for easy reference.

6. In some situations the use of gender-specific pronouns may be appropriate, but most standard form agreements apply to transactions with men, women, and transgender persons. Use of the plural rather than the singular can avoid the problem of choice of gender, but the plural does not always fit the context. (In the Owens Chemical contract, for example, it would be inappropriate to use the plural to refer to Contractors since the agreement is with an individual salesperson.) Some contracts use the male pronoun with a general statement that the male form is intended to include the female, but this form can give the impression of male dominance. With a short agreement like this one, the best approach may be to avoid pronouns altogether.

7. The obligation of sales personnel to devote full time and to use their best efforts on behalf of the Company was not mentioned by the client but was included by the drafter on the assumption that these provisions reflect the client's desires. Any provision that the drafter includes based on the drafter's view of what the client probably wants should be discussed with the client before the agreement is executed. See the letter to the client that follows the Model Agreement.

8. Owens has said that the Company has a problem with sales representatives selling outside their territories. Drafting a clause to deal with this issue may appear to be a simple task, but it is not. Owens's customers may have more than one place of business; companies may also move or open additional places of business. How should the agreement deal with the fact that a customer may be physically located in more than one territory? Your tasks as a drafter are first to identify the problem and then to draft a solution that is compatible with the client's desires and business operation.

The agreement uses blanks for provisions that vary among the sales personnel. It is also common to group individual variations in an appendix to the standard form agreement.

9. Is the meaning of "gross sales" clear or is a definition needed? For example, are returns or credits deducted in determining the amount of gross sales to which the commission applies? This point should be raised with the client. The more general point is that operative terms in the agreement often need to be defined. When the agreement contains a number of definitions, the contract should contain a separate definitional paragraph.

10. Is the date for payment consistent with company practice?

11. Under federal income tax law, whether a person is treated as an employee or an independent contractor depends on a number of factors, especially whether the employer has the right to control the day-to-day activities of the Contractor. See Employment Status — Employee v. Independent Contractor (BNA) No. 391-2d (1993). See also Anna Deknatel & Lauren Hoff-Downing, ABC on the Books and in the Courts: An Analysis of Recent Independent Contractor and Misclassification Statutes, 18 U. Pa. J. L. & Soc. Change 53 (2015), for a broader discussion of issues related to employee or independent contractor classification.

5. *Expenses and Benefits.* Contractor shall be responsible for all expenses involved in performing duties under this agreement and shall not be entitled to any employee benefits, such as Social Security, workers' compensation, or insurance.

6. *Liability.* The work to be performed under this contract will be performed entirely at Contractor's risk. For the duration of this contract, Contractor will carry personal liability insurance naming Company as an additional insured in the following amount: _____. Contractor agrees to indemnify and hold the company harmless against any liability or loss arising from Contractor's negligence.[12]

7. *Duration and Termination.* This agreement shall continue for one year from its execution. It shall be automatically renewed for additional one-year periods unless either party gives written notice of termination at least three (3) months before the anniversary of the execution of this agreement.[13] Provided, however, either party may terminate this agreement at any time for good cause.

8. *Entire Agreement.* This document constitutes the entire agreement between the parties. No agreements between the parties are binding on them unless incorporated in a writing signed by both parties. This agreement may be modified only in writing signed by both parties.[14]

In witness whereof,[15] the parties have executed[16] this agreement on the day and year first written above.

---

12. Paragraph 6 raises the issues of the lawyer's role in drafting and of the fairness of the agreement. The client has not mentioned the need for sales personnel to carry insurance or for indemnification against liability. The lawyer certainly has an ethical obligation to raise the issue of insurance with the client because the absence of such insurance could pose a substantial financial risk to the client and because it would not be unreasonable for sales personnel to be required to carry insurance.

The indemnification clause, however, is a different matter. Does the client really need the additional protection of an indemnification clause from sales personnel? If so, how broadly should the clause be drafted? Should it indemnify the Company against any loss resulting from the negligence of the salesperson, or should it protect the Company against any liability arising from the actions of the salesperson, whether negligent or not? As noted above, a lawyer may not draft a clause that is illegal or fraudulent, but this broad clause clearly does not violate those restrictions. Should the lawyer, therefore, include any provision that protects the client's interests, or should the lawyer strive to draft an agreement that reasonably protects the client's interests without overreaching?

One possible answer to this question is that the lawyer should draft the agreement to protect the client to the maximum extent possible but also should discuss with the client the advantages and disadvantages of the provisions in question so that the client can make an informed decision. The difficulty with this approach is that the client will often turn to the lawyer for advice about what should be included. In addition, human inertia being what it is, the provision that the lawyer initially drafts will be more likely to remain in the agreement.

The drafter of this agreement has included an indemnification clause that the drafter believes reasonably protects the client's interest but without overreaching. The clause, therefore, is limited to negligence by the salesperson. Do you agree with this approach? Or do you consider it inconsistent with the lawyer's fiduciary obligations to this client?

13. The automatic renewal clause avoids the necessity of additional paperwork to renew the contract each year, but the Company should be made aware of the requirement to give three months' written notice if it wishes to terminate a salesperson at the end of any year.

14. This merger clause is intended to invoke the application of the parol evidence rule and to prevent oral modifications.

15. This is a standard conclusion to a contract but could easily be eliminated.

16. Witnesses to a contract are not required for the validity of a contract but may be desirable if there is any possibility of a later dispute about execution or terms of the contract. Given the nature of this contract, witnesses seem unnecessary.

Certain contracts, particularly contracts involving real estate, may be recorded in public records if one of the parties wishes to give public notice of the existence of the contract. To be recorded, however, a contract must meet statutory requirements regarding number of witnesses, one of whom must be a "notary public" or other similar officer legally authorized to witness the execution of documents under oath. Since this contract will not be recorded, notarization is unnecessary.

Many older contracts stated that they were executed "under seal" or "L.S." (locus sigilli). The significance of the seal has largely disappeared in modern times. In some jurisdictions, execution under seal may have the benefit of lengthening the statute of limitations for suit for breach of the agreement, but this is a fairly minor point.

CONTRACTOR: OWENS CHEMICAL, INC.

_____   By: _____

                                         Authorized Agent[17]

V. COUNSELING THE CLIENT

Once the attorney has prepared a draft of the contract, the attorney will then submit the draft to the client for review. Typically, the lawyer will do this with an accompanying cover letter pointing out the principal provisions in the agreement along with questions that the attorney would like the client to consider.

                                           September 15, 2017

Mr. Tom Owens
Owens Chemical, Inc.
218 Local Street
Your Town, YS 91128

Dear Tom:

I enclose for your review a draft Independent Contractor Agreement for your sales personnel. Please consider the following points and questions as you review the agreement.

1. *Description of Work.* I included a provision stating that salespeople will devote their "full time" to Company sales. Is this satisfactory? Do you have or expect to have any part-timers? Do you have any sales representatives who also represent other chemical companies?

The provision also states that sales personnel will use their best efforts on behalf of the Company. Under paragraph 7 you can terminate any salesperson for good cause, which would include failure to use best efforts. You can also terminate a salesperson at the end of any year for any reason provided you give three months' written notice.

2. *Territory.* I drafted the territory clause to try to deal with the problem you mentioned about salespeople who contact customers outside their territories. A possible difficulty is that your customers may have places of business in several territories. This clause uses the principal place of business of a customer to define the territory in which the customer is located. Let's discuss this to determine if it meets your needs.

3. *Commission.* As you mentioned, the commission is based on 6 percent of gross sales. Should we define "gross sales"? Are there any deductions that

---

17. Whenever a corporation or other business entity is a party to an agreement, the authority of the agent who is signing the agreement on its behalf should be verified. This may be done by a certification from the secretary of the entity that the official has authority to act on behalf of the entity either under the bylaws or other governing document of the entity, or by virtue of a resolution adopted by the governing body of the entity (the board of directors of a corporation, for example). The president of a corporation normally has implied or inherent authority to execute contracts that are reasonably necessary for the corporation to take any formal action.

should be made from gross sales, like returns or credits, for the purpose of determining commissions? Is payment of the commission on the 15th of the month for the previous month's sales consistent with your practice?

4. *Relationship of Parties.* This paragraph confirms that sales personnel are independent contractors. Under federal and state law, a salesperson will be treated as an independent contractor if the employer is concerned only about results and does not control the day-to-day activities of the sales personnel. This is a factual question. Despite what the agreement says, if you do try to control or direct the day-to-day activities of your personnel, they will no longer be independent contractors. Be aware of this fact as you conduct your business.

5. *Expenses and Benefits.* This confirms that the Company has no obligation to reimburse sales personnel for expenses or to provide any benefits.

6. *Liability.* We did not discuss the question of liability, but I have drafted a clause requiring sales personnel to carry insurance and also providing that sales personnel must indemnify the Company for any liability arising from their negligence. Do you need or want this protection, or do you simply want to rely on your own insurance? In any event, you should check with your insurance company to make sure your insurance covers the Company for any actions of its sales personnel.

7. *Duration and Termination.* The term of the agreement is one year, and the agreement automatically renews for additional one-year periods unless written notice of termination is given by either party three months before the end of any one-year period. The agreement may be terminated at any time for good cause. Are there any specific forms of misconduct that the agreement should specify as grounds for discharge?

8. *Entire Agreement.* This is a standard provision requiring that any modifications or additions to the agreement be in writing. The purpose of this clause is to reduce or eliminate disputes about the terms of the agreement. If you decide that change or modification of the agreement is necessary, you should reduce the provision to writing and have it signed by both the Company and the Contractor.

Other points to consider.

I did not include in the agreement a covenant not to compete. Do you want to consider including such a clause? For example, the agreement might prohibit a salesperson who leaves the Company from contacting any customer of the Company on behalf of a competitor of the Company for a designated period, such as one year. Courts sometimes refuse to enforce covenants not to compete, so if you wish to pursue this idea, we will need to discuss it further.

The agreement provides that if a salesperson learns of a potential customer outside the salesperson's territory, the salesperson will promptly notify the Company. Do you want to give sales personnel an incentive to make such contacts, such as giving them a referral fee if a sale results?

We did not discuss your preferences regarding governing law or dispute resolution. As Owens Chemical expands its sales force and client base, disputes may arise that woud not obviously be governed by the law of this state. It is quite common to include a provision selecting the law of a particular state to govern any dispute arising out of an agreement. Would you like me to include such a clause? How about an arbitration or other alternative dispute resolution clause?

These are fairly standard and, if properly drafted, courts will enforce them to divert litigation to a less costly, more expedient forum. Would you like me to include such a clause?

After you have had a chance to review the draft, give me a call so that we can discuss revisions and consider any suggestions you may have.

Best regards,

Helen T. Partner, Esq.

VI. BIBLIOGRAPHY

Given the importance of drafting, law schools are devoting increasing attention to the subject. In the past few years a number of fine books on drafting have been published. These include the following:

Scott Burnham, Drafting and Analyzing Contracts (4th ed. 2016)
Thomas R. Haggard, Contract Law from a Drafting Perspective (2002)
George W. Kuney, The Elements of Contract Drafting (4th ed. 2014)
Sue Payne, Basic Contract Drafting Assignments: A Narrative Approach (2010)
Tina L. Stark, Drafting Contracts: How and Why Lawyers Do What They Do (2nd ed. 2013)